T0189500

Lecture Notes in Computer Science 13655

More information about this series at https://link.springer.com/bookseries/558

Yuan Xu · Hongyang Yan · Huang Teng ·
Jun Cai · Jin Li (Eds.)

Machine Learning for Cyber Security

4th International Conference, ML4CS 2022
Guangzhou, China, December 2–4, 2022
Proceedings, Part I

Editors
Yuan Xu
School of Computing and Informatics
University of Louisiana at Lafayette
Lafayette, IN, USA

Hongyang Yan
Institute of Artificial Intelligence
and Blockchain
Guangzhou University
Guangzhou, China

Huang Teng
Institute of Artificial Intelligence
and Blockchain
Guangzhou University
Guangzhou, China

Jun Cai
Guangdong Polytechnic Normal University
Guangzhou, China

Jin Li
Institute of Artificial Intelligence
and Blockchain
Guangzhou University
Guangzhou, China

ISSN 0302-9743 ISSN 1611-3349 (electronic)
Lecture Notes in Computer Science
ISBN 978-3-031-20095-3 ISBN 978-3-031-20096-0 (eBook)
https://doi.org/10.1007/978-3-031-20096-0

This Springer imprint is published by the registered company Springer Nature Switzerland AG
The registered company address is: Gewerbestrasse 11, 6330 Cham, Switzerland

Preface

The Fourth International Conference on Machine Learning for Cyber Security (ML4CS 2022) was held in Guangzhou, China, during December 2–4, 2022. ML4CS is a well-recognized annual international forum for AI-driven security researchers to exchange ideas and present their works.

The conference received 367 submissions. Committee accepted 100 regular papers and 46 short papers to be included in the conference program. It was single blind during the paper review process, and there are two reviews per paper at least. The proceedings contain revised versions of the accepted papers. While revisions are expected to take the referees comments into account, this was not enforced and the authors bear full responsibility for the content of their papers.

ML4CS 2022 was organized by Guangdong Polytechnic Normal University, Pazhou Lab, and Sun Yat-sen University. The conference would not have been such a success without the support of these organizations, and we sincerely thank them for their continued assistance and support.

We would also like to thank the authors who submitted their papers to ML4CS 2022, and the conference attendees for their interest and support. We thank the Organizing Committee for their time and effort dedicated to arranging the conference. This allowed us to focus on the paper selection and deal with the scientific program. We thank the Program Committee members and the external reviewers for their hard work in reviewing the submissions; the conference would not have been possible without their expert reviews. Finally, we thank the EasyChair system and its operators, for making the entire process of managing the conference convenient.

September 2022

Xiaochun Cao
Jin Li
Jun Cai
Huang Teng
Yan Jia
Min Yang
Xu Yuan

Organization

General Chairs

Xiaochun Cao	Sun Yat-sen University, China
Jin Li	Guangzhou University, China
Jun Cai	Guangdong Polytechnic Normal University, China
Teng Huang	Guangzhou University, China

Program Chairs

Yan Jia	Peng Cheng Laboratory, China
Min Yang	Fudan University, China
Xu Yuan	University of Louisiana at Lafayette, USA

Track Chairs

Machine Learning Based Cybersecurity Track

Wei Wang	Beijing Jiaotong University, China
Yu-an Tan	Beijing Institute of Technology, China

Big Data Analytics for Cybersecurity Track

Xuyun Zhang	Macquaire University, Australia
Wenchao Jiang	Guangdong University of Technology, China

Cryptography in Machine Learning Track

Xinyi Huang	Fujian Normal University, China
Joseph K. Liu	Monash University, Australia

Differential Privacy Track

Changyu Dong	Newcastle University, UK
Tianqing Zhu	University of Technology Sydney, Australia

Data Security in Machine Learning Track

Zheli Liu	Nankai University, China
Zuoyong Li	Minjiang University, China

Adversarial Attacks and Defenses Track

Qian Wang	Wuhan University, China
Kai Chen	Institute of Information Engineering, Chinese Academy of Sciences, China

Security and Privacy in Federated Learning Track

Lianyong Qi	Qufu Normal University, China
Tong Li	Nankai University, China

Explainable Machine Learning Track

Sheng Hong	Beihang University, China

Security in Machine Learning Application Track

Tao Xiang	Chongqing University, China
Yilei Wang	Qufu Normal University, China

AI/Machine Learning Security and Application Track

Hao Peng	Zhejiang Normal University, China

Workshop Chair

Wei Gao	Yunnan Normal University, China

Publication Chair

Di Wu	Guangzhou University, China

Publicity Chair

Zhuo Ma	Xidian University, China

Steering Committee

Xiaofeng Chen	Xidian University, China
Iqbal Gondal	Federation University, Australia
Ryan Ko	Waikato University, New Zealand
Jonathan Oliver	Trend Micro, USA
Islam Rafiqul	Charles Sturt University, Australia
Vijay Varadharajan	University of Newcastle, Australia
Ian Welch	Victoria University of Wellington, New Zealand
Yang Xiang (Chair)	Swinburne University of Technology, Australia
Jun Zhang (Chair)	Swinburne University of Technology, Australia
Wanlei Zhou	Deakin University, Australia

Program Committee

Silvio Barra	University of Salerno, Italy
M. Z. Alam Bhuiyan	Guangzhou University, China
Carlo Blundo	University of Salerno, Italy
Yiqiao Cai	Huaqiao University, China
Luigi Catuogno	University of Salerno, Italy
Lorenzo Cavallaro	King's College London, UK
Liang Chang	Guilin University of Electronic Technology, China
Fei Chen	Shenzhen University, China
Xiaofeng Chen	Xidian University, China
Zhe Chen	Singapore Management University, Singapore
Frédéric Cuppens	IMT Atlantique, France
Changyu Dong	Newcastle University, UK
Guangjie Dong	East China Jiaotong University, China
Mohammed EI-Abd	American University of Kuwait, Kuwait
Wei Gao	Yunnan Normal University, China
Dieter Gollmann	Hamburg University of Technology, Germany
Zheng Gong	South China Normal University, China
Zhitao Guan	North China Electric Power University, China
Zhaolu Guo	Chinese Academy of Sciences, China
Jinguang Han	Queen's University Belfast, UK
Saeid Hosseini	Singapore University of Technology and Design, Singapore
Chingfang Hsu	Huazhong University of Science and Technology, China
Haibo Hu	The Hong Kong Polytechnic University, Hong Kong
Teng Huang	Guangzhou University, China
Xinyi Huang	Fujian Normal University, China

Wenchao Jiang	Guangdong University of Technology, China
Lutful Karim	Seneca College of Applied Arts and Technology, Canada
Hadis Karimipour	University of Guelph, Canada
Sokratis Katsikas	Open University of Cyprus, Cyprus
Neeraj Kumar	Thapar Institute of Engineering and Technology, India
Kangshun Li	South China Agricultural University, China
Ping Li	South China Normal University, China
Tong Li	Naikai University, China
Wei Li	Jiangxi University of Science and Technology, China
Xuejun Li	Anhui University, China
Kaitai Liang	University of Surrey, UK
Hui Liu	University of Calgary, Canada
Wei Lu	Sun Yat-sen University, China
Xiaobo Ma	Xi'an Jiaotong University, China
Fabio Martinelli	IIT-CNR, Italy
Ficco Massimo	Second University of Naples, Italy
Weizhi Meng	Technical University of Denmark, Denmark
Vincenzo Moscato	University of Naples, Italy
Francesco Palmieri	University of Salerno, Italy
Fei Peng	Hunan University, China
Hu Peng	Wuhan University, China
Lizhi Peng	Jinan University, China
Umberto Petrillo	Sapienza University of Rome, Italy
Lianyong Qi	Qufu Normal University, China
Shahryar Rahnamayan	University of Ontario Institute of Technology, Canada
Khaled Riad	Guangzhou University, China
Yu Sun	Guangxi University, China
Yu-An Tan	Beijing Institute of Technology, China
Zhiyuan Tan	Edinburgh Napier University, UK
Ming Tao	Dongguan University of Technology, China
Donghai Tian	Beijing Institute of Technology, China
Chundong Wang	Tianjin University of Technology, China
Ding Wang	Peking University, China
Feng Wang	Wuhan University, China
Hui Wang	Nanchang Institute of Technology, China
Jianfeng Wang	Xidian University, China
Jin Wang	Soochow University, China

Licheng Wang	Beijing University of Posts and Telecommunications, China
Lingyu Wang	Concordia University, Canada
Tianyin Wang	Luoyang Normal University, China
Wei Wang	Beijing Jiaotong University, China
Wenle Wang	Jiangxi Normal University, China
Sheng Wen	Swinburne University of Technology, Australia
Yang Xiang	Swinburne University of Technology, Australia
Run Xie	Yibin University, China
Xiaolong Xu	Nanjing University of Information Science & Technology, China
Li Yang	Xidian University, China
Shao-Jun Yang	Fujian Normal University, China
Zhe Yang	Northwestern Polytechnical University, China
Yanqing Yao	Beihang University, China
Xu Yuan	University of Louisiana at Lafayette, USA
Qikun Zhang	Beijing Institute of Technology, China
Xiao Zhang	Beihang University, China
Xiaosong Zhang	Tangshan University, China
Xuyun Zhang	Macquarie University, Australia
Yuan Zhang	Nanjing University, China
Xianfeng Zhao	Chinese Academy of Sciences, China
Lei Zhu	Huazhong University of Science and Technology, China
Tianqing Zhu	China University of Geosciences, China

Track Program Committee - AI/Machine Learning Security and Application

Hao Peng (Chair)	Zhejiang Normal University, China
Meng Cai	Xi'an Jiaotong University, China
Jianting Ning	Singapore Management University, Singapore
Hui Tian	Huaqiao University, China
Fushao Jing	National University of Defense Technology, China
Guangquan Xu	Tianjin University, China
Jun Shao	Zhejiang Gongshang University, China

Contents – Part I

Contents – Part II

Contents – Part III

Traditional Chinese Medicine Health Status Identification with Graph Attention Network

Amin Fu[1], Jishun Ma[1], Chuansheng Wang[2], Changen Zhou[3], Zuoyong Li[4(✉)], and Shenghua Teng[1(✉)]

[1] College of Electronic and Information Engineering, Shandong University of Science and Technology, Qingdao 266590, China
shteng@sdust.edu.cn

[2] Department of Automatic Control Technical, Polytechnic University of Catalonia, Barcelona 08034, Spain

[3] Research Base of Traditional Chinese Medicine Syndrome, Fujian University of Traditional Chinese Medicine, Fuzhou 350122, China

[4] Fujian Provincial Key Laboratory of Information Processing and Intelligent Control, College of Computer and Control Engineering, Minjiang University, Fuzhou 350121, China
fzulzytdq@126.com

Abstract. The Traditional Chinese Medicine Health Status Identification plays an important role in TCM diagnosis and prescription recommendation. In this paper, we propose a method of Status Identification via Graph Attention Network, named SIGAT, which captures the complex medical correlation in the symptom-syndrome graph. More specifically, we construct a symptom-syndrome graph in that symptoms are taken as nodes and the edges are connected by syndromes. And we realize automatic induction of symptom to state element classification by using the attention mechanism and perceptron classifier. Finally, we conduct experiments by using hamming loss, coverage, 0/1 error, ranking loss, average precision, macro-F1 score, and micro-F1 score as evaluation metrics. The results demonstrate that the SIGAT model outperforms comparison algorithms on Traditional Chinese Medicine Prescription Dictionary dataset. The case study results suggest that the proposed method is a valuable way to identify the state element. The application of the graph attention network classification algorithm in TCM health status identification is of high precision and methodological feasibility.

Keywords: Graph attention network · Multi-label classification · TCM health status identification

1 Introduction

With the development of emerging medical technology, people's demand for medical treatment has translated into health demand. Since China has gradually

Y. Xu et al. (Eds.): ML4CS 2022, LNCS 13655, pp. 1–14, 2023.
https://doi.org/10.1007/978-3-031-20096-0_1

entered the center of the world stage, TCM has received national attention and benefits people all over the world [18]. The rapid development of big data and artificial intelligence in recent years has made traditional Chinese medicine more intelligent [7]. The theory of TCM state identification effectively promotes clinical treatment, and the induction of state elements is the key to TCM diagnosis and treatment. The state element is a generalization of the local or overall functions and conditions of the human body, and is the key to grasping the state of human health [1]. The theory of health state identification is based on the theory of Traditional Chinese Medicine. It is a process that identifies the location, nature, degree, and other state elements of the disease according to the four-diagnosis information such as observation, auscultation and olfaction, inquiry, and pulse feeling and palpation [6,20]. State elements can be divided into two types: disease location (such as stomach, spleen, etc.) and disease (such as heat, cold, etc.) [5]. The essence of the state element is to summarize the characteristics of the human body's Yin and Yang conflict state under specific conditions, including the physiological and pathological characteristics of the disease, the type of cold and heat deficiency and excess of the disease, and the environment's cold, heat, summer and dampness characteristics [1].

Traditional status identification methods aim to classify state elements based on symptoms. There are two types of state elements induction methods. One is based on traditional machine learning methods, such as multi-label learning with label-specific features (LIFT) based on generic attributes, multi-label learning K nearest neighbor (ML-KNN), rank support vector machines (Rank SVM), and other methods [15,17]. The second is the deep learning method based on the graph neural network. Since the dialectical relationship among TCM symptoms, state elements, and syndromes can be concretized through graph representation learning, this paper uses the graph attention network to realize the task of state element induction.

In this paper, we propose a graph attention network-based method for TCM health status identification, named SIGAT. More specifically, SIGAT captures complex medical correlations between nodes and edges for graph representation learning. We construct a symptom-syndrome graph in this model by using a graph attention network and a perceptron classifier to inductive state elements. Then we conduct comparative experiments based on several different machine learning methods and demonstrate that SIGAT achieves higher state element multi-label classification precision, laying a foundation for further research. The contributions of this paper are as follows:

- We develop a graph representation based on Traditional Chinese Medicine health status identification, where symptoms are regarded as nodes and syndromes are regarded as edges in a symptom-syndrome graph.
- We propose a graph attention network framework for Traditional Chinese Medicine health status identification, named the SIGAT model. Different from previous methods, we build a graph attention mechanism architecture along with a perceptron classifier for multi-label classification.

- We conduct extensive experiments on real-world datasets and demonstrate the feasibility and effectiveness of the proposed SIGAT compared with other machine learning methods.

2 Related Work

The state element induction work based on status identification theory can be defined as single-label classification and multi-label classification in the field of artificial intelligence [16]. The accuracy of single-label classification is low due to the rough abstraction of the features of TCM symptoms, in this paper, the status factor induction task is defined as a multi-label classification problem. The features of the symptom's characterization parameters are used as input, and the state element is used as the output label of the model. In addition, every prescription record has one or more status elements, so it is more reasonable to define the task as a multi-label classification problem.

In recent years, the task of multi-label text classification originated from deep learning techniques of text classification. And large numbers of graph neural network embedding techniques have been proposed for multi-label text classification tasks [3]. The Graph Attention Network proposed by Veličković et al. [14] introduces the attention mechanism into the spatial domain-based graph neural network [8]. The network is trained by aggregating the features of neighbor nodes, and the feature representation of the central node is updated, which improves the generalization ability of the model [14]. Through the attention mechanism, the graph attention network enables each neighbor node to learn different attention weight parameters and achieves a more efficient feature extraction ability by achieving effective aggregation of neighbor nodes [11]. Attention mechanisms have been shown to be effective in many domains [9]. In the task of state element classification, not all symptoms and syndromes contribute to the classification results, and the attention mechanism enables different symptoms to play a moderating role in the final node representation, thereby improving the classification accuracy.

3 Methods

In this section, we introduce the graph attention network for TCM health status identification called SIGAT, as shown in Fig. 1. The SIGAT model is mainly divided into three modules: TCM graph construction module, attention layer construction module, and state element prediction module.

3.1 TCM Graph Constrcuction Module

Firstly, we introduce the graph construction based on TCM state identification knowledge. We define the number of TCM prescriptions as M, and define the symptom set as V, where the number of symptoms is N. Let E stand for syndrome. Y is the set of state elements, and the number of state elements is L. For

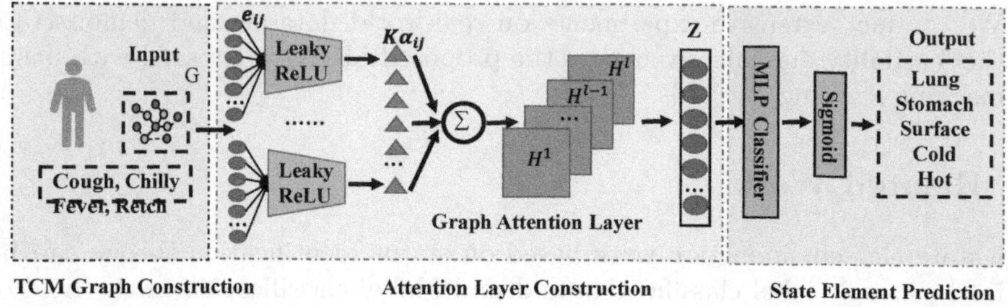

Fig. 1. The framework of the proposed SIGAT model.

every TCM prescription, symptom, syndrome, and state element are multi-hot coded into a vector. As shown in Fig. 2, the graph data we constructed is a series of interconnected nodes representing symptoms, and the edge relationship of the TCM syndrome type structure contains the TCM state identification theory. In the symptom-syndrome graph, the symptom node correlation is represented by the interconnected edge relation 1, that is, the two symptoms exist in the same syndrome. If the unconnected edge relationship between two nodes is 0, it indicates that these are two unrelated symptom nodes. The solid line in the graph is the symptom with solar typhoid syndrome as the edge, and the connection of the dotted line is due to other syndromes. We define a graph structure $G = (V, E)$, where the set of symptoms nodes is V, and the edge set of syndromes is E. Every symptom node contains unique features, F is the initial feature of the node. $X = \{\boldsymbol{x}_1, \boldsymbol{x}_2, \ldots, \boldsymbol{x}_N\}$ is the multi-hot vector of prescription symptoms.

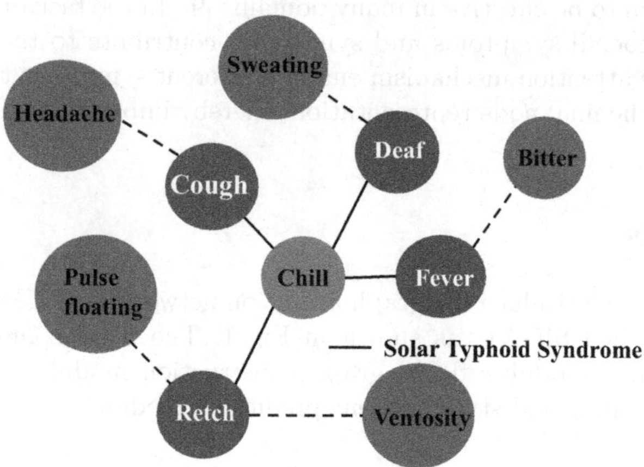

Fig. 2. Symptom-syndrome graph for TCM state identification.

3.2 Attention Layer Construction Module

The main idea of the graph attention network is that the generation of any node feature in the graph needs to pay attention to the contribution degree of its different nodes. After learning the correlation between this central node and other adjacent nodes, we assign different weight coefficients to all nodes [14]. This section first introduces a single graph attention layer and then stacks multiple graph attention layers to construct the SIGAT model.

Calculation of Attention Coefficient. Let the input of the graph attention layer be the feature H of all nodes, where N is the total number of nodes (symptoms). The goal of this layer is to aggregate neighbour information of nodes to obtain new node feature representation [14]. Firstly, the attention coefficient of a single node i is calculated. Assuming that the central node i has an adjacent point $j \in N_i$, which are WH_i and WH_j respectively after linear transformation, the attention coefficient of the adjacent node j to the node i is:

$$e_{ij} = a\left([WH_i \| WH_j]\right), j \in N_i. \tag{1}$$

W is a shared parameter of linear mapping, which enhances the features of nodes, $[\cdot\|\cdot]$ concatenates the transformed features of nodes i and j. Here, $a(\cdot)$ stacks the concatenated higher-dimensional features to a real number. Obviously, through the learnable parameter W and mapping $a(\cdot)$, e_{ij} represents the importance of adjacent node j to the new features of central node i, and the correlation between nodes i and j is learned.

When node i has multiple adjacent points, we normalize the correlation coefficient to avoid the problem that the attention coefficient is too large and is not conducive to training [10]. Meanwhile, in order to generalize the fitting ability of the model, the nonlinear activation function can be added to the linearly changed value as $LeakyReLU(\cdot)$, and the final attention coefficient calculation formula is:

$$\alpha_{ij} = LeakyReLU(e_{ij})\frac{exp(e_{ij})}{\sum_{k \in N_i} exp(e_{ik})}. \tag{2}$$

Then, the weighted summation of neighbour node features is performed to obtain new node features:

$$H_i = \sigma(\sum_{j \in N_i} \alpha_{ij} W H_j). \tag{3}$$

H_i is the new feature output by the graph attention layer that incorporates neighbourhood information for every node i, and $\sigma(\cdot)$ is the activation function. As described above, the features of a single layer of graph attention layer can be obtained.

Multiple Attention Mechanism. Using k independent attention mechanisms, feature information of different subspaces can be obtained. In every graph attention layer, K independent transformation matrices W^k are calculated. We aggregate the attention information of multiple subspaces, which is calculated in parallel according to Eq. (3), and then we concatenate the obtained results again:

$$H_i = \sigma(\frac{1}{k}\sum_{i=1}^{k}\sum_{j\in N_i}\alpha_{ij}^{(k)}W^{(k)}H_j), \tag{4}$$

where $\alpha_{ij}^{(k)}$ is the weight coefficient calculated by the K transformation matrix W^k, which cause H_i to have higher dimensions $(1, kd')$. So it can only be used as a middle layer and not an output layer. For the output layer, one aggregation approach is the weighted average of each attention mechanism H'.

Attention Layer Polymerization. After obtaining the attention coefficients of the single-layer symptom node and its adjacent nodes above, the model aggregates multiple graph attention layers to obtain the final node embedding representation:

$$H_i^{(l)} = \sigma(\sum_{j\in N_i}\alpha_{ij}^{(l)}W^{(l)}H_j^{(l-1)})(1 < l < P), \tag{5}$$

where l represents the number of network layers and the feature H of the first layer is the initial feature $H^{(0)} = F$. The graph attention layer aggregates the features of symptom neighbour nodes to the central symptom nodes, and it learns new node feature expressions by using the nodes connection strategy based on the graph. Finally, the embedding of a symptom group is defined as Z. The fusion of all symptoms in a symptom group is expressed as the following formula:

$$Z = \sigma(XH_i^{(P)}). \tag{6}$$

3.3 State Element Prediction Module

After using the graph attention mechanism to obtain the graph embedding representation Z of symptoms and syndromes, the perceptron classifier and sigmoid function are set in the output layer, and every neuron corresponds to a label:

$$y = Sigmoid(WZ), \tag{7}$$

where, W is the trainable weight parameter, and $Sigmoid(\cdot)$ is the activation function that converts the output value into probability. The cross-entropy loss function [2,4] is used in network training as follows:

$$Loss = -\frac{1}{L}\sum_{i=1}^{L}(y_i\log_2(y_i') + (1-y_i)\log_2(1-y_i'). \tag{8}$$

There, $y_i \in \{0,1\}$ represents the true value of prescription sample, $y_i' \in [0,1]$ is the predicted probability value. L is the number of state elements.

4 Experiments

In this section, we introduce the experimental setups and analyze the experimental results.

4.1 Experimental Setup

Dataset. The data set used in this paper is collated from the Large Dictionary of Prescriptions. The dataset includes 2685 diagnosis and treatment prescriptions, 298 symptoms, 69 status elements, and 747 syndromes. The information statistics and examples are shown in Table 1.

Table 1. Dataste information statistics.

Traditional Chinese Medicine Prescription Dictionary			Counts
Prescription	Dajianzhong Decoction	Yiqi sanfeng Decoction	2685
Symptoms	Shortness of breath, Hot flash, Asthma, Cough	Heaviness in waist, Aversion to wind, Adiapneustia, Headache	298
Syndrome	Spleen and stomach Yang deficiency	Superficies tightened By wind cold	747
State Elements	Yang deficiency, Stomach, Spleen, Cold	Qi deficiency, Kidney, Wet, Hot	69

Implementation. The implementation of our method is based on the deep learning framework of PyTorch. All experiments are run on NVIDIA 1650Ti GPU with 4 GB memory and a Windows 10 operating system. Adaptive moment estimation (Adam) is used to minimize the final objective function with a learning rate of 1.5×10^{-4}, batch size of 8, and weight decay of 1×10^{-8}.

Comparison Algorithm. The following machine learning methods are selected to compare with the proposed SIGAT:

(1) Support Vector Machines (SVM): The kernel function of the support vector machine is set to a gaussian kernel, the kernel coefficient is 0.3, and the penalty coefficient of the relaxation coefficient is set to 3.
(2) Bayesian Network (NB): The naive bayes classifier of the multivariate bernoulli model binarizes (maps to boolean values) the threshold of sample features, with the smoothing parameter set to 1.

(3) K Nearest Neighbors (KNN): The number of neighbours used in the query is 10, and the nearest 10 points are selected with the size of the ball tree and KD tree constructed to 3.
(4) Random Forests (RF): We set the number of decision trees in the forest is 10, and the minimum number of samples needed to divide internal nodes is 2. The minimum number of samples needed to be on leaf nodes is set to 1.

Evaluation Metrics. Performance evaluation for multi-label classification is complicated, and the prediction result of each instance is a set of labels. We define the total number of prescription samples in the dataset of the Traditional Chinese Medicine Prescription Dictionary as M. The total state element label set is defined as Y, and the total number of categories is defined as L. For any sample x_i, Y_i' represents the predicted label set, and Y_i represents the true label set corresponding to the sample. And $r_i(\lambda)$ stands for the ranking position of label λ among all predicted labels. In this paper, we employ 7 different metrics, which are widely used to evaluate the performance of classifiers.

Hamming loss (HLoss) is used to measure the number of misclassified labels. Δ calculates the commission errors and omission errors between the true labels and predicted results. Hamming loss represents the proportion of wrong samples in all labels [12], which is defined as follows:

$$\text{HLoss} = \frac{1}{M}\sum_{i=1}^{M}\frac{1}{L}|Y_i \Delta Y_i'|. \tag{9}$$

Coverage indicates that the prediction results of the state element label are sorted from probability and the average value of the probability values requires to cover the true labels [19]. And $\max_{\lambda\in Y_i} r_i(\lambda)$ is the ranking of true labels among the predicted labels. Similarly, a small value indicates high network prediction performance. The calculation formula is as follows:

$$\text{Coverage} = \frac{1}{M}\sum_{i=1}^{M}\max_{\lambda\in Y_i} r_i(\lambda) - 1. \tag{10}$$

0/1 error indicates the number of irrelevant labels with the highest ranking in the ranking labels of the prediction results [13]. In prescription sample x_i, $argmax(r_i(\lambda))$ is the top-ranked label. When the prediction label λ is not in Y_i, the prediction result is wrong, then $\delta(\lambda) = 1$. In the same way, when the prediction is correct, $\delta(\lambda) = 0$. A small 0/1 error indicates better network prediction performance as follows:

$$0/1 \text{ Error} = \frac{1}{M}\sum_{i=1}^{M}\delta(argmax(r_i(\lambda)), \lambda \notin Y_i). \tag{11}$$

Ranking loss (RLoss) is the number that the probability ranking $r_i(\lambda_b)$ of irrelevant label λ_b is higher than the probability $r_i(\lambda_a)$ of the related label λ_a.

Y_i is the relevant label set in the true prescription, but $\bar{Y}_i$ is the label that is not relevant to the prescription [13]. The low the ranking loss, the few unrelated labels are predicted to the front, which means the higher the prediction accuracy of the true relevant labels as follows:

$$\text{RLoss} = \frac{1}{M}\sum_{i=1}^{M}\frac{1}{|Y_i||\bar{Y}_i|}|(\lambda_a,\lambda_b): r_i(\lambda_a) > r_i(\lambda_b), (\lambda_a,\lambda_b) \in Y_i \times \bar{Y}_i|. \tag{12}$$

Average precision (AP) refers to the average probability that in the ranking labels of the predicted prescription, the label of the predicted sample in front is also the truly related label Y_i. For the predicted label λ', $r_i(\lambda')$ is the probability ranking of the predicted samples, and $r_i(\lambda)$ is the ranking of the true label of the samples. The calculation formula is as follows:

$$\text{AP} = \frac{1}{M}\sum_{i=1}^{M}\frac{1}{|Y_i|}\sum_{\lambda\in Y_i}\frac{|\lambda' \in Y_i | r_i(\lambda') \le r_i(\lambda)\ |}{r_i(\lambda)}. \tag{13}$$

Macro-F1 focuses on the difference between state element labels. we first calculate Macro-P and Macro-R for all classes, then calculate Macro-F1 as follows:

$$\text{Macro-P} = \frac{1}{\text{L}}\sum_{\text{i}=1}^{\text{L}}\text{P}_\text{i} = \frac{1}{\text{L}}\sum_{\text{i}=1}^{\text{L}}\frac{\text{TP}}{\text{TP}+\text{FP}}, \tag{14}$$

$$\text{Macro-R} = \frac{1}{\text{L}}\sum_{\text{i}=1}^{\text{L}}\text{R}_\text{i} = \frac{1}{\text{L}}\sum_{\text{i}=1}^{\text{L}}\frac{\text{TP}}{\text{TP}+\text{FN}}, \tag{15}$$

$$\text{Macro-F1} = \frac{2\text{Macro-P}\cdot\text{Macro-R}}{\text{Macro-P}+\text{Macro-R}}. \tag{16}$$

Micro-F1 ignores the difference between labels and establishes the global confusion matrix without classifying every instance in the data set. We calculate Micro-P and Micro-R for all labels, resulting in Micro-F1:

$$\text{Micro-P} = \frac{\sum_{\text{i}=1}^{\text{L}}\text{TP}_\text{i}}{\sum_{\text{i}=1}^{\text{L}}\text{TP}_\text{i}+\sum_{\text{i}=1}^{\text{L}}\text{FP}_\text{i}}, \tag{17}$$

$$\text{Micro-R} = \frac{\sum_{\text{i}=1}^{\text{L}}\text{TP}_\text{i}}{\sum_{\text{i}=1}^{\text{L}}\text{TP}_\text{i}+\sum_{\text{i}=1}^{\text{L}}\text{FN}_\text{i}}, \tag{18}$$

$$\text{Micro-F1} = \frac{2\text{Micro-P}\cdot\text{Micro-R}}{\text{Micro-P}+\text{Micro-R}}. \tag{19}$$

4.2 Experimental Results and Analysis

In this section, we demonstrate the effectiveness of the proposed SIGAT method by presenting quantitative results and contrasting them with comparison algorithms for TCM status identification. In addition, we analyze ablation studies and case studies of state element classification.

TCM Status Identifiaction. Table 2 shows the different training ratios of the dataset to evaluate our method, including 50%, 60%, 70%, 80% and 90%, and the rest are used as test data, respectively. The maximum macro-F1 is 37.79% when the proportion of the training set is 90%. When the training set is 80%, the hamming loss of SIGAT network training is least to 0.1060 and the 0/1 error is least to 0.2486. When the proportion of the training set is 70%, the coverage is least to 21.9862 and the ranking loss is least to 0.0858. The maximum average precision is 65.92%, and the maximum micro-F1 score is 58.29%.

Table 2. Results of SIGAT model carried out on different training ratios set.

Training ratio	HLoss	Coverage	RLoss	0/1 Error	AP	Macro-F1	Micro-F1
90%	0.1108	22.2100	0.0946	0.2500	0.6499	**0.3779**	0.5811
80%	**0.1060**	23.3618	0.0933	**0.2486**	0.6569	0.3094	0.5759
70%	0.1101	**21.9862**	**0.0858**	0.2594	**0.6592**	0.3460	**0.5829**
60%	0.1089	22.0839	0.0884	0.2799	0.6439	0.3127	0.5601
50%	0.1120	22.0636	0.0870	0.2897	0.6436	0.3332	0.5658

The experimental results in Table 3 show that the proposed SIGAT significantly outperforms the compared machine learning methods. For example, given 80% training data, SIGAT has the smallest coverage, ranking loss, and 0/1 error compared to SVM, NB, KNN, and RF, with an increase of 2%–10%, 1%–13%, and 6%–10% in average precision, macro-F1, and micro-F1, respectively.

Table 3. Experiment results of comparison algorithms.

Algorithm	HLoss	Coverage	RLoss	0/1 Error	AP	Macro-F1	Micro-F1
SVM	**0.0985**	25.0317	0.1018	0.2998	0.6348	0.3000	0.5118
NB	0.1003	25.4380	0.1018	0.2810	0.6392	0.2176	0.4605
KNN	0.1026	39.1174	0.1830	0.2991	0.5735	0.1712	0.3761
RF	0.1043	45.2436	0.2153	0.3370	0.5592	0.2840	0.4718
SIGAT	0.1060	**23.3618**	**0.0933**	**0.2486**	**0.6569**	**0.3094**	**0.5759**

Ablation Study. We evaluate the contributions of the graph attention layer construction module with the ablation studies: 1. MLP as the baseline model for 80% training dataset; 2. The number of attentional heads; 3. The number of graph attention layers.

According to Fig. 3, SIGAT outperforms MLP on various metrics. Experimental results show that graph attention performs better in terms of average precision, macro-F1 and micro-F1, and lower in ranking loss and 0/1 error. This shows that the embedded graph attention layer module plays an important role in SIGAT, and this component is effective. Therefore, it indicates that SIGAT integrates the features of symptoms and syndromes through graph representation learning, which further verifies the importance of embedding syndromes in the model for the classification of state elements.

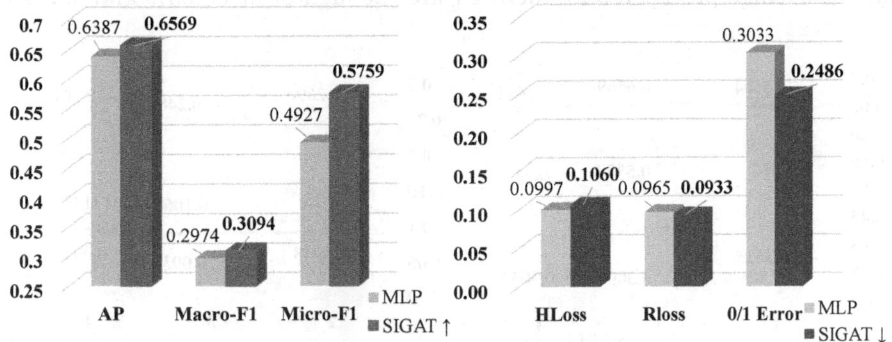

Fig. 3. The effectiveness of SIGAT model compared with MLP.

To learn the graph feature of TCM data and reduce the calculation time, Fig. 4 shows the influence of different attentional heads, that is, K takes different values on the performance of the SIGAT model. The attentional heads K determine how many times the model calculates the data attention weights. The more heads, the more computationally expensive the model is, and the longer it takes. It can be seen from the experimental results that when the number of heads of attentional heads is 4, the performance of the model reaches the optimal value. It indicates that too many heads lead to over-fitting of the network. Not only fails to achieve better results but also increases the amount of calculation and training time.

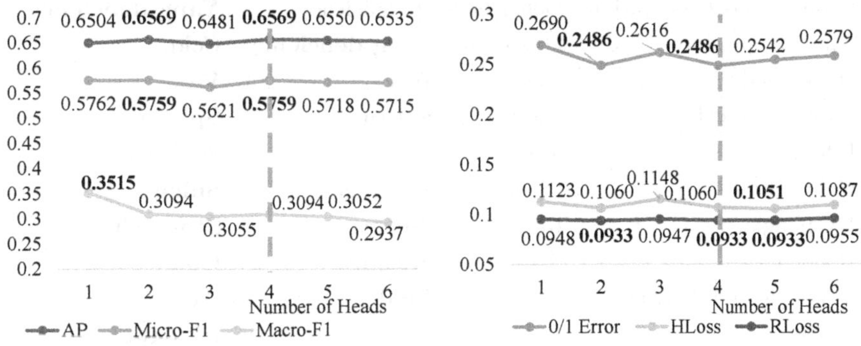

Fig. 4. The influence of the number of attentional heads.

Nodes of the graph attention network collect information from neighbouring nodes. The first layer collects the information of the first-order neighbours, and the second layer collects the information of the second-order neighbours. The experimental results in Fig. 5 show that setting the graph attention layer to 3 is the optimal parameter for SIGAT. The hamming loss, ranking loss, and 0/1 error rates reached the lowest value of 0.1060, 0.0933, and 0.2486 respectively. And the average precision and micro-F1 are the highest at 65.69% and 59.59%.

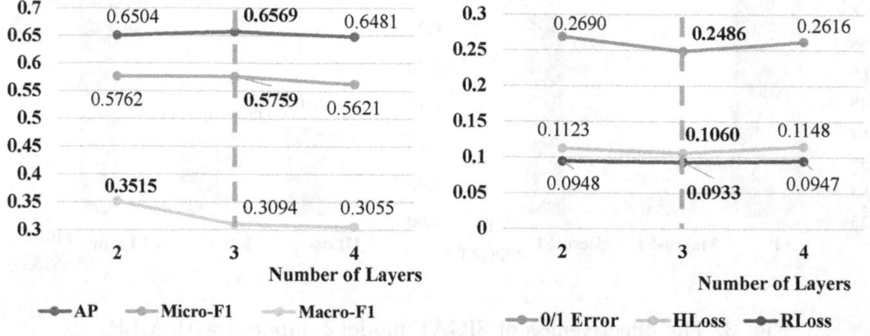

Fig. 5. The influence of the number of graph attention layer.

Case Study. Table 4 shows two prediction cases of SIGAT, the model correctly predicts the bolded state elements. In the first case, three state elements in the label are correct. There is one misreported state element: Qi deficiency. In the second case, four state elements in the label are all predicted by SIGAT correctly. These results suggest that SIGAT has substantial practical value.

Table 4. State elements predicted by SIGAT.

Symptoms	Syndrome	Ground-Truth	Prediction
Spontaneous perspiration, Thin sloppy stool, Heavy body, Aversion to cold, Edema	Deficiency Of spleen And Kidney Yang	Qi deficiency, **Yang deficiency,** **Wet,** **Spleen**	**Yang deficiency,** Cold, **Wet,** **Spleen,** Surface
Cold Limbs, Dysphagia, Headche, Vomiting and diarrhea, Nausea	Phlegm Retention Syndrome	**Stomach,** **Spleen,** **phlegm,** **Cold**	**Spleen,** **Stomach,** **Cold,** Wet, **Phlegm**

5 Conclusion

In this paper, we propose a graph attention network for health state identification based on TCM knowledge, called SIGAT. We define symptoms as nodes and syndrome as edges in this model. In SIGAT, automatic induction of TCM symptoms to state elements is realized with relatively high average precision, macro-F1 score, and micro-F1 score. And we implement state element classification with low hamming loss, coverage, 0/1 error, and ranking loss. The application of graph attention network classification algorithm in TCM health status identification contributes to computer-assisted diagnosis and treatment. In future work, we will consider other better composition methods to achieve a more accurate prediction of state elements, and we will also consider other work such as syndrome classification and herbal medicine recommendations.

Acknowledgments. This work is partially supported by National Natural Science Foundation of China (61972187), Natural Science Foundation of Fujian Province (2020J02024).

References

1. Chen, S., Wang, Y.: Analysis of TCM health management mode with status identification as core. Asia-Pacific Tradit. Med. **15**(11), 165–166 (2019)
2. Fan, H., Zhang, F., Wang, R., Huang, X., Li, Z.: Semi-supervised time series classification by temporal relation prediction. In: Proceedings of the IEEE International Conference on Acoustics, Speech and Signal Processing, pp. 3545–3549 (2021)
3. Fan, H., et al.: Heterogeneous hypergraph variational autoencoder for link prediction. IEEE Trans. Pattern Anal. Mach. Intell. **44**(8), 4125–4138 (2021). https://doi.org/10.1109/TPAMI.2021.3059313
4. Fan, H., Zhang, F., Xi, L., Li, Z., Guanghai, L., Xu, Y.: LeukocyteMask: an automated localization and segmentation method for leukocyte in blood smear images using deep neural networks. J. Biophotonicse 12(7) (2019)
5. Feng, S.: Classical prescriptions syndrome differentiation based on symptomatic response. China J. Tradit. Chinese Med. Pharm. **36**(1), 22–26 (2021)
6. Li, C., Yang, X., Gan, H., Lai, X., Changen, Z., Chen, M.: China journal of traditional Chinese medicine and pharmacy. Asia-Pacific Tradit. Med. **26**(6), 1351–1355 (2011)
7. Liang, W., Lin, X., Yu, J., Min, L., Li, C.: Big database of real world promotes health management of traditional Chinese medicine into artificial intelligence era. China J. Tradit. Chinese Med. Pharm. **33**(4), 1213–1215 (2018)
8. Liu, J., Xie, Y.: Collaborative filtering recommendation algorithm based on graph attention network representation learning. Comput. Syst. Appl. **31**(4), 273–280 (2022)
9. Nie, T.: Research on short text classification based on graph attention networks. Northeast Normal University (2021)
10. Pan, M.: Research on social recommender system based on graph attention network. Northeast Normal University (2021)
11. Shi, Y., Zhou, K., Li, S., Zhou, M., Liu, W.: Heterogeneous graph attention network for food safety risk prediction. J. Food Eng. **323**, 111005 (2022)

12. Song, Z., Li, Y., Li, D., Li, S.: Multi-label classification of legal text with fusion of label relations. Pattern Recogn. Artif. Intell. **35**(2), 185–192 (2022)
13. Tsoumakas, G., Katakis, I., Vlahavas, I.: Mining multi-label data. In: Data Mining and Knowledge Discovery Handbook, pp. 667–685 (2010)
14. Veličković, P., Cucurull, G., Casanova, A., Romero, A., Lio, P., Bengio, Y.: Graph attention networks. In: Proceedings of the International Conference on Learning Representations (2017)
15. Xin, J.: Research of health status identification algorithm based on TCM theory of state. Fujian University of Traditional Chinese Medicine (2021)
16. Xin, J., Li, S., Zhang, J., Lei, H., Candong, L.: Dicovery of identification method of traditional Chinese medicine health status. China J. Tradit. Chinese Med. Pharm. **34**(7), 3151–3153 (2019)
17. Xin, J., Zhang, J., Li, S., Li, C.: Research on multi-label classification methods for the identification of health state in traditional Chinese medicine. China J. Tradit. Chinese Med. Pharm. **34**(9), 3952–3955 (2019)
18. Xu, J., et al.: Rules of traditional Chinese medicine state identification based on artificial intelligence algorithm. J. Tradit. Chinese Med. **61**(3), 204–208 (2020)
19. Zhang, M., Wu, L.: Lift: multi-label learning with label-specific features. IEEE Trans. Pattern Anal. Mach. Intell. **37**(1), 107–120 (2015)
20. Zhao, W., Lu, W., Li, Z., Zhou, C., Fan, H., Yang, Z.: TCM herbal prescription recommendation model based on multi-graph convolutional network. J. Ethnopharmacol. **297**, 115109 (2022)

Flexible Task Splitting Strategy in Aircraft Maintenance Technician Scheduling Based on Swarm Intelligence

Bowen Xue[1], Huifen Zhong[1], Junrui Lu[1,2], Tianwei Zhou[1], and Ben Niu[1](✉)

[1] College of Management, Shenzhen University, Shenzhen 518060, China
drniuben@gmail.com

[2] Greater Bay Area International Institute for Innovation, Shenzhen University, Shenzhen 518060, China

Abstract. Working overtime is a problem that airlines and maintenance technicians pay great attention to and have not been effectively solved. To alleviate this phenomenon as well as save the maintenance cost and time, this paper introduces a flexible task splitting strategy (FTSS) into the original aircraft maintenance technician scheduling (AMTS) model and presents a novel model called AMTS-FTSS. In AMTS-FTSS, one maintenance task can be completed by multiple multi-skilled maintenance technicians. When the maintenance task needs to be completed over time, it can be flexibly split, and the splitting standard is controlled by the flexible time. Finally, ant colony optimization, particle swarm optimization, bacterial foraging optimization, and artificial bee colony algorithms and their variants are used to verify the effectiveness and universality of FTSS. The experimental results show that compared with the AMTS model, AMTS-FTSS can save the maintenance cost and time in most circumstances.

Keywords: Flexible task splitting strategy · Aircraft maintenance technician scheduling · Swarm intelligence algorithm

1 Introduction

Proper scheduling and control of fatigue levels of maintenance technicians are the requirements of the civil aviation administration for airlines, which provides an essential guarantee for the safety and high-quality development of civil aviation [1].

The early literature on aircraft maintenance technician scheduling (AMTS) mainly focused on scheduling maintenance teams, which spanned a long maintenance cycle and did not involve specific maintenance task assignment [2]. Then, Gang et al. [3] refined the aircraft maintenance technician scheduling to assign specific maintenance tasks and simplified the problem to a maintenance task that only needs one maintenance technician to complete. On this basis, Qin et al. [4] and Niu et al. [5] conducted further research. Qin et al. [4] combined maintenance staff scheduling with aircraft allocation to build a two-stage aircraft maintenance joint scheduling model. Niu et al. [5] improved the assignment mode of aircraft maintenance technicians and built a distributed aircraft

Y. Xu et al. (Eds.): ML4CS 2022, LNCS 13655, pp. 15–26, 2023.
https://doi.org/10.1007/978-3-031-20096-0_2

maintenance technician scheduling model. However, few studies can consider the urgent problems in aircraft maintenance technician scheduling, such as overtime work and high fatigue levels of maintenance technicians.

Therefore, based on the research of Niu et al. [5], this paper designs an aircraft maintenance technician scheduling model more suitable for the actual maintenance scenario. In this model, the maintenance technicians have the attribute of multi-skills. One maintenance task is no longer limited by the number of maintenance technicians but can be assigned to multiple maintenance technicians to complete together. In addition, to alleviate the overtime work of maintenance technicians, this paper proposes a flexible task splitting strategy for the scheduling model, namely AMTS-FTSS.

Finally, as the research models in this paper are multi-dimensional, complex, and multi-constraint nonlinear models, this paper uses the swarm intelligence optimization algorithms suitable for NP-hard problems as the solution methods. At the same time, in order to verify the effectiveness of AMTS-FTSS in controlling cost and saving time, this paper applies eight common swarm intelligence algorithms to solve the models, including artificial ant colony optimization (ACO) [6], particle swarm optimization (PSO) [7], comprehensive learning particle swarm optimizer (CLPSO) [8], hybrid firefly and particle swarm optimization (HFPSO) [9], phasor particle swarm optimization (PPSO) [10], bacterial foraging optimization (BFO) [11], bacterial colony optimization (BCO) [12], and artificial bee colony (ABC) [13] algorithms.

The remainder of this paper is organized as follows. Section 2 explains the definitions of aircraft maintenance technician scheduling and proposes the flexible task splitting strategy. The formulations of our proposed model are given in Sect. 3. In Sect. 4, eight swarm intelligence algorithms are briefly introduced, and the encoding scheme is presented. Section 5 displays the experiments and results analysis, after which the whole paper is concluded in Sect. 6.

2 Problem Definition and Flexible Task Splitting Strategy

Aircraft maintenance technician scheduling (AMTS) mainly focuses on the practical assignment of aircraft maintenance technicians for maintenance tasks to save maintenance costs and time. Besides, it is a dynamic process involving aircraft, shift, maintenance task, maintenance technician, etc. The whole scheduling process mainly depends on the completion progress of the maintenance task sequence.

2.1 Problem Description

The execution of aircraft maintenance work is often guided by cost control and time-saving. When an aircraft arrives at the maintenance hangar, it begins to be repaired. Each aircraft has a fixed task sequence, and each maintenance task has requirements for license levels and numbers of maintenance technicians holding each license level. Each aircraft is equipped with an independent maintenance team, including multiple maintenance technicians with multiple license levels. During the scheduling process, technicians shall be assigned to each maintenance task in turn according to the arrival time of each aircraft. The implementation of technician assignment shall be carried out in strict accordance with the requirements of maintenance tasks on the number and license level of technicians. Among them, technicians with higher license levels can replace technicians with lower license levels to complete maintenance tasks.

2.2 Flexible Task Splitting Strategy

In the technician assignment process, different technicians may spend different times completing the same maintenance task. Therefore, the work progress of the task sequence depends on the technician scheduling scheme, and the exact maintenance shift of maintenance tasks cannot be predicted, leading to the technicians working overtime for some complex and time-consuming tasks. In order to alleviate the problem of overtime work, this section proposes a flexible task splitting mechanism. It introduces the technician exchange method on this basis in order to save maintenance time. Then the model can be called an aircraft maintenance technician scheduling model with a flexible task splitting strategy (AMTS-FTSS).

At the end of maintenance shift t, if maintenance task s has not been completed, it is necessary to consider whether task s needs to be split and give the reasonable assignment of maintenance technicians. This kind of tasks can be defined in formula (1), where rt_{ism_1} is the time required for technician m_1 to complete task s of aircraft i, and st_{is} is the start time of task s of aircraft i.

$$rt_{ism_1} > H \cdot t - st_{is}, \forall i \in A, \forall m_1 \in M_i, \forall s \in S_i, \forall t \in T \tag{1}$$

In particular, if the start time of this task is slightly earlier or its estimated end time is slightly later than the end time of shift t, it can be considered not to split this task. In other words, the time threshold range can be set according to the needs of the actual scenario to split the maintenance tasks satisfying formula (1) flexibly.

Then, the time threshold range is set to $[H \cdot t - f, H \cdot t + f]$, where H represents the length of a shift and f is called the flexible time to adjust this range. When a maintenance task spans two shifts and its start time or estimated end time is outside this range, it is necessary to split the maintenance task into subtasks s_1 and s_2. Therefore, the conditions for a flexible task splitting strategy include formulas (2) and (3).

$$st_{is} < H \cdot t - f, \forall i \in A, \forall m_1 \in M_i, \forall s \in S_i, \forall t \in T \tag{2}$$

$$st_{is} + rt_{ism_1} > H \cdot t + f, \forall i \in A, \forall m_1 \in M_i, \forall s \in S_i, \forall t \in T \tag{3}$$

2.3 Technician Assignment Methods

As mentioned in Sect. 2.2, if maintenance task s is split, there will be two subtasks, i.e., s_1 and s_2. The time left for subtask s_1 is fixed, which is represented by lt_{ist}, and the calculation of lt_{ist} is shown in formula (4).

$$lt_{ist} = H \cdot t - st_{is} \tag{4}$$

Specifically, s_1 and s_2 have the same requirements for maintenance technicians as task s. Then, another group of technicians m_2 should be chosen for task s. Generally, the time required for technicians m_2 to complete task s is different from m_1, and it can also be understood that the work efficiencies of technicians m_1 and m_2 are distinctive. Therefore, there may be a case that the maintenance task s does not need to be split when replacing technicians m_1 with m_2, i.e., $rt_{ism_2} + st_{is} \leq H \cdot t + f$.

Except for the above circumstance, in order to save maintenance time, it is necessary to assign technicians m_1 and m_2 to subtasks s_1 and s_2 according to the work efficiency and the estimated maintenance time of task s. Obviously, there are two assignment methods, which are illustrated as follows.

No Technician Exchange Method. With this method, technicians m_1 are assigned to subtask s_1 and technicians m_2 are assigned to subtask s_2. At the end of shift t, when subtask s_1 is finished, the work progress of task s can be represented by lt_{ist}/rt_{ism_1}, then the left work progress for technicians m_2 is $(1 - lt_{ist}/rt_{ism_1})$. After that, the maintenance time of task s with no technician exchange method is:

$$mt_{is}^{0} = lt_{ist} + \left(1 - lt_{ist}/rt_{ism_1}\right) \cdot rt_{ism_2} \tag{5}$$

Technician Exchange Method. With this method, technicians m_2 are assigned to subtask s_1 and technicians m_1 are assigned to subtask s_2. Compared with the no technician exchange method, this method exchanges the sequence of technicians m_1 and m_2. Thus, at the end of shift t, the work progress of task s is lt_{ist}/rt_{ism_2}. Then the left work progress for technicians m_1 is $(1 - lt_{ist}/rt_{ism_2})$. Similarly, the maintenance time of task s with the technician exchange method is shown in formula (6).

$$mt_{is}^{1} = lt_{ist} + \left(1 - lt_{ist}/rt_{ism_2}\right) \cdot rt_{ism_1} \tag{6}$$

Then, by comparing the maintenance time obtained by the above two methods, the method with the shortest maintenance time is selected as the final technician assignment method, and the following assignment principles are obtained. Finally, the flowchart of aircraft maintenance technician scheduling with the flexible task splitting strategy is demonstrated in Fig. 1.

- If $0 < lt_{ist} \leq \frac{rt_{ism_1} \cdot rt_{ism_2}}{rt_{ism_1} + rt_{ism_2}}$, then $mt_{is}^{0} \leq mt_{is}^{1}$, and no technician exchange method is applied, the maintenance time mt_{is} of task s is equal to mt_{is}^{0}.
- If $\frac{rt_{ism_1} \cdot rt_{ism_2}}{rt_{ism_1} + rt_{ism_2}} < lt_{ist} \leq H$, then $mt_{is}^{0} > mt_{is}^{1}$, and the technician exchange method is applied, the maintenance time mt_{is} of task s is equal to mt_{is}^{1}.

3 Model Design and Formulations

In this section, the objective and constraints of the AMTS-FTSS model are given. The variables and their meanings are shown in Table 1.

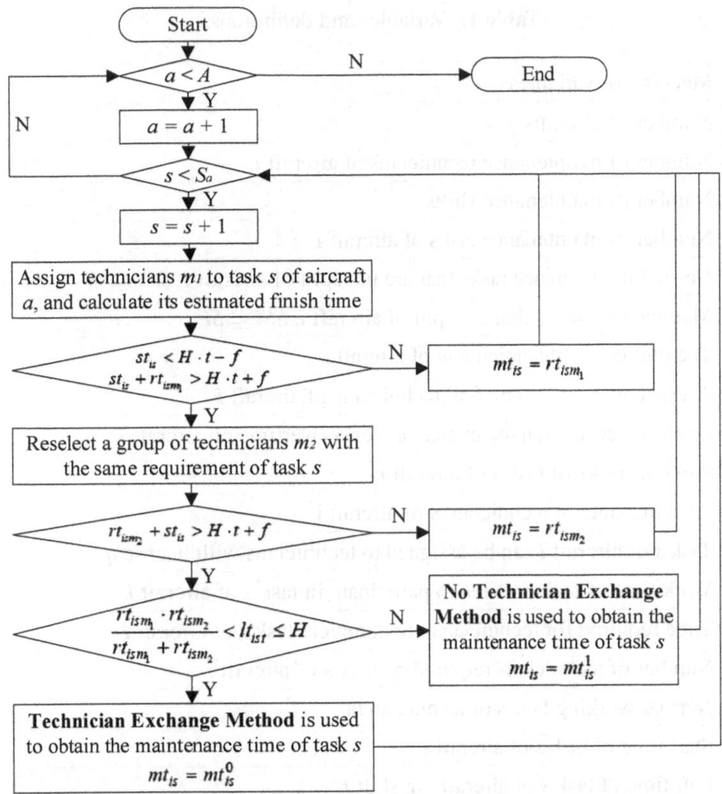

Fig. 1. Flowchart of aircraft maintenance technician scheduling with flexible task splitting strategy.

3.1 Objective Formulation

The optimization objective of this model is to minimize the total cost, including labor cost, overtime cost, and workload fairness cost, as shown in formula (7). Where, wt_{ism} represents the maintenance time of technician m participating in the task s of aircraft i, λ_{im} represents the unit cost of technician m on aircraft i, OC_{im} represents the overtime cost of technician m on aircraft i, and avg_i is the average working time of aircraft i.

$$\min \sum_{i \in A} \left(\sum_{s \in S_i} \sum_{m \in M_i} wt_{ism} \cdot \lambda_{im} + \sum_{m \in M_i} OC_{im} + \frac{1}{|M_i|} \sqrt{\sum_{s \in S_i} \left[\sum_{m \in M_i} kmis \cdot (wt_{ism} - avg_i) \right]^2} \right) \tag{7}$$

3.2 Constraints Formulation

First, as shown in constraints (8) and (9), only the aircrafts parking in the maintenance hangar can be repaired. Maintenance tasks on aircraft that have not arrived or have left

Table 1. Variables and definitions.

Variables	Meaning of variables
A	Number of aircrafts
M_i	Number of maintenance technicians of aircraft i
T	Number of maintenance shifts
Si	Number of maintenance tasks of aircraft i
SNi	Normal maintenance tasks that are not split of aircraft i, $SNi \subseteq Si$
SSi	Maintenance tasks that are split of aircraft i, $SSi \subseteq Si$
λim	The unit cost of technician m of aircraft i
avg_i	Average working time of all technicians of aircraft i
OC_{im}	Overtime cost when technician m works overtime on aircraft i
$PSis$	Previous tasks of task s of aircraft i
$wsim$	Working state of technician m of aircraft i
$Aqis$	Task s of aircraft i can be assigned to technicians with license q
wt_{ism}	Work time of technician m to participate in task s of aircraft i
rt_{ism}	Time required for technician m to complete task s of aircraft i
rm_{is}	Number of technicians required by task s of aircraft i
nm	Normal working hours of technician m
st_{is}	Start time of task s of aircraft i
lt_{ist}	Left time of task s of aircraft i in shift t
f	Flexible time
H	Length of a shift
mt_{is}	Maintenance time of task s of aircraft i
mt_{is}^0, mt_{is}^1	Maintenance time of task s of aircraft i with no technician exchange approach and with technician exchange approach, respectively
AT_i	Arrival time of aircraft i
qm	Whether technician m holding license level q, $q \in \{1, 2, 3\}$
in_i	Whether aircraft i has entered the maintenance hangar
out_i	Whether aircraft i has left the maintenance hangar
$kmis$	Whether technician m participates in task s of aircraft i
tis	Whether task s of aircraft i can be implemented
fis	Whether task s of aircraft i is complicated

the hanger cannot be performed. Then, constraint (10) represents that maintenance tasks can be performed only after their previous maintenance tasks have been finished. Next, constraints (11)–(15) mean that only the maintenance tasks that can be performed can be assigned to maintenance technicians, and the assignment of technicians should not only meet the technician requirements of maintenance tasks, but also consider the limitation of maximum workload. Finally, formula (16) defines the maintenance time of a normal task s of aircraft i. Formula (17) defines the maintenance time of task s of aircraft i which is split.

$$t_{is} \leq 1 - in_i, \forall i \in A, \forall s \in S_i \tag{8}$$

$$t_{is} \leq 1 - out_i, \forall i \in A, \forall s \in S_i \tag{9}$$

$$tis \leq \frac{1}{|PSis|} \cdot \sum_{s' \in PS_{is}} fis', \forall i \in A, \forall s \in S_i \tag{10}$$

$$kmis \leq t_{is}, \forall i \in A, \forall s \in S_i \tag{11}$$

$$kmis \leq wsim, \forall i \in A, \forall m \in M_i, \forall s \in S_i \tag{12}$$

$$kmis \leq qm \cdot Aqis, \forall i \in A, \forall m \in M_i, \forall s \in S_i \tag{13}$$

$$\sum_{m \in M_i} k_{mis} = rm_{is}, \forall i \in A, \forall s \in S_i \tag{14}$$

$$\sum_{s \in S_i} kmis \cdot wt_{ism} \leq nm, \forall i \in A, \forall m \in M_i \tag{15}$$

$$mt_{is} = k_{mis} \cdot rt_{ism}, \forall i \in A, \forall m \in M_i, \forall s \in SN_i \tag{16}$$

$$mt_{is} = \begin{cases} k_{mis} \cdot mt_{is}^0, \text{ if } 0 < lt_{ist} \leq \dfrac{rt_{ism_1} \cdot rt_{ism_2}}{rt_{ism_1} + rt_{ism_2}} \\ k_{mis} \cdot mt_{is}^1, \text{ if } \dfrac{rt_{ism_1} \cdot rt_{ism_2}}{rt_{ism_1} + rt_{ism_2}} < lt_{ist} \leq H \end{cases}, \forall i \in A, \forall m_1, m_2 \in M_i, \forall s \in SS_i \tag{17}$$

4 Swarm Intelligence Algorithms and Solution Encoding

This section briefly introduces several representativeswarm intelligence algorithms and gives the encoding scheme used to connect the mathematical model with the solution algorithms.

4.1 Swarm Intelligence Algorithms

Swarm intelligence algorithms mainly simulate the social behaviors of natural organisms, such as the foraging behavior of ant colony, bacteria colony and bird colony, and the honey-collecting behavior of bees. Common swarm intelligence algorithms include artificial ant colony optimization (ACO) algorithm, particle swarm optimization (PSO) algorithm, bacterial foraging optimization (BFO) algorithm, bee colony (ABC) algorithm, etc.

Ant Colony Optimization. Dorigo et al. [6] first proposed ant colony optimization algorithm by simulating the path-finding behavior of ants. In this algorithm, the information interaction between ant individuals is carried out through the pheromones, and the optimal solution is found through a positive feedback mechanism.

Particle Swarm Optimization. Inspired by the regularity of bird predation behavior, Kennedy et al. [7] proposed the particle swarm optimization algorithm, which achieves the swarm optimal through collective cooperation. Following Kennedy, a series of improved PSO algorithms have been put forward, e.g., CLPSO [8], HFPSO [9], and PPSO [10].

Bacterial Foraging Optimization. Bacterial foraging optimization algorithm is designed by Passino [11], which imitates the foraging behavior of E. Coli in the human intestine. It mainly includes three operators, i.e., chemotaxis, reproduction, and extinction. On this basis, Niu et al. [12] presented the bacterial colony optimization (BCO) algorithm.

Artificial Bee Colony Optimization. Artificial bee colony algorithm was proposed by Karaboga [13] based on the honey collection behavior of bee colony. In this algorithm, the bees carry out different activities and realize the information exchange of the bee colony, so as to find the optimal solution to the problem.

4.2 Encoding Scheme

From Sect. 4.1, we can see that the swarm intelligence algorithms often realize the optimizing process through continuously updating individual positions in the swarm. Therefore, an encoding scheme is supposed to be designed to realize the transformation from individual positions to technician assignment. Figure 2(a) gives the initial position of an individual, where the value of each dimension is between 0 and 1. Figure 2(b) indicates the encoding scheme for the model parts, where the gray parts represent unqualified technicians, and the corresponding dimensions are set to "0"; The blue parts mean the technicians selected according to the random principle, and the corresponding dimensions are set to "1".

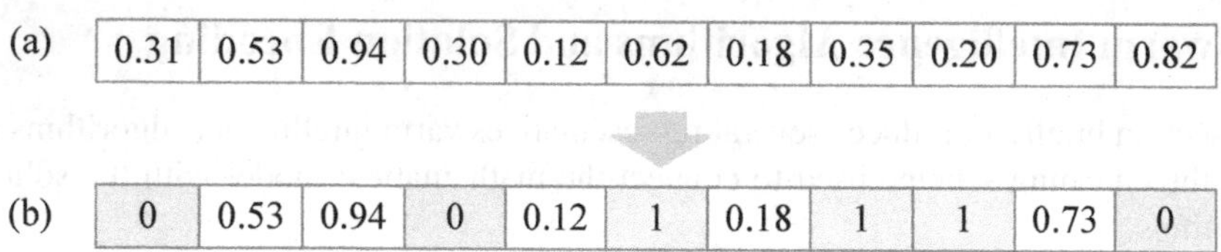

Fig. 2. Encoding scheme. (Color figure online)

5 Experiments and Comparisons

To prove the effectiveness of flexible task splitting strategy in aircraft maintenance technician scheduling model, this section makes a comparative verification using eight swarm intelligence algorithms.

5.1 Experimental Settings

The simulation data of our experiments comes from the enterprise research, including the number of aircrafts, the arrival time of each aircraft, the number of maintenance technicians at all levels equipped for each aircraft, and the number of maintenance tasks for each aircraft, as shown in Table 2. Each maintenance shift lasts 8 h, and the first shift of a day starts at 00:00. The time required for each technician to complete a maintenance task follows a random distribution between 0–6.5 h. The flexible time f is set to 0.2 h.

Table 2. Experimental simulation data.

A	AT_i	M_i	S_i
A1	4:00	13 (5, 6, 2)	6
A2	5:15	14 (3, 5, 6)	9
A3	8:00	8 (3, 3, 2)	4
A4	9:36	9 (4, 3, 2)	4
A5	10:00	11 (2, 4, 5)	7
A6	12:00	9 (4, 3, 2)	3
A7	16:00	11 (3, 5, 3)	8

Then, this paper uses eight algorithms, i.e., ACO, PSO, CLPSO, HFPSO, PPSO, BFO, BCO, and ABC, to compare AMTS and AMTS-FTSS models based on the same data. The population size of eight algorithms is set to 50 with a maximum fitness evaluation time of 2000. The detailed parameter setting of each algorithm is as follows.

- In ACO, $Q = 1$, $\alpha = 0.3$, $\rho = 0.1$.
- In PSO, $c_1 = c_2 = 2$, $v_{max} = 0.8$, $w = 0.9$.
- In CLPSO and PPSO, $v_{max} = 100$, $v_{min} = -100$.
- In HFPSO, $c_1 = c_2 = 1.49445$, $v_{max} = 1$.
- In BFO, $N_c = 100$, $N_s = 4$, $N_{re} = 5$, $N_{ed} = 2$, $P_{ed} = 0.25$.
- In BCO, $N_c = 100$, $N_s = 4$, $P_{ed} = 0.25$, $C_{start} = 0.2$, $C_{end} = 0.01$.
- In ABC, $a = 1$, $L = 13920$.

5.2 Experiments and Results

In order to verify the effectiveness of the flexible task splitting strategy in the aircraft maintenance technician scheduling concerning cost controlling, ACO, PSO, CLPSO, HFPSO, PPSO, BFO, BCO, and ABC algorithms are applied to both AMTS and AMTS-FTSS models. Figure 3 presents the convergence curves of the eight algorithms on the average total cost in AMTS and AMTS-FTSS models. Table 3 gives the optimal solutions of eight algorithms on both the total cost and the maintenance time in AMTS and AMTS-FTSS models.

From Fig. 3 and Table 3, it can be seen that for the AMTS model, these swarm intelligence algorithms and their variants have similar effects on problem-solving. While in the AMTS-FTSS model, the performance gap between different algorithms increases. Among those eight algorithms, ACO is the best in cost control, followed by BFO and CLPSO, and ABC is the worst. Besides, the maintenance time in the AMTS-FTSS model is shorter than that in the AMTS model in most cases, which is optimized by the technician assignment methods. Generally, using the AMTS-FTSS model can lower total cost than the AMTS model while shortening the maintenance time.

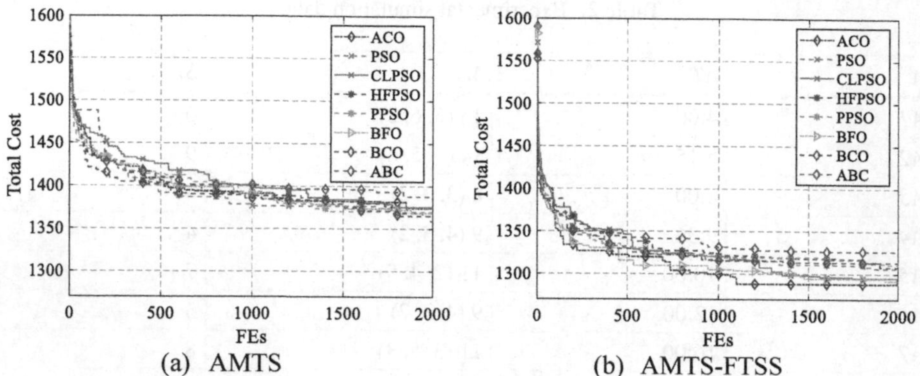

Fig. 3. Convergence curves of eight algorithms in AMTS and AMTS-FTSS models.

Table 3. Optimal solutions of obtained by eight algorithms.

Algorithms	Total cost			Average maintenance time		
	AMTS	AMTS-FTSS	Gap	AMTS	AMTS-FTSS	Gap
ACO	1281.00	1235.57	−3.55%	15.14	13.39	−11.57%
PSO	1303.18	1282.25	−1.61%	14.72	13.96	−5.20%
CLPSO	1316.60	1230.45	−6.54%	14.91	13.98	−6.20%
HFPSO	1306.54	1272.72	−2.59%	14.31	14.14	−1.20%
PPSO	1313.09	1279.95	−2.52%	15.43	13.88	−10.05%
BFO	1306.75	1196.54	−8.43%	14.81	12.90	−12.85%
BCO	1308.31	1278.30	−2.29%	13.66	14.16	3.66%
ABC	1290.95	1286.07	−0.38%	15.13	14.75	−2.51%

Then, another six groups of experiments are designed to verify the impact of different flexible time values on the effectiveness of the flexible task splitting strategy. The flexible time values of each group of experiments are $f \in \{0.0, 0.1, 0.2, 0.3, 0.4, 0.5\}$. Each group of experiments is run by eight algorithms 10 times, respectively. The average optimal total costs obtained by each algorithm in each group of experiments are recorded, as shown in Fig. 4. It can be concluded that with the increase of f, the total cost shows a fluctuating upward trend. However, it has different performances in different algorithms. For example, when PSO and HFPSO algorithms are used, the fluctuation ranges are large, while when BFO, BCO, and PPSO are used, the fluctuation ranges are small.

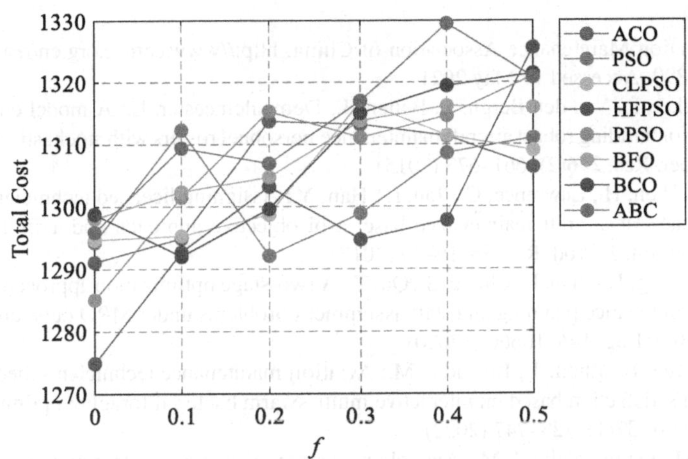

Fig. 4. Impact of flexible time on the total cost.

6 Conclusions

This paper improves the aircraft maintenance technician scheduling model with a flexible task splitting strategy. In this strategy, some complex and time-consuming maintenance tasks are split into two or more subtasks. Then, a flexible time is set to adjust the time range of normal tasks, and tasks need to be split. Besides, a technician assignment method is designed to control the maintenance time. By verifying eight mainstream swarm intelligence algorithms, the experimental results indicate that our proposed AMTS-FTSS model can effectively reduce the total cost and the maintenance time. Additionally, flexible time can help the managers conveniently adjust the total cost in a small range according to their maintenance demand.

In future work, we will focus on the swarm intelligence algorithms that perform well in the improved model from the experimental results, including BFO, ACO, etc., and present an algorithm more suitable for solving the AMTS-FTSS model.

Acknowledgment. The study is supported by The National Natural Science Foundation of China (Nos. 71971143, 61703102), Major Project of Natural Science Foundation of China (No. 71790615), Integrated Project of Natural Science Foundation of China (No. 91846301), Social Science Youth Foundation of Ministry of Education of China (Nos. 21YJC630052, 21YJC630181), Key Research Foundation of Higher Education of Guangdong Provincial Education Bureau (No. 2019KZDXM030), Natural Science Foundation of Guangdong Province (Nos. 2020A1515010749, 2020A1515010752), Guangdong Basic and Applied Basic Research

Foundation (No. 2019A1515110401), and Natural Science Foundation of Shenzhen City (No. JCYJ20190808145011259), Guangdong Province Innovation Team (No. 2021WCXTD002).

References

1. Civil Aviation Maintenance Association of China. http://www.camac.org.cn/read.php?cid=7&id=11899. Accessed 17 May 2021
2. De Bruecker, P., Van den Bergh, J., Beliën, J., Demeulemeester, E.: A model enhancement heuristic for building robust aircraft maintenance personnel rosters with stochastic constraints. Eur. J. Oper. Res. **246**(2), 661–673 (2015)
3. Gang, C., Wen, H., Lawrence, C., Tan, L., Han, Y.: Assigning licenced technicians to maintenance tasks at aircraft maintenance base: a bi-objective approach and a Chinese airline application. Int. J. Prod. Res. **55**, 19–20 (2017)
4. Qin, Y., Zhang, J., Chan, F., Chung, S., Qu, T.: A two-stage optimization approach for aircraft hangar maintenance planning and staff assignment problems under MRO outsourcing mode. Comput. Ind. Eng. **146**, 106607 (2020)
5. Niu, B., Xue, B., Zhou, T., Kustudic, M.: Aviation maintenance technician scheduling with personnel satisfaction based on interactive multi-swarm bacterial foraging optimization. Int. J. Intell. Syst. **37**(1), 723–747 (2022)
6. Dorigo, M., Gambardella, L.M.: Ant colony system: a cooperative learning approach to the traveling salesman problem. IEEE Trans. Evol. Comput. **1**, 53–66 (1997)
7. Kennedy, J., Eberhart, R.: Particle swarm optimization. In: Proceedings of ICNN 1995 - International Conference on Neural Networks, vol. 4, pp. 1942–1948. IEEE (1995)
8. Liang, J.J., Qin, A.K., Suganthan, P.N., Baskar, S.: Comprehensive learning particle swarm optimizer for global optimization of multimodal functions. IEEE Trans. Evol. Comput. **10**(3), 281–295 (2006)
9. Aydilek, I.: A hybrid firefly and particle swarm optimization algorithm for computationally expensive numerical problems. Appl. Soft Comput. **66**, 232–249 (2018)
10. Ghasemi, M., Akbari, E., Rahimnejad, A., Razavi, S.E., Ghavidel, S., Li, L.: Phasor particle swarm optimization: a simple and efficient variant of PSO. Soft. Comput. **23**(19), 9701–9718 (2019)
11. Passino, K.: Biomimicry of bacterial foraging for distributed optimization and control. IEEE Control Syst. Mag. **22**(3), 52–67 (2002)
12. Niu, B., Wang, H.: Bacterial colony optimization. Discrete Dyn. Nat. Soc. **2012**, 698057 (2012)
13. Karaboga, D.: An idea based on honey bee swarm for numerical optimization. Technical report-TR06, Erciyes University, Engineering Faculty, Computer Engineering Department, Turkey (2005)

Privacy Preserving CSI Fingerprint Device-Free Localization

Tianxin Huang[1], Lingjun Zhao[2], Zeyang Dai[3], Liang Lin[1], and Huakun Huang[1,4](✉)

[1] School of Computer Science and Cyber Engineering, Guangzhou University, Guangzhou, China
huanghuakun@gzhu.edu.cn
[2] School of Software Engineering, Sun Yat-sen University, Zhuhai, China
[3] Greater Bay Area Institue of Precision Medicine, Guangzhou, China
[4] Guangdong Provincial Key Laboratory of Building Energy Efficiency and Application Technologies, Guangzhou University, Guangzhou, China

Abstract. Device-Free Localization (DFL) method based on wireless signal fingerprint is a mainstream indoor location method at present. The main concerns in this field are location accuracy and complexity of computing, while the problem of privacy protection is easily neglected. Since the leakage of wireless signal data is likely leading to the leakage of location information, this paper proposes a privacy-preserving Channel State Information(CSI) fingerprint device-free localization method based on federated learning(PPDFL). Through federated learning, each client trains a local model using the collected local data and then transmits the trained parameters to the server. The server consolidates these parameters and then distributes the resulting parameters to each client for local model's updating. After several rounds of training and updating, each client ends up with a fully trained model. Compared with the existing DFL methods, this method would not share the data of each client, and only transmits model parameters between server and client, thus achieving the effect of privacy protection. Several experiments are performed to prove the effectiveness of the proposed PPDFL.

Keywords: Device-free localization · Channel state information · Privacy preserving · Federated learning

1 Introduction

With the development of the internet of things, needs of localization-related services are rising. It has been arising extensive attention to indoor localization from both academia and industry. In the past localization technologies, targets often need to wear hardware devices of certain specifications for effective localization, such as GPS, RFID [1] and Bluetooth [2]. In some real scenarios, such as people trapped in a fire, burglars breaking into homes, elderly people in need of care, device-based localization is difficult to implement. In recent years, it has been

Y. Xu et al. (Eds.): ML4CS 2022, LNCS 13655, pp. 27–39, 2023.
https://doi.org/10.1007/978-3-031-20096-0_3

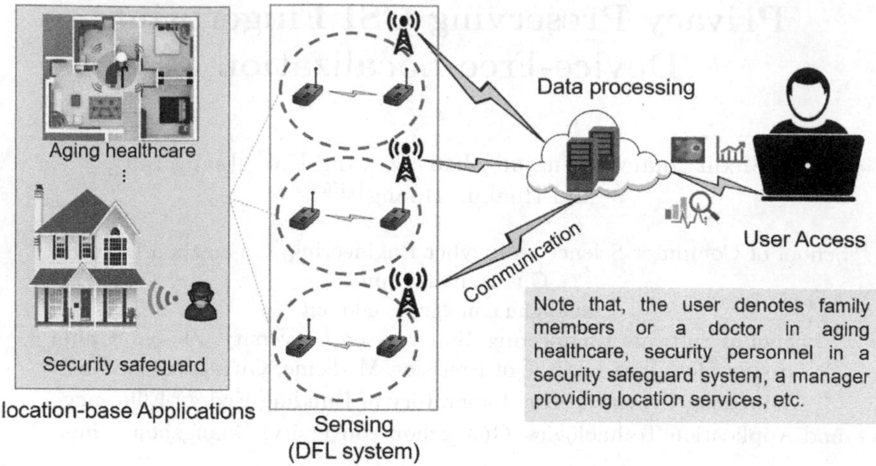

Fig. 1. Basic model of a DFL system based on wireless sensing networks

found that a target without any localization device can be located by using the influence of the target on the surrounding wireless signals. As described in Fig. 1, use sensor to acquire data in the wireless signal network, and then the collected data is sent to the server for data processing. After data processing, location information can be obtained for user access. This technique is called device-free localization (DFL), DFL technology has gradually become a research hotspot in the field of localization [3–5].

Received Signal Strength (RSS) is a kind of information extracted from the wireless signal, which can express the attenuation of the wireless signal in the propagation process. RSS is easy to obtain and has low requirements for the hardware equipment. At present, there have been many studies to implement DFL using RSS [6–8]. [6] introduced a new Bayesian filter that solves the divergence problem of the traditional Bayesian filter and constructs a localization system with both high localization accuracy and robustness. [7] obtained the principal components of the measured RSS data by Principal Component Analysis (PCA), overcomes the problem of data imbalance, and calculated the probability of the target at each reference point based on a logistic regression model. Zhao et al. [8] constructs the RSS information into an image, which converts the DFL problem into an image classification problem. They designed a three-layer convolutional autoencoder neural network to perform unsupervised feature extraction on the original signal and classification. This system achieves high localization accuracy and strong robustness to noisy data.

Although, the current RSS-based DFL can achieve high localization accuracy in simple environments, the performance of RSS-based DFL will decline significantly in a complex indoor environment due to the influence of the multipath effect and shadow fading [9–11]. Fortunately, researchers can obtain CSI from commercial network cards by modifying wireless network card drivers [12,13].

CSI is more fine-grained than RSS, which can represent the channel state of each sub-carrier of wireless link in the Orthogonal Frequency Division Multiplexing (OFDM) system. In complex indoor environments, CSI can better represent the changes in wireless links.Wang et al. proposed DeepFi [14]. DeepFI trains the weights of the network as fingerprints and uses probabilistic methods to predict target locations, which can effectively reduce localization errors. Zhou et al. applied Deep Neural Network (DNN) for CSI fingerprint localization [15]. It employed DNN to model the relationship between CSI fingerprint and location coordinates of the positioning area, and then realized accurate localization through regression method. Dang et al. [16] adopt Wavelet Domain Denoising for CSI amplitude, and use deconvolution and linear transform to remove the random offset of CSI phase, which enables CSI data to more fully reflect localization characteristics.

Through the use of artificial neural network, CSI fingerprint based DFL can achieve accurate localization. Meanwhile, training neural networks and building a fingerprint database need to collect a large amount of CSI data. Generally, centralized learning is adopted for model training, where the WiFi devices would not train the neural network model locally after collecting CSI fingerprint. Instead, the data is transferred to the centralized server. The server collects a large number of CSI fingerprints and trains a global model. This kind of approach has significant communication costs and potential data leakage risks.

With the development of DFL technology, data privacy issues related to DFL become very important [17]. If someone steals a user's CSI information, it is highly likely that the user's location information will be leaked through DFL technology. For solving these problems, we propose a CSI fingerprint localization system based on federated learning [18]. There are multiple clients in the system for CSI data collection. Each client uses the local-collected data samples to train the model and transmits the model parameters to the server after the training. The server consolidates all the parameters passed by the client and comes up with a global model. Finally, each client updates the local model according to the parameters of the global model. Through multiple rounds of training, integration and updating, each client can get a local model with high evaluation accuracy. Because there is no data sharing among clients and server in the whole training procedure, thus protecting the location information.

In addition to privacy protection, this method can also solve the problems of poor data quality and unbalanced sample quantity. Poor sample quality means that the client only collects CSI samples from some locations, this scenario is very common in practical applications. Due to the missing of samples in some locations, the accuracy of the model trained by the client would be limited. Unbalanced sample quantity means that the client collects a large number of samples from some locations and a small number of samples from other locations. In both scenarios, the proposed method achieves good results. When the server integrates all the model parameters, the database of each client will complement each other. Through the cooperation of clients, the influence of poor quality of samples and unbalanced sample quantity can be weakened, and each client in the system can obtain a well-trained model.

The major contributions of this article are summarized as follows:

- We propose a privacy-preserving DFL(PPDFL) system based on CSI fingerprint and federated learning. The server would not obtain the overall data fingerprint database, but integrates the models from each client and transmits it to each client to prevent user data leakage thus achieving the effect of privacy protection.
- We conducted experiments in real experimental scenarios and collected a large amount of CSI data to construct our data set. Experiments are also performed to evaluated the effectiveness of our proposed method.
- Through experiments, it is verify that the PPDFL system can still achieve high accuracy even under specific conditions, including unbalanced sample quantity and poor quality of samples, i.e., samples missing in some locations.

The remainder of the paper is organized as follows. Section 2 introduces some theories and our proposed system model. Section 3 conducts the performance evaluation. Finally, Sect. 4 shows the conclusion of this study.

2 Theories and System

2.1 Channel State Information

OFDM is a kind of multi carrier modulation. It transmits signals through multiple subcarriers, and the signals on each subcarrier have corresponding signal strength and phase. CSI can represent the channel state of each subcarrier in wireless link, including multipath effect, signal scattering and shadow fading, etc. At present, CSI can be obtained on commercial wireless network cards by modifying network interface card driver. In this way, amplitude and phase information in the subcarrier can be easily obtained.

Compared with RSS, CSI is more sensitive to environmental changes. In an OFDM system, the WiFi channel model can be defined as follows:

$$\vec{Y} = CSI \cdot \vec{X} + \vec{N}, \tag{1}$$

where $\vec{Y}$ represents the received signal vector, $\vec{X}$ represents the sent information vector, $\vec{N}$ represents the additive White Gaussian noise, and CSI represents the channel frequency response.

The channel frequency response of the subcarrier is a complex value, defined as follows:

$$CSI_i = |CSI_i| e^{j \angle CSI_i}, \tag{2}$$

where $|CSI_i|$ represents the amplitude of the i-th subcarrier, and $\angle CSI_i$ represents the phase value of the i-th subcarrier.

2.2 Artificial Neural Network

In our DFL system, several reference points would be selected in the experimental area, and each reference point represents a potential position. In the off-line phase, CSI data are collected when the target stands at each reference point, and CSI fingerprint database is constructed. In the on-line testing phase, CSI test data is collected in real time, and the collected CSI test data is employed to compared with the fingerprint database. Deterministic or probabilistic methods are used to find the fingerprint most similar to the test data, so as to obtain the location of the positioning target. According to the characteristics of the data, the problem of fingerprint comparison can be transformed into a classification problem, and artificial neural network can be well qualified for this task.

We design a three layers neural network. CSI data is taken as the input of the neural network, as in general cases, the output of one layer is employed as the input of the next layer to perform nonlinear mapping calculation of features:

$$A_s = f\left(\boldsymbol{wx} + \boldsymbol{b}\right), \tag{3}$$

where s is the encoding result of the s-th sample, $\boldsymbol{w}$ and $\boldsymbol{b}$ represent the weight and bias of the connection respectively, and x represents the input from the previous layer. $f(\cdot)$ represents a nonlinear activation function, and rectified linear unit(ReLu) is used as the activation function in our system. ReLu is defined as follows, with z representing the input:

$$f\left(\boldsymbol{z}\right) = max\left(0, \boldsymbol{z}\right) \tag{4}$$

In the classification stage, softmax is used as a classifier to estimate the probability of each category. In our work, each category corresponds to each reference point in the experimental area. Cross-entropy loss is used as the loss function.

$$E\left(\boldsymbol{w}, \boldsymbol{b}\right) = \frac{1}{N}\sum_{i=1}^{N} y_i \times log\left(y_i'\left(\boldsymbol{w}, \boldsymbol{b}\right)\right) \tag{5}$$

$\boldsymbol{w}$ and $\boldsymbol{b}$ represent network parameters, y_i and y_i' represent real label of the samples and prediction results of the model, respectively. The above equation shows the error between the predicted results and the labels. By minimizing the loss function through stochastic gradient descent(SGD) and back propagation algorithms, the parameters of the network can be optimized and the prediction accuracy of the network can be improved to the optimal or local optimal.

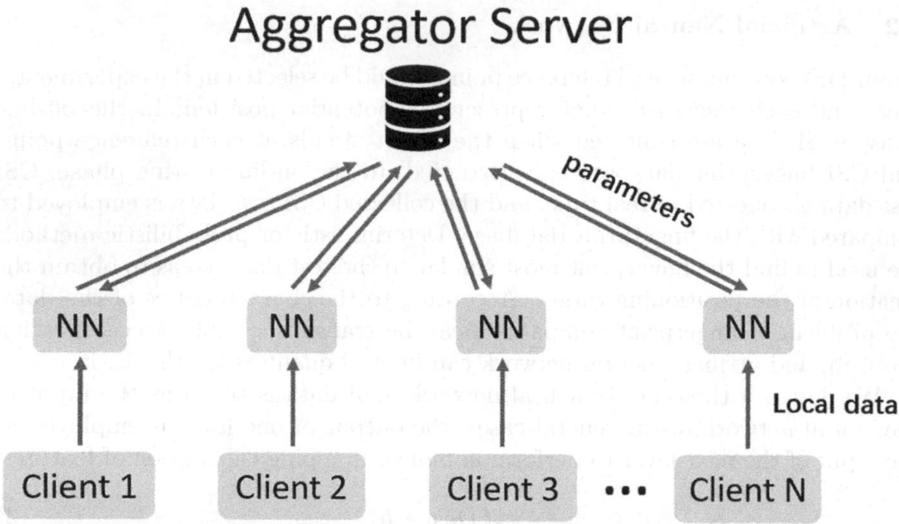

Fig. 2. The basic structure of our system, NN represents the local model of each client.

2.3 Federated Learning

The localization scheme mentioned in Sect. 2.2 employ centralized training in the server. In detail, the neural network model is trained on the server and then distributed to each client after training process is completed. Although such a scheme can achieve good localization accuracy, the system is implemented under a centralized management structure, it requires frequent data transmission between the server and each client. Therefore, there is a communication burden and a certain risk of leaking client data.

Federated Learning Framework. What we propose is a distributed learning method that can protect privacy of user data. Figure 2 represents the basic structure of our system, which includes three clients and one server. In this figure, each client trains a local model with their local data. After completing a round of learning, all the clients send their local trained models to the server. Server integrates the received models to come up with a global model, and then distributed the global one to each client. Finally, each client replaces the local model with the global model. This training process will be repeated for several rounds until the model converges. To be specific, each training round consists of the following four steps:

(a) First, each client has an independent data set, they separately train their local models according to Eq. (3) and (4). In each local model, weight parameters are updated according to the gradient $\nabla \mathbf{g_L}$, which is calculated as:

$$\nabla \mathbf{g_L} = \frac{\delta E(\mathbf{W})}{\delta \mathbf{W}}, \tag{6}$$

Algorithm 1. PPDFL

Input: Real time signal of CSI
Output: Target position
Initialize the server site to wait for collecting local models when r = 0
while $r \leq T$ **and** do not converge **do**
    Train local model in each client according to Eq. (3) and Eq. (4)
    $\nabla \mathbf{g}_L \leftarrow \frac{\delta E(\mathbf{W})}{\delta \mathbf{W}}$ /* Calculate local gradient
    $W' = W - \eta \nabla \mathbf{g}_L$ /* Update the local model
    Send W' from each client to server for updating the global model
    $W_s = \frac{1}{n}\sum_{i=1}^{n} W'_i$ /* Update global model
    $W_c = W_s$ /* Update local model
end while
Evaluate target location according to the trained models

$$W' = W - \eta \nabla \mathbf{g}_L, \tag{7}$$

where W is the weight before the update, W' denotes the updated weight, and η denotes the learning rate.

(b) After updating the local model weight parameters, each client sends the weight parameters to the server.

(c) The server integrates all the model weight parameters uploaded by client and creates a global weight parameter by following the process described below:

$$W_s = \frac{1}{n}\sum_{i=1}^{n} W'_i, \tag{8}$$

where W_s denotes the weight of the server global model, W'_i is weight of the i-th client's local model, n is the number of clients.

(d) When the client receives the global weight parameters sent by the server, it replaces the local model weight parameters with the received global ones. The parameters are updated as follows:

$$W_c = W_s, \tag{9}$$

where W_c represents the weight parameter of the updated local model of the client.The pseudocode of the system is shown in Algorithm 1.

3 Performance Evaluation

3.1 Experimental Configurations

We conducted the experiment in a 4m × 5m living room. Fig 3 illustrates the schematic diagram of the experimental environment. As shown in this figure, we selected 26 reference points in the experimental scene, with a distance of 0.5m between each reference point. Two MiniPCs equipped with Intel5300 network card were used, one for sending WIFI signals and the other for receiving WIFI

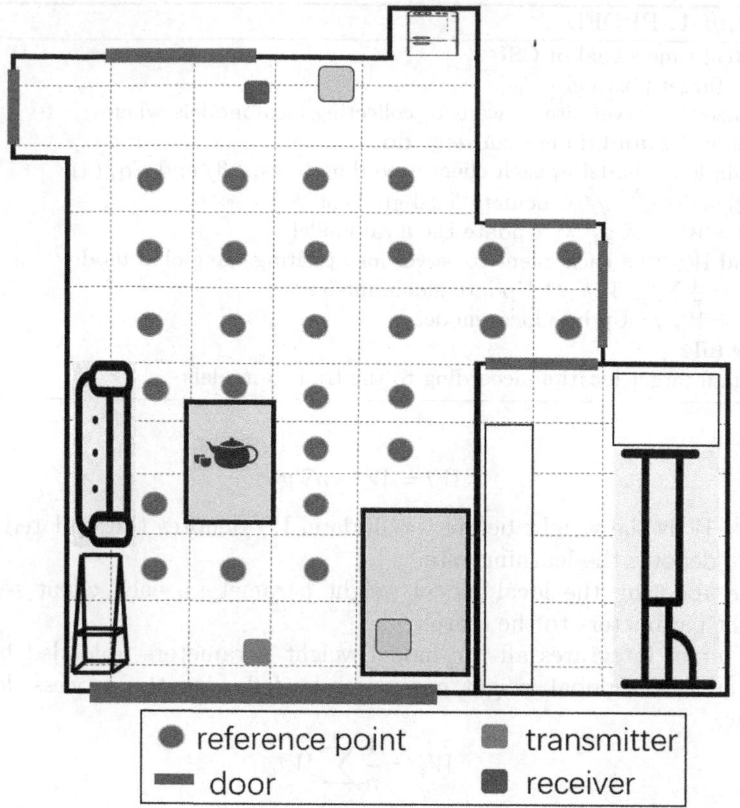

Fig. 3. Schematic diagram of the experimental environment

signals, as shown in Fig. 4 and Fig. 5. By placing targets at each reference point for CSI data collection, we established a CSI data set containing reference points of all locations.

The experimental scenario contains a total of 26 reference points, which means that dataset contains samples of 26 categories. To simulate the scenario of poor data quality, we built different database for each of the three clients, so that each client lacked some categories of samples. Taking the number of sample categories lacked on the client as variable, in this paper, the experiment is conducted when each client lacks samples from 8, 10, 12, 14 and 16 categories.

In the case of unbalanced sample quantity, each client has samples of all categories, but the number of samples for each category is random. To simulated this scenario, in the following experiments, 1–10 samples are randomly selected from each category to build the local sample database for each client.

Comparison methods: (1) Local training. Clients construct a local sample database, and trains a neural network model using this database; (2) Centralized learning. Clients collect CSI data and transmit it to server. And server uses all

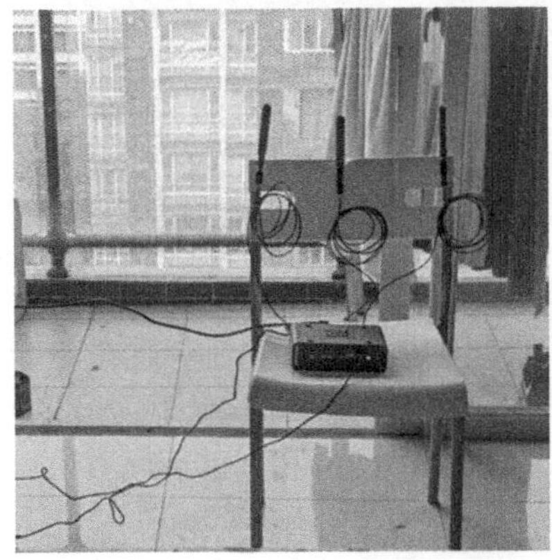
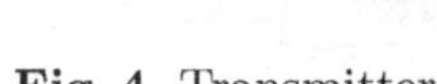

Fig. 4. Transmitter

Fig. 5. Receiver and monitor

the data sent by clients to construct a sample database and trains a neural network model using this database.

Metric: We use localization accuracy to evaluate the effectiveness of our proposed system. Localization accuracy is defined as the percentage of correct localization results to all localization results.

3.2 Experimental Results and Discussion

To demonstrate the superior performance of the proposed PPDFL, we performed experiments on data with poor quality and data with unbalanced quantity.

Experiments on Poor-quality Data. Figure 6(a) to Fig. 6(c) show the evaluation accuracy comparison with different training rounds on the proposed PPDFL, centralized learning and local learning, i.e., models trained by client 1, client 2 and client 3, respectively. Note that the results are obtained under the condition of poor sample quality, where 8, 12 and 16 categories of data samples are missing. It is obvious that when the missing number of categories is less than 12, almost half of the whole categories, the proposed PPDFL could obtain similar or equal accuracy of the centralized learning. Moreover, our proposal could always perform much better than local learning, no matter model trained by client 1, client 2 or client 3.

To further illustrate the performance of the PPDFL on poor-quality data, we summarized all the comparison results in Table 1. When the number of missing categories in the client sample database is 8, the federated learning method proposed by us can achieve 100% accuracy, which is consistent with the accuracy of centralized learning and about 30% higher than the accuracy of local training. When 10 categories and 12 categories are missing, the accuracy of federated learning is similar with centralized learning, and about 39% and 42% higher than

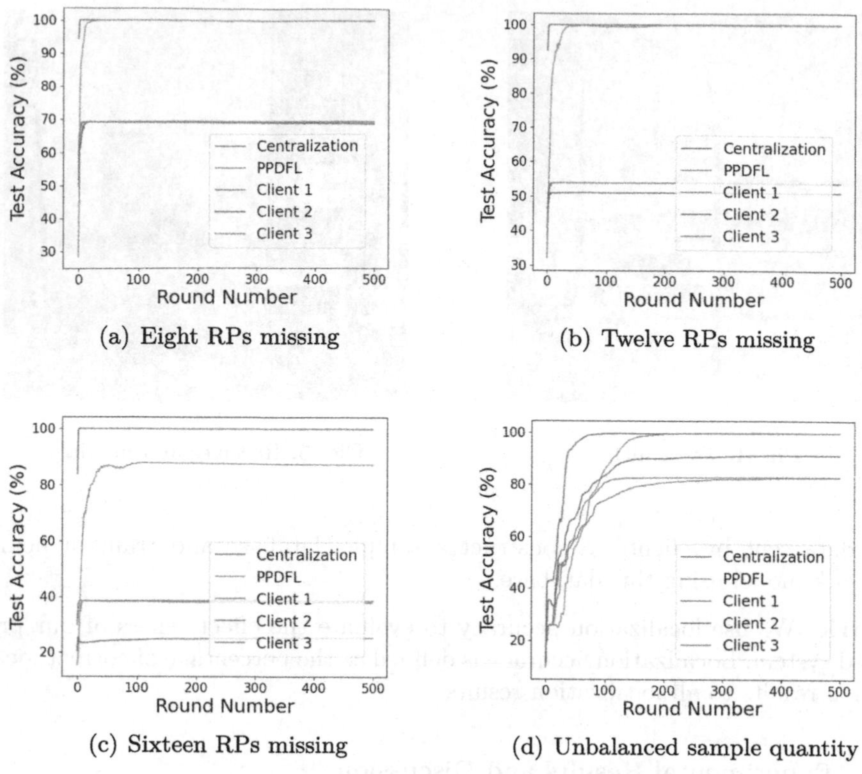

(a) Eight RPs missing

(b) Twelve RPs missing

(c) Sixteen RPs missing

(d) Unbalanced sample quantity

Fig. 6. Accuracy comparison on PPDFL, centralized learning, and local learning with different training round under the condition of poor sample quality and unbalanced sample quantity. Figure 6(a)-6(c) show the evaluation accuracy when 8, 12 and 16 sample categories are missing in the case of poor sample quality. Figure 6(d) represents the evaluation accuracy in the case of unbalanced sample quantity. Note: RP is short for reference point.

local training, respectively. When 14 categories and 16 categories are missing, the accuracy of federated learning dropped to 96.85% and 89.08%, respectively, about 51% and 42% higher than local training. It can be proved that in the case of poor data quality, the proposed system can complement each client sample database, so as to obtain high recognition accuracy. However, if the number of missing categories is too many, the performance of federated learning will decline sharply, which shows that this complementary effect is limited.

Experiments on Unbalance-Quantity Data. Figure 6(d) shows the evaluation accuracy comparison with different training rounds on the proposed PPDFL, centralized learning and local learning. Different with the aforementioned figures, this figure shows the results obtained under the condition of unbalanced number of data samples. It is clear that the centralized learning could always get the highest localization accuracy of 100% even the training round is

Table 1. Accuracy comparison on PPDFL, centralized learning, and local learning under the condition of each client lacking samples of 8, 10, 12, 14 and 16 categories.

	8	10	12	14	16
Centralization	**100%**	**100%**	**100%**	**100%**	**100%**
PPDFL	**100%**	**99.31%**	**99.92%**	**96.85%**	**89.08%**
Client 1	**69.23%**	**61.50%**	**53.62%**	**45.42%**	**37.50%**
Client 2	**68.77%**	**60.42%**	**50.50%**	**39.35%**	**24.31%**
Client 3	**69.23%**	**61.54%**	**53.85%**	**46.04%**	**38.42%**

small. However, compared with centralized learning, our proposed PPDFL could also achieve a high localization accuracy of 99%, a very similar results with centralized learning, after enough number of training rounds. Different with our proposal, the models trained through local learning, no matter which client, could only obtain accuracy between 80% and 90%, which is much lower than the PPDFL. It can be concluded that the PPDFL system proposed in this paper has a certain effect when the number of data samples is not balanced. Based on the considerable performance of PPDFL, the future work will focus on exploiting the advantages of DFL technology on fields of energy efficiency [19] and metaverse world [20,21].

4 Conclusion

For privacy protection, we propose a CSI fingerprint localization system based on federated learning. Based on the theory of federated learning, the server and client in the localization system can train model by transferring model parameters, avoiding transmission or sharing of private data among the server and all the clients. It can solve the potential privacy problems. In addition, we design and perform a DFL system in a real apartment and construct several different real-world CSI-based indoor DFL databases. We also verify the effectiveness of the proposed method through a large number of experiments. Experimental results show that the PPDFL system can achieve high localization accuracy by integrating the data characteristics of all client databases in the cases of poor data quality and unbalanced sample quantity.

Acknowledgment. This work was supported in part by the National Natural Science Foundation of China under Grant 62001126, in part by the GuangDong Basic and Applied Basic Research Foundation (Project No. 2021A1515110455), and in part by China Postdoctoral Science Foundation (Project No. 2021M693617), and the Science and Technology Program of Guangzhou (Project No. 202201010348, 202201020184).

References

1. Motroni, A., Buffi, A., Nepa, P.: A survey on indoor vehicle localization through RFID technology. IEEE Access **9**, 17921–17942 (2021)

2. Pušnik, M., Galun, M., Šumak, B.: Improved bluetooth low energy sensor detection for indoor localization services. Sensors **20**(8), 2336 (2020)
3. Zhang, K., Tan, B., Ding, S., Li, Y., Li, G.: Device-free indoor localization based on sparse coding with nonconvex regularization and adaptive relaxation localization criteria. Int. J. Mach. Learn. Cybern., 1–15 (2022)
4. Shit, R.C., et al.: Ubiquitous Localization (UBILOC): a survey and taxonomy on device free localization for smart world. IEEE Commun. Surv. Tutorials **21**(4), 3532–3564 (2019)
5. Zhao, L., et al.: Indoor device-free passive localization with DCNN for location-based services. J. Supercomput. **76**(11), 8432–8449 (2020)
6. Kaltiokallio, O., Hostettler, R., Patwari, N.: A novel Bayesian filter for RSS-based device-free localization and tracking. IEEE Trans. Mobile Comput. **20**(3), 780–795 (2019)
7. Lee, K., Ahn, H., You, K.: Device free localization using prior correction based logistic regression. IEEE Wireless Commun. Lett. (2022)
8. Zhao, L., Huang, H., Li, X., Ding, S., Zhao, H., Han, Z.: An accurate and robust approach of device-free localization with convolutional autoencoder. IEEE Internet Things J. **6**(3), 5825–5840 (2019)
9. Yang, Z., Zhou, Z., Liu, Y.: From RSSI to CSI: indoor localization via channel response. ACM Comput. Surv. (CSUR) **46**(2), 1–32 (2013)
10. Huang, H., Han, Z., Ding, S., Chunhua, S., Zhao, L.: Improved sparse coding algorithm with device-free localization technique for intrusion detection and monitoring. Symmetry **11**(5), 637 (2019)
11. Zhao, L., et al.: Block-sparse coding-based machine learning approach for dependable device-free localization in IoT environment. IEEE Internet Things J. **8**(5), 3211–3223 (2020)
12. Halperin, D., Hu, W., Sheth, A., Wetherall, D.: Tool release: gathering 802.11 n traces with channel state information. ACM SIGCOMM Comput. Commun. Rev. **41**(1), 53–53 (2011)
13. Han, Z., Wang, Z., Huang, H., Zhao, L., Su, C.: WiFi-based indoor positioning and communication: empirical model and theoretical analysis. Wireless Commun. Mobile Comput. 2022 (2022)
14. Wang, X., Gao, L., Mao, S., Pandey, S.: CSI-based fingerprinting for indoor localization: a deep learning approach. IEEE Trans. Veh. Technol. **66**(1), 763–776 (2016)
15. Zhou, R., Hao, M., Lu, X., Tang, M., Fu, Y.: Device-free localization based on CSI fingerprints and deep neural networks. In: 2018 15th Annual IEEE International Conference on Sensing, Communication, and Networking (SECON), pp. 1–9. IEEE (2018)
16. Dang, X., Tang, X., Hao, Z., Liu, Y.: A device-free indoor localization method using CSI with Wi-Fi signals. Sensors **19**(14), 3233 (2019)
17. Han, Z., et al.: CNN-based attack defense for device-free localization. Mobile Inf. Syst. 2022 (2022)
18. McMahan, B., Moore, E., Ramage, D., Hampson, S., y Arcas, B.A.: Communication-efficient learning of deep networks from decentralized data. In: Singh, A., Zhu, J., (eds) Proceedings of the 20th International Conference on Artificial Intelligence and Statistics, volume 54 of Proceedings of Machine Learning Research, 20–22 Apr, pp. 1273–1282. PMLR (2017)
19. Huang, H., et al.: Optimum insulation thicknesses and energy conservation of building thermal insulation materials in Chinese zone of humid subtropical climate. Sustain. Cities Soc. **52**, 101840 (2020)

20. Huang, H., Zeng, X., Zhao, L., Qiu, C., Wu, H., Fan, L.: Fusion of building information modeling and blockchain for metaverse: a survey. IEEE Open J. Comput. Soc. (2022)
21. Yang, Q., Zhao, Y., Huang, H., Xiong, Z., Kang, J., Zheng, Z.: Fusing blockchain and AI with metaverse: a survey. IEEE Open J. Comput. Soc. **3**, 122–136 (2022)

A Novel Blockchain-MEC-Based Near-Domain Medical Resource Sharing Model

Haichao Wu, Xiaoming Liu, and Wei Ou(✉)

School of Cyberspace Security (School of Cryptology), Hainan University, Haikou 570228, Hainan, China
ouwei@hainanu.edu.cn

Abstract. Current medical information systems face important security issues in the transmission and storage of medical data, especially since there is currently no research related to the security of medical resource sharing in near-domain networks. Most of the medical data is transmitted through an insecure environment without encryption, and there is a risk of interception and tampering. In addition, lots of medical data is uploaded to the cloud platform for storage without processing, which is inefficient. Therefore, this paper proposes a near-domain medical resource sharing scheme based on block-chain and Multi-access Edge Computing (MEC). The approach makes use of device-to-device (D2D) communication technologies to make data sharing between medical devices safer and more efficient. The MEC is used to process medical data, which is encrypted and decrypted using the ShangMi cryptographic algorithms. Finally, the blockchain is used to ensure data security and tamper resistance. Through the simulation experiment, the performance test results show that the scheme meets the performance index, and the security analysis results show that the scheme can provide security. It offers a novel approach to the secure and trustworthy sharing of medical and health data and intelligent processing of that data.

Keywords: Blockchain · MEC · Near-domain network · Medical resource sharing · D2D · ShangMi cryptographic algorithms

1 Introduction

Medical resource sharing has ushered in a new era, and the interconnection of medical information has become a trend. Medical resource sharing has ushered in a new era, and the interconnection of medical information has become a trend. The deep integration of the Internet of Things, 5G, artificial intelligence, big data, and other new generation of intelligent technologies with various industries in recent years. However, numerous issues remain in the field of medical resource sharing, particularly in the area of near-domain medical resource sharing, which has yet to be researched. How to securely transmit, process, and use these data, as well as how to better protect patient privacy, has become a serious problem facing near-domain medical resource sharing.

Y. Xu et al. (Eds.): ML4CS 2022, LNCS 13655, pp. 40–56, 2023.
https://doi.org/10.1007/978-3-031-20096-0_4

In the development of near-domain medical resource sharing, it provides a more dependable and secure connection for data sharing across medical devices, D2D communication technology will increasingly replace Bluetooth and WLAN. When compared to typical wireless transmission technologies such as Bluetooth and WLAN, D2D technology is distinguished by the use of authorized telecommunication carrier frequency channels. It can ensure that the interference environment is controlled and data transfer is more reliable. Bluetooth communication requires manual user matching, and WLAN communication requires user-defined access point (AP) settings before communication. However, D2D communication does not, it makes the access process easier and faster and satisfies a large amount of information interaction between smart devices [1].

The important security issues currently faced by traditional medical information systems in near-domain medical resource sharing are reflected in the following areas:

1. The security of medical data transmission. Medical equipment is connected to each other in the existing medical resource sharing system mostly by short-range communication technologies based on ISM bands, such as WLAN or Bluetooth [2]. The patient's confidential information is transmitted without encryption in these unsafe situations, posing a significant security risk to the users. Furthermore, if a hacker gains access to the system and tampers with the data, a substantial amount of medical data will be rendered useless for research.
2. The storage security of medical data. At present, medical resources are mostly stored in the cloud platform for resource transfer [3], which cannot guarantee the trustworthiness of third parties. It is also difficult to prevent illegal modification and loss of users' private data, and there are issues such as data traceability and incredibility.
3. The problem of medical data processing. A large number of intelligent terminal devices in hospitals will produce a large amount of medical data. These data must be integrated and processed by computer before they can be used for future research.
4. The problem of access control of medical data. Medical data includes patient privacy. How to configure the user roles of the system and assign relevant permissions to prevent the leakage or improper use of medical data to the greatest extent. This has become a challenge.
5. The problem of sharing medical data across hospitals. Medical data is part of a hospital's digital assets, and it has some research and economic value. The key difficulty that needs to be solved to promote resource sharing among hospitals is how to fairly share the benefits and get each hospital to agree [4].

Based on the current situation, this paper proposes a near-domain medical resource sharing scheme based on blockchain and MEC. The scheme adopts D2D communication technology, blockchain technology, and MEC to solve the security problems of medical data transmission and storage, provide a more secure and open connection for data sharing between medical devices, and realize more secure and efficient near-domain medical resource sharing. It realizes the goal of promoting medical digitalization and improving the security of medical data sharing.

The rest of the paper is organized as follows. The second part presents current technology research in medical resource-sharing security. The third part presents the proposed architecture. The module of the proposed system is analyzed in the fourth part. The fifth part presents the experimental results and analysis. Finally, the sixth part concludes the paper.

2 Related Works

Foreign research on the combination of blockchain and healthcare information security started earlier. Q Xia proposed MeDShare, a system to solve the problem of sharing healthcare data in a trustless environment among custodians of healthcare big data. The system is based on blockchain and provides data sourcing, auditing, and control for shared medical data in cloud repositories between big data entities. MeDShare keeps an eye on organizations that access data from data hosting platforms to see if they're being used maliciously. All data transfers and sharing between entities, as well as all actions done on the MeDShare system, are documented in a tamper-proof way in MeDShare. Smart contracts and access control methods are used in the architecture to effectively track data activity and revoke access to the offending entity when a violation is identified [5]. Dubovitskaya presented a framework for organizing and exchanging EMR data for cancer patient care that ensures privacy, security, availability, and fine-grained access control. This research has the potential to speed up EMR sharing, improve medical decision-making, and lower overall costs [6]. Tharaka Hewa suggested a blockchain-based multi-access edge computing (MEC) and service architecture that uses lightweight ECQV (Elliptic Curve Qu-Vanstone) certificates for real-time data privacy, integrity, and authentication between IoT and MEC [7].

The research of this in China began late, but with vigorous attempts to digitize healthcare and specific laws to foster the growth of blockchain, an increasing number of scholars are devoting themselves to research in this area. Based on the improved practical Byzantine fault-tolerant consensus mechanism, Dong Daying et al. proposed an electronic medical record sharing model that enables user-defined personalized access control policies through access control. It partly solves the problem of weak information security in the current electronic medical record sharing [8]. Using the ideas of decentralization and blockchain architecture, Xiong et al. presented a novel distributed electronic medical record management system based on Ethernet smart contracts to establish a secure and interoperable system. That can allow the secure sharing of medical data [9]. Jian Xu et al. proposed a method that combines blockchain technology and cryptography with asymmetric encryption technology and applied the characteristics of asymmetric encryption technology to blockchain technology. It effectively realizes the simplification of the cross-domain sharing process of medical records [10]. In studying the problem of combining blockchain and MEC, Wei Chen proposes a blockchain-based D2D-assisted multi-access edge computing architecture (BD-MEC) for resource sharing. In BD-MEC, a game-theoretic-based offloading decision for multi-user scenarios is proposed to meet the needs of different users considering factors such as delay, energy consumption, and payment overhead [11].

3 Structure

The overall organization of the proposed scheme in this paper is shown in Fig. 1, which is designed with a four-layer structure, including the device layer, MEC layer, blockchain layer, and application layer. The roles of each layer are explained in detail in the following section:

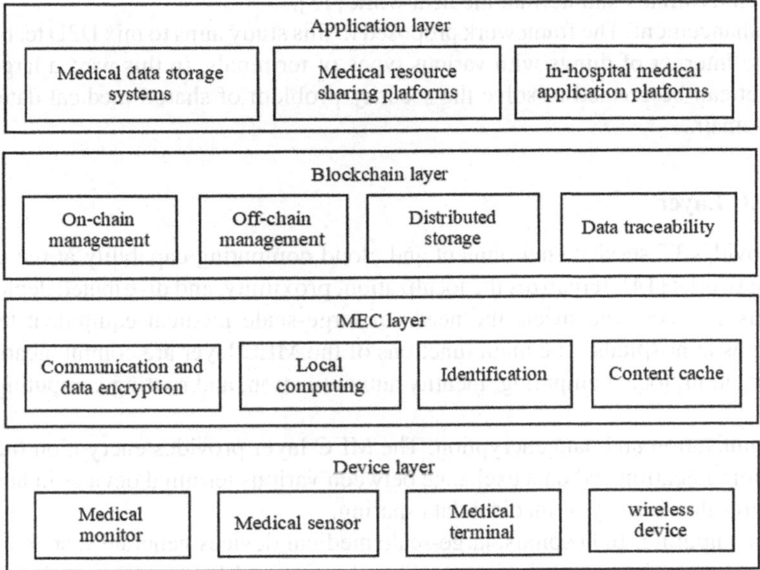

Fig. 1. Our structure

3.1 Device Layer

The device layer uses D2D technology to connect all smart devices in the hospital's near-field network for communication, including data collectors, medical sensors, medical terminals, and so on. It allows the devices to safely communicate data. There are three main functions that are accomplished:

- Local service. Medical data is sent directly from the device to the device, bypassing the network (e.g. core network). Through the D2D discovery feature, the hospital's smart devices can be connected to other smart devices in the surrounding region, and data transmission between proximate smart devices can be accomplished using the D2D communication function. The local data transmission takes advantage of D2D's near-domain feature and data pass-through feature, which saves a lot of spectrum. This way avoids the situation of uploading a lot of medical data to the Internet without processing. It also relieves a lot of pressure on operators' core networks and spectrum resources [12].
- Emergency communications. When natural disasters such as earthquakes strike, the traditional communication network infrastructure is frequently disrupted, and the network goes down. This can be a substantial impediment to medical care, and D2D communications can help to overcome this issue. When the communication network

infrastructure is destroyed, it is still possible to establish an end-to-end wireless communication network based on D2D connections between medical devices, i.e., an Ad Hoc network based on multi-hop D2D. It can ensure smooth wireless communication between terminals and normal medical work [13].

- IoT Enhancement. The framework proposed in this study aims to mix D2D technology and the Internet of things with various types of terminals. In this way, a large-scale Internet can be created to solve the security problem of shared medical data in the near domain.

3.2 MEC Layer

MEC provides IT service environment and cloud computing capability at the edge of mobile networks [14]. It realizes the localization, proximity, and distributed deployment of various services, and meets the needs of large-scale medical equipment terminal connections in hospitals. The main functions of the MEC layer are communication and data encryption, local computing, identity authentication, and routing computing.

- Communication and data encryption. The MEC layer provides encryption functions for communication and data exchange between various terminal devices in hospitals. It ensures the security of medical data sharing.
- Local computing. In hospitals, large-scale medical devices generate vast amounts of medical data, which must be integrated and processed before they can be used for further research. The cost of uploading these large-scale medical data directly to the cloud server is very high and the transmission efficiency will be very low. The MEC layer, on the other hand, can perform local computation for this data in close proximity, lowering computation, and transmission costs while increasing computation efficiency.
- Identity verification. The device nodes that join the blockchain need to upload complete device information [15]. Only the devices that have been verified by the MEC layer can access resources and share resources with other devices. This effectively prevents third-party or hacker intrusion and ensures data security and privacy.
- Content Cache. Edge computing technology is dedicated to providing IT service resources at the edge of the wireless access network. By allocating the appropriate computing and storage space as well as bandwidth resources, it can provide low-latency services to medical terminals and reduce the pressure on the wireless access network. The content caching and distribution based on edge computing is an important aspect of achieving MEC. User traffic can be unloaded locally by deploying a MEC server in the base station and storing suitable material in the server. At this time, a close MEC server delivers services without passing through the network layer and requests services from a data center at the far end of the Internet [16]. This can help relieve network congestion by reducing transmission delay.

3.3 Blockchain Layer

The blockchain layer ensures the security of medical data storage while providing a tamper-evident and traceable mechanism. The cost and efficiency of storing all data on the blockchain will be relatively low due to the massive volume of data generated by medical device terminals. Therefore, the blockchain layer in this paper's structure uses an on-chain/off-chain storage method. The original data is transferred to an off-chain storage system for storage. But the pointer or index pointing to the original data's location is stored in the block body. The original medical data is saved on an off-chain storage server, and a unique identifier for the original data storage site is generated and stored in the blockchain system using particular rules. The original data is accessible in the off-chain storage system based on this unique identity when data access is conducted. This technique ensures file storage efficiency and security.

3.4 Application Layer

The application layer is built on blockchain and MEC. It allows third-party apps or medical applications, such as medical data storage systems, medical resource sharing platforms, and medical application platforms, to be integrated into the platform. It can implement a simple open network capability and expand the network's functionality.

4 Module

Figure 2 depicts the model described in this article. Among them, medical terminal devices (such as monitors, workstations, sensors, etc.) are interconnected through multi-hop D2D to transmit medical data. Relay nodes connect these medical end devices to the base station. Then it sends the medical data to the MEC for processing. After processing the data, the MEC performs two tasks: one, it returns the data to the base station, and the other, it uploads the data to the blockchain.

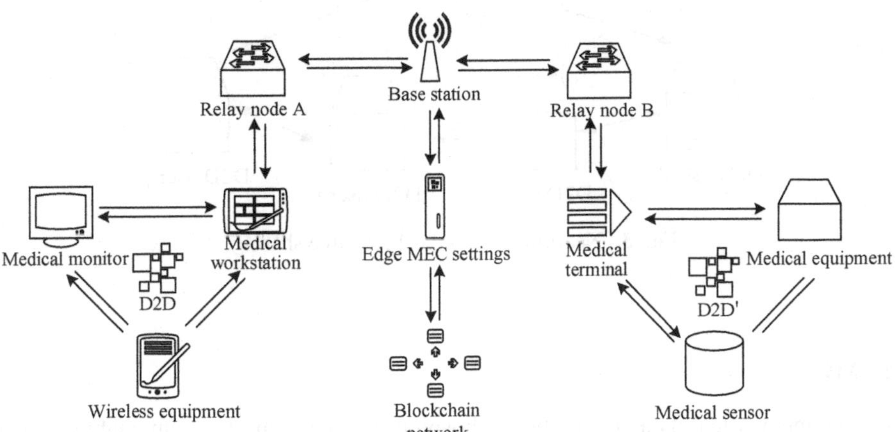

Fig. 2. Near-domain medical resource sharing

4.1 D2D Communication

The D2D module allows terminals in the hospital's near-domain network to communicate directly with one another. Once a D2D communication link has been established in a communication network, speech or data can be transmitted without the need for the base station's intervention [17]. This decreases data strain on the communication system's base station and core network, improves spectrum usage and throughput, expands network capacity, and ensures that the communication network runs more flexibly, intelligently, and efficiently. Direct data resource sharing and transmission by near-domain medical devices enhance resource circulation speed and usage and improve data security. Also, it can minimize the danger of information leakage and hacker assaults. This is how the process works: First, the medical user device initiates a session request. Second, the gateway service detects the source and destination of the data and determines that the devices are in the same or adjacent area. Third, the medical user device initiates a session request. The base station node determines whether or not a D2D connection can be created by testing the channel quality. The base station node creates the connection via control if the device has D2D capability. The device's wireless network and D2D resource allocation remain under the control of the base station node after D2D is formed. Medical equipment communicates with one another directly through the D2D network, bypassing the base station node (Fig. 3).

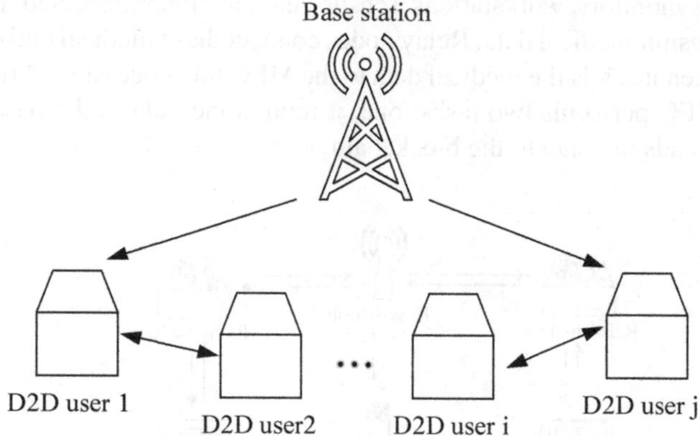

Fig. 3. Near-domain medical resource sharing

4.2 MEC

For the huge medical data created by the hospital, the MEC module can enable greater performance in local computation and network transmission. In terms of access control [18], the MEC module uses an authentication technique that solves the problem of two-way security authentication with the terminal while also protecting resources from unauthorized access. The authentication protocol is divided into four phases: initial phase, user registration phase, server registration phase, and authentication phase. It is based on the Hash function and asymmetric cryptosystem. The authentication process employs symmetric key encryption and decryption. The following is a description of the authentication procedure.

- Initialization phase. The registration center creates its own public and private keys, as well as reveals its own public key.
- User registration phase. Before using the MEC server's services, the user must first register as a legitimate user with the registration center. The user sends the registration center a registration request, and the registration center generates a master key for the user. A secure channel is used to communicate between the user and the registration center.
- Server registration phase. The MEC server creates a public-private key pair of its own and sends the public key to the registration center. The registration center assigns the MEC server identity and signs it with its own private key before sending it to the MEC server, which does not need to be kept hidden.
- Authentication phase. When a user requests a service from the MEC server, the closest MEC server receives the request and asks the registration center to verify the user's identity. If it does, it generates and delivers a shared key between the MEC server and the user to the MEC server. After authentication, the session key is determined by the user and the MEC server.

To strengthen data storage security and limit the danger of privacy exposure, the MEC module employs the SM4 algorithm to encrypt the original data before storing it in the off-chain server [19]. The data storage address and file are hashed using the SM3 hash function, and then the hash value is stored in the blockchain, thus ensuring data tamper-proofness.

4.3 Blockchain

The blockchain module is used to upload significant amounts of medical data to the blockchain for storage and sharing with other devices in the near-domain network. When data is stored before the MEC module platform processes cached packets, it is first stored off-chain, and then the hash address and file hash of the file is stored in the Hyperledger Fabric blockchain [20]. If resource sharing is required, the endpoint device submits a data sharing request, launches the Hyperledger Fabric blockchain, and queries the smart contract ID and file hash address. If it exists, it signifies that the data is saved on the blockchain and can be shared, and it then uses the file hash address to query and acquire the medical device's stored data. If the hash address does not exist, the necessary data will not be found. Simultaneously, you may compare the file hash saved in Hyperledger Fabric to the file hash saved in the original data to see if the file has been tampered with or lost (Fig. 4).

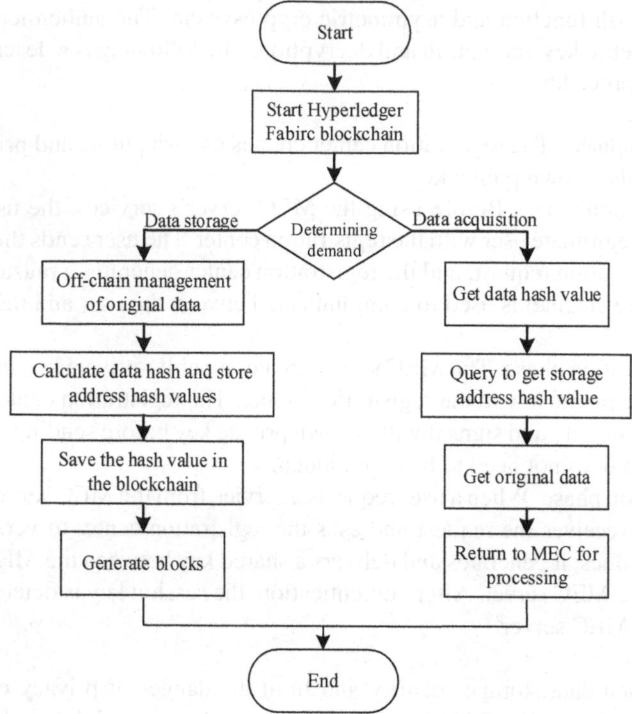

Fig. 4. Near-domain medical resource sharing

5 Experiment and Analysis

5.1 Experimental Environment

In the experimental evaluation, we employed a virtual machine simulation as the MEC server and the thread group under test as the IoT nodes, which represent medical devices and sensors. The IoT-MEC connection is formed using the Message Queue Telemetry Transport (MQTT) protocol [21]. Fabric is used to create nodes to store data for blockchain testing. The experiment's purpose is to gather data for analysis in order to assess the system's MEC and blockchain modules, both of which must meet performance requirements.

We leveraged a real-world dataset from the GMS.gov repository to apply the approach presented in this research. A general standardized survey of central hemodialysis patients (including data such as patient number, network, facility name, dialysis status, time, and so on), ranging in size from 100 KB to 5 MB. These data can be kept in medical equipment connected to a nearby domain network. They're shared as resources via the D2D communication module. Also, they can be centrally uploaded to the MEC server for encryption or decryption, as well as being kept on the blockchain.

The hardware configurations are shown in Table 1, the software configuration is shown in Table 2.

Table 1. Hardware server configurations

Configuration items	Performance test environment
CPU	Intel i5-7300HQ 2.50 GHz
MEM	16.00 GB
SSD	256G
Operating system and version	centOS7
Database system and version	MySQL5.7.27

Table 2. Software configurations

Category	Environment
Dependency library	SM3, SM4, MQTT
Hyperledger Fabric	2.1.0
Jmeter	5.4.3
Hyperledger Caliper	2.0.0

5.2 Experimental Content

In the experimental part, our work is divided into two parts: performance testing and security analysis. To simulate the tasks of the MEC module including MQTT, Encrypt, and HTTP request, we utilize Jmeter to construct a test thread group. After that, we have the experiment's performance results as well as the system's resource usage for analysis. For the blockchain performance test, we use caliper to design the test environment and parameters and get the results through a data chaining stress test. Finally, we draw a conclusion by comparing our findings to the available indices.

Next, we carry out a safety analysis mainly from two aspects: Consortium blockchain and cryptographic mechanism. Through theoretical analysis, our scheme meets the problem of medical resources in the near-domain network.

5.3 Result

MEC Performance

- Performance indicators (Table 3)

Table 3. Performance indicators

Items	Value
Average transaction response time	≤3 s
TPS	≥200
Error rate	=0%
CPU utilization	<70%
Memory utilization	<75%
Physical disk utilization	<70%
Network throughput	<60%

- Test results

1. Summary report

We used Jmeter to test the MEC simulation nodes and analyze the results. As shown in the figure, the stress test using Jmeter collects the results and generates a summary report. The number of samples executed, the average value, the error rate, the throughput, and the received and sent packet rates are all provided in this section (Table 4).

Table 4. Summary of statistical results

Label	#Samples	Average	Error%	Throughput	Received KB/sec	Send KB/sec	Avg Bytes
MQTT	150	224	0.67%	117.6/s	334.22	49.63	2909.0
Encrypt	150	81	0.00%	125.4/s	1334.47	93.46	10895.5
HTTP request	150	73	0.67%	123.5/s	400.88	92.42	3325.0
Total	450	125	0.44%	289.0/s	1611.57	184.55	5709.8

This information is obtained by simulating 150 queries per node for a total of 450 requests. The total error rate is 0.44%, and the total throughput is 289.0/s. The average reaction time is 126 ms. In the meantime, the MQTT throughput is 117.6 ms/s, the encryption throughput is 125.4 ms/s, and the HTTP request throughput is 123.5 ms/s.

2. Response time (Fig. 5)

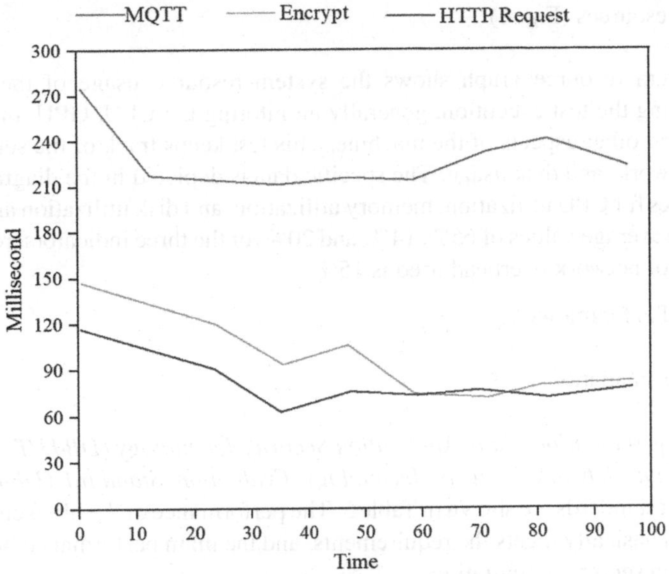

Fig. 5. Response time

As shown in the graph above, MQTT response time is 240 ms on average, while HTTP Request and Encrypt response time is 100 ms on average. The curve is typical and essentially stable under 300 ms, showing that the server can react to requests and produce results in a reasonable amount of time.

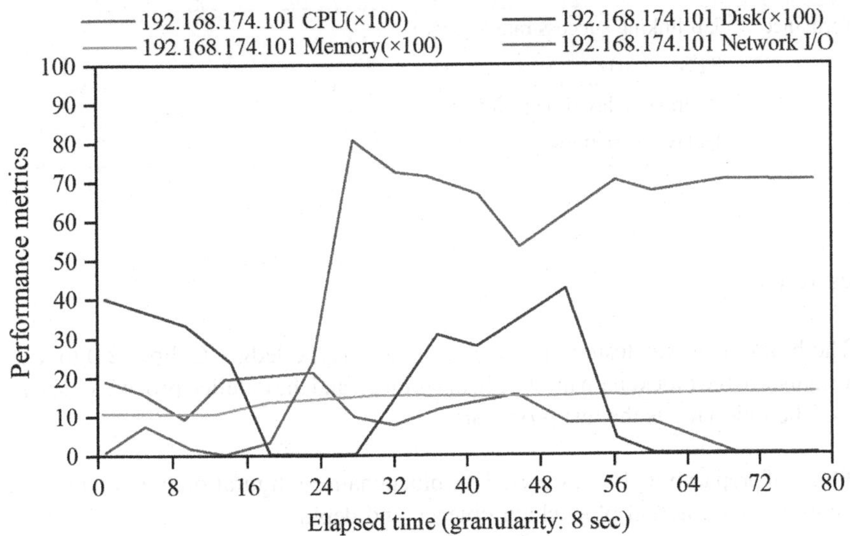

Fig. 6. Resource utilization monitoring

3. System resources (Fig. 6)

The system resource graph shows the system resource usage of the monitored machine during the test execution, generally monitoring the CPU, GPU, memory, network, disk and other aspects of the machine. This test keeps track of the server's CPU, memory, network, and disk usage. The specific data is depicted in the diagram above.

The curves for CPU utilization, memory utilization, and disk utilization are relatively smooth, with average values of 65%, 14%, and 20% for the three indicators, respectively. The amount of network overhead used is 15%.

Blockchain Performance

- Evaluation standards

According to the *Blockchain Application Security Technology (DB43/T 1842–2020)* and *Blockchain Network Security Technology Evaluation Standard (DB43/T 1840–2020)*, the test standards are shown in Table 5. The performance of the blockchain module in our system basically meets the requirements, and the main performance bottleneck is the blockchain server configuration.

Table 5. Blockchain test standards

Items	Requirements
Stress	The number of transactions received every second is nearly identical to the number of uploads, and the upload success rate exceeds 95%
Stability	Low-load operation with no system breakdown
Performance	Up-linking success rate (>95%)
	TPS(>200)
	Average delay time (<0.5 s)
	Delay (<1000 ms)

- Test result

The blockchain was tested and analyzed using Hyperledger Caliper 2.0 to test the performance of the blockchain module in the project, and the detailed process is described below. The following is the test procedure:

1. Phase of preparation: First, we used the blockchain configuration file to establish and configure the internal blockchain objects, and deployed smart contracts according to the setup parameters. Then Caliper starts the monitoring object to keep track of the back-end blockchain system's resource utilization.

2. Phase of testing: In this phase, the main process will execute tests based on our configuration file and generate tasks based on the defined load. Then, they are assigned to the procedure of the customer terminal. Finally, the system will keep track of each client's performance statistics for the next analysis.
3. Phase of reporting: In this phase, Caliper will evaluate the data of all client processes and create results for each cycle of testing.

After the test, the HTML report of data uplink test statistics is shown in Fig. 7.

Performance metrics for dataUpload

Name	Succ	Fail	Send Rate (TPS)	Max Latency (s)	Min Latency (s)	Avg Latency (s)	Throughput (TPS)
dataUpload	6865	0	231.9	0.04	0.01	0.01	231.9

Resource utilization for dataUpload

Resource monitor: docker

Name	CPU% (max)	CPU% (avg)	Memory(max) [MB]	Memory(avg) [MB]	Traffic In [MB]	Traffic Out [MB]	Disc Write [KB]	Disc Read [B]
dev-peer0.org1.example.com-basic_1.0-c33244dbf2796675f675bad53b619f8225e0b52f636c68be4607146769039362	35.55	14.29	52.1	51.9	11.5	4.01	0.00	0.00
dev-peer0.org2.example.com-basic_1.0-c33244dbf2796675f675bad53b619f8225e0b52f636c68be4607146769039362	1.20	0.10	47.3	47.2	0.0389	0.0153	0.00	0.00
dev-peer0.org2.example.com-sacc_1.0-5562f868f6fd43ff8873f403aa52bc6928161fec933065d0b81e2193f6038bd0	0.01	0.00	6.43	6.43	0.000584	0.000584	0.00	0.00
dev-peer0.org1.example.com-sacc_1.0-5562f868f6fd43ff8873f403aa52bc6928161fec933065d0b81e2193f6038bd0	0.01	0.00	6.43	6.43	0.000584	0.000584	0.00	0.00
cli	0.00	0.00	12.3	11.7	0.00	0.00	0.00	0.00
peer0.org2.example.com	3.42	2.15	124	123	0.190	0.128	709	0.00
peer0.org1.example.com	50.53	22.68	150	149	13.6	21.4	709	0.00
orderer.example.com	0.80	0.14	29.2	28.5	0.100	0.194	714	0.00

Fig. 7. Blockchain test report

5.4 Analysis

- Performance

As for the MEC test, the following table shows the statistics obtained from the Jmeter test (Table 6).

According to the test report, the system has a 100% success rate, a TPS of 231.9, a maximum delay of 0.04 s, a minimum delay of 0.01 s, and an average demo of 0.01 s. This test can generally carry the daily concurrency and concurrency number based on the data, and it is also less than the target value based on other data. We can see from the CPU usage rate that the CPU usage rate is high, which can improve the server's performance standard.

As for the blockchain test, through the test report, we got the failure rate, TPS, average delay, and hardware utilization. Compared with the test standard of blockchain, our system has passed the stress test, and the success rate has reached more than 95%. The system runs at a low load without breakdown. And all the measured data meet the performance indicators, but the CPU utilization is high, so the hardware performance needs to be improved.

Table 6. Test results

Items	Value
Average transaction response time	165 ms
Success rate	99.56%
TPS	289
Number of concurrent	150
CPU usage	65%
Memory usage	14%
Physical disk usage	20%
Network usage	15%

- Security

Consortium Blockchain. To promote data privacy and integrity, a blockchain is constructed utilizing the consortium blockchain Fabric. The consortium blockchain has greater privacy protection capability, and only members who join this medical resource sharing alliance are able to perform block verification and medical information access. In this way, a regulated group is formed, which greatly promotes the sharing of medical resources, trust, and privacy protection. Encrypted medical resources are uploaded to the blockchain in a certain format, and network organizations update the distributed ledger using a unified consensus method. To maintain the confidentiality of medical resources and prevent tampering with evidence, the process employs encryption for data verification. Medical data stored in a distributed manner on the blockchain is recorded in its entirety and can be retrieved via transaction hashes, allowing for data traceability.

Cryptographic Mechanism. When the data is stored and preserved under the chain, it is encrypted using the SM4 method to enhance the danger of its security and privacy being compromised. Also, the SM3 hash algorithm is used to hash the data storage addresses and files, and the hash values are then put on the blockchain, assuring data integrity. As a result, the ShangMi cryptographic methods guarantee total security during resource sharing while also improving the data's reliability and security.

6 Conclusion

We propose a secure sharing scheme for near-domain medical device resources based on blockchain and MEC in this paper, which employs D2D communication, MEC, and blockchain to ensure data security and privacy, and secure resource sharing. According to our analysis, it can ensure the security of medical device resource sharing in the near-domain network, guarantee data storage security and patient privacy, and provide autonomous and controllable medical resource sharing. The following are some of the flaws in this paper: To begin with, hospitals have a wide range of medical equipment, and the format of the data provided by these devices might vary. Thus determining how to standardize the interaction of various devices is a topic that has to be thoroughly investigated. Second, in terms of sharing medical resources in the near-domain, this study focuses on creating medical device connections in a single hospital and achieving medical resource sharing and storage. Integrating and sharing the medical resources of many hospitals is difficult. In fact, numerous different hospitals are strewn around the globe, making resource integration and synchronization difficult. In terms of adaptability for cross-chain data sharing, the model described in this paper has to be improved.

This paper's subsequent work focuses on a variety of topics. First, we will continue to improve the scheme proposed in this paper and form partnerships with hospitals to test the model proposed in the scheme in a real-world setting; second, we will use cross-chain technology and other methods in future research. And we try to integrate the medical resources of multiple hospitals in order to achieve secure medical resource sharing across different blockchains.

References

1. Guo, J., Ma, J., Li, X., et al.: An attribute-based trust negotiation protocol for D2D communication in smart city balancing trust and privacy. J. Inf. Sci. Eng. **33**(4), 1007–1023 (2017)
2. Zhang, Y., Zhang, G.: Overview of the application of medical Internet of things. Internet Things Technol. **9**(1), 91–94 (2019)
3. Fan, W., Zhao, D., Wang, S.: Design and implementation of regional medical information sharing platform based on cloud computing. Mil. Med. (4), 257–260 (2015)
4. Linyuanmo, X., Wen, H., et al.: Research on intelligent medical system based on cloud computing and Internet of things technology. Wirel. Internet Technol. **16**(18), 16–18 (2019)
5. Xia, Q.I., Sifah, E.B., Asamoah, K.O., et al.: MeDShare: trust-less medical data sharing among cloud service providers via blockchain. IEEE Access **5**, 14757–14767 (2017)
6. Dubovitskaya, A., Xu, Z., Ryu, S., et al.: Secure and trustable electronic medical records sharing using blockchain. In: AMIA Annual Symposium Proceedings, vol. 2017, pp. 650–659. American Medical Informatics Association (2017)
7. Hewa, T., Braeken, A., Ylianttila, M., et al.: Multi-access edge computing and blockchain-based secure telehealth system connected with 5G and IoT. In: GLOBECOM 2020-2020 IEEE Global Communications Conference, pp. 1–6. IEEE (2020)
8. Dong, D., Wang, X.: Research on electronic medical record sharing based on blockchain. Comput. Technol. Dev. **29**, 121–125 (2019)
9. Xiong, Z., Zhou, W.: Research on electronic medical records based on blockchain technology. China Digit. Med. **14**(1), 64–66 (2019)
10. Mei, Y.: Research on blockchain method for secure storage of medical records. J. Jiangxi Normal Univ. **41**(5), 481–487 (2017)
11. Feng, Y., Wei, A., Han, Z., Li, X., Song, B.: Research on the national health information platform based on blockchain technology. China Digit. Med. **2019**(06), 24–26 (2019)
12. Chen, W., Huo, R., Wang, S., et al.: Block chain based D2D assisted MEC resource sharing architecture. J. Beijing Univ. Posts Telecommun. **44**(5), 1–9 (2021)
13. Wang, L.: Research on resource optimization algorithm of mobile medical D2D network based on power control. University of Electronic Science and Technology of China (2018)
14. Yang, X., Zhao, H.: Multi-access edge computing MEC technology and service development strategy. Mob. Commun. **43**(1), 29–33 (2019)

15. Chen, L., Liu, Z., Wang, Z.: Research on heterogeneous terminal security access technology in edge computing scenario. In: 2019 11th International Conference on Measuring Technology and Mechatronics Automation (ICMTMA), pp. 472–476. IEEE (2019)
16. He, W., Su, Y., Huang, L., et al.: Research on streaming media cache optimization based on mobile edge computing. In: 2018 13th International Conference on Computer Science & Education (ICCSE), pp. 1–6. IEEE (2018)
17. Wu, R., Xin, X., Zou, S.: Research and implementation of regional medical information sharing platform. J. Med. Inform. **32**(1), 19–23 (2011)
18. Ali, B., Gregory, M.A., Li, S.: Multi-access edge computing architecture, data security and privacy: a review. IEEE Access **9**, 18706–18721 (2021)
19. Wu, Y., Ma, R., Zou, C., et al.: ACARS data protection technology based on state secret algorithm. Inf. Secur. Res. **7**(4), 342–350 (2021)
20. Alshalali, T., M'Bale, K., Josyula, D.: Security and privacy of electronic health records sharing using hyperledger fabric. In: 2018 International Conference on Computational Science and Computational Intelligence (CSCI), pp. 760–763. IEEE (2018)
21. Xu, K., Ding, Q.: An Internet of things communication gateway based on MQTT protocol. Instrum. Technol. **2019**(1), 1–4 (2019)

Pairwise Decomposition of Directed Graphic Models for Performing Amortized Approximate Inference

Peng Lin[1], Changsheng Dou[1](✉), Nannan Gu[1], Zhiyuan Shi[2], and Lili Ma[1]

[1] School of Statistics, Capital University of Economics and Business, Beijing 100070, China
{linpeng,douchangsheng,nngu,malili}@cueb.edu.cn
[2] Onfido Research London, 3 Finsbury Avenue, London EC2M 2PA, UK
zhiyuan.shi@onfido.com

Abstract. Exact inference for large directed graphic models (known as Bayesian networks (BN)) is difficult as the space complexity grows exponentially in the tree-width of the model. Approximate inference, such as generalized belief propagation (GBP), is used instead. GBP treats inference as an energy function optimization problem. The solution is found using iterative message passing, which is inefficient and convergent problematic. Recent progress on amortized technique for GBP is an attractive alternative solution that can optimize the energy function using (deep) neural networks, requiring no message passing. Despite being efficient, the amortized technique for GBP is so far only applied to undirected graphic models with specific structures and factors, with no guarantee of the approximation quality for general models. This is because the energy function to be amortized is defined by a region graph that is ad-hoc and difficult to construct. To ensure the amortized technique for GBP is applied to BN inference for practical use, we propose (i) A new pairwise conversion (PWC) algorithm converts all the conditional probability distributions in the BN into pairwise factors to facilitate neural network parameterization and the region graph construction. (ii) An improved loop structured region graph (LSRG) algorithm to generate a valid region graph satisfying desired region properties. (iii) The energy function defined by the PWC-LSRG region graph can be directly amortized using (deep) neural networks and yield sensible approximations. Experiments show that the proposed amortized PWC-LSRG algorithm improves significantly in accuracy and efficiency compared to conventional algorithms.

Keywords: Amortized technique · Neural network · Pairwise decomposition · Directed graphic models · Belief propagation

1 Introduction and Motivation

Directed graphic models, also known as Bayesian networks (BN) [1], encode causal and dependent information among random variables. Therefore, BN is considered a nature-inspired graphic tool for human probabilistic reasoning [2]. In recent years, applications

Y. Xu et al. (Eds.): ML4CS 2022, LNCS 13655, pp. 57–71, 2023.
https://doi.org/10.1007/978-3-031-20096-0_5

driven by BN modeling have increased rapidly in medical, finance, forensics, biology, cybersecurity [3], law [4], etc. Meanwhile, the BN scale also grows in the number of variables and the complexity of the model, making exact probabilistic inference methods, such as the Junction tree algorithm [5], intractable. One must rely on approximate methods instead.

One important class of approximate inference is variational inference (VI) [6] and its alternative generalized belief propagation (GBP) [7]. VI and GBP are both optimization-based methods, which turn the original inference problem into an optimization problem subject to relaxed space complexity constraints. VI is an analytical solution requiring specific knowledge from the user. It is efficient but not as accurate as GBP for most inference tasks. GBP is an iterative message-passing procedure to minimize the objective function. It is convenient for automated inference when all continuous variables are discretized [8] into discrete variables. However, the objective function determines GBP's accuracy, which involves constructing a region graph that is ad-hoc and difficult for users.

Representative region graph algorithms involve iterative joint graph propagation (IJGP) [9], loop structured region graph (LSRG) [10], and triplet region construction (TRC) [11]. The TRC is a hybrid algorithm using both structural and factor information of the model and is more accurate than IJGP and LSRG under bounded cluster size. However, one limitation of TRC is that it is designed explicitly for BNs, so not directly applicable to Markov networks. In contrast, LSRG and IJGP use structural information only and apply to general forms of factors.

Although the space complexity for GBP is low, running GBP message passing is inefficient for large models as it is iterative and sensitive to numerical issues. Recent progress on graph neural network (GNN) [12, 13] and amortized technique [14–16] for GBP solve this issue by avoiding the GBP message passing using reparametrized neural networks. The GNN methods directly map the message passing nodes used in GBP into neural network nodes; hence the simulation is an analogy to the message passing. In contrast, the amortized technique for GBP is more efficient, directly minimizing the objective function by training a (deep) neural network with GBP constrained information. The output of the (deep) neural network is the marginal belief. This technique is called amortizing because the parameters of interest are amortized by neural network parameters. Despite being promising, both GNN and amortizing (for GBP) are so far only applied to undirected graphic models, such as the Markov random fields (MRF), with only pairwise and singleton factors. This is because general MRFs is assumed to be decomposable into pairwise MRFs. Except that, the accuracy of both GNN and amortizing depend on how GBP energy function is defined, specifically, how the region graph is constructed.

Therefore, using the amortized technique (for GBP) for BN inference involves resolving two critical issues: (i) fill the gap between Markov random field (MRF) and BN with the proper factor conversion method, thus existing amortized technique and region graph construction algorithms can be applied. (ii) improve the region graph construction method to ensure sensible approximations for BNs.

This paper assumes all discrete BNs given continuous variables can be discretized [8]. Motivated by the efficiency gained using amortized technique for GBP and the success of region graph construction for specific undirected graphic models, we propose a new amortized approximate inference algorithm for BN inference tasks. The novelty of this work is fourfold:

1. Normally, the amortized technique for GBP is applied to the undirected graphic models. We propose using it for BN inference systematically.
2. We propose a new pairwise conversion (PWC) algorithm generally applicable to conditional probability distributions in BNs, facilitating both the neural network parameterization and region graph construction.
3. We propose an improved loop structured region graph algorithm (LSRG) by incorporating node ordering information in a BN, resulting in more accurate region graph-based approximations than others.
4. Both 2 and 3 can be used independently. Combining 1–3 we obtain an amortized PWC-LSRG algorithm, which achieved significant improvement in efficiency and convergence compared to conventional BN inference algorithms.

The paper is organized as follows. Section 2 introduces the related BN inference methods. Section 3 develops our proposed amortized PWC-LSRG algorithm. Section 4 carries out the experiments, and Sect. 5 concludes the paper.

2 BNs and Inference Methods

2.1 BNs and Exact Inference

In this section, we review the BN notations we will use in the paper and describe why it is sufficient to solve the BN inference problem using a complete BN structure.

A BN is a directed acyclic graph (DAG) $G = \langle \boldsymbol{V}, \boldsymbol{E} \rangle$, with nodes $\boldsymbol{V} = \{1, \ldots, m\}$ representing random variables and a set of edges $\boldsymbol{E} = \{(s, t) : s, t \in \boldsymbol{V}\}$. For each $i \in \boldsymbol{V}$, X_i is a random variable.

Two variables X_i, X_j are *conditional independent* (CI) given $\boldsymbol{K} \subseteq \boldsymbol{V} \backslash \{i, j\}$, noted $X_i \perp X_j | X_{\boldsymbol{K}} : P\big(X_i = x_i | X_j = x_j, X_{\boldsymbol{K}} = x_{\boldsymbol{K}}\big) = P(X_i = x_i | X_{\boldsymbol{K}} = x_k)$. The key property of a BN is the *ordered Markov property* which defines an ordering π_V for nodes such that a node only depends on its immediate parents, $X_i \perp X_{pred(i)} | X_{pa(i)}$, where $pa(i)$ are the parents of node i and $pred(i)$ are the predecessors of i. A conditional probability distribution (CPD) is associated with each node, depending on its parent nodes, if there are any. The BN represents the joint distribution, p of the random variables as the product (chain rule factorization) of its CPDs:

$$p(X_1, \ldots, X_m | G) = \prod\nolimits_{i=1}^{m} p(X_i | X_{pa(i)}), \tag{1}$$

where each term $p(X_i | X_{pa(i)})$ is a CPD. The number of variables involved in a CPD is the *CPD size*.

In the worst case, there are no CI assumptions in the BN; the BN graph is a complete DAG with m nodes, i.e., every pair of nodes is connected by a directed edge. Performing inference on such a BN graph represents the worst-case space complexity $O(K^m)$ if each node has K states and is usually intractable for exact methods.

Theoretically, any BN model can be represented by a complete BN (by removing CI assumptions). Hence, any algorithm that performs efficient inference for complete BN models will also be efficient for arbitrary BN models. Therefore, it is sufficient to find an approximate inference algorithm that is efficient for complete BN models; hence, this is the focus of the rest of the paper.

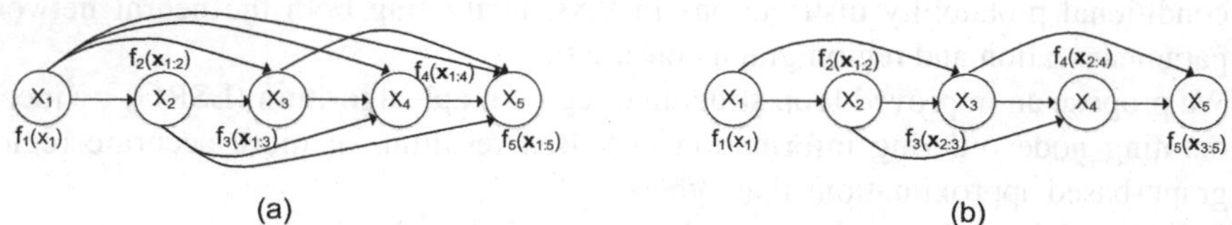

Fig. 1. (a) a 5-dimensional complete BN G with the CPDs list aside each node; (b) a 5-dimensional sparse BN.

Each CPD $p(X_i|X_{pa(i)})$ in a complete DAG G is a function of the variables it contains, $p(X_i|X_{pa(i)}) \sim f_i(X_{1:i})$, as shown in Fig. 1(a). In Fig. 1(b), the BN contains CI information, so the number of connected edges is less than (a). However, BN (a) suffices to represent the BN (b) by setting the redundant edges with uniform distribution.

Theorem 1. Any sparse BN G of m nodes can be converted to an equivalent m dimensional complete BN G', with the equivalence $p(G) = p(G')$.

Proof. We can always set CPD for the edge in G' that is missed in G a uniform distribution. Then following the chain rule (1), such uniform CPDs will not change the joint distribution of the BN.

Theorem 1 ensures that we can always convert a sparse BN to its complete BN format, ensuring we obtain a unified representation for all BNs.

To perform exact inference for BNs, we use the Junction tree (JT) algorithm [5]. The JT construction involves moralization, triangulation, and node elimination processes. The moralization converts the BN G to an undirected graph (also known as Markov network) by connecting an edge (X_i, X_j) if there is an edge between X_i and X_j in BN G, or if X_i and X_j are parents of the same child node. The added edge between the parents that share the same child node is called a *moral edge*. The undirected graph is called triangulated if every cycle of length strictly greater than 3 possesses a chord. After performing these steps, we can obtain a maximal spanning tree as a JT if the triangulation is optimal. Each vertex in the JT is a cluster containing a set of BN variables. The space complexity of the JT is measured by the maximum cluster size -1, called the *tree-width* of a BN. The maximum cluster size controls the space complexity and is lower bounded by the maximum CPD size.

We must rely on approximate inference when exact inference is intractable for high tree-width BNs. We need first to reduce the CPD size of the BN to a minimum level so that the cluster size can be reduced in approximate methods. Then, we can further reduce the maximum cluster size using region graph-based methods.

2.2 Generalized Belief Propagation and Region Graph

Belief propagation (BP) [7] is a relatively simple approximate inference algorithm capturing only singleton interactions among variables in an undirected graph model. It converts the BN to a Markov network (MN) by using moralization and transforming the CPDs $p(X_i|X_{pa(i)})$ into factors $\varphi_a(X_a)$, in which X_a are variables in the factor φ_a, and the length of $|X_a|$ equals the factor size.

We can then express the joint distribution of the BN $p(X_1, \ldots, X_m)$ using a factor graph representation, which is a bipartite graph connecting the factor nodes a ($a \in \Phi$, with Φ be all factors in the MN) and the variable nodes i ($i = 1, \ldots, m$). The $p(X_1, \ldots, X_m)$ can then be expressed as:

$$p(X_1, \ldots, X_m) = \frac{1}{Z} \prod\nolimits_{a=1}^{\Phi} \varphi_a(X_a), \tag{2}$$

where Z is the normalization constant or partition function. Using Boltzmann's law [7], we can formularize (2) as the probability of a non-physical system at state $\boldsymbol{x}$, $p(X = \boldsymbol{x}) = (1/Z(T)) \cdot e^{-E(\boldsymbol{x})/T}$. Here T is the temperature and $E(X = \boldsymbol{x}) = -\sum_{a=1}^{\Phi} \ln \varphi_a(X_a)$ is the energy term of the system at state $\boldsymbol{x}$. The partition function $Z(T)$ is calculated as $Z(T) = \sum_{\boldsymbol{x} \in \boldsymbol{S}} e^{-E(\boldsymbol{x})/T}$, where $\boldsymbol{S}$ is the space of all possible states of the system.

When $Z(T)$ cannot be computed exactly, we can use a belief $b(X)$ to construct an approximation:

$$\mathcal{F}_{BFE}(b) = U(b) - H(b) = -\ln Z + D(b||p), \tag{3}$$

where $\mathcal{F}_{BFE}(b)$ is the Bethe free energy (BFE) [7], $U(b) = \sum_{\boldsymbol{x} \in \boldsymbol{S}} b(\boldsymbol{x}) E(\boldsymbol{x})$ and $H(b) = -\sum_{\boldsymbol{x} \in \boldsymbol{S}} b(\boldsymbol{x}) \ln b(\boldsymbol{x})$ are variational energy and variational entropy respectively. When the Kullback-Leibler distance $D(b||p) = 0$ the BFE achieves its minimal and recovers the partition function Z. Therefore minimizing $\mathcal{F}_{bethe}(b)$ approximates $-\ln Z$ when $D(b||p) \neq 0$. The beliefs contain limited information exchange in the factor graph representation since the factor nodes are only connected to singleton variable nodes, so only singleton node interactions are captured.

Compared to BP, GBP is more general as it allows higher-ordered node interactions during the approximation. This is achieved by using a region graph instead of a factor graph. For an undirected graphic model with joint distribution $p(X_1, \ldots, X_m)$, , (2) is rewritten as:

$$p(X_1, \ldots, X_m) = \frac{1}{Z} \prod\nolimits_{r \in R} \phi_r(X_r), \tag{4}$$

where R is a collection of subsets of variables $\boldsymbol{V}$; we call each $r \in R$ a *region*. Associated with each region r is a non-negative function $\phi_r(X_r)$. A *region graph* G_R is a directed graph in which each vertex $v \in G_R$ corresponding to a region r. We say v_p is an *ancestor* of v_c if $v_c \subset v_p$. If $v_p \rightarrow v_c$ is a directed edge, v_p is a *parent* of v_c.

Different from BP which optimizes the BFE, GBP optimizes the Kikuchi cluster free energy (KFE) [7] function. Optimizing the KFE involves defining a factored energy function regarding entropies over all regions as an approximation of $\mathcal{F}_{KFE}$, and enforcing a set of regions to obey consistency on the local polytope (rather than global marginal polytope). The key components are:

1. Define a collection of R-pseudo-beliefs $\{b_r(X_r), r \in R\}$.
2. Construct a constrained minimization problem of the form:

$$\{p_r(X_r)\} \cong \{b_r^*(X_r)\} := arg \min_{\{b_r(X_r) \in L_R\}} \mathcal{F}_{KFE}(\{b_r(X_r)\}), \tag{5}$$

$$\mathcal{F}_{KFE}(\{b_r(X_r)\}) := \sum_{r \in R} c_r \left\{ \sum_{X_r} b_r(X_r) E_r(X_r) + \sum_{X_r} b_r(X_r) \ln(b_r(X_r)) \right\}, \tag{6}$$

where the Lagrangian term $\mathcal{L}_R$ in (5) ensures belief consistency between parent-to-child regions, and the value in the belief is normalized:

$$\mathcal{L}_R := \Big\{ \{b_r(X_r), r \in R\} : \forall r, u \in R \; s.t. \; u \subset r, \sum_{X_{r \setminus u}} b_r(X_r) = b_u(X_u), \\ and \; \forall \, u \in R, \sum_{X_u} b_r(X_u) = 1 \Big\}. \tag{7}$$

The term E_r in (6) represents the energy associated with each region r. $c_r = 1 - \sum_{\hat{r} \in Ancestor(r)} c_{\hat{r}}$ is counting number of each region, given $c_{\hat{r}}$ is degrees of freedom for the region $\hat{r}$.

Optimizing (6) with constraints (7) can be achieved by using GBP message passing. The benefit of using the Kikuchi approximation is that we can use a collection of bounded-sized regions in Eqs. (5)–(7) to avoid the exponentially sized clusters in exact methods.

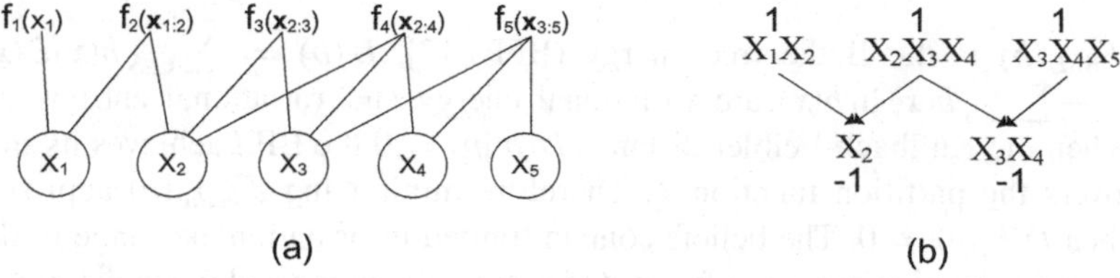

Fig. 2. (a) factor graph G_f and (b) CVM region graph G_R of Fig. 1(b) BN

The cluster variation method (CVM) [7] is used to construct a region graph, ensuring each node is counted exactly once. The CVM is a multi-level region graph with the first level regions, called the *outer regions*, absorbing all factors in the factor graph. The subsequent levels of regions are *inner regions*, which intersect the previous level regions. All outer regions use a default counting number 1, and all inner region counting numbers are calculated using the counting number definition. Figure 2 compares a factor graph G_f and a CVM region graph G_R for Fig. 1(b) BN. The CVM region graph encodes higher-ordered interactions among variables than the factor graph. So, region graph-based methods can be more accurate than factor graph-based methods.

The CVM region graph is determined when the outer regions are defined. However, CVM does not define the outer regions. The loop structured region graph (LSRG) [10] is a well-known outer region selection algorithm that selects outer regions solely based on the model structure information. The merit of LSRG is that it satisfies two important region properties: maxent-entropy normal and tree-robustness. The maxent-normal requires that if a constrained region-based free energy approximation is valid, the corresponding region-based entropy achieves its maximum when all the beliefs are uniform. This property can be easily achieved by following the CVM algorithm.

The tree-robustness requires that a structured region graph can be reduced so that inference on any spanning tree of G is exact. Therefore, the LSRG selects cycle faces from an undirected graph model G as outer regions by ensuring any spanning tree of G runs exactly under these selected outer regions. Apparently, this property is difficult to satisfy for general structured models. So, the LSRG [10] defined the outer regions that satisfy the tree-robustness for two typical graph structures: the grid MN and the complete MN, in which each edge of the MN encodes a pairwise factor. The LSRG selects outer regions for a complete MN as follows: (i) choose a root node i as the starting point. (ii) from node i create a spanning tree of the MN, with the off-tree edges (j, k). (iii) create (i, j, k) as the outer regions.

The LSRG is promising but has several limitations when applying it to BNs. BN is a directed graph model, so choosing which node as the root node is undefined by LSRG. The cycle size found by LSRG is not equal, presenting difficulties in controlling the space complexity.

3 Amortized BN Inference

Section 3.1 derives the pairwise conversion algorithm for BN CPDs. Section 3.2 presents an improved LSRG algorithm bespoke for BNs. Finally, Sect. 3.3 constructs the amortized PWC-LSRG algorithm.

3.1 Pairwise Decomposition of CPDs

Reducing the CPD size can be achieved from either the factor or the CPD level. Representing methods are binary factorization (BF) [11, 17] and MRF decomposition [18]. The BF reduces the CPD size by introducing intermediate nodes to ensure each node connects no more than two parent nodes. The MRF decomposition [18] can decompose the general MN factors into pairwise factors by introducing an auxiliary node, with the new pairwise factors defined as the fraction power of the original factor. This method is inconvenient to apply to BN when the CPD size is large.

Our proposed pairwise decomposition method is a two-step hybrid algorithm. We use BF to reduce the CPD size to three initially. Then for each triplet CPD, we decompose it into three pairwise CPDs and two associated hidden pairwise factors. The process is exact. The joint distribution of the BN is then expressed as the product of all pairwise factors.

We binary factorize the BN G by adding intermediate nodes and obtaining an equivalent BF model G', in which every node has at most two parent nodes. Equivalence means that the BF model G' can always rebuild the CPDs in the BN G through intermediate nodes. It has been proved in [11] that the BF process is exact for discrete BNs, so any ordered joint distributions defined on the same variables between G and G' are the same. The benefit of using the BF algorithm is to ensure the CPD size is no larger than three.

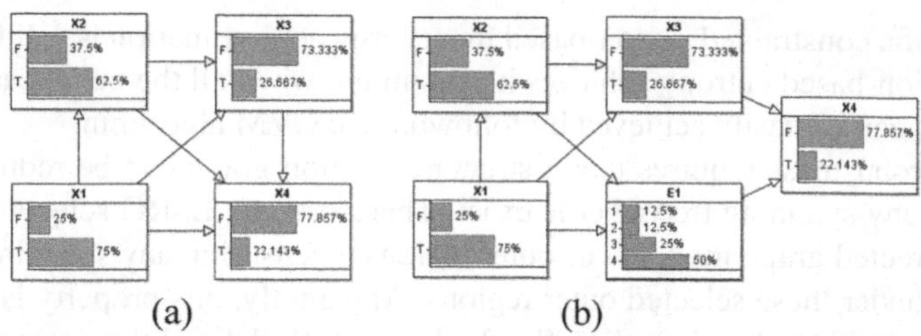

Fig. 3. (a) a 4-dimensional complete discrete BN G with all binary variables; (b) a binary factorized BN G' of (a). The singleton marginal distributions are obtained using the JT algorithm in AgenaRisk [19].

Figure 3 presents the BF algorithm for factorizing a 4-dimensional complete BN G into its BF model G'. In general, the CPD for the added intermediate node E has the form:

$$p\left(E = e_{ij} | X = x_p, Y = y_q\right) = \begin{cases} 1 \; if \; p = i \; and \; q = j \\ 0 \qquad\qquad otherwise \end{cases}, \tag{8}$$

where X, Y are parents of E, x_p $(p = 1, \ldots, m_1)$ and y_q $(q = 1, \ldots, m_2)$ are node states, and e_{ij} $(i = 1, \ldots, m_1, j = 1, \ldots, m_2)$ is an $m_1 \times m_2$ CPD matrix for E.

Following (8), we can always obtain a binary factorized BN, with a maximum CPD size of three.

In general, for a triplet CPD $p(X_3|X_1, X_2)$ with the associated possible pairwise CPDs $p(X_1|X_{pa(1)})$ and $p(X_2|X_{pa(2)})$, we can introduce an intermediate node Z with the settings in (9) to decompose $p(X_3|X_1, X_2)$ into pairwise CPDs. The scope of Z is the Cartesian product: $\mathcal{S}(Z) = \mathcal{S}(X_1) \times \mathcal{S}(X_2) \times \mathcal{S}(X_3)$. Therefore, $Z = z_j$ $(j = 1, \ldots, |\mathcal{S}(Z)|)$ takes the value of all assignments of (X_1, X_2, X_3). We have:

$$\begin{cases} p(Z) = \varphi_{123}(X_1, X_2, X_3), \\ p\left(X_1 = x_1 | Z = z_j\right) = 1, \; if \; x_1 \subset assignment \; j \\ p\left(X_2 = x_2 | Z = z_j\right) = 1, \; if \; x_2 \subset assignment \; j \\ p\left(X_3 = x_3 | Z = z_j\right) = 1, \; if \; x_3 \subset assignment \; j \end{cases}, \tag{9}$$

where $\varphi_{123}(X_1, X_2, X_3)$ is the function of $p(X_3|X_1, X_2)$. Due to the complementary property of the CPD, other entries not in (9) are set to zero. Because (9) adds new connections $Z \rightarrow X_1$ and $Z \rightarrow X_2$ for constructing the new CPDs, the original CPDs $p(X_1|X_{pa(1)})$ and $p(X_2|X_{pa(2)})$ cannot be explicitly represented in the BN. So, they are set as hidden pairwise factors (as opposed to CPDs) in the inference phase. Note that we cannot multiply the CPD $p(X_1|X_{pa(1)})$ into $p(X_1|Z)$ as that breaks the pairwise factor constraint.

Figure 4 shows an example using (9). The CPD $p(C|A, B)$ in (a) G does not associate with pairwise CPDs for the parent nodes A and B, so we simply introduce a new node Z_0 in (b) $\widehat{G}$ following (9). Node C is then disconnected to A and B and connects to Z_0 instead. Similarly, we need to introduce a new node Z_1 to decompose the CPD $p(F|D, E)$ in (b). The CPD $p(F|D, E)$ is associated with two pairwise CPDs $p(D|B)$ and $p(E|C)$, which are set as hidden pairwise factors, shown as dashed edges in (b). After exact inference, both (a) G and (b) $\widehat{G}$ produced identical marginal results.

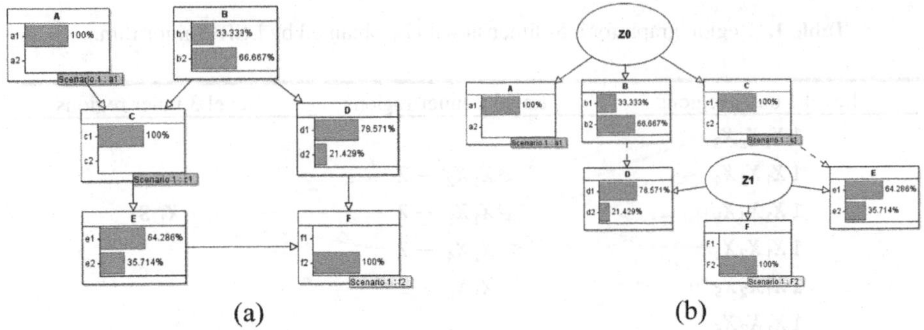

Fig. 4. (a) a binary factorized BN G; (b) pairwise converted BN $\widehat{G}$ of G. The dashed edges represent hidden CPDs.

Proposition 1. The pairwise conversion (PWC) (9) is an exact procedure to convert BN G into its equivalent pairwise representation BN $\widehat{G}$.

Proof. The CPD $p\big(X_1 = x_1 | Z = z_j\big) = 1$ in (9) can be viewed as an indicator function, which means taking the relevant values in $\varphi_{123}(X_1, X_2, X_3)$. So multiplying all the CPDs in (9) and integrating Z out, we end up with $\varphi_{123}(X_1, X_2, X_3)$, equaling $p(X_3|X_1, X_2)$. The hidden pairwise factors are BN CPDs. Therefore, our pairwise converted BN $\widehat{G}$ does not change the chain rule (1) for BN G, hence $p\Big(\widehat{G}\Big) = p(G)$.

3.2 LSRG Algorithm with Node Ordering

Given a pairwise converted BN $\widehat{G}$ we can apply LSRG directly to its moralized graph. However, the LSRG does not consider the node ordering information of the BN, resulting in less optimal region graph constructions. To improve that, we introduce a node ordering π using the BN $\widehat{G}$ and produce a complete BN $\widehat{G}_\pi$ following the ordering π. LSRG will select regions directly from $\widehat{G}_\pi$.

The **node ordering** π is defined as $\pi := \{X_1 \rightarrow, \ldots, \rightarrow X_m\}$ for the m variables in $\widehat{G}$, where for any X_j that is the successor to X_i, $X_j \notin X_{pa(i)}$.

Following the definition of π we can define node ordering for Fig. 4(b) $\widehat{G}$ with $\pi := \{Z_0 \rightarrow A \rightarrow B \rightarrow C \rightarrow Z_1 \rightarrow D \rightarrow E \rightarrow F\}$ and obtain an 8-dimensional complete BN $\widehat{G}_\pi$ (model accessible at [20]), with the pairwise CPD not contained in $\widehat{G}$ a uniform distribution. Since every pair of nodes in $\widehat{G}_\pi$ are connected, the structure of $\widehat{G}_\pi$ is the same to its moralized graph. We can therefore choose Z_0 as the root node for LSRG to obtain the outer regions conveniently. Note that all outer region size is limited to size three regardless of how large the tree-width of the BN is.

To give a relatively simple example of our improved LSRG region graph, we consider a 5-dimensional $\widehat{G}_\pi$, i.e., shown in Fig. 1(a) with the node ordering already defined as $\pi := \{X_1 \rightarrow X_2 \rightarrow X_3 \rightarrow X_4 \rightarrow X_5\}$. Assuming all CPDs are pairwise and singletons, the joint distribution $p(X_1, \ldots, X_5) = \frac{1}{Z} \prod_{(i,j) \in \boldsymbol{E}} \varphi_{ij}\big(X_i, X_j\big) \prod_{i \in V} \varphi_i(X_i)$. The improved LSRG region graph is shown in Table 1.

Table 1. Region graph for a 5-dimensional $\widehat{G}_{\pi}$ obtained by LSRG algorithm.

Level 1 outer regions	Level 2 inner regions	Level 3 inner regions
1 $X_1X_2X_3$		
1 $X_1X_3X_4$	X_1X_2 −2	
1 $X_1X_4X_5$	X_1X_3 −2	X_1 3
1 $X_1X_2X_4$	X_1X_4 −2	
1 $X_1X_2X_5$	X_1X_5 −2	
1 $X_1X_3X_5$		

In Table 1, the region counting numbers are listed aside from each region. The root node is X_1. The inner regions are obtained using the CVM algorithm. It can be verified that this region graph satisfies the tree-robustness property so that the approximation will be sensible. It is possible to remove some outer regions to increase efficiency since not all edges are connected in the BN. This can be achieved by removing outer regions such that all involved edges are unregularized.

We proposed an improved LSRG algorithm directly applicable to BN inference problems. Furthermore, the energy function defined by this improved LSRG region graph can be amortized using a (deep) neural network to receive performance gains.

3.3 Amortizing

Amortizing [14–16] means using neural network-based methods to minimize the BFE or KFE function. The parameters in the BFE/KFE are amortized by alternatively optimizing the neural network parameters. It has been shown [7, 16] that the KFE is superior to the BFE, provided that the region graph is well defined, no matter whether the function is minimized by GBP message passing or neural networks. Therefore, we omit the BFE and its associated amortizing formulas for brevity. Minimization of the KFE using amortized technique involves the following steps:

1. Given an n-level region graph G_R, predict the region beliefs for outer regions $b_r(r \in R_{level1})$ by:

$$b_r(\boldsymbol{x}_r; \boldsymbol{\omega}) = \text{softmax}(\boldsymbol{f}(G_R, r; \boldsymbol{\omega})), \tag{10}$$

   where $\mathbf{f}(G_R, r; \boldsymbol{\omega})$ is a vector of scores for all variable configurations in region r, produced by a neural network with parameters $\boldsymbol{\omega}$. The b_r is then predicted by using a SoftMax function of the neural network.

2. Compute the inner region beliefs $b_u(u \in R_{level2:n})$ by:

$$b_u(\boldsymbol{x}_u; \boldsymbol{\omega}) = \frac{1}{|R_{pa(u)}|} \sum\nolimits_{r_p \in R_{pa(u)}} \sum\nolimits_{\boldsymbol{x}_p \setminus \boldsymbol{x}_u} b_p(\boldsymbol{x}_p; \boldsymbol{\omega}), \tag{11}$$

where $R_{pa(u)}$ denotes all the parent regions of u, and $|\cdot|$ is the length of the set. Equation (11) means that the inner region belief is the average over the same subset of all the parent region beliefs.

3. The constrained KFE objective is then minimized as:

$$\min_{\omega} \mathcal{F}_{KFE}(\{b_r(x_r)\}) + \gamma \sum\nolimits_r \sum\nolimits_{r_p \in R_{pa(r)}} d\left(b_r, \sum\nolimits_{x_p \setminus x_r} b_p(x_p; \omega)\right), \quad (12)$$

where γ is a tuning parameter and $d(\cdot, \cdot)$ is a L_2 distance measuring the mismatch between the current and the estimated belief for determining convergence.

The input of the neural network are pairwise factors of the MN, and the region graph constraints are used as penalties. So, the amortized technique for GBP can be viewed as consuming a region graph and outputting the beliefs as predictions. So far, only specific MRFs with pairwise and singleton factors are studied under amortized techniques for GBP, such as the Ising model [15] and the complete MN model [16].

Specifically, each node X_i is undergone a Transformer [21] layer to obtain a hidden node representation h_i, which is associated with a learnable embedding vector e_i. If the outer region size is 2, the pairwise belief for a region $r_{i,j}$ is obtained by applying an affine layer followed by a softmax function: $b_{ij}(x_i, x_j) = \mathrm{softmax}\left(\mathbf{W}\left[\mathrm{h_i}, \mathrm{h_j}\right] + \mathrm{b}\right)$.

Since all CPDs are converted into pairwise factors and the region graph is obtained by our improved LSRG algorithm, the PWC-LSRG region graph with the associated factors can directly fit into the amortized inference framework (10) (11) (12). The resulting amortized PWC-LSRG algorithm is given in Table 2.

Table 2. Amortized PWC-LSRG algorithm

Input: a discrete BN $\boldsymbol{G}$ with CPD for each variable $\boldsymbol{X_i}$ $(\boldsymbol{i} = \mathbf{1}, \ldots, \boldsymbol{m})$.
Output: Marginals of $\boldsymbol{G}$.

01: obtain binary factorized BN $\boldsymbol{G_1} \leftarrow \boldsymbol{BF}(\boldsymbol{G})$, with variables $\boldsymbol{X_j}$ $(\boldsymbol{j} = \mathbf{1}, \ldots, \boldsymbol{m_1})$;
02: initialize a BN $\widehat{\boldsymbol{G}} = \boldsymbol{G_1}$;
03: **for** each CPD $\boldsymbol{p}(\boldsymbol{X_j}|\boldsymbol{X_{pa(j)}})$ in $\widehat{\boldsymbol{G}}$:
04: **if** $|\boldsymbol{p}(\boldsymbol{X_j}|\boldsymbol{X_{pa(j)}})| = \mathbf{3}$:
05: add an intermediate node $\boldsymbol{Z}$ with the CPD defined in (9) and reconnect all nodes;
06: convert $\boldsymbol{p}(\boldsymbol{X_{pa(j)}}|\boldsymbol{X_{pa(pa(j))}})$ as hidden pairwise factors in $\widehat{\boldsymbol{G}}$;
07: **end If** #4; **end for** #3;
08: define a node ordering $\boldsymbol{\pi}$ for all variables $\boldsymbol{X_k}$ $(\boldsymbol{k} = \mathbf{1}, \ldots, \boldsymbol{m_2})$ in $\widehat{\boldsymbol{G}}$
09: convert $\widehat{\boldsymbol{G}}$ to its corresponding complete BN $\widehat{\boldsymbol{G}}_{\boldsymbol{\pi}}$;
10: choose the first node in $\boldsymbol{\pi}$ as the root node;
11: select outer regions $\boldsymbol{R_{level1}}$ using the LSRG algorithm for $\widehat{\boldsymbol{G}}_{\boldsymbol{\pi}}$;
12: build the region graph $\boldsymbol{G_R} = \boldsymbol{CVM}(\boldsymbol{R_{level1}})$ and assign all the pairwise factors into relevant outer regions;
13: train a (deep) neural network by consuming $\boldsymbol{G_R}$ using (10) (11) (12);
14: output marginal beliefs using (10) for $\widehat{\boldsymbol{G}}_{\boldsymbol{\pi}}$;
15: **return** the marginals of $\boldsymbol{X_i}$ in $\boldsymbol{G}$ by marginalizing irrelevant variables from the beliefs in 14

4 Evaluations

4.1 Validation of the PWC Algorithm

The testing environment is Java 1.8, i5-9400H. We use Fig. 4 BN, the well-known Student [1], and Grid [1] BNs for the testing. All these tests can be accessed online [20]. Each test BN is associated with two observations, and the CPDs are randomly generated. The testing purpose is to validate that the PWC sub-algorithm is exact.

Table 3. log$p(e)$ Comparison of G and its pairwise converted BN $\widehat{G}$ using JT inference.

BNs	log$p(e)$ of G	log$p(e)$ of $\widehat{G}$	Abs. diff.
Figure 4 BN (m = 6, t.w. 2)	−1.4579	−1.4579	0
Student (m = 8, t.w. 3)	−1.6478	−1.6478	0
3 × 3 Grid (m = 9, t.w. 3)	−1.8457	−1.8457	0

We use the probability of evidence log$p(e)$ [1] for the testing as log$p(e)$ reflects the overall accuracy of the BN when given observations. Table 3 shows that the results obtained by using BN $\widehat{G}$ is the same with which obtained by G under the JT inference. These tests also empirically validated the Proposition 1.

4.2 Validation of the PWC-LSRG Region Graph

The testing environment is Java 1.8, i5-9400H. We use the BNs in 4.1 and two more well-known BNs, Asia [4] and HMM [1], for the testing. The testing purpose is to validate that the region graph generated by PWC-LSRG yields sensible approximations under GBP message passing.

Table 4. log$p(e)$ Comparison of PWC-LSRG with competing algorithms.

BNs	JT (exact)	BP (diff.)	IJGP (diff.)	PWC-LSRG (diff.)
Fig. 4 BN	-1.111	2.90E-07	2.90E-07	2.90E-07
Asia	-0.959	2.01E-13	0	3.69E-12
Student	-0.590	9.91E-11	2.19E-11	2.64E-10
2x3 HMM	-1.410	7.58E-10	1.39E-09	9.72E-11
5x5 Grid	-0.320	0.002792	0.003036	1.50E-04

Table 4 shows the exact results obtained by JT and the absolute difference for all approximate algorithms. The PWC-LSRG outperforms other approximate algorithms on accuracy as BP and IJGP degrade significantly when the tree-width increases. For example, they are considerably worse than PWC-LSRG on the 5 × 5 Grid ($t.w. = 5$), shown with results in orange.

4.3 Validation of the Amortized PWC-LSRG Algorithm

Next, the testing environment is Python 3.9, Apple Silicon M1-Max. The testing purpose is to validate the efficiency gains obtained by using amortized PWC-LSRG algorithm (code accessible at [20]).

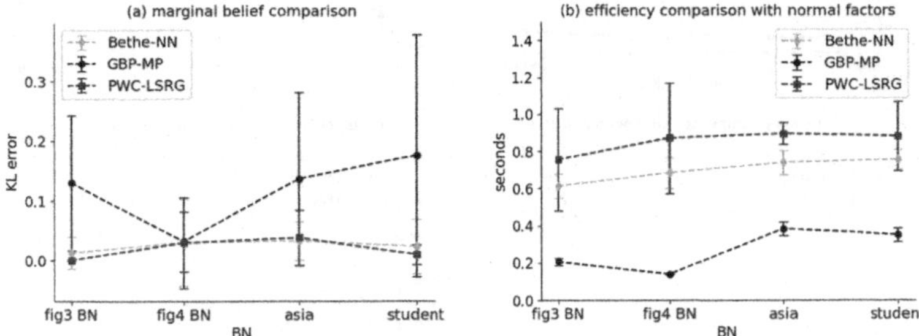

Fig. 5. Compares the accuracy using (a) singleton marginal belief and efficiency (b) for three competing algorithms: Bethe-NN [15], GBP-MP [7], and amortized PWC-LSRG.

We conduct tests on low and high tree-width BNs respectively, as shown in Fig. 5 and 6. As all BN inputs for PWC-LSRG are complete BNs $\widehat{G}_{\pi}$. To improve efficiency, we can remove unnecessary regions generated by PWC-LSRG for sparse BNs in Fig. 5. The competing algorithms are amortized Bethe energy neural network (Bethe-NN) [15], and GBP message passing with CVM region graph (GBP-MP) [7]. Both Bethe-NN and amortized PWC-LSRG use the same (deep) neural network layers (Attention + two residual layers + SoftMax) for fairness. The different values of the tuning parameter γ in (12) can influence the accuracy of the amortized PWC-LSRG, but we set $\gamma = 3$ for all tests for simplicity. In Fig. 5(a) the amortized PWC-LSRG achieved the best accuracy for singleton marginal beliefs over randomly generated CPDs, but is the slowest algorithm, as shown in (b). This is because the number of variables is small in these tests, and the message passing algorithm is slightly more efficient than amortized technique. Still, all algorithms complete the tests under 1 s.

Next, for high tree-width BN tests, we use randomly generated CPDs for complete BNs $\widehat{G}_{\pi}$ from 4 to 16 variables, hence the tree-width increases from 3 to 15. Although the number of variables is not large, in practice, most BNs won't exceed the tree-width 15, thus the test is challenging. Figure 6 error bar results of mean and std. are obtained using 20 instances for each sub-figure. It is expected that PWC-LSRG has outperformed the other two algorithms in accuracy, as shown in (a) (b) for log$p(e)$ and marginal beliefs because its region graph is superior to others. The efficiency of amortized PWC-LSRG is about four times faster than GBP-MP using both normal (*uniform* [0, 1]) and extreme (near zero and one) CPDs, as shown in (c) and (d). We can expect a further improvement in efficiency by using powerful GPU processors. The Bethe-NN is slightly more efficient than PWC-LSRG in extreme CPD cases, given it consumes a factor graph rather than a region graph, thus trading accuracy with efficiency.

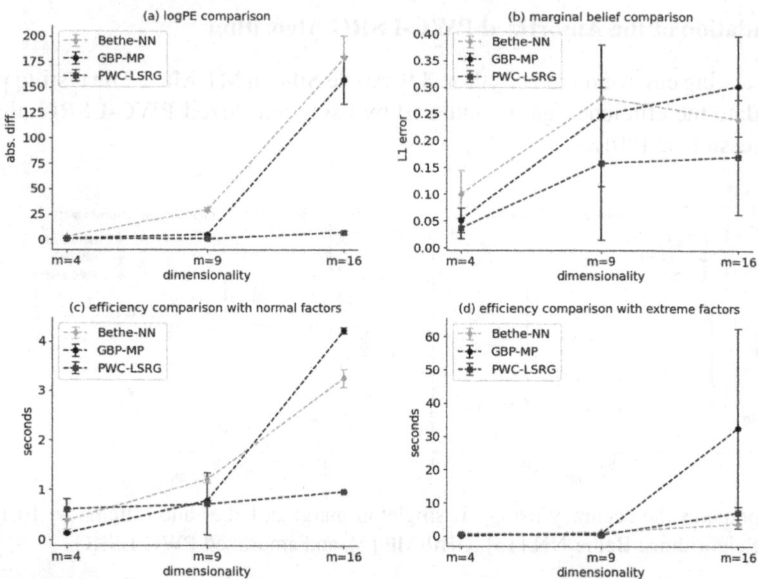

Fig. 6. 2×2 figure box comparing the accuracy (a) (b) and efficiency (c) (d) for three competing algorithms: Bethe-NN [15], GBP-MP [7], and amortized PWC-LSRG.

5 Conclusion and Future Works

We empirically validated that our proposed PWC-LSRG region graph is more accurate than the competing algorithms. More importantly, based on the pairwise decomposition and improved region graph construction, the PWC-LSRG optimization for the KFE function can be directly amortized using (deep) neural networks, avoiding the iterative message passing and obtaining good convergence property. The efficiency gain is significant. Future work will remove the unnecessary outer regions during the region graph construction phase to apply this algorithm to large BNs.

Acknowledgment. This work was partly supported by the Special Fund for Fundamental Scientific Research of the Beijing Colleges in CUEB No. QNTD202109. We acknowledge Agena, Ltd. for software support.

References

1. Koller, D., Friedman, N.: Probabilistic Graphical Models - Principles and Techniques. MIT Press, Cambridge (2009)
2. Pearl, J.: Causality. Cambridge University Press, Cambridge (2009)
3. Wang, J., Neil, M., Fenton, N.: A Bayesian network approach for cybersecurity risk assessment implementing and extending the FAIR model. Comput. Secur. **89**, 101659 (2020)
4. Fenton, N., Neil, M.: Risk Assessment and Decision Analysis with Bayesian Networks. CRC Press, Boca Raton (2018)

5. Lauritzen, S.L., Spiegelhalter, D.J.: Local computations with probabilities on graphical structures and their application to expert systems. J. R. Stat. Soc. Ser. B **50**, 157–224 (1988)
6. Beal, M.J.: Variational Algorithms for Approximate Bayesian Inference. The Gatsby Computational Neuroscience Unit. University College London, London (2003)
7. Yedidia, J.S., Freeman, W.T., Weiss, Y.: Constructing free-energy approximations and generalized belief propagation algorithms. IEEE Trans. Inf. Theory **51**, 2282–2312 (2005)
8. Neil, M., Tailor, M., Marquez, D.: Inference in hybrid Bayesian networks using dynamic discretization. Stat. Comput. **17**, 219–233 (2007)
9. Mateescu, R., Kask, K., Gogate, V., Dechter, R.: Join-graph propagation algorithms J. . Artif. Intell. Res. **37**, 279–328 (2010)
10. Gelfand, A., Welling, M.: Generalized belief propagation on tree robust structured region graphs. In: UAI 2012: Proceedings of the Twenty-Eighth Conference on Uncertainty in Artificial Intelligence, pp. 296–305 (2012)
11. Lin, P., Neil, M., Fenton, N.: Improved high dimensional discrete bayesian network inference using triplet region construction. J. Artif. Intell. Res. **69**, 231–295 (2020)
12. Yoon, K., et al.: Inference in probabilistic graphical models by graph neural networks. In: Sixth International Conference on Learning Representations (ICLR) Workshop (2018)
13. Zhang, Z., Wu, F., Lee, W.S.: Factor graph neural network. In: Thirty-Fourth Conference on Neural Information Processing Systems, pp. 8577–8587 (2020)
14. Srikumar, V., Kundu, G., Roth, D.: On amortizing inference cost for structured prediction. In: Proceedings of the 2012 Joint Conference on Empirical Methods in Natural Language Processing and Computational Natural Language Learning, pp. 1114–1124. Association for Computational Linguistics (2012)
15. Wiseman, S., Kim, Y.: Amortized Bethe free energy minimization for learning MRFs. In: Thirty-Third Conference on Neural Information Processing Systems, pp. 15520–15531 (2019)
16. Liu, D., Thobaben, R., Rasmussen, L.K.: Region-based energy neural network for approximate inference. arXiv preprint arXiv:2006.09927 (2020)
17. Neil, M., Chen, X., Fenton, N.: Optimizing the calculation of conditional probability tables in hybrid Bayesian networks using binary factorization. IEEE Trans. Knowl. Data Eng. **24**, 1306–1322 (2012)
18. Wainwright, M.J., Jordan, M.I.: Graphical models, exponential families, and variational inference. Found. Trends Mach. Learn. **1**, 1–305 (2008)
19. Agena Ltd. AgenaRisk. https://www.agenarisk.com
20. Lin, P.: Amortized BN inference. https://github.com/penglin17/amortizedBNinference
21. Vaswani, A., et al.: Attention is all you need. In: Advances in Neural Information Processing Systems, vol. 30, pp. 5998–6008 (2017)

VDDL: A Deep Learning-Based Vulnerability Detection Model for Smart Contracts

Fan Jiang[1], Yuanlong Cao[1], Jianmao Xiao[1](✉), Hui Yi[1], Gang Lei[1], Min Liu[1], Shuiguang Deng[2], and Hao Wang[1]

[1] School of Software, Jiangxi Normal University, Nanchang, China
jm_xiao@jxnu.edu.cn

[2] College of Computer Science, Zhejiang University, Hangzhou, China

Abstract. With the widespread use of smart contracts in various fields, the research on smart contract vulnerability detection has increased yearly. Most of the previous research work is based on symbol detection and comparison with expert-defined error patterns to analyze the possible vulnerabilities of smart contracts. The accuracy and performance of such methods are generally low. In response to this problem, this paper proposes an efficient smart contract vulnerability detection model VDDL (Vulnerability Detection Based on Deep Learning). VDDL uses a multi-layer bidirectional Transformer architecture as the model architecture, involving a multi-head attention mechanism and a masking mechanism. A multi-head attention mechanism is applied in the encoder-decoder layer. The masking mechanism randomly masks the input tokens and combined with the context to predict the masked tokens, a deep bidirectional representation for training is realized. Furthermore, VDDL incorporates CodeBERT, a large bimodal pre-trained model for natural and programming languages, to improve training performance. We collected 47,038 smart contracts as datasets for model training and testing. In the end, the accuracy of VDDL reached 92.35%, the recall reached 81.43%, and the F1-score reached 86.38%, which can efficiently detect possible loopholes in smart contracts.

Keywords: Blockchain · Deep learning · Smart contract · Transformer · Vulnerability

1 Introduction

Smart contract is a computer protocol that disseminates, verifies, or executes contracts in an information-based manner. This concept was proposed by Nick Szabo in 1995. With the advent of Bitcoin, distributed ledger technology (aka blockchain) was proposed, implementing smart contract technology possible. Ethereum [1] combines smart contracts with blockchain for the first time, realizing smart contracts in a true sense. Ethereum is by far the most famous smart contract platform.

Smart contracts have involved more than 10 billion dollars worth of value in various fields, which has greatly stimulated hackers to attack. For example, in the famous DAO incident, hackers exploited the reentrancy vulnerability to attack the DAO contract and

Y. Xu et al. (Eds.): ML4CS 2022, LNCS 13655, pp. 72–86, 2023.
https://doi.org/10.1007/978-3-031-20096-0_6

stole USD 60 million worth of ether on the Ethereum platform. This event directly led to the decision of the Ethereum community to make a hard fork, and the hard fork was successful.

In addition, because of the anonymity of the public chain platform, it is challenging to trace the origin of the attacker. And smart contracts are immutable and cannot be modified after deployment on the chain. Even if you want to update the contract, you can only do so by deploying a new contract and transferring funds. Therefore, it is a very critical process to perform security vulnerability detection on smart contracts before they are deployed on the chain.

There are many tools for vulnerability detection of smart contracts. Luu et al. [2] proposed Oyente, the first tool for security analysis of smart contracts, which uses dynamic symbolic execution techniques for security vulnerability detection. Feist et al. [3] proposed the Slither tool, a static analysis framework implemented by converting the solidity smart contract language into an intermediate representation of SlithIR. Tsankov et al. [4] proposed Securify, a scalable, fully automated security analyzer for smart contracts. Brent et al. [5] proposed Vandal, a security analysis framework for Ethereum smart contracts that includes an analysis pipeline to convert Ethereum Virtual Machine (EVM) bytecodes into logical semantic relationships. Reference [6] provides Mythril, a security analysis tool for EVM bytecode. It uses symbolic execution, SMT resolution, and taint analysis to detect various security vulnerabilities. [7] proposed ZEUS, a tool that leverages abstract interpretation and symbolic model checking, along with the power of CHC, to determine verification conditions quickly. Chang et al. [8] provided Scompile, a tool for detecting vulnerabilities in Ethereum smart contracts based on symbolic execution, which improved the detection efficiency by optimizing the selection of paths. Jiang et al. [9] proposed ContractFuzzer, which uses a fuzzing method to detect vulnerabilities in Ethereum smart contracts. Liu et al. [10] proposed ReGuard, a tool for vulnerability detection of Ethereum smart contracts based on fuzzing, mainly to detect reentrancy vulnerabilities. Gao et al. [11] proposed EasyFlow, a tool that detects error types that are integer overflows. EasyFlow can not only distinguish contracts into security contracts and contracts with overflow vulnerabilities but also automatically generate transactions that trigger integer overflow vulnerabilities. Reference [12] proposes a static analysis framework, Orisis, based on symbolic execution and taint analysis, which can detect integer overflow-type vulnerabilities in Ethereum smart contracts. The input to this tool is the bytecode or source code of the smart contract, which can be compiled to bytecode. Most of these tools are based on conventional methods such as symbolic execution and expert-defined error patterns, and there are not many ML-based(based on machine learning) vulnerability detection tools with better performance. In response to this problem, this paper proposes a high-performance smart contract vulnerability detection model based on deep learning, named VDDL (Vulnerability Detection Based on Deep Learning).

VDDL uses a multi-layer bidirectional Transformer architecture as the model architecture, which involves a multi-head attention mechanism and a masking mechanism. A multi-head attention mechanism is applied in the encoder-decoder layer. The encoder contains a self-attention layer. The masking mechanism enables training deep bidirectional representations by simply masking a certain percentage of input tokens at random and predicting the masked tokens. VDDL uses 47,038 smart contracts collected and processed as a dataset, combined with a large-scale bimodal pre-training model CodeBERT for training. The Accuracy, Recall, and F1-score of the final model surpasses other traditional ML-based methods.

The main contributions of this paper are as follows:

- Proposed a high-performance smart contract vulnerability detection model based on deep learning: VDDL. A multi-layer bidirectional Transformer architecture is used as the model architecture, involving a multi-head attention mechanism and a masking mechanism. VDDL can efficiently detect possible vulnerabilities in smart contracts.
- Collected a large number of smart contract source code data sets from Etherscan, marked 47,038 smart contracts, and performed data cleaning and slicing on them. We make the dataset public on GitHub for relevant researchers to use.

The remainder of this paper is organized as follows: Sect. 2 presents related work. Section 3 introduces the architecture of the VDDL model method and describes it in detail from the perspectives of Extraction, Training, and Prediction. Section 4 introduces the deployment of our project and the comparison with other smart contract vulnerability detection tools. Section 5 is the conclusion and future work of this paper.

2 Related Work

Vulnerability detection of smart contracts has always been a very popular research direction. Early vulnerability detection tools were mainly implemented by experts defining error patterns. With the widespread use of machine learning in natural language processing, several ML-based vulnerability detection tools for smart contracts have gradually emerged, which have improved in terms of accuracy compared to others.

Most of the previous research work is based on symbol detection and comparison with expert-defined error patterns to analyze the possible vulnerabilities of smart contracts. Luu et al. [2] proposed Oyente, the first tool for security analysis of smart contracts, which uses dynamic symbolic execution techniques for security vulnerability detection. The input is the bytecode of the smart contract, which can detect four types of error modes: Transaction-Ordering Dependence, Timestamp Dependence, Mishandled Exceptions, and Reentrancy Vulnerability. Feist et al. [3] proposed a tool called Slither, a static analysis framework implemented by converting the solidity smart contract language into an intermediate representation of SlithIR. This tool can be used to automatically detect vulnerabilities, automatically detect code optimization, improve users' understanding of contracts and assist in code review. Tsankov et al. [4] proposed a tool called Securify, a scalable and fully automated smart contract security analyzer. It can prove whether the behavior of the contract is safe for a given property. Brent et al. [5] proposed Vandal, which is a security analysis framework for Ethereum smart contracts, which includes an analysis pipeline to convert Ethereum Virtual Machine (EVM) bytecodes into logical semantic relationships. Then use the logic specification written in Soufflé language to carry out the security analysis work. Mythril [6] is a security analysis tool for EVM bytecode. It detects security vulnerabilities in smart contracts built for Ethereum, Hedera, Quorum, Vechain, Roostock, Tron, and other EVM-compatible blockchains. It uses symbolic execution, SMT resolution, and taint analysis to detect various security vulnerabilities. It is also used in the MythX security analysis platform (in conjunction with other tools and techniques). Kalra et al. [7] proposed a vulnerability detection tool ZEUS that utilizes abstract interpretation and symbolic model checking, which utilizes abstract interpretation and symbolic model checking, as well as the power of CHC to determine verification conditions quickly. Chang et al. [8] provided Scompile, a tool for detecting vulnerabilities in Ethereum smart contracts based on symbolic execution, which improved the detection efficiency by optimizing the selection of paths. The tool takes Ethereum bytecode as input, builds a control flow graph, and enumerates all paths. Identifying a currency-related path and scoring it according to whether it violates a pre-defined security property. Then use symbolic execution to filter out infeasible critical paths, and finally present the inspection results and related paths to the user. Jiang et al. [9] proposed ContractFuzzer, the first tool for vulnerability detection of Ethereum smart contracts using a fuzzing approach. It first analyzes the application binary interface (ABI) of the smart contract, parses information such as function parameter types, randomly generates test cases to call the contract according to the parsed relevant information, and obtains the contract execution log by monitoring the EVM, and analyzes it. These logs are used to report security breaches. Liu et al. [10] proposed ReGuard, a tool for vulnerability detection of Ethereum smart contracts based on fuzzing, mainly to detect reentrancy vulnerabilities. The implementation method of ReGuard is to detect after translating source code or byte code into C++ language. Gao et al. [11] proposed EasyFlow, a tool that detects error types that are integer overflows. EasyFlow can not only distinguish contracts into security contracts and contracts with overflow vulnerabilities but also automatically generate transactions that trigger integer overflow vulnerabilities. Torres [12] proposed a static analysis framework Orisis based on symbolic execution and taint analysis, which can detect integer overflow type vulnerabilities in Ethereum smart contracts. The input to the tool is the bytecode or source code of the smart contract, where the source code can be compiled into bytecode.

In recent years, research on the application of machine learning to vulnerability detection of smart contracts has gradually emerged. Compared with vulnerability detection tools based on symbolic execution and expert-defined error patterns, ML-based vulnerability detection tools have improved in terms of accuracy and other metrics.

Gao et al. [13] proposed SmartEmbed, the first tool to use machine learning techniques in smart contract vulnerability detection. The tool applies two embedding algorithms: word2vec and FastText. Through embedding learning, the normalized word spacing between codes can be obtained, so that the similarity between different smart contracts can be detected. Finally, they judged whether the smart contract has security risks by comparing it with the collected vulnerability error pattern code base. Liu et al. [14] combined graph neural networks and expert knowledge to implement vulnerability detection work. They transformed source code and data flow semantics into contract graphs and designed a node elimination phase to normalize the graph. Then a novel message propagation network is used to extract graph features from the normalized graph summary, and the graph features are combined with the designed expert mode to generate the final detection system. Qian et al. [15] proposed the use of sequence models for reentrancy detection tasks, applying the effectiveness of deep neural networks to smart contract vulnerability detection. A key contract fragment representation and sequential model (i.e., BLSTM-ATT) is proposed to learn more informative features at the source code level and even contract fragment level. Zhuang [16] proposed a fully automatic vulnerability analyzer for smart contracts. Compared to existing methods, we explicitly model the fallback mechanism of smart contracts, consider rich dependencies among program elements, and explore the possibility of using novel graph neural networks for vulnerability detection. Tann et al. [17] proposed the use of LSTM for sequential learning of smart contract weaknesses, which allows us to detect new attack trends relatively quickly, leading to more secure smart contracts.

The accuracy and performance of methods based on symbolic execution and expert verification are generally low. Although the accuracy and performance of ML-based methods have improved, there is still a lot of room for improvement. Aiming at this problem, this paper proposes a high-performance deep learning-based smart contract vulnerability detection model VDDL.

3 Model

3.1 Overview

As shown in Fig. 1, the VDDL model is divided into Extraction, Training, and Prediction. In Extraction, the data is processed to obtain a labeled data set that can be used for training, and finally, 47038 processed labeled smart contract data sets are obtained. In Training, a multi-layer bidirectional Transformer architecture is used as the model architecture, and the architecture involves a multi-head attention mechanism and a masking mechanism. Using the collected 47038 smart contracts as a dataset and combining with the large-scale bimodal pre-training model CodeBERT for training, the VDDL model available in the final prediction stage is obtained. In Prediction, the trained VDDL model is used for prediction operation, and the prediction result is obtained.

3.2 Extraction

The goal of the Extraction is to obtain a processed dataset that can be used for training. This process has two sub-steps: dataset collection and data processing.

During the dataset collection process, we used the crawler tool [18] to scrape 47038 smart contracts from Etherscan [19]. In the data processing stage, we use the SmartCheck tool [20] to label the contract dataset and perform manual verification on the test set. Different from other smart contract vulnerability detection tools, this tool has higher precision, can detect different types of errors, and gives the error type, which can assist verification well. For ease of understanding, we give examples of two of the most common security vulnerabilities below: re-entrancy and integer overflow.

Re-entrancy: The reentrancy attack vulnerability is a type of security vulnerability with a high-risk factor. The most notorious event in the history of Ethereum, "The DAO", is the reentrancy attack exploited. The incident led to hackers stealing about 60 million dollars worth of ether.

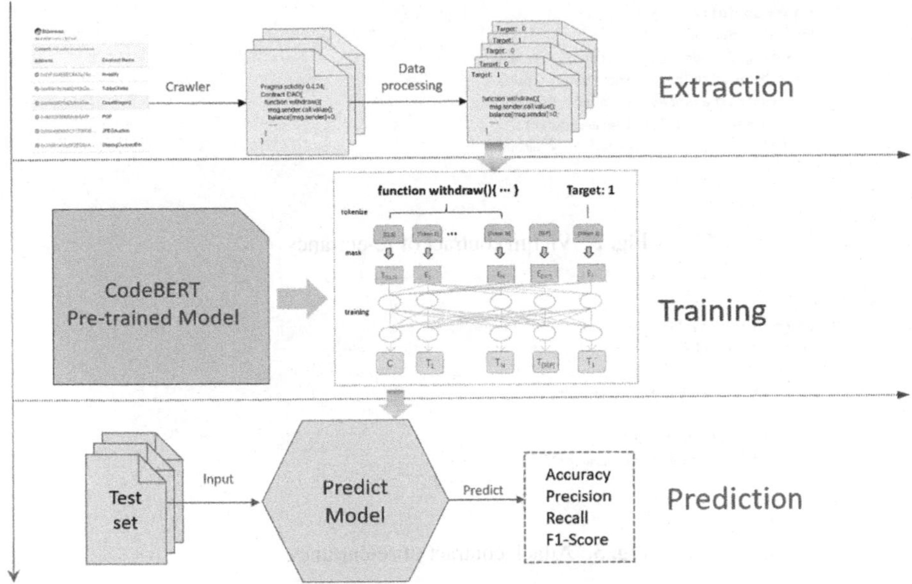

Fig. 1. An overview of our model

This vulnerability usually occurs in the process of transferring money to an external user address, which is caused by the external user address recursively calling the same function of the contract. There is a fallback function without a function name and parameters in the Ethereum smart contract by default. This function is automatically triggered when a transfer is received. When the contract transfer operation modifies the contract storage state variable operation, it may be subject to reentrancy attacks because the attacker can inject a malicious fallback function to call the same function of the contract again.

An example of vulnerable code for a reentrancy attack is shown in Fig. 2, where the code snippet represents a victim contract that can be used to withdraw funds. There is a *withdraw* function in the contract for the receiver to withdraw funds. Line 5 checks whether the balance of the contract have sufficient balance, and if the balance is sufficient, the amount is transferred to the receiver (line 6), and the receiver's balance on line 7 is subtracted by the corresponding transfer amount.

The attacker contract code is shown in Fig. 3. The attacker first calls the *withdraw* of the victim's contract in the fourth line to retrieve the funds. The sixth line is the above *fallback* function without a function name. When the transfer is received, the function will be triggered automatically, and the *withdraw* function will be called again to withdraw money. Because the transfer operation bit in the victim contract is before the account balance is modified, the *fallback* function in Fig. 3 can repeatedly call the withdraw function to withdraw money, and the transfer operation will not stop until the victim contract balance is empty or the gas is consumed.

Integer Overflow: The Ethereum Virtual Machine (EVM) has an integer overflow problem. For example, if the decimal number 256 is stored in the variable of uint8, since the

```
pragma solidity ^0.4.0;
contract Victim {
  mapping ( address = > uint ) balances ;
  function withdraw (uint amount) public {
    require(balances[msg.sender]>=amount);
    msg.sender.call.value(amount)();
    balances [ msg . sender ] -= amount;
  }
}
```

Fig. 2. Victim contract of re-entrancy

```
pragma solidity ^0.4.0;
contract Attack{
  function transfer(){
    victim.withdraw(this.amount);
  }
  function payable(){
    victim.withdraw(this.amount);
  }
}
```

Fig. 3. Attack contract of re-entrancy

maximum value stored in uint8 is 255 in decimal, an overflow will occur, and the final result will become 0.

In the BEC incident, the attacker only needs to construct $amount = 2 \times 2^{255}$ to successfully issue additional BEC, and the final result has resulted in the market value of nearly 900 million US dollars of BEC being almost zero.

As shown in Fig. 4, it is a code example with an integer overflow security vulnerability. The fifth line is the vulnerable code. The attacker only needs to construct a number with a value of 2^{256}, an integer overflow will occur after the amount is stored, the actual value of the amount is stored as 0, and the deducted amount in line 8 is 0, thus realizing the generation of Additional issuance of coins.

The above process is an example of a reentrancy attack and an integer overflow. We mark smart contracts that contain both error types or other error types as positive.

```
1  pragma solidity ^0.4.0;
2  contract Fund{
3    funtion Transfer(){
4      uint cnt = _receivers.length;
5      uint256 amount = uint256(cnt) *_value;
6      require(cnt>0&&cnt<=20);
7      require(_value>0&&balances[msg.sender] >= amount)
8      balances[msg.sender] = balances[msg.sender].sub(amount);
9      for(uint i = 0; i < cnt; i++){
10       balances[_receivers[i]] = balances[_receivers[i]].add(_value);
11       Transfer(msg.sender, _receivers[i], _value);
12     }
13     return true;
14   }
15 }
```

Fig. 4. Victim contract of Integer overflow

After labeling, we split the dataset. If the data set granularity of the smart contract is set to the contract level, the granularity will be too large, and some large contracts may even contain thousands of lines of code. If it is divided into rows, the granularity of the dataset will be too small, because a single line of code does not have logical semantic relationships. Therefore, we segment the smart contract data set into function levels in the data segmentation process. At the same time, we believe that if a contract is positive, all functions in it are related, so all functions under the contract are set to be positive. Then, we get the final dataset by removing redundant blank lines and useless annotations that would affect the training results.

3.3 Training

VDDL is inspired by BERT [21] and RoBERTa [22], using a multi-layer bidirectional Transformer architecture as the model architecture. In order to improve the performance and accuracy of training, VDDL incorporates the model trained by CodeBert [23] and uses the 47038 smart contract datasets processed and cleaned in the extraction process for training to obtain the final model. The architecture of VDDL mainly includes the attention mechanism and the masking mechanism.

3.3.1 Embedding and Masking

The process of Embedding is achieved by word segmentation and adding tags. The first token of each sequence after embedding is always a special classification token ([CLS]). The final hidden state corresponding to this token is used as the aggregated sequence representation for the classification task. Sentence pairs are packed into a single sequence. We distinguish sentences in two ways. First, we separate them with a special marker ([SEP]). For example, the *withdraw* function in the code of Fig. 2 in Sect. 3.2, others have security holes, so the corresponding label is 1 (positive). Then, the embedding process corresponding to this function is shown in Fig. 5.

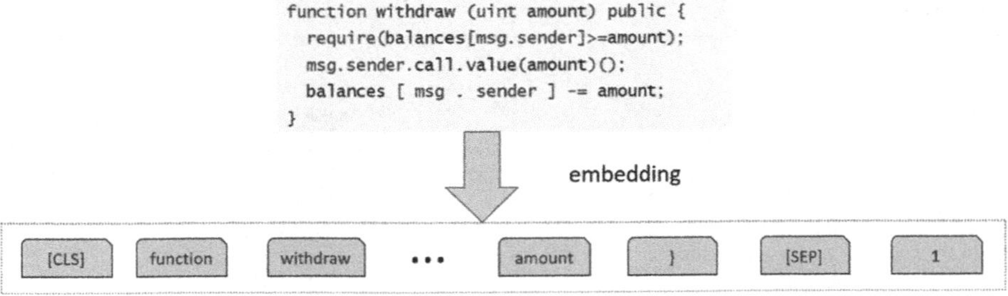

Fig. 5. An example of embedding

The Masking mechanism is to enable bidirectional training of the opcode output after embedding. Standard conditional language models can only be trained left-to-right or right-to-left, while bidirectional conditional will allow each word to see itself indirectly, and the model can easily predict the target word context in multiple layers, so bidirectional training is better than one-way training. Deep bidirectional representations can be trained by simply masking a percentage of input tokens at random, and then predicting those masked tokens. This process is called the Cloze task [24]. In [21], this task was renamed masked language model (MLM). In this case, the final hidden vector corresponding to the mask tokens is fed to the output softmax on the vocabulary, as in the standard language model (LM).

Through such a process, the process of bidirectional pre-training can be obtained. The process of masking words is achieved by modifying the words into [MASK] tokens. In order to enhance the matching between different pre-trained models, in addition to using [MASK] to replace the words to be masked, a small part of the words are replaced by random words and original words respectively.

3.3.2 Attention

After embedding and masking, the opcodes are fed into a multi-head attention layer [25] for learning and feature extraction. The structure of the attention function is shown on the left in Fig. 6, where Q is the query, K is the key, and V is the value. The key value corresponding to the key can be queried through the Query function. The values after embedding in Sect. 3.3.1 correspond to these key values. Q, K, and V are all vectors. Output is a weighted sum of values, where the weight assigned to each value is calculated by the query's compatibility function with the corresponding key.

The calculation formula of the attention output function is as follows:

$$\text{Output} = \text{Attention(Q, K, V)} = \text{softmax}\left(\frac{QK^T}{\sqrt{d_k}}\right) \quad (1)$$

The input consists of the query and key of dimension d_k and the value of dimension d_v. The computed dot product queries all keys, divides each key by $\sqrt{d_k}$, and then applies the softmax function to get the weights of the values. Then apply the softmax function to get the weights of the values. The attention function for a set of queries is computed simultaneously and packed into the matrix Q. Keys and values are also packed into matrices K and V.

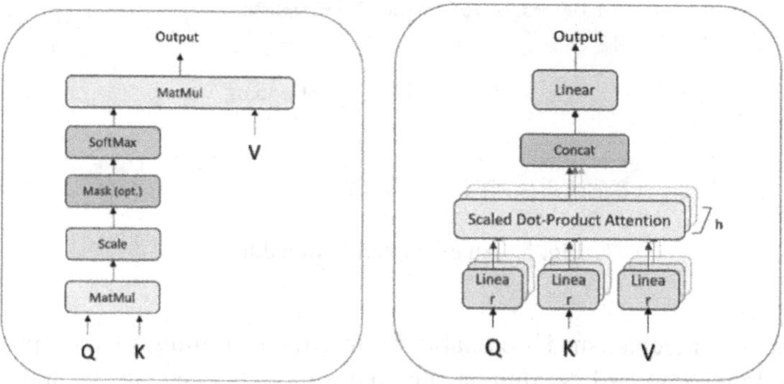

Fig. 6. Scaled dot-product attention (left) and multi-head attention (right)

The multi-head attention layer performs the same self-attention network computation as above. The difference is that each $head_i$ projects the input vectors Q, K, and V through different linear transformations to maintain the independent vector weight matrix of each *head*, thereby generating different attention vector matrices. Finally, the vectors generated by each head are superimposed and concatenated to form a vector matrix containing all attention head information. The multi-head attention network structure used by the model is shown on the right in Fig. 6; it improves the performance of the attention layer and extends the model's ability to focus on different locations. The output of the multi-head attention layer is calculated as follows:

$$\text{OutPut} = \text{MultiHead}(Q, K, V) = \text{Concat}(head_1, \ldots, head_h)W^O \tag{2}$$

$$\text{Where } head_i = Attention\left(QW_i^Q, KW_i^K, VW_i^V\right) \tag{3}$$

where the projections are parameter matrices $W_i^Q \in R^{d_{model} \times d_k}$, $W_i^K \in R^{d_{model} \times d_k}$, $W_i^V \in R^{d_{model} \times d_k}$, $W^O \in R^{d_{model} \times hd_v}$.

3.4 Prediction

The prediction stage is to use the trained VDDL model for prediction operation. The test set is the complete smart contract code. In this part, the contract-level dataset is sliced into function-level datasets using the data slicing function in the data extraction phase.

Using the VDDL model to predict the split test set, the final prediction result report can be obtained. The result report includes Predict result, Accuracy, Precision, Recall, and F1-Score. The Predict result is the prediction result corresponding to the test set. The latter four are evaluation indicators, the Accuracy is the proportion of correct samples in the total samples, the Precision is the proportion of correct positive samples in the positive samples (P) and the detection result is positive, and the recall rate is a measure of coverage, representing the meaning F1-score is an indicator used to measure the accuracy of the binary classification model by the proportion of all positive samples detected. It takes into account both the precision and recall of the classification model.

4 Experiment and Evaluation

4.1 Dataset

We used the crawler tool [18] to scrape 47038 smart contracts from Etherscan. The data were then labeled using smartcheck, an existing smart contract vulnerability detection tool, and manually verified on the test set. Among them, the number of contracts with security risks is 9380. The data we collected are shown in Table 1.

For the convenience of reading and indexing, we set the data structure of the dataset to the structure shown in Table 2. "idx" is the index number of each function. "idx" has two functions, one is to facilitate reading, and the other is that in the process of dividing the data set according to the ratio of 8:1:1, "idx" provides the unique positioning of the function. "contract name" is the name of the contract. The "function contact" stores the

Table 1. Collected data

Type	Numbers
Contract	47038
Vulnerable contracts	9380
Functions	684790

specific code of the function, which is the main content of the data set, and the data used for training is this part of the content. One "contract name" corresponds to multiple "function content", and one "function content" corresponds to one "contract name". "target" is the label for the function.

Table 2. Data set structure

idx	Contract name	Function content	Target
1	AccountRegistry.sol	function transferFrom(){ … }	0
2	AccountRegistry.sol	function transfer(){ … }	0
3	GasToken2.sol	function makeChild(){ … }	1
.	.	.	.
.	.	.	.
.	.	.	.
684790	Lottery.sol	Function buy(){ … }	1

4.2 Experimental Setup

The environment used in this paper is based on PyTorch1.8, and the GPU version used is NVIDIA Tesla V100. All experimental environments are shown in Table 3.

Table 3. Environment

Software and Hardware	Configuration
Operating system	Ubuntu 18.04
GPU	NVIDIA Tesla V100
CPU	Quad-core
PyTorch	1.8
CUDA	11.0

(*continued*)

Table 3. (*continued*)

Software and Hardware	Configuration
Python	3.9.7

4.3 Evaluation Metrics

We used accuracy (%), Recall (%), and F1-score (%) as metrics to evaluate the performance of VDDL. Each evaluation metric is detailed as follows: Accuracy is the sum of true positives (TP) and true negatives (TN) divided by the sum of TP, TN, false positives (FP), and false negatives (FN), and is the total accuracy of the sample.

$$\text{Accuracy} = \frac{TP + TN}{TP + TN + FP + FN} \tag{4}$$

Precision is the proportion of correct samples and the detection result is a positive sample (P). Precision is required in calculating Recall and F1-score. Its calculation formula is:

$$\text{Precision} = \frac{TP}{TP + FP} \tag{5}$$

Recall is a measure of coverage, which represents the proportion of all positive samples detected. Its calculation formula is:

$$\text{Recall} = \frac{TP}{TP + FN} \tag{6}$$

F1-score is an indicator used to measure the accuracy of the binary classification model. It takes into account both the precision and recall of the classification model. Its calculation formula is:

$$F1_{score} = 2 \cdot \frac{precision \cdot recall}{precision + recall} \tag{7}$$

4.4 Parameter Influence

In this section, we compare the effects of different parameters on the experimental performance. As shown in Figure in the top half of Fig. 7, it is the effect of batch size on performance. The abscissa is epoch, which is the number of training rounds. The ordinate is the value of the loss function. The lower the loss value, the better the training effect and the higher the accuracy. When the batch_size is 32, the loss value of the whole process is lower than the loss value when the batch_size is 16, so the effect is better when the batch_size is 32.

As shown in the bottom half of Fig. 7, it is the effect of learning rate on performance. The abscissa of the left picture is epoch, and the ordinate is the loss value; the abscissa of the right picture is epoch, and the ordinate is precision.

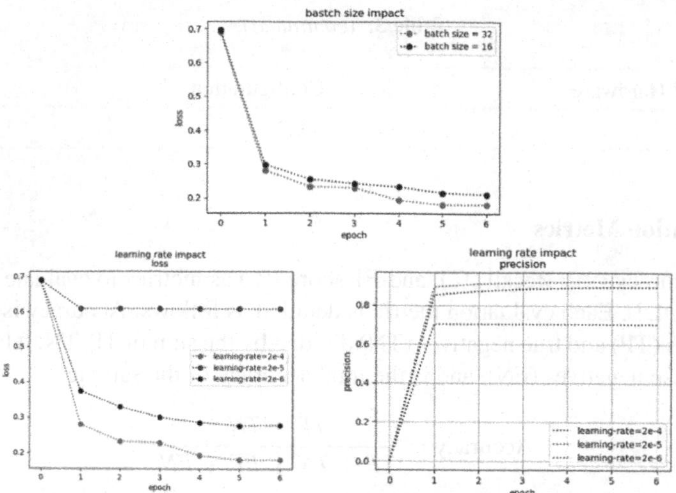

Fig. 7. Batch size impact (upper) and learning rate impact (lower)

We compared the learning rate of $2e^{-4}, 2e^{-5}, 2e^{-6}$. We found that when the learning rate is $2e^{-5}$, the loss function has the lowest value and the highest precision. This means that the efficiency is highest at this time.

Above all, it works best when the batch_size is 32 and the learning rate is $2e^{-5}$.

4.5 Comparison with ML-Based Methods

As shown in Table 4, we compared the VDDL tool with the logistic regression algorithm, the Naive Bayes algorithm, and the random forest algorithm. Since Accuracy and Precision have similar meanings (both represent the accuracy of detection results), and Precision has been reflected in Recall and F1-score, we only list the Accuracy value here. Through comparison, it can be found that the accuracy, recall, and F1-score of VDDL are all higher than those of conventional ML-based models. The accuracy is 92.35%, the recall is 81.43%, and the F1-score is 86.38%. If the security vulnerabilities of smart contracts are not detected, they may be attacked after they are deployed on the chain, which will bring very serious consequences. The recall rate reflects the ratio of all positive samples detected. The recall rate of VDDL greatly exceeds that of other ML-based methods, which is very beneficial for the detection of smart contract vulnerabilities with extremely high-security requirements.

In addition to the comparison with the traditional ML-based methods mentioned above, we also compare with TextRNN, one of the best works on AI-based classification problems. We used this paper's data set and test set to train and test TextRNN, and finally compare the Accuracy, Recall, and F1-score of VDDL to be 1.63%, 1.97%, and 2.74% higher than TextRNN, respectively.

These comparisons prove that the VDDL method can effectively detect possible security vulnerabilities in smart contracts.

Table 4. Comparative experimental results of ML methods

Methods	Accuracy (%)	Recall (%)	F1-score (%)
Logistic regression	88.25	66.48	77.12
Naive Bayes	88.84	70.47	79.00
Random Forest	91.22	76.60	83.86
VDDL	**92.35**	**81.43**	**86.38**

5 Conclusion and Future Work

In this paper, we propose a high-performance smart contract vulnerability detection model: VDDL, which uses a multi-layer bidirectional Transformer architecture as the model architecture. The architecture involves the attention mechanism and the masking mechanism. The model incorporates CodeBERT, a large bimodal pre-trained model for natural and programming languages, to improve training performance. We collected 47,038 smart contracts as datasets for model training and testing. The accuracy of our model's prediction of smart contract vulnerabilities detection reaches 92.35%, the Recall reaches 81.43%, and the F1-score reaches 86.38%, which can efficiently detect possible smart contract vulnerabilities. For future work, we will investigate extending our model to bytecode-only smart contracts and adapting the model idea to clone detection.

Acknowledgement. This work was supported by the National Natural Science Foundation of China (NSFC) under Grant No. 61962026, and by the Natural Science Foundation of Jiangxi Province under Grant No. 20192ACBL21031, and by the Foundation of Jiangxi Educational Committee (GJJ210338).

References

1. Ethereum. Website (2015). https://github.com/ethereum/go-ethereum
2. Luu, L., Chu, D.H., Olickel, H., et al.: Making smart contracts smarter. In: Proceedings of the 2016 ACM SIGSAC Conference on Computer and Communications Security, pp. 254–269 (2016)
3. Feist, J., Grieco, G., Groce, A.: Slither: a static analysis framework for smart contracts. In: 2019 IEEE/ACM 2nd International Workshop on Emerging Trends in Software Engineering for Blockchain (WETSEB), pp. 8–15. IEEE (2019)
4. Tsankov, P., Dan, A., Drachsler-Cohen, D., et al.: Securify: practical security analysis of smart contracts. In: Proceedings of the 2018 ACM SIGSAC Conference on Computer and Communications Security, pp. 67–82 (2018)
5. Brent, L., Jurisevic, A., Kong, M., et al.: Vandal: a scalable security analysis framework for smart contracts. arXiv preprint arXiv:1809.03981 (2018)
6. Mythril. Website (2018). https://github.com/ConsenSys/mythril
7. Kalra, S., Goel, S., Dhawan, M., et al.: ZEUS: analyzing safety of smart contracts. In: NDSS, pp. 1–12 (2018)

8. Chang, J., Gao, B., Xiao, H., Sun, J., Cai, Y., Yang, Z.: sCompile: critical path identification and analysis for smart contracts. In: Ait-Ameur, Y., Qin, S. (eds.) ICFEM 2019. LNCS, vol. 11852, pp. 286–304. Springer, Cham (2019). https://doi.org/10.1007/978-3-030-32409-4_18
9. Jiang, B., Liu, Y., Chan, W.K.: ContractFuzzer: fuzzing smart contracts for vulnerability detection. In: 2018 33rd IEEE/ACM International Conference on Automated Software Engineering (ASE), pp. 259–269. IEEE (2018)
10. Liu, C., Liu, H., Cao, Z., et al.: ReGuard: finding reentrancy bugs in smart contracts. In: 2018 IEEE/ACM 40th International Conference on Software Engineering: Companion (ICSE-Companion), pp. 65–68. IEEE (2018)
11. Gao, J., Liu, H., Liu, C., et al.: EASYFLOW: keep ethereum away from overflow. In: 2019 IEEE/ACM 41st International Conference on Software Engineering: Companion Proceedings (ICSE-Companion), pp. 23–26. IEEE (2019)
12. Torres, C.F., Schütte, J., State, R.: Osiris: hunting for integer bugs in ethereum smart contracts. In: Proceedings of the 34th Annual Computer Security Applications Conference, pp. 664–676 (2018)
13. Gao, Z., Jiang, L., Xia, X., et al.: Checking smart contracts with structural code embedding. IEEE Trans. Softw. Eng. **47**, 2874–2891 (2020)
14. Liu, Z., Qian, P., Wang, X., et al.: Combining graph neural networks with expert knowledge for smart contract vulnerability detection. arXiv preprint arXiv:2107.11598 (2021)
15. Qian, P., Liu, Z., He, Q., et al.: Towards automated reentrancy detection for smart contracts based on sequential models. IEEE Access **8**, 19685–19695 (2020)
16. Zhuang, Y., Liu, Z., Qian, P., et al.: Smart contract vulnerability detection using graph neural network. In: IJCAI, pp. 3283–3290 (2020)
17. Tann, W.J.W., Han, X.J., Gupta, S.S., et al.: Towards safer smart contracts: a sequence learning approach to detecting security threats. arXiv preprint arXiv:1811.06632 (2018)
18. etherscan_verified_contracts. Website (2018). https://github.com/thec00n/etherscan_verified_contracts
19. Etherscan. Website (2015). https://etherscan.io
20. Tikhomirov, S., Voskresenskaya, E., Ivanitskiy, I., et al.: SmartCheck: static analysis of ethereum smart contracts. In: Proceedings of the 1st International Workshop on Emerging Trends in Software Engineering for Blockchain, pp. 9–16 (2018)
21. Devlin, J., Chang, M.W., Lee, K., et al.: BERT: pre-training of deep bidirectional transformers for language understanding. arXiv preprint arXiv:1810.04805 (2018)
22. Liu, Y., Ott, M., Goyal, N., et al.: RoBERTa: a robustly optimized BERT pretraining approach. arXiv preprint arXiv:1907.11692 (2019)
23. Feng, Z., Guo, D., Tang, D., et al.: CodeBERT: a pre-trained model for programming and natural languages. arXiv preprint arXiv:2002.08155 (2020)
24. Taylor, W.L.: "Cloze procedure": a new tool for measuring readability. J. Q. **30**(4), 415–433 (1953)
25. Vaswani, A., Shazeer, N., Parmar, N., et al.: Attention is all you need. In: Advances in Neural Information Processing Systems, vol. 30 (2017)

Robust Remote Sensing Scene Classification with Multi-view Voting and Entropy Ranking

Jinyang Wang[1,2], Tao Wang[1,2(✉)], Min Gan[2(✉)], and George Hadjichristofi[3]

[1] Fujian Provincial Key Laboratory of Information Processing and Intelligent Control, College of Computer and Control Engineering and International Digital Economy College, Minjiang University, Fuzhou 350108, China
twang@mju.edu.cn

[2] College of Computer and Data Science, Fuzhou University, Fuzhou 350108, China
aganmin@aliyun.com

[3] Department of Computer Science and Engineering, European University Cyprus, Nicosia 1516, Cyprus

Abstract. Deep convolutional neural networks have been widely used in scene classification of remotely sensed images. In this work, we propose a robust learning method for the task that is secure against partially incorrect categorization of images. Specifically, we remove and correct errors in the labels progressively by iterative multi-view voting and entropy ranking. At each time step, we first divide the training data into disjoint parts for separate training and voting. The unanimity in the voting reveals the correctness of the labels, so that we can train a strong model with only the images with unanimous votes. In addition, we adopt entropy as an effective measure for prediction uncertainty, in order to partially recover labeling errors by ranking and selection. We empirically demonstrate the superiority of the proposed method on the WHU-RS19 dataset and the AID dataset.

Keywords: Remote sensing scene classification · Deep convolution neural network · Noisy labels · Multi-view voting · Entropy ranking

1 Introduction

Remotely sensed imagery is an important means to acquire information about the Earth with wide applications in geography, land surveying, ecology, and oceanography, among others. Particularly, remote sensing (RS) scene classification is a fundamental task in RS image analytics that classifies each image into a predefined set of semantic categories. As large-scale RS image datasets become more easily accessible, it has recently been feasible to train effective Deep Convolutional Neural Networks (DCNNs) for the task.

One of the key limitations of training DCNNs for RS scene classification, however, is that a large amount of manual labeling is required, in order to train

Y. Xu et al. (Eds.): ML4CS 2022, LNCS 13655, pp. 87–98, 2023.
https://doi.org/10.1007/978-3-031-20096-0_7

models with good generalization abilities. Commercial imaging companies are collecting hundreds of terabytes of new satellite images every day; it is virtually impossible to manually label even a fraction of the ever-expanding image data. One possible remedy to this dilemma would be the use of labels obtained through crowd-sourcing platforms. However, it would be difficult to eliminate labeling errors even with label voting or aggregation. In addition, labels obtained through other channels such as automated labeling methods or auxiliary information, such as user-generated labels could also be error-prone, as manual verification of the labels is time-consuming. In this paper, we address the problem of training DCNNs on datasets with noisy labels. Here, labels being "noisy" means that some of the images in the datasets are incorrectly categorized. Conventionally, training DCNNs with noisy labels would inevitably lead to a rapid degradation of model performance. From a model learning perspective, it would be ideal if we could train models that are robust to label noise. Importantly, this would suggest that the learning algorithms are more secure against deliberated attacks such as label manipulation, which is a vital consideration in the security of machine learning algorithms.

In this work, we propose a robust remote sensing scene classification method with iterative multi-view voting and entropy ranking. Our method is able to deal with noisy labels by progressively removing and rectifying labeling errors. Specifically, at each time step, we first divide the training data into disjoint parts for separate training and voting. The unanimity in the voting reveals the correctness of the labels, so that we can train a strong model with only the images with unanimous votes. In addition, we adopt entropy as an effective measure for prediction uncertainty, in order to partially recover labeling errors by ranking and selection. By performing the above steps repeatedly, the quality of the labeling and the trained models is gradually improved. The main contributions of our method are two-fold: 1) We propose a simple yet effective method for robust scene classification of remotely sensed images. The two main steps, multi-view voting and entropy ranking, are complementary and enhance each other. Specifically, multi-view voting provides a way to identify errors in labels, and entropy ranking could then partially rectify these errors based on prediction uncertainty. 2) Our method provides a general framework for robust learning, and works easily with different deep models. Also, experiments on two public datasets, WHU-RS19 and AID, demonstrate the efficacy of the proposed method.

The rest of the paper is organized as follows. Sect. 2 briefly reviews recent work on deep learning-based image classification with noisy labels, as well as those for remote sensing scene classification. Section 3 describes the proposed method in detail, followed by experimental evaluation results in Sect. 4 and closing remarks in Sect. 5.

2 Related Work

Many deep learning-based methods have been proposed to solve the problem of label noise in generic image classification. For example, Wang *et al.* [15]

proved that on the "simple" classes, the cross-entropy learning criterion will over-fit noisy labels. To address this issue, the authors proposed anti-noise reverse cross-entropy, a method of symmetric cross-entropy learning. Xia *et al.* [17] approached the problem by making a distinction between critical and non-critical parameters. The effect of noisy labels is scaled down by applying different rules for these two types of parameters. Another closely related work from Kaneko *et al.* [5] proposed label-noise robust Generative Adversarial Networks (GANs), which trained a noise transition model to extract knowledge from clean labels even in the presence of noise. In addition, Huang *et al.* [4] proposed O2U-net to detect noisy labels through parameter adjustments. Specifically, the network can be transferred from the over-fitting state to the under-fitting state cyclically, during which the normalized average loss of a sample is recorded for the identification of label noise. Vahdat [13] proposed a conditional random field that represents the relationship between noisy and clean labels in a semi-supervised setting. Furthermore, Cordeiro *et al.* [1] divided the training data into clean and noisy sets in an unsupervised manner, followed by semi-supervised learning to minimize the empirical vicinal risk (EVR). They demonstrated the importance of the accuracy of the unsupervised classifier and the the size of the training set to minimize the EVR. Consequently, a new algorithm, termed LongReMix, was proposed. Unlike existing work, in this paper we propose to refine noisy labels in an iterative fashion by multi-view voting and entropy ranking.

In the realm of RS image classification, there have also been some recent attempts to address the problem of label noise. For instance, Kang *et al.* [6] used the negative Box-Cox transformation to downplay the effect of noisy labels, and proposed a robust normalized softmax loss. Li *et al.* [10] used multi-view CNNs to correct errors in labels, and proposed an error-tolerant deep learning method, in addition to an adaptive multi-feature collaborative representation classifier to improve classification quality. Tu *et al.* [12] designed a covariance matrix representation-based noisy label model. Li *et al.* [8] combined ordinary learning and complementary learning as the latter can reduce the probability of learning misinformation. Being closest to our work, Li *et al.* [9] proposed a robust scene classification method based on multi-view voting. Our work differs from theirs as we use entropy as an important additional predictor for label correctness. In particular, we propose a way to rectify the labels of images with non-unanimous votes, which is not possible with their method. Also, the entropy ranking method we proposed provides performance improvements in addition to multi-view voting at different label noise ratios on two public datasets.

3 Our Approach

In this paper, we propose an approach to RS scene classification that is robust to label noise. Given an initial training set with noisy labels, we perform iterative refinement via multi-view voting and entropy ranking to produce a cleaner dataset with fewer incorrect labels. Our method is based on two key observations: 1) images with correct labels tend to receive unanimous votes when we

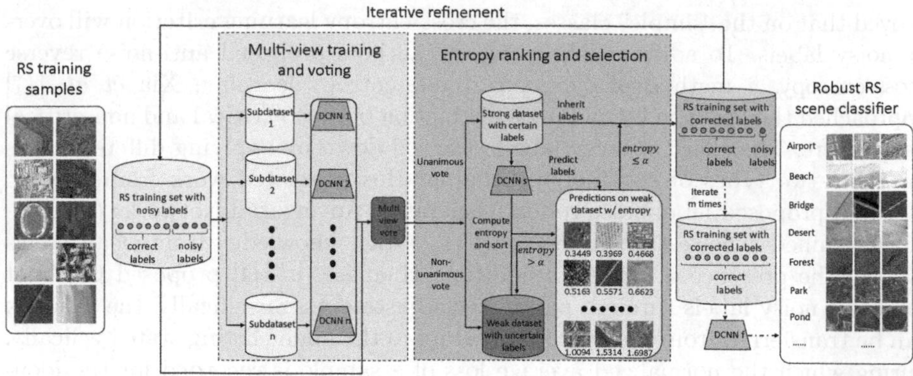

Fig. 1. Robust remote sensing scene classification via iterative multi-view voting and entropy ranking. In each iteration, the dataset with noisy labels is divided into disjoint subsets for multi-view training and voting (shown in the blue rectangle). Based on voting unanimity, the dataset is split into a strong dataset with certain labels and a weak dataset with uncertain labels. A DCNN is trained with the strong dataset and based on its prediction entropy, confident samples with lower entropy are further added into the strong dataset (shown in the gray rectangle). The above steps are carried out several times to produce a final training set. See Sect. 3 for details. (Color figure online)

split the original dataset into multiple subsets to perform multi-view voting, and 2) the entropy of predictions can be used as an additional predictor for label correctness. Thus, we refine our dataset in an iterative fashion with both multi-view voting and entropy ranking. The overall process is illustrated in Fig. 1.

More specifically, we take two steps for dataset refinement in each iteration: 1) multi-view training and voting (shown in the blue rectangle in Fig. 1), and 2) entropy ranking and selection (shown in the gray rectangle in Fig. 1). All the cylinders in Fig. 1 represent training datasets, the green dots in the cylinders represent correctly labeled images, and the red dots represent incorrectly labeled images. In the multi-view training and voting step, we split the training set into n disjoint subsets to train n DCNNs. Based on the predictions from these DCNNs, the original dataset with noisy labels can be divided into a strong dataset and a weak dataset. The samples in the strong dataset are those with consistent votes across all n DCNN models, and the weak dataset contains samples with inconsistent voting results. In the entropy ranking and selection step, a portion of noisy labels is converted into correct labels. This is done by training a DCNN on the strong dataset and evaluating its prediction entropy on the weak dataset. Here, entropy is used as an effective measure of label correctness. Samples with lower prediction entropy (with their labels converted according to the most likely class in prediction) are further added into the strong dataset, to produce a cleaner output dataset for the current iteration. After M iterations, a dataset with the lowest proportion of incorrect labels will be obtained, and a DCNN is trained

Algorithm 1: The proposed algorithm with multi-view voting and entropy ranking.

Input: Dataset with noisy labels $\mathcal{D}$. Semantic classes $\mathcal{C}$.
Iterative refinement with M iterations:
for $m = 1 : M$ **do**
  Divide the dataset $\mathcal{D}_m$ ($\mathcal{D}_1 = \mathcal{D}$. $\mathcal{D}_m = \mathcal{D}^s_{m-1}$ if $m > 1$) into n disjoint parts: $\mathcal{S}_1 \cap \mathcal{S}_2 \cap \cdots \cap \mathcal{S}_n = \emptyset$, $\mathcal{D} = \mathcal{S}_1 \cup \mathcal{S}_2 \cup \cdots \cup \mathcal{S}_n$
  for $\mathcal{S}_j = \mathcal{S}_1 : \mathcal{S}_n$ **do**
    Train a Deep Convolutional Neural Network (DCNN) with $\mathcal{S}_j$
    return $DCNN_j$
  for $DCNN_t = DCNN_1 : DCNN_n$ **do**
    for $(\mathbf{x}_i, y_i)$ *in* $\mathcal{D}_m$ **do**
      Predict the label $z_i^t = \arg\max_{c \in \mathcal{C}} p_{DCNN_t}(\mathbf{x}_i = c)$ for each image
  for $(\mathbf{x}_i, y_i)$ *in* $\mathcal{D}_m$ **do**
    If $z_i^1 = z_i^2 = \cdots = z_i^n$: label the image accordingly and place the image into strong dataset $(\mathbf{x}_i, y_i) \rightarrow \mathcal{D}^s$
    Else : place the image into weak dataset $\mathbf{x}_i \rightarrow \mathcal{D}^w$
  Train strong $DCNN_s$ with $\mathcal{D}^s$
  for $\mathbf{x}_i$ *in* $\mathcal{D}^w$ **do**
    Calculate the entropy of $E^w(\mathbf{x}_i)$
    If $E^w(\mathbf{x}_i) \leq \alpha$: predict label $\hat{y}_i$ with $DCNN_s$ and place the image into strong dataset $(\mathbf{x}_i, \hat{y}_i) \rightarrow \mathcal{D}^s$
  Output dataset for the current iteration $\mathcal{D}^s_m = \mathcal{D}^s$
Train a final model $DCNN_f$ with $\mathcal{D}^s_M$
return $DCNN_f$

---

with this dataset to obtain a robust classification model. We summarize the main procedure of our algorithm in Algorithm 1.

The rest of this section is organized as follows. In Subsects. 3.1 and 3.2, we describe details in the multi-view training and voting step and the entropy ranking step, respectively. Subsection 3.3 provides details on the iterative refinement.

3.1 Multi-view Training and Voting

For datasets containing noisy labels, it has been shown that the negative impact of noisy labels can be effectively mitigated by splitting the dataset into several parts and training them separately. Here we follow the multi-view training and voting method outlined in [9] while removing the training of a post-hoc Support Vector Machine (SVM) [14] for simplicity considerations.

More formally, denote the input RS image as $\mathbf{x} \in \mathbb{R}^{H \times W \times 3}$ and $y \in \mathcal{C}$ its corresponding semantic class label, where $\mathcal{C} = \{1 \ldots C\}$ is the label space. At the beginning of training, we are given an input dataset $\mathcal{D} = \{(\mathbf{x}_i, y_i)\}_{i=1}^N$ whose labels may be partially incorrect. In addition, denote $\mathcal{D}_m$ as the input training set at the m-th iteration of our algorithm. The total number of iterations is M (see Subsect. 3.3). Naturally we have $\mathcal{D}_1 = \mathcal{D}$. Apart from $\mathcal{D}_m$, the iteration number m is omitted below for notation simplicity. In each iteration, we split $\mathcal{D}_m$ into n disjoint parts, i.e., $\mathcal{S}_1 \cap \mathcal{S}_2 \cap \cdots \cap \mathcal{S}_n = \emptyset$, $\mathcal{D}_m = \mathcal{S}_1 \cup \mathcal{S}_2 \cup \cdots \cup \mathcal{S}_n$. Next, n DCNNs are trained on $\mathcal{S}_1, \mathcal{S}_2, \cdots \mathcal{S}_n$, respectively, so as to obtain $DCNN_1$, $DCNN_2$, $\cdots$, $DCNN_n$. We use these DCNN models to make predictions on all RS images in $\mathcal{D}_m$, and if the prediction results of all models for a given image $\mathbf{x}$ are consistent, the image is placed in the strong dataset $\mathcal{D}^s = \{(\mathbf{x}_i, y_i)\}_{i=1}^{K}$. Otherwise, we remove the label corresponding to this image and place it into the weak dataset $\mathcal{D}^w = \{\mathbf{x}_i\}_{i=K+1}^{N}$. We note that, once an image is placed into the weak dataset $\mathcal{D}^w$, it shall remain in $\mathcal{D}^w$ across iterations such that the number of images in $\mathcal{D}^s$ and $\mathcal{D}^w$ should always add up to N. However, as we will show in Sect. 3.2, the strong dataset $\mathcal{D}^s$ and consequently the quality of the model trained on $\mathcal{D}^s$ will improve over time. Therefore, images in $\mathcal{D}^w$ may be moved back to $\mathcal{D}^s$ at a later time. In the above, $\mathbf{x}_i$ represents the i-th image in the strong dataset, y_i represents the predicted label of the i-th image, N represents the number of images in the entire training set.

Figure 2 illustrates the voting process. In the top row and the bottom row are images and their corresponding labels. The trapezoidal blocks in the middle represent the trained DCNN models after splitting the dataset. The arrows between the images and the DCNNs indicates that each image will get predictions from all DCNNs, and the arrows between the DCNNs and the labels indicate the predictions by voting. If the votes are unanimous, then the image will be added into the strong dataset. Otherwise, the corresponding image will be added into the weak dataset (images shown with red border in the top row, and also with a cross by their corresponding labels in the bottom row).

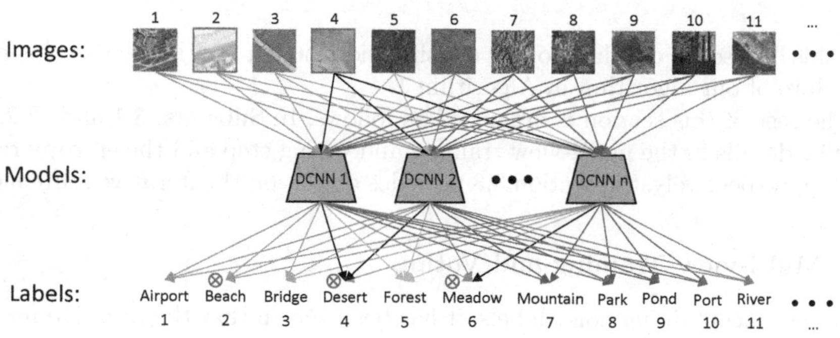

Fig. 2. Example of the multi-view voting process. All images are jointly predicted by all DCNN models. Depending on whether the votes are unanimous or non-unanimous, we sort the images into a strong dataset (images with unanimous votes) and a weak dataset (images with non-unanimous votes, marked with red borders and a cross next to the corresponding labels). Lines with different colors represent the training and prediction paths for different training images. See text for details. (Color figure online)

3.2 Entropy Ranking

After we obtain $\mathcal{D}^s$ with the steps outlined in the previous section, we can train a strong DCNN model $DCNN_s$ with $\mathcal{D}^s$. We note that this DCNN will likely be trained with cleaner labels, so that its predictions will less likely be affected by label noise. In this regard, we further evaluate the predictions of $DCNN_s$ on the weak dataset $\mathcal{D}^w$, in the hope that we can additionally recover some images from $\mathcal{D}^w$. Here, we use entropy as a proxy for prediction certainty, i.e., we only choose images receiving a low entropy in the prediction by $DCNN_s$.

Specifically, given an image from the weak dataset $\mathbf{x}_i \in \mathcal{D}^w$, denote $p(\mathbf{x}_i = c)$ as the output probability for the c-th class by $DCNN_s$, the entropy $E^w(\mathbf{x}_i)$ can be written as:

$$E^w(\mathbf{x}_i) = -\sum_{c \in \mathcal{C}} p(\mathbf{x}_i = c) \log p(\mathbf{x}_i = c) \quad (1)$$

We then sort the entropy for all images in $\mathcal{D}^w$ in ascending order, and take a hyperparameters α as the entropy threshold. Specifically, we move the image from the weak dataset into the strong dataset if the prediction entropy of an image is not greater than α. If α is lower, we only move images with high prediction certainty from the weak dataset to the strong dataset, potentially missing some images with correct predictions as a result. If α is higher, we move more images into the strong dataset, resulting in a higher chance of incorrect labels in the strong dataset. In practice, the value of α is chosen empirically (see discussion in Subsect. 4.2). The process above can be written as:

$$\mathcal{D}^w = \mathcal{D}^w \backslash \mathbf{x}_i, \ (\mathbf{x}_i, \hat{y}_i) \rightarrow \mathcal{D}^s, \quad \text{if } E^w(\mathbf{x}_i) \leq \alpha \quad (2)$$

where $\mathcal{D}^w = \mathcal{D}^w \backslash \mathbf{x}_i$ means that we remove $\mathbf{x}_i$ from $\mathcal{D}^w$ and $(\mathbf{x}_i, \hat{y}_i) \rightarrow \mathcal{D}^s$ indicates that we add $(\mathbf{x}_i, \hat{y}_i)$ into $\mathcal{D}^s$. Here, $\hat{y}_i = \arg\max_{c \in \mathcal{C}} p(\mathbf{x}_i = c)$ is the maximum a posteriori (MAP) estimate provided by $DCNN_s$, as the truth label y_i may be noisy and hence not used.

3.3 Iterative Refinement

In practice, the multi-view voting results may be partially incorrect and that noisy labels could sometimes be included in the strong dataset $\mathcal{D}^s$. This problem can be alleviated by performing the steps in Sect. 3.1 and Sect. 3.2 in an iterative fashion and gradually improving the quality of the strong dataset. Specifically, denote $\mathcal{D}^s_{m-1}$ as the strong dataset we obtained at the end of the previous iteration. We let this strong dataset be the input dataset in the next iteration, i.e., $\mathcal{D}_m = \mathcal{D}^s_{m-1}$. In our experiments, we found that the iterative refinement of $\mathcal{D}^s$ is particularly important when the proportion of noisy labels is large. We set the total number of iterations to $M = 3$ empirically as it provides the largest performance gain in most cases.

4 Experiments and Discussions

In this section, we use two widely used public RS image datasets to demonstrate the efficacy of the proposed noise-tolerant robust RS scene classification method. In the following, we first describe the details of the datasets and our implementation, and then present results and discussions.

4.1 Datasets

WHU-RS19 dataset [11]. The WHU-RS19 dataset has a total of 1,005 images, which belong to 19 different classes. The size of each image is 600 × 600 pixels. Following [9], we use 50% of the images for training and the remaining 50% for testing.

Aerial Image Datasets (AID) dataset [16]. The AID dataset has a total of 10,000 images, which belong to 30 different classes. The number of images per class is between 200 and 500, and the size of each image is 600 × 600 pixels. Again, we use 50% of the images for training and the remaining 50% for testing following [9].

4.2 Implementation Details

In our experiments, we introduce random errors from 10% to 50% (at 10% interval) of the original correct labels, in order to create varying levels of label noise. We use a 50-layer ResNet [3] pretrained on ImageNet [2] for all DCNNs. In the preprocessing step, all images are resized to 256 × 256 pixels. We use Adam [7] as the optimizer with learning rate set to 0.001. Each DCNN is trained for 50 epochs with the standard cross-entropy loss. We implement our method with PyTorch, and all the experiments were run on a single NVIDIA GeForce RTX 2080 Ti GPU.

In order to ensure fairness of the experiments, in the initial training set, the proportion of label noise in each class is consistent with the proportion of label noise in the entire training set, and the noisy labels are randomly distributed. The hyperparameter M, which is the number of iterations, is chosen empirically. Specifically, we perform experiments with different noise ratios, i.e., 10%, 20%, 30%, 40%, and 50%. For each noise ratio, we perform 10 different noise distribution experiments. Following [9], two DCNN views(i.e., $n = 2$) are used to validate our method, and we will try more cases in subsequent works. Finally, the average of the results is taken to choose the number of iterations M. We present the average accuracy results we obtained in Fig. 3. It is clear that $M = 3$ works best and we use this value throughout our experiments. In particular, increasing M beyond 3 may lead to over-fitting to the label noise so it may even lead to a degradation of performance. Another important hyperparameter α, which is the entropy threshold for recovering images from the weak dataset, is chosen by grid search. We present an example in Fig. 4 that shows a typical value of 1.5 for α on the WHU-RS19 dataset.

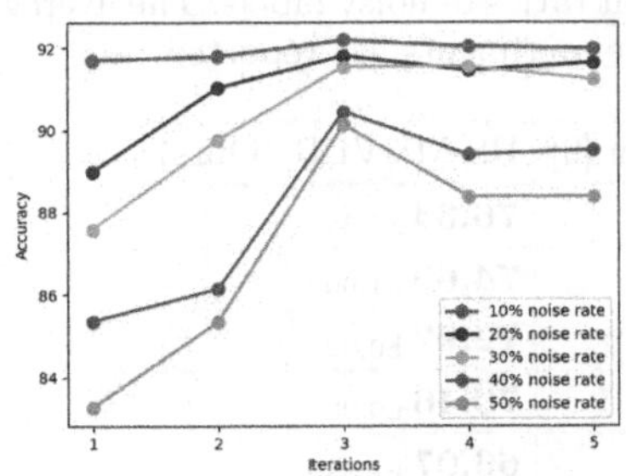

Fig. 3. Classification accuracy *vs.* number of iterations M on the WHU-RS19 dataset under varying label noise ratios.

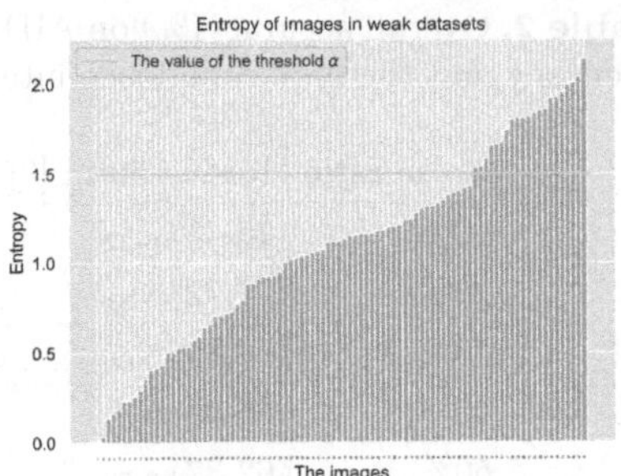

Fig. 4. An example entropy distribution in the weak dataset on the WHU-RS19 dataset (40% noise ratio, 2nd iteration).

4.3 Results

We present the quantitative results of our experiments in Tables 1 and 2. Table 1 shows the experimental evaluation results on the WHU-RS19 dataset. Table 2 shows the experimental evaluation results on the AID dataset. It is clear that our method, Remote Sensing Multi-View Voting and Entropy Ranking (RS-MVVER), is superior to the competing method by a clear margin. We note that while the accuracy improvements may seem small in some cases, our method provides consistent improvements at all noise ratios. In addition, even a small improvement is important for remote sensing scene classification which may involve images of critical infrastructures, and we generally want the results to be as accurate as possible. Specifically, we compare our method against two baseline methods: ResNet-50 [3] and RS-ETDL [9]. We note that the latter is a strong baseline method that also uses multi-view voting for learning from noisy labels in remote sensing scene classification. The results suggest that both multi-view voting and entropy ranking can positively impact model performance.

Table 1. Overall accuracy(%) on WHU-RS19 using different ratios of noisy labels. The average accuracy and the 95% confidence interval across 10 experiments are reported.

Noise ratio	ResNet50 in [3]	RS-ETDL in [9]	RS-MVVER (Ours)
10%	$91.35_{\pm 1.42}$	$91.79_{\pm 2.22}$	$\mathbf{92.18}_{\pm 0.72}$
20%	$88.65_{\pm 1.36}$	$89.74_{\pm 1.88}$	$\mathbf{91.80}_{\pm 1.38}$
30%	$87.12_{\pm 2.63}$	$88.91_{\pm 1.96}$	$\mathbf{91.53}_{\pm 0.31}$
40%	$83.27_{\pm 1.58}$	$88.71_{\pm 1.45}$	$\mathbf{90.45}_{\pm 1.24}$
50%	$82.12_{\pm 3.14}$	$89.10_{\pm 3.57}$	$\mathbf{90.13}_{\pm 3.09}$

Table 2. Overall accuracy(%) on AID using different ratios of noisy labels. The average accuracy and the 95% confidence interval across 5 experiments are reported.

Noise ratio	ResNet50 in [3]	RS-ETDL in [9]	RS-MVVER (Ours)
10%	$75.45_{\pm 0.37}$	$75.78_{\pm 0.32}$	$\mathbf{76.34}_{\pm 0.38}$
20%	$71.72_{\pm 0.31}$	$73.93_{\pm 0.54}$	$\mathbf{74.60}_{\pm 1.00}$
30%	$68.89_{\pm 0.68}$	$71.40_{\pm 0.85}$	$\mathbf{72.97}_{\pm 0.92}$
40%	$66.39_{\pm 0.39}$	$70.34_{\pm 0.23}$	$\mathbf{70.46}_{\pm 0.23}$
50%	$62.37_{\pm 0.72}$	$65.12_{\pm 0.56}$	$\mathbf{66.07}_{\pm 1.33}$

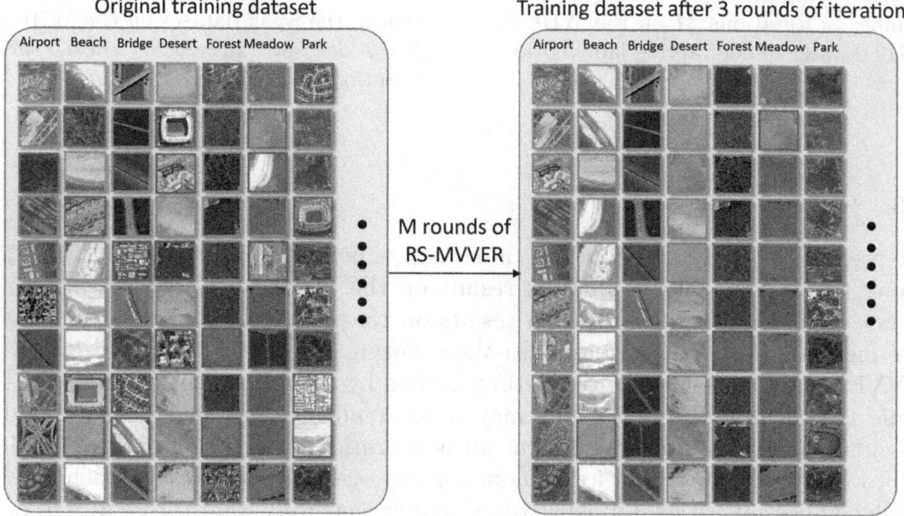

Fig. 5. Dataset before and after M rounds of iterative refinement (40% noise ratio on the WHU-RS19 dataset). Images with red borders represent the wrongly labeled ones in the original training data set, and images with green borders represent the correctly labeled ones. After 3 rounds of iterations, we can clearly see that the noisy labels are greatly reduced. (Color figure online)

Finally, we present a qualitative example of the iterative refinement to the dataset. Figure 5 shows an example of the iterative refinement process of the WHU-RS19 dataset. The original dataset has 40% noisy labels, and the number of noisy labels are either eliminated or greatly reduced for most classes after 3 rounds of iterative refinement. We note that the iterative refinement is performed during training, so that it does not impact evaluation performance. In our experiments, a single training iteration takes 15 and 60 minutes on the WHU-RS19 and the AID dataset, respectively. This is acceptable as the training is performed offline.

5 Conclusion

In this paper, we propose a robust remote sensing scene classification method with multi-view voting and entropy ranking that can deal with training datasets containing noisy labels. Our method begins with splitting the original training dataset into disjoint parts and training a set of multi-view classifiers. Next, we use multi-view voting followed by entropy ranking to sort images into a strong dataset and a weak dataset. By iteratively perfoming the steps above, we can obtain a cleaner dataset with much fewer noisy labels. Experiments on two public datasets, WHU-RS19 and AID, show that our method compares favorably with competing methods. We hope that our method could provide some new insights and a better starting point for future work on this topic. In particular, we would like to explore incorporating knowledge from images in the weak dataset or additional unlabeled images into our learning objectives.

Acknowledgment. This work is supported by NSFC (61703195), Fujian NSF (2022J011112) and Fuzhou Technology Planning Program (2021-ZD-284).

References

1. Cordeiro, F.R., Sachdeva, R., Belagiannis, V., Reid, I., Carneiro, G.: LongReMix: robust learning with high confidence samples in a noisy label environment. arXiv preprint arXiv:2103.04173 (2021)
2. Deng, J., Dong, W., Socher, R., Li, L.J., Li, K., Fei-Fei, L.: ImageNet: a large-scale hierarchical image database. In: 2009 IEEE Conference on Computer Vision and Pattern Recognition, pp. 248–255. IEEE (2009)
3. He, K., Zhang, X., Ren, S., Sun, J.: Deep residual learning for image recognition. In: Proceedings of the IEEE Conference on Computer Vision and Pattern Recognition, pp. 770–778 (2016)
4. Huang, J., Qu, L., Jia, R., Zhao, B.: O2U-Net: a simple noisy label detection approach for deep neural networks. In: Proceedings of the IEEE/CVF International Conference on Computer Vision, pp. 3326–3334 (2019)
5. Kaneko, T., Ushiku, Y., Harada, T.: Label-noise robust generative adversarial networks. In: Proceedings of the IEEE/CVF Conference on Computer Vision and Pattern Recognition, pp. 2467–2476 (2019)
6. Kang, J., Fernandez-Beltran, R., Duan, P., Kang, X., Plaza, A.J.: Robust normalized softmax loss for deep metric learning-based characterization of remote sensing images with label noise. IEEE Trans. Geosci. Remote Sens. **59**(10), 8798–8811 (2020)
7. Kingma, D.P., Ba, J.: Adam: a method for stochastic optimization. arXiv preprint arXiv:1412.6980 (2014)
8. Li, Q., Chen, Y., Ghamisi, P.: Complementary learning-based scene classification of remote sensing images with noisy labels. IEEE Geosci. Remote Sens. Lett. **19**, 1–5 (2021)
9. Li, Y., Zhang, Y., Zhu, Z.: Learning deep networks under noisy labels for remote sensing image scene classification. In: IGARSS 2019–2019 IEEE International Geoscience and Remote Sensing Symposium. pp. 3025–3028. IEEE (2019)

10. Li, Y., Zhang, Y., Zhu, Z.: Error-tolerant deep learning for remote sensing image scene classification. IEEE trans. cybern. **51**(4), 1756–1768 (2020)
11. Sheng, G., Yang, W., Xu, T., Sun, H.: High-resolution satellite scene classification using a sparse coding based multiple feature combination. Int. J. Remote Sens. **33**(8), 2395–2412 (2012)
12. Tu, B., Kuang, W., He, W., Zhang, G., Peng, Y.: Robust learning of mislabeled training samples for remote sensing image scene classification. IEEE J. Selected Top. Appl. Earth Obs. Remote Sens. **13**, 5623–5639 (2020)
13. Vahdat, A.: Toward robustness against label noise in training deep discriminative neural networks. In: Advances in Neural Information Processing Systems, vol. 30 (2017)
14. Vapnik, V.: The nature of statistical learning theory. Springer Science & Business Media (1999)
15. Wang, Y., Ma, X., Chen, Z., Luo, Y., Yi, J., Bailey, J.: Symmetric cross entropy for robust learning with noisy labels. In: Proceedings of the IEEE/CVF International Conference on Computer Vision, pp. 322–330 (2019)
16. Xia, G.S., et al.: AID: a benchmark data set for performance evaluation of aerial scene classification. IEEE Trans. Geosci. Remote Sens. **55**(7), 3965–3981 (2017)
17. Xia, X., et al.: Robust early-learning: hindering the memorization of noisy labels. In: International Conference on Learning Representations (2020)

Visualized Analysis of the Emerging Trends of Automated Audio Description Technology

Lingqian Zheng[1] and Xinrong Cao[2(✉)]

[1] College of Foreign Languages, Minjiang University, Fuzhou, China
[2] College of Computer and Control Engineering, Minjiang University, Fuzhou, China
cxrxmu@163.com

Abstract. Automated audio description has provided groundbreaking solutions to audio description production and delivery and has been one of the core topics of audio description studies. Based on the data collected from the Web of Science database, this article uses the visualized analysis software of CiteSpace to analyze the progress and development of automated audio description technology. It is found that the main keywords include computer vision, natural language processing, video captioning and deep learning, among which video captioning is at the core of the emerging trend of automated audio description, facilitated by deep learning, such as CNN, RNN, LSTM and their improvements. Knowledge-guided and data-driven learning methods may be possible solutions for computer understanding and generation of human-like description of videos.

Keywords: Automated audio description · CiteSpace · Computer vision · Natural language processing · Deep learning

1 Introduction

According to the statistics of the World Health Organization, "at least 2.2 billion people around the world have a vision impairment" [1]. Services for accessibility is of great significance to meet the needs of all users, including the visually impaired, and to promote human rights. Audio description (AD), also known as video description [2], is a service for audiovisual or media accessibility. It refers to "the visual made verbal" [3], meaning the verbal description of images or visual information in audio-visual materials for those who are unable to access it themselves. Its application scenarios include films, television programs, theatrical performances, museum exhibitions, sports programs, etc. At present, AD is mainly produced and delivered by human resources, which is of high cost and low efficiency, limiting the scope of its production and delivery. Automated AD has provided groundbreaking solutions to description generation and visual content retrieval and has been one of the core topics of AD research.

Automated AD refers to automatic generation of natural language sentences that describe the contents of a given video [4], which involves understanding the semantics of a video and then generating human-like descriptions of the video [5]. As the shared research focus of media accessibility, audiovisual translation and computer science,

Y. Xu et al. (Eds.): ML4CS 2022, LNCS 13655, pp. 99–108, 2023.
https://doi.org/10.1007/978-3-031-20096-0_8

automated AD broadens the scope of computer vision and natural language processing studies, enabling the visual content to be delivered to different types of audiences in innovative and diversified approaches. However, few studies have systematically discussed the progress and development of automated AD and its applications. In view of this, this paper, based on the data collected from the Web of Science database and using the visualized analysis software of CiteSpace, discusses the hot spots and emerging trends of automatic AD technology, in a bid to provide references for the theoretical development and application of automatic AD.

2 Data Collection

Data of this study were derived from the core databases, including SSCI, A&HCI, SCI, ESCI, CPCI-S, CPCI-SSH, BKCI-SSH (Book Citation Index-Social Sciences & humanities), BKCI-S (Book Citation Index-Science), of the Web of Science database. In order to ensure the comprehensiveness of the retrieved data, the terms of "audio descri*" or "video descri*" are used for cross search in titles, abstracts and author keywords. "*" indicates that words such as "description", "described", "describing" and "descriptor" can be retrieved. After filtering out record types of editorials, news and reports, as well as records irrelevant to AD technology, by the time of retrieval (April 30, 2022), a total of 270 records and 7290 cite references were collected. The 270 records include 102 journal articles, 165 conference papers and 3 book chapters. The software of CiteSpace is used for generation and visualization of co-occurrence, co-citation and time zone networks, etc., so that the general trends and critical points in the development of AD studies can be depicted.

3 Data Analysis

3.1 Brief Description of the General Trends

Figure 1 shows that the first record of AD technology studies appeared in 1996, but it was until 2009 that the studies began to attract growing attention. The number of records increased significantly since 2016, and has been maintained at a high level in recent years. 2016 is the year when Alpha Go the AI defeated the world champion and greatly enhanced studies of deep learning. Deep learning has facilitated new achievement in image recognition, thus enabling fast development in computer vision, which may be the possible reason behind the surge of literature since 2016.

According to result analysis of the Web of Science database, the research areas mainly include Engineering, Computer Science, Imaging Science Photographic Technology and so on, showing obvious interdisciplinary features.

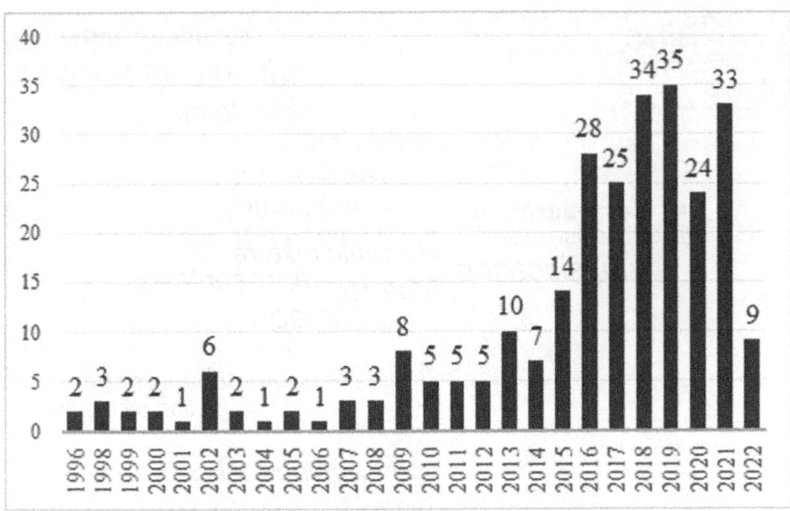

Fig. 1. Brief description of the general trend

3.2 Most Active Topic Analysis

Figure 2 shows the keyword co-occurrence and clustering networks generated by CiteSpace. The Modularity Q value is 0.877 and the Mean Silhouette value is 0.948, indicating that the clustering network structure is significant and the clustering results are reasonable. Keyword frequency is an important indicator of hotspot analysis. Table 1 lists the main co-occurred keywords in each cluster, and marks the top 10 high-frequency keywords with an asterisk (*). The "Year" column represents the average year of keyword co-occurrence in each cluster.

All the keywords are divided into seven clusters. Cluster #0 focuses on video description with the main keywords of computer vision and natural language processing. The average year of the cluster is 2016, indicating that the topics of this cluster are relatively novel. The average years of Cluster #1, #2, #3, #6, with the cluster labels of video representation, activity recognition, video descriptor and video accessibility respectively, are before 2016, meaning that these are relatively early topics.

The average years of Cluster #4 and Cluster #5 are both 2018, which means that the keywords in the two clusters are the hot spots of automated AD. Cluster #4 and Cluster #5 are closely related, with the high-frequency keywords of convolutional neural network (CNN), deep learning, video captioning and video to text. Video to text is the main task of video captioning, which is one of the most important components in the production and delivery of automated AD. Deep learning, including CNN and other networks, helps improve the performance of video captioning.

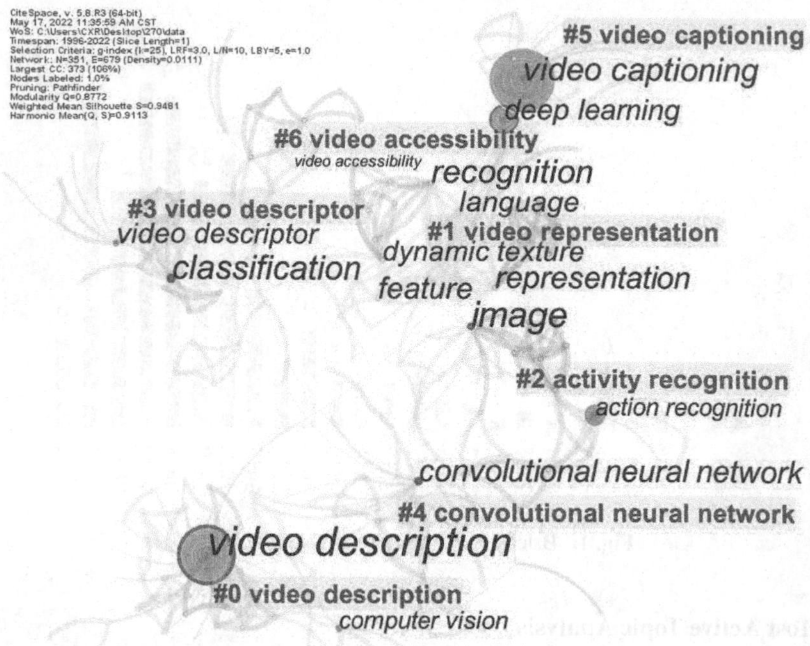

Fig. 2. Keyword co-occurrence and clustering networks

Table 1. List of keyword clustering information (*: high-frequency keywords).

No	Quantity	Year	Clustering label	Main co-occurrence keywords
#0	43	2016	Vidoe description	Video description*; computer vision*; audio description; natural language processing
#1	30	2015	Video representation	Video representation; dynamic texture*; graph neural networks; spatio-temporal action detection; texture extraction
#2	28	2014	Activity recognition	Activity recognition; optical flow; action recognition*; human activity
#3	26	2015	Video descriptor	Video descriptor*; video classification*

(*continued*)

Table 1. (*continued*)

No	Quantity	Year	Clustering label	Main co-occurrence keywords
#4	25	2018	Convolutional neural network	Convolutional neural network*; feature representation; feature encoding; temporal-spatial features
#5	20	2018	Video captioning	Deep learning*; video captioning*; video to text; multi-task; multimodal
#6	18	2015	Video accessibility	Machine learning; human action recognition; video accessibility*; generators; benchmark testing

3.3 Research Trend Analysis

Figure 3 shows the keyword time zone network, also known as the theme path network, generated by CiteSpace. Keyword time zone network can be used to analyze the significantly increase of keywords, so as to depict the development trend of automated AD technology.

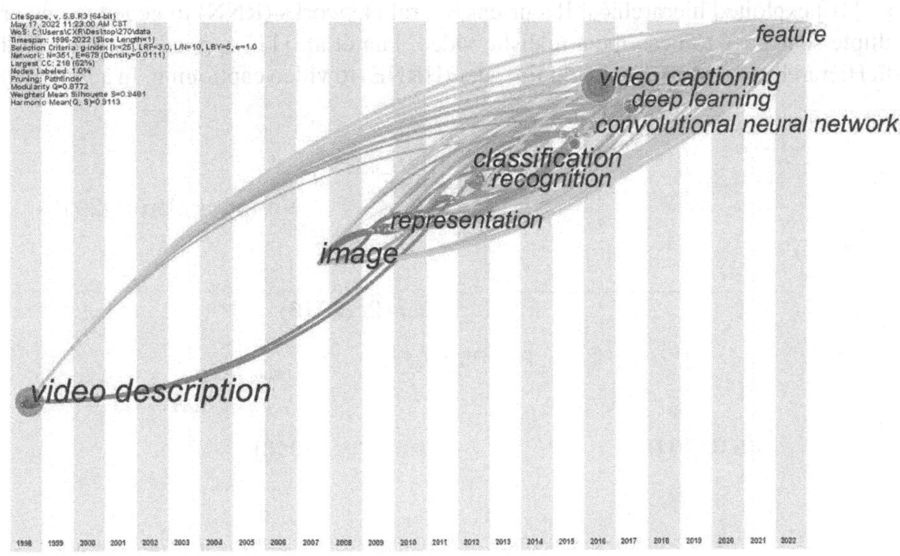

Fig. 3. Keyword time zone network

As can be seen from the figure, keywords in the earlier years include representation, recognition and classification. In 2016 and 2017, video captioning, deep learning and convolutional neural network (CNN) appeared as keywords in automated AD studies.

Among them, video captioning has been the most frequently used keywords in later records of literature. With the biggest nod size. Deep learning, with CNN as one of the core methods, has been applied in video captioning to handle the complexities and challenges of automatically describing video content with natural language.

3.4 Knowledge Base Analysis

Highly cited references constitute the knowledge base of AD studies. The co-citation network is shown in Fig. 4. Table 2 lists 7 references with co-citation frequency of more than 40 times.

The 7 references appeared in two top conferences in computer vision studies, IEEE International Conference on Computer Vision (ICCV) in 2015 and IEEE Conference on Computer Vision and Pattern Recognition (CVPR) in 2015 and 2016, which indicated that computer vision may be the core impulse to the development of automated AD.

These highly cited references are related to deep learning, image recognition and metrics. Firstly, deep learning has gained great attention because of their superior performance and the availability of high-speed computing resources [13]. Among 7 highly cited articles, 4 are related to deep learning, discussing how to design and use various neural networks to transform video to text. Venugopalan et al. [6] proposed a novel end-to-end and sequence-to-sequence model to generate captions for videos. Pan et al. [8] designed a novel unified framework with Long Short-Term Memory (LSTM) to enforce the relationship between the semantics of the entire sentence and visual content. Yu et al. [10] exploited hierarchical Recurrent Neural Networks (RNN) to generate one or multiple sentences to describe a realistic video. Pan et al. [11] applied a new method with Hierarchical Recurrent Neural Encoder (HRNE) to video captioning. In addition to

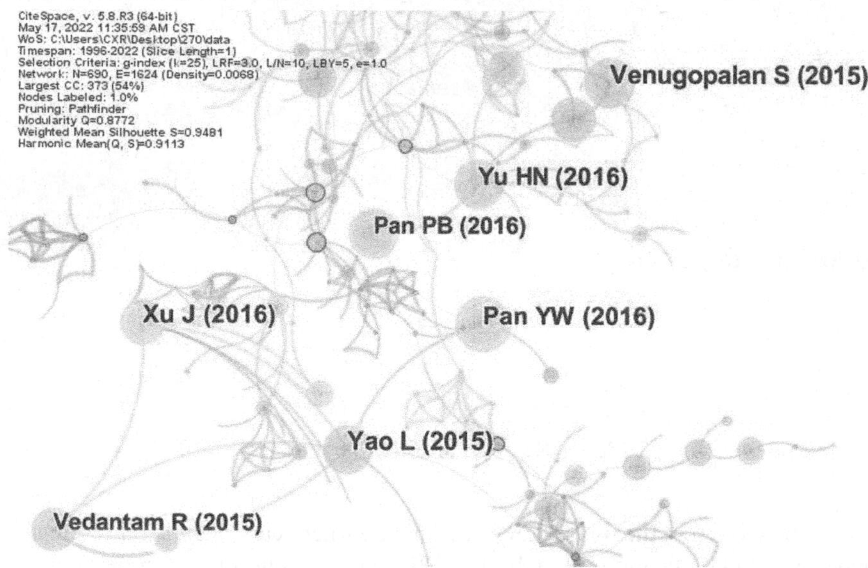

Fig. 4. Literature co citation Atlas

the technologies of static image recognition, dynamic temporal structure can be useful in video description. Yao et al. [7] proposed an approach that took into account both the local and global temporal structure of videos in description production.

Moreover, for AD production facilitated by deep learning, it is challenging to evaluate the quality of descriptions. Xu et al. [9] presented a new large-scale video benchmark for video understanding, and Vedantam et al. [12] proposed a novel paradigm, CIDEr, which performed better than existing metrics in capturing human judgment of consensus.

Table 2. List of highly cited documents.

No	Highly cited literatures	Author	Source	Year
1	Sequence to Sequence – Video to Text [6]	Venugopalan S	ICCV	2015
2	Describing Videos by Exploiting Temporal Structure [7]	Yao L	ICCV	2015
3	Jointly Modeling Embedding and Translation to Bridge Video and Language [8]	Pan YW	CVPR	2016
4	MSR-VTT: A Large Video Description Dataset for Bridging Video and Language [9]	Xu J	CVPR	2016
5	Video Paragraph Captioning Using Hierarchical Recurrent Neural Networks [10]	Yu HN	CVPR	2016
6	Hierarchical Recurrent Neural Encoder for Video Representation with Application to Captioning [11]	Pan PB	CVPR	2016
7	CIDEr: Consensus-based image description evaluation [12]	Vedantam R	CVPR	2015

4 Discussion

The interest in audiovisual content description technologies is in the recent surge to meet the needs of the blind and partially sighted audiences [3]. As is found in active topic analysis, computer vision and natural language processing are among the main keywords in the co-occurrence cluster of the biggest size, Cluster #0. Automatic description of the contents of a static image or a video is an interdisciplinary problem that requires joint efforts in the studies of computer vision and natural language processing [14]. The keyword of video captioning, appeared in 2016, is among the hot spots of automated AD, which is mainly facilitated by deep learning, such as and CNN, RNN, LSTM and their improvements.

Although a good number of literatures focused on automatic generation of descriptions, it is still an intricate task for computers [5]. The automatic description of static images remains challenging in terms of accuracy, completeness and robustness [15]. Descriptions of moving images and visual storytelling pose additional challenges in terms of temporality, including co-referencing [16] and other features of narrative continuity [17].

Real-world videos often have complex dynamics [6], so dynamic information is more important than static information in video description [18]. The methods for generating video descriptions should be sensitive to temporal structure. Venugopalan et al. [6] proposed a novel end-to-end sequence-to-sequence model to generate captions for videos. The model was able to learn the temporal structure of the sequence of frames as well as the sequence model of the generated sentences, i.e., a language model. Li et al. [7] proposed an approach that successfully takes into account both the local and global temporal structures of videos to produce descriptions. Yu et al. [10] presented an approach that exploits hierarchical Recurrent Neural Networks (RNN) to tackle the video captioning problem. It exploited both temporal and spatial attention mechanisms to selectively focus on visual elements during generation. Pan et al. [11] proposed a new approach to exploit temporal information of videos with deep convolutional neural networks for video representation.

Moreover, most existing approaches of computer vision and natural language processing generate words locally based on given words and the visual content, while the relationship between the semantics of sentences and the visual content is not holistically exploited. As a result, the generated sentences may be contextually correct but semantically illogical and incoherent [8].

To enforce the relationship between the semantics of the entire sentence and visual content, Pan et al. [8] presented a novel unified framework, which could simultaneously explore the learning of LSTM and visual-semantic embedding. Huang et al. [19] proposed a video scenario description system to select relevant semantic features and translate them into the corresponding video descriptions. Vinyals et al. [14] presented a generative model based on a deep recurrent architecture to generate the fluence natural sentences to describe an image. Naik et al. [20] proposed a LSTM model integrated with an attention mechanism, which enabled the decoder to perceive and focus on relevant objects and correlate the visual context and language content for producing semantically correct captions. In addition, Ahmed et al. [21] proposed an attention-based encoder-decoder model for describing the video in textual format. However, this direct visual to textual translation ignored the rich intermediate description, such as objects, scenes and actions. Liu et al. [22] provided a solution by proposing a Hierarchical & Multimodal Video Caption (HMVC) model, which transferred external knowledge by latent semantic discoveries to generate complex and helpful complementary cues.

In addition to temporality and semantic information, it is also important to measure the agreement between machine-generated descriptions with that of humans. The datasets should contain both the adequate visual diversity and complexity of linguistic structures. However, current evaluation metrics fall short of measuring the agreement between machine generated descriptions with that of humans. Therefore, evaluation of the quality of descriptions has proven to be challenging [4].

It is worth noting that although many literatures have established various models of deep learning for video captioning, the match of visual features and language models has yet to be perfect, which needs further exploration.

5 Conclusion

Studies of automated AD is of great significance and value for the blind and the visually impaired to gain video accessibility. Based on the data collected from the Web of Science database and facilitated by the visualized analysis software of CiteSpace, this article discusses the hot spots and emerging trends of automatic AD technology. It is found that automated AD technology is an interdisciplinary topic of areas such as Engineering, Computer Science and Imaging Science Photographic Technology. The main keywords include computer vision, natural language processing, video captioning, deep learning, CNN and video to text. Among them, video captioning, one of the most important components in the process of production, is at the core of the emerging trend of automated AD, facilitated by deep learning.

At present, there are still huge challenges for video captioning. The description of dynamic images and visual stories brings additional challenges about timeliness. A possible solution is to fully combine the dynamic information in the technological design for static images. Deep learning, such as CNN, RNN and LSTM, has become the main method to solve such problems. These networks and their improved schemes have enhanced the performance of video captioning and contributed to the implementation and application of automated AD. Moreover, since the deep learning models relying on large number of datasets are unable to cover the complexity of the real world, knowledge-guided and data-driven learning methods may be used in the future studies to improve the performance of the algorithm, thus contributing to the development and application of automated AD.

Acknowledgement. This work was supported in part by Humanities and Social Sciences Fund of the Ministry of Education (21YJC740082), Project of the 14th Five Year Plan of Education Studies, Fujian Province (FJJKBK21-197).

References

1. WHO. World Report on Vision. Geneva: World Health Organization (2019). https://www.who.int/publications/i/item/9789241516570
2. Frazier, G.: The autobiography of Miss Jane Pitman: an all-audio adaptation of the teleplay for the blind and visually handicapped. Unpublished M.A. thesis, San Francisco State University (1975)
3. Braun, S., Starr, K.: Innovation in Audio Description Research. Routledge, New York (2021)
4. Aafaq, N., Mian, A., Liu, W., et al.: Video description: a survey of methods, datasets, and evaluation metrics. ACM Comput. Surv. (CSUR) **52**(6), 1–37 (2019)
5. Khurana, K., Deshpande, U.: Video question-answering techniques, benchmark datasets and evaluation metrics leveraging video captioning: a comprehensive survey. IEEE Access **9**, 43799–43823 (2021)
6. Venugopalan, S., Rohrbach, M., Donahue, J., et al.: Sequence to sequence-video to text. In: The IEEE International Conference on Computer Vision 2015, pp. 4534–4542. IEEE, Santiago (2015)
7. Yao, L., Torabi, A., Cho, K., et al.: Describing videos by exploiting temporal structure. In: The IEEE International Conference on Computer Vision 2015, pp. 4507–4515. IEEE, Santiago (2015)

8. Pan, Y., Mei, T., Yao, T., et al.: Jointly modeling embedding and translation to bridge video and language. In: The IEEE Conference on Computer Vision and Pattern Recognition 2016, pp. 4594–4602. IEEE, Las Vegas (2016)
9. Xu, J., Mei, T., Yao, T., et al.: MSR-VTT: a large video description dataset for bridging video and language. In: The IEEE Conference on Computer Vision and Pattern Recognition 2016, pp. 5288–5296. IEEE, Las Vegas (2016)
10. Yu, H., Wang, J., Huang, Z., et al.: Video paragraph captioning using hierarchical recurrent neural networks. In: The IEEE Conference on Computer Vision and Pattern Recognition 2016, pp. 4584–4593. IEEE, Las Vegas (2016)
11. Pan, P., Xu, Z., Yang, Y., et al.: Hierarchical recurrent neural encoder for video representation with application to captioning. In: Proceedings of the IEEE Conference on Computer Vision and Pattern Recognition 2016, pp. 1029–1038. IEEE, Las Vegas (2016)
12. Vedantam, R., Lawrence Zitnick, C., Parikh, D.: CIDEr: consensus-based image description evaluation. In: The IEEE Conference on Computer Vision and Pattern Recognition 2015, pp. 4566–4575. IEEE, Boston (2015)
13. Dilawari, A., Khan, M.U.G., Farooq, A., et al.: Natural language description of video streams using task-specific feature encoding. IEEE Access **6**, 16639–16645 (2018)
14. Vinyals, O., Toshev, A., Bengio, S., et al.: Show and tell: a neural image caption generator. In: Proceedings of the IEEE Conference on Computer Vision and Pattern Recognition 2015, pp. 3156–3164. IEEE, Boston (2015)
15. Husain, S.S., Bober, M.: Improving large-scale image retrieval through robust aggregation of local descriptors. IEEE Trans. Pattern Anal. Mach. Intell. **39**(9), 1783–1796 (2016)
16. Rohrbach, A., Rohrbach, M., Tang, S., et al.: Generating descriptions with grounded and co-referenced people. In: The IEEE Conference on Computer Vision and Pattern Recognition 2017, pp. 4979–4989. IEEE, Honolulu (2017)
17. Huang, T.H., Ferraro, F., Mostafazadeh, N., et al.: Visual storytelling. In: The Conference of the North American Chapter of the Association for Computational Linguistics: Human Language Technologies 2016, pp. 1233–1239. Association for Computational Linguistics, San Diego (2016)
18. Yadav, N., Naik, D.: Generating short video description using Deep-LSTM and attention mechanism. In: International Conference for Convergence in Technology (I2CT) 2021, pp. 1–6. IEEE (2021)
19. Huang, Y.F., Shih, L.P., Tsai, C.H., et al.: Describing video scenarios using deep learning techniques. Int. J. Intell. Syst. **36**(6), 2465–2490 (2021)
20. Naik, D., Jaidhar, C.D.: Semantic context driven language descriptions of videos using deep neural network. J. Big Data **9**(1), 1–22 (2022)
21. Ahmed, S., Saif, A.F.M.S., Hanif, M.I., et al.: Att-BiL-SL: attention-based Bi-LSTM and sequential LSTM for describing video in the textual formation. Appl. Sci. **12**(1), 317 (2021)
22. Liu, A.A., Xu, N., Wong, Y., et al.: Hierarchical & multimodal video captioning: discovering and transferring multimodal knowledge for vision to language. Comput. Vis. Image Underst. **163**, 113–125 (2017)

Anomaly Detection for Multi-time Series with Normalizing Flow

Weiye Ning[1(✉)], Xin Xie[1], Yuhui Huang[1], Si Yu[1], Zhao Li[1], and Hao Yang[2]

[1] School of Information Engineering, East China Jiaotong University, Nanchang 330013, China
niniye1998@163.com

[2] State Grid Jiangxi Electric Power Co Ltd Electric Power Research Institute, Nanchang 330013, China

Abstract. Various interconnected devices and sensors of cyber-physical systems interact with each other in time and space, and the multiple time series generated have interdependent implicit correlations and highly nonlinear relationships. Determining how to model the multiple time series and search anomaly measures through feature selection is the key to anomaly detection. Aiming at the complex interdependence between multi-time series, this paper proposes an anomaly detection model GNF, which applies a Bayesian network to model the structural relationships of multiple time series, and introduces a dependency encoder to obtain the representations of interdependency between multiple time series. Assuming that the anomalies are distributed in the low density area, the joint probability density of the time series can be decomposed into the product of conditional densities, and the data corresponding to the final low density is judged as abnormal. We have conducted experiments on real world datasets and demonstrated the effectiveness of GNF in anomaly detection.

Keywords: Anomaly detection · Multi-time series · Normalizing flow

1 Introduction

With the rapid growth of interconnected devices and sensors in cyber-physical systems, real-world systems involve more and more interconnected sensors. The interconnected sensors in the system influence and interact with each other. The data change of one sensor may cause the whole changes in system data, which means there is some kind of implicit relationship between the sensors. The implicit relationship represents the intricate interdependence among multi-time series, which is difficult to model. Therefore, determining how to model the implicit dependencies and obtain anomaly measures through feature selection [1] is the current challenge and topic worthy of further study in the field of multiple time series for anomaly detection.

Due to the lack of labels in the data, as well as the unpredictability and high variability of anomalies, the problem of anomaly detection is often viewed as an unsupervised learning problem. In the past few years, many classic unsupervised methods have been

Y. Xu et al. (Eds.): ML4CS 2022, LNCS 13655, pp. 109–117, 2023.
https://doi.org/10.1007/978-3-031-20096-0_9

developed, such as density-based methods [2], linear model-based methods [3], distance-based methods [4] and classification models [5]. However, these methods are insufficient for highly nonlinear relations in many real-world systems. Recently, graph neural networks (GNN) [6] have been widely used to deal with nonlinear topological relations, and these methods include graph convolutional networks (GCN) [7] and graph attention networks (GAT) [8]. When obtaining the intricate interdependence between time series through graphs, how to use this interdependence for anomaly detection of multi-time series has become a problem to be solved.

Thereby, we propose an anomaly detection model GNF, which uses a Bayesian network [9] to model the structural relationship between variables, thereby obtaining a representable graph adjacency matrix, then decomposes the joint probability density of nodes into the product of the conditional densities, finally model uses the normalizing flow for density estimation to make anomaly judgments. The contributions of the paper are as follows:

(1) We introduce a dependency encoder to capture the interdependence between multi-time series and introduce the interdependence into a normalizing flow for density estimation.

(2) We propose a model that combines graph structure and normalizing flow, which decomposes the joint probability density of time series and introduces normalizing flow to achieve the purpose of anomaly detection.

2 Related Work and Theory

2.1 Anomaly Detection

The purpose of anomaly detection is to detect abnormal samples that deviate from most of the data. Most of the current supervised anomaly detection methods rely on ready-made training datasets and labels. The only way to detect anomalies is to obtain normal data labels for training, which has a large limitation. In contrast, the unsupervised anomaly detection methods do not need to consider the labels of the input samples and only need to use normal samples for training, so that the model learns the data distribution of normal samples. According to the anomaly judgment criteria, they can be roughly divided into density estimation methods, clustering-based methods, and reconstruction-based methods.

For density estimation methods, the DAGMM model proposed by Zong [10] et al. combines an auto-encoder with a Gaussian mixture model, which can obtain latent representations from the auto-encoder, and use a Gaussian mixture model for density estimation. For cluster-based methods, the SVDD [11] model and the DeepSVDD [12] model try to cluster the representations of normal data into clusters, while the distance of the input instance to the cluster center represents the final outlier. Reconstruction-based methods detect anomalies by reconstruction errors, and the LSTM-VAE model proposed by Park [13] et al. uses long short-term memory (LSTM) to model series relations and a variational auto-encoder (VAE) to reconstruct the input data, and finally detect anomalies by reconstruction error. The OmniAnomaly proposed by Su [14] et al. further extends the LSTM-VAE by normalizing flow, it models the time dependence and randomness of time series and uses reconstruction probabilities for anomaly detection. The InterFusion proposed by Li [15] et al. models the interdependencies between multiple time series by a hierarchical VAE with two stochastic latent variables and uses the reconstruction error as the anomaly score.

2.2 Bayesian Network

Bayesian network [16] is a probabilistic graph model whose network topology is a directed acyclic graph (DAG). Each node in the DAG represents a random variable, and the directed edge between the nodes represents the "dependencies" between the random variables. If there is a directed edge between the two nodes, it means that there is a point-to-point "causal relationship" between the two nodes. The conditional probability represents the strength of the relationship between nodes. Therefore, this structure can decompose the joint probability density of the graph node into the product of the conditional density, making the joint probability density after decomposition easier to parameterize, calculate and evaluate.

Let X^i represents a random variable, then a Bayesian network with the number of n variables is a DAG with variables as nodes. Let A represents the weighted adjacency matrix of a DAG, if X^j is the parent node of X^i, then $A_{ij} \neq 0$, otherwise $A_{ij} = 0$. According to the properties of Bayesian networks, the joint probability density of the multiple time series can be calculated as the product of the conditional density of all nodes. Therefore, the joint distribution density of time series $X = (X^1, \ldots, X^n)$ is:

$$p(X^1, \ldots, X^n) = \prod_{i=1}^{n} p(X^i | pa(X^i)) \tag{1}$$

Which $pa(X^i) = \{X^j : A_{ij} \neq 0\}$ represents the parent node of X^i.

2.3 Normalizing Flow

Normalizing flow is a kind of generative model for learning the underlying distribution of data samples, normalizing complex data distributions to "standard distribution" by a series of invertible and differentiable transformations. Dinh [17] et al. proposed Real-NVP, a normalizing flow framework for density estimation. Then Papamakarios [18] et al. extended and improved it by stacking multiple autoregressive models, building a normalizing flow model MAF (Masked Autoregressive Flow) with the advantage of expressive power and fast computational speed. Rasul [19] et al. combined the conditional normalizing flow with the autoregressive model for dynamically modeling multivariate time series, this method supports a large number of underlying data distributions and can be extended to thousands of time series.

A normalizing flow is a map about vector-valued reversible which can normalize the distribution of x to a "base distribution", namely $f(x) : \mathbb{R}^D \rightarrow \mathbb{R}^D$ and $x \in \mathbb{R}^D$ denotes a D-dimensional random variable. Let $z = f(x)$ and the probability density function is $q(z)$, according to the variational formula, the logarithm density of x can be expressed as:

$$logp(x) = logq(f(x)) + log|det \nabla_x f(x)| \tag{2}$$

In addition, the normalizing flow can be enhanced by the conditional information $h \in \mathbb{R}^d$ with different dimensions, and the enhanced normalizing flow becomes the conditional normalizing flow, which is denoted as $f : \mathbb{R}^D \times \mathbb{R}^d \rightarrow \mathbb{R}^D$. Combining with Eq. (2), the logarithmic density of x with h as the conditional information can be denoted as:

$$logp(x|h) = logq(f(x;h)) + log|det\nabla_x f(x;h)| \tag{3}$$

3 Method

3.1 Overall Framework

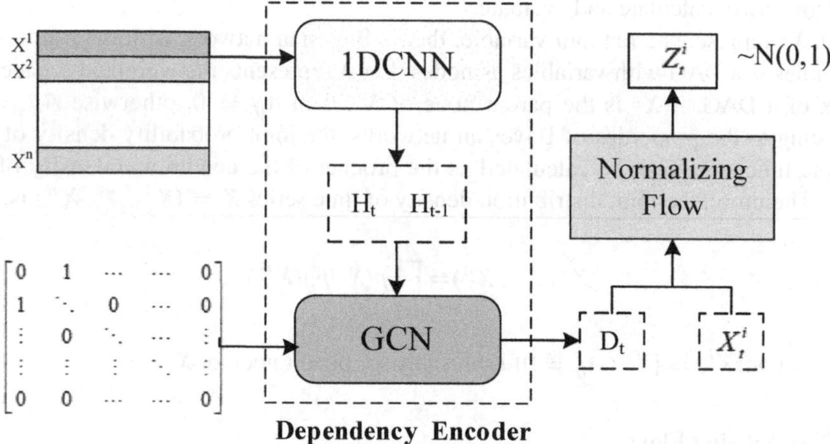

Fig. 1. The overall framework of the GNF

We propose an anomaly detection model GNF, the overall framework proposed in this paper is shown in Fig. 1. The main idea of the GNF is to use a Bayesian network to model the structural relationship between variables and to use normalizing flow for density estimation. For time series $X = (X^1, \ldots, X^n)$, and $X^i \in \mathbb{R}^{D\times T}$, the model decomposes the time series density $p(X)$, then uses a graph-based dependency encoder to parameterize the conditional probabilities resulting from the decomposition, and finally introduces a normalizing flow for density estimation.

For the multiple time series $X = (X^1, \ldots, X^n)$, where $X^i \in \mathbb{R}^{D\times T}$, the structural relationship between variables is modeled by the Bayesian network to obtain a representable graph adjacency matrix $A \in \mathbb{R}^{n\times n}$. . A differentiable constraint is imposed to ensure that the corresponding graph is a directed acyclic graph (the constraint of A corresponding to the DAG can be expressed as a differentiable equation). The joint density of multiple time series $p(X)$ is decomposed into conditional density along the time dimension and sequential dimension. In the conditional density calculation, a dependency encoder is designed to capture the interdependencies between series. The interdependencies are introduced into the normalizing flow as conditional information for density estimation. The GNF needs to learn both the graph adjacency matrix A and the conditional normalizing flow to obtain Z, which is a random variable with a "simple distribution" similar to the anisotropic Gaussian distribution.

3.2 Dependency Encoder

Since the node history information is arbitrary in length, a one-dimensional convolutional neural network is used to map multi-time steps to a fixed-length vector. Inspired by the success of GCN [7] in aggregating the representations of neighboring nodes, a graph convolutional layer is added to aggregate the hidden state of parent nodes for dependence encoding. The graph convolutional layer generates the corresponding dependence vector $D_t = (d_t^1, ..., d_t^n)$ for the time series at time t by formula (4):

$$D_t = ReLU(AH_tW_1 + H_{t-1}W_2) \cdot W_3 \tag{4}$$

where $H_t = (h_t^1, \ldots, h_t^n)$ contains all hidden states, $W_1 \in \mathbb{R}^{d \times d}$ and $W_2 \in \mathbb{R}^{d \times d}$ are denoted as the parameters used to aggregate the feature vector of the parent node and the parameter used to aggregate the feature vector of the node history information respectively, while $W_3 \in \mathbb{R}^{d \times d}$ is an extra transformation to improve the representation of dependence features.

3.3 Anomaly Detection

The interdependence vector $D_t = (d_t^1, ..., d_t^n)$ is obtained by the encoder, and then the normalizing flow $f : \mathbb{R}^D \times \mathbb{R}^d \to \mathbb{R}^D$ with d_t^i as conditional information is introduced for density estimation. According to formula (3), the logarithmic conditional density of X_t^i can be written as:

$$logp(X_t^i|pa(X^i)_{1:t}, X_{1:t-1}^i) = logp(X_t^i|d_t^i) = logq(f(X_t^i; d_t^i)) + log|det\nabla_{X_t^i}f(X_t^i; d_t^i)| \tag{5}$$

where $q(z)$ is the standard distribution with $z \in \mathbb{R}^D$. The conditional normalizing flow f can be Real NVP [17] or MAF [18]. The logarithmic density of the time series X can be obtained:

$$logp(X) = \sum_{i=1}^{n}\sum_{t=1}^{T}\left[logq(f(X_t^i; d_t^i)) + log|det\nabla_{X_t^i}f(X_t^i; d_t^i)|\right] \tag{6}$$

In addition to the density of the whole series, the conditional density $logp(X^i|pa(X^i))$ can also be obtained. The density calculated is used as a measure, where a lower density indicates a more likely anomaly which suggests that abnormal behaviors could be traced to individual series.

4 Experiment

4.1 Dataset

To evaluate the effectiveness of GNF, we conduct experiments on a water system dataset. The Secure Water Treatment dataset (SWaT) [20] was collected from an operational water treatment testbed coordinated with the Singapore Public Utility Board. The dataset collected recordings of 51 sensors for 11 days at a frequency of one second, of which 496800 samples were collected under the normal scenario for the first 7 days and 449919 samples were collected under the attacked scenario for the last 4 days. There were 36 attacks in total, generating about 12% abnormal data.

4.2 Experimental Detail

We implement experiments on NVIDIA Tesla V100 GPU. The overall code framework of the GNF is based on Pytorch. We use MAF with 6 flow blocks as normalizing flow. For parameters, we set the initial learning rate of the adjacency matrix and the neural network parameters to 0.001 and choose the hyper-parameter that yields the highest logarithmic density on the validation set.

4.3 Experimental Metrics

An intuitive comparison is made by calculating the AUC (Area Under Curve) values and drawing the corresponding ROC curves. The AUC represents the area enclosed with the coordinate axis under the ROC curve and it ranges between 0.5 and 1, the closer to 1, the higher the authenticity of the method. The specific results are shown in Table 1 and Fig. 2.

4.4 Baselines

EncDecAD [21]: This method trained an LSTM-based autoencoder and used the reconstruction error as the anomaly metric.

DeepSVDD [12]: This method contained the minimization of the volume of the hypersphere represented of the data, and samples far from the center of the hypersphere were considered as anomalies.

ALOCC [22]: This method was based on a generative adversarial network, which learned to reconstruct normal samples through a generator and identified anomalies through a discriminator.

DROCC [23]: This method learned a robust representation of the data and identified anomalies through adversarial training.

DeepSAD [24]: This method extended DeepSVDD to a semi-supervised loss term for training.

4.5 Experimental Result

For anomaly detection, the proportion of abnormal samples in the whole dataset is relatively low, thus, the positive and negative data samples are not balanced. In this case, it is reasonable to evaluate the performance of the model by calculating the AUC value. In this paper, the AUC value is calculated on the SWaT dataset, and the specific results are shown in Table 1.

Table 1. The AUC values of various methods

Dataset	EncDecAD	DeepSVDD	ALOCC	DROCC	DeepSAD	GNF
SWaT	76.5	69.1	76.7	74.4	75.9	85.6

Table 1 shows the AUC values of each baseline method and GNF, comparing GNF with various baseline methods, from which it can be seen that: (1) GNF can more effectively exploit the interdependence between time series, resulting in substantial improvements in anomaly detection. (2) GNF confirms the advantage of using probability density for anomaly detection. (3) GNF can also achieve good results when labels are scarce.

In addition to calculating the AUC values of each method, we also plot the ROC curve for each method in Fig. 2. It can be seen from Fig. 2 that the curve of GNF is superior to other curves.

From Table 1 and Fig. 2, the following conclusions can be drawn: (1) The model GNF in this paper can more effectively exploit the interdependencies of constituent sequences, making substantial improvements in anomaly detection. (2) The GNF significantly outperforms the single-class model, confirming that using probability density for anomaly

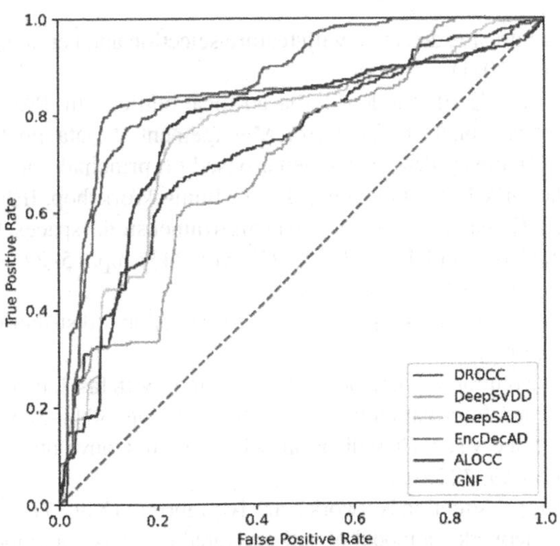

Fig. 2. The ROC curves of various methods.

detection is effective and feasible. (3) The performance of GNF is also better than that of semi-supervised methods, which rely on labels for supervised training (especially when labels are scarce), showing that GNF can also achieve good results when labels are scarce.

5 Conclusion

We propose an anomaly detection method for multiple time series, called GNF. The GNF uses Bayesian networks to model the structural relationships between multiple time series. We design an encoder to summarize the conditional information required for the normalizing flow to density estimation. And the conditional information is introduced to the conditional normalizing flow for density estimation, and finally detecting anomalies by identifying samples with low density.

The experimental comparisons on the SWaT have demonstrated the effectiveness and feasibility of combining Bayesian networks and normalizing flows. The AUC scores on the SWaT dataset also outperformed the other comparison methods. However, connecting more series as input will increase the complexity of training and make it difficult to train the parameters to the optimum, resulting in a decrease in effectiveness. This will be a potential direction of improvement in the future.

Acknowledgments. This paper is supported by the National Natural Science Foundation of China, under Grant No. 62162026, the Science and Technology Key Research and Development Program of Jiangxi Province, under Grant No. 20202BBEL53004 and the Science and Technology Project supported by the Education Department of Jiangxi Province, under Grant No. GJJ210611.

References

1. Wu, C.: Enhancing intrusion detection with feature selection and neural network. Int. J. Intell. Syst. **36**, 3087–3105 (2021)
2. Breunig, M.M.: LOF: identifying density-based local outliers. In: Proceedings of the 2000 ACM SIGMOD International Conference on Management of Data, pp. 93–104 (2000)
3. Shyu, M.: A novel anomaly detection scheme based on principal component classifier. In: Proc Icdm Foundation & New Direction of Data Mining Workshop. IEEE (2003)
4. Angiulli, F., Pizzuti, C.: Fast outlier detection in high dimensional spaces. In: Elomaa, T., Mannila, H., Toivonen, H. (eds.) PKDD 2002. LNCS, vol. 2431, pp. 15–27. Springer, Heidelberg (2002). https://doi.org/10.1007/3-540-45681-3_2
5. Sch¨olkopf, B.: Estimating the support of a high-dimensional distribution. Neural Comput. **13**(7), 1443–1471 (2001)
6. Defferrard, M.: Convolutional neural networks on graphs with fast localized spectral filtering. In: Advances in Neural Information Processing Systems, pp. 3844–3852 (2016)
7. Kipf, T.N.: Semi-Supervised Classification with Graph Convolutional Networks. arXiv preprint arXiv:1609.02907 (2016)
8. Veliˇckovi´c, P.: Graph Attention Networks. arXiv preprint arXiv:1710.10903 (2017)
9. Pearl, J.: Bayesian networks: a model of self-activated memory for evidential reasoning. In: Proceedings of the 7th Conference of the Cognitive Science Society (1985)

10. Zong, B.: Deep autoencoding gaussian mixture model for unsupervised anomaly detection. In: International Conference on Learning Representations (2018)
11. Tax, D.M.J.: Support vector data description. Mach. Learn. (2004)
12. Ruff, L.: Deep one-class classification. In: International Conference on Machine Learning (2018)
13. Park, D.: A multimodal anomaly detector for robot-assisted feeding using an LSTM-based variational autoencoder. IEEE Robot. Autom. Lett. (2018)
14. Su, Y.: Robust anomaly detection for multivariate time series through stochastic recurrent neural network. In: Proceedings of the 25th ACM SIGKDD International Conference on Knowledge Discovery & Data Mining (2019)
15. Li, Z.: Multivariate time series anomaly detection and interpretation using hierarchical inter-metric and temporal embedding. In: Proceedings of the 27th ACM SIGKDD Conference on Knowledge Discovery & Data Mining, pp. 3220–3230 (2021)
16. Pearl, J.: Bayesian networks: a model of self-activated memory for evidential reasoning. In: Proceedings of the 7th Conference of the Cognitive Science Society, pp. 329–334 (1985)
17. Dinh, L.: Density estimation using Real NVP. arXiv preprint arXiv:1605.08803 (2016)
18. Papamakarios, G.: Masked autoregressive flow for density estimation. In: Advances in Neural Information Processing Systems (2017)
19. Rasul, K.: Multivariate Probabilistic Time Series Forecasting via Conditioned Normalizing Flows. ArXiv (2020)
20. Mathur, A.P., Tippenhauer, N.O.: SWaT: a water treatment test bed for research and training on ICS security. In: 2016 International Workshop on Cyber-physical Systems for Smart Water Networks (CySWater). IEEE, pp. 31–36 (2016)
21. Pankaj, M.: Lstm-based encoder-decoder for Multi-sensor Anomaly Detection. arXiv preprint arXiv:1607.00148 (2016)
22. Mohammad, S.: Deep end-to-end one class classifier. IEEE Trans. Neural Netw. Learn. Syst. **32**(2), 675–684 (2020)
23. Sachin, G.: Drocc: deep robust one-class classification. In: International Conference on Machine Learning, pp. 3711–3721. PMLR (2020)
24. Ruff, L.: Deep semi-supervised anomaly detection. In: International Conference on Learning Representations (2020)

Encrypted Transmission Method of Network Speech Recognition Information Based on Big Data Analysis

Yanning Zhang(✉)

Beijing Polytechnic, Beijing 100016, China
witgirl316@126.com

Abstract. Voice is the medium of language. With the development and popularization of network technology, voice has also become the main carrier of network information. Because the network is open to a certain extent, it poses a great threat to the security of network information transmission. Therefore, a research on encrypted transmission method of network speech recognition information based on big data analysis is proposed. Preprocess network speech signals (sampling, quantization, filtering, pre emphasis, windowing and framing, endpoint detection, etc.), extract network speech signal features based on big data analysis technology, apply hidden Markov model to obtain network speech recognition information, build information encryption model PKI, effectively combine symmetric encryption algorithm and asymmetric encryption algorithm, and formulate encryption and decryption steps of speech recognition information. Thus, the encrypted transmission of network speech recognition information is realized. The experimental data show that the minimum value of the network speech recognition information acquisition time of the proposed method is 10.09s, and the maximum proportion of successful speech recognition information encryption is 97%, which fully proves that the proposed method has better information encryption transmission effect.

Keywords: Big data analysis technology · Network voice · Speech recognition · Information encryption · Information transmission · Secure transmission

1 Introduction

Language is a unique skill different from other animals. As the medium of language, speech plays a unique role in the process of information dissemination and emotional expression [1]. Nowadays, all aspects of our life are gradually surrounded by the network. Due to the continuous strengthening of the informatization of the national economy and the emergence of new network industries such as e-commerce, the network has become more and more indispensable in the normal operation of our daily life. Users are no longer only satisfied with the initial voice business and data business, but the business they need begins to show diversification. A variety of application services such as wireless medical treatment, online ticket purchase, online banking, distance education and so on have sprung up in our lives and won our favor. Because the wireless

Y. Xu et al. (Eds.): ML4CS 2022, LNCS 13655, pp. 118–132, 2023.
https://doi.org/10.1007/978-3-031-20096-0_10

channel can transmit or store many sensitive information on the wireless platform, with the popularity of such new services, we need higher security of network resources. Therefore, with the continuous expansion of the network, the security problems have hindered the development of the network to some extent. How to ensure the privacy of network information, avoid personal privacy exposure, and ensure the rights and interests of users will become a topic of great research value in the network field. People's trust in the network can make the business widely promoted. On the contrary, if we look at the network information security problem with a negative attitude, the new business development of the network will stagnate. Therefore, only by gaining the trust of users can we earn rich market profits.

The reason why the network can be used by users is because of the existence of signaling interaction or data transmission. However, the wireless signal is open, which makes it possible for other unintended receivers to receive its signal. People, when receiving the same frequency, can easily eavesdrop or tamper with information that does not belong to them, so the security of information transmission is worrying. However, due to the inherent insufficiency of user terminal equipment in terms of storage, computing, etc., many security technologies in cutting-edge networks cannot be promoted in the network, and encryption algorithms with complex computation and large storage cannot be used. In addition, because network resources are inherently scarce, network resources cannot be occupied by lengthy and cumbersome control signaling. The improvement of network security technology is limited by various practical problems. Because the security of mobile user information on the network cannot be guaranteed and is vulnerable to malicious attacks by illegal elements, it is very likely that users or the network will suffer loss of profits [2].

Reference [3] proposes a speech information encryption transmission method based on Logistic mapping and random noise, which divides speech into left and right channels, randomly encrypts each channel, and then synthesizes a complete encrypted speech. By adding random noise, the anti attack ability and transmission stability are improved. Reference [4] proposes a speech information encryption transmission method based on cascaded chaotic system. First, the speech signals are grouped. Secondly, the order of fractional Fourier transform is obtained by using chaotic system, and the corresponding order of each group of data changes dynamically. Then, the sampled fractional Fourier discrete transform with low computational complexity is used to obtain the corresponding fractional domain spectral data of each group. Finally, the cascaded chaotic system is used to encrypt the data of each fractional domain in turn, so as to realize the overall encrypted transmission of voice signals. Reference [5] proposes a voice information encryption transmission method based on the combination of time-domain analysis and fast correlation method. On the basis of establishing a two-stage synchronization model and based on the time-domain feature analysis of sinusoidal signals, a post verification algorithm is designed to achieve synchronous signal capture. Through the correlation calculation of LFM signal, the synchronous deviation compensation algorithm is designed to realize the encrypted transmission of voice signal. Although the above method can realize the encrypted transmission of voice signals, there are some deficiencies in the success rate of encryption.

Network speech is a data form widely used in the network today, and its accurate recognition and encryption transmission play a vital role. Therefore, a network speech recognition information encryption transmission method based on big data analysis is proposed. The characteristics of network speech signals are extracted based on big data analysis technology, and the steps of speech recognition information encryption and decryption are formulated by effectively combining symmetric encryption algorithm and asymmetric encryption algorithm. Thus, the encrypted transmission of network speech recognition information is realized.

2 Network Voice Preprocessing

Network speech signal preprocessing consists of sampling, quantization, filtering, pre emphasis, windowing and framing, endpoint detection and other steps, which are introduced below.

The network speech signal sequence is composed of a group of continuously changing analog quantities, but the computer can only save and analyze binary digital quantities, so the first step is to sample and quantify the speech signal sequence to convert it into binary digital quantities, and then send it to the computer for storage and subsequent processing. Sampling means to collect the analog value of the analog signal according to a set frequency, that is, a very short time interval. Quantization means that according to the analog voltage value collected during the sampling operation, the method of hierarchical quantization is adopted to divide the variation range of all voltage values into several intervals, divide the analog voltage value samples falling into a certain interval into one category, and set their corresponding quantization values. "Sampling frequency" refers to the number of samples of the amplitude of the sound signal collected in each second after digitizing the analog voice signal waveform, and its unit is generally kHz (kilohertz). The number of quantized data bits (also called the quantization level) refers to the range of values that each sampling point can cover, usually 8-bit, 12-bit, 16-bit and other quantized data bits, of which 8-bit word length quantization belongs to low-quality quantization and 16-bit word length quantization belongs to high-quality quantization, and 16-bit word length quantization is the most commonly used quantization data bit. Before using the recording software on the computer to record the voice signal, set the sampling frequency, quantization bits, and channels, so that the voice signal can be stored in the computer in digital form. The speech signal obtained above contains noise, and a corresponding filter needs to be designed to filter the noisy speech to eliminate the noise.

Pre emphasis is usually used in the process of network speech signal processing, that is, after the network speech signal is sampled, a first-order high pass filter is added to minimize the effect of glottic pulse, leaving only the channel part, and then the channel parameters are analyzed.

Pre emphasis belongs to the first-order high pass filter, which can raise the high-frequency part of the speech signal. It needs to be programmed in the software to achieve this purpose. Its function expression is:

$$H(z) = 1 - \mu z^{-1} \tag{1}$$

In formula (1), $H(z)$ represents the expression of the pre-emphasis function; μ represents the pre-emphasis coefficient, and the value range is usually between 0.9 and 1.0; z represents the pre-emphasis processing target.

Set the original network voice signal as $s(n)$, then after pre-emphasis processing it is:

$$s'(n) = s(n) - \mu s(n-1) \tag{2}$$

In formula (2), $s'(n)$ represents the VoIP signal after pre-emphasis processing; $s(n-1)$ represents the $n-1$ original VoIP signal.

Speech signals are non-stationary and time-varying signals, but in a relatively short time span (10–30 ms), it is generally considered to be stationary and not time-varying. It is precisely because of this characteristic of speech signals that they are often regarded as "quasi-steady-state" signals. This "quasi-steady state" feature runs through the entire process of speech signal analysis and processing, forming a "short-term analysis technology" for speech signals.

In the short-time analysis technology, the speech signal is usually cut into several small segments. This operation is called "frame division", and the frame length is generally 10–30 ms. Speech signal is a signal that changes with time, and its characteristic parameters hardly change in a very short time span, so it is analyzed as a steady-state signal, but changes will occur outside this very short time span. Therefore, when dividing frames, partial overlap is often set between two adjacent frames to ensure the smooth transition between frames. The displacement of the next frame relative to the previous frame can be expressed by frame displacement. The specific operation is to realize the purpose of framing by convoluting the movable window function with the speech signal with a limited length:

$$s_w(n) = s'(n) * w(n) \tag{3}$$

In formula (3), $s_w(n)$ represents the framing result of the network voice signal; $w(n)$ represents the window function.

Window function usually has low-pass property. Different selection of window function will lead to different bandpass width and spectrum omission. Window functions widely used in digital signal processing tasks include rectangular window, Haining window and Hamming window. When selecting the window function, two factors need to be considered: on the one hand, the main lobe width B of the spectrum should be as narrow as possible to make the transition band steep; On the other hand, the first side lobe attenuation A should be as large as possible to make the energy converge. Inside the main lobe. The characteristics of the three window functions are shown in Table 1.

As shown in Table 1, Δw is the angular frequency resolution when the spectrum is obtained. Looking at Table 1, it can be found that among the three window functions, the main lobe width of the rectangular window function is the narrowest, but its first side lobe attenuation is the smallest, which means that its spectrum will be higher than that of the two other window functions. Functions are missing a lot. The main lobe width of the Hamming window is relatively narrow, but its first side lobe attenuation is the largest. In the analysis and processing of speech signals, it is necessary to select the appropriate window function according to different actual situations. In the field of

Table 1. Window function characteristic table

Window function	Main lobe width	First side lobe attenuation
Rectangular window	$0.89\Delta w$	13 dB
Haining window	$1.44\Delta w$	32 dB
Hamming window	$1.30\Delta w$	43 dB

speech recognition, the Hamming window is the most widely used. In this paper, the Hamming window function is used when windowing and framing the speech signal.

At present, there are many endpoint detection algorithms, such as endpoint detection based on double threshold method, endpoint detection based on energy zero ratio and energy entropy ratio, etc. Considering the real-time and computational complexity of speech recognition task, this paper selects the double threshold method based on short-term average energy and short-term average zero crossing rate for endpoint detection. Its basic principle is that Chinese is composed of vowels and consonants. Vowels contain vowels, and vowels contain a lot of energy. Vowels contain consonants, and the frequency of consonants is very high, so we can use short-term average energy to find vowels, using the short-time average zero crossing rate to find the initial consonants, we can find the whole Chinese syllable [6]. The solution steps of the algorithm are as follows:

Step 1: Assume that the sampled voice sample time-domain signal sequence is $s(n)$, the window function is $w(n)$, and the i frame voice signal obtained after pre-emphasis, windowing and framing is $y_i(n)$, $1 \leq i \leq f_n$, and f_n are the total frames after framing.

Step 2: Calculate the short-term energy of the speech signal $y_i(n)$ in the i frame, and the mathematical expression is:

$$E(i) = \sum_{n=0}^{L-1} y_i^2(n),\ 1 \leq i \leq f_n \tag{4}$$

In formula (4), $E(i)$ represents the short-term energy of the network voice signal; L represents the frame length.

Step 3: Calculate the short-term average zero-crossing rate of the i frame speech signal $y_i(n)$, the formula is:

$$\begin{cases} Z(i) = \frac{1}{2}\sum_{n=0}^{L-1} \left|\mathrm{sgn}[y_i(n)] - \mathrm{sgn}[y_i(n-1)]\right| \\ \mathrm{sgn}[x] = \begin{cases} 1 & x \geq 0 \\ -1 & x < 0 \end{cases} \end{cases} \tag{5}$$

In formula (5), $Z(i)$ represents the short-term average zero-crossing rate of the network speech signal; $\mathrm{sgn}[\cdot]$ represents the sign function; x represents the target object of the sign function.

Determine a suitable threshold T_2 from the short-term energy curve of speech and select a suitable threshold T_1 on the average energy curve to preliminarily determine the starting point and end point of the effective speech segment; Then, according to the short-term average zero-crossing rate Below a certain threshold T_3, the starting point and the ending point position of the valid speech segment are further determined. At the same time, in view of the fact that there is a small duration of silence between two syllables when the speech signal is uttered, which represents the stagnation between syllables, that is, it will be judged only after it is lower than the threshold T_3 and meets this small duration. The end of the effective speech segment is actually equivalent to increasing the size of the tail syllable of the effective speech segment. The research uses the vad function for endpoint detection, but the three thresholds of T_1, T_2 and T_3 in this program are all fixed values, which cannot be changed with different signals, and this function is only suitable for detecting pure speech. Obviously, the voice recorded under laboratory conditions contains less noise, so the vad function is modified in this paper. The flowchart of the modified vad function is shown in Fig. 1.

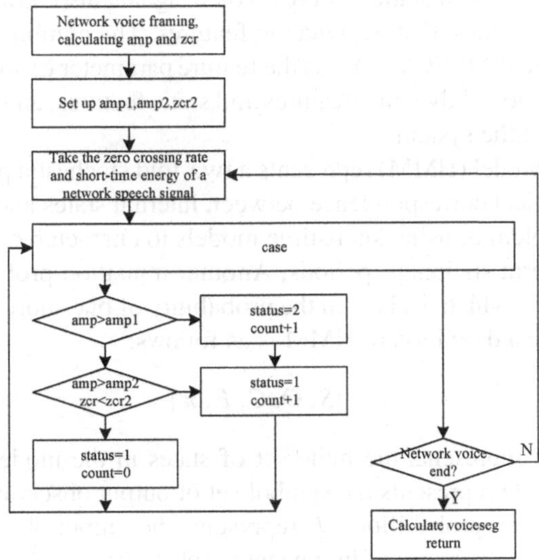

Fig. 1. Vad function flow chart

The above process completes the preprocessing of network speech (sampling, quantization, filtering, pre emphasis, windowing and framing, endpoint detection), and lays a solid foundation for subsequent network speech recognition.

The network speech signal is generated by exciting the channel models with different shapes. The characteristics of the speech signal can be obtained by using the parameters estimated from the channel shape or model to complete speech recognition. The basic concept of all pole linear prediction model is that a speech signal can be approximated by a linear combination of several speech samples in the past. By minimizing the sum of squares of error values between actual speech sampling and linear prediction sampling, a group of prediction coefficients that can be uniquely determined is called linear prediction coefficients [7].

The linear prediction cepstral coefficient (LPCC) is the cepstral domain representation of the linear prediction coefficient LPC.

Mel frequency cepstral coefficients have been widely used in recent years, and the MFCC parameters are used to obtain better identification results than the LPCC parameters. The calculation steps are as follows: determine the number of points of each frame of speech sampling sequence, perform pre-emphasis processing on each frame sequence, and then undergo discrete FFT transformation, take the square of the modulo to obtain the discrete power spectrum, and calculate the discrete power spectrum obtained after passing through M bandpass filters, obtain M parameters P_m, calculate the natural logarithm of P_m, obtain L_m, calculate its discrete cosine transform to obtain D_m, take D_k as the MFCC parameter, and k in this paper is an integer from 1 to 12.

The human ear is more sensitive to the dynamic characteristics of speech, which can be described by the difference between MFCC and LPCC as parameters, that is ΔMFCC and ΔLPCC.

To sum up, in addition to static features, voice signals also have transient features between consecutive frames, that is, dynamic features. The combination of LPCC and ΔLPCC or MFCC and ΔMFCC is used as the feature parameter of speech, which makes the effective combination of dynamic features and static features, and can better improve the recognition rate of the system.

Hidden Markov Model (HMM) represents a two-fold stochastic process: one is used to describe the statistical correspondence between internal states and observations, and it deals with the problem of using short-time models to characterize the transient characteristics of short-term stationary periods; Another transition probability distribution used to describe states, which deals with the probability of one short-term plateau to the next. The mathematical definition of HMM is as follows:

$$\lambda = \{S, O, C, F, \pi\} \tag{6}$$

In formula (6), S represents the finite set of states in the model, denoted as $S = \{S_i | i = 1, 2, \cdots, N\}$; O represents the symbol set of output observations; C represents the set of state transition probabilities; F represents the output observations the set of probabilities; π represents the set of initial state probabilities of the system.

According to the HMM shown in formula (6), the network speech recognition information can be obtained, which is abbreviated as $X = \{X_i | i = 1, 2, \cdots, n\}$, providing support for the subsequent construction of information encryption model.

3 Encrypted Transmission of Speech Recognition Information

Based on the above obtained network speech recognition information, an information encryption model PKI is constructed, which lays a solid foundation for the subsequent implementation of information encryption transmission.

PKI technology uses public key theory to build information security transmission system, and provides a more secure and convenient information transmission channel using public key. It is a unified technical framework that uses public key cryptography to provide data encryption and digital signature services in an open network environment.

PKI provides a system that supports centralized and automated key management and key distribution. The purpose of establishing PKI is to manage the keys, certificates for encryption and digital signatures, and the trust relationship between various institutions resulting therefrom. PKI system is composed of basic components such as public key cryptography, digital certificate, certificate authority (CA) and system security policy. It is a comprehensive system for verifying the identity of users who hold keys. A PKI system consists of CAs, policy and technical standards, and necessary laws. Its establishment will promote the application of public key cryptosystem in the Internet [8].

The most important security technology in PKI technology includes two aspects: public key encryption technology and digital signature technology. Public key encryption technology can provide the confidentiality of information and an effective means of access control. It ensures the confidentiality of data. Digital signature technology provides us with an effective method of mutual authentication between network communications, a reliable means to ensure the integrity of information in the process of communication, and an effective mechanism to prevent mutual repudiation after the end of communication.

To establish a PKI network security environment with practical use value, the following basic conditions must be met:

- Able to issue digital certificates based on public key cryptosystem;
- Access environment and channels with digital certificates;
- Able to invalidate the certificate;
- Realize key backup and recovery;
- Support non-repudiation digital signature;
- Automatic update of public key pairs and digital certificates;
- Archive management of public key pairs;
- Supports cross-certification of digital certificates, etal.

X.509 provides a PKI structure for authenticating X.500 services, the X.500 standard for providing directory services in large computer networks. An X.500 directory entity can represent any entity in the real world. Each entity is assigned a globally unique name (DN) by X.500. This is similar to the phone book we often use, as long as the DN of the entity is given, the detailed information of the entity can be found. An example diagram of the X.500 directory is shown in Fig. 2.

Based on the above information encryption model - PKI, effectively combine symmetric encryption algorithm and asymmetric encryption algorithm to encrypt speech recognition information, so as to improve the security of network speech recognition information transmission.

The idea of encrypted transmission of network speech recognition information is as follows:

Before encrypted transmission of network speech recognition information, the sender first obtains the public key PK encrypted by RSA of the receiver; Then, at the sending end, the original network speech recognition information plaintext P is encrypted with Logistic chaotic encryption key K, and the encrypted network speech recognition information ciphertext H is obtained; At the same time, the sender encrypts the chaotic key K with the public key PK of the receiver to obtain the key ciphertext H; Finally, during data transmission, the ciphertext H and the key ciphertext CK are packaged together and transmitted to the receiver through a secure channel.

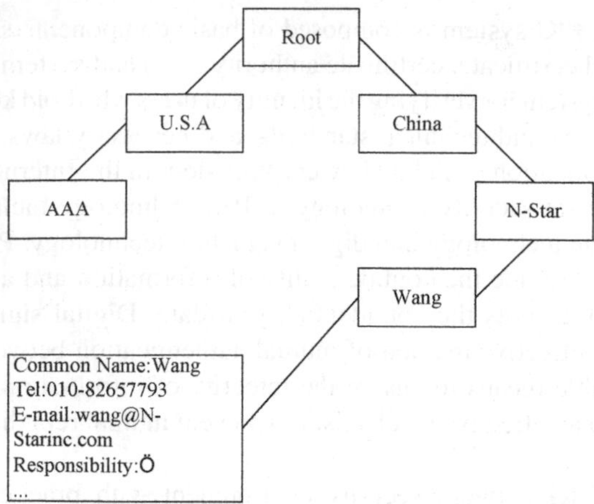

Fig. 2. Example of X.500 Directory

After receiving the data packets of the ciphertext H and the key ciphertext CK, the receiver uses the private key SK to perform RSA decryption on the key ciphertext CK, obtains the chaotic decryption key K of the Logistic mapping, and decrypts the ciphertext H.

During the network transmission of data, when a third-party attacker intercepts ciphertext H and key ciphertext CK through a packet capture tool, since the attacker does not have the recipient's private key SK, the key ciphertext CK cannot be decrypted correctly The key K is obtained, so that the ciphertext H cannot be decrypted. Therefore, the security of information during encrypted transmission can be guaranteed.

The hybrid algorithm can not only solve the security problems of key transmission and key distribution management in chaotic algorithm in practical application, but also solve the problems of slow encryption speed and low efficiency in RSA algorithm [9].

The specific encryption steps of network speech recognition information are as follows:

Step 1: Read the set of network speech recognition information to be encrypted. Obtain the sample data sequence P and sampling frequency f_s of the network speech recognition information. At this time, the data type of P is a double-precision floating point type. Generally, the sampling frequency of the network speech recognition information is 44100 Hz. Since the value range of the read network speech recognition information is in [0, 255], the network speech recognition information is converted into an 8-bit unsigned integer and mapped in the range of [0, 255], which is recorded as the network speech recognition information plaintext sequence P'.

Step 2: Set key parameters. Logistic mapping sets control parameters δ_1 and δ_2, initial values x_0 and y_0, and pre-iteration times N_1 and N_2 as key parameters. It can be known from the relevant basic knowledge that the value range of the initial values x_0 and N_2 of the Logistic map is $x_0, y_0 \in (0, 1)$. When $\delta \in (3.5699456, 4]$, the system enters a chaotic state.

Step 3: Generate two sets of Logistic chaotic sequences. The key parameters: control parameters δ_1, δ_2, initial values x_0, y_0 and the number of pre-iterations are replaced from N_1, N_2 into the Logistic mapping formula to iteratively generate chaotic sequences J, Q. In order to prevent transient effects, set the chaotic system pre-iteration N_1 and N_2 times, that is, remove the values of the previous N_1 and N_2 iterations, which can increase the key space and obtain a more stable random sequence, so that the generated sequence value presents a good appearance. Pseudo-randomness. Arrange the first group of chaotic sequences J in ascending order, and record the new sequence J' after sorting.

Since the value range of the chaotic sequence Q generated by the logistic map is in the range of [0, 1], the decimal non-integer cannot be XORed, so the chaotic sequence Q generated by the second group of logistic map iterations is mapped to an integer whose value range is [0, 255]. Data, the chaotic password sequence Q' is obtained.

The formula for calculating J' and Q' is

$$\begin{cases} [J', Index] = sort(J) \\ Q' = unit8(floor(Q \times 256)) \end{cases} \tag{7}$$

In formula (7), *Index* represents the corresponding position index information of the new sequence J' in the chaotic sequence J; *sort* represents the function expression of the chaotic sequence J in ascending order.

Step 4: perform position transformation. The network speech recognition information plaintext P' is arranged according to the position index *Index* of J' in ascending order of chaotic sequence J, the position of the network speech recognition information sequence is scrambled, and the network speech recognition information sequence P'' after position transformation is output;

Step 5: perform XOR encryption. The position transformed network speech recognition information sequence P'' and chaotic sequence Q' are XOR computed to obtain the encrypted network speech recognition information, which is transmitted accordingly.

The decryption process of the network speech recognition information file by the receiver is the reverse process of encryption. The receiver uses the private key to correctly decrypt the key ciphertext to obtain the key parameters of the Logistic chaotic system. Then use the correct key parameters to control parameters δ_1, δ_2, initial values x_0, y_0 and pre-iteration times N_1, N_2, to obtain the same chaotic sequence used in chaotic encryption. The chaotic sequence and the encrypted network speech recognition information sequence are solved according to the inverse process of the encryption algorithm to obtain the original network speech recognition information [10].

The decryption steps of network speech recognition information file are as follows:

Step 1: read the network speech recognition information file to be decrypted. Convert the sample sequence V of the network speech recognition information file to be decrypted into an eight bit unsigned integer, and record it as the network speech recognition information ciphertext V';

Step 2: obtain key parameters. The receiver uses the private key to decrypt the key parameters through RSA algorithm;

Step 3: Generate two sets of Logistic chaotic sequences. Substitute the key parameter into the Logistic map for iteration. Generate chaotic sequences J and Q, and update them to J' and Q';

Step 4: Perform an inverse XOR operation. Perform an XOR operation on the decrypted network speech recognition information ciphertext V' and the chaotic sequence Q' to obtain the XOR decrypted network speech recognition information ciphertext P'';

Step 5: perform reverse position transformation. The XOR decrypted network speech recognition information ciphertext P'' is inversely transformed according to the position index *Index* after the first group of logistic chaos J is arranged in ascending order to obtain the network speech recognition information sequence P' after the inverse position transformation decryption;

Step 6: get the decrypted network speech recognition information file. Convert the decrypted integer data of network speech recognition information into double precision floating-point type, and then save the encrypted network speech recognition information file.

The above process realizes the encrypted transmission of network speech recognition information, and gives the decryption steps of network speech recognition information, which provides a more effective method support for network information security.

4 Experiment and Result Analysis

4.1 Experiment Preparation Stage

In order to verify the application performance of the proposed method, a network speech recognition information encryption transmission experiment is designed. The experimental preparation is the key and premise to ensure the smooth progress of the experiment. The experimental preparation stage is set according to the experimental needs, including the determination of the best pre weighting coefficient and the setting of experimental conditions.

Among them, the pre emphasis coefficient is the key parameter that affects the network speech processing, so its optimal value is determined. The relation curve between the pre emphasis coefficient and the network speech processing efficiency obtained through the test is shown in Fig. 3.

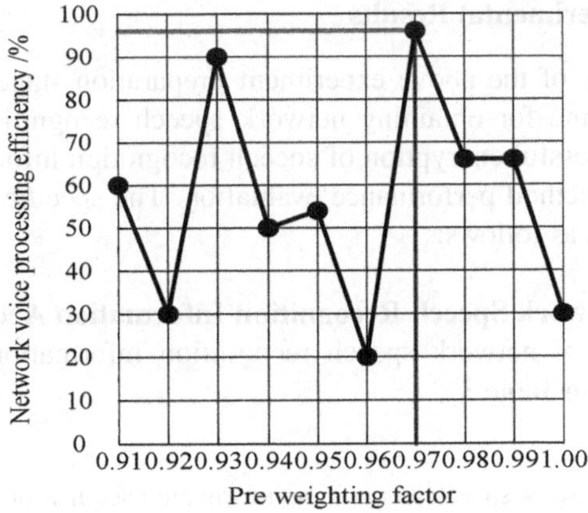

Fig. 3. Schematic diagram of the relationship between pre-emphasis coefficient and network voice processing efficiency

As shown in Fig. 3, when the pre emphasis coefficient is 0.97, the network speech processing efficiency reaches the maximum value of 96%, so the best pre emphasis coefficient is determined to be 0.97.

In order to improve the accuracy of the experimental conclusion, 10 different experimental conditions are set, as shown in Table 2.

Table 2. Experimental conditions table

Experimental condition number	VoIP number /strip	The proportion of information encryption needs
1	561	56.23%
2	450	45.01%
3	351	62.31%
4	485	72.09%
5	700	55.25%
6	615	41.02%
7	438	65.30%
8	389	49.87%
9	456	50.31%
10	378	62.04%

The above process completes the determination of experimental parameters and the setting of experimental conditions, which provides convenience for the smooth progress of subsequent experiments.

4.2 Analysis of Experimental Results

Based on the contents of the above experiment preparation stage, the experiment is conducted, and the time for obtaining network speech recognition information and the proportion of successful encryption of speech recognition information are selected as the indicators for method performance evaluation. The specific analysis process of experimental results is as follows:

Time Analysis of Network Speech Recognition Information Acquisition
The acquisition time of network speech recognition information obtained through experiments is shown in Table 3.

Table 3. Network speech recognition information acquisition timetable

Experimental condition number	Suggest a way	Maximum limit
1	10.23 s	20.15 s
2	15.46 s	25.49 s
3	11.28 s	24.78 s
4	15.46 s	23.02 s
5	15.30 s	25.48 s
6	12.02 s	26.12 s
7	15.49 s	30.12 s
8	15.40 s	20.14 s
9	11.28 s	30.48 s
10	10.09 s	21.04 s

As shown in Table 3, the acquisition time of network speech recognition information obtained by applying the proposed method is less than the given maximum limit, and the minimum value reaches 10.09 s.

Analysis of the Successful Proportion of Speech Recognition Information Encryption
The success rate of speech recognition information encryption obtained through experiments is shown in Fig. 4.

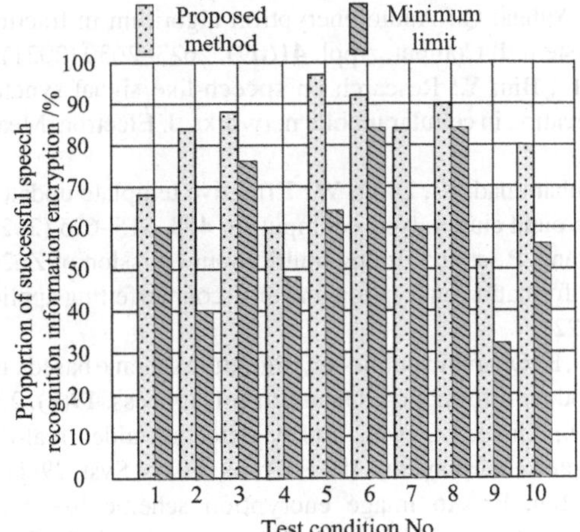

Fig. 4. Schematic diagram of the percentage of successful encryption of speech recognition information

As shown in Fig. 4, the proportion of successful encryption of speech recognition information obtained by applying the proposed method is greater than the given minimum limit, and the maximum value reaches 97%.

The above experimental data show that the acquisition time of network speech recognition information obtained by the proposed method is less than the given maximum limit, and the proportion of successful encryption of speech recognition information is greater than the given minimum limit, which fully proves the effectiveness and feasibility of the proposed method.

5 Conclusion

This research introduces big data analysis technology and proposes a new network speech recognition information encryption transmission method, which shortens the network speech recognition information acquisition time and improves the successful proportion of speech recognition information encryption. It can provide a more effective method support for network speech recognition information encryption transmission, and also provide a certain reference for information encryption transmission related research.

References

1. Li, F., Xiaojian, W.: Intelligent network communication terminal information security simulation method. Comput. Simul. **37**(5), 86–90 (2020)
2. Liu, S., Wang, S., Liu, X., Gandomi, A.H., Daneshmand, M., Muhammad, K., De Albuquerque, V.H.C.: Human memory update strategy: a multi-layer template update mechanism for remote visual monitoring. IEEE Trans. Multimedia, **23**, 2188–2198 (2021)
3. Qing, W., Tao, L., Lei, W.C., Baoxiang, D.: An improved Logistic mapping and random noise voice encryption method. J. Natl. Sci. Heilongjiang Univ. **37**(02), 240-246 (2020)

4. Liyun, X., Tao, Y., Yuhua, Q.: Audio encryption algorithm in fractional domain based on cascaded chaotic system. J. Comput. Appl. **41**(09), 2623–2630 (2021)
5. Tikui, Z., Sensen, L., Bin, Y.: Research on speech-like signal synchronization scheme of encrypted communication in cellular mobile networks. J. Electron. Measure. Instrum. **34**(01), 163-170 (2020)
6. Liu, S., Liu, D., Muhammad, K., Ding, W.: Effective template update mechanism in visual tracking with background clutter. Neurocomputing **458**, 615–625 (2021)
7. Gao, D., Ma, K., Wang, P., et al.: Tuning multicolour emission of Zn2GeO4: Mn phosphors by Li+ doping for information encryption and anti-counterfeiting applications. Dalton Trans. **51**(2), 553–561 (2022)
8. Xin, X., Yang, Q., Li, F.: Quantum public-key signature scheme based on asymmetric quantum encryption with trapdoor information. Quantum Inf. Process. **19**(8), 233 (2020)
9. Shuai, L., Shuai, W., Xinyu, L., et al.: Fuzzy detection aided real-time and robust visual tracking under complex environments. IEEE Trans. Fuzzy Syst. **29**(1), 90–102 (2021)
10. Li, X., Zhou, L., Tan, F.: An image encryption scheme based on finite-time cluster synchronization of two-layer complex dynamic networks. Soft. Comput. **26**(2), 511–525 (2021)

A Lightweight NFT Auction Protocol for Cross-chain Environment

Hongyu Guo, Mao Chen, and Wei Ou(✉)

School of Cyberspace Security (School of Cryptology), Hainan University, Haikou 570228, Hainan, China
ouwei@hainanu.edu.cn

Abstract. The NFT market has been booming in recent years. In 2021, digital artist Pak's newest creation, The Merge, fetched US$91.8 million on Nifty Gateway. Since then, many NFT owners have turned to auctions to gain more profits through their collections. Ethereum covers the majority of NFT transactions at the moment. However, it will be hard for them to make profits if they have only one way to sell. To settle this situation, we propose an auction protocol for NFTs which works in a cross-chain environment. We design our protocol by using hash time lock and adding strategies to control users' malicious behaviors. We also optimize the cross-chain asset exchange process to ensure both auction and exchange are successful. Through testing in Ethereum and FISCO BCOS networks, the experimental results show that our scheme is capable of completing auctions in heterogeneous blockchain networks and maintaining low communication costs. The transactions can be confirmed in an average of 4 blocks, and the contract strategies will filter out invalid transactions. We also do additional experiments to prove that our protocol can resist reentrancy.

Keywords: Non-fungible token · Electronic auction · Cross chain · Asset swap

1 Introduction

Non-fungible token (NFT [1]) is a type of cryptocurrency and was firstly proposed in Ethereum Improvement Proposals (EIP-721 [2]). Unlike the traditional ones, NFT is unique, which means it cannot be exchanged equivalently. When an NFT is minted, it also records information about its owner, the time it was minted, etc. It can be traded, but it cannot be split or replaced. This type of token is now widely used to prove the ownership of virtual assets such as images, videos, etc. It emphasizes the unique characteristics that attract the creator's

This work was supported in part by the Hainan Provincial Natural Science Foundation of China (621RC508), Henan Key Laboratory of Network Cryptography Technology (LNCT2021-A16), the Science Project of Hainan University (KYQD(ZR)-21075).

Y. Xu et al. (Eds.): ML4CS 2022, LNCS 13655, pp. 133–146, 2023.
https://doi.org/10.1007/978-3-031-20096-0_11

and the public's attention, indicating the asset's potential value. Collins Dictionary has also selected "NFT" as its word of the year for 2021, reflecting its influence to a certain extent. According to Forbes, the NFT market generated more than $23 billion in volume in 2021, which is an explosive increase from 2020 that has been sustained to date. However, some investors see the NFT market in 2021 as a speculative bubble likely to collapse quickly. However, to this day (May 2022), the NFT market remains highly active. Although the overall volume of transactions has decreased, the number of transactions has increased rather than decreased, which indicates that the value of a single NFT is rising. Compared to NFT, bitcoins and tokens generated based on ERC-20 are homogeneous. For example, the first bitcoin block was mined by Satoshi Nakamoto, who received the bitcoin reward for that block. However, this earliest bitcoin is now lost in the Bitcoin network and is no different from the bitcoin generated by the block just mined. Smart contracts manage NFTs, and over 97% of NFT smart contracts are deployed in the Ethereum leading network. However, the thousandfold return on its increasing market draws vast attention worldwide. Due to the staggering growth volume, the Ethereum network can no longer meet the needs of all users. Those who own NFTs wish that they can trade their NFTs in other blockchain networks, which involve the technologies of cross-chain asset exchange and electronic auction.

First, to solve the problem of blockchain data silos, researchers have developed several ways to realize the exchange of assets or information between different blockchain networks. The existing cross-chain approaches are divided into four basic methods [3]: notary schemes, sidechains/relays, hash-locking, and distributed private key control. The notary mechanism is essentially a kind of intermediary, and this mutually trusted intermediary verifies and forwards cross-chain messages. In a sidechain scheme, miners need to use Simplified Payment Verification (SPV) to verify transactions on other chains, resulting in a soft fork of the main chain that does not easily support cross-chain exchange. Hash-locking technology, the idea of which is to create a micro-payment channel to lock deposits for a specific time, has been applied to the Lightning Network. However, it allows malicious users to request transactions frequently but refuses to redeem them, resulting in some tokens being locked for a long time. In the distributed private key control scheme, multiple verifiers realize currency exchange based on secure multi-party computation and threshold signature technology. Tesseract [4] is a system that utilizes a Trusted Execution Environment (TEE), SGX. However, the trading accounts of all clients of that project are managed by SGX, which is of significant risk.

In terms of the electronic auction, blockchain and secure multi-party computation play an active role, especially in reverse auctions [5] and double auctions [6]. Traditional auctions are managed by a central auction service structure called the auctioneer. It coordinates the auction process and holds most of the data and power. Nevertheless, it can also lead to severe consequences when the auctioneer act maliciously. Through blockchain, users can participate in an auction without any auctioneers. As long as the corresponding contracts are deployed, users need no one to trust. Furthermore, researchers have proposed sealed-bid schemes using secure multi-party computation. The MPC protocol allows multiple users to perform collaborative computing under mutual distrust leaking their privacy. However, such schemes are usually very complex and can hardly be used in existing blockchain networks. At present, there is very little research on the cross-chain auction protocol. According to our investigation, AucSwap [7] proposed a cross-chain asset swap protocol based on the Vickrey [8] auction model, which has the characteristics of atomicity and decentralization. However, its experimental environment is limited to homogeneous Ethereum, and it cannot overcome the shortcomings of the Vickrey auction model itself. As a second-price auction model, it cannot defend against joint attacks by bidders nor maximize the auctioneer's revenue. To address such issues, we propose a lightweight auction protocol aiming at NFT, which works in a cross-chain environment. We use hash time lock contracts to achieve cross-chain asset transfer, which makes it efficient and decentralized. Smart contracts conduct the process of the bidding parts, and bidding strategies are included in the contracts to enhance the support of blockchains and simplify the auction procedure. The experiment results show that our scheme is competent for isomorphic and heterogeneous cross-chain auctions and requires less communication cost. The main contributions are listed as follows:

- By using atomic exchange technology, we propose an NFT auction protocol for cross-chain conditions. It does not need any third-party trusted auctioneers, thereby preventing the harm of user collusion.
- The auction process is conducted during the asset exchange to ensure the interests of both parties. As long as the auction successes, the cross-chain asset exchange is bound to implement.
- We use blockchain anonymity to protect the user's identity and temporarily lock the user's amount in the smart contract to ensure that the user cannot deny it.
- We provide some interfaces to help users learn essential information about the bidding process, such as the highest bid at now and which address will benefit from it. We completed the tests in the Ethereum-Ethereum and Ethereum-FISCO BCOS environments, respectively, which proved that our protocol has a certain tolerance for heterogeneous cross-chain environments and achieved a good performance at 509.8TPS.

The rest of the paper is organized as follows: We summarize the related works in Sect. 2 and then illustrate our method in Sect. 3. Section 4 does the experiment evaluation, and the final part discusses the conclusion.

2 Related Works

2.1 Cross-Chain Schemes

There are currently four mainstream cross-chain schemes, including a notary scheme mechanism, relay chain/side chain, hash time lock, and distributed private key control.

Notary Scheme. The notary scheme is a technical framework created based on the Interledger [9] protocol, similar to the real-world intermediary mechanism. This mechanism assumes that the two sides of a transaction cannot trust each other and introduces a third party trusted by both sides of the transaction to act as a notary. The notary scheme is divided into single-signature notary scheme, multi-signature notary scheme, and distributed signature notary scheme. The single-signature notary scheme operates with relatively high processing efficiency, which is the simplest but also the model with the highest risk of a single point of failure. This system has the problem of centralization. The security of the central node is the key to the system's stability; once the notary itself is maliciously attacked, the transaction becomes untrustworthy, and the whole system will have a security vulnerability. The distributed signature notary scheme uses the idea of secure multi-party computing [10], which is more secure but more challenging to implement.

Sidechains and Relays. BTC-Relay [11] is the first sidechain of Bitcoin [12] and Ethereum [13]. In a sidechain mechanism, a sidechain is another blockchain system with a completely independent function. Then the sidechain can actively sense and act on information from the main chain. A sidechain is essentially a cross-blockchain solution that enables the transfer of digital assets from one blockchain to another. The concept of sidechaining first appeared in Bitcoin, and now its representatives are Cosmos [14] and Polkadot [15]. Sidechain technology allows for the transfer of assets between Bitcoin and other currencies, allowing users to use assets they already own by accessing the new cryptocurrency system. Because the sidechain system is independent of the main chain, technological innovation on the sidechain is not hindered. At the same time, the damage to the sidechain does not affect the performance and security of the main chain.

Hash-Locking. Hash locking is a technical implementation model proposed in the Lightning Network, widely used in the Lightning Network technical architecture. The Lightning Network is a typical application of hash locking technology, essentially a mechanism to perform zero-confirmation transactions using HTLC securely. Herlihy M et al. [16] propose a hash-locking scheme to support asset exchange between two chains. Two users from different chains who need to exchange can each exchange assets on their blockchain using hash time-locked contracts.

Distributed Private Key Control. Distributed private key control is a technology through private key generation and control technology. This technology maps cryptocurrency assets to a chain with built-in asset templates based on blockchain protocols. And then deploy smart contracts based on cross-chain transaction information to create cryptocurrency assets. Fusion [17], for example, uses distributed key generation algorithms and threshold signature technology in cryptography to ensure the security of cross-chain assets. All nodes participating in the system consensus decide the locking and unlocking of assets in the cross-chain process. Therefore, no node or a few nodes jointly have the right to use the assets in the process.

2.2 Blockchain-Based Electronic Auction

The decentralized, tamper-evident, and open and transparent features of blockchain are beneficial to solving the traditional auction scenario of problems, such as un-trustworthy tripartite. Therefore, many researchers try to deploy electronic auctions in blockchain [18,19] networks to conduct them. Existing blockchain-based e-auction protocols can be broadly classified into two categories:

The first solution is to rely on digital currency. In this type of solution, the logic in a smart contract is often used to manage the entire auction process. Bidders are given a limited time to bid by providing a deposit held in a smart contract that handles the auction process. At the end of the bidding period, the contract compares all the bids and determines the winner, seizes the winner's funds, and returns the deposit to the others. Since the blockchain address does not reflect the bidder's real identity, this scheme has certain anonymity. However, this makes it difficult to expose or punish malicious bidders. In addition, bidders generally use digital currency to bid through transactions so that the blockchain network can guarantee that they cannot double-spend or reverse their bids. However, the amount of the bid is publicly transparent and less private.

If they do not rely on digital currency, auctions are generally conducted by sending cryptographic values, such as those electronic auction schemes based on secure multi-party computation [20]. These schemes [21,22] rely on cryptographic techniques such as group signatures and homomorphic encryption to enable anonymous and verifiable auctions between semi-trusted entities. Since there is no need to send digital currency directly, this scheme avoids some financial risk, but the winning bidder may renege after winning the auction and not send the money. In addition, because it relies on more cryptographic technologies and the protocols are more complex, cause corresponding computational overhead is significantly increased. It will make it challenging to be implemented on a large scale in existing blockchain networks.

2.3 Cross-Chain NFT

In multi-chain development, cross-chain has become a hot spot for market and academic research. NFT is also blooming on multiple chains, but cross-chain NFT is still an immature concept. In 2021, the NFT cross-chain exchange protocol ENVELOP went live and currently supports public chains such as Ethereum, Cryptocurrency Smart chain, and Polygon. ENVELOP's approach is to store the original NFT as a cryptocurrency or other NFT, that is, to encapsulate the original NFT in a new NFT until the owner decides to open the NFT. After opening it (like opening an envelope), the owner of the original NFT can sell, store or repackage the NFT.

Although the Ethereum leading network is often congested, it is still the preferred rooting place for NFT players. Because it has the most active NFT market, the latest and most exciting things generally appear here, and the best liquidity is also here. For example, it can be observed from Etherscan that Gh0stly, a chain that can store NFTs, only called the function of traverseChains nine times within a month. This means that only nine transfers of NFTs from the Ethereum leading network to this chain occurred during this period. This shows that the public does not yet accept the current scenario of cross-chain NFTs, and ordinary users tend to transfer their NFTs through auctions or sales in Ethereum.

3 Cross-Chain Auction Protocol

3.1 Protocol Illustration

The protocol consists of three contracts and implements the following functions, and Fig. 1 describes its process.

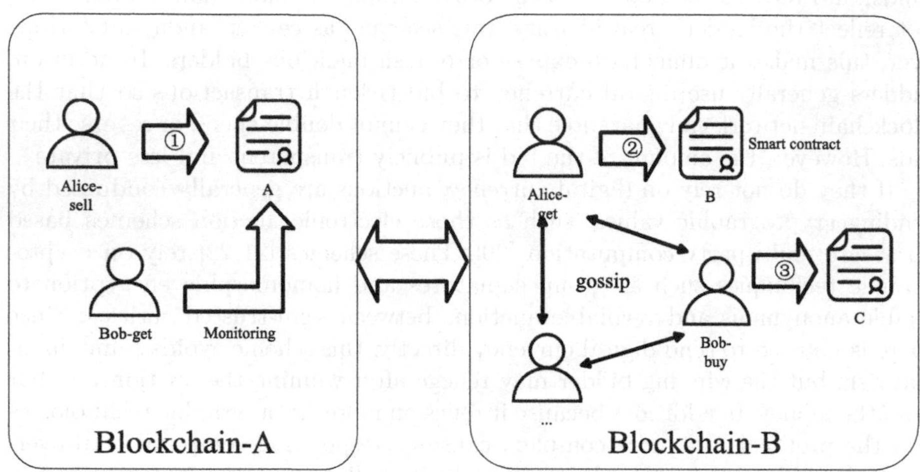

Fig. 1. The process of the protocol.

Step 1: First, the seller passes a random string z, and the Hash encrypts this string to generate a Hash(z). According to Hash (z), the hash time lock contract (HTLC) can be written to lock the NFT assets on the account and deployed on the Ethernet. And then broadcast to the whole network to prove the authenticity of the NFT assets. The transaction deadline in the HTLC can be set to half an hour after the auction end. And then, if a user on the blockchain can provide the secret z before the deadline, the user can access the NFT assets. **Step 2:** The seller sends an auction request across the blockchain to all users on the blockchain (including Ethereum and FISCO BCOS) via Algorithm 1. The initialization parameters require the input of the auctionend (up to three hours) and the beneficiary address. **Step 3:** Once the bidder receives auction information, the user can make an offer through Algorithm 2 before the end of the auction. The price offered must be an actual bid based on the available assets, and all unrealistic bids will be denied service. **Step 4:** The user can obtain the address of the user with the highest current bid and the current highest price through the function in the bidding contract. If the previous bid is surpassed, the previous bid can be retrieved through Algorithm 3. Users can determine whether to continue with a new round of bidding based on the current situation. **Step 5:** The seller receives the information and offer of the highest bidder after the auction ends and broadcasts the results of that auction. **Step 6:** After the auction ends, the winner is asked to generate the corresponding HTLC for asset exchange. The winner can base on the auction's price bid and the seller's HTLC to deploy the NFT asset to generate the contract.

3.2 NFT Locking Process

The first step in the protocol is that sellers need to lock the NFT they wish to auction to a specific contract. Assuming that user A owns an NFT on chain A, the contract address of its minting is Contract address A. Through this address, any user can find the current state information of the NFT, including who minted it, the current owner, and whether the NFT is in the state of sale.

3.3 NFT Auction Process

The auction process of NFT is the core process of this protocol. The seller sends an auction request to the B chain (another chain) and creates a corresponding contract. The transaction is spread in the blockchain network. And then, interested buyers can interact with the contract account generated by the transaction to compete for bidding. The buyer sends the bid amount as a transaction to the contract during the bidding process. To filter out invalid offers, the logic inside the contract will reject all bids that are less than the current highest bid. In addition, by interacting with the contract, users can view the current maximum bid amount at any time and adjust their bids. The sender can call the interface to retrieve the deposit if the bid is not accepted. Because the flow of money in the blockchain is open and transparent, each user can verify the legitimacy of the entire process by querying the transaction data of the contract.

Algorithm 1. Auction Contract Setup

```
Input: auctionend, profots, price
Output: transactionStatus, contractAddress
  if auctionend ≤ 10800 then
     set bidding.time = block.timestamp + auctionend
     if len(profits) == 42 then
        set beneficiary = profits
        set startingPrice = price
     end if
  end if
  return contractAddress
```

Algorithm 1 describes the initial parameters required to deploy the contract, including auctionend, profits, and price. Among them, "auctionend" represents the time when the auction ends we need to initialize, and the "auctionend" must be no more than three hours. Profits said that we need to enter the address of the NFT holder (the address of the NFT owner on different chains is subject to the actual situation) and determine whether the address is legal. Next, the seller needs to enter the expected price for the NFT. After the deployment is successful, the status information of the current contract (whether the deployment is successful or not), the transaction hash, and the contract address will be displayed.

Algorithm 2. Bid for NFT

Input: amount
Output: transactionStatus

```
while auctionend > time.Now do
  while amount > highestBid do
    if highestBid != startingPrice then
      returnsBid[highestBidder]+= highestBid
    end if
    highestBidder = msg.sender
    highestBid = amount
  end while
end while
```

When users bid for NFT, they will first enter a price they think is reasonable or call the function with the highest bid to query the highest bid of the current auction as a basis for bidding. In Algorithm 2, the timestamp of the current bid auction is compared with the timestamp of the end of the auction. If the period of the current transaction is during the auction period, the current user bid amount and the highest auction price will be judged. Suppose it is greater than the current highest bid price. In that case, the highest bid price will be mapped to the address of the highest bidder first and wait for the bidder to call up the bid amount manually. Because of the grammatical feature of solidity, when the user's bid is automatically returned to the account, the malicious contract can intercept the user's assets by calling the function body. Therefore, the amount after the bid is exceeded must be manually retrieved by the user to ensure security. And then, the address of the highest bidder will be changed to the address of the current user. Correspondingly, the highest price is also changed to the price offered by the current user.

When the user's bid is exceeded, the bid amount will be placed in the mapping of its address, and the user needs to call the function to retrieve the bid amount manually. When calling the function, the user does not need to enter the address where he wants to withdraw the amount. The function body will judge whether the user's address and the input address are consistent. Only when the addresses are consistent can the amount be withdrawn. Then it will determine whether

Algorithm 3. Withdraw

```
Input: accountAddress
Output: transactionStatus
  if address != msg.sender then
    set amount = returnsBid[address]
    if amount > 0 then
      set returnsBid[address] = 0
      if !address.send(amount) then
        returnsBid[address] = amount
      end if
    end if
  end if
```

there is an amount in the current address map and if so, it will first clear the amount in the address map. This is because, as part of accepting the call, the receiver can call the function again before 'send' returns, so first, set the amount in the address map to zero). And then send the corresponding amount to the current user's address.

3.4 Asset Exchange

Since NFT can only be deployed on Ethereum, for a successful bidder, the user's blockchain is first determined (Ethereum or FISCO BCOS, accounts for receiving assets differ on different chains). Assets can then be exchanged via HTLC. According to the traditional hash time lock method, the buyer and seller must create a hash time lock contract with the exact string. However, in our protocol, the seller has deployed the hash time lock contract before the auction, and the hash string Hash(z) is hosted in the auction contract. When the seller successfully deploys a hash time lock contract that locks the NFT assets, the smart contract will broadcast to the entire network. All users participating in the auction have received this network broadcast and confirmed the NFT assets before the bidding starts. The buyer actively calls a function to deposit the bids into the hash time lock contract after the auction ends. The seller performs two confirmations when it detects the presence of the same contract:

4 Experiment and Analysis

4.1 Experiment Setup

In order to verify and evaluate the cross-chain auction protocol for NFT proposed in this paper, we wrote the corresponding Solidity smart contracts to implement the logic process on the Ethereum private network and FISCO BCOS.

We built an Ethereum private network and deployed the NFT on the Ethereum test network. As you can see from Fig. 2, there are few accounts on each blockchain, and each user controls at least one account. We conducted

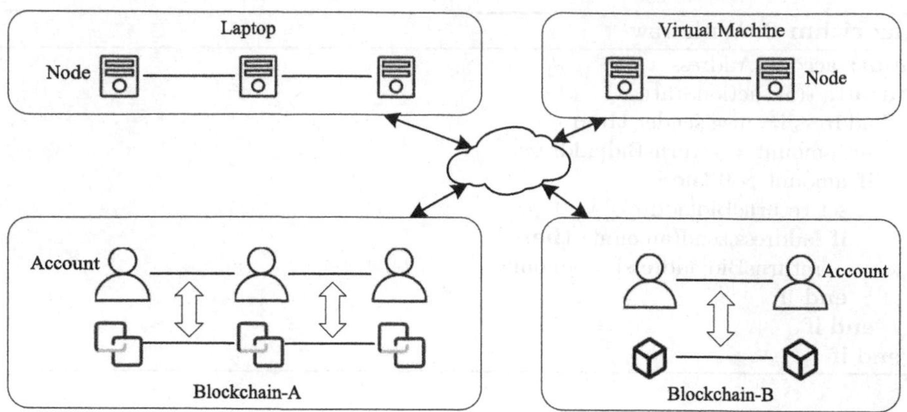

Fig. 2. Network topology for cross-chain auction experiment.

experiments on a laptop (CPU: i7-11800h, memory: DDR4 3200 8G*2, 500G SSD) and ran a few light nodes on virtual machines. After that, we also built up a FISCO BCOS network to simulate heterogeneous conditions. The data of transactions were recorded on the blockchain, and we exported it into tables. We implemented two experiments to test our protocol: the Ethereum-Ethereum cross-chain auction and the Ethereum-BCOS cross-chain auction. In each experiment, the NFT is always deployed in one Ethereum, and the auction contract will be initiated in another test chain. Finally, the exchange of cross-chain assets will be completed through the hash time lock contracts. We analyze and evaluate the performance and security of the protocol from the following aspects: transaction completion time, bid strategy control, heterogeneous cross-chain tolerance, and comparison with existing schemes. We first conduct the Ethereum-Ethereum cross-chain auction. There are four users in this process, one of which created the auction contract, and the rest can bid freely. During this process, we first manipulate the users to bid and withdraw legally and test the availability of the interfaces provided in the contracts. Then we focus on several key issues. For example, we let some users use reentrancy while he calls to see if our scheme can resist it.

Moreover, we also send some carefully designed transactions to examine the effectiveness of our bidding strategy. When the auction ends, we will also check if the cross-chain asset exchange succeeds. The block number and time are recorded so that we can see the efficiency of our protocol. The following experiment occurs in the Ethereum-BCOS networks, and the auction is completed in the FISCO BCOS network. There are four groups of users, and their asset changes are similar to those in the former experiment. In the BCOS network, there are few interfaces currently implemented. We first deploy asset contracts in the BCOS network, register enough assets for each user, and then finish the auction. The bidding and withdrawal operations of the auction are simulated. It is a method by which money can transfer from one account to another. We collect the experiment results and do the work of calculation and comparison.

4.2 Results

These are the transaction records for the first Ethereum-Ethereum cross-chain auction. There are four users in the auction process, among which user1 is the initiator of the auction, who creates the bidding contract and sets the auction duration. The other three users can bid continuously. For the convenience of analysis, we take the first transaction block as the initial block height and time when processing data. It can be seen that the entire auction lasted for 1532 s, and 21 transactions were completed during the period, which does not reflect the performance of the network because the bidding needs to be manually initiated by users. Most of the time, we are waiting for users to bid. The user interacts with the contract to send quotations through Bid. After the contract accepts a new quotation, it will update the current highest quotation and the address of the current highest quotation user. The purpose of providing these two interfaces is to facilitate users to view the current highest valid quotation to adjust their quotation strategy and avoid invalid quotations. Our protocol does not limit the address from which the quotation is initiated, except for the limit on the quotation amount. Moreover, the contract provides an interface to query the address of the auction initiator, which is. By comparing the address with the highest bid address, the user can know whether the auction initiator is trying to raise the price, making it difficult to cheat maliciously (Table 1).

Table 1. The Ethereum-Ethereum cross-chain auction details.

Transaction number	Block number	Timestamp	From	Value	Method	Status
1	0	0	user1	0	contract created	success
2	5	75	user2	10	bid	success
3	12	180	user3	10	bid	fail
4	14	210	user3	50	bid	success
5	18	270	user4	99	bid	success
6	20	300	user4	100	bid	success
7	22	330	user4	99	withdraw	success
8	26	390	user2	10	withdraw	success
9	29	390	user2	123	bid	success
10	31	465	user3	50	withdraw	success
11	33	495	user3	144	bid	success
12	37	555	user3	0	withdraw	success
13	39	585	user4	100	withdraw	success
14	42	630	user4	500	bid	success
15	48	720	user4	0	withdraw	success
16	53	795	user4	0	withdraw	success
17	67	1005	user3	144	withdraw	success
18	75	1125	user1	0	auctionEnd	fail
19	86	1292	user1	500	auctionEnd	success
20	88	1322	user2	123	withdraw	success

It can be seen from transactions 2 and 3 that user2 and user3 have sent the exact quotation successively because the quotation strategy of this agreement does not accept all quotations lower than the current highest quotation. Hence, transaction 3 fails, and the corresponding quotation is also invalid. Users can also send bids consecutively, as long as the later bid is higher than the previous one, such as transactions 5 and 6. Once an offer is sent, the corresponding amount is temporarily held in the contract, and all but the current highest bid can be withdrawn, whether the auction is in progress (transactions 7, 8, etc.) or has ended (transactions 20, 21). When the contract returns the user's invalid quotation, it does not transfer again. However, it directly returns the quotation through the function "revert" to circulate the user's funds safely and quickly. Users with insufficient funds can retrieve the original invalid quotations and then submit quotations again (transactions 8, 9), which effectively increases the flexibility of capital flow. At the end of the bidding process, we complete the exchanges of cross-chain assets through hash time lock contracts. Assume that the accounts of both parties to the swap are Alice and Bob in Fig. 1, and both have accounts for receiving and transferring assets. In our protocol, since the buyer's funds will be locked in the bidding contract, the auctioneer must lock the NFT asset to a specific contract before the auction, assuming its original image is ε and the locking time is t_1. After the auction, the winner generates a hash time lock contract with the same original image by calling "auctionEnd", passing in the hash string and locking time t_2. (It is required that $t_1 \gg t_2$ to ensure that the auction and exchange have enough time to proceed). At this time, A can obtain the auction revenue by offering the secret, and B can also obtain the NFT assets on another blockchain (Table 2).

Table 2. Testing results of transfer in the Ethereum-BCOS cross-chain auction.

Name	Succeed	Fail	SendRate (TPS)	Maxlatency (ms)	Minlatency (ms)	Avglatency (ms)	TPS
Transfer	10000	0	976.7	18.35	10.35	12.23	509.8

It can be seen from the table that on the BCOS network, the Send Rate (TPS) of the method based on this protocol is 976.7, of which a total of 10,000 transactions were sent, 10,000 times were successfully verified without failure, and the average delay in verifying transactions was 12.23 ms, which can maintain good performance.

5 Conclusion

In this paper, we combine the process of hash locking and cross-chain auction to designing a decentralized protocol to complete the cross-chain auction of NFT assets. The scheme has no third-party auctioneer and can filter invalid bids through in-contract strategies. Through testing in Ethereum-Ethereum and

Ethereum-BCOS, it can be proved that our protocol is compatible with a heterogeneous cross-chain environment, with an average of 4 blocks to confirm transactions. We also reached 509.8 TPS in the Ethereum-BCOS network. Nevertheless, there are still some shortcomings in our work, such as not being able to run on blockchains that do not support solidity; the degree of automation of the protocol is not high. It can be seen from the table that on the BCOS network, the Send Rate (TPS) of the method based on this protocol is 976.7, of which a total of 10,000 transactions were sent, 10,000 times were successfully verified without failure, and the average delay in verifying transactions was 12.23 ms, which can maintain good performance.

Our next step will try to implement secret auctions in a cross-chain environment. Since the transaction amount on the blockchain is publicly queryable, it is difficult to hide the bid amount. There are some secret bidding schemes based on secure multi-party computation. However, due to the anonymity of blockchain identities, users participating in the auction can choose to bid a high price to influence the auction and refuse to pay at the payment stage. Even if the address is blocked, malicious users can create new addresses at a small cost. Therefore, for the secret bid-ding protocol adapted to the blockchain, more research is needed on overcoming the contradiction between secret bidding and denial of payment.

Acknowledgements. This work was supported in part by the Hainan Provincial Natural Science Foundation of China (621RC508), Henan Key Laboratory of Network Cryptography Technology (LNCT2021-A16), the Science Project of Hainan University (KYQD(ZR)-21075).

References

1. Wang, Q., Li, R., Wang, Q., Chen, S.: Non-fungible token (NFT): overview. Evaluation, Opportunities and Challenges. arXiv (2021)
2. Entriken, W., Shirley, D., Evans, J., Sachs, N.: EIP-721: ERC-721 non-fungible token standard. Ethereum Improvement Proposals (721) (2018)
3. Deng, L., Chen, H., Zeng, J., Zhang, L.-J.: Research on cross-chain technology based on sidechain and hash-locking. In: Liu, S., Tekinerdogan, B., Aoyama, M., Zhang, L.-J. (eds.) EDGE 2018. LNCS, vol. 10973, pp. 144–151. Springer, Cham (2018). https://doi.org/10.1007/978-3-319-94340-4_12
4. Smith, R.: An overview of the tesseract OCR engine. In: Ninth International Conference on Document Analysis and Recognition (ICDAR 2007), vol. 2, pp. 629–633. IEEE (2007)
5. Gumussoy, C.A., Calisir, F.: Understanding factors affecting e-reverse auction use: an integrative approach. Comput. Hum. Behav. **25**(4), 975–988 (2009)
6. Liu, L., Du, M., Ma, X.: Blockchain-based fair and secure electronic double auction protocol. IEEE Intell. Syst. **35**(3), 31–40 (2020)
7. Liu, W., Wu, H., Meng, T., Wang, R., Wang, Y., Xu, C.Z.: AucSwap: a Vickrey auction modeled decentralized cross-blockchain asset transfer protocol. J. Syst. Architect. **117**, 102102 (2021)
8. Ausubel, L.M., Milgrom, P., et al.: The lovely but lonely Vickrey auction. Combin. Auctions **17**, 22–26 (2006)

9. Neisse, R., et al.: An interledger blockchain platform for cross-border management of cybersecurity information. IEEE Internet Comput. **24**(3), 19–29 (2020)
10. Chaofan, Y., Wang, L., Zhou, A., Zhang, N., Tian, H., Xiao, J.: Method and apparatus for performing multi-party secure computing based-on issuing certificate. US Patent 11,038,699, 15 June 2021
11. Chow, J.: BTC relay. BTC-relay (2016)
12. Nakamoto, S.: Bitcoin: a peer-to-peer electronic cash system. Decentralized Bus. Rev. 21260 (2008)
13. Wood, G., et al.: Ethereum: a secure decentralised generalised transaction ledger. Ethereum Proj. Yellow Pap. **151**(2014), 1–32 (2014)
14. Scoville, N., et al.: The cosmic evolution survey (COSMOS): overview. Astrophys. J. Suppl. Ser. **172**(1), 1 (2007)
15. Wood, G.: Polkadot: vision for a heterogeneous multi-chain framework. White Pap. **21**, 2327–4662 (2016)
16. Herlihy, M.: Atomic cross-chain swaps. In: Proceedings of the 2018 ACM Symposium on Principles of Distributed Computing, pp. 245–254 (2018)
17. Yang, G., Zang, C., Chen, J., Guo, D., Zhang, J.: Distributed fusion cross-chain model and architecture. IET Blockchain (2022)
18. Sánchez, D.C.: Raziel: private and verifiable smart contracts on blockchains. arXiv preprint arXiv:1807.09484 (2018)
19. Galal, H.S., Youssef, A.M.: Verifiable sealed-bid auction on the ethereum blockchain. In: Zohar, A., et al. (eds.) FC 2018. LNCS, vol. 10958, pp. 265–278. Springer, Heidelberg (2019). https://doi.org/10.1007/978-3-662-58820-8_18
20. Lindell, Y.: Secure multiparty computation. Commun. ACM **64**(1), 86–96 (2020)
21. David, B., Gentile, L., Pourpouneh, M.: FAST: fair auctions via secret transactions. In: Ateniese, G., Venturi, D. (eds.) ACNS 2022. LNCS, vol. 13269, pp. 727–747. Springer, Cham (2022). https://doi.org/10.1007/978-3-031-09234-3_36
22. Shi, R.H.: Anonymous quantum sealed-bid auction. IEEE Trans. Circ. Syst. II express briefs **69**(2), 414–418 (2021)

A Multi-scale Framework for Out-of-Distribution Detection in Dermoscopic Images

Zhongzheng Huang[1,2], Tao Wang[1,2,3,4(✉)], Yuanzheng Cai[2], and Lingyu Liang[5]

[1] College of Computer and Data Science, Fuzhou University, Fuzhou 350108, China

[2] Fujian Provincial Key Laboratory of Information Processing and Intelligent Control, College of Computer and Control Engineering and International Digital Economy College, Minjiang University, Fuzhou 350108, China
twang@mju.edu.cn

[3] The Key Laboratory of Cognitive Computing and Intelligent Information Processing of Fujian Education Institutions, Wuyi University, Wuyishan 354300, China

[4] Fujian Yilian-Health Nursing Information Technology Co. Ltd., Fuzhou 350003, China

[5] School of Electronic and Information Engineering, South China University of Technology, Guangzhou 510641, China

Abstract. The automatic detection of skin diseases via dermoscopic images can improve the efficiency in diagnosis and help doctors make more accurate judgments. However, conventional skin disease recognition systems may produce high confidence for out-of-distribution (OOD) data, which may become a major security vulnerability in practical applications. In this paper, we propose a multi-scale detection framework to detect out-of-distribution skin disease image data to ensure the robustness of the system. Our framework extracts features from different layers of the neural network. In the early layers, rectified activation is used to make the output features closer to the well-behaved distribution, and then an one-class SVM is trained to detect OOD data; in the penultimate layer, an adapted Gram matrix is used to calculate the features after rectified activation, and finally the layer with the best performance is chosen to compute a normality score. Experiments show that the proposed framework achieves superior performance when compared with other state-of-the-art methods in the task of skin disease recognition.

Keywords: Out-of-distribution detection · Dermoscopic images · Skin disease recognition

1 Introduction

Skin is the largest organ of the human body, and skin diseases contributed 1.79% to the global burden of disease measured in disability-adjusted life years [11].

Y. Xu et al. (Eds.): ML4CS 2022, LNCS 13655, pp. 147–159, 2023.
https://doi.org/10.1007/978-3-031-20096-0_12

Therefore, computer-aided monitoring, diagnosis and management of skin diseases are of wide interest to the medical imaging community. In particular, deep learning has been recently used in this field for the task of automatic diagnosis of skin diseases [6]. Typically, deep neural networks assume that the training set and the test set are of the same set of classes [7]. However, in real-life applications, the recognition system often needs to detect some images that do not belong to the training classes [16]. In this case, conventional systems may generate high confidence in some images without skin diseases. In addition, it is important for these systems to identify irrelevant images (e.g., animal pictures with color similar to that of skin lesions). Failure to do so weakens the security of a skin disease identification system and adversely affects its use in general.

In order to address the above problem, out-of-distribution (OOD) detection methods in deep learning are proposed to reduce the error rate of the model by identifying in advance whether the input image is an OOD sample [9]. In broad terms, existing OOD detection methods can be categorized into density-based, distance-based and classification-based [32]. In particular, classification-based OOD detection methods judge whether a sample is OOD by using a classifier to classify the extracted features [18]. Inspired by the success of multi-scale detection models in object detection [34], we design a classification-based multi-scale detection framework to further improve OOD detection performance. First, we use different classifiers for the features extracted from different layers of the network. In the shallow layers, we choose one-class SVM for classification, which does not require a large amount of data to train a good classifier and hence fits the task of skin disease detection with a relatively small amount of data; in the penultimate layer, we choose an adapted Gram matrix that calculates the correlation between the ID features and the OOD features, and finally obtain a relatively accurate detection score. In addition, in order to obtain features that are closer to the well-behaved distribution for computation, we add a rectified activation operation after feature extraction for each layer of the model, which selects the final feature by comparing it with a preset threshold and sending it to the classifier corresponding to the current layer. Our main contributions are as follows:

- We propose a multi-scale detection framework that integrates one-class SVM and adapted Gram matrix to detect and compare features at different layers of the deep neural network, and then selects the layer with the best performance to compute the final normality score.
- We introduce a rectified activation operation after each deep neural network layer to produce a well-behaved distribution for the subsequent feature classifiers.
- We compare our method with recently proposed OOD detection methods on multiple datasets and models, and the results show that our method is able to achieve the state-of-the-art in most settings.

2 Related Work

2.1 Out-of-Distribution Detection

In recent years, out-of-distribution detection has been widely studied in the field of image classification. For example, Zaeemzadeh et al. [33] show that embedding in-distribution (ID) data into a low-dimensional space can make OOD data easier to detect. If the probability of the test data occupying an area with ID data is 0, it belongs to OOD. Zisselman et al. [36] introduce a method of learning residual distribution from base Gaussian distribution for building flow structures. Serrà et al. [27] observe that generative models are ineffective for OOD detection, and they use an estimate of input complexity to obtain OOD scores. Yang et al. [31] propose a semantically coherent OOD detection benchmark, and design a framework for extracting features with unsupervised dual grouping, which enriches semantic information while improving the classification of ID data and the detection of OOD data.

2.2 Out-of-Distribution Detection in Skin Images

Due to the high-level of inter-class similarity and intra-class variation in dermoscopic image classification [17], OOD detection for skin images has also been studied. For example, Li et al. [15] propose an OOD detection algorithm that fuses deep neural networks and parametric-free isolation forest. Bagchi et al. [2] use an ensemble model to classify in-distribution data and design a CS-KSU module collection to detect OOD data. Roy et al. [24] propose a new HOD loss and find that the use of recent representation learning methods and a suitable ensemble strategy can significantly improve performance, and then finally introduce a cost matrix to estimate the downstream clinical impact. Kim et al. [13] add perturbations to the data to maximize the variance of the OOD samples and apply subset scanning in the latent space representation. Mohseni et al. [21] design a network called BinaryHeads capable of simultaneously classifying ID/OOD data. Unlike existing work, we propose a multi-scale detection framework that integrates one-class SVM and adapted Gram matrix for OOD detection in skin images.

3 Method

In this section, we first introduce a rectified one-class support vector machine to detect OOD data from the output of early network layers, and then use the adapted Gram matrix to detect OOD data from the penultimate network layer. Additionally, we adopt a multi-scale detection framework to integrate the above techniques and further improve the ability of the neural network for detecting out-of-distribution samples. See Fig. 1 for an overview of the proposed method.

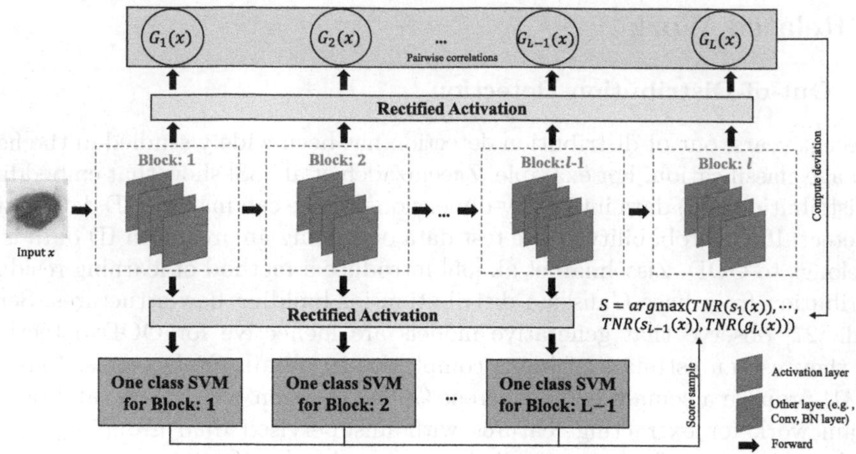

Fig. 1. The overview framework of the proposed multi-scale OOD detection framework.

3.1 Rectified One-Class Support Vector Machine

Inspired by [1], we also regard the OOD detection of skin images as an one-class classification problem, and use an one-class Support Vector Machine (SVM) to analyze the shallow features of the images after passing them through the neural network. One-class SVM aims to find a hyperplane in the vector space, so that the hyperplane is the farthest from the zero point, and all normal data (in-distribution data) are on the same side of the hyperplane. Therefore, one-class SVM can produce good results in the detection of out-of-distribution data. In addition, because the high-dimensional features generated by deep neural networks will have a negative impact on one-class SVM, we reduce its dimension in the width and height dimensions, following [1]:

$$f_k^l(x) = \frac{1}{w * h} \sum_{i=1}^{w} \sum_{j=1}^{h} |f_{ijk}^l| \tag{1}$$

where $f_k^l(x)$ denotes the k-th feature map at the l-th layer given input x. w, h are the width and height of the feature map, f_{ijk}^l is the (i, j, k)-th element of $f^l(x)$.

Since the main purpose of out-of-distribution detection is to make the model only confident in the samples within the distribution, we introduce rectified activation [29] in order to further improve the detection accuracy and to reduce the frequency of high confidence predictions of out-of-distribution data. By setting a threshold c in the feature extraction layer, the output of layer $f(x)$ is compared with c: $V = min(f(x), c)$, where V is the value to be fed into the classifier. We choose the activation layers of the backbone network as the feature extraction layer, so that the features can be resued for computing the adapted Gram matrix, as outlined in the next subsection. Specifically, we add a rectified activation operation to the output of each layer to make the activation pattern closer to the actual distribution, and then send it to the one-class SVM at the corresponding layer.

3.2 Adapted Gram Matrix

Gram matrix is proposed by [26] and used for out-of-distribution detection, and the adapted Gram matrix is improved by [22] for the skin cancer classification task. Here, we begin by revisiting the procedure for computing the Gram matrix. First, we obtain the relationship between the features of layer l through a p-order matrix, which is written as: $G_l^p = (r_l^p r_l^{pT})$. Here, G is the Gram matrix, r is the representation of the l-th layer, and additional regularization is performed to make all the values of G in $(0, 1)$, so as to ensure that each maximum and minimum value is calculated from the same interval. At the same time, in order to reduce the complexity of the algorithm, the above features are obtained only in the activation layers of the network, and $p = 1$ (effective for skin disease classification). Next, in the training set, a maximum and a minimum value are determined according to G:

$$\begin{aligned} \lambda_l^p &= min[G_l^p(f(x))] \\ \Lambda_l^p &= max[G_l^p(f(x))] \end{aligned} \tag{2}$$

where $f(\cdot)$ represents the network, and x is the input image. In practice, we use the row-wise sum of G_l^p for computing the maximum and minimum values, as proposed in [22].

Finally, when an unknown image inputs, the distribution deviation between the unknown image and data in the distribution (i.e., the training set) can be calculated with normalization using the previously saved maximum and minimum values:

$$\delta(\lambda, \Lambda, G) = \begin{cases} 0, & \lambda \leq G \leq \Lambda \\ \frac{\lambda - G}{|\lambda|}, & G < \lambda \\ \frac{G - \Lambda}{|\Lambda|}, & G > \Lambda \end{cases} \tag{3}$$

$$g(x) = \sum_{l=1}^{L} \sum_{k=1}^{K} \frac{\delta(\lambda_l^p[k], \Lambda_l^p[k], G_l^p(f(x))[k])}{E_{Va}[\delta_l]} \tag{4}$$

where $g(\cdot)$ denotes the output of the adapted Gram matrix in different layers, k denotes the k-th feature map of a certain layer, $E_{Va}[\delta_l]$ denotes the expected deviation at layer l computed on the validation set. The deviation value can be compared with the threshold determined by the percentile of the total deviation to judge whether a sample is ID or OOD. We also introduce the rectified activation in penultimate layer which can make the output of the activation layer closer to the true distribution, and also make the total deviation of the adapted Gram matrix closer to the well-behaved case.

3.3 Multi-scale Detection Framework

The design of a multi-scale network is widely used in the field of object detection [19,35], among other computer vision tasks. For large objects, its semantic information will appear in the feature maps at deeper layers; for small objects, the semantic information appears in the feature maps at shallow layers. Inspired by this, we design a multi-scale detection framework using different OOD detection approaches mentioned above at different network layers to further improve the ability of our model for recognizing out-of-distribution samples. In the early layers, rectified one-class support vector machine is used for out-of-distribution detection. When the image is in the penultimate layer of the network, we use the adapted Gram matrix. In our multi-scale detection framework, the final ID/OOD classification result of an image x depends on the performance of the two methods above on different out-of-distribution datasets. We choose our final normality score computing layer S by the maximum TNR (True Negative Rate) of the one-class SVM and the adapted Gram matrix at every layer:

$$\mathrm{TNR} = \frac{\mathrm{TN}}{\mathrm{TN} + \mathrm{FP}} \tag{5}$$

$$S = \underset{s_1,\dots,s_{L-1},g_L}{\arg\max}\ [TNR(s_1(x)), \cdots, TNR(s_{L-2}(x)), TNR(s_{L-1}(x)), TNR(g_L(x))] \tag{6}$$

where TN is the number of true negatives and FP is the number of false positives, $s_l(\cdot)$ denotes output of the one-class SVM at the l-th layer and $g_L(\cdot)$ denotes the output of the adapted Gram matrix at the L-th layer. It should be noted that our method requires an OOD dataset available at training in order to compute TNR. When OOD data are not available, we could use empirical values of S for a specific model such as those listed in Table 1. The final ID/OOD classification result will be produced by comparing the output with a threshold θ:

$$D(x) = \begin{cases} 1, & S(x) > \theta \\ 0, & S(x) < \theta \end{cases} \tag{7}$$

where $D(\cdot)$ represents the final ID/OOD classification result. If the normality score of an input x is greater than θ, it belongs to ID. It should be noted that the results of the same out-of-distribution dataset are generated by the same chosen network layer. In the experiments that follow, θ is set to 0.95.

4 Experiments

4.1 Setup

ID/OOD Datasets. In our experiments, ISIC 2019 [3,4,30] is regarded as the ID dataset, which consists of eight different categories of skin diseases, with a total of 25331 images. The division and preprocessing of the dataset are consistent with [22]. In addition, we use the following six non-overlapping OOD datasets for detection, with example images shown in Fig. 2:

Imagenet. Contains 3000 images randomly sampled from ImageNet [5] test set.

NCT. There are 9 classes in the original NCT-CRC-HE-7K [12] dataset. The data used for detection are 150 randomly sampled human colorectal cancer (CRC) images from each class.

BBOX. It contains 2025 skin disease images with bounding boxes after successful segmentation by U-net trained on the ISIC 2017 segmentation dataset [23].

BBOX70. The acquisition method of this dataset is the same as that of BBOX, but the bounding box will cover 70 % of the whole skin lesion.

Derm-Skin. It contains 1565 images selected from ISIC 2019. These images belong to the area that does not contain lesions after cropping.

Clinical. Contains 723 healthy skin images collected from social networks.

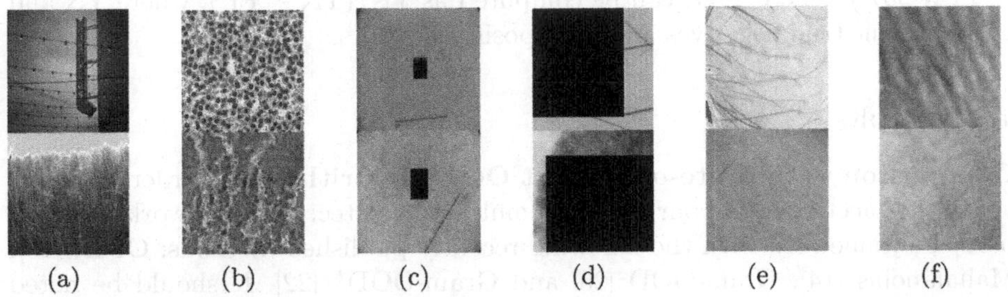

Fig. 2. Samples of six non-overlapping datasets as OOD data for detection. From (a) to (f): Imagenet, NCT, BBOX, BBOX70, Derm-skin, Clinical.

Pre-trained Models and Parameters. For a fair comparison, we directly use the model pre-trained on the ISIC 2019 training set used by [22] as our backbone network, including DenseNet-121 [10], MobileNet-v2 [25], ResNet-50 [8] and VGGNet-16 [28]. All models are optimized using the Adam algorithm. The initial learning rate is set to 0.0001 and the batch size is set to 40. Among them, the learning rate is decreased by a factor of 0.2 after the model failed to optimize the validation loss for 15 consecutive epochs. The balanced accuracy of the four pre-trained models on the ISIC 2019 test set are 82.3%, 81.2%, 82% and 82.5% respectively.

As for the one-class SVM, we use RBF kernel for training and set ν to 0.001, which is consistent with the experimental setting of [1]. We select the output layer with the highest TNR as the network layer used to calculate the normality score. The output layers corresponding to each out-of-distribution dataset and the backbone network are shown in Table 1. Under four different models, the rectified activation operation thresholds used for the adapted Gram matrix are 1.0, 0.8, 0.6 and 0.7, while the rectified activation operation thresholds for one-class SVM are all set to 1.0.

Table 1. Layer selected for calculating the normality score corresponding to each out-of-distribution dataset and network backbone.

Model	Selected layer					
	Imagenet	NCT	BBOX	BBOX70	Derm-skin	Clinical
DenseNet-121	25	39	13	9	3	74
MobileNet-v2	18	25	19	10	2	24
ResNet-50	13	8	16	5	1	10
VGGNet-16	8	8	9	1	2	13

Evaluation Metrics. We adopt three evaluation metrics commonly used in out-of-distributin detection: area under the ROC curve (AUROC) [26]; the maximum achievable classification accuracy across all possible thresholds in distinguishing among in-distribution and out-of-distribution samples (Detection Accuracy) [26]; true negative rate when the true positive rate is as high as 95% (TNR @ TPR 95%), where TNR can be computed as TN/(TN + FP), where TN and FP represent true negatives and false positives [26].

4.2 Results

Comparison with State-of-the-Art OOD Algorithms. In order to better verify the effectiveness of our proposed multi-scale detection framework, we compare the framework with the following recently published methods: ODIN [16], Mahalanobis [14], Gram-OOD [26] and Gram-OOD* [22]. It should be noted that ODIN and Mahalanobis have been fine-tuned on the OOD dataset. Also, our method requires OOD data during training in order to choose the best-performing layer for OOD classification. See Fig. 3 for a detailed performance analysis when we choose different layers. In particular, Gram-OOD* with rectified activations is a special case in our method (i.e., choosing the penultimate layer with the adapted Gram matrix) that still offers a competitive performance.

As shown in Table 2, the performance of our framework exceeds that of other recently published methods under most settings. For the evaluation metric TNR @ TPR 95%, our framework has an obvious advantage, being 5.6%, 2.1%, 3.5%, and 3.6% higher than Gram-OOD* with rectified activation on average using different models, showing that our framework can better distinguish in distribution (ID) data and out-of-distribution (OOD) data based on the shallow neural network layers. The results of ODIN and Baseline show that the traditional method of using the Softmax function for out-of-distribution detection is not suitable for difficult classification tasks such as skin disease anomaly detection.

Impact of Selecting Different Layers. In Fig. 3, we present the results of out-of-distribution detection based on the features extracted from different network layers. On the whole, BBOX70 and NCT datasets perform more stably when we extract features from different network layers. Only in the deeper networks will

Table 2. Comparison with state-of-the-art methods in out-of-distribution detection using different backbone networks and datasets.

Model	OOD set	AUROC	Detection accuracy	TNR @ TPR 95%
		Baseline/ODIN/Mahalanobis/Gram-OOD/Gram-OOD* (w/rectified activation)/Ours		
DenseNet -121	ImageNet	59.1/83.8/99.9/97.0/97.3/**99.3**	56.6/78.1/99.1/92.0/93.0/**96.6**	9.30/50.0/99.9/80.7/86.0/**97.7**
	NCT	36.7/82.0/98.9/99.4/99.4/**100.**	50.1/75.0/98.7/97.1/98.1/**99.7**	1.44/32.5/98.7/98.9/99.9/**100.**
	BBOX	77.3/90.6/98.3/98.1/97.5/**99.4**	69.8/83.7/95.3/94.5/93.6/**97.3**	27.9/68.8/94.8/88.0/88.2/**98.4**
	BBOX70	89.4/99.8/100./99.7/99.8/**100.**	84.9/98.1/99.9/99.0/99.2/**99.9**	36.6/99.3/100./99.9/100./**100.**
	Derm-skin	74.4/86.8/96.2/96.5/**96.6**/96.4	67.3/78.3/89.7/90.9/91.0/**91.4**	22.8/46.2/81.4/78.0/81.8/**87.5**
	Clinical	72.5/69.5/96.1/96.6/96.3/**98.1**	67.3/65.8/90.1/91.1/91.1/**92.9**	18.5/25.2/81.7/82.8/84.6/**90.7**
MobileNet -v2	ImageNet	61.9/86.8/99.7/97.2/98.4/**99.6**	58.5/81.8/98.5/92.1/94.5/**97.3**	12.4/36.6/99.8/84.3/92.6/**98.8**
	NCT	75.7/72.2/99.9/99.4/99.7/**100.**	68.2/69.9/99.3/97.4/98.9/**99.4**	25.4/33.3/100./99.3/100./**100.**
	BBOX	56.3/95.3/99.3/97.3/98.8/**99.8**	56.2/90.0/95.6/94.4/97.0/**98.5**	6.70/71.9/96.3/86.9/98.6/**100.**
	BBOX70	72.6/97.9/99.9/99.8/99.9/**100.**	68.1/96.0/99.8/99.0/99.5/**99.9**	13.4/92.9/100./100./100./**100.**
	Derm-skin	65.1/79.4/92.6/94.2/**94.7**/93.5	59.8/71.8/86.1/87.1/**88.4**/87.3	18.8/40.8/64.2/66.7/75.2/**79.4**
	Clinical	62.9/78.3/97.6/95.3/96.3/**96.8**	59.6/71.7/92.6/89.6/**90.7**/89.8	14.2/27.8/85.5/77.9/83.5/**84.4**
ResNet -50	ImageNet	60.1/83.9/99.9/97.9/97.9/**99.5**	57.6/77.0/99.2/92.9/93.2/**96.9**	8.50/49.2/99.9/86.6/87.4/**98.2**
	NCT	67.4/93.3/99.9/99.8/99.9/**100.**	64.6/86.0/99.6/98.4/99.0/**99.9**	8.40/70.2/100./99.9/100./**100.**
	BBOX	69.7/74.5/99.8/97.9/99.4/**99.6**	65.1/69.7/98.0/94.2/**97.5**/97.4	11.7/34.9/99.6/88.4/**99.2**/98.7
	BBOX70	71.6/99.7/99.9/99.9/100./**100.**	72.2/97.9/99.9/99.5/99.7/**99.8**	8.90/99.2/100./100./100./**100.**
	Derm-skin	72.1/87.2/96.0/**96.1**/95.1/95.0	66.8/80.2/89.7/**90.1**/88.5/89.5	14.8/57.9/81.1/74.8/73.9/**83.8**
	Clinical	62.0/71.4/95.1/97.2/**97.4**/96.9	59.7/67.0/88.9/91.2/**91.8**/90.7	8.30/23.6/73.4/84.7/85.9/**86.4**
VGGNet -16	ImageNet	46.6/82.9/99.4/96.3/95.3/**98.5**	50.6/79.0/98.0/90.2/90.5/**94.2**	5.90/25.1/99.3/77.6/81.3/**93.3**
	NCT	57.4/72.1/99.2/99.6/99.8/**100.**	55.5/69.5/98.9/97.9/99.0/**99.4**	10.7/16.6/99.2/99.7/100./**100.**
	BBOX	74.9/86.9/99.9/97.9/98.4/**99.0**	67.4/81.3/98.6/94.0/95.1/**95.5**	30.3/64.6/99.8/86.5/94.0/**95.7**
	BBOX70	81.7/99.9/100./99.9/100./**100.**	83.1/99.2/99.9/99.7/99.7/**99.8**	5.40/99.0/100./100./100./**100.**
	Derm-skin	67.1/93.1/91.4/96.0/93.6/**96.1**	61.4/87.1/83.6/89.8/89.4/**91.9**	21.1/78.6/65.8/79.8/80.6/**88.6**
	Clinical	66.3/72.4/97.2/**95.7**/93.8/95.4	62.1/68.3/91.6/**89.8**/89.1/87.3	15.0/31.3/84.3/80.7/**81.1**/80.9

there be the same performance degradation problem as in other datasets, and the possible reason is that it is easier to classify ID/OOD data on these datasets, and the obvious embeddings may be affected as the network grows deeper. On the other four datasets, there are intense performance fluctuations when we extract features from different layers, proving the importance of choosing an appropriate layer for feature extraction. Furthermore, even if the adapted Gram matrix offers a competitive performance as already shown in Table 2 (see Gram-OOD* with rectified activations), in most cases it does not provide superior performance with the datasets and models we tested. Besides, we visualize a few examples of the feature embeddings extracted from different layers of the neural network. As Fig. 4 shows, the layer for computing the normality score selected by Eq. 6 separates ID/OOD data points with a wider margin when compared to the penultimate layer.

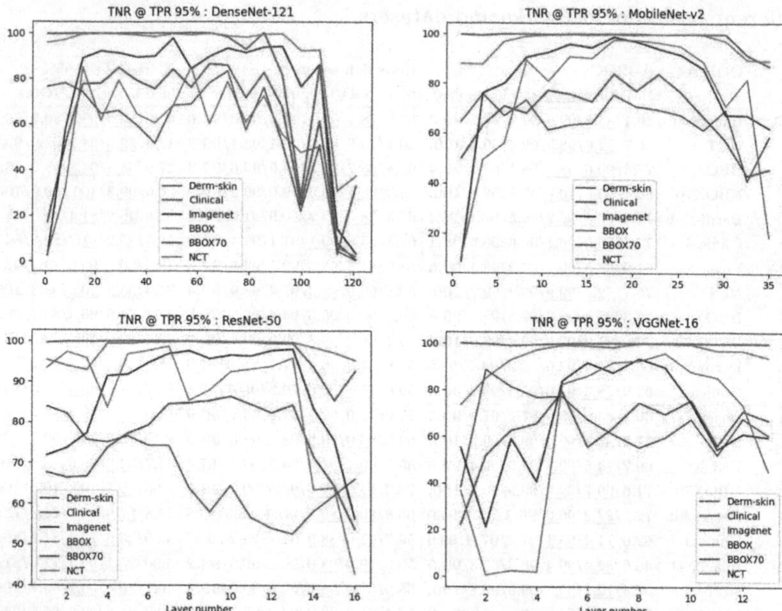

Fig. 3. Influence of layer selected to compute the normality score on TNR @ TPR 95% with different models after smoothing.

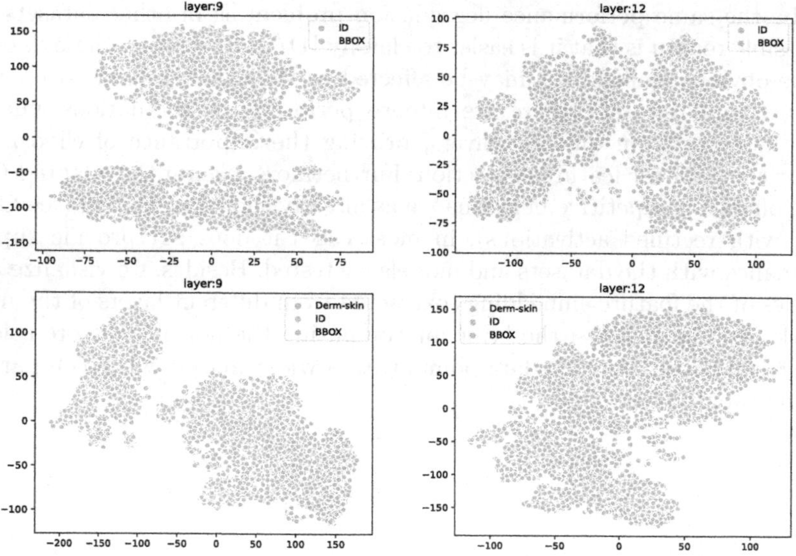

Fig. 4. t-SNE [20] visualization of features extracted from the layer selected for computing the normality score (layer 9) and the penultimate layer (layer 12).

5 Conclusion

In this paper, to enhance the security of skin disease identification systems, we investigate the classification-based out-of-distribution detection problem in dermoscopic images. Specifically, we propose a multi-scale detection framework that uses different classifiers at the various layers of the neural network to detect and compare feature embeddings, and select the layer with the best performance to compute a normality score. In addition, we adopt a rectified activation operation before feeding features into classifiers to ensure that the features are closer to a well-behaved distribution. We hope that our modest attempt could provide some useful insights for future research on out-of-distribution detection in skin images and beyond.

Acknowledgment. This work is supported by NSFC (61703195), Fujian NSF (2022J011112, 2020J01828), Guangdong NSF (2019A1515011045), Science and Technology Program of Guangzhou (202102020692), the Open Program of The Key Laboratory of Cognitive Computing and Intelligent Information Processing of Fujian Education Institutions, Wuyi University (KLCCIIP2020202), the Open Fund of Fujian Provincial Key Laboratory of Information Processing and Intelligent Control, Minjiang University (MJUKF-IPIC202102), the CAAI-Huawei MindSpore Open Fund, and Fuzhou Technology Planning Program (2021-ZD-284).

References

1. Abdelzad, V., Czarnecki, K., Salay, R., Denounden, T., Vernekar, S., Phan, B.: Detecting out-of-distribution inputs in deep neural networks using an early-layer output. arXiv preprint arXiv:1910.10307 (2019)
2. Bagchi, S., Banerjee, A., Bathula, D.R.: Learning a meta-ensemble technique for skin lesion classification and novel class detection. In: Proceedings of the IEEE/CVF Conference on Computer Vision and Pattern Recognition Workshops, pp. 746–747 (2020)
3. Codella, N.C., et al.: Skin lesion analysis toward melanoma detection: a challenge at the 2017 international symposium on biomedical imaging (ISBI), hosted by the international skin imaging collaboration (ISIC). In: 2018 IEEE 15th International Symposium on Biomedical Imaging (ISBI 2018), pp. 168–172. IEEE (2018)
4. Combalia, M., et al.: BCN20000: dermoscopic lesions in the wild. arXiv preprint arXiv:1908.02288 (2019)
5. Deng, J.: A large-scale hierarchical image database. In: 2009 Proceedings of IEEE Computer Vision and Pattern Recognition (2009)
6. Esteva, A., et al.: Dermatologist-level classification of skin cancer with deep neural networks. Nature **542**(7639), 115–118 (2017)
7. Goodfellow, I., Bengio, Y., Courville, A.: Deep Learning. MIT Press, Cambridge (2016)
8. He, K., Zhang, X., Ren, S., Sun, J.: Deep residual learning for image recognition. In: Proceedings of the IEEE Conference on Computer Vision and Pattern Recognition, pp. 770–778 (2016)
9. Hendrycks, D., Gimpel, K.: A baseline for detecting misclassified and out-of-distribution examples in neural networks. arXiv preprint arXiv:1610.02136 (2016)

10. Huang, G., Liu, Z., Van Der Maaten, L., Weinberger, K.Q.: Densely connected convolutional networks. In: Proceedings of the IEEE Conference on Computer Vision and Pattern Recognition, pp. 4700–4708 (2017)
11. Karimkhani, C., et al.: Global skin disease morbidity and mortality: an update from the global burden of disease study 2013. JAMA Dermatol. **153**(5), 406–412 (2017)
12. Kather, J.N., et al.: Predicting survival from colorectal cancer histology slides using deep learning: a retrospective multicenter study. PLoS Med. **16**(1), e1002730 (2019)
13. Kim, H., Tadesse, G.A., Cintas, C., Speakman, S., Varshney, K.: Out-of-distribution detection in dermatology using input perturbation and subset scanning. In: 2022 IEEE 19th International Symposium on Biomedical Imaging (ISBI), pp. 1–4. IEEE (2022)
14. Lee, K., Lee, K., Lee, H., Shin, J.: A simple unified framework for detecting out-of-distribution samples and adversarial attacks. Adv. Neural Inf. Process. Syst. **31**, 7167–7177 (2018)
15. Li, X., Lu, Y., Desrosiers, C., Liu, X.: Out-of-distribution detection for skin lesion images with deep isolation forest. In: Liu, M., Yan, P., Lian, C., Cao, X. (eds.) MLMI 2020. LNCS, vol. 12436, pp. 91–100. Springer, Cham (2020). https://doi.org/10.1007/978-3-030-59861-7_10
16. Liang, S., Li, Y., Srikant, R.: Enhancing the reliability of out-of-distribution image detection in neural networks. arXiv preprint arXiv:1706.02690 (2017)
17. Liu, Q., Yu, L., Luo, L., Dou, Q., Heng, P.A.: Semi-supervised medical image classification with relation-driven self-ensembling model. IEEE Trans. Med. Imaging **39**(11), 3429–3440 (2020)
18. Liu, W., Wang, X., Owens, J., Li, Y.: Energy-based out-of-distribution detection. Adv. Neural. Inf. Process. Syst. **33**, 21464–21475 (2020)
19. Liu, Y., Zhang, X.Y., Bian, J.W., Zhang, L., Cheng, M.M.: SAMNet: stereoscopically attentive multi-scale network for lightweight salient object detection. IEEE Trans. Image Process. **30**, 3804–3814 (2021)
20. Van der Maaten, L., Hinton, G.: Visualizing data using t-SNE. J. Mach. Learn. Res. **9**(11), 2579–2605 (2008)
21. Mohseni, M., Yap, J., Yolland, W., Razmara, M., Atkins, M.S.: Out-of-distribution detection for dermoscopic image classification. arXiv preprint arXiv:2104.07819 (2021)
22. Pacheco, A.G., Sastry, C.S., Trappenberg, T., Oore, S., Krohling, R.A.: On out-of-distribution detection algorithms with deep neural skin cancer classifiers. In: Proceedings of the IEEE/CVF Conference on Computer Vision and Pattern Recognition Workshops, pp. 732–733 (2020)
23. Ronneberger, O., Fischer, P., Brox, T.: U-net: convolutional networks for biomedical image segmentation. In: Navab, N., Hornegger, J., Wells, W.M., Frangi, A.F. (eds.) MICCAI 2015. LNCS, vol. 9351, pp. 234–241. Springer, Cham (2015). https://doi.org/10.1007/978-3-319-24574-4_28
24. Roy, A.G., et al.: Does your dermatology classifier know what it doesn't know? Detecting the long-tail of unseen conditions. Med. Image Anal. **75**, 102274 (2022)
25. Sandler, M., Howard, A., Zhu, M., Zhmoginov, A., Chen, L.C.: MobileNetV 2: inverted residuals and linear bottlenecks. In: Proceedings of the IEEE Conference on Computer Vision and Pattern Recognition, pp. 4510–4520 (2018)
26. Sastry, C.S., Oore, S.: Detecting out-of-distribution examples with in-distribution examples and gram matrices. arXiv preprint arXiv:1912.12510 (2019)

27. Serrà, J., Álvarez, D., Gómez, V., Slizovskaia, O., Núñez, J.F., Luque, J.: Input complexity and out-of-distribution detection with likelihood-based generative models. arXiv preprint arXiv:1909.11480 (2019)
28. Simonyan, K., Zisserman, A.: Very deep convolutional networks for large-scale image recognition. arXiv preprint arXiv:1409.1556 (2014)
29. Sun, Y., Guo, C., Li, Y.: ReAct: out-of-distribution detection with rectified activations. Adv. Neural Inf. Process. Syst. **34**, 144–157 (2021)
30. Tschandl, P., Rosendahl, C., Kittler, H.: The ham10000 dataset, a large collection of multi-source dermatoscopic images of common pigmented skin lesions. Sci. Data **5**(1), 1–9 (2018)
31. Yang, J., et al.: Semantically coherent out-of-distribution detection. In: Proceedings of the IEEE/CVF International Conference on Computer Vision, pp. 8301–8309 (2021)
32. Yang, J., Zhou, K., Li, Y., Liu, Z.: Generalized out-of-distribution detection: a survey. arXiv preprint arXiv:2110.11334 (2021)
33. Zaeemzadeh, A., Bisagno, N., Sambugaro, Z., Conci, N., Rahnavard, N., Shah, M.: Out-of-distribution detection using union of 1-dimensional subspaces. In: Proceedings of the IEEE/CVF Conference on Computer Vision and Pattern Recognition, pp. 9452–9461 (2021)
34. Zhang, H., Sun, M., Li, Q., Liu, L., Liu, M., Ji, Y.: An empirical study of multi-scale object detection in high resolution UAV images. Neurocomputing **421**, 173–182 (2021)
35. Zhang, P., et al: Multi-scale vision longformer: a new vision transformer for high-resolution image encoding. In: Proceedings of the IEEE/CVF International Conference on Computer Vision, pp. 2998–3008 (2021)
36. Zisselman, E., Tamar, A.: Deep residual flow for out of distribution detection. In: Proceedings of the IEEE/CVF Conference on Computer Vision and Pattern Recognition, pp. 13994–14003 (2020)

Swarm Intelligence for Multi-objective Portfolio Optimization

Li Chen[1], Yongjin Wang[1,2], Jia Liu[1], and Lijing Tan[3(✉)]

[1] College of Management, Shenzhen University, Shenzhen 518060, China
[2] Greater Bay Area International Institute for Innovation, Shenzhen University, Shenzhen 518060, China
[3] School of Management, Shenzhen Institute of Information Technology, Shenzhen 518172, China
mstlj@163.com

Abstract. This paper employs five classical multi-objective swarm intelligence algorithms to solve portfolio optimization (PO) problem with background returns. The potential investment ratio is considered as an individual. In the experiments, we consider five different PO cases. The simulation results show that multi-objective evolutionary algorithm based on decomposition (MOEA/D) and weighted optimization framework (WOF) perform significantly better than the other four in solving the high-dimensional objective problem, and WOF obtains a more uniform solution to the high-dimensional problem.

Keywords: Swarm intelligence · Multi-objective · Portfolio optimization

1 Introduction

Portfolio optimization (PO) is that people invest the assets and maximize the returns of a certain level of risk or minimize the risks of a certain level of return according to the established return target and risk tolerance. Markowitz, an American economist, proposed the precise definition of risk and return based on Mean-Variance portfolio theory [1] for the first time by using mathematical analysis. Scholars put forward more sophisticated PO models based on this theory, which consider all kinds of constraints of real-world investments like liquidity risk, market risk [2]. It can be seen from previous research that swarm intelligence optimization algorithms, such as particle swarm optimization (PSO) [3] and bacterial forging optimization (BFO) [4], are better than traditional mathematical optimization methods in solving PO problem.

In simple terms, multi-objective optimization problems refer to that many problems in real life are composed of multiple goals that conflict with each other and affect each other. These goals cannot reach the optimal state at the same time. We usually try to make these goals reach the optimal state in a certain area.

In this paper, we use five classical swarm intelligence algorithms to solve five different dimensions of PO problems. The IGD of five swarm intelligence algorithms is collected to find their convergence and divergence. In addition, we also plot their pareto

Y. Xu et al. (Eds.): ML4CS 2022, LNCS 13655, pp. 160–169, 2023.
https://doi.org/10.1007/978-3-031-20096-0_13

solutions in the graph so as to see the advantages and disadvantages and uniformity of their solutions. Through the analysis of the figure and table, we can see the performance of these swarm intelligence algorithms in solving PO problems of different dimensions and find certain rules.

The rest of this paper is discussed in the following order. In Sect. 2, we introduce five classical swarm intelligence algorithms. In Sect. 3, the mathematical model of PO problem is constructed, followed by the experimental results of five classical algorithms on different dimensions of PO problems in Sect. 4. Finally, we draw the conclusion in Sect. 5.

2 Swarm Intelligence for Multi-objective Optimization

2.1 Multi-objective Optimization Model

Multi-objective optimization refers to making optimal decisions by trade-offs between two or more conflicting optimization objectives. Its solutions are generally in the form of unspecified nodes or sets, so the task of multi-objective optimization is to find as many optimal solutions as possible. The mathematical model of a multi-objective optimization problem containing n decision variables and m objective functions takes the following form:

$$miny = F(x) = f(f1(x), f2(x), f3(x) \ldots fm(x)) \tag{1}$$

$$s.t.\begin{cases} gi(x) \leq 0, i = 1, 2 \ldots q \\ hj(x) = 0, j = 1, 2 \ldots p \\ x = (x1, x2 \ldots xn) \in X \in R^n \\ y = (y1, y2 \ldots yn) \in Y \in R^n \end{cases} \tag{2}$$

where $x = (x1, x2 \ldots xn)$ is the decision variable and $y = (y1, y2 \ldots yn)$ is the objective function. The objective function F contains n objectives, q inequality constraints, and p equation constraints. In multi-objective optimization problems, people often use the concept of dominance, its definition and related concepts will be given here:

Pareto dominates. For a multi-objective optimization problem, it can be assumed that there are two feasible solutions xi and xj. If and only if the following formula is true, xi can be said to be superior to xj, denoted as $xi < xj$.

$$\forall m = \{1, 2, \ldots, k\}, fm(xi) \leq fm(xj) \tag{3}$$

$$\exists n = \{1, 2, \ldots, k\}, fn(xi) < fn(xj) \tag{4}$$

Pareto noninferior optimal solution. $X^* \in \Omega$ is a Pareto non-inferior optimal solution, which has the following formula,

$$\exists x, F(x) < F(x*) \tag{5}$$

Pareto noninferior optimal solution set.

$$P* = \{x \in \Omega |, \exists x \in \Omega, F(x') < F(x)\} \tag{6}$$

Pareto frontier.

$$Pareto = \{F(x) = (f1(x), fx(x), \ldots fk(x)) | x \in P*\} \tag{7}$$

In the past, mathematical models for solving multi-objective optimization problems include linear weighting method, ideal point method, hierarchical sequence method and so on. Linear weighting, also known as utility maximization. Its basic principle is to adopt a certain method to form a relative relation between all objectives and the objective utility function, and then determine the influence function by measuring the relative weight of all objectives in the whole objective and transform the multi-objective optimization problem into a single objective optimization problem model in the final stage. Ideal point method is to be evaluated object as a multiple assessment by the reaction of its overall situation the target from a certain point selected in high dimensional space, assessment will translate into the evaluation object in the high-dimensional space adjacent points in the judgment or order, this requires a reference point in advance, as the criterion to evaluate the object the stand or fall of the adjacent point to judge. Generally speaking, back to the test points have positive ideal points and negative ideal points, from the positive ideal point the closer the better, and from the negative ideal point the farther the better; Stratified sequence method refers to all the target a arranged according to their degree of importance, and then calculate the first one of the most important goal of optimal prediction solution, then a goal before guarantee according to their importance degree of classification as solving ways, this loop, until finally it is concluded that the least important of the optimal prediction solution set a target of, or to find the optimal prediction algorithm.

2.2 Swarm Intelligence

Swarm Intelligence simulate the behavior of groups of insects, herd, birds and fish, which search for food in a cooperative manner with each member of the group constantly changing the direction of its search by learning from its own experience and the experience of other members. Any kind of algorithm or distributed problem solving strategy inspired by insect swarms or other animal social behavior mechanisms is swarm intelligence. In this paper, we will focus on five classical swarm intelligence optimization algorithms. They are Nondominated sorting genetic algorithm II(NSGAII) [5], Strength Pareto evolutionary algorithm 2(SPEA2) [6], Multiobjective evolutionary algorithm based on decomposition (MOEA/D) [7], Multi-objective particle swarm optimization(MOPSO) [8] and Weighted optimization framework (WOF) [9]. The core of each algorithm can be described as follows:

The Nondominated Sorting Genetic Algorithm II. NSGA is based on genetic algorithm and Pareto optimal concept. The main difference between NSGA and the basic genetic algorithm is that it performs rapid non-dominated sorting on individuals before selection operation, increasing the probability of excellent individuals being retained, while selection, crossover, mutation and other operations are no different from the basic genetic algorithm. Through the research and test of many scholars, NSGA is better than the traditional multi-objective genetic algorithm. However, in practical application, it is found that NSGA still has some disadvantages, such as a large amount of algorithm calculation, no application of elite strategy, and the need to specify the sharing radius artificially.

NSGAII is an improvement on NSGA. Compared with the NSGA, NSGAII uses a fast non-dominated sorting method, which reduces the computational complexity of the algorithm from $O(mN^3)$ to $O(mN^2)$, making the computational time of the algorithm greatly reduced. NSGAII uses an elite strategy to merge parent individuals with child individuals for non-dominated sorting, which makes the search space larger, and generates the next generation parent population in the order of the individuals with higher priority are selected in order when generating the next-generation parent population, and the individuals of the same level are selected using crowding degree to ensure that the best individuals can have a higher probability of being retained. Finally, NSGAII replaces the fitness sharing strategy, which requires a specified sharing radius, with the crowding degree method, and uses it as a criterion for selecting the best individuals among siblings, which ensures the diversity of individuals in the population and facilitates the selection, crossover and mutation of individuals throughout the interval.

The Strength Pareto Evolutionary Algorithm 2. SPEA2 is an improvement on SPEA. SPEA exist the following problems: the first is in the process fitness assignment of SPEA, be same file members dominate populations of individual fitness, this means that when an external file contains only one member, no matter whether there is a dominant relationship between individual species, all the individual species have the same fitness value, in this case, the SPEA is similar to random search; Second, SPEA can reduce the size of the non-inferior solution set in the clustering analysis, but it may mistakenly delete some individuals that must be saved in the non-inferior solution set, which affects the diversity of the algorithm. However, SPEA2 improves SPEA in three aspects: fitness assignment, individual density calculation method and external file maintenance. Today, SPEA2 has been widely used in multi-objective optimization problems. For example, the improved SPEA2 based on local search is applied in the path planning of mobile robots. SPEA2 based on adaptive selection evolutionary operator is used to solve the workshop scheduling problem. In order to improve the performance of the algorithm, the neighbor propagation algorithm was propagated into SPEA2 and so on.

The Multiobjective Evolutionary Algorithm Based on Decomposition. The essence of MOEA/D is to decompose a multi-objective problem into multiple scalar quantum problems to solve simultaneously. Before MOEA/D, the idea of solving the multi-objective problem was to assign a weight to each objective to indicate its importance, and through this weight, the multi-objective problem was transformed into a single-objective optimization problem. As a result, only one solution can be obtained in each run. Obviously, it is impossible for a multi-objective optimization problem to have only one solution that simultaneously satisfies all objective optimizations. Therefore, a set of different weight vectors is used to decompose the multi-objective optimization problem into a set of single-objective optimization problems to solve it simultaneously.

In this way, the solutions of each single objective problem correspond to different points on the Pareto frontier respectively, which is also a set of optimal solutions of the multi-objective optimization problem. For faster population convergence, each individual is assigned a weight vector. At the same time, a neighboring weight vector replacement strategy is used, that is, each individual (weight vector) and several neighboring individuals (weight vector) will be compared and optimized. Its advantages are reflected in the following aspects: The first is to ensure that there are good solutions in a group, it adopts information sharing strategy and maintains the diversity of individuals; The second point is to optimize the corresponding target by using each scalar aggregation function without considering the conflicts between the targets, which is beneficial to the distribution of fitness and the maintenance of diversity. Third, due to its low computational complexity, evenly distributed solutions can be generated in small populations.

The Multi-objective Particle Swarm Optimization. The MOPSO incorporating the Pareto competition mechanism proposed by C. A. Coello Coello and M. S. Lechuga in 2002 is a very classical approach to solve multi-objective problems. Its basic idea is to find the optimal solution by collaboration and information sharing among individuals in a population, and it has the characteristics of both evolutionary computation and group intelligence.

As for PSO, MOPSO has five major improvements: The first one is the optimization of velocity update formula, introducing a contraction factor; The second point is the update of position and the handling of transgression; Thirdly, the disturbance factor is added to solve the problem of fast convergence into local optimum. Fourthly, the adaptive grid algorithm is applied to improve the convergence and diversity of the algorithm. The last one is the archiving method of MOPSO; In MOPSO, after the population has been updated, it is archived through the following three steps: the first step is the first round of screening based on the dominance relationship, where bad solutions are removed and the remaining ones are added to the archive; The second step is to conduct a second round of filtering according to the dominant relationship in the archive, remove the inferior solution, and calculate the position of the archived particles in the grid. The final step is to filter against an adaptive grid up to the threshold when the number of archives exceeds the archive threshold. Remeshing. Although MOPSO has been widely applied in the field of industrial multi-objective optimization, it still has disadvantages such as high computational complexity, low universality, poor convergence, and poor performance in solving the problem of high-dimensional multi-objective PO.

The Weighted Optimization Framework. Based on the existing meta-heuristic algorithm, WOF can perform more efficient search in a smaller space by simplifying N variables into R variables. In WOF, we change the original decision variable into the optimization weight W, so that the optimal solution contains only a small search space. Then the remaining functions are re-evaluated, and the original decision variables are optimized so as to obtain a more diversified solution set. However, because the evolution numbers of weight optimization and original optimization are fixed, and only one search operator is used in WOF, it may perform well in solving some large-scale high-dimensional problems but may not always be effective in solving various large-scale multi-objective optimization problems.

3 Swarm Intelligence for Portfolio Selection Problems

3.1 Portfolio Selection Model

In the actual PO problem model, in addition to the return of the project itself, investors also need to consider the return brought by external uncertain factors, such as the stock price rise caused by market economic fluctuations. We take this as inspiration and add background return into the model as a way of return. Without considering short sales, the model is established as follows:

$$MinF(x) = Min[\frac{1}{f(x)}, g(x)] \tag{8}$$

$$s.t. \begin{cases} \sum_{i=1}^{n} Xi = 1 \\ Xi > 0 \end{cases} \tag{9}$$

The return function $f(x)$ and risk function of investors $g(x)$ are constructed as follows.

$$f(x) = \sum_{i=1}^{n} [\alpha Ri + (1 - \alpha)KiRi - Pi]Xi \tag{10}$$

$$g(x) = \sum_{\substack{i=1 \\ j=1}}^{n} \sigma ijXiXj \tag{11}$$

Suppose that investors invest funds in d assets. α represents the percentage of return generated by the project itself. Let *Xi* be equal to the proportion of the investment in class d assets, *Ri* be the expected return of asset i, *Ki* be the correlation coefficient between securities and markets, *Pi* be the fixed cost ratio, σij be the covariance of *ri* and *rj*.

3.2 Encoding

In this paper, we treat each individual generated in the algorithm as the potential portfolio ratio. Each individual (*Xi*) denotes the proportion of the investor's holdings of asset i. d dimension represents d kinds of assets. The fitness function is calculated by Eq. (8). According to non-dominated sorting, we can select the best individual of PO.

4 Experiments and Discussions

In this paper, five classical swarm intelligence algorithms are selected and compared in solving PO problem. We will look at the performance of five swarm intelligence optimization algorithms in different d assets. All the algorithms presented in this paper were coded in MATLAB language and run on an Intel Core i7 processor with 1.8 GHz CPU speed.

4.1 Definition of Experiments

In the experiment, we assume that an investor has ten assets to invest in, and the original ratio of each asset is equal to 0.1, and the sum of the initial ratios of each asset is 1. The population of swarm intelligence is 100 and the number of iterations is 100. Refer to the relevant information we set up the related parameters are shown as follow:

$$\begin{cases} \alpha = 0.5 \\ Ki = 0.8 \\ Pi = 0.0070 \end{cases}$$

In total, we set up five different d assets as shown as follow:

$$d = [5, 10, 20, 30, 50]$$

$$R1 = [0.1721, 0.3157, 0.1064, 0.0735, 0.1572]$$

$$R2 = [0.2606, 0.2775, 0.2453, 0.1670, 0.2186, 0.1847, 0.1468, 0.0929, 0.1385, 0.1782]$$

$$R3 = [0.0598, 0.2619, 0.0132, 0.0417, 0.0020, 0.2855, 0.0703, 0.0815, 0.0575, 0.0909,$$
$$0.2338, 0.0160, 0.0013, 0.0064, 0.1091, 0.1377, 0.0025, 0.1876, 0.0099, 0.1201]$$

$$R4 = [0.2111, 0.0354, 0.0003, 0.0935, 0.0273, 0.045, 0.2049, 0.0214, 0.1511, 0.03632,$$
$$0.1687, 0.0113, 0.3225, 0.2650, 0.1082, 0.2614, 0.1081, 0.1039, 0.2159, 0.0255,$$
$$0.2141, 0.0069, 0.0306, 0.0671, 0.0618, 0.1148, 0.1328, 0.0991, 0.0008, 0.1132]$$

$$R5 = [0.0062, 0.0105, 0.0757, 0.3185, 0.1002.0.1874, 0.3884, 0.0460, 0.1305, 0.2100,$$
$$0.0425, 0.0798, 0.0098, 0.0052, 0.0510, 0.0503, 0.2750, 0.4185, 0.2899, 0.1187,$$
$$0.3572, 0.1361, 0.0261, 0.1531, 0.0786, 0.1326, 0.0765, 0.0610, 0.1409, 0.1402,$$
$$0.0042, 0.1231, 0.0068, 0.0140, 0.0124, 0.0014, 0.2805, 0.1153, 0.3247, 0.0046,$$
$$0.0239, 0.1196, 0.0275, 0.1019, 0.3693, 0.3749, 0.1191, 0.0276, 0.1492, 0.0431]$$

Table 1. The average IGD metric obtained by 10runs for the test functions

Algorithms	d = 5	d = 10	d = 20	d = 30	d = 50
NSGAII	**2.7333**	3.5661	5.5475	5.6188	4.5930
SPEA2	2.7389	3.6218	5.6272	5.4839	4.5121
MOEA/D	**2.7333**	**3.1890**	**3.1763**	**3.2361**	**2.5197**
MOPSO	2.7341	3.5104	5.6488	5.6662	4.7040
WOF	**2.7333**	3.2482	3.5802	**3.3490**	**2.7702**

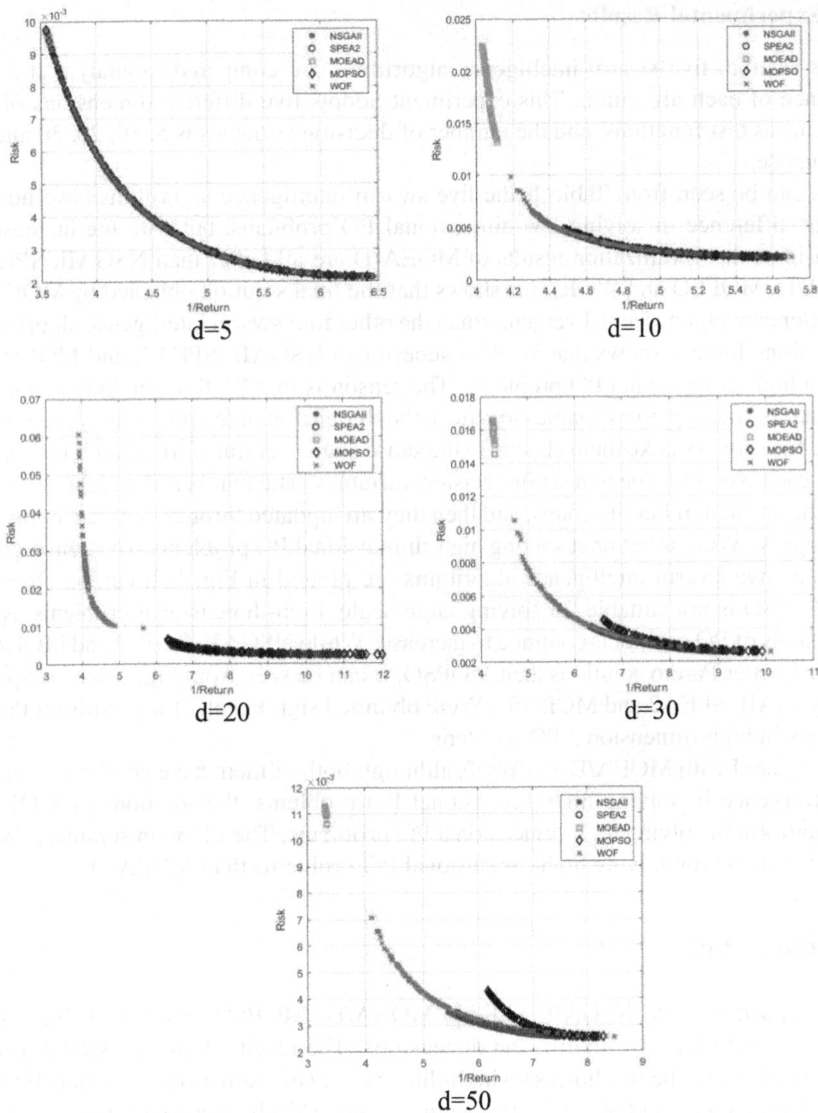

Fig. 1. The convergence curve offive algorithms

The average IGD metric obtained by five algorithms of d = 5, d = 10, d = 20, d = 30 and d = 50 of 10 runs are given in Table 1. The best results are showed in bold. Figure 1 presents the convergence curves of the five algorithms of five different dimensions of PO problem.

4.2 Experimental Results

In this section, five swarm intelligence algorithms are compared to analyze the performance of each algorithm. This experiment adopts five different dimensions of PO problems as test functions, and the number of decision variables is 5, 10, 20, 30 and 50 in sequence.

As can be seen from Table 1, the five swarm intelligence algorithms have no significant difference in solving low-dimensional PO problems, but with the increase of dimensions, the optimization results of MOEA/D are all better than NSGAII, SPEA2, MOEA/D, MOPSO and WOF. This shows that the final solution obtained by MOEA/D has better convergence and divergence than the other four swarm intelligence algorithms. In addition, Table 1 shows that WOF is superior to NSGAII, SPEA2, and MOPSO in solving high-dimensional PO problems. The reason is that WOF essentially changes a large part of the decision variables to reduce the dimension of the problem by transforming the function to make them change to the same degree. A transformation function can assign each weight value to a set of decision variables. The number of weight vectors is the same as the number of groups, and then they are updated through separate optimization steps, so WOF is better at solving high-dimensional PO problems. The convergence curves of five swarm intelligence algorithms are plotted in Fig. 1. It can be observed that MOPSO is not suitable for solving large-scale, high-dimensional problems as the dimensions of PO problems continue to increase. While NSGAII, SPEA2 and MOEA/D obtained better Pareto solutions than MOPSO, it can be seen from Fig. 1 that compared with NSGAII, SPEA2 and MOEA/D, WOF obtained significantly more uniform Pareto solutions in high-dimensional PO problems.

Compared with MOEA/D and WOF, although both of them have good convergence and divergence in solving high-dimensional PO problems, the solutions of WOF are more uniform in solving high-dimensional PO problems. Therefore, in summary, WOF is more suitable for solving high-dimensional PO problems than MOEA/D.

5 Conclusion

In this paper, we use NSGAII, SPEA2, MOEA/D, MOPSO, WOF to solve multi-objective PO problems with different dimensions. The results show that MOEA/D and WOF are obviously better choices for high-dimensional investment optimization. Further research may focus on how to determine the relationship between background returns and project actual returns to propose a new investment optimization model. According to the comparison results, MOEA/D and WOF algorithms perform better than NSGAII, MOPSO and SPEA2 for high-dimensional PO models. The next step is to refine the better performing algorithm and use it to solve more complex models.

Acknowledgement. The work was supported by The Natural Science Foundation of Guangdong Province (No. 2020A1515010752).

References

1. Markowitz, H.: Portfolio selection. J. Finance **7**(1), 77–91 (1952)
2. Niu, B., Xue, B., Li, L., Chai, Y.: Symbiotic multi-swarm PSO for portfolio optimization. In: Huang, D.-S., Jo, K.-H., Lee, H.-H., Kang, H.-J., Bevilacqua, V. (eds.) ICIC 2009. LNCS, vol. 5755, pp. 776–784. Springer, Heidelberg (2009)
3. Yin, X., Ni, Q., Zhai, Y.: A novel particle swarm optimization for portfolio optimization based on random population topology strategies. In: Tan, Y., Shi, Y., Buarque, F., Gelbukh, A., Das, S., Engelbrecht, A. (eds.) ICSI-CCI 2015. LNCS, vol. 9140, pp. 164–175. Springer, Heidelberg (2015)
4. Niu, B., Bi, Y., Xie, T.: Structure-redesign-based bacterial foraging optimization for portfolio selection. In: Huang, D.-S., Han, K., Gromiha, M. (eds.) ICIC 2014. LNCS, vol. 8590, pp. 424–430. Springer, Cham (2014). https://doi.org/10.1007/978-3-319-09330-7_49
5. Deb, K., Pratap, A., Agarwal, S., Meyarivan, T.: A fast and elitist multiobjective genetic algorithm: NSGA-II. J. Trans. Evol. Comput. **6**(2), 182–197 (2022)
6. Zitzler, E., Laumanns, M., Thiele, L.: SPEA2: improving the strength pareto evolutionary algorithm. In: Proceedings of the Conference on Evolutionary Methods for Design, Optimization and Control with Applications to Industrial Problems, pp. 95–100 (2001)
7. Zhang, Q., Li, H.: MOEA/D: a multiobjective evolutionary algorithm based on decomposition. J. Trans. Evol. Comput. **11**(6), 712–731 (2007)
8. Coello Coello, C.A., Lechuga, M.S.: MOPSO: a proposal for multiple objective particle swarm optimization. In: Proceedings of the IEEE Congress on Evolutionary Computation, pp.1051–1056 (2002)
9. Zille, H., Ishibuchi, H., Mostaghim, S., Nojima, Y.: A framework for large-scale multiobjective optimization based on problem transformation. J. Trans. Evol. Comput. **22**(2), 260–275 (2018)

Research on Secure Cloud Storage of Regional Economic Data Network Based on Blockchain Technology

Huiling Liu(✉)

School of Finance and Economics, Guangzhou Huali Vocational College of Science and Technology, Guangzhou 511325, China
hlxy7892022@163.com

Abstract. In order to provide secure network storage space for regional economic data and ensure the integrity, correctness and security of regional economic data, a secure cloud storage method for regional economic data network based on blockchain technology is proposed. According to the distribution of regional economic data network nodes, the relevant network model is constructed. Under this model, the regional economic data are collected in real time, and the preprocessing of the collected data is realized through the two steps of data removal and normalization. The blockchain technology is used to determine the data storage structure, encrypt and process the regional economic data, and realize the secure cloud storage of the regional economic data network in combination with the identity authentication mechanism. The experimental results show that compared with the traditional methods, the data loss and the proportion of tampered data are reduced by 7.32 GB and 16.15% respectively, and the storage task execution time of the optimized cloud storage method is higher. It shows that this method can solve the problems existing in the traditional cloud storage of regional economic data network security, maximize the storage security of regional economic data, and make outstanding contributions to the rapid development of the field of data security.

Keywords: Blockchain Technology · Regional Economic Data · Data Network · Data Security · Cloud Storage

1 Introduction

Regional economy refers to the part of the national economy distributed in various administrative regions. Its formation is the result of regional division of labor [1]. Regional economy can provide theoretical basis for the international strategy, regional economic and cultural development strategy of contemporary countries, and provide all-round theoretical basis for economic and cultural development, design and planning. Cloud storage technology is a business developed on the basis of cloud computing technology. Through computer cluster technology, distributed technology and grid technology, cloud storage will work together with a large number of different types of storage devices

Y. Xu et al. (Eds.): ML4CS 2022, LNCS 13655, pp. 170–184, 2023.
https://doi.org/10.1007/978-3-031-20096-0_14

through specific communication protocols and software integration, provide users with remote data storage and access services, and can provide convenient data management services. However, in the process of network storage of regional economic data, it will be attacked by illegal users, resulting in the loss and tampering of stored data, resulting in the decline of data security. Aiming at the problem of secure cloud storage of regional economic data network, some scholars have defined the network architecture of SDN, built a process spatial data center platform through controllers, interface protocols and key technologies of data area, expanded the spatial data storage space by using HBase, logically corresponded the organization type to the geographical characteristics of spatial data, reduced the number of disk access to the storage space, and organized raster image data according to the quadtree method. At the same time, quadtree encodes each grid image to complete the secure cloud storage of multi process spatial data. There are also some studies that regard the key administrator as a semi trusted third party, build a new system model and security model, improve the algorithm of encrypting data by using the key administrator, and propose a user cloud data security storage protocol based on the semi trusted third party, so as to realize data security cloud storage.

Therefore, in order to provide a safe network storage space for regional economic data and ensure the integrity, correctness and security of regional economic data, a secure cloud storage method of regional economic data network based on blockchain technology is proposed. According to the node distribution of the regional economic data network, build the relevant network model, collect the regional economic data in real time, remove and normalize the duplicate data, and make the ciphertext obey the uniform distribution by adding entropy in the ciphertext in the process of duplicate data removal, so as to ensure the security in the process of duplicate data removal. Block chain technology is used to determine the data storage structure, that is, data blocks are combined into a chain structure in chronological order, and cryptology algorithm is used to collectively maintain the reliability of the database in the way of distributed accounting. On this basis, the regional economic data is encrypted and processed through five steps: key generation, key encryption, plaintext transmission, cloud encryption and cloud decryption, so as to ensure the high reliability and security of the data. Combined with the identity authentication mechanism, the secure cloud storage of the regional economic data network is realized. This method can solve the problems of mutual trust and data security in the traditional cloud storage of regional economic data network security, and maximize the storage security of regional economic data, which has a prominent contribution to the rapid development of the field of data security.

2 Design of Secure Cloud Storage Method for Regional Economic Data Network

The number of terminals in the system is M, U is the set of dynamic data information codes in the system, the sub-element u_i in set U includes the corresponding dynamic data information codes, and displays the status of regional economic digital files [2]. Assuming that the probability of an attacker arriving in the time interval $[t, t + \Delta t]$ is $p(\Delta t)$, therefore, at time $t + \Delta t$, the probability that the regional economic data is attacked by n attackers is:

$$p_n(t + \Delta t) = p_n(t)(1 - \mu\Delta t) + o(\Delta t)\frac{p_n(t + \Delta t) - p_n(t)}{\Delta t} \quad (1)$$

where, μ represents the risk factor for the operation of regional economic data, and $o(\Delta t)$ represents the probability that the regional economic documents will be tampered with or forged many times under the conditions of safe operation. The centralized database storage mode adopts a combination of security means such as access control, access authentication, information encryption, digital watermarking and other traditional cryptography methods, which can improve the system security storage performance to some extent, but it can not avoid the potential vulnerabilities that may exist in the system and the security threats caused by malicious destruction by staff, so it can not fundamentally solve the security problem of dynamic data storage. Therefore, a method to optimize the dynamic data storage mechanism based on blockchain technology is proposed.

2.1 Building a Regional Economic Data Network Model

The construction of regional economic data network model is divided into three parts, namely, the process creation of application layer protocol, the creation of network nodes and the construction of regional economic data network topology. According to the network layered structure of TCP/IP, the typical node model is shown in Fig. 3.

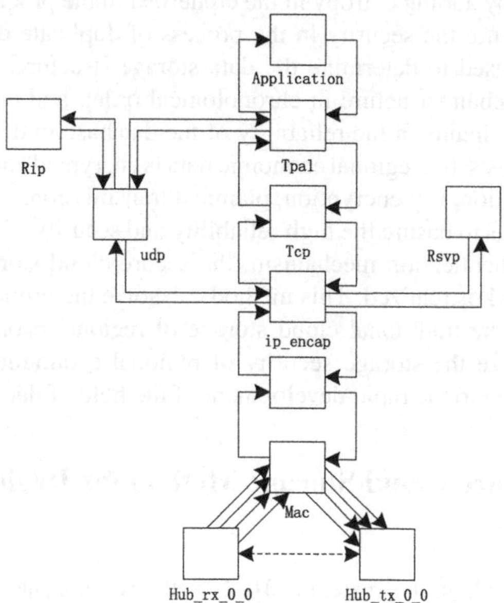

Fig. 1. Distribution of nodes in regional economic data network

By analyzing Fig. 1, we can see that various applications are defined in the application module of the application layer, such as database, email, FTP, HTTP, etc., which use TCP protocol, while those such as videoconferencing, voicetransport, etc. use UDP protocol. Therefore, there is a tpal module in the application layer and rip layer, which is used to provide a unified interface between various applications and different transmission protocols. It is equivalent to an adapter, which configures corresponding transmission protocols for different applications [4]. The designed device nodes include an application layer protocol module, a UDP module, a tcp routing protocol encapsulation module, an ip routing protocol module, an arp address resolution protocol module, a mac module, a group of transceivers, and two hub modules. The network model describes the communication system at a higher level, and the communication equipment and communication links together constitute the topology model of the communication system. The network model describes the location of nodes in the network, the connections between nodes and the configuration of nodes. The network model can include one or more nodes or sub-networks, and the size and scope of the network model can also be determined according to actual design requirements. According to the actual situation of the above-mentioned regional economic data network node distribution, it is assumed that the nodes in the network are relatively evenly distributed in the range of 100 m × 100 m. Each scenario designed here is composed of device nodes of equal priority, which can create the topology of the data network.

2.2 Collect and Process Regional Economic Data

Set multiple measuring points in the constructed regional economic data network model, and use hardware equipment to collect regional economic data according to the process shown in Fig. 2.

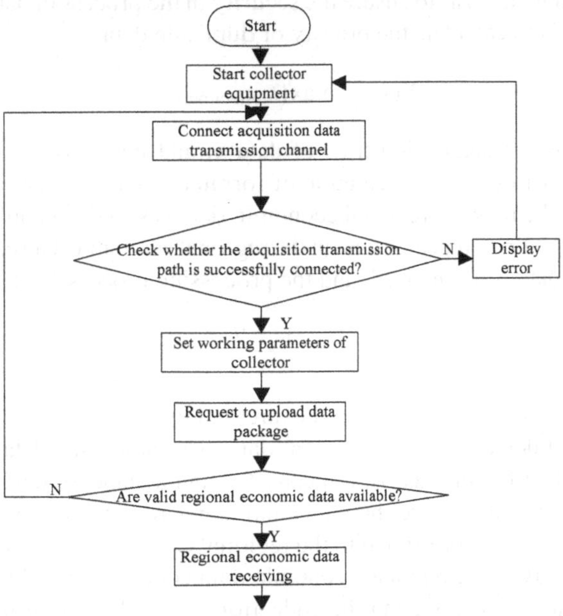

Fig. 2. Flow chart of regional economic data collection

In cloud storage system, data deduplication technology can save hard disk space and network transmission bandwidth by detecting and preventing redundant data uploading. The cloud storage system model includes at least two entities: the data holder and the cloud storage server. In the data upload phase, the data holder interacts with the cloud storage server to check the repeatability by means of electronic tag index. If there is duplicate data in the server, the cloud storage server only retains a copy of the data and returns a pointer to the copy to the data uploader. The data uploader can use the pointer to retrieve the data. The secure data deduplication scheme requires the system to be able to perform data deduplication on encrypted data, which belongs to the secure multi-party computing problem [5]. Before uploading the data, the encryption operation shall be carried out first to ensure the confidentiality of the data. At the same time, the encrypted data shall be able to be detected by the repeatability check. Data holders need to complete data identity authentication, Ownership Authentication and other operations without divulging their privacy and data information, and prevent malicious attacks by storage servers and other participants in the cooperation process of data outsourcing. Use formula (3) to judge whether there is duplicate data in the initially collected regional economic data.

$$r(x_i, x_j) = \sqrt{(x_i - x_j)^2} \tag{2}$$

In the formula, x_i and x_j are any two data in the initial regional economic data, respectively. If the calculation result of formula (2) is higher than the set threshold r_0, it is determined that the data x_i and x_j are duplicate data, and one of the data needs to be deleted. By adding entropy $H(C) = n\log|Y|$ to the ciphertext, where n represents the length of the ciphertext and Y represents the ciphertext letter string, so that the ciphertext is uniformly distributed, so as to ensure the security in the process of data deduplication.

Use formula (3) to calculate the priority of duplicate data.

$$Y(x) = \max(t_{\text{collection,x}}) \tag{3}$$

where $t_{\text{collection,x}}$ is the acquisition time of data x, and max() is the maximum value solution function. Through the calculation of formula (3), the historical duplicate data is eliminated, and the updated regional economic data is saved. According to the above process, the elimination of repeated data in the regional economic data can be completed. On this basis, the data is normalized, and the processing process can be expressed as:

$$x^* = \frac{x - \mu}{\sigma} \tag{4}$$

The normalization processing method expressed by formula (4) is to normalize the mean and standard deviation of the original data. The processed data conformed to a standard normal distribution, that is, a mean of 0 and a standard deviation of 1. Variables μ and σ in formula (4) are the mean and standard deviation of all sample data, respectively, and x and x^* correspond to the regional economic data samples before and after normalization [6]. The regional economic data collected in real time is processed according to the above process, and the collection and collection results that meet the quality requirements are obtained.

2.3 Use Blockchain Technology to Determine the Storage Structure of Economic Data

In the case of considering privacy, throughput and resource consumption, the blockchain type is selected, and the blockchain framework Ethereum is selected in the optimally designed cloud storage method to build a blockchain for storing data. Therefore, a private chain based on the Ethereum platform Geth client using the Clique consensus algorithm is used. During the blockchain construction process, determine how many nodes there are in the network, use the Geth command to create an Ethereum account for each node, and use the tool puppeth that comes with Geth to generate the configuration file genesis.json of the genesis block. The configuration file specifies the ID of the blockchain network, the consensus algorithm used, and the amount in the account. Use the configuration file genesis.json to initialize each node in the network, fill in the information of all nodes in the network into the static-nodes.json file, and put this file into the working root directory of each node for use in the network nodes discover each other.Start all nodes in the network in turn. The startup parameters specify the remote call port of the node and the specific service to be started by remote call, and prohibit the node from being discovered by nodes outside the network. The constructed blockchain is composed of multiple block bodies, and each block is composed of two parts: block header and block body. The basic structure of the data block is shown in Fig. 3.

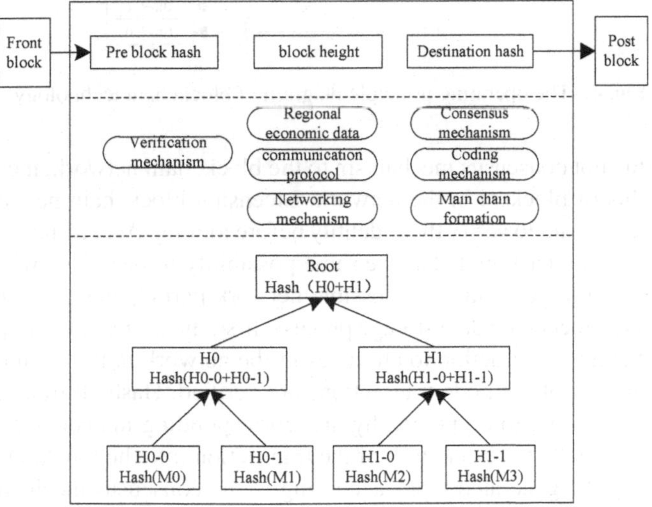

Fig. 3. Block structure diagram of regional economic data

Block headers are used to link to previous blocks to ensure the integrity of the blockchain. Each block header contains information such as version number, parent hash value, Merkle root, timestamp, random number, and target hash. A block contains all the valuable transactions that occurred during the creation of a verified block. Each block contains the parental Hash value, that is, the Merkle root of all transactions in the previous block, so that each block is connected in a certain order; the timestamp is the approximate time when the block was generated; the block The IDs of this block in the chain system are organized according to the MerkleTree structure, and at the bottom are all the valuable transactions in the block [7]. Each transaction gets a hash value after hash encryption. Then, the obtained Hash values are combined in pairs until the ID of this block is finally obtained, which is the Merkle root of the current block. It is precisely because of this ring-connected working mode that the blockchain has strong anti-tampering and anti-attack properties. The operation of the blockchain generally includes the steps of request submission, transaction verification, new block generation and consensus mechanism. Figure 4 shows the operation process of the blockchain technology.

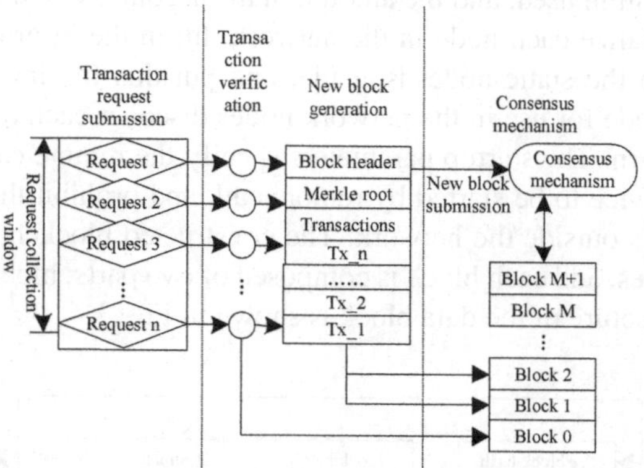

Fig. 4. The operating principle diagram of blockchain technology

Applying the pot consensus mechanism to the blockchain network, it can determine the mining rights of blockers in the network. Licensing blockchain networks requires any intended participant to verify their identity before joining. According to the principle of fair lottery system, each node has the same possibility to become a winner. The pot mechanism gives a large number of possible network participants an equal chance to win. In the actual blockchain data storage process, first, the user sends a request, and the system sends the new transaction to all nodes in the network in the form of broadcast. After more than half of the node transactions are verified, Hash all transactions in the time period T according to cryptography and corresponding mathematical principles, add the timestamp and the target Hash of the transaction into the block. Other nodes in the system verify the generated block according to the consensus mechanism settings. If all transaction information in the block is valid and passes the system verification, the system will recognize the transaction information of the block, and the accounting node will connect the block information to the tail of the original blockchain [8]. Then, the system broadcasts the information recorded in the blockchain, and the internal nodes of the system synchronize the new blockchain information to their own information base.Finally, all nodes move on to create the next block, and the Merkle root of this block will be recorded as the hash value of the parent block in the block header of the new block. In the cloud storage method of dynamic data, the block chain terminal is obtained from the block packaged by the terminal set Z_i, any participant is the same as the verifier, and the block verification result submitted between Z_j and Z_i is represented by C_{ij}, and the result is The following conditions need to be met:

$$C_{ij} = \begin{cases} 1 \\ -1 \end{cases} \tag{5}$$

The verification of formula (5) shows that it is legal for Z_i to submit a block under the result of 1, but it is illegal for Z_j to submit a block under the result of 2. Through the above method, the block storage structure and storage authority of economic data are determined. Among them, the smart contract is shown in Fig. 5.

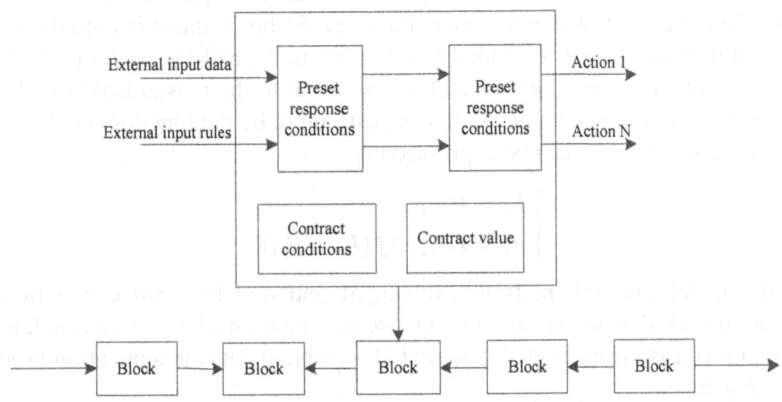

Fig. 5. Smart contract

2.4 Regional Economic Data Encryption

In order to ensure the security of regional economic data network cloud storage, it is necessary to encrypt the real-time storage data. The secure storage process of regional economic data includes five steps: key generation, key encryption, plaintext transmission, cloud encryption and cloud decryption. The client logs in to the ECS and uploads the encryption and decryption public key:

$$\text{Key}_{\text{public}} = \text{e}^{a} \bmod \text{P} \tag{6}$$

Among them, mod$(\cdot)$ represents the remainder function, and the calculation result is the generated public key, e and P are the randomly selected large prime numbers and small prime numbers, respectively, and a is the random number whose value is in the interval [1, P]. After receiving the public key, the cloud server generates the encryption and decryption private key through the key generation algorithm. The mathematical formula is as follows:

$$K = \begin{cases} Key_{Y}^{a}, Y \in J \\ Key_{X}^{b}, X \in F \end{cases} \tag{7}$$

In formula (7), b is both a random number in [1, P], which represents the random number of the receiving end, and J and F are the sets of the receiving end and the transmitting end respectively [9]. The client uploads the plaintext M of the data to be encrypted. After receiving the plaintext data, the cloud server encrypts the plaintext data through a data encryption algorithm, and encrypts the key at the same time to protect the security of the key. The obtained plaintext and ciphertext are respectively for:

$$\begin{cases} Q = \mathrm{Enc}_k(M) \\ M = \mathrm{Dec}_k(Q) \end{cases} \tag{8}$$

where $\mathrm{Enc}_k()$ and $\mathrm{Dec}_k()$ are the encryption function and the decryption function, respectively. The DES algorithm is selected to perform encryption processing of all regional economic data in the cloud storage space. First, the 64-bit plaintext is initially replaced with IP, and then the output is divided into two parts, L_0 and V_0, each of which is 32 bits. Then the obtained two parts L_0 and V_0 are input to the Feistel network, the right half R_i will be sent to the function, and the result output by the function will be XORed with L_i. The above process can be expressed as:

$$\begin{cases} L_i = R_{i-1} \\ R_i = L_{i-1} \oplus f(R_{i-1}, K_i) \end{cases} \tag{9}$$

Finally, the left and right parts are exchanged, and after 16 iterative operations, L_{16} and R_{16} are obtained as inputs, and the inverse permutation IP-1 is performed, and the final output result is the encrypted plaintext. The remote data authentication process is shown in Fig. 6.

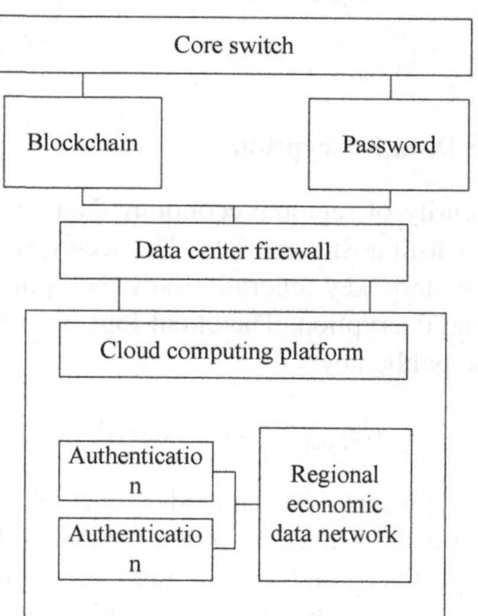

Fig. 6. Schematic diagram of remote data authentication

According to the authentication method shown in Fig. 6, the data encryption storage method is provided with two-level authentication, namely, the legal person authentication to which the data belongs and the data authentication. The identity verification of the legal person to which the data belongs can ensure that the data will not be called by other personnel at will and ensure the security of the data.

Realize the secure cloud storage of regional economic data network.

With the support of blockchain technology, the secure cloud storage framework of regional economic data network is shown in Fig. 7.

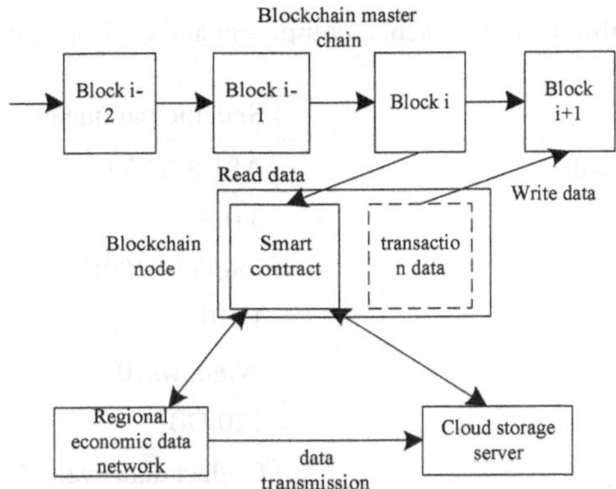

Fig. 7. Block diagram of regional economic data network security cloud storage

In the actual storage execution process, first the depositor submits a request for data encryption storage on any terminal with blockchain technology, and then the blockchain technology submits the request to the database management center, which queries and retrieves whether the depositor has stored data. If so, it calls out the storage space sequence. If not, it creates a data storage space, and the blockchain management center sends back the storage space address. Secondly, the blockchain technology verifies the data identity of the stored data, and generates a unique information point and the basic attributes of the data to be stored. After the data authentication process, the data is encrypted and controlled through the blockchain technology, the access control decision is made, and the decision result is returned to the data authentication center [10]. Finally, the blockchain technology encrypts and stores the data provided by the user according to the authentication instructions and encryption control instructions. Each user in the blockchain corresponds to a public key address as the identity certificate for data storage and logout. The identity key and storage serial number of the storer manage and maintain the permissions to ensure the security of remote data encryption storage.

3 Experiment Analysis of Cloud Storage Effect Test

In order to verify the storage effect of the secure cloud storage method of regional economic data network based on blockchain technology, an effect test experiment is designed. The experimental process covers such key processes as data encryption and decryption, file storage and access, and blockchain data reading and writing. Through the comparison with the traditional row column hybrid storage method of regional economic data network security cloud storage, the application advantages of the optimization design method are reflected.

3.1 Configure the Experimental Environment

The experimental equipment and environment are shown in Table 1.

Table 1. Experimental equipment and environment

Project	Specific parameters
Computer version and model	ASUS X550
Image net dataset version	3.0.3
CPU	Intel i7-9700K
Memory	1 GB
operating system	Windows10
Hard disk capacity	120 GB
Data sampling frequency	Collect data every 2 s
Simulation software	Matlab R2014a

The experimental environment of the cloud storage effect test experiment consists of three industrial PCs, a laptop, data collectors and various network peripherals. Using the above equipment, a data monitoring system is deployed using the tools related to the Hyperledger Fabric blockchain project. The laptop is used as a client to receive sensor data collected from the regional economic data network. The certificate and key services in the network are provided by the Fabric CA blockchain project, a sub-project of Hyperledger Fabric. After the device is deployed, the configuration files of each node need to be prepared before the network runs.

3.2 Prepare Regional Economic Data Samples

According to the above method, the preparation results of all regional economic data during the study period can be obtained. The total amount of regional economic data prepared in the experiment is 430.0 GB.

3.3 Generate Data Security Storage Tasks

In order to ensure the reliability of the experimental results and avoid the impact of accidental events on the experimental results, multiple data storage tasks are set in the experiment. The specific generation of storage tasks is shown in Table 2.

Table 2. Data security storage task description table

Store the task number	Data sources	Data storage address	Data storage/GB
S01	173.102.44.01	Cloud storage 1	22.65
S02	173.102.44.05	Cloud storage 1	30.45
S03	173.102.44.02	Cloud storage 1	55.60
S04	173.102.44.14	Cloud storage 2	36.80
S05	173.102.44.06	Cloud storage 2	65.00
S06	173.102.44.11	Cloud storage 3	72.40
S07	173.102.44.23	Cloud storage 3	80.00
S08	173.102.44.12	Cloud storage 3	67.10

During the experimental test, the designated regional economic data samples are input to the client to perform the corresponding cloud storage tasks.

3.4 Introducing Malicious Nodes

In order to test the security of cloud storage data, malicious nodes are introduced into the regional economic data network environment. When there are malicious nodes in the network, the attacks that information may suffer in the transmission process are divided into the following three types: data theft, data tampering and data fraud. Other network operation processes such as data transmission and collection are not considered, and only the network data storage process of regional economic data is concerned. After the regional economic data storage process and storage are completed, three malicious attacks are carried out. The attack method is a combination of data theft and data tampering, and the intensity and form of each attack are the same.

3.5 Set Cloud Storage Effect Test Indicators

This experiment is tested from two aspects of storage security and storage task execution efficiency. According to the set data attack type, the integrity and correctness of cloud storage data are verified, and the amount of storage data loss and the proportion of tampered data are set. These indicators are used as quantitative test indicators of storage security, and the numerical results are:

$$\begin{cases} N_{loss} = N_{\text{storage}} - N_{\text{actual}} \\ \eta = \dfrac{N_{\text{Tampering}}}{N_{\text{storage}}} \times 100\% \end{cases} \tag{10}$$

In the formula, N_{storage}, N_{actual} and $N_{\text{Tampering}}$ respectively represent the theoretical storage data volume, the actual storage data volume and the tampered data volume in the stored data. The calculation shows that the greater the loss of stored data and the higher the proportion of tampered data, the lower the storage security of the corresponding method. In addition, the quantitative test index of the execution efficiency of the storage task is the execution time of the storage task, and the numerical results are as follows:

$$\Delta T = t_{\text{complete}} - t_{\text{input}} \quad (11)$$

The variables t_{complete} and t_{input} in the above formula are the successful storage time of regional economic data and the input time of the storage task, respectively. It is calculated that the shorter the execution time of the storage task, the higher the storage efficiency of the corresponding cloud storage method.

3.6 Experimental Process and Result Analysis

In the experiment, the traditional regional economic data network security cloud storage method based on row-column hybrid storage is set as the comparison method of the experiment, and the execution result of the comparison storage method is obtained according to the above process. By reading the relevant data, the test results reflecting the security of the cloud storage method are obtained, as shown in Table 3.

Table 3. Cloud storage security test data sheet

Store the task number	Data security cloud storage method based on Quadtree		Data security cloud storage based on semi trusted third party		A secure cloud storage method for regional economic data network based on blockchain technology	
	N_{actual}/GB	$N_{\text{Tampering}}$/GB	N_{actual}/GB	$N_{\text{Tampering}}$/GB	N_{actual}/GB	$N_{\text{Tampering}}$/GB
S01	17.03	6.47	17.63	6.53	21.58	0.88
S02	20.6	8.72	20.12	8.86	30.21	0.52
S03	48.83	7.03	48.12	6.33	55.04	0.16
S04	26.77	9.46	26.12	9.12	36.36	0.81
S05	55.36	8.29	55.18	8.13	63.87	0.34
S06	64.15	8.62	64.16	8.28	71.62	0.29
S07	73.15	6.29	73.09	6.76	79.06	0.41
S08	59.66	7.51	59.11	7.52	66.28	0.37

Substituting the data in Table 3 into Eq. 10, the average storage data loss of the optimized design cloud storage method and the tampered data ratio indicator test results are 0.74 GB and 1.26%. In addition, through the calculation of formula (11), the test result of the execution time of the storage task is obtained, as shown in Fig. 8.

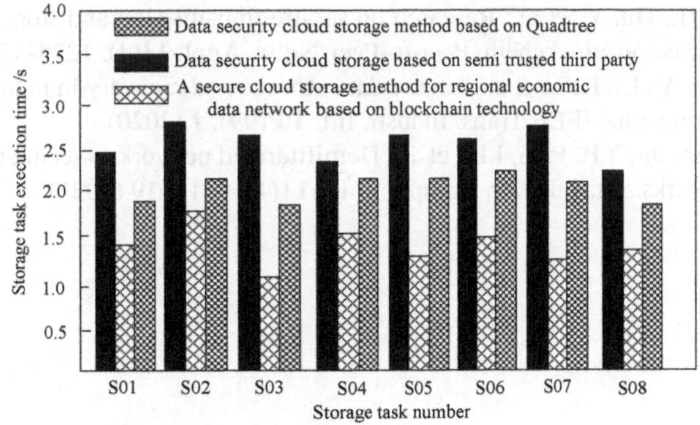

Fig. 8. Data network security cloud storage efficiency test results

It can be seen from Fig. 8 that the optimized design of the secure cloud storage method of regional economic data network based on blockchain technology has shorter storage task execution time and higher task execution efficiency.

4 Conclusion

In the context of cloud storage, how to ensure the security of big data is a very important issue. Data security is not only to protect the data content, but also to protect the structure status information, customer access information, mode and other information of the data. The combination of blockchain and cloud storage technology makes full use of the advantages of the two technologies. It is a new application mode of cloud data storage, point-to-point transmission, consensus mechanism, encryption algorithm and other computer technologies. It solves the problems of mutual trust and data security among multiple points, provides security guarantee for cloud storage of regional economic data network, and has broad application prospects.

References

1. Liu, S., Liu, D., Muhammad, K., Ding, W.: Effective template update mechanism in visual tracking with background clutter. Neurocomputing **458**, 615–625 (2021)
2. Liu, S., et al.: Human memory update strategy: a multi-layer template update mechanism for remote visual monitoring. IEEE Trans. Multimedia **23**, 2188–2198 (2021)
3. Shuai, L., Shuai, W., Xinyu, L., et al.: Fuzzy detection aided real-time and robust visual tracking under complex environments. IEEE Trans. Fuzzy Syst. **29**(1), 90–102 (2021)
4. Huang, C., Zhan, L.: Research on encryption simulation of attributes based on cloud LabDatabase resource cloud storage. Comput. Simul. **37**(5), 115–118 (2020). 123
5. Wang, J., Chen, W., Wang, L., et al.: Data secure storage mechanism of sensor networks based on blockchain. Comput. Mater. Continua **65**(3), 2365–2384 (2020)
6. Teng, L., Li, H., Yin, S., et al.: A modified advanced encryption standard for data security. Int. J. Netw. Secur. **22**(1), 112–117 (2020)
7. Ning, J., Huang, X., Susilo, W., et al.: Dual access control for cloud-based data storage and sharing. IEEE Trans. Dependable Secure Comput. **PP**(99), 1 (2020)

8. Hou, R., Liu, H., Hu, Y., et al.: Research on secure transmission and storage of energy IoT information based on Blockchain. Peer-to-Peer Netw. Appl. **13**(4), 1225–1235 (2020)
9. Liang, W., Fan, Y., Li, K.C., et al.: Secure data storage and recovery in industrial blockchain network environments. IEEE Trans. Industr. Inf. **PP**(99), 1 (2020)
10. Alvarez, J., Zamora, Y.P., Pina, I.B., et al.: Demilitarized network to secure the data stored in industrial networks. Int. J. Electr. Comput. Eng. **11**(1), 611–619 (2021)

Data Leakage with Label Reconstruction in Distributed Learning Environments

Xiaoxue Zhang[1], Xiuhua Zhou[1], and Kongyang Chen[2,3,4](✉)

[1] School of Computer Science and Cyber Engineering, Guangzhou University, Guangzhou, China

[2] Institute of Artificial Intelligence and Blockchain, Guangzhou University, Guangzhou, China
kychen@gzhu.edu.cn

[3] Pazhou Lab, Guangzhou, China

[4] Jiangsu Key Laboratory of Media Design and Software Technology, Jiangnan University, Wuxi, China

Abstract. Distributed learning is commonly applied for the high demands of computation resources while training models with large-scale data. However, existing solutions revealed that it may lead to information leakage of private data. Attackers are able to reconstruct data via minimizing the difference between shared gradients and fake gradients that are produced by themselves. This is so-called data leakage attack from gradients. We find that, in many cases, such attack can only obtain random noises or extreme fuzzy information, which are quite different from the raw data. To deal with this problem, we exploit the gradient updates as well as their labels during the parameter-server training, and discover significant information losses during the label coding. Thus, in our method, we reconstruct the labels of samples with a fine-grained method, and we recover the raw inputs with these processed labels. We test our method on different datasets (i.e. CIFAR100 dataset and solid color images) and obtained the reconstructed results which are obviously clearer than the ones of the state-of-the-arts. The results prove the effectiveness of our algorithm in fixing defects to some extent as well. Extensive experiments are also conducted to explore defense strategies against data leakage.

Keywords: Distributed learning · Label reconstruction · Data privacy

1 Introduction

Large-scale deep learning is gaining more and more attention for its benefits in generalization and high performance, which is now widely used in computer vision and natural language processing [5,7,10]. However, large-scale deep learning suffers from the high demands of computation resources, time-consuming training process, and potential data leakage risk during the data transmission. To solve these problems, distributed learning is introduced, which partitions and

Y. Xu et al. (Eds.): ML4CS 2022, LNCS 13655, pp. 185–197, 2023.
https://doi.org/10.1007/978-3-031-20096-0_15

distributes the training tasks to different nodes for computation. The distributed learning process is not finished yet, and an extra aggregation process is required. In general, distributed training can be divided into two categories: a centralized manner and a decentralized manner. In a centralized manner, participants train their shadow models with private data and send weights or gradients to a central parameter server for further aggregation. While in a decentralized manner, the participant sends weights or gradients to the neighboring one instead of a central one.

It is recognized that sending gradients, rather than raw data, for aggregation is safe. However, a recent study shows that a method named *Deep Leakage from Gradients* (DLG) [12], which is able to reconstruct training data through shared gradients. In this method, the dummy data is randomly initialized by the attacker and then optimize the dummy data via minimizing the difference between the dummy gradients and the real gradients until convergence. For further improvement, [11] exposed the relationship between labels and the positive or negative symbols of the loss gradient, and proposed the algorithm of label reconstruction, which reduced iterations of DLG. Although these previous studies have proved the possibility of stealing data through gradients leakage, there are non-trivial problems in practice. The main problem we found is that some specific data sets (i.e., solid color pictures) are hard to be reconstructed by previous algorithms. Existing methods can only obtain random noises or very fuzzy information, which is far from piratical usages.

In order to address the above problems, we propose a simple but highly effective approach, named Data Leakage with Label Reconstruction (DLLR). The main idea of our approach is to perform specific processing over labels to extract as much information from data as possible, which has been validated to be effective in recovering special data sets. Extensive empirical experiments show the efficiency of our methods over the state of the arts.

Our contributions can be summarized as follows:

1. We identify the deficiency of the previous methods, which makes them totally fail to work in particular situations.
2. We propose a deep data reconstruction attack with fine-grained labels and experiment results demonstrate its superiority over other approaches.

The rest of this paper is structured as follows: In Sect. 2, we point out the limitations of previous work. In Sect. 3, we present the detailed procedure about how we extract information from labels. In Sect. 4, our experiments are demonstrated. Section 5 discusses some defense strategies. Section 6 is a general description of related work. Finally, Sect. 7 concludes our paper.

2 Motivation

Previous work has fully confirmed that it is achievable to reconstruct data through the shared gradients in distributed training. [12] propose a corresponding method named Deep Leakage from Gradients(DLG). In this method, the attacker first randomly initializes a fake sample that contains the fake input and the fake label and then feeds the fake sample into the shadow model to obtain the fake gradients by gradient descent. Then match the fake gradients with the real gradients obtained by the victim model by adjusting the fake sample. When the algorithm converges, the attacker can successfully reconstruct the private data.

However, there is potential improvement in practical applications via using DLG. Of all problems, the poor performance of reconstruction is obvious. It is more challenging to reconstruct pictures that contain solid color parches and CT images.

For example, Fig. 1 demonstrates the reconstruction process of solid-color images. While trying to recover the yellow pictures, the results acquired by multiple iterations with repeated adjustment of hyperparameters such as the learning rate are still full of random noise, signifying the total failure of reconstruction.

3 Method

3.1 Overview

There are limitations in the application scenarios of the existing data reconstruction methods with shared gradients. Specifically, even if there is a large difference between the reconstructed data and the real data, the optimization of reconstruction can not be continued. For example, even though it is impossible to distinguish the background color in recovered pictures, the updating process of some solid-color images is terminated immediately after obtaining the correct one-hot label, leaving a large amount of noise.

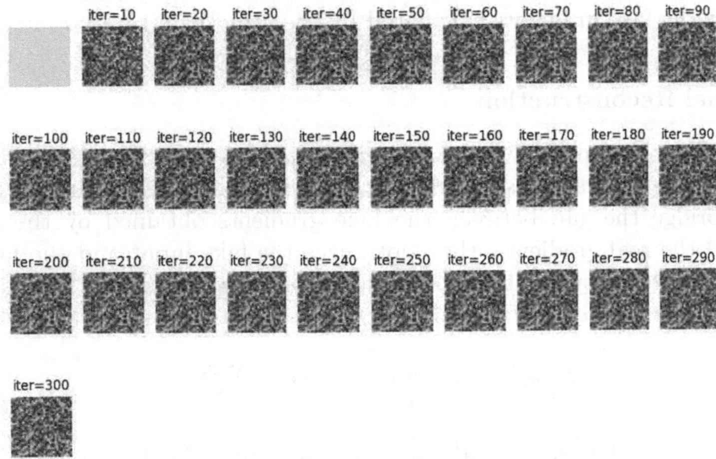

Fig. 1. Reconstruction of solid color picture (Color figure online)

According to the above, we propose a deep data reconstruction method with fine-grained labels. Our method focuses on extracting more iteration information from labels to make the reconstructed data more complete and accurate. Figure 2 is an overview of our algorithm.

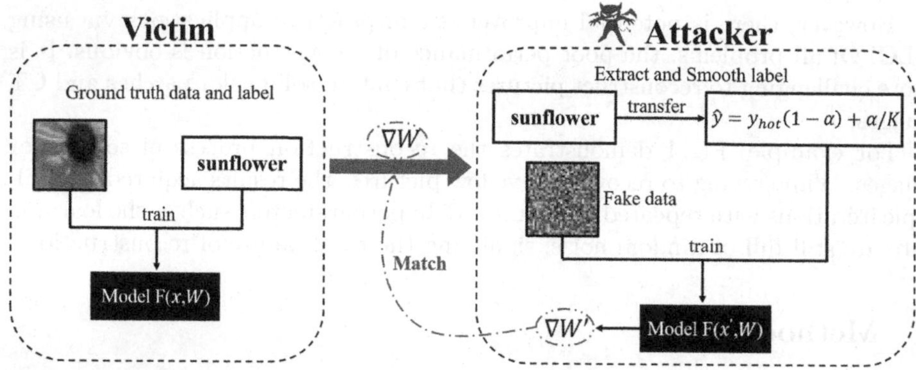

Fig. 2. Overview of our algorithm

The attacker steals the label of the victim's data by using the label reconstruction method [11] and converts the label into the form of one-hot code. Then, smooth the one-hot labels by the hyperparameters, which provides the information between fine-grained labels and data. After that, the processed labels and randomly initialized fake inputs are fed into the attacker model to calculate the model weight gradients. The data reconstruction is realized by continuously minimizing the gradient difference between the shared gradients of the victim model and the fake gradients calculated by the attacker.

3.2 Label Reconstruction

It is possible to steal the victim's gradients and reconstruct its private data with the usage of gradients for the attacker in distributed training [12]. The attacker bridge the gap between the fake gradients obtained by the attacker model and the real gradients, then optimizes the fake input and the fake label randomly generated by itself. The objective function value of data reconstruction is continuously reduced as follows:

$$x'^*, y'^* = \underset{x', y'}{\arg\min} \quad \|\nabla \mathbf{W}' - \nabla \mathbf{W}\|^2 \tag{1}$$

where x' is the fake input randomly initialized from $\mathbf{N}(0,1)$, y' is the corresponding fake label. $\nabla \mathbf{W}'$ is the fake gradient calculated by attacker with the fake input, while $\nabla \mathbf{W}$ is the real gradient. The specific process of the algorithm is as follows.

1. The attacker steals the real gradients $\nabla\mathbf{W}$ of the victim model $\mathbf{F}$:

$$\nabla\mathbf{W} \leftarrow \partial loss(F(x, \mathbf{W}), y)/\partial\mathbf{W} \tag{2}$$

2. The attacker randomly initializes the fake data, that is, random initialization of the fake input x′ and the fake label y′:

$$x' \leftarrow \mathbf{N}(0,1),\ y' \leftarrow \mathbf{N}(0,1) \tag{3}$$

3. The attacker feeds the fake data into the shadow model and trains to acquire the fake gradients $\nabla\mathbf{W}'$:

$$\nabla\mathbf{W}' \leftarrow \partial loss(F(x', \mathbf{W}), y')/\partial\mathbf{W} \tag{4}$$

4. Use gradients difference to adjust the fake data reversely with multiple attempts of changing learning rate α, which is helpful to control the updating amplitude:

$$x' \leftarrow x' - \alpha\nabla_{x'}\|\nabla\mathbf{W}' - \nabla\mathbf{W}\|^2 \tag{5}$$

$$y' \leftarrow y' - \alpha\nabla_{y'}\|\nabla\mathbf{W}' - \nabla\mathbf{W}\|^2 \tag{6}$$

5. Repeat steps (3) and (4) until the gradients difference approaches convergence.

In order to reduce iterations of data reconstruction, [11] et al. implements label reconstruction algorithm before data reconstruction. As shown in Fig. 3, the corresponding ground-truth labels are obtained directly from the shared gradient by revealing the relationship between specific labels and the positive or negative symbols of the loss gradients for each output.

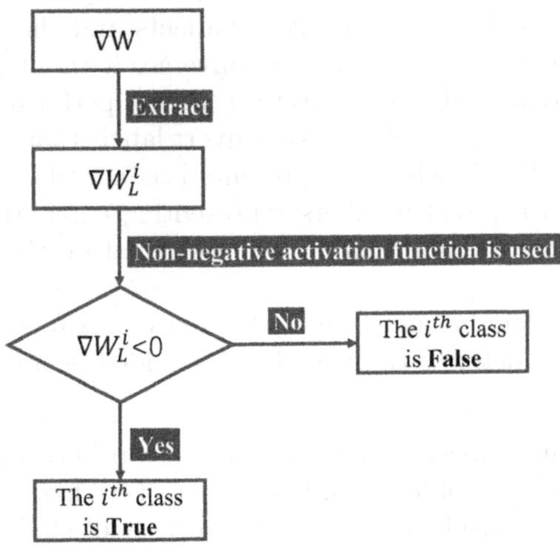

Fig. 3. Overview of label reconstruction

Considering multi-class classification tasks, the model is generally trained with the usage of the cross-entropy loss function for one-hot labels. Then, the gradients between the prediction value y and the loss $l(x, c)$ can be expressed as:

$$g_i = \begin{cases} -1 + \frac{e^{y_i}}{\sum_j e^{y_j}} & \text{if y = c,} \\ \frac{e^{y_i}}{\sum_j e^{y_j}} & \text{else.} \end{cases} \tag{7}$$

y = $[y_1, y_2, ...]$ denotes the outputs of model, which is the probability of predicting as i^{th} class. When $-1 < g_i < 0$, the correct label should be class **i**, otherwise, it should not be class **i**. Thus, it seems to be straightforward to extract the ground-truth labels by observing the positive and negative values of g_i. However, the shared gradients, derived partially from the model weights, do not contain them in some cases, which makes the direct acquisition of labels hindered.

$\nabla \mathbf{W}_L^i$, the gradients of $l(x, c)$ of the weights $\mathbf{W}_L^i$, can be formulated as:

$$\nabla \mathbf{W}_L^i = g_i \cdot a_{L-1} \tag{8}$$

where a_{L-1} is the unit value of the layer that is the previous one of the output layer. If the activation function value is non-negative and $\nabla \mathbf{W}_L^i < 0$, g_i take negative value and the ith class is the ground-truth label. A detailed description of equations (7) and (8) is introduced in iDLG [11], thus it is no need to be repeated here. Since the shared gradients contain the gradient vector $\nabla \mathbf{W}_L^i$, label reconstruction is reasonable to be implemented and the accuracy is up to 100% which has been verified in [11].

3.3 Label Smoothing

One-Hot Label. It is known that the image background has little effect on label prediction. When the target object of the fake input is successfully reconstructed, the difference between the fake gradients and the real gradients will be extremely close to zero. The algorithm converges without recovering the pictures'background. To alleviate this limitation, we will perform specific processing over labels after label reconstruction. We convert labels that are stolen by iDLG into one-hot labels. The labels are represented as encoded vectors instead of direct outputs which are real numbers representing categories. This approach can provide more accurate information when calculating the gradients at each backpropagation.

However, the problem has not been addressed yet. A further smoothing process, where hyperparameter to the hard label is added, is applied.

Smooth. The one-hot labels ignore the relationship between labels and data, which leads to the missing of learning knowledge of background details of data. For example, it is more likely to misclassify samples of class "plane" as "bird" than the samples of other classes. Similar classes of data deserve special treatment. It is neglected by one-hot labels, leading to an arbitrary model and a poor performance. Similarly, when using DLG to recover data over one-hot labels, DLG tends to focus only on the target objects, ignoring the background information of images.

Label smoothing addresses the deficiency of the lack of supervised signals in classification tasks. The distribution after label smoothing is equivalent to adding noise to the true distribution, avoiding the model being overconfident about the correct labels. The label vector after smoothing is formulated as following:

$$\hat{y}_i = y_{hot}(1 - \alpha) + \alpha/\mathbf{K} \tag{9}$$

where $\mathbf{K}$ is the total number of classes and α is a small hyperparameter. The label prediction can also be written as:

$$\hat{y}_i = \begin{cases} 1 - \alpha \ \mathrm{if\,i} = \mathrm{target}, \\ \alpha/\mathbf{K} \ \mathrm{else}. \end{cases} \tag{10}$$

4 Experiment

In this section, We compare DLG with our methods over the same datasets. The experiments are based on Pytorch platform. LeNet and L-BFGS with learning rate of 0.1, 0.5 and 1 are used as data reconstruction models and iteration optimizers. Regarding the datasets, we used MNIST dataset, CIFAR100 dataset and solid color pictures. First, we demonstrate the superiority of our algorithm over DLG algorithm. Then, we present the reconstruction effects of our algorithm and DLG on pre-trained models.

4.1 Over Special Datasets

To verify the improvement in the data restoration achieved by our method, we perform DLG and our approach on the same dataset. The model we selected is LeNet with weights randomly initialized from Gaussian distribution. Private data can be reconstructed by continuously optimizing fake inputs and fake labels to match the fake gradients with the real gradients. Only a single image is to be recovered at a time.

Figure 4 displays the effects of DLG and our method over pure color pictures. The DLG shows that there are still a lot of noises in the recovered data after 390 iterations. (see the upper image). In contrast, our method shows that the reconstructed data gets close to the original one after fewer iterations (see the lower image).

4.2 On Pretrained Model

The pre-trained model is applied for data reconstruction to simulate the occasion where the client's shadow model could be stolen by an attacker at any time during the training process. Considering the image classification tasks, we observe the effects of executing the data reconstruction attack (i.e. DLG and DLLR)

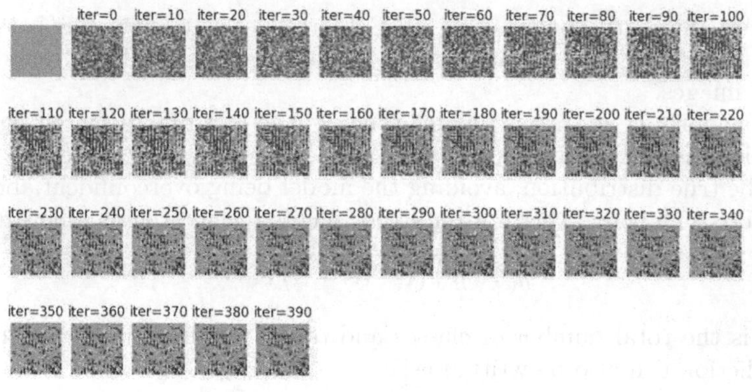

(a) DLG

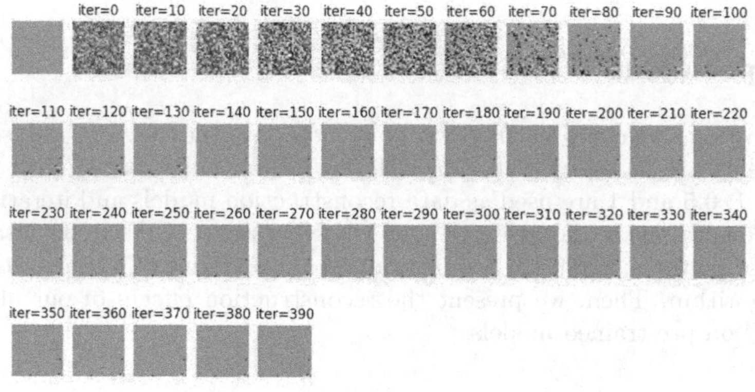

(b) DLLR

Fig. 4. Solid color picture (green) reconstruction (Color figure online)

over the pre-trained model and the initial model. As we discovered, DLG algorithm performs badly while conducting on pre-trained models, which hinders its application in real-world scenarios.

To explore whether our method can improve the above deficiency, we perform comparison experiments of DLG and DLLR. We train the LeNet model for the classification task of MNIST and CIFAR100. After each training epoch, 1000 pictures are randomly selected as validation set and further to be reconstructed. The ratio of the number of successfully recovered images to the total number of images is regarded as the recovery rate. As shown in Fig. 5, our method makes progress to solve the problem that poor recovery effects are acquired over pre-trained models.

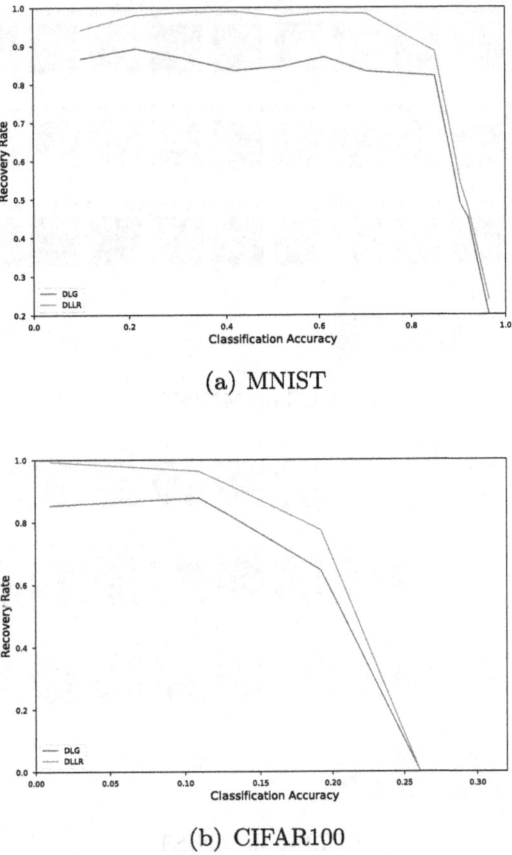

(a) MNIST

(b) CIFAR100

Fig. 5. Reconstruction result on pretrained model

5 Defense Methods

To prevent deep leakage from gradients, the most direct strategy is to add perturbations to the shared gradients. Perturbations like random noise can be considered to decrease the accuracy of data reconstruction. In this section, we proposed two types of experiments: add noise and do not add noise to gradients. It works if the number of successfully recovered images drops. Otherwise, this defense strategy is invalid.

Figure 6 and Fig. 7 show the results of adding Gaussian noise, which prove that the Gaussian noise can effectively prevent DLG attack and DLLR.

6 Related Work

Distributed Training: To meet the computational demands of deep learning, a new training manner named distributed training is introduced [1]. It distributes the training task to multiple devices to complete the computational task in a limited time. Distributed training can be divided into central distributed

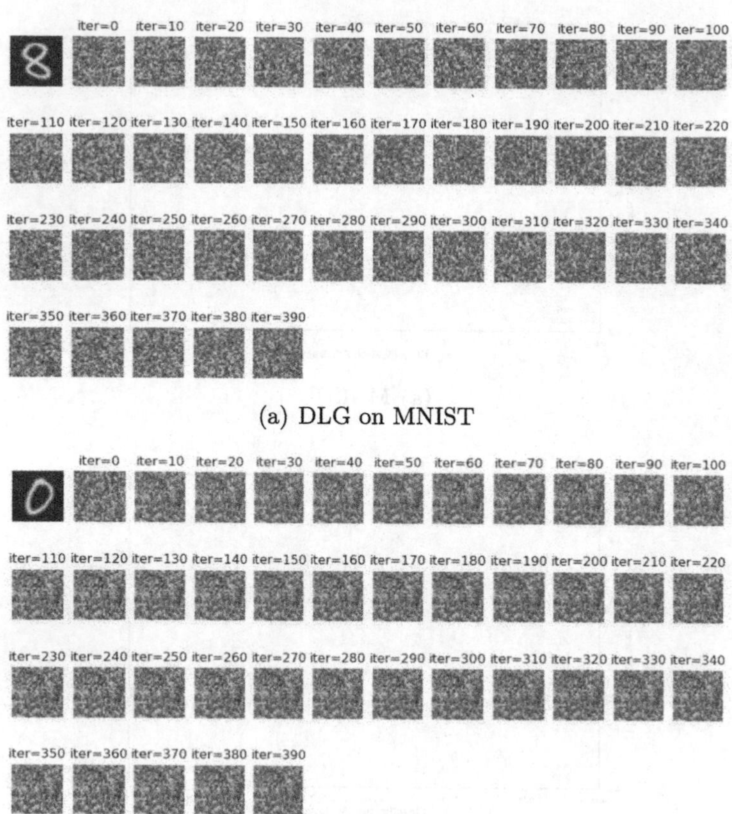

(a) DLG on MNIST

(b) DLLR on MNIST

Fig. 6. Add Gaussian noise for MINST

training and fully distributed training. The former is orchestrated by a central server, while the latter does not. For centralized distributed training, [6] et al. demonstrated the superiority of scalability and full utilization of computational resources of the training framework that fuses the training intermediate media (weight values, gradients) from each client for iterative updates on a central server, and then feeds the updated model back to the clients. For fully distributed training, [4] proposes to perform fusion updates by sending the training intermediate media to neighboring nodes without a central server and verifies that this approach has better performance in the case of uneven distribution of data. Distributed training can also be divided into these two categories: weights-sharing manner [3] and gradient-sharing manner [8]. In the latter case, nodes share only gradients and later achieve self-update by gradient confusion, while in the former case, they exchange model weights. Specifically, weights-sharing manner is commonly practiced in the medical field for the extreme sensitivity of patient's privacy.

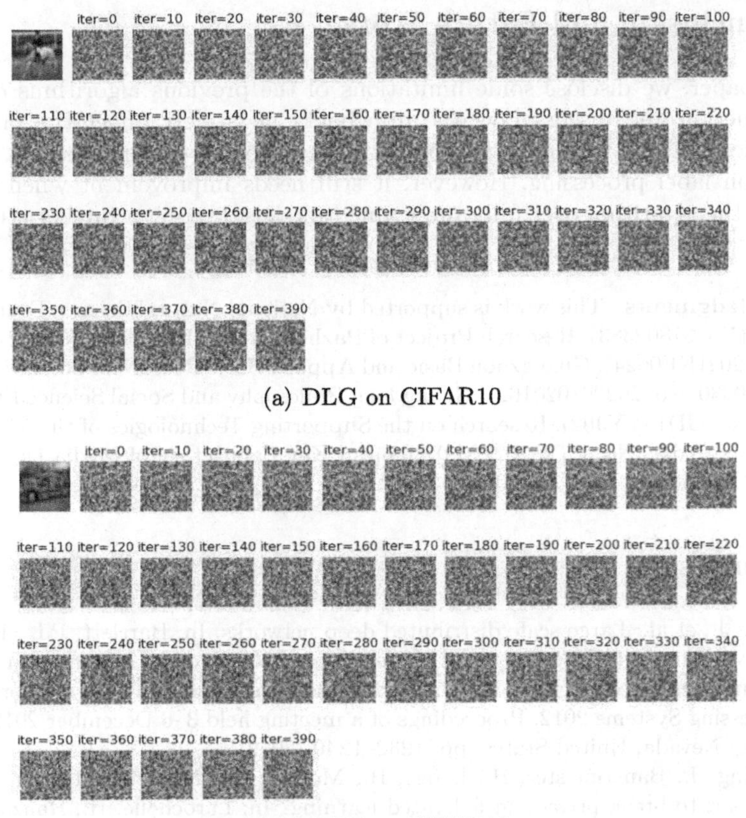

(a) DLG on CIFAR10

(b) DLLR on CIFAR10

Fig. 7. Add Gaussian noise for CIFAR10

Data Reconstruction: The work on reconstructing private data in distributed training has attracted growing attention. Various studies about it have been already conducted. An innovative approach was first proposed by [12] et al. First, the dummy data is randomly initialized and then fed into the shadow model to obtain the dummy gradients. Then they optimize the dummy data by minimizing the difference between the dummy gradients and the real gradients until convergence. For further improvement, [11] proposed to reconstruct labels before reconstructing data. While the above algorithms are more advantageous in single picture reconstruction, [9] et al. are more concerned about improving the quality of data reconstruction performed on batches of images. They achieve superior results in reconstructing multiple images at once by adding regular terms and so on. In addition to focusing on data itself, the research led by [2] focuses more on the threats of gradient leakage in a specific training scenario, federated learning. In contrast to other studies, our work focuses on further improving the accuracy of data reconstruction.

7 Conclusion and Future Work

In this paper, we disclose some limitations of the previous algorithms of data reconstruction and discuss how the drawbacks negatively affect the practical applications. Then we propose a novel method to solve these defects, which focuses on label processing. However, it still needs improvement when implementing the algorithm over fully pre-trained models, leaving a further study for us.

Acknowledgments. This work is supported by National Natural Science Foundation of China (No. 61802383), Research Project of Pazhou Lab for Excellent Young Scholars (No. PZL2021KF0024), Guangzhou Basic and Applied Basic Research Foundation (No. 202201010330, No. 202201020162), Guangdong Philosophy and Social Science Planning Project (No. GD19YYJ02), Research on the Supporting Technologies of the Metaverse in Cultural Media (No. PT252022039), Jiangsu Key Laboratory of Media Design and Software Technology (No. 21ST0202).

References

1. Dean, J., et al.: Large scale distributed deep networks. In: Bartlett, P.L., Pereira, F.C.N., Burges, C.J.C., Bottou, L., Weinberger, K.Q. (eds.) Advances in Neural Information Processing Systems 25: 26th Annual Conference on Neural Information Processing Systems 2012. Proceedings of a meeting held 3–6 December 2012, Lake Tahoe, Nevada, United States, pp. 1232–1240 (2012)
2. Geiping, J., Bauermeister, H., Dröge, H., Moeller, M.: Inverting gradients - how easy is it to break privacy in federated learning? In: Larochelle, H., Ranzato, M., Hadsell, R., Balcan, M., Lin, H. (eds.) Advances in Neural Information Processing Systems 33: Annual Conference on Neural Information Processing Systems 2020, NeurIPS 2020, 6–12 December 2020, virtual (2020)
3. Goyal, P., et al.: Accurate, large minibatch SGD: training imagenet in 1 hour. CoRR abs/1706.02677 (2017)
4. Hegedűs, I., Danner, G., Jelasity, M.: Gossip learning as a decentralized alternative to federated learning. In: Pereira, J., Ricci, L. (eds.) DAIS 2019. LNCS, vol. 11534, pp. 74–90. Springer, Cham (2019). https://doi.org/10.1007/978-3-030-22496-7_5
5. Kooi, T., et al.: Large scale deep learning for computer aided detection of mammographic lesions. Medical Image Anal. **35**, 303–312 (2017)
6. Li, M., et al.: Scaling distributed machine learning with the parameter server. In: Flinn, J., Levy, H. (eds.) 11th USENIX Symposium on Operating Systems Design and Implementation, OSDI 2014, Broomfield, CO, USA, 6–8 October 2014, pp. 583–598. USENIX Association (2014)
7. O'Mahony, N., et al.: Deep learning vs. traditional computer vision. In: Arai, K., Kapoor, S. (eds.) CVC 2019. AISC, vol. 943, pp. 128–144. Springer, Cham (2020). https://doi.org/10.1007/978-3-030-17795-9_10
8. McMahan, B., Moore, E., Ramage, D., Hampson, S., Arcas, B.A.: Communication-efficient learning of deep networks from decentralized data. In: Singh, A., Zhu, X.J. (eds.) Proceedings of the 20th International Conference on Artificial Intelligence and Statistics, AISTATS 2017, 20–22 April 2017, Fort Lauderdale, FL, USA. Proceedings of Machine Learning Research, vol. 54, pp. 1273–1282. PMLR (2017)

9. Yin, H., Mallya, A., Vahdat, A., Alvarez, J.M., Kautz, J., Molchanov, P.: See through gradients: image batch recovery via gradinversion. In: IEEE Conference on Computer Vision and Pattern Recognition, CVPR 2021, virtual, 19–25 June 2021, pp. 16337–16346. Computer Vision Foundation/IEEE (2021)
10. Young, T., Hazarika, D., Poria, S., Cambria, E.: Recent trends in deep learning based natural language processing. IEEE Comput. Intell. Mag. **13**(3), 55–75 (2018)
11. Zhao, B., Mopuri, K.R., Bilen, H.: IDLG: improved deep leakage from gradients. CoRR abs/2001.02610 (2020)
12. Zhu, L., Liu, Z., Han, S.: Deep leakage from gradients. In: Wallach, H.M., Larochelle, H., Beygelzimer, A., d'Alché-Buc, F., Fox, E.B., Garnett, R. (eds.) Advances in Neural Information Processing Systems 32: Annual Conference on Neural Information Processing Systems 2019, NeurIPS 2019, 8–14 December 2019, Vancouver, BC, Canada, pp. 14747–14756 (2019)

Analysis Method of Abnormal Traffic of Teaching Network in Higher Vocational Massive Open Online Course Based on Deep Convolutional Neural Network

Haiying Chen[1] and Jiahui Zou[2(✉)]

[1] Department of Public Courses, Tianmen Vocational College, Tianmen 431700, China
[2] Tianmen Vocational College, Tianmen 431700, China
jhdbfd87@163.com

Abstract. The running security and stability of massive open online course's teaching network directly affect the implementation process of massive open online course's teaching tasks. In order to provide valuable reference data for the management and maintenance of the network, this paper puts forward an analysis method of abnormal traffic of higher vocational massive open online course's teaching network based on deep convolution neural network. According to the structure of the teaching network of massive open online course in higher vocational colleges, a network model is built. Under this model, the flow data is collected, and the preprocessing of the initial flow data is completed through data cleaning, standardized conversion and clustering. The deep convolution neural network is established, and the characteristics of network traffic data are extracted through back propagation iteration. After discrete detection and feature matching, the abnormal traffic in the teaching network of higher vocational massive open online course is detected, and the visual analysis results are obtained. Compared with the traditional network abnormal traffic analysis method, it is found that the detection error and missed detection rate of the optimized design method are reduced by 3.75MB and 1.02% respectively, the accuracy of traffic abnormal type analysis is increased by 1%, and the analysis speed is obviously improved.

Keywords: Deep Convolution Neural Network · Teaching in Massive Open Online Course · Teaching Network · Abnormal Flow Analysis

1 Introduction

Massive open network course teaching is a kind of large-scale open network course, which is an online course for the public to learn through the network through open educational resources [1]. Under the influence of the big environment, massive open online course teaching is chosen by many users because it is not limited by time and space.

At present, the teaching of massive open network courses in higher vocational colleges has been put into practical teaching work, and the online number and concentration

Y. Xu et al. (Eds.): ML4CS 2022, LNCS 13655, pp. 198–212, 2023.
https://doi.org/10.1007/978-3-031-20096-0_16

of students have increased significantly, which provides a great challenge for the operation of the teaching network of massive open network courses in higher vocational colleges. In order to ensure the stability of the teaching network of massive open network courses and reduce the negative influence of illegal users on the teaching network, it is necessary to put forward an analysis method of abnormal traffic of massive open network courses.

At present, the mainstream research direction is network abnormal traffic analysis method based on machine learning or support vector machine. The main advantage of this method is that the normal traffic can be distinguished even if the data set containing not only normal traffic but also various attacks is used for training. However, these algorithms seem to be accurate only when the number of normal transmissions in the data set far exceeds the number of attacks. Through the application, it is found that the existing network abnormal traffic analysis methods are applied to the detection and management of massive open network teaching network in higher vocational colleges, and there are obvious problems such as low analysis accuracy. Therefore, the deep convolution neural network algorithm is introduced.

The deep convolution neural network and its algorithm are applied to the analysis method of abnormal network traffic of massive open network course teaching in higher vocational colleges, so as to improve the analysis accuracy of abnormal network traffic and indirectly improve the stability and security of massive open network course teaching network in higher vocational colleges.

2 Analysis Method Design of Abnormal Traffic in Teaching Network of Higher Vocational Education in Massive Open Online Course

2.1 Constructing Massive Open Online Course Teaching Network Model in Higher Vocational Education

The construction of massive open online course teaching in higher vocational colleges adopts C.S network structure, which requires loading a client program. Figure 1 shows the basic structure of massive open online course teaching network in higher vocational colleges.

The traffic changes of some links in the network can accurately reflect the traffic changes of the whole network, and such links are called critical links. In order to facilitate the collection of traffic data of massive open online course teaching network in higher vocational colleges, the key links of the network are determined by calculating the utilization ratio of links in the performance parameters of the network [2]. The utilization rate reflects the degree of channel utilization, and the channel resources with high utilization rate can be fully utilized. The utilization rate of network links can be expressed as:

$$u(a) = \frac{l(a)}{C(a)} \tag{1}$$

Variables $l(a)$ and $C(a)$ in the above formula represent the load and capacity of the network link, respectively. In the process of traffic data collection of massive open online

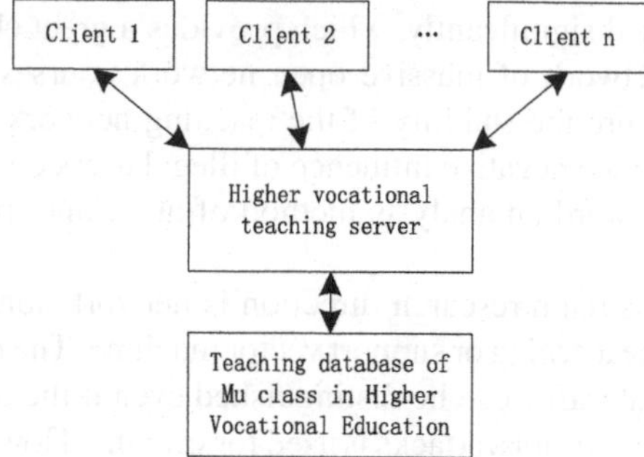

Fig. 1. Structure diagram of teaching network in higher vocational massive open online course

course teaching network in higher vocational colleges, the link whose utilization rate is higher than 0.8 is selected as the collection object.

2.2 Collecting Traffic Data of Teaching Network in Higher Vocational Massive Open Online Course

Set up measuring points in the key links of the teaching network model of massive open network courses in higher vocational colleges, and install sensor devices at the measuring points to complete the collection of real-time network traffic data. The NetFlow method is used to collect network traffic data. The real-time data collected from the source device of NetFlow and the subsequent data flow statistics are stored in the cache of NetFlow. Just input the operation instruction, you can view the network traffic data information exported to NetFlow collector, and prepare for the next analysis and processing of network traffic data. Figure 2 shows the flow data collection process of massive open online course teaching network in higher vocational colleges.

In the process of actual traffic data collection, the functions in NetFlow technology are used to search for available host network cards in the whole teaching network of higher vocational massive open online course. Whenever a network card is found, it can be added to the local network card linked list, and the way of adding it is to the end. Look for the newly added network card at the end of the network card linked list. If you can't find it, it means that the network card has not been added successfully. You can choose to find it again. If you successfully query in the network card linked list, this step is to open the network card just queried in the network card linked list. If you successfully open the network card, you will go to the next step smoothly. If you fail to open the network card, you will automatically jump back to the stage of querying in the network card linked list [3]. Capture the data packets in the successfully opened network card. The capture tool can use the pcap_dispatch function in the network packet capture database libpcap to capture. During the capture process, check whether the network card is in the running state, which supports the capture process to continue. If the network card is in a stagnant state during the detection, return to the beginning stage of capturing data packets.

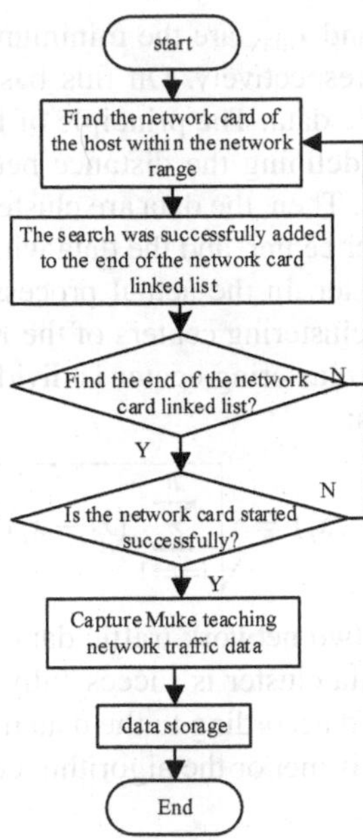

Fig. 2. Flow chart of traffic data collection of teaching network in massive open online course

2.3 Pre-processing of Teaching Network Traffic Data in Massive Open Online Course Higher Vocational Education

The pre-processing of teaching network traffic data in massive open online course is divided into three parts, namely, removing dirty data, standardizing data and clustering data. Dirty data is the acquisition error caused by hardware, software or transmission failure. Dirty data will pollute the traffic matrix. Determining and removing dirty data can reduce the error rate of traffic matrix estimation by a large order of magnitude. The threshold filtering method is adopted to denoise the initially collected network traffic data, and the processing process can be expressed as follows:

$$x = \begin{cases} x_{\text{initial}} & \text{if } x_{\text{initial}} \in A \\ 0 & \text{otherwise} \end{cases} \tag{2}$$

x_{initial} is the initially collected network traffic data, A is the set threshold range, and x is the processing result of the dirty data removal step. For continuous feature attributes, the measurement methods of each attribute are different. The attribute values can be standardized to eliminate the influence of attribute measurement differences on the algorithm. Data normalization is used to scale the value of a feature to a specific confidence interval and eliminate the deviation of the original data without modifying the statistical characteristics of the feature [4]. Methods The data were normalized by normalization, and different characteristic classes were divided into uniform orders of magnitude. The results of data normalization are as follows:

$$x' = \frac{x - x_{\min}}{x_{\max} - x_{\min}} \tag{3}$$

In the above formula, $x_{\min}$ and $x_{\max}$ are the minimum and maximum values in the collected network traffic data, respectively. On this basis, the K-means algorithm is used to cluster the network traffic data. The principle of K-means algorithm is to show the similarity between data by defining the distance between data and the similarity coefficient between data indexes. Then, the data are clustered according to the degree of similarity according to the cluster center, and the data with high similarity to the cluster center can be assigned to a cluster. In the actual processing process, several data are randomly selected as the initial clustering centers of the K-means clustering algorithm, and the data closest to an initial clustering center is divided into a group. The distance calculation formula is as follows:

$$d(x_i, x_j) = \sqrt{\sum_{i=j=1}^{n} \left(x_i - x_j\right)^2} \tag{4}$$

Equations x_i and x_j are any two network traffic data, and n is the data sample size to be clustered. Every time a data cluster is successfully divided, the cluster center of this cluster should be recalculated according to the data in the cluster. Repeat the above steps until the number of cycles is met or the algorithm converges.

2.4 Extracting Traffic Characteristics Using Deep Convolution Neural Network

Convolution network model is a multi-layer feedforward neural network composed of convolution layer and pool layer. Convolution layer is used to obtain local features, while pool layer is mainly used to reduce the dimensions of features, so as to retain the features that are important for target decision, while removing unimportant and redundant features [5]. Figure 3 shows the constructed deep convolution neural network.

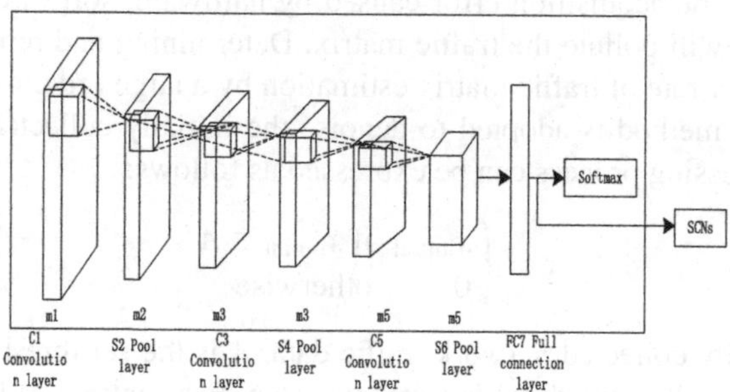

Fig. 3. Schematic diagram of deep convolution neural network

The feature of convolution layer in deep convolution neural network is realized by convolution operation specified by the feature map of the upper layer through convolution kernel, which slides down and to the left in turn along the left edge and the upper edge on the feature map. The calculation process of convolution kernel is as follows:

$$y_{\text{convolution}} = f\left(\sum_{i \in M_j} y_i^{l-1} \otimes k_{ij}^l + b_j^l\right) \tag{5}$$

where $y_{\text{convolution}}$ and y_i^{l-1} represent the input of the i feature of the l layer and the output of the i feature layer of the previous layer, respectively, k_{ij}^l and b_j^l correspond to the number of features of the $l-1$ layer and the offset of the j channel of the current layer. The symbol ⊗ represents convolution operation, and $f()$ is the activation function of convolution neural network. Its expression is:

$$f(x) = \frac{1}{1+e^{-x}} \tag{6}$$

The operation of pooling layer also divides the original feature data into $n \times n$ non-overlapping area by sliding the window. There are two main pooling methods: maximum pooling and average pooling [6]. In these two methods, the original data is reduced by $n \times n$ by averaging or maximizing the regional data. The formula of pooling is:

$$y_{\text{Pooling}} = f\left(\omega \text{down}\left(x_i^{l-1}\right)\right) + b_j^l \tag{7}$$

In the above formula, ω is the weight coefficient, b_j^l is the bias term of the pool layer, and down() is the pool function. In addition, the fully connected layer usually appears behind the last pool layer or convolution layer, and each neuron is connected with all the neurons in the upper layer. Its calculation formula is:

$$h_{w,b}(x) = f\left(W^{\mathrm{T}}x + b\right) \tag{8}$$

In formula 8, x is the input of neurons, $h_{w,b}(x)$ is the output of neurons, and W^{T} and b are the input weight matrix and offset vector respectively. In the process of feature extraction of teaching network traffic data in higher vocational massive open online course, it is necessary to use the constructed deep convolution neural network for back propagation, that is, compare the output results with the expected results, stop all learning processes when the deviation meets the requirements, and run the back propagation algorithm when it does not. That is, through the iteration of the gradient descent method, all the superparameters in the network calculate the partial derivatives of the loss function respectively, and the calculated better parameters are used to replace the original superparameters [7]. Figure 4 shows the back propagation learning process of deep convolution neural network.

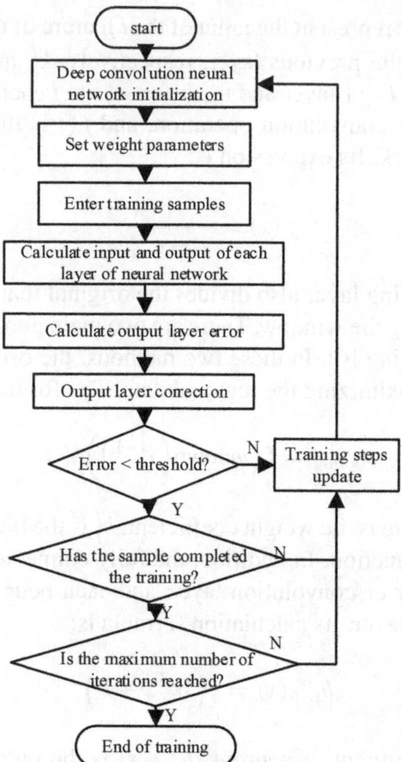

Fig. 4. Flow chart of back propagation of deep convolution neural network

Using the above-mentioned constructed deep convolution neural network and its propagation algorithm, the collected and processed traffic data of massive open online course teaching network in higher vocational education is transmitted to the neural network as input data, and the characteristics of network traffic data are extracted from time domain [8]. The extraction results of traffic peak characteristics are as follows:

$$\tau_p = \max(X) \tag{9}$$

Where X is the network traffic data set and max() is the maximum solution function. Similarly, the extraction results of kurtosis feature, waveform feature and pulse feature can be obtained as follows:

$$\begin{cases} \tau_q = \dfrac{\sum_{i=1}^{n} x_i^4}{n} \\ \tau_b = \dfrac{x_{rms}}{x_{avg}} \\ \tau_m = \dfrac{x_{\max}}{x_{avg}} \end{cases} \tag{10}$$

In the above formula, x_{rms}, x_{avg} and $x_{\max}$ respectively correspond to the peak value, average value and root mean square value of network traffic data. Finally, all the extracted network traffic data features are fused to obtain the comprehensive feature extraction result of network traffic data.

2.5 Detect Abnormal Phenomenon of Network Traffic Data

From two aspects: the discrete points of network traffic data and the correlation coefficient of abnormal data, it is determined whether there is any abnormal phenomenon in the current teaching network traffic in higher vocational massive open online course. In order to achieve a good outlier detection effect and reduce the running cost of the algorithm as much as possible, we found the strongly correlated data sets, and then discarded all the data that did not belong to the strongly correlated data sets to form a high-quality anomaly detection training data set [9]. A DSNOD outlier detection method is proposed. DSNOD outlier detection is to cluster data sets based on distance to form a number of initial clusters, and then judge outliers according to the density between generated clusters, and consider whether they are outliers from two aspects: distance and density. The calculation results of data cluster density are as follows:

$$\rho(C_i) = count\left(\mu\left(C_i, C_j\right) \geq \mu_0\right) \tag{11}$$

Where μ_0 is the threshold for judging whether two data points are similar, $\mu\left(C_i, C_j\right)$ represents the similarity between data cluster C_i and data cluster C_j, and $count()$ is the counting function. Through the above methods, we can get the detection results of discrete points of teaching network traffic in higher vocational massive open online course, and use them as the detection results of abnormal traffic. In addition, according to different types of network anomalies, the change characteristics of corresponding network traffic can be set, and the correlation coefficient between them can be calculated by Formula 12.

$$\lambda = |\tau_{set} - \tau_{com}|^2 \tag{12}$$

τ_{set} and τ_{com} are the set abnormal network traffic characteristics and the real-time traffic comprehensive characteristics extracted by deep convolution neural network. If the calculation result of Formula 12 is higher than λ_0, it is determined that there is a correlation between them, that is, there is abnormal traffic in the teaching network of massive open online course in higher vocational education, otherwise it is determined that there is no abnormal phenomenon in the current teaching network of massive open online course in higher vocational education.

2.6 Realize Network Abnormal Traffic Analysis

According to the measured data of the network, the whole network and traffic flow are modeled correctly, the parameters for evaluating the network performance are calculated, and a large number of performance parameters are analyzed, and performance conclusions are drawn, such as global performance statistics of the network, performance statistics of network nodes, traffic and delay of network links, etc. [10]. In addition to the abnormal network traffic judgment results, the abnormal network traffic analysis results also need to display: the current network abnormal traffic type, the elephant traffic identification results, and mark the abnormal traffic. Use Formula 12 to calculate the standard features of different types of traffic, and select the abnormal traffic type corresponding to the feature with the highest correlation coefficient as the abnormal type of current network traffic. According to the standard deviation of the average value, the threshold value is set as the average flow value of OD flow recorded in each period of a week plus N times the mean square deviation. If the current observed value deviates from the threshold value obviously, we consider the flow in this period as abnormal flow.

3 Comparative Experimental Analysis

The abnormal flow analysis method of massive open online course teaching network based on deep convolution neural network is applied to the teaching work of massive open online course in a higher vocational college, and the optimized design method is tested. Through the operation of the method, its analysis performance is evaluated, and compared with the traditional analysis method, the performance advantage of the optimized design method is reflected.

3.1 Configure the Research Object of Massive Open Online Course Teaching Network in Higher Vocational Education

This experiment chooses a higher vocational college as the experimental background. The teaching network of massive open online courses in higher vocational colleges covers a number of campuses connected by optical fibers, adopts gigabit backbone network, and has a huge user base and huge network traffic. Moreover, each router has NetFlow function, and a high-performance host specially collects and processes the raw traffic measurement data sent by the router. In the massive open network courses, there are 1371 students, 58 teachers and a server in the teaching network of higher vocational colleges. Hardware configuration of the client is XeonSiliver4210@2.2GHzCPU, 64GB memory and NVIDIATeslaP100 graphics card. The main test computer has built-in KaliLinux2019 operating system, TensorFlow and Keras software framework based on Python3.6.

3.2 Prepare a Sample of Teaching Network Traffic Data in Massive Open Online Course of Higher Vocational Education

In order to test the analysis results of different abnormal traffic analysis methods more fairly, different abnormal traffic analysis methods need to test the same set of data sets, so that the results can be comparable. Start the configured higher vocational massive open online course teaching network, and use the hardware equipment to obtain the sample preparation results of traffic data under normal conditions, as shown in Fig. 5.

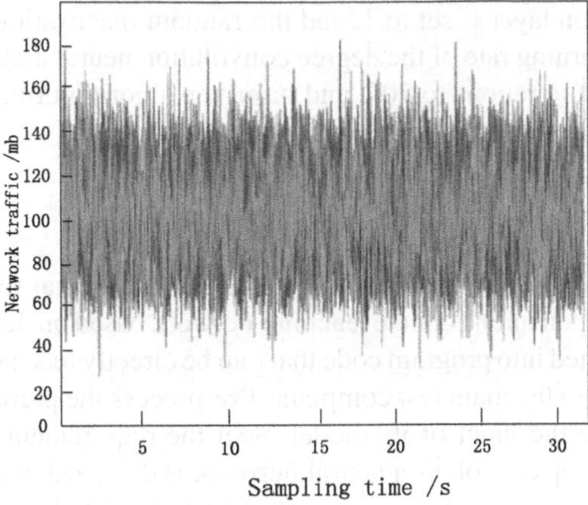

Fig. 5. Waveform diagram of normal flow data of massive open online course teaching network

Use the data in Fig. 5 as the standard to judge whether the network traffic is normal. On this basis, the attack programs were imported into several student clients, which resulted in abnormal teaching network traffic. The preparation of abnormal traffic data samples is shown in Table 1.

Table 1. Sample of abnormal traffic data of teaching network in massive open online course

Exception User Number	User IP Address	Data Exception Type	Generate Abnormal Flow Quantity/MB
1	10.128.254.004	Collective anomaly	135.72
2	10.128.254.002	Point anomaly	18.94
3	10.128.254.015	Context exception	86.23
4	10.128.254.117	Collective anomaly	178.25
5	10.128.254.164	Point anomaly	21.61

In order to ensure the reliability of the experimental results, two experimental scenarios are set in the test experiment. The five abnormal users shown in Table 1 are scenario 1, and 25 abnormal users are set in scenario 2, and the corresponding abnormal flow data sample preparation results are obtained according to the above method.

3.3 Input that Running Parameter of the Deep Convolution Neural Network Algorithm

The deep convolution neural network requires the input data format to be (None,None,118), which means that countless pieces of traffic data after data preprocessing are input, and the dimensions of each piece of data are 118 dimensions. The step size in the convolution layer is set to 1, and the random inactivation rate value is set to 0.5. Set the initial learning rate of the degree convolution neural network to 0.01 and the maximum number of iterations to 200, and input the algorithm running parameters set above into the experimental environment.

3.4 Describe the Test Process of Comparative Experiment

Using coding tools, the optimized analysis method of abnormal traffic flow in higher vocational massive open online course teaching network based on deep convolution neural network is converted into program code that can be directly read and run by computer, and then imported into the main test computer. Pre-process the prepared network traffic data sample to make the input of its model meet the requirements. According to the proposed model, a deep convolution neural network is designed, and the training set in the prepared data set is input into the network for training. At first, the learning rate of the network is set to 0.01, and then with the increasing number of iterations, the learning rate is dynamically reduced to gradually increase the accuracy rate. According to the training results, debug and change other super parameters of the network, and repeat the above steps continuously until the training results reach the ideal state. At this point, the network model training is finished. Finally, the analysis result of abnormal traffic of massive open online course teaching network in higher vocational colleges is output, as shown in Fig. 6.

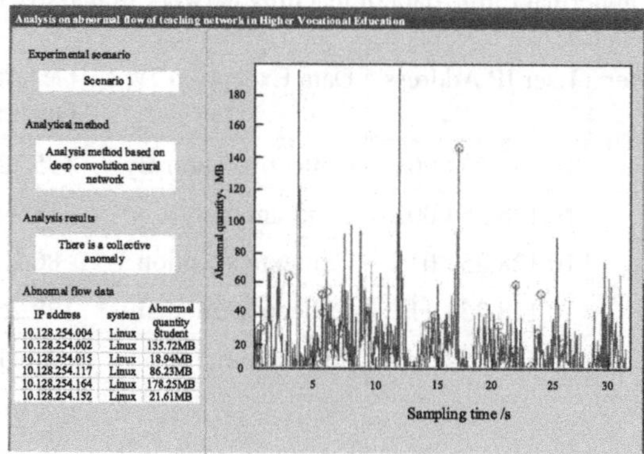

Fig. 6. Analysis result of abnormal flow output by design method

In order to form the experimental comparison, the traditional network abnormal traffic analysis method based on machine learning is set as the experimental comparison method, and the prepared data set is substituted into the comparison method to get the corresponding analysis results. In the actual testing process, it is required that the data samples processed by the comparison method and the experimental method are the same, so as to ensure the uniqueness of experimental variables to the greatest extent.

3.5 Set Performance Test Index of Network Abnormal Traffic Analysis

In this experiment, the accuracy and speed of network abnormal traffic analysis are tested respectively, and three indicators are set to reflect the accuracy of the analysis method, namely, detection error, missed detection rate and analysis accuracy rate of network abnormal traffic types. The numerical results of detection error and missed detection rate of network abnormal traffic are as follows:

$$\begin{cases} \varepsilon = \left|N_{\text{ab}} - N_{\text{out,ab}}\right| \\ \eta_{loss} = \dfrac{\varepsilon}{N_{all}} \times 100\% \end{cases} \tag{13}$$

Equations N_{ab}, $N_{\text{out,ab}}$ and N_{all} are the actual flow anomaly, the flow anomaly shown in the analysis results and the total amount of flow data samples. The numerical results of the accuracy of network traffic anomaly type analysis are as follows:

$$\eta_{\text{type}} = \frac{N_{suc}}{N_{all}} \times 100\% \tag{14}$$

Equation N_{suc} shows the correct flow value of abnormal type analysis. It is concluded that the higher the index value of detection error and missed detection rate of traffic anomaly, the lower the accuracy of network traffic anomaly type analysis, indicating the lower the accuracy of the corresponding analysis method. In addition, the test index of the analysis speed is the output time of the analysis result, which can be directly obtained by retrieving the background data of the method operation. The shorter the output time of the analysis result calculated, the faster the analysis speed of the corresponding method is proved.

3.6 Comparison of Experimental Results and Analysis

Through the statistics of relevant data, the test results of detection error and missed detection rate of abnormal flow are obtained, as shown in Table 2.

By substituting the data in Table 2 into Formula 13, it is calculated that the average detection error and average missed detection rate of network abnormal traffic based on machine learning are 5.55GB and 1.48% respectively, while the average detection error and average missed detection rate of optimized design method are 1.80GB and 0.46% respectively. In addition, through the calculation of Formula 14, the test result of the accuracy of network traffic anomaly type analysis is obtained, as shown in Table 3.

Through the average calculation, it is found that the average accuracy of abnormal traffic type analysis of the network abnormal traffic analysis method based on machine learning and the optimization design method of massive open online course teaching network in higher vocational colleges are 98.78% and 99.78% respectively. To sum up, compared with the traditional network abnormal traffic analysis method, the optimization design method has higher analysis accuracy. In addition, the test and comparison results of response speed of analysis methods are shown in Fig. 7.

It can be seen intuitively from Fig. 7 that the output time of the abnormal traffic analysis method of optimized design teaching network is shorter, that is, it has more advantages in response speed.

Table 2. Test results of abnormal quantity detection error and missed detection rate

Experimental Scene	Number of Experiments	Total Amount of Data Samples/MB	Actual Flow Anomaly/MB	Network Abnormal Traffic Analysis Method Based on Machine Learning Outputs Abnormal Traffic/MB	Optimize the Abnormal Flow Analysis Method of Massive Open Online Course Teaching Network in Higher Vocational Education, and Output the Abnormal Flow/MB
Scene 1	1	200	98	95.6	97.5
	2	200	104	101.5	103.2
Scene 2	1	500	244	238.9	243.7
	2	500	275	262.8	269.4

Table 3. Test results of accuracy of traffic anomaly type analysis

Experimental Scene	Number of Experiments	Accuracy of Network Abnormal Traffic Analysis Based on Machine Learning/%	Optimize the Accuracy Rate of Traffic Anomaly Type Analysis of the Abnormal Traffic Analysis Method of Massive Open Online Course Teaching Network in Higher Vocational Colleges./%
Scene 1	1	99.2	99.6
	2	98.3	99.8
Scene 2	1	99.0	99.9
	2	98.6	99.8

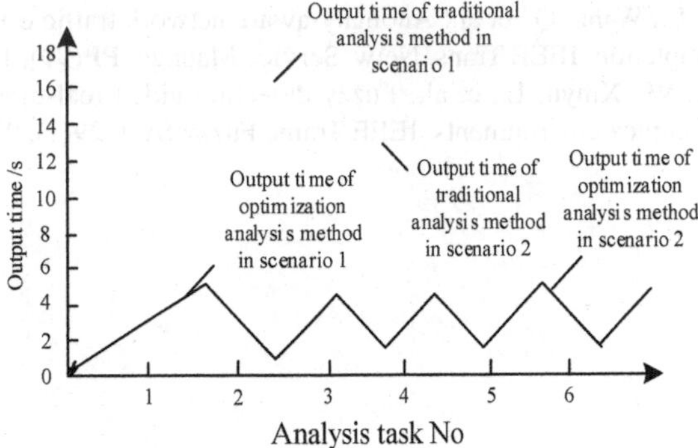

Fig. 7. Comparison curve of abnormal traffic analysis speed of teaching network

4 Concluding Remarks

In the special period, massive open online course teaching has become the main teaching method in higher vocational colleges. Through the design and optimization of network abnormal traffic analysis method, it provides an auxiliary tool for the management and maintenance of massive open online course teaching network in higher vocational colleges, which has high practical significance.

Aknowledgement. Scientific research project of Hubei Vocational and Technical Education Association: Research on innovative teaching mode of deep integration of information technology and higher vocational mathematics under the background of Mooc. (Project No.: ZJGB2021061).

References

1. Zhang, L., Geng, J., Wang, S., et al.: Purification simulation of integrated network abnormal traffic based on feature library recognition. Comput. Simul. **37**(7), 363–367 (2020)
2. Liu, S., Liu, D., Muhammad, K., Ding, W.: Effective template update mechanism in visual tracking with background clutter. Neurocomputing **458**, 615–625 (2021)
3. Ding, P., Li, J., Wang, L., et al.: HYBRID-CNN: an efficient scheme for abnormal flow detection in the SDN-based smart grid. Secur. Commun. Netw. **2020**(4), 1–20 (2020)
4. Monshizadeh, M., Khatri, V., Gamdou, M., et al.: Improving data generalization with variational autoencoders for network traffic anomaly detection. IEEE Access **PP**(99), 1 (2021)
5. Liu, S., Wang, S., Liu, X., Gandomi, A.H., Daneshmand, M., Muhammad, K.: Human memory update strategy: a multi-layer template update mechanism for remote visual monitoring. IEEE Trans. Multimedia **23**, 2188–2198 (2021)
6. Wang, Y.N., Wang, J., Fan, X., et al.: Network traffic anomaly detection algorithm based on intuitionistic fuzzy time series graph mining. IEEE Access **PP**(99), 1 (2020)
7. Zhang, S.T., Lin, X.B., Wu, L., et al.: Network traffic anomaly detection based on ML-ESN for power metering system. Math. Probl. Eng. **2020**(1), 1–21 (2020)
8. Hwang, R.H., Peng, M.C., Huang, C.W., et al.: An unsupervised deep learning model for early network traffic anomaly detection. IEEE Access **8**, 30387–30399 (2020)

9. Wang, Q., Chen, L., Wang, Q., et al.: Anomaly-aware network traffic estimation via outlier-robust tensor completion. IEEE Trans. Netw. Service Manage. **PP**(99), 1 (2020)
10. Shuai, L., Shuai, W., Xinyu, L., et al.: Fuzzy detection aided real-time and robust visual tracking under complex environments. IEEE Trans. Fuzzy Syst. **29**(1), 90–102 (2021)

Spatio-Temporal Context Modeling for Road Obstacle Detection

Xiuen Wu[1,2], Tao Wang[2,3(✉)], Lingyu Liang[4,5,6(✉)], Zuoyong Li[2], and Fum Yew Ching[7]

[1] College of Computer and Data Science, Fuzhou University, Fuzhou 350108, China
[2] Fujian Provincial Key Laboratory of Information Processing and Intelligent Control, Minjiang University, Fuzhou 350108, China
twang@mju.edu.cn
[3] The Key Laboratory of Cognitive Computing and Intelligent Information Processing of Fujian Education Institutions, Wuyi University, Wuyishan 354300, China
[4] School of Electronic and Information Engineering, South China University of Technology, Guangzhou 510641, China
eelyliang@scut.edu.cn
[5] Ministry of Education Key Laboratory of Computer Network and Information Integration, Southeast University, Nanjing 211189, China
[6] Guangdong Artificial Intelligence and Digital Economy Laboratory (Pazhou Lab Guangzhou), Guangzhou 510320, China
[7] School of Computer Sciences, University of Sciences (USM), Penang 11800, Malaysia

Abstract. Road obstacle detection is an important problem for vehicle driving safety. In this paper, we aim to obtain robust road obstacle detection based on spatio-temporal context modeling. Firstly, a data-driven spatial context model of the driving scene is constructed with the layouts of the training data. Then, obstacles in the input image are detected via the state-of-the-art object detection algorithms, and the results are combined with the generated scene layout. In addition, to further improve the performance and robustness, temporal information in the image sequence is taken into consideration, and the optical flow is obtained in the vicinity of the detected objects to track the obstacles across neighboring frames. Qualitative and quantitative experiments were conducted on the Small Obstacle Detection (SOD) dataset and the Lost and Found dataset. The results indicate that our method with spatio-temporal context modeling is superior to existing methods for road obstacle detection.

Keywords: Object detection · Road obstacles · Spatio-temporal context · Optical flow

1 Introduction

The performance of object detection algorithms has been significantly improved in recent years, largely due to the success of models based on deep convolutional

Y. Xu et al. (Eds.): ML4CS 2022, LNCS 13655, pp. 213–227, 2023.
https://doi.org/10.1007/978-3-031-20096-0_17

neural networks [1–6]. In addition, object detection algorithms have been widely used in a spectrum of practical application scenarios. Among them, obstacle object detection in road scenes is a crucial ability for self-driving vehicles. If we can detect the obstacle in front of the vehicle ahead of time and maneuver around it, traffic collisions and consequent injuries, death, and property damage can be avoided.

Despite its significance in driving safety, road obstacle detection is much more challenging than generic object detection. Firstly, road obstacles can be very small especially when viewed from distance. This poses challenges to modern deep learning-based object detectors as they usually operate at fixed levels of the spatial pyramid. While we could potentially train specialized detectors for small-scale object detection, these algorithms would require additional computational budget due to the increased feature resolution. In addition, visual cues from road obstacles can be weak or ambiguous due to motion blur, illumination variation, occlusion, etc. This is particularly the case when the objects are either small or distant, or both. As humans, we overcome these difficulties by constantly focusing on road conditions while driving. An experienced driver will even know what kind of obstacles are more likely to appear at which part of the scene, and pay extra attention to these regions accordingly. Therefore, it would be ideal if an object detection method could reason about the presence of obstacles in a similar fashion.

In this work, we aim to improve state-of-the-art road obstacle detectors with spatio-temporal context. For example, by analyzing the spatial context, we can discover that the obstacles are usually located on the road surface and mainly in front of the vehicle. Therefore, we adopt a data-driven approach to extract the location of obstacles and the road layout from training images to build a scene layout model, so that our detector can focus more on the objects on the road surface and eliminate the irrelevant false positives from the background region. In addition, temporal cues are also important for road obstacle detection. Sometimes, an object is detectable in one frame, but will become undetectable in the next frame due to adverse factors such as motion blur, illumination changes, or partial occlusion. Therefore, we could exploit the temporal information in consecutive frames to further assist object detection. Specifically, we use optical flow [7] to transfer object cues from one frame to another. We note that, in our case, the obstacles and the vehicle are both moving while driving. Therefore, when computing the optical flow between the preceding and the following frames, the flow may be too noisy. Therefore, we propose a method based on object region selection, which only calculates the optical flow of the region around the detected objects. This not only removes the complex background, but also reduces the computational complexity. See Fig. 1 for a high-level overview of our method. The contribution of this work is four-fold:

- We propose to integrate spatial and temporal context into state-of-the-art object detection algorithms based on deep learning to improve detection accuracy for road obstacles.

- Based on the spatial context of the obstacles and roads, we construct an interpretable and effective data-driven road scene layout model.
- Based on the temporal context, we track the detected objects via optical flow to assist their detection in the subsequent frames. In particular, we propose an optical flow calculation method based on object region selection.
- We empirically demonstrated the superiority of our method over state-of-the-art object detection methods on the Small Obstacle Detection (SOD) dataset [8] and the Lost and Found dataset [9].

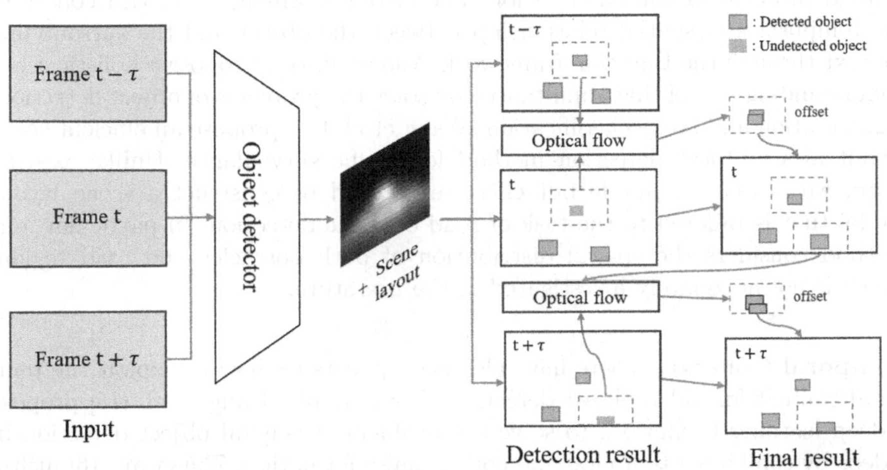

Fig. 1. Overview of our method. Given an input sequence of images, our method first integrates the spatial context by building a scene layout model that reasons about the spatial distribution of obstacles and road region. We then calculate the optical flow of the detected object region in two adjacent frames, so as to obtain the object position offset between them. The spatial and temporal contexts are both integrated into the final detection results.

2 Related Work

Object Detection. State-of-the-art methods for object detection are mainly based on Convolutional Neural Networks (CNNs). On a broad level, these algorithms can be categorized into two-stage detectors and one-stage detectors. The two-stage detectors mainly follow the R-CNN [4] pipeline that includes the object proposal stage and the detection stage. The original R-CNN uses CNNs for object classification on object proposals generated by selective search [10]. However, it is too slow for real-time applications due to the repeated computations of convolutional features for each proposal. Fast R-CNN [11] is faster than R-CNN because it performs feature extraction for object classification only once for all the region proposals. Furthermore, Faster R-CNN [5] combines object proposal and classification into an unified model, so as to improve the efficiency of the network and allow end-to-end training. On the other hand, the YOLO series [1–3] is a classic example of one-stage detectors, which frames object detection as a regression problem. YOLO can directly predict the bounding boxes and the object categories without proposal generation and region refinement, so it is better suited for real-time applications. In this work, we choose Faster RCNN [5] and YOLOv5 [3] as our baseline object detectors and explore how to improve their results with spatio-temporal context.

Spatial Context. Modeling the spatial context for object detection is a well-studied problem in computer vision. For instance, Zhang et al. [12] construct the temporal and spatial relationship between the object and the surrounding context through the Bayesian framework. Yao et al. [13] propose a holistic scene understanding model that simultaneously solve the problems of object detection, segmentation and scene classification. Wang et al. [14] propose an efficient scene layout aware object detection method for traffic surveillance. Unlike existing work, we propose a simple but effective method to construct a scene layout model that is tailored to the task of road obstacle detection. In particular, our method considers the spatial distribution of both obstacles and road region, which is not adequately investigated in the literature.

Temporal Context. There have also been papers on how to exploit the temporal context for video object detection. For example, Kang et al. [15] propose a deep learning framework to solve the problem of general object detection in videos by combining temporal and contextual information. Zhu et al. [16] utilize optical flow to propagate feature across frames to avoid costly feature extraction for non-key frames. Galteri et al. [17] propose a closed-loop framework that uses the object detection results on the previous frame to feed back to the proposal algorithm to improve detection accuracy. Again, our approach differs from these methods as we specifically consider the challenging scenario of road obstacle detection in autonomous driving, and that we propose a method based on object region selection that limits the adverse impact of background noise.

Road Obstacle Detection. In recent years, a lot of work has been done on road obstacle detection. Kyutoku et al. [18] propose a method based on image subtraction, which mainly uses the difference between the road surface region of the present and past in-vehicle camera images to detect obstacles. Levi et al. [19] propose to treat the obstacle detection problem as a column-wise regression problem, and then use CNN to solve it. Leng et al. [20] present a method that utilizes the U-V disparity map and contextual information to detect obstacles. Our work differs from the methods above in the sense that we integrate a cross-image spatial context model of the obstacles and the road into object detection, in addition to the temporal cues between consecutive frames to more accurately detect objects.

3 Method

In this work, we propose a general framework for integrating the spatio-temporal context into object detection, and it works with any object detection algorithm that outputs bounding boxes. Firstly, the object detection results are obtained through the detector, and then a spatial context score is calculated for the position of each bounding box using the scene layout model. This score is combined with the detection to suppress the false positives in the background. Finally, the object is tracked through the optical flow, so as to provide additional support for object hypotheses in frames with weaker visual cues. The overall process is shown in Fig. 1.

More formally, suppose at time t we have an image I_t as input. Let the object hypothesis be $x \in X$, where X is the object pose space. To simplify the notation, we assume each hypothesis is $x = (x_c, b_s, b_r, o)$ where $x_c = (b_x, b_y)$ is the image coordinate location of the object center, $b_s = (b_w, b_h)$ a scale, b_r an aspect ratio and $o \in O$ a target class. Note that each x now implies a bounding box as well. Object detection algorithms define a scoring function $S_D(x)$ for each valid object hypothesis x. For example, in Faster RCNN, this score is usually obtained via a multi-class softmax score on a convolutional feature map f_{CNN},i.e., $S_D(x) = \frac{exp(f_{CNN}(x))}{\sum_{o \in O} exp(f_{CNN}(x))}$. We propose an additional scene layout score $S_L(x)$ for any given object hypothesis x. The final detection score is a weighted sum of the two scores:

$$S(x) = S_D(x) + \theta S_L(x) \tag{1}$$

where θ is a hyperparameter for the relative importance between the two terms.

In addition, as the image of the current frame is I_t, we define the image of the next frame as $I_{(t+\delta)}$. Likewise, for a given object hypothesis x in the current frame, the bounding box generated by optical flow tracking in the next frame is denoted as $x_{(t+\delta)}$. For the bounding box generated by optical flow, we define its scoring function in Eq. 4.

3.1 Scene Layout Construction

We obtain the spatial context information in the road scene by constructing the scene layout, and then use the obtained contextual information to provide regularization to the detection results. For the locations with high probability of obstacles, a higher detection score is given, so as to enhance the confidence of the objects that are difficult to detect on the road. In addition, by modeling the spatial distribution of roads, we can quickly eliminate the false positives outside the road region. Therefore, we build the scene layout based on the spatial distribution of both the obstacles and the road, as outlined below.

Obstacle Distribution. In autonomous driving, the spatial distribution of obstacles shows strong regularity, because we will usually focus on the objects in front of the vehicle as they potentially affect our driving safety. Due to the

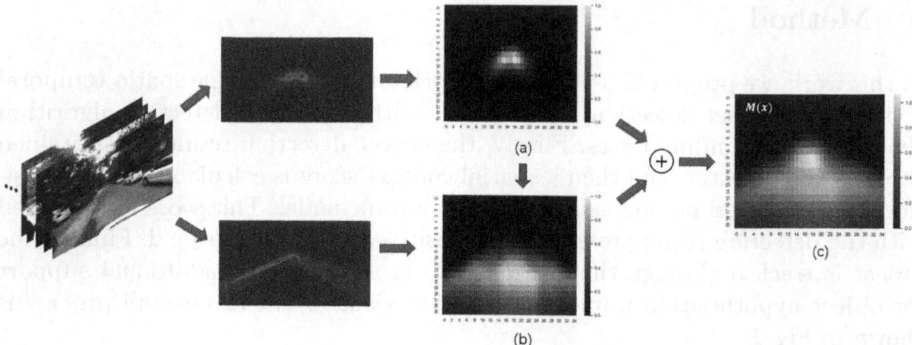

Fig. 2. Scene layout construction. We derive data-driven 2D distributions of obstacles and roads from the training set. (a) Obstacle distribution heat map. (b) Road distribution heat map. (c) The scene layout obtained by combining obstacle distribution and road distribution.

distance of these objects, they may be small and their visual cues may be weak due to motion blur, illumination, or partial occlusion. Therefore, the detector often gives low confidence for these objects and they cannot be reliably detected in practice. To address the above problem, we derive statistics on the distribution of obstacles in the training set. We first obtain all the ground truth bounding boxes in the training set and take all their center points to obtain a 2D spatial distribution in the form of a heat map. The results are shown in Fig. 2 (a). The distribution of obstacles in the image shows a strong regularity, which is mainly concentrated in the center of the image. Therefore, we use this distribution as prior information to regularize the object detection results.

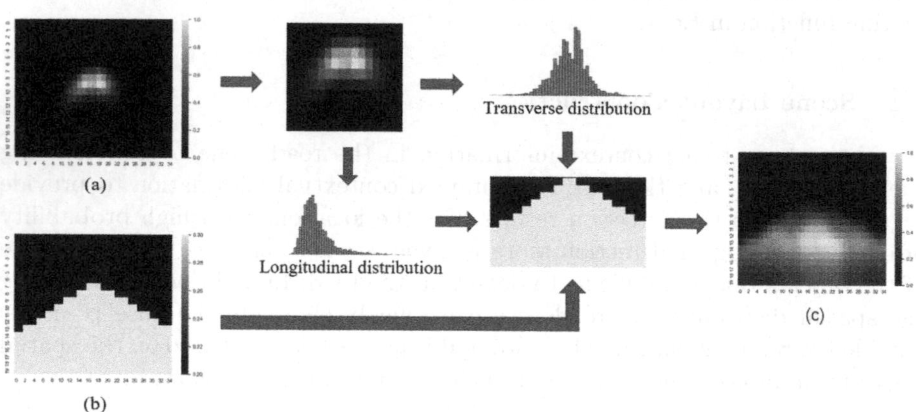

Fig. 3. An example of road distribution. (a) Obstacle distribution heat map. (b) Road region. (c) Road distribution obtained by spreading out the obstacle distribution along transverse and longitudinal directions in the road region.

Road Distribution. In addition, the road distribution is obtained to further assist the construction of the scene layout model, so that the obstacles in the road can be effectively detected, and the false positives outside the road region can be appropriately ignored. We note that both the SOD dataset and the Lost and Found dataset provide road segmentation annotations, so we could easily obtain the road contour in the training set. To obtain the final road contour, we take several points along the road contour in each image to obtain an average road contour across multiple images. Since the obstacle distribution we obtained in the previous step can be unevenly distributed in the road region, here we propose a method to spread out the obstacle distribution to the entire road region. Specifically, according to the distribution of obstacles, different weights are given along the transverse and longitudinal directions in the road region, respectively. The process is illustrated in Fig. 3. It can be seen that for our daily driving scenarios, the road gradually opens up from far to near, and is roughly in the shape of a pyramid. Also, we note that it is possible to design more complex road models for diverse driving scenarios, but the current model is sufficient for the relatively simple road distribution in the datasets we use in this paper.

Scene Layout Aware Detection. The obstacle distribution and road distribution are added up and then normalized to obtain the final scene layout, as shown in Fig. 2 (c). Afterwards, we can generate a score $S_L(x)$ for each object hypothesis x using the scene layout. Then we can combine the score of object hypothesis x obtained from the object detector $S_D(x)$ with the scene layout score $S_L(x)$ to obtain the final score $S(x)$. Specifically, the definition of $S_L(x)$ is as follows:

$$S_L(x) = \begin{cases} -1 & M(x) < 0.15 \\ 0 & 0.15 < M(x) < 0.6 \\ \alpha e^{M(x)} + b & M(x) \geq 0.6 \end{cases} \tag{2}$$

Here $S_L(x)$ is the scene layout score of object x. $M(x)$ is the score based on the location of object x in the scene layout that includes both obstacle and road distributions, α is a variable parameter to adjust the score of the scene layout, and b is a fixed bias value of the scene layout score.

According to Eq. 2, we assume that when the score $M(x) < 0.15$, the object is outside the road distribution, which is considered a false positive. When the score is $0.15 < M(x) < 0.6$, we consider that the object is within the road region but close to the boundary, so there will be no change to the detection score. When the score $M(x) \geq 0.6$, it is considered that the object appears at a position that we are most likely to detect the obstacles, and the score is increased accordingly.

3.2 Obstacle Tracking with Optical Flow

Here, we use the Lucas-Kanade (LK) method [7] to calculate the optical flow between two consecutive frames, and note that other methods may also be used. Specifically, we consider two frames from time t to $t + \delta$, in order to achieve the tracking of the detected objects. In general, LK method is based on the following three assumptions: (1) the brightness of the tracked part of the object in the scene remains basically unchanged; (2) the motion is relatively slow relative to the frame rate; (3) adjacent points on the same surface in a scene should have similar motion. In addition, the image pyramid is introduced to improve its performance. By reducing the size of the image, the moving speed of the object in the image is relatively reduced, so that the object with faster moving speed can be tracked with better quality.

While detecting and tracking road obstacles, the assumptions above may not be met due to constantly changing motion, illumination, partial occlusion, etc. Therefore, instead of calculating the optical flow for the entire scene, we focus on the vicinity where an object is detected. As such, we can eliminate the unnecessary distractions from other parts of the scene, as illustrated in Fig. 4. The specific steps are as follows:

Step1. The detector is used to detect the obstacles, obtain the detection results of the preceding and the following frames, and select the detections with scores $S_D(x) > 0.3$ in the preceding frame.

Step2. To judge whether the detection is missed in the following frame, we define a search area A_r in the following frame by enlarging the detection bounding box of the detected object. The definition of the search area A_r is given as:

$$A_r(x) = (b_x, b_y, \alpha b_w + \tau, \beta b_h + \tau) \tag{3}$$

where α and β are the adjustment coefficients of the selected area width and height respectively. τ represents the initial size of the area. Here, $\alpha > 1$, $\beta > 1$, and $\tau > 0$ as we only enlarge the bounding box to define the search area.

Step3. If the obstacle is missed in the following frame (i.e., no bounding box for the same obstacle category within $A_r(x)$), we crop out the search area given in step 2 in both the preceding and the following frames, and obtain image corners in the cropped area using the Shi-Tomasi corner detection algorithm [21], and select the feature corners located on the detected object.

Step4. The Lucas Kanade optical flow method is then used to track the feature corners in the cropped area, in order to obtain the offset of the feature corners in the two frames before and after.

Step5. We transfer the bounding boxes in the previous frame to the following frame through the obtained offset. Again, this happens only when the obstacle is missed in the following frame.

3.3 Spatio-temporal Aware Detection

Based on the spatial and temporal context modeling above, we combine them in the final inference process. Firstly, the obstacles in the input image are detected

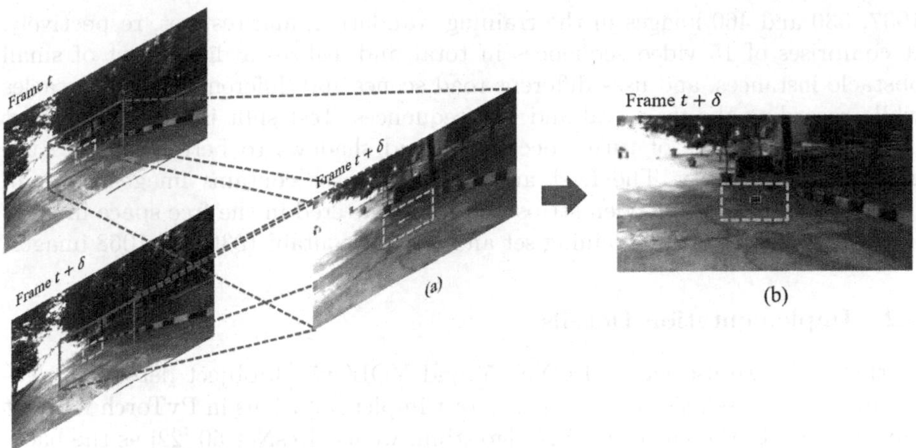

Fig. 4. Obstacle tracking with optical flow. The orange dashed box indicates the object area used to calculate the optical flow of adjacent frames. (a) The yellow and pink lines represent the offset of the object. (b) The blue box indicates the bounding box overlaid from the preceding frame. The green box indicates the bounding box obtained by optical flow tracking in the following frame. Best viewed in electronically, zoomed in.

by the detector, and then the scene layout model is used to process the detection results to remove the incorrect detections outside the road scene distribution, and strengthen the confidence of small or weak obstacles in the road region (see Sect. 3.1.). Secondly, the bounding box of missed detections in the road region is recovered by obstacle tracking and bounding box transfer (see Sect. 3.2). Finally, in order to avoid false positives, we calculate the score of the recovered bounding boxes in combination with the scene layout model. Our final score function is written as follows:

$$S(x_{(t+\delta)}) = S(x) - (\lambda \log M^2(x_{(t+\delta)}) + b) \tag{4}$$

where $S(x_{(t+\delta)})$ is the score function for object $x_{(t+\delta)}$ generated by optical flow tracking. $M(x_{(t+\delta)})$ is the location score of $x_{(t+\delta)}$ in the scene layout (see Sec. 3.1). λ is a variable parameter used to adjust the score of the scene layout model. b is a bias, giving a fixed initial score to the scene layout model. If the score $S(x_{(t+\delta)}) < 0.3$, we treat the recovered bounding box as invalid and remove it.

4 Experiments

4.1 Datasets

Our experiments are carried out on two public datasets: the Small Obstacle Detection (SOD) dataset [8] and the Lost and Found dataset [9], for evaluating the efficacy of the method. There are 2927 images in the SOD dataset, including

1937, 530 and 460 images in the training, validation, and test set, respectively. It comprises of 15 video sequences in total and utilizes a diverse set of small obstacle instances, and uses different road scenes and different sets of obstacles while recording the train, val and test sequences. Test split is kept to be most challenging in terms of turns, occlusions and shadows to better evaluate the generalization ability. The Lost and Found dataset contains images of small items, such as cargo, wooden strips and toys scattered in the free space in front of the car. Among them, training set and test set contain 1036 and 1068 images.

4.2 Implementation Details

In this work, we use Faster RCNN [5] and YOLOv5 [3] object detection algorithms as our baselines. We use their latest implementations in PyTorch without any changes. In the Faster RCNN algorithm, we use ResNet-50 [22] as the backbone network, SGD as the optimizer, and use a minibatch size of 8. A total of 30 epochs were trained. The learning rate starts from 0.006, and the learning rate decreases to one-third of the original every 5 epochs. We also use the ImageNet [23] pre-trained model for network initialization. In addition, we use feature pyramid networks (FPN) [24] in order to learn high quality multi-scale feature representations. In the YOLOv5 algorithm, we use the yolov5l6 network structure, and use the MS-COCO [25] pre-trained model to initialize the network weight. SGD is used as the optimizer, and the minibatch size is set to 8. A total of 100 epochs are trained, and the epoch with the best validation results is selected. In addition, for the search area in Eq. 3, we set $\alpha = 2$, $\beta = 3$, $\tau = 30$ and $\tau = 40$ for SOD and Lost and Found, respectively.

4.3 Experimental Results

Metrics. Following common practice [25,26], we use average precision (AP) to evaluate the detection algorithm. Specifically, true positives (TP) represent the number of positive objects correctly detected, false positives (FP) represent the number of background regions incorrectly marked as objects, false negatives (FN) represent the number of positive objects not detected, and recall and precision are calculated according to Eqs. 5 and 6.

$$Recall = \frac{TP}{TP + FN} \tag{5}$$

$$Precision = \frac{TP}{TP + FP} \tag{6}$$

Given recall and precision at varying detection score thresholds, we could plot the precision-recall curve of the test results, and the average accuracy (AP) represents the area between the curve and the coordinate axes. In addition, we evaluate results computed at varying Intersection over Union (IoU) [26] thresholds, i.e., AP values at 50%, 75% IoU and the average of AP from 50% to 95% IoU (at 5% IoU interval) as the evaluation metrics.

Results. Taking Faster RCNN and YOLOv5 as our baselines, the experimental results obtained by adding the scene layout model (SL), the obstacle tracking with optical flow (OF) and the combination of the two methods are shown in Table 1.

Table 1. The ablation study on SOD dataset. **SL:** Scene layout. **OF:** Optical flow tracking. Note that our method improves performance both the Faster RCNN and the YOLOv5 baselines.

Method	AP_{50}	AP_{75}	AP	AP_S	AP_M	AP_L
Faster RCNN	48.4	21.8	24.6	22.8	57.3	23.3
Faster RCNN+SL	50.9	**22.2**	25.3	23.1	59.9	23.3
Faster RCNN+OF	49.8	22.0	25.0	23.0	57.5	23.3
Faster RCNN+SL+OF	**52.6**	22.1	**25.7**	**23.4**	**60.1**	**23.3**
YOLOv5	57.8	27.7	30.7	29.3	57.7	27.3
YOLOv5+SL	58.3	27.8	30.9	29.2	57.9	27.1
YOLOv5+OF	58.9	**27.9**	31.1	29.4	**58.2**	**28.9**
YOLOv5+SL+OF	**59.4**	27.7	**31.2**	**29.6**	58.1	27.9

Taking AP_{50} as an example, the average precision is increased by 2.5% and 1.4% when the scene layout (SL) model and object tracking with optical flow (OF) method are used separately with Faster RCNN, which demonstrates the efficacy of the two methods. Combining these two methods provides a significant improvement by 4.2%. For YOLOv5, the scene layout model provides a modest improvement of 0.5%. However, object tracking with optical flow provides a considerable improvement of 1.1%. Combining these two methods provides the largest improvement of 1.6%. We also present some qualitative results in Fig. 5, which clearly show that our method is able to eliminate false positives while being able to detect distant obstacles with weak visual support.

In addition, due to the much larger time interval between adjacent image frames in the Lost and Found dataset, the temporal smoothness between two adjacent frames is poor. Therefore, in this dataset, we only use the scene layout model. The quantitative results we obtained are summarized in Table 2. It can be seen that AP_{50} is increased by 0.9% when the scene layout model is used. We also show some qualitative results in Fig. 6, demonstrating the ability of our method to remove false positives, while boosting the scores of obstacles in the scene layout detected by Faster RCNN.

Table 2. Results with and without scene layout model on Lost and Found dataset.

Method	AP_{50}	AP_{75}	AP	AP_S	AP_M	AP_L
Faster RCNN	65.4	39.9	38.3	28.7	52.0	67.0
Faster RCNN+SL	**66.3**	**40.4**	**38.7**	**28.8**	**52.7**	**67.9**

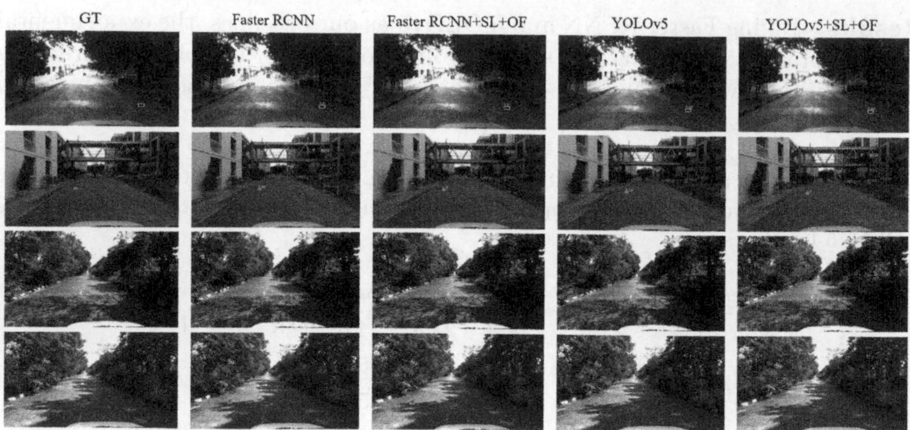

Fig. 5. Example detection results on the test set of the SOD dataset. Columns: **GT:** Input image with ground-truths overlaid. **Faster RCNN:** Detections with Faster RCNN. **Faster RCNN+SL+OF:** Detections with Faster RCNN+Scene Layout+Optical Flow. **YOLOv5:** Detections with YOLOv5. **YOLOv5+SL+OF:** Detections with YOLOv5+Scene Layout+Optical Flow. Red boxes are false positives, green boxes are true positives. Detection score threshold is 0.05. Best viewed electronically, zoomed in.

Fig. 6. Example detection results on the test set of the Lost and Found dataset. Columns: **GT:** Input image with ground-truths overlaid. **Faster RCNN:** Detections with Faster RCNN. **Faster RCNN+SL:** Detections with Faster RCNN+Scene Layout. Red boxes are false positives, green boxes are true positives. Detection score threshold is 0.05. Best viewed electronically, zoomed in.

The computational efficiency of our method is also acceptable for practical applications. Taking the baseline Faster RCNN algorithm on SOD dataset as an example, the average inference time per image is about 61 ms on a single nVIDIA RTX 3080 Ti. The inference time does not change when we introduce the spatial context, as the parameters in the scene layout model can be calculated in advance and used directly in the inference phase. Then, with the optical flow tracking added, the processing time increases to 89 ms per image. It should be noted that because we adopt the optical flow calculation method based on region selection to eliminate unnecessary computations in a large part of the image, the additional computational budget for the temporal context is reduced to only 28 ms per image.

Based on the analysis above, both the spatial context and the temporal context improve final detection performance when used alone, and their combination produces the best detection results. These results validate the efficacy of the proposed method.

5 Conclusion

In this paper, we proposed a novel method to detect road obstacles by integrating the spatial and temporal context. Specifically, we derive the spatial distribution of obstacles and the road with a data-driven approach to build a scene layout model, and propose an obstacle tracking method based on optical flow and object region selection to encode temporal smoothness while suppressing the adverse impact of background noise. Our experiments show significant improvements in object detection accuracy compared to state-of-the-art baseline detectors. As a general framework for spatio-temporal context modeling, our method can work with other object detection algorithms not mentioned in this paper. In the future, we plan to further integrate spatio-temporal context modeling into deep models to allow for end-to-end training of a unified model.

Acknowledgment. This work is partially supported by NSFC (61972187, 61703195), Fujian NSF (2022J011112, 2020J02024), the Open Program of The Key Laboratory of Cognitive Computing and Intelligent Information Processing of Fujian Education Institutions, Wuyi University (KLCCIIP2020202), and the Research Startup Fund of Minjiang University (MJY19021). Lingyu Liang is supported by Science and Technology Program of Guangzhou (202102020692), the Open Fund of Ministry of Education Key Laboratory of Computer Network and Information Integration (Southeast University) (K93-9-2021-01), the Open Fund of Fujian Provincial Key Laboratory of Information Processing and Intelligent Control (Minjiang University) (MJUKF-IPIC202102), Guangdong NSF (2019A1515011045) and CAAI-Huawei MindSpore Open Fund.

References

1. Redmon, J., Divvala, S., Girshick, R., Farhadi, A.: You only look once: unified, real-time object detection. In: Proceedings of the IEEE Conference on Computer Vision and Pattern Recognition, pp. 779–788 (2016)

2. Redmon, J., Farhadi, A.: Yolo9000: better, faster, stronger. In: IEEE Conference on Computer Vision & Pattern Recognition, pp. 6517–6525 (2017)
3. Jocher, G., et al.: ultralytics/yolov5: v5. 0-yolov5-p6 1280 models aws supervise. ly and youtube integrations. Zenodo 11 (2021)
4. Girshick, R., Donahue, J., Darrell, T., Malik, J.: Rich feature hierarchies for accurate object detection and semantic segmentation. In: Proceedings of the IEEE Conference on Computer Vision and Pattern Recognition, pp. 580–587 (2014)
5. Ren, S., He, K., Girshick, R., Sun, J.: Faster r-cnn: Towards real-time object detection with region proposal networks. Adv. Neural Inf. Process. Syst. **28** (2015)
6. Cai, Z., Vasconcelos, N.: Cascade r-cnn: delving into high quality object detection. In: Proceedings of the IEEE Conference on Computer Vision and Pattern Recognition, pp. 6154–6162 (2018)
7. Bouguet, J.Y., et al.: Pyramidal implementation of the affine lucas kanade feature tracker description of the algorithm. Intel Corpor. **5**(1–10), 4 (2001)
8. Singh, A., Kamireddypalli, A., Gandhi, V., Krishna, K.M.: Lidar guided small obstacle segmentation. In: 2020 IEEE/RSJ International Conference on Intelligent Robots and Systems (IROS), pp. 8513–8520. IEEE (2020)
9. Pinggera, P., Ramos, S., Gehrig, S., Franke, U., Rother, C., Mester, R.: Lost and found: detecting small road hazards for self-driving vehicles. In: 2016 IEEE/RSJ International Conference on Intelligent Robots and Systems (IROS), pp. 1099–1106. IEEE (2016)
10. Uijlings, J.R., Van De Sande, K.E., Gevers, T., Smeulders, A.W.: Selective search for object recognition. Int. J. Comput. Vis. **104**(2), 154–171 (2013)
11. Girshick, R.: Fast r-cnn. In: Proceedings of the IEEE International Conference on Computer Vision, pp. 1440–1448 (2015)
12. Zhang, K., Zhang, L., Liu, Q., Zhang, D., Yang, M.-H.: Fast visual tracking via dense spatio-temporal context learning. In: Fleet, D., Pajdla, T., Schiele, B., Tuytelaars, T. (eds.) ECCV 2014. LNCS, vol. 8693, pp. 127–141. Springer, Cham (2014). https://doi.org/10.1007/978-3-319-10602-1_9
13. Yao, J., Fidler, S., Urtasun, R.: Describing the scene as a whole: Joint object detection, scene classification and semantic segmentation. In: 2012 IEEE Conference on Computer Vision and Pattern Recognition, pp. 702–709. IEEE (2012)
14. Wang, T., He, X., Su, S., Guan, Y.: Efficient scene layout aware object detection for traffic surveillance. In: Proceedings of the IEEE Conference on Computer Vision and Pattern Recognition Workshops, pp. 53–60 (2017)
15. Kang, K., et al.: T-cnn: tubelets with convolutional neural networks for object detection from videos. IEEE Trans. Circ. Syst. Video Technol. **28**(10), 2896–2907 (2017)
16. Zhu, X., Xiong, Y., Dai, J., Yuan, L., Wei, Y.: Deep feature flow for video recognition. In: Proceedings of the IEEE Conference on Computer Vision and Pattern Recognition, pp. 2349–2358 (2017)
17. Galteri, L., Seidenari, L., Bertini, M., Del Bimbo, A.: Spatio-temporal closed-loop object detection. IEEE Trans. Image Process. **26**(3), 1253–1263 (2017)
18. Kyutoku, H., Takahashi, T., Mekada, Y., Ide, I., Murase, H.: On-road obstacle detection by comparing present and past in-vehicle camera images. In: MVA, pp. 357–360. Citeseer (2011)
19. Levi, D., Garnett, N., Fetaya, E., Herzlyia, I.: Stixelnet: A deep convolutional network for obstacle detection and road segmentation. In: BMVC, vol. 1, p. 4 (2015)

20. Leng, J., Liu, Y., Du, D., Zhang, T., Quan, P.: Robust obstacle detection and recognition for driver assistance systems. IEEE Trans. Intell. Transp. Syst. **21**(4), 1560–1571 (2019)
21. Tommasini, T., Fusiello, A., Trucco, E., Roberto, V.: Making good features track better. In: Proceedings. 1998 IEEE Computer Society Conference on Computer Vision and Pattern Recognition (Cat. No. 98CB36231), pp. 178–183. IEEE (1998)
22. He, K., Zhang, X., Ren, S., Sun, J.: Deep residual learning for image recognition. In: Proceedings of the IEEE Conference on Computer Vision and Pattern Recognition, pp. 770–778 (2016)
23. Deng, J., Dong, W., Socher, R., Li, L.J., Li, K., Fei-Fei, L.: Imagenet: a large-scale hierarchical image database. In: 2009 IEEE Conference on Computer Vision and Pattern Recognition, pp. 248–255. IEEE(2009)
24. Lin, T.Y., Dollár, P., Girshick, R., He, K., Hariharan, B., Belongie, S.: Feature pyramid networks for object detection. In: Proceedings of the IEEE Conference on Computer Vision and Pattern Recognition, pp. 2117–2125 (2017)
25. Lin, T.Y., et al.: Microsoft COCO: common objects in context. In: Fleet, D., Pajdla, T., Schiele, B., Tuytelaars, T. (eds.) ECCV 2014. LNCS, vol. 8693, pp. 740–755. Springer, Cham (2014). https://doi.org/10.1007/978-3-319-10602-1_48
26. Everingham, M., Van Gool, L., Williams, C.K., Winn, J., Zisserman, A.: The pascal visual object classes (voc) challenge. Int. J. Comput. Vis. **88**(2), 303–338 (2010)

A Survey of Android Malware Detection Based on Deep Learning

Dianxin Wang(✉), Tian Chen, Zheng Zhang, and Nan Zhang(✉)

Beijing Institute of Technology, Beijing 100081, China
{dianxinw,chentian20,zhangzheng}@bit.edu.cn, nanzhang611@126.com

Abstract. Android malware poses a serious threat to cyberspace security, and many researchers are committed to researching fast and effective methods for Android malware detection. However, the latest Android malware usually uses escape techniques such as code obfuscation, so the traditional machine learning methods gradually become invalid. In recent years, deep learning has been gradually applied in the field of Android malware detection due to its powerful data processing and feature representation capabilities, and has achieved convincing performance. This paper conducts a review and research on the related achievements of Android malware detection based on deep learning in recent years, and classifies Android malware detection methods according to different characteristics and different networks. At the same time, a systematic introduction on deep learning model algorithms, such as RNN, CNN, Attention Mechanism, etc., is made. Besides, we analyze most commonly used datasets and evaluation indicators. The outcomes of this paper can provide a more comprehensive overview for researchers in the field, aiming to inspire researchers to make more and better achievements in Android malware detection.

Keywords: Malware detection · Android system · Deep learning · Neural network

1 Introduction

The open source of the Android operating system has brought a large number of users, thus making the Android system occupies the vast majority of the intelligent systems marketing, while it comes a large number of malicious code attacks against the Android platform. Since February 2022, researchers have found a 500% surge in the spread of mobile malware in Europe, and the vast majority come from Android devices. There are a wide variety of Android malware, which brings a huge threat to user privacy, financial security and many other aspects. Therefore, it is an urgent and challenging task to propose an efficient method to detect Android malware.

In recent years, researchers have initially proposed the use of machine learning methods for Android malware detection, and achieved quite good results

Y. Xu et al. (Eds.): ML4CS 2022, LNCS 13655, pp. 228–242, 2023.
https://doi.org/10.1007/978-3-031-20096-0_18

[1–4]. Deep learning is a branch of machine learning and has shown strong development potential in many fields. Unlike traditional machine learning, deep learning methods can automatically extract feature when inputting raw data, and can learn feature representations from raw data with almost no priori. In 2014, deep learning tools were first applied to Android malware detection and demonstrated excellent performance [5]. Subsequently, more and more researchers have developed Android malware detection models or frameworks based on various deep learning algorithms.

This paper studies the state-of-art Android malware detection based on deep learning, and makes a useful exploration for the application of deep learning technology in the field of Android malware detection. It will provide reference for the security protection of mobile terminal equipment and promote the development of mobile security and information security.

The main contributions of this paper are: a. From different perspectives, we analyze and summarize the latest research results of Android malware detection methods, based on different characteristics and different networks. b. We compare and analyze the commonly used datasets and evaluation indicators of malware detection in an intuitive way.

The structure of this paper is as follows. Section 1 introduces the research background and necessity of Android malware detection based on deep learning, as well as the main contributions of this paper. Section 2 introduces the background knowledge of malware detection, including the main structure of Android applications, the main deep learning model algorithms and the process of Android malware detection based on deep learning. Section 3 analyzes and summarizes the latest research results of Android malware detection methods in recent years, based on different characteristics and different network classification methods. Section 4 compares and analyzes a variety of commonly used malware detection datasets. Section 5 introduces the current commonly used evaluation indicators system in malware model detection. Section 6 summarizes the main research content and results of this paper.

2 Android Malware Detection Based on Deep Learning

2.1 Android Application Structure

Android application package(APK) are developed by Java language, and the Java bytecode is compiled into the classes.dex (Dalvik Executable, DEX) file, which contains all Dalvik bytecodes and other possible .jar files from third-party libraries. The file is packaged together with the Manifest, resource files and generate to the APK file finally. We divide these resource files into 3 parts, AndroidManifest.xml, Classes.dex and others.

AndroidManifest.xml is a file in XML format that stores data such as package name, required permissions, one or more parts definition, min and max versions supported and link libraries etc.

Classes.dex is an executable file that stores Dalvik bytecode that can be executed on the Dalvik Virtual Machine (DVM). The .smali file and .jar file can be obtained by decompiling the classed.dex file. Features such as String and API calls can be extracted from the .smali file, and the java source code can be obtained from the .jar file after further decompiling.

Others assets/ contains the App's assets. **META-INF/** contains the signing and authentication of the APK. **lib/** stores the compiled native library, suffixed with .so. **res/** includes resource documents that are not compiled into resources.arsc. **resource.arsc** is the compiled binary resource file.

2.2 Deep Learning Model Algorithms

TextCNN. TextCNN [6] is a text classification model proposed by Kim in 2014 based on changes to the input of the convolutional neural network. There is no difference between TextCNN and the traditional CNN model. Its model structure mainly includes 4 layers: input layer, convolution layer, maximum pooling layer and softmax output layer. In this model, each input sequence is a k-dimensional vector (padded if necessary), and each input comes as a series of n sequences; thus each input is a feature map of $n \times k$ dimensions. After this, a max-timeout pooling operation is applied on the feature map, taking the feature corresponding to the filter with the highest value, which aims at capturing the most important features.

RNN. The traditional neural network is usually a top-down hierarchical network structure. The information flow can only be transmitted from top to bottom along the network structure, thus, it cannot remember some important previous information. To solve this problem, Recursive Neural Network (RNN) came into being. It has a cyclic network structure, which can maintain a certain amount of memory for contextual information and memorize the more important content learned before, but the RNN network has a serious long-term dependence problem, that is, when the input sequence interval is long, the RNN is difficult to connect to the relevant information.

LSTM. Long short-term memory (LSTM) network [7] refers to a special recurrent neural network architecture whose appearance improves the long-term dependency problem of RNN networks. An LSTM network contains forget gate layer, input gate layer, output gate layer, and neuron state. The forget gate layer decides which information to be discarded and sends the remaining information to the neurons; the input gate layer decides which information to be saved in the input to the neuron; the output gate layer determines the output information based on the current state of the neuron.

Attention Mechanism. Attention Mechanism was proposed in the literature [8] in 2014, which is a major breakthrough in the field of deep learning. It originated from the study of human vision, and it has been widely used in machine learning applications such as machine translation, sentiment classification, automatic summarization, automatic question answering, and dependency analysis. Suppose $X = [X_1, X_2, ..., X_N]$, which means N input information. In consideration of saving computing resources, it has no necessary to let the neural network process all N input information, but only need to pay attention on those related to the task.

2.3 Android Malware Detection Process Based on Deep Learning

Android malware detection based on deep learning mainly includes two stages: training and detection. In the training phase, first perform feature extraction, then obtain the features of all samples and input them to the model for training, and finally output the trained model file. In the detection phase, extract the unknown samples' same features as the training phase, and then input them into the trained classification. The detector obtains the final detection result to determine whether the sample is malicious or benign.

3 Research Progress

With the improvement and development of deep learning technology theory, researchers gradually use deep learning methods to detect Android malware. For the convenience of research, we classify and summarize the existing Android malware schemes based on different characteristics and different networks.

3.1 Android Malware Detection Based on Different Characteristics

Deep learning-based detection can generally be divided into three methods according to the different characteristics used: static analysis, dynamic analysis, and hybrid analysis, as shown in Fig. 1. Static analysis does not require running code, and has the advantages of low computing cost and low power consumption. However, it cannot identify applications that spread malicious behaviors through obfuscated code and dynamic loading etc. Dynamic detection technology aims to identify malicious behavior by running applications, which can detect the dynamic loading process in the running of the program and record the behavior of the program, but it has the problems of high resource consumption and low code coverage. The hybrid analysis combines the advantages of both.

Static Analysis. Analyzing the existing Android malware detection methods based on static features comprehensively, it can be divided into feature-based detection, API call-based detection, Opcode call-based detection, binary code-based detection, graph network-based detection and meta information-based detection. Then we introduce them in detail.

Permission-Based Android Malware Detection. Permissions are a security mechanism proposed by Google for component access between applications and to restrict some security-sensitive items within applications. Therefore, researchers often use permissions as a feature to detect Android malware [9–12]. MADFU [13] is a new method to detect Android malware based on feature uncertainty.

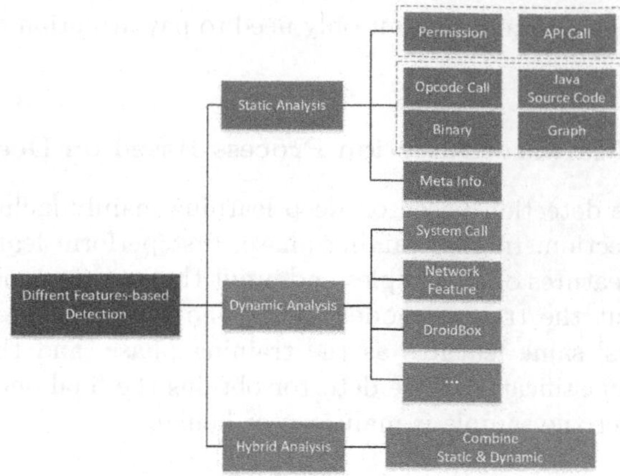

Fig. 1. Android malware detection based on different characteristics

MADFU extracts 24 dangerous permissions from the application, and then uses the MCMC algorithm to calculate the uncertainty value of permissions in malicious APP detection. Finally, classification is based on the permissions that contributed more. Booz et al.

API Calls-Based Android Malware Detection. Malware detection based on API behavior analysis extracts the sequence of API calls of executable programs through reverse engineering, and extracts features from statistical representations or dependencies of API calls. Li et al. [14] from Tsinghua University developed a deep neural network-based system that applies static features such as required permissions and API calls, to train a model to classify Android malware from benign malware. The experiments on Drebin achieves an F1-Score of 95.64%. Reference [15] is the first attempt to build a malware detection system for Android using CNN. The authors use sequences of API calls as features and use CNNs and long short-term memory (LSTM) models to accomplish classification tasks. Experiments show that this method outperforms traditional methods based on N-grams. Hou et al. [16,17] extracted API calls from the smali code of the application and assigned the extracted API calls belonging to the same method into one block as a feature. MalDozer [18] uses the sequence of the original API method as static features, and uses deep learning methods to identify malicious samples and attribute their families. Large-scale experiments show that MalDozer is efficient in malware detection.

Opcode Call-Based Android Malware Detection. Malware detection based on opcode semantic analysis extracts the opcode sequence of the executable program through disassembly, and then characterizes it and extracts features. Finally, it uses the deep learning methods to detect the opcode features of the malware. Previous work [19–24] has demonstrated that the semantic information contained in opcode can also be used as a feature to detect Android malware. To classify the Android malware family efficiently, the authors [25] use sensitive opcode sequences, such as opcodes, sensitive APIs, STRs, and operations. Additionally, oversampling techniques are used to improve efficiency. Experiment result has high accuracy and AUC. Millar et al. [26] propose DANdroid, which is a mobile malware detection model that uses deep learning to classify applications. DANdroid utilizes opcodes, permissions and API calls. The experiment on Drebin shows that the F1-Score using the CNN algorithm is as high as 97.3%. Op2Vec [27] proposes the first state-of-the-art dataset for end-to-end Android malware detection.

Java Source Code-Based Android Malware Detection. Reference [28] uses code cloning technology to detect Android malware. This method uses NiCad tool for code cloning as a signature, and then finds similar malware in other malicious code, and achieves a detection accuracy rate as high as 96.88%. ROCKY [29] adopts NLP technique to analyze the decompiled source code, it defines three types of tokens by frequency, and utilizes the common token sequence to train the classifier. ANDRE [30] is a novel weakly labeled malware clustering method that combines Virustotal's AV vendors raw labels, code similarity, and metadata information to learn source code representations.

Binary-Based Android Malware Detection. IMCFN [31] converts raw binary files of malware to color images, a fine-tuned CNN architecture is used to detect and identify malware families. The main setup in MDMC [32] is to convert malware binary files to Markov images according to the byte transfer probability matrix, and then use deep convolutional neural networks for Markov image classification. DexRay [33] converts the DEX files' bytecode of application into grayscale "vector" images and feeds them to a 1D convolutional neural network model. Reference [34] uses a CNN network to learn the features of malware directly from Dalvik bytecode, and achieves a detection accuracy of 93%.

Graph Network-Based Android Malware Detection. Malware detection based on control flow and data flow analysis uses reverse technology to extract the opcodes and behaviors of executable programs, and builds Data Flow Graphs (DFG) and Control Flow Graphs (CFG) according to the input/output relationship and calling relationship between operations and behaviors. In addition to these two graphs, there are other graphs such as Program Dependency Graph (PDG) and Code Property Graph (CPG). Reference proposes an extended version of the CDGDroid [35] method, which uses the combination of CFG and DFG as features, uses graph embedding technology to encode graphs into vectors, and finally uses deep learning methods to complete malware detection and family classification. The detection performance exceeds Drebin, CDGDroid and some other detection methods. GDroid [36] is the first study to explore the application of graph neural networks in the field of malware classification, they map Apps and APIs to a large heterogeneous network, and then transform the original malware classification problem into a node classification problem. Experiments show that GDroid can effectively achieve to the highest detection accuracy of 98.99%, and the false positive rate is less than 1%, which is better than existing methods. FamDroid [37] uses general static features combined with API relational network as new features, and then designs an adaptive weighted integration classifier. It achieves the purpose of accurate malware family classification.

Meta Information-Based Android Malware Detection. Reference [38] proposes and develops a novel semantic-perception method that can improve the accuracy of identifying malicious mobile applications in large-scale datasets and effectively reduce the analytical processing runtime. DeepIntent [39] synergistically combines program analysis and deep learning to detect intent-behavior differences in mobile applications. Applying a parallel co-attention mechanism, it combines icons with the context of icon widgets, and detects the intention. The technique can find behavioral differences by calculating and summarizing the abnormal scores for each permission used by the icon widget.

Dynamic Analysis. Dynamic features are mainly analyzed based on system call, network traffic, CPU, battery information, data network, system resource, user interaction, process reporting and other features. In addition, dynamic analysis tools such as DroidBox are also commonly used to extract features. Among these, the most commonly used one is system call analysis. Although network traffic analysis is effective in Android malware detection, it requires a large number of datasets for analysis and processing, and requires in-depth familiarity with network architecture, so it is not sought after by researchers. Additionally, there are not many useful features that can be extracted, such as CPU data and battery information, so they are often used as assistant methods.

Ananya et al. propose Sysdroid [40], a system call-based dynamic analysis method and a new feature selection method to improve the performance of the classifier. Experimental results on different classifiers show that the accuracy is between 95% and 99%. De-LADY [41] is an efficient framework based on recording dynamic behavior logs. Experiments including 13,533 applications from different categories show that the accuracy is 98.08% and the F-measure is 98.84%. SeqMobile [42] achieves a detection accuracy of 97.85% using a method combining dynamic sequence features with a customized deep neural network on various Android devices. The authors [43] treat system calls as sequences of natural language in order to extract semantic information. Based on the similarity scores, two LSTM models are trained to classify unknown applications. Reference [44] uses dynamic analysis for the first time to extract features such as system calls, network traffic, and request permissions during application running, and then extracts features of application components through static analysis. The final detection accuracy reaches to 95% through DNN. Reference [45] designes a two-layer classification model, in which the second layer uses a deep learning model based on CACNN to detect the network traffic characteristics of Android samples. MEGDroid [46] is a novel model-driven framework to generate events for dynamic analysis of Android malware.

Hybrid Analysis. DroidDetector [47] is a deep learning based Android malware detection engine. About 192 features are obtained from dynamic and static application analysis to distinguish benign and malware applications. The tool claims to achieve a detection accuracy of 96.76%, which is much higher than traditional machine learning techniques. Xu et al. [48] proposes HADM, the features extracted during static analysis are transformed into vector-based representations, while the features extracted during dynamic analysis are transformed into vector-based and graph-based representations. Deep learning techniques are used to train a neural network for each vector set. Finally, a hierarchical multi-kernel learning technique is applied to combine the different kernel learning results of different features to improve the classification accuracy. According to the authors, their model is too weak to fight against code obfuscation techniques because dynamic analysis is guided by the results obtained by static analysis. eDSDroid [49] uses static and dynamic analysis to identify malware which targeting the communication between applications. Specifically, in the first stage, static analysis detects information leakage, while dynamic analysis is used to help eliminate false positives in the first stage. The disadvantageous is that their method has only been evaluated on a small corpus of applications. DL-Droid [50] is an automated dynamic analysis framework employing deep learning. Within experiments on over 30,000 applications on real devices, the results show that DL-Droid can achieve better performance when only dynamic features and mixed features are used.

3.2 Android Malware Detection Based on Different Networks

Deep learning is a branch of machine learning. The Android malware detection based on deep learning are mainly divided into different detection methods based on CNN, RNN/LSTM, DBN, AE network and other networks.

CNN Based Android Malware Detection. Reference [51] selects malware-related API features and explores the structural relationship between these APIs, and then maps them to a matrix as the API-based input feature map for training a CNN-based classifier. Zhao et al. [52] from Northeastern University propose and evaluate a deep CNN-based offline tool that uses opcode sequences as application features to improve the security of Android systems. The authors of [53] use raw opcode sequences originating from Android applications as features, and traditional neural networks are used to detect Android malware. ByteDroid [54] is a CNN-based automatic Android malware detection system that can automatically learn malware features. It performs well in unknown samples and can resist many popular obfuscation techniques. Liang et al. [55] treat the sequence of system calls as text processing, then use a CNN to train this feature and achieve a detection accuracy of 93.16%.

RNN Based Android Malware Detection. Reference [56] uses a recurrent LSTM layer to convert Android permission sequences into features through word embeddings, which are used to capture the semantic knowledge of Android application permission sequences in a high-dimensional embedding feature space. Reference [57] compares the ability of RNN network and LSTM network to detect Android malware. The features are extracted under the static and dynamic methods respectively. The final results show that the LSTM model outperforms the RNN model in the setting of 5-fold cross-validation. Reference [58] designs an Android malware detection model based on LSTM model, which uses one-hot for feature encoding and ADAM optimizer for 1000 rounds of training. The experimental results show that it achieves a maximum detection accuracy of 95.3% under a large number of sample data sets. Reference [59] creates an activity sequence according to the time sequence of the target application, which contains API calls and internal function calls etc. The LSTM model achieves an F1-score of 98.5%.

DBN Based Android Malware Detection. Droid-sec [5] is the first deep learning-based Android malware detection method, which uses hybrid analysis based on DBN to detect Android malware. The evaluation shows that Droid-sec achieves 96% detection accuracy. DroidDeep [60] first extracts five different types of static features from different numbers of applications. The DBN model is used to learn features, and finally the SVM algorithm is used to classify these samples. According to the results, the accuracy of DroidDeep reaches 99.4%, and the detection performance exceeds that of two traditional machine learning models, DroidAPIMiner and Fest [61]. A new version of DroidDeep [62] improves detection performance. DroidVecDeep [63] uses static analysis to extract various features such as permissions and sensitive API calls, and uses Random Forest (RF) [64] for dimensionality reduction and feature selection and finally uses word2vec to convert these features into numerical vectors and uses DBN network to complete classification.

AE Network Based Android Malware Detection. Reference [65] proposes a deep AE network with two hidden layers, and experiments improve that the F1-score and recall values of this method are 64.3% and 93% respectively. These results outperform three other baseline models-the first logistic regression model trained directly on the original feature set, the second model proposed in [66], and the third CNN model proposed in [67]. Hou et al. [68] propose an Android malware detection system named Deep4MalDroid, which uses the Linux kernel system call graph as features. Finally, it achieves 93.68% classification accuracy under experiments on a dataset containing 3000 applications using stacked autoencoders as classifiers.

Other Network Models Based Android Malware Detection. A CNN-based fusion model is proposed in reference [69], which uses multiple feature types for Android malware detection. Due to the different types of information presented in different features, each sub-model is trained separately. Each sub-model is a CNN network that captures important information for a specific feature type. Unfortunately, the interpretability of the proposed fusion CNN model is poor. A hybrid Android malware detection model consisting of CNN and deep AE is proposed in reference [70] to ensure high accuracy and good efficiency. That is, employing multiple CNNs and deep AEs can guarantee high detection accuracy and model efficiency respectively. Reference [71] is the first deep learning-based multimodal approach. The authors define two new efficient feature representation methods.

4 Datasets Analysis

This section mainly introduces the commonly used datasets for Android malware detection, as shown in Table 1.

Table 1. Dataset analysis

Datasets	Main characteristic
Drebin	Provided by MobileSandbox project, 5560 Apps, 179 malware families, 2010–2012
AndroZoo	Includ GooglePlay App market, contains 5,781,781 different APKs
Kharon	A set of fully reversed and documented malware, help evaluate research experiments
Android Malware Dataset (AMD)	Contains 24,553 samples, 71 malware families, 2010–2016
AndroidMalGenome	Over 1200 malware samples, 2010–2011, cover most Android malware families
PRAGuard	Obfuscate MalGenomeand Con-tagio Minidump datasets, contains 10,479 samples
DroidCollector	Provides .apk (8,000 benign and 8,860 malware) and .pcap files, has research articles

5 Evaluation Indicators

The main indicators used to evaluate the Android malware detection performance of the deep learning model are the detection accuracy rate (Accuracy), the detection precision rate (Precision), the detection recall rate (Recall), the F1 value (F1-score), AUC (Area Under Curve) and ROC curve (Receiver Operating Characteristic Curve), as shown in Table 2.

Table 2. Evaluation indicators

Indicators	Defination
True Positive(TP)	Number of malware identified correctly
True Negative(TN)	Number of benign classified correctly
False Positive(FP)	Number of benign misclassified as malware
Frue Negative(FN)	Number of malware misidentified as benign
Accuracy	$Accuracy = \frac{TP+TN}{TP+FP+TN+FN}$
Precision	$Precision = \frac{TP}{TP+FP}$
Recall	$Recall = \frac{TP}{TP+FN}$
F1-score	$F1 - score = 2 \times \frac{Precision \times Recall}{Precision + Recall}$
FPR	$FPR = \frac{FP}{FP+TN}$
TPR	$TPR = \frac{TP}{TP+FN}$
AUC	$AUC = \frac{1}{2}\left(\frac{TP}{TP+FP} + \frac{TN}{TN+FN}\right)$
ROC curve	The horizontal axis is FPR, the vertical axis is TPR, and the area under the curve is AUC

6 Conclusion

In this paper, we talk about classification and research on the related achievements of deep learning Android malware detection based on different characteristics and different networks in recent years. In the future, more new artificial intelligence methods can be used to identify malware, and we should also strengthen the analysis and traceability of detected and intercepted malicious attacks. At the same time, this work needs taking a great step on the complex application fields of Internet of Thing (IoT), Mobile Cloud Computing (MCC) and Cyber-Physical Systems (CPS).

References

1. Arp, D., Spreitzenbarth, M., Hubner, M., et al.: Drebin: effective and explainable detection of android malware in your pocket. In: NDSS, vol. 14, pp. 23–26 (2014)
2. Mariconti, E., Onwuzurike, L., Andriotis, P., et al.: Mamadroid: detecting android malware by building Markov chains of behavioral models. arXiv preprint arXiv:1612.04433 (2016)
3. Aafer, Y., Du, W., Yin, H.: DroidAPIMiner: mining API-level features for robust malware detection in android. In: Zia, T., Zomaya, A., Varadharajan, V., Mao, M. (eds.) SecureComm 2013. LNICST, vol. 127, pp. 86–103. Springer, Cham (2013). https://doi.org/10.1007/978-3-319-04283-1_6
4. Yang, C., Xu, Z., Gu, G., Yegneswaran, V., Porras, P.: DroidMiner: automated mining and characterization of fine-grained malicious behaviors in android applications. In: Kutyłowski, M., Vaidya, J. (eds.) ESORICS 2014. LNCS, vol. 8712, pp. 163–182. Springer, Cham (2014). https://doi.org/10.1007/978-3-319-11203-9_10

5. Yuan, Z., Lu, Y., Wang, Z., et al.: Droid-sec: deep learning in android malware detection. In: Proceedings of the 2014 ACM Conference on SIGCOMM, pp. 371–372 (2014)
6. Kim, Y.: Convolutional neural networks for sentence classification. In: Proceedings of the 2014 Conference on Empirical Methods in Natural Language Processing (EMNLP), Doha, Qatar. Association for Computational Linguistics, pp. 1746–1751 (2014). http://aclanthology.org/D14-1181
7. Hochreiter, S., Schmidhuber, J.: Long short-term memory. Neural Comput. **9**(8), 1735–1780 (1997)
8. Bahdanau, D., Cho, K., Bengio, Y.: Neural machine translation by jointly learning to align and translate. arXiv preprint arXiv:1409.0473 (2014)
9. Lee, W.Y., Saxe, J., Harang, R.: SeqDroid: obfuscated android malware detection using stacked convolutional and recurrent neural networks. In: Alazab, M., Tang, M.J. (eds.) Deep Learning Applications for Cyber Security. ASTSA, pp. 197–210. Springer, Cham (2019). https://doi.org/10.1007/978-3-030-13057-2_9
10. Fereidooni, H., Conti, M., Yao, D., et al.: Anastasia: android malware detection using static analysis of applications. In: 2016 8th IFIP International Conference on New Technologies, Mobility and Security (NTMS), Larnaca, Cyprus. IEEE (2016)
11. Pengwei, L., Yuqian, J., Feiyang, X., et al.: A strong adversarial android malicious code detection method based on deep learning. Chin. J. Electron. **48**(8), 1502 (2020)
12. Laudanna, S., Visaggio, C.A., et al.: GANG-MAM: GAN based engine for modifying android malware. arXiv preprint arXiv:2109.13297 (2021)
13. Yuan, H., Tang, Y.: MADFU: an improved malicious application detection method based on features uncertainty. Entropy **22**(7), 792 (2020)
14. Li, D., Wang, Z., Xue, Y.: Fine-grained android malware detection based on deep learning. In: 2018 IEEE Conference on Communications and Network Security (CNS), Beijing, China, pp. 1–2. IEEE (2018)
15. Nix, R., Zhang, J.: Classification of android apps and malware using deep neural networks. In: 2017 International Joint Conference on Neural Networks (IJCNN), Anchorage, AK, USA, pp. 1871–1878. IEEE (2017)
16. Hou, S., Saas, A., Chen, L., et al.: Deep neural networks for automatic android malware detection. In: Proceedings of the 2017 IEEE/ACM International Conference on Advances in Social Networks Analysis and Mining 2017, pp. 803–810 (2017)
17. Hou, S., Saas, A., Ye, Y., Chen, L.: DroidDelver: an android malware detection system using deep belief network based on API call blocks. In: Song, S., Tong, Y. (eds.) WAIM 2016. LNCS, vol. 9998, pp. 54–66. Springer, Cham (2016). https://doi.org/10.1007/978-3-319-47121-1_5
18. Karbab, E.B., Debbabi, M., Derhab, A., et al.: Maldozer: automatic framework for android malware detection using deep learning. Digit. Investig. **24**, S48–S59 (2018)
19. Feng, R., Chen, S., Xie, X., et al.: Mobidroid: a performance-sensitive malware detection system on mobile platform. In: 2019 24th International Conference on Engineering of Complex Computer Systems (ICECCS), Los Alamitos, CA, USA, pp. 61–70. IEEE (2019)
20. Pektaş, A., Acarman, T.: Learning to detect android malware via opcode sequences. Neurocomputing **396**, 599–608 (2020)
21. Sharif, A., Nauman, M.: Function identification in android binaries with deep learning. In: 2019 Seventh International Symposium on Computing and Networking (CANDAR), Nagasaki, Japan, pp. 92–101. IEEE (2019)

22. Xu, K., Li, Y., Deng, R.H., et al.: Deeprefiner: multi-layer android malware detection system applying deep neural networks. In: 2018 IEEE European Symposium on Security and Privacy (EuroS&P), London, UK, pp. 473–487. IEEE (2018)
23. Zhu, D., Ma, Y., Xi, T., et al.: FSNet: android malware detection with only one feature. In: 2019 IEEE Symposium on Computers and Communications (ISCC), Barcelona, Spain, pp. 1–6. IEEE (2019)
24. Yan, J., Qi, Y., Rao, Q.: LSTM-based hierarchical denoising network for android malware detection. Secur. Commun. Netw. (2018)
25. Jiang, J., Li, S., Yu, M., et al.: Android malware family classification based on sensitive opcode sequence. In: 2019 IEEE Symposium on Computers and Communications (ISCC), Barcelona, Spain, pp. 1–7. IEEE (2019)
26. Millar, S., McLaughlin, N., Martinez del Rincon, J., et al.: Dandroid: a multi-view discriminative adversarial network for obfuscated android malware detection. In: Proceedings of the Tenth ACM Conference on Data and Application Security and Privacy, pp. 353–364 (2020)
27. Khan, K.N., Khan, M.S., Nauman, M., et al.: OP2VEC: an opcode embedding technique and dataset design for end-to-end detection of android malware. arXiv preprint arXiv:2104.04798 (2021)
28. Chen, J., Alalfi, M.H., Dean, T.R., et al.: Detecting android malware using clone detection. J. Comput. Sci. Technol. **30**(5), 942–956 (2015)
29. Mateless, R., Rejabek, D., Margalit, O., et al.: Decompiled APK based malicious code classification. Futur. Gener. Comput. Syst. **110**, 135–147 (2020)
30. Zhang, Y., Sui, Y., Pan, S., et al.: Familial clustering for weakly-labeled android malware using hybrid representation learning. IEEE Trans. Inf. Forensics Secur. **15**, 3401–3414 (2019)
31. Vasan, D., Alazab, M., Wassan, S., et al.: IMCFN: image-based malware classification using fine-tuned convolutional neural network architecture. Comput. Netw. **171**, 107138 (2020)
32. Yuan, B., Wang, J., Liu, D., et al.: Byte-level malware classification based on Markov images and deep learning. Comput. Secur. **92**, 101740 (2020)
33. Daoudi, N., Samhi, J., Kabore, A.K., Allix, K., Bissyandé, T.F., Klein, J.: DexRay: a simple, yet effective deep learning approach to android malware detection based on image representation of bytecode. In: Wang, G., Ciptadi, A., Ahmadzadeh, A. (eds.) MLHat 2021. CCIS, vol. 1482, pp. 81–106. Springer, Cham (2021). https://doi.org/10.1007/978-3-030-87839-9_4
34. Xiao, X., Yang, S.: An image-inspired and CNN-based android malware detection approach. In: 2019 34th IEEE/ACM International Conference on Automated Software Engineering (ASE), San Diego, CA, USA, pp. 1259–1261. IEEE (2019)
35. Zhiwu, X., Ren, K., Song, F.: Android malware family classification and characterization using CFG and DFG. In: 2019 International Symposium on Theoretical Aspects of Software Engineering (TASE), Guilin, China, pp. 49–56. IEEE (2019)
36. Gao, H., Cheng, S., Zhang, W.: GDroid: android malware detection and classification with graph convolutional network. Comput. Secur. **106**, 102264 (2021)
37. Zhao, L., Wang, J., Chen, Y., et al.: Famdroid: learning-based android malware family classification using static analysis. arXiv preprint arXiv:2101.03965 (2021)
38. Sun, B., Ban, T., Chang, S.C., et al.: A scalable and accurate feature representation method for identifying malicious mobile applications. In: Proceedings of the 34th ACM/SIGAPP Symposium on Applied Computing, pp. 1182–1189 (2019)
39. Xi, S., Yang, S., Xiao, X., et al.: Deepintent: deep icon-behavior learning for detecting intention- behavior discrepancy in mobile apps. In: Proceedings of the 2019

ACM SIGSAC Conference on Computer and Communications Security, pp. 2421–2436 (2019)
40. Ananya, A., Aswathy, A., Amal, T., et al.: Sysdroid: a dynamic ML-based android malware analyzer using system call traces. Clust. Comput. **23**(4), 2789–2808 (2020)
41. Sihag, V., Vardhan, M., Singh, P., et al.: De-lady: deep learning based android malware detection using dynamic features. J. Internet Serv. Inf. Secur. (JISIS) **11**(2), 34–45 (2021)
42. Feng, R., Lim, J.Q., Chen, S., et al.: Seqmobile: a sequence based efficient android malware detection system using RNN on mobile devices. arXiv preprint arXiv:2011.05218 (2020)
43. Xiao, X., Zhang, S., Mercaldo, F., et al.: Android malware detection based on system call sequences and LSTM. Multimedia Tools Appl. **78**(4), 3979–3999 (2019)
44. Alshahrani, H., Mansourt, H., Thorn, S., et al.: DDefender: android application threat detection using static and dynamic analysis. In: 2018 IEEE International Conference on Consumer Electronics (ICCE), Las Vegas, NV, USA, pp. 1–6. IEEE (2018)
45. Feng, J., Shen, L., Chen, Z., et al.: A two-layer deep learning method for android malware detection using network traffic. IEEE Access **8**, 125786–125796 (2020)
46. Hasan, H., Ladani, B.T., Zamani, B.: MEGDroid: a model-driven event generation framework for dynamic android malware analysis. Inf. Softw. Technol. **135**, 106569 (2021)
47. Yuan, Z., Lu, Y., Xue, Y.: Droiddetector: android malware characterization and detection using deep learning. Tsinghua Sci. Technol. **21**(1), 114–123 (2016)
48. Xu, L., Zhang, D., Jayasena, N., Cavazos, J.: HADM: hybrid analysis for detection of malware. In: Bi, Y., Kapoor, S., Bhatia, R. (eds.) IntelliSys 2016. LNNS, vol. 16, pp. 702–724. Springer, Cham (2018). https://doi.org/10.1007/978-3-319-56991-8_51
49. Tuan, L.H., Cam, N.T., Pham, V.H.: Enhancing the accuracy of static analysis for detecting sensitive data leakage in android by using dynamic analysis. Clust. Comput. **22**(1), 1079–1085 (2019)
50. Alzaylaee, M.K., Yerima, S.Y., Sezer, S.: Dl-droid: deep learning based android malware detection using real devices. Comput. Secur. **89**, 101663 (2020)
51. Huang, N., Xu, M., Zheng, N., et al.: Deep android malware classification with API-based feature graph. In: 2019 18th IEEE International Conference on Trust, Security and Privacy in Computing and Communications/13th IEEE International Conference on Big Data Science and Engineering (TrustCom/BigDataSE), Rotorua, New Zealand, pp. 296–303. IEEE (2019)
52. Zhao, L., Li, D., Zheng, G., et al.: Deep neural network based on android mobile malware detection system using opcode sequences. In: 2018 IEEE 18th International Conference on Communication Technology (ICCT), Chongqing, China, pp. 1141–1147. IEEE (2018)
53. McLaughlin, N., Martinez del Rincon, J., Kang, B., et al.: Deep android malware detection. In: Proceedings of the Seventh ACM on Conference on Data and Application Security and Privacy, pp. 301–308 (2017)
54. Zou, K., Luo, X., Liu, P., Wang, W., Wang, H.: ByteDroid: android malware detection using deep learning on bytecode sequences. In: Han, W., Zhu, L., Yan, F. (eds.) CTCIS 2019. CCIS, vol. 1149, pp. 159–176. Springer, Singapore (2020). https://doi.org/10.1007/978-981-15-3418-8_12
55. Liang, H., Song, Y., Xiao, D.: An end-to-end model for android malware detection. In: 2017 IEEE International Conference on Intelligence and Security Informatics (ISI), Beijing, China, pp. 140–142. IEEE (2017)

56. Vinayakumar, R., Soman, K., Poornachandran, P.: Deep android malware detection and classification. In: 2017 International Conference on Advances in Computing, Communications and Informatics (ICACCI), Cham, pp. 1677–1683. IEEE (2017)
57. Vinayakumar, R., Soman, K., Poornachandran, P., et al.: Detecting android malware using long short- term memory (LSTM). J. Intell. Fuzzy Syst. **34**(3), 12771288 (2018)
58. Huang, S.J., Zhao, J.W., Liu, Z.Y.: Cost-effective training of deep CNNs with active model adaptation. In: Proceedings of the 24th ACM SIGKDD International Conference on Knowledge Discovery & Data Mining, pp. 1580–1588 (2018)
59. Oak, R., Du, M., Yan, D., et al.: Malware detection on highly imbalanced data through sequence modeling. In: Proceedings of the 12th ACM Workshop on Artificial Intelligence and Security, pp. 37–48 (2019)
60. Su, X., Zhang, D., Li, W., et al.: A deep learning approach to android malware feature learning and detection. In: 2016 IEEE Trustcom/BigDataSE/ISPA, Tianjin, China, pp. 244–251. IEEE (2016)
61. Zhao, K., Zhang, D., Su, X., et al.: Fest: a feature extraction and selection tool for android malware detection. In: 2015 IEEE Symposium on Computers and Communication (ISCC), Larnaca, Cyprus, pp. 714–720. IEEE (2015)
62. Su, X., Shi, W., Qu, X., et al.: Droiddeep: using deep belief network to characterize and detect android malware. Soft. Comput. **24**(8), 6017–6030 (2020)
63. Chen, T., Mao, Q., Lv, M., et al.: Droidvecdeep: android malware detection based on word2vec and deep belief network. KSII Trans. Internet Inf. Syst. (TIIS) **13**(4), 2180–2197 (2019)
64. Louppe, G., Wehenkel, L., Sutera, A., et al.: Understanding variable importances in forests of randomized trees. In: Advances in Neural Information Processing Systems, vol. 26 (2013)
65. He, N., Wang, T., Chen, P., et al.: An android malware detection method based on deep autoencoder. In: Proceedings of the 2018 Artificial Intelligence and Cloud Computing Conference, pp. 88–93 (2018)
66. Chen, L., Zhang, M., Yang, C.Y., et al.: Poster: semi-supervised classification for dynamic android malware detection. In: Proceedings of the 2017 ACM SIGSAC Conference on Computer and Com- munications Security, pp. 2479–2481 (2017)
67. Yakura, H., Shinozaki, S., Nishimura, R., et al.: Malware analysis of imaged binary samples by convolutional neural network with attention mechanism. In: Proceedings of the Eighth ACM Conference on Data and Application Security and Privacy, pp. 127–134 (2018)
68. Hou, S., Saas, A., Chen, L., et al.: Deep4maldroid: a deep learning framework for android malware detection based on linux kernel system call graphs. In: 2016 IEEE/WIC/ACM International Conference on Web Intelligence Workshops (WIW), Omaha, USA. IEEE (2016)
69. Zhu, D., Xi, T., Jing, P., et al.: A transparent and multimodal malware detection method for android apps. In: Proceedings of the 22nd International ACM Conference on Modeling, Analysis and Simulation of Wireless and Mobile Systems, pp. 51–60 (2019)
70. Wang, W., Zhao, M., Wang, J.: Effective android malware detection with a hybrid model based on deep autoencoder and convolutional neural network. J. Ambient. Intell. Humaniz. Comput. **10**(8), 3035–3043 (2019)
71. Kim, T., Kang, B., Rho, M., et al.: A multimodal deep learning method for android malware detection using various features. IEEE Trans. Inf. Forensics Secur. **14**(3), 773–788 (2018)

Information Encryption Transmission Method of Automobile Communication Network Based on Neural Network

Chunhua Kong[1(✉)], Kai Ma[2], and Jiatong Wei[1]

[1] College of Automotive Engineering, Jilin Communications Polytechnic, Changchun 130012, China
13596157766@163.com

[2] Jilin Communications Polytechnic, Changchun 130012, China

Abstract. In order to ensure the information security of automobile communication network, an encryption transmission method of automobile communication network information based on neural network is proposed. Use neural network to generate random key to encrypt vehicle communication network information. Design encryption transmission scheme, including data encryption module, dynamic key generation module and data transmission module. The encrypted transmission scheme is used to transmit the ciphertext of the vehicle communication network information to the other end. The results show that compared with des and RSA encryption methods, the proposed method has shorter encryption time and higher key sensitivity, indicating that the proposed encryption transmission method is more efficient and secure.

Keywords: Neural network · Automobile communication network · Information encryption transmission method

1 Introduction

Security requirements of on-board network in the wireless communication scenario of on-board network, there are "one to many" data transmission scenarios such as vehicle, vehicle infrastructure and infrastructure infrastructure. In order to ensure the data security of users, data encryption can be carried out for users and systems. The vehicle or equipment nodes in the on-board network system often have different attributes, and a vehicle can be described by an attribute set. In many scenarios, users hope that only vehicles or devices that meet certain specific attributes can decrypt the ciphertext they send.For example, in a city car network, Alice, the driver of the taxi software company "DiDi", drives to Shanghai People's Square, and wants to send information such as speed, passenger load, mileage, parking space, etc. to other nearby companies of the same company. Vehicles or devices that do not meet these conditions cannot decrypt their own messages. In addition, due to the large number of vehicle terminals, strong mobility, and limited computing, storage, and communication capabilities of vehicle equipment, people hope that the encryption scheme in VANET is efficient. Most of the

Y. Xu et al. (Eds.): ML4CS 2022, LNCS 13655, pp. 243–256, 2023.
https://doi.org/10.1007/978-3-031-20096-0_19

existing VANET data encryption schemes use group encryption technology. Due to the high dynamics of the vehicle network, it is not ideal in practical applications. Its construction and maintenance consume a lot of system overhead, and its application effect is not good. In recent years, more and more researchers have begun to study the security of vehicle network data transmission, and are actively developing encryption schemes with better application effects. Ru Tian et al. proposed a privacy protection method for network data transmission based on RSA and Paillier [1]. The method first collects data, and then sends a data packet transmission request to neighboring nodes through the node itself to confirm the demand, completes the establishment of the network data transmission model, and then obtains the network ciphertext entropy through the public and private keys of RSA. The multiplicative homomorphic property uses the public and private keys to obtain the entropy of the network ciphertext, so that the server can receive the data information, encrypt the constants in the data, and obtain the ultimate privacy protection. Although this method enhances the privacy protection of network data to a certain extent, its robustness is not strong, and it is difficult to encrypt and transmit a large amount of data. Fan et al. [2] proposed a wireless communication encryption scheme for measurement, transmission and control systems based on the DES algorithm, which ensures the reliability of encryption by adding variable redundancy codes to the plaintext data; The random identification code is embedded between the two, so that the structure of the communication data is effectively hidden, and it provides support for the receiver to recover the data. This method can complete data encryption well, but it is a group encryption method, which consumes too much key management and is difficult to maintain. Based on the above background, this paper proposes an encrypted transmission method of vehicle communication network information based on neural network. Aiming at the problems of low efficiency and imperfect function of the existing vehicle networking encryption scheme, this paper introduces the neural network technology, and studies the information encryption transmission method suitable for the vehicle communication network.

2 Research on Encrypted Transmission of Vehicle Communication Network Information

2.1 Information Encryption of Automotive Communication Network Based on Neural Network

A neural network is a computer model whose structure essentially mimics the human brain to acquire knowledge and generate skills. In this paper, the neural network is introduced into the vehicle data encryption transmission, which needs to involve the relevant theoretical knowledge of neural cryptography. Neural cryptography mainly studies the application of stochastic algorithms, especially neural network algorithms in cryptanalysis and encryption. Neural network is self-adaptive and self-training, after research, most of the encryption algorithm can be realized by the three-layer forward neural network of artificial neural network, and because the artificial neural network is a parallel computing way, and more advanced, so its operation speed is fast and extremely difficult to crack. The basic structure of neural network is shown in Fig. 1.

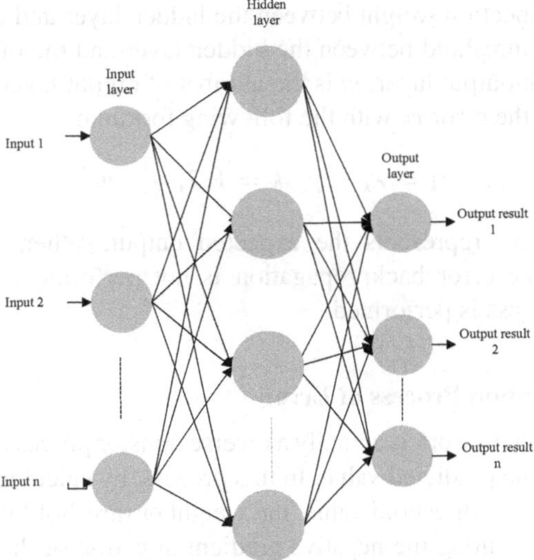

Fig. 1. Neural network structure

The standard artificial neural network algorithm includes two aspects: one is forward propagation, that is, for the input signal; On the other hand, for the error between the predicted value and the expected value, that is, back propagation. The following describes the specific algorithm process of these two processes.

2.1.1 Forward Propagation Process

Step 1: initial network. Assign a random number in the interval $(-1, 1)$ to each connection weight, set the error function, and give the calculation accuracy value and the maximum learning times.

Step 2: calculate the hidden layer. The calculation formula is as follows:

$$\beta_j = f\left(\sum_{i=1}^{n} w_{ij}x_i - \phi_j\right), j = 1, 2, \cdots, l \tag{1}$$

In the formula, x_i is the input vector; w_{ij} is the connection weight between the input layer and the hidden layer; ϕ_j is the threshold of the hidden layer; β_j is the output of the hidden layer; l is the number of nodes in the hidden layer; f is the activation function of the hidden layer.

The third step: output layer calculation. The calculation formula of the output layer is as follows:

$$\gamma_k = f\left(\sum_{j=1}^{m} \beta_j w_{jk} - \varphi_k\right), k = 1, 2, \cdots, m \tag{2}$$

where, w_{jk} is the connection weight between the hidden layer and the output layer, and φ_k is the connection threshold between the hidden layer and the output layer; γ_k is the output of BP network output layer; m is the number of output layer nodes.

Step 4: calculate the error r_k with the following formula:

$$r_k = \lambda_k - \gamma_k, k = 1, 2, \cdots, m \tag{3}$$

In the formula, λ_k represents the expected output. When r_k is less than the set error function, the error backpropagation is not performed, otherwise the error backpropagation process is performed.

2.1.2 Back Propagation Process of Error

The principle of neural network is actually a reverse transfer process of the error between the actual value and the predicted value. In this process, by calculating the derivative of the error to the weight or threshold value, the weight or threshold value is continuously adjusted and corrected along the negative gradient direction of the derivative until the final output error (the sum of squares of the error between the actual value and the predicted value) is within the allowable range. Compared with other traditional methods, the first obvious advantage of BP neural network method is that unlike other methods, the final mathematical model must be obtained. The rules trained by the neural network are hidden in the network and reflected through the network parameters finally modified.

The most important property of neural networks is their generalization performance, which ensures that when systems pass inputs they have not seen before, they can produce satisfactory results. This property allows neural networks to be used in many scenarios. It is easy to compute y_k from x_k, assuming that x_k represents the input of the network and y_k represents the output of the network. However, if the output y_k is known, it is difficult to calculate the network input x_k corresponding to the output. Due to this characteristic of the neural network, a neural network can be used to generate a hash function. Another important feature of neural networks is parallel implementation, each layer is parallel so they can implement certain functions independently. A special property of neural network is chaos, which is caused by the nonlinear structure of the network, so in the case of nonlinear and complex, the output value depends on the input value, because of this confusing feature, neural network is more suitable for password design.

The artificial neural network realizes a mapping relationship from input to output. After the neural network is trained, the network will enter a stable state. At this time, for a certain input, the neural network will output a certain value according to a certain nonlinear operation rule. Therefore, the neural network system is used to generate the key stream, which can make the encryption have the characteristics of "one scrambling codebook at a time". In order to improve the complexity of the function module that makes the network input values not repeated, greatly improve the complexity of the algorithm and the periodicity of the key sequence, the model uses the transformation processing algorithm to transform the key sequence generated by the neural network to generate random seeds, thus forming an extremely secure encryption mode.

Of course, before use, you must first design or select a neural network, and initialize the network and learning parameters, such as determining the number of neurons in each layer, initial weights, the number of neurons in the input and output layers, the number of layers in the hidden layer and More sample values, and then train the network to make it have strong classification ability. In addition, according to the number of neurons in the input layer and the output layer, the number of plaintext sequences to be encrypted each time should be determined. Finally, the network should be trained after the end. The parameters of "secret" are used for network parameters in the encryption and decryption process.

Designing a cryptosystem based on neural network is a very complex system engineering. Encryption designers not only need to understand the topology of neural network and other key technologies, but also need to have the knowledge of weight adaptive iteration and encryption and decryption system. In the cryptosystem based on neural network, the bit error rate should be as small as possible under the condition of ensuring security. The application of neural network in cryptography requires many important artificial neural network technologies. These technologies include the following:

- Tree Parity Machine (TPM) is used for exchanging synchronization state as a key on the input and output of both communication parties, and exchanging keys through a public channel to generate a public key system.
- The chaotic logic mapping neural network is applied in cryptography, both parties use the neural network as the input of the logic mapping to generate the output bits to be learned.
- Use generalized regression neural network (General Regression Neural Network, GRNN) to carry out the encryption and decryption process based on three layers, in which the input data is 3 bits and the output data is 8 bits.
- Train backpropagation NN as public key and Boolean as private key.
- Use the time-varying time-delay chaotic hopfield neural network to generate the binary sequence and encrypt it as the random switching function of the chaotic map.
- The chaotic dynamic behavior generated by the neural network based on the chaotic generator is used as the public key.
- A Pseudo Random Number (PRN) generator based on neural network is applied to stream cipher as a key generator.
- Using chaotic neural network to generate chaotic sequence as the tripartite key of cryptography (the combination of initial conditions and control parameters).
- Using the weight matrix of Layer Recurrent Neural Network (LRNN) to generate pseudo-random numbers as keys.
- Use the initial weights of the trained neural network as a symmetric key.

In the neural network encryption model based on the above neural network, for an initial random seed G_i, G_i is also the input of the neural network when encryption starts. The neural network will generate a pseudo-random number F_i matching the plaintext, and F_i will be the random key. The output sequence and plaintext generated by the neural network are used for XOR operation to generate ciphertext, and the output key sequence is treated as a new random seed. The encryption and decryption model based on neural network is shown in Fig. 2 [3].

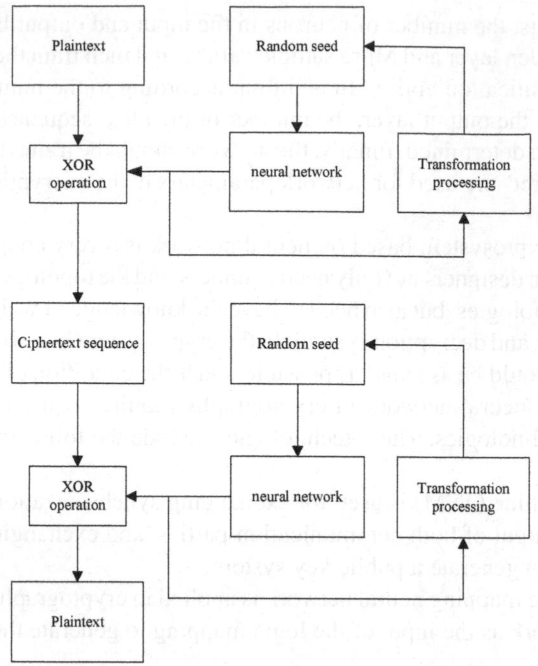

Fig. 2. Encryption and decryption model based on neural network

(1) After the neural network enters a stable state, for a certain input sequence, the neural network will output a certain output sequence according to some nonlinear operation rules.
(2) The output value generated by the neural network is transformed and then input into the neural network as the next random seed. In the transformation processing algorithm, the key sequence can be divided into two parts of equal ratio bits, and the termination condition in the genetic algorithm is determined as a certain evolutionary algebra. After the transformation processing algorithm, the periodicity of the key sequence tends to infinity, so that the input values of the neural network do not repeat. During each encryption and decryption, the initial random seed is different, and the generated ciphertext is also different [4].
(3) The ciphertext sequence is obtained by exclusive or operation between plaintext sequence and key sequence.

$$B_i = F_i \otimes B'_i \tag{4}$$

In the formula, B_i represents the ciphertext; F_i represents the random key output by the neural network; B'_i represents the plaintext, that is, the vehicle communication network information.

2.2 Information Transmission of Vehicle Communication Network

In the traditional car communication information transmission mode, the sender sends the information to the receiver, which is directly transmitted to the Internet network, and then reaches the receiver. In this process, the information sent will be exposed on the Internet, which is easy to be stolen, and there are insecure factors. In this study, the content of network transmission is encrypted, and based on the principle of Socket network communication, a neural network algorithm for encrypted transmission of communication information is proposed [5]. Under this scheme, the transmitted data is encrypted data, which can prevent bad attempts from stealing the information in the information network. After the artificial neural network encryption algorithm is used to encrypt the data, it is difficult to crack the data and obtain the real information of the user, which ensures the security of the communication information, improves the operation efficiency and reduces the resource consumption. Users only need to set a few parameters to achieve data encryption, simple operation, with good scalability, can be promoted in the current and future network applications.

In order to maintain the freshness of the key and improve the security of the automotive communication network, a dynamic encrypted transmission scheme is designed to transmit the encrypted information safely in the encrypted channel. The designed encryption transmission scheme needs to meet three necessary conditions: data encryption module, dynamic key generation module and data transmission module [6].

(1) The function of the data encryption module is to encrypt the power dispatching information to be transmitted. This step has been implemented in the previous section and will not be described in this section;
(2) The dynamic key generation module requires that in the process of information transmission, a dynamic key is generated between the power master device and the slave device to maintain the consistency of both ends;

According to the encryption function, the shared key is the key component of encryption, and the update condition of the shared key is set by using the dynamic key. It is known that traditional encrypted transmission involves two protocols, DNP3 and Modbus, among which Modbus protocol is the most widely used. Therefore, the characteristics and rules of this protocol will not be described in detail in this paper, but the DNP3 protocol rules will be started [7]. DNP3 information transmission rule: Within the specified time, the sender sends control commands from the power supply scheduling information. If the sender does not receive the expected response, the transmission fails and the application layer scheduling information needs to be sent again. The expected dynamic key designed in this study is generated by monitoring the correctly transmitted information, and there is no additional overhead in parsing the data link, so the transmission random number can be used as the basis for generating a new dynamic key [8].

The automobile communication network information needs to attach a random number encrypted by the shared key when sending the ciphertext, in which the random number sequence of E_{CN} and E_{SN} slave station equipment CN and master station equipment SN, and use M to control the key update frequency; counter indicates the count value.

The dynamic key generation process is the cipher text sent by the slave device CN to the master device SN. The time threshold is preset. When the time threshold is reached, if the response message cannot be received all the time, it needs to be re-sent; the master device SN uses the shared Decrypt the key, temporarily store the generated random number string, and send a response message to the slave device CN; after CN receives the response message, it automatically updates E_{CN}, increases counter, and continues to send ciphertext to SN. The master device uses the shared key K to obtain a random number, sends a message to the slave device, and then compares it with the last temporarily stored random number. When the two are completely consistent, it means that the data is repeated; otherwise, update E_{SN} and increase counter. When counter = M, recalculate the dynamic key of the slave device, and use the key as the dynamic key in the power transmission network. At this time, the master device and the slave device continuously update the dynamic key, and the shared key needs to be consistent with the dynamic key, so the hash value of the slave device CN is calculated and the key is sent [9]. Then the update equation of the shared key is

$$J_t = M\left(T_t + J_{t-1}\right) \tag{5}$$

where, J_t represents the shared key at time t; T_t represents the dynamic key at time t; J_{t-1} represents the shared key at time $t - 1$.

(3) The data transmission module uses the dynamic key in the encrypted transmission to update the shared key in real time. The module includes two sub modules: sending and receiving information and information processing. The functions of these two modules are shown in Table 1.

Table 1. Composition and function of data transmission module

Module name	Basic function
Sending and receiving information sub module	Send information in a certain format to and receive information from the central controller
Information processing sub module	Responsible for information processing, such as processing registration process, event information, processing information sent by the central controller to the main firewall and sending information to the central controller

- Send and receive information

The information sending and receiving module mainly includes two processes, as shown in Table 2.

Table 2. Information sending and receiving module process

Procedure name	msgsend	msgget
Function	Send message	Receive information
Input	Send socket, message header, message body, message body length, encryption mark, encryption key, key length	Accept message socket, message header, message body, message body size
Output	Bytes sent	Success: 1, failure: 0

Note: msgsend is responsible for sending the encrypted information to the central controller. The information type is indicated by the encryption mark, which can be 0, 4 or 8. The information is sent in the form of plaintext and ciphertext encrypted by the random key generated by the neural network algorithm. Msgget receives the information sent back by the central controller, decrypts the information if necessary, and obtains the plaintext.

- information processing module

The information processing sub module mainly includes four processes to complete different functions. As shown in Table 3.

The scheme realizes three links: data encryption module, dynamic key generation module and data transmission module, thus completing the design of dynamic encryption transmission scheme [10]. So far, the design of information encryption transmission method for automotive communication network based on neural network has been completed.

3 Method Testing and Analysis

In order to verify the reliability of the neural network-based vehicle communication network information encryption transmission method proposed in this study, the following comparative experiments are designed. Take the method in this paper as the test group A, the method based on DES to realize information security transmission as the test group B, and the RSA-based encryption method as the test group C. The effectiveness of different methods is judged by comparing the security and self-healing properties of the vehicle communication network after applying different information encryption transmission methods.

3.1 Experiment Preparation

Select an automobile communication network information as the test object to simulate and set different types of network attacks. The attack types simulated in the experiment include eavesdropping attack, malicious injection attack and counterfeiting attack. The basic information of the three attacks is shown in Table 4.

As shown in the table above, there are three common types of attacks, namely, data theft, malicious intrusion, and counterfeiting, respectively, so that data cannot be

Table 3. Information processing sub-module process

Procedure name	LinMsgProc	Reg2Center	Send Alive ACK	KeepAliveProc
Function	Process information from the central controller	Process registration process	Send confirmation information of keeping alive	Keep alive process treatment
Input	Connected socket	Central controller address, central controller port	Central controller ID number	Central controller ID number
Output	None	Success: 0 failure: −1	None	None

Note: Lin Msg Proc: responsible for processing the information sent by the central controller. If the central controller requires re-registration, the re-registration process will be started; if the central controller requires to send a keep-alive confirmation message to the central controller, the keep-alive will be sent. Confirm the information. Reg2Center: Connect to the central controller and send the registration information to the central controller. If it fails, it will indicate the registration failure in the system log, and successfully copy the obtained information to the shared storage structure, obtain the public key sent by the central controller, and then use the public key. The key used for encryption and data transmission of the central controller, and the encrypted key is sent to the central controller again. Send Alive ACK: Responsible for sending keep-alive confirmation information; Keep Alive Proc: Connect to the central controller, exit if the central controller fails to keep alive, otherwise send keep-alive information to the central controller, if the central controller's keep-alive confirmation information is obtained, set the survival flag of the central controller, and register if the re-registration information of the central controller is obtained. The information processing module realizes the transfer of information between the main firewall and the central controller by calling the sub-processes of sending and receiving information in the sending and receiving modules, including the registration and keep-alive processes.

Table 4. Statistics of different attack characteristics

Label	Number of nodes	Affected path/piece	Critical impact path/piece
Eavesdropping attacks	125	225	58
Malicious injection attack	214	230	125
Impersonation attack	21	33	75

encrypted and transmitted. When the power grid transmits power dispatching information, the above three types of attacks are injected at the same time. Combined with the above test environment, the security of the automotive communication network is tested after the application of different encryption methods, so as to judge different application performance.

3.2 Neural Network Parameter Settings

See Table 5.

Table 5. Basic parameters of neural network

Name	Parameter
Enter the number of layer nodes	26
Number of hidden layer nodes	35
Number of output layer nodes	5
Input layer and hidden layer connection weights	0.5
Connection weights of hidden layer and output layer	0.8
Hidden layer threshold	0.01
Output layer threshold	0.002
Target accuracy of neural network	0.001
Learning rate	0.05
Neuron excitation function	Sigmoid function
Maximum training times	1000

3.3 Neural Network Training

The network error training curve is obtained by training the network, as shown in Fig. 3.

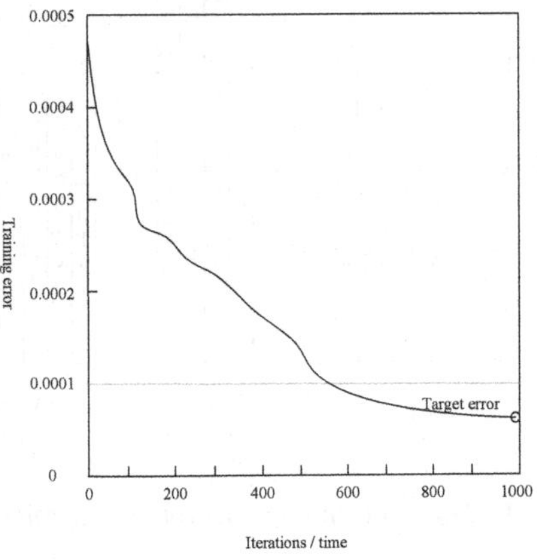

Fig. 3. Neural network training results

As can be seen from Fig. 3, when the neural network algorithm is used, the network error obtained by the final training is far less than 0.0001, which does not reach the set target error, and has been trained to the set maximum number of training steps. It can be seen that the neural network has good performance and can be used in the formal test.

3.4 Method Performance Evaluation Indicators

3.4.1 Encryption Time-Consuming

Due to the large amount of data in automotive communication network information, there are higher requirements for data encryption time and encryption efficiency in practical applications. In this paper, five information samples of different sizes are selected to be encrypted on Matlab, and the encryption time required for using the DES-based encryption method and the RSA-based encryption method for the information samples of different sizes is tested.

3.4.2 Key Sensitivity Analysis

Considering the validity of key replacement, the secure encryption algorithm should be highly sensitive to key change, and the key should have avalanche phenomenon. When any bit of the key or plaintext changes, more than half of the bits in the ciphertext will change accordingly. Therefore, the stronger the key sensitivity, the higher the security of the method.

3.5 Method Performance Test Results

3.5.1 Encryption Time-Consuming

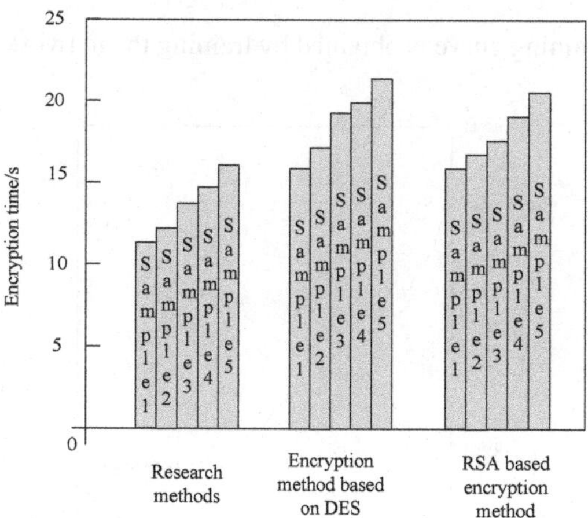

Fig. 4. Time-consuming encrypted transmission

As can be seen from Fig. 4, compared with DES based encryption method and RSA based encryption method, the encryption time under the application of the research method is lower, indicating that the effect of the research encryption transmission method is higher.

3.5.2 Key Sensitivity

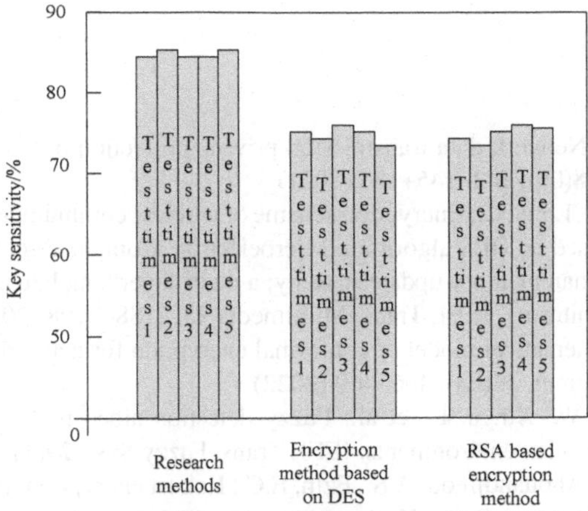

Fig. 5. Key Sensitivity

It can be seen from Fig. 5 that the key sensitivity of the des-based encryption method and the rsa-based encryption method is low, both less than 80%, which means that the security of the data encryption transmission method is low, and the encryption of the studied algorithm is low. The key sensitivity is higher, all above 80%, which indicates that the encryption transmission method studied is more secure.

4 Conclusion

To sum up, with the rapid development and wide application of on-board network, the security of its data transmission has been paid more and more attention. The traditional encryption scheme can not adapt to the dynamics of vehicle network and the limitations of vehicle equipment performance. In recent years, the research on encryption has made rapid development. The research on its security and efficiency makes the application of encryption system more and more close to reality. Combined with the characteristics of the vehicle network and the research results of the existing encryption technology, this paper proposes an encryption transmission method based on neural network for the vehicle network, which effectively ensures the security of the data transmission process of the power grid, and provides a reliable protection means for the information encryption transmission when there is an attack. The application of encryption transmission method based on neural network in vehicle network security is still immature, and there are still problems worth studying in the future: the revocation mechanism for users in vehicle network in this paper is realized by maintaining an revocation list by an authority, which needs to be updated regularly. Vehicles in vehicle network are highly dynamic, and their system changes are frequent. This paper has not yet put forward an appropriate standard for the list update cycle, which can be further studied in the future in combination with the actual data and models of the on-board network.

Acknowledgement. Innovation team of automobile service engineering in cold area, Fund number: 2019-5.

References

1. Tian, M., Yu, T.: Network data transmission privacy protection based on RSA and paillier. Comput. Simul. **38**(06), 142–145+183 (2021)
2. Jun-hao, F., Bo, C., Long, C.: Encryption scheme of wireless communication in missile launch control system based on DES algorithm. Microelectron. Comput. **35**(11), 134–138 (2018)
3. Liu, S., et al.: Human memory update strategy: a multi-layer template update mechanism for remote visual monitoring. IEEE Trans. Multimedia **23**, 2188–2198 (2021)
4. Yumei, Z.: A mathematical model of conformal encryption for network data based on block cipher. Comput. Simul. **39**(03), 466–469 (2022)
5. Shuai, L., Shuai, W., Xinyu, L., et al.: Fuzzy detection aided real-time and robust visual tracking under complex environments. IEEE Trans. Fuzzy Syst. **29**(1), 90–102 (2021)
6. Ametepe, A.F.X., Ahouandjinou, A.S., Ezin, E.C.: Robust encryption method based on AES-CBC using elliptic curves Diffie-Hellman to secure data in wireless sensor networks. Wirel. Netw. **28**(3), 991–1001 (2022)
7. Liu, S., Liu, D., Muhammad, K., Ding, W.: Effective template update mechanism in visual tracking with background clutter. Neurocomputing **458**, 615–625 (2021)
8. Obaid, Z.K., Saffar, N.: Image encryption based on menezes vanstone elliptic curve cryptosystem. Solid State Technology **63**(3), 5256–5265 (2020)
9. Abdulwahid, M.M., Basil, N.: Review on chaotic theory using DNA encoding with image encryption. Informatica **2**(1), 14–19 (2021)
10. Liu, Y., Li, B., Zhang, Y., et al.: A Huffman-based joint compression and encryption scheme for secure data storage using physical unclonable functions. Electronics **10**(11), 1267 (2021)

Explanation-Guided Minimum Adversarial Attack

Mingting Liu[1], Xiaozhang Liu[2(✉)], Anli Yan[1], Yuan Qi[2], and Wei Li[2]

[1] School of Cyberspace Security, Hainan University, Hainan 570228, China
[2] School of Computer Science and Technology, Hainan University, Hainan 570228, China
lxzh@hainanu.edu.cn

Abstract. Machine learning has been tremendously successful in various fields, rang-ing from image classification to natural language processing. Despite it has been gained ubiquitous, its application in high-risk domains has been hindered by the opacity of its decision-making, i.e., users do not understand the reason for the given prediction result. To circumvent this limitation, explainable artificial intelligence (XAI) is being developed from multiple perspectives and at multiple levels. However, the auxiliary information provided by XAI helps to build a trust bridge between users and models, while inevitably increasing the risk of the model being attacked. In this paper, we prove that explanation information has a certain risk of attack on the model, and to explore how the adversary can use explanation information to reduce the attack dimension. Our proposed attack method can reduce the perturbation range to a certain extent, i.e., the adversary can add perturbation in a very small range. It can ensure the distortion and success rate at the same time, reduce the perturbation amplitude, and obtain the adversary samples that can not be discernible by human eyes. Extensive evaluations results show that the explanation information provided by XAI provides a set of sensitive features for the adversary. On the CIFAR-10 dataset, the scope of our attack is 90% smaller than the C&W attack, while maintaining a similar success rate and distortion. At the same time, we verify that our method can still achieve good attack effect even in black box.

Keywords: Machine learning · Explanation model · Adversarial example attack

1 Introduction

Machine learning(ML) continues to evolve in visual tasks. For instance, in image classification and detection, the classification accuracy of the model increases gradually. Machine learning models have been gradually applied in various realistic tasks and sensitive fields, such as intelligent medical treatment and unmanned driving, etc. [6,24–26]. However, the trust crisis of developing ML has always existed [11,13]. One of the key technologies to improve human trust in ML model

Y. Xu et al. (Eds.): ML4CS 2022, LNCS 13655, pp. 257–270, 2023.
https://doi.org/10.1007/978-3-031-20096-0_20

is explainable artificial intelligence (XAI). Although XAI alleviates the problem of model credibility, the auxiliary information it provides users divulges more privacy. Meanwhile, we have witnessed a corresponding increase in concern about ML explanation methods being used to guide attacks against machine learning models. In this paper, we focus on the insidious issue of adversarial attack.

There are many adversarial example attacks, including feature-based and gradient-based [5,12] attacks. Researchers pay attention to query budget, attack success rate, perturbation range, and other indicators in adversarial example attacks [14,17,19]. In the field of adversarial example attack, researchers pay attention to query cost, attack effect, interference range and other indicators.However, existing adversarial example attacks focus on reducing the query budget, but do not pay attention to the disturbance may be excessive, which may be detected by human eyes. Furthermore, the creation of a small number of perturbed hostile images may provide new insights into the geometric characteristics and overall behavior of ML model in high-dimensional space [14]. We believe that the minimal perturbation image may be beneficial to avoid defensive detection.

Due to the complexity of the model, the adversary cannot control the selection of sensitive features when carrying out adversarial example attacks. To this end, in this paper, we leverage the model explanations to carry out minimal feature adversarial attack against the ML model. Our attack is to create adversarial examples through the features provided by model explanations. In the field of image classification, we focus on the intuitive information brought by visual interpretation to the adversary, i.e., the model explanation provided by feature-based interpreters – LIME and Shap Value.

Shap Value explanatory tool [1] provides the contribution of images to decision-making as the model explanation, which intuitively reveals important feature. LIME is a model-agnostic explanation method. Its goal is to filter a small group of effective features mainly using ML interpretability tools. We evaluate our attack against machine learning models trained on widely used image classification datasets i.e., MNIST and CIFAR-10 datasets. In all the research models, we find that model explanations provide an attack range for adversary, the attack success rate does not decrease, and the perturbation range is smaller while ensuring the distortion rate.

To sum up, our contributions are:

We find that the explanatory information provided by interpretability is beneficial in guiding the creation of minimum adversarial examples.

Using visual interpretation information division to narrow the attack range, the adversary can ensure the distortion rate and attack with a smaller perturbation rate, but not reduce the success rate.

According to different interpreters, we comprehensively evaluate the attack success rate, distortion rate and attack pixel ratio for finite pixel attack with limited pixel by interpreter in two datasets.

2 Related Work

2.1 Adversarial Example Attack

Since 2014, when Szegedy et al. proposed the adversarial example, the research on adversarial attack has experienced a boom, and a variety of attack methods have emerged. Adversarial attack algorithms can be divided into three categories: attack based on gradient iteration, attack based on GAN and attack based on optimization. Papernot et al. [12] only added disturbance to 4.02% of the input features in the adversarial image generated by Jacobi significance graph method to achieve good attack effect, but the visual effect of this method is not good. Suet al. [14] used the differential evolution algorithm to iteratively modify each pixel to generate sub-images, and compared with the parent image. The sub-image with the best attack effect was retained according to the selection criteria to realize the adversarial attack. The C&W attack method proposed by Carlini and Wagner [5] is based on Adam optimization to carry out gradient iteration, which is one of the strongest first-order attacks at present. Moosavi-dezfooli et al. [9] generated minimum specifications to counter perturbation through iterative calculation, i.e., Deepfool attack. Universal Adversarial Perturbations [8]can generate disturbances that attack any image implementation, and these disturbances are also almost invisible to humans; Andriushchenko et al.'s black box attack based on score and independent of local gradient information [18]; Andrew et al. used natural evolution strategy to carry out black box adversarial attacks, reducing the query by 2–3 orders of magnitude [23]. Du et al. proposed the concept of minimum adversarial examples [19]. ZOO attack [17] is the first attempt at gradient-free black box attack, which uses zero-ladder algorithm and symmetric difference quotient to evaluate the gradient of the i-th component of DNN, but the query cost generated by this method is huge. AutoZoom [2] improved on the basis of ZOO, using average random global gradient estimation for the first time, and using dimensionality reduction algorithm to reduce the dimension of the sample before the attack, which greatly reduced the query cost. However, when using encoder and decoder dimensionality reduction, it would take too much time, and the disturbance space was the whole image. One pixel attack [14] is a rare study of adding disturbance to a limited number of pixels. However, the limitation of this method lies in search. The larger the image size is, the worse the effect is, and the query cost is also high.

2.2 Privacy Risk of Model Explanations

In recent years, the safety risk of model interpretability has been gradually noticed by researchers. Shokri et al., for the first time, successfully carried out member inference attack and data set reconstruction attack on the model using case-based explainable information [7]. In addition, Ulrich AağVodji et al. [3] used the information provided by the counterfactual interpretability method to construct model extraction attacks. Smitha Milli et al. [10] used gradient-based model interpretation information to carry out model theft attack on the model.

Giorgio Severi et al. [15] studied the advantages of self-interpreting machine learning model in back-door poisoning attacks. In model authentication technology, Somesh Jha et al. [8] used explainable artificial intelligence technology to reveal the inefficiency of the underlying classification model and provide a new method to attack the authentication system. Abderrahmen et al. designed the EG-Booster attack method by us-ing explanatory machine learning technology. The EG-Booster attack method uses predictive interpretation based on feature model to guide the production of countermeasure samples [4]. Abderahmen's goal is similar to ours, except that our goal is to use interpretive information to carry out small scale attacks. Zhao et al. developed a multi-mode transposed CNN architecture to reconstruct private images from data interpretation for model inversion attacks [16].

3 Method

In this study, post-hoc explanatory tools are used to extract a small group of sensitive features and attack the sensitive features, so as to achieve a great success rate by changing a few pixels. In order to achieve the research objective of this study, this study is divided into two stages (see Fig. 1): First, the post-hoc explanatory technologies are selected to explain the model prediction, and the features that are beneficial to the current prediction are obtained. We extract these features and set them as the finite space of perturbation. Then, we add perturbations to the extracted sensitive feature design, and use Adam optimizer to accelerate the selection of optimal perturbations. In the following, we describe the selection of explanatory tools, the selection of attack methods, and the details of specific attack models.

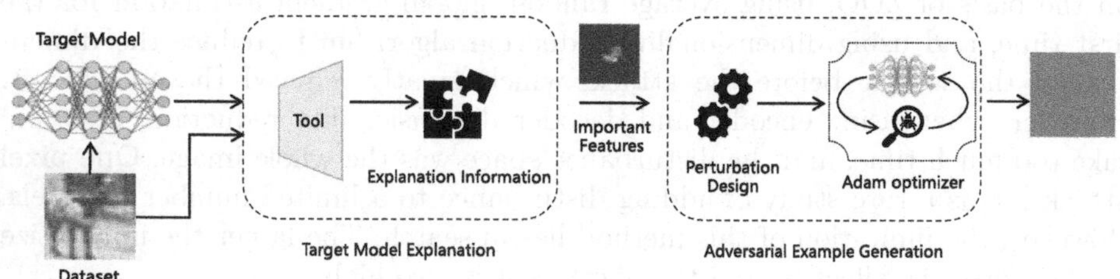

Fig. 1. Explanation-Guided minimum adversarial attack overview.

3.1 Model Independent Explanations

Explanatory techniques of models are developing in multiple levels and diversified, mainly divided into ante-hoc explanation and post-hoc explanation.

Visual explanation technique is mostly used in the field of computer vision, such as Grad-CAM interpretation method [20], Score-CAM visual interpretation method [21], LIME interpretation method [13] and counterfactual explanations method [22] etc. Our goal is to extract sensitive features from interpretable information. In order to reduce the relationship with the model and make our approach unconstrained in model selection, we tend to choose interpretive techniques that are model-independent. Therefore, we relax the requirements of the interpreter on the model, and choose model-independent post-interpretability, so that the means of obtaining the interpreter is model-independent. In this article, we choose two popular post-hoc explanatory techniques -ÍC LIME explainability technique and Shap Value explainability technique.

LIME Explanation. PRibeiro et al. [13] proposed LIME interpreter in 2016. LIME interpreter is a local interpretability model algorithm applied to black box models of text classes and image classes. With the increasing complexity of models, it is difficult to obtain globally usable interpretation models. Thus, the author focuses on local approximation to the underlying model to generate the interpretation. The principle is that the perturbation instance generates a data set D (which we obtained by transforming a sample data), and we expect the prediction results of the simple D-single model on the new data set to be similar to the prediction results of the complex model on the data set. A locally faithful linear model is obtained based on data set D, and the result is explanatory when feature pixels with higher weight are obtained by fitting the model. In other words, when the model classifies samples into certain categories with a certain confidence score, the interpreter returns features that are favorable to the score.

Shap Value Explanation. The innovation of Shap Value is the combination of Shapley Value and LIME. The concept of Shapley Value is derived from game theory, which requires one game and multiple players. Shapley Value is used to quantify each player's contribution to the game. As mentioned above, LIME uses a linear model of local fidelity to obtain high-weight local features as interpretation results. The goal of SHAP Value is to interpret the judgment results of the model by calculating the contribution of each feature in variable X to prediction and quantifying the contribution of feature to model prediction.

3.2 Adversarial Example Attack

Among the adversarial example attack algorithms, most of the strongest attacks are white box attacks, among which PGD and C&W are one of the strongest attack algorithms. In essence, both types of attacks are gradition-based attacks. Different from FGSM attacks, PGD and C&W attacks focus on maximizing the attack effect by taking one small step at a time. In C&W attacks, optimization algorithm Adam is added to speed up convergence. JSMA attack algorithm uses Jacobian matrix filtering to change few feature pixels and achieves high attack success rate. Inspired by the C&W and JSMA attacks, we use interpreters to define the attack scope, design a new attack algorithm to limit the attack dimension, and then adversarial attack the model. In order to make our attack model suitable for both white box attack and black box attack, we combine the popular white box attack and black box attack.

C&W Attack. C&W attack takes adversarial examples as a variable, and the author expresses the problem of attack success as a constraint minimization problem, whose objective function is:

$$\begin{aligned} &minimize \quad D(x, x+\delta) + c \cdot f(x+\delta) \\ &suchthat \quad x+\delta \in [0,1]^2 \end{aligned} \tag{1}$$

c stands for regularization coefficient, and $f(\cdot)$ is the loss function of deep learning, reflecting the success of attack. After comparing seven loss functions, Carlin and Wagner choose a loss function that is most conducive to attack:

$$f(x,t) = max\{max_{i \neq t}[F(x)]_i - [F(x)]_t, -k\} \tag{2}$$

Carlin and Wagner proposed three norm attacks. L_0 attack is based on L_2 attacks, which uses L_2 attack to remove unnecessary pixel perturbations and obtain the minimum set of necessary pixel perturbations.

Unconstrained Black Box Attack. Chen et al. [17] modified the parameters required by the white box of C&W attack formula, oriented the problem to the black box attack, and modified the problem description and loss function to make them irrelevant to the internal structure of the model. The constraint problems after modification are as follows:

$$min_{x \in [0,1]} Dist(x, x_0) + \lambda \cdot Loss(F(x), t) \tag{3}$$

where λ is the regularization coefficient, which is similar to c in C&W attack. $Loss(F(x), t)$ is the loss function, and $min_{x \in [0,1]} Dist(x, x_0)$ is the distance between the antagonistic image and the original image. The author modified the loss function as:

$$Loss(F(x), t) = max\{log[F(x)_i] - max_{t \neq i} log[F(x)]_t, 0\} \tag{4}$$

The logits output of the neural network is processed by $log(\cdot)$ to reduce the significant advantage of the label class while maintaining the numerical order of the classification probability.

3.3 Explanation-Guided Minimum Adversarial Attack Algorithm

Our goal is to limit the attack scope with interpretive information so that the distortion rate can be guaranteed while reducing the scope of adding perturbation. Inspired by C&W attack and ZOO attack, in order to unify the attack

Algorithm 1. Explanation-Guided Minimum Adversarial Attack Algorithm

Input: $F(\cdot)$, $Exp(F(\cdot),\cdot)$, x_0, Q
Output: Adversarial Example
$Exp(x) \longleftarrow x_0$
$mask = Exp(F(x_0), x_0)$ //The explanatory tools outputs explain. information
$[m] = one[mask]$ //Use explanatory information to obtain sensitive features.
$\delta = tanh([m]) + 1 - x_0$
while Q **do**
  $x^* = \frac{1}{2}(tanh([m]) + 1) - x_0$
  $f(x^*, t) = max\{log[F(x^*)_i] - max_{t \neq i} log[F(x^*)]_t, 0\}$
  $Loss = minDist(x^*, x_0) + \lambda \cdot f(x^*, t)$
  The Adam optimizer speeds up to δ
End While

and generally apply to white box attack and black box attack, we modify the loss function to the loss function in black box state. We demonstrate that the adversarial attack based on interpreted information can be applied not only to white box attack but also to black box attack. The contribution points of model decisions are obtained by explanatory techniques, and sensitive points are quickly found. These sensitive features are fixed as disturbance space to attack the model. Compared with C&W attack, our attack reduces the iterative process of continuous iteration of L_2 attack during L_0 attack. For L_2 attack, our method also reduces the number of disturbed pixels, so that the proportion of attack pixels decreases. And compared to the JSMA attack, we use gradient optimization to achieve a similar effect to the Jacobi matrix attack, and our attack is more visually advantageous. Our attack algorithm formula is expressed as:

$$\begin{gathered}\delta = \frac{1}{2}(tanh(\omega_n) + 1) - x_n \\ min_{x \in [0,1]} Dist(x, x_0) + \lambda \cdot f(\frac{1}{2}(tanh(\omega_n) + 1)) \\ where \quad f(x^{'}) = max\{log[F(x)_i] - max_{t \neq i} log[F(x)]_t, 0\}\end{gathered} \tag{5}$$

Optimization Algorithm Setting. In the white box attack, Adam algorithm obtains the internal gradient of the model for optimization. In the black box attack, the gradient information cannot be obtained deeply inside the model, so we set a new Adam algorithm gradient information, which is derived from the new loss function. We express the gradient formula of the optimizer as:

$$\mathbf{g} = \frac{f(\mathbf{x} + \beta \mathbf{u})}{\beta} \cdot \mathbf{u} \tag{6}$$

$\beta > 0$ is A smoothing parameter, $\mathbf{u}$ is A unit vector, and $f(\cdot)$ is the loss function. In Algorithm 1, the $F(\cdot)$ is the model to be attacked, x_0 is the input sample, $Exp(\cdot)$ is the model interpreter, Q is the maximum number of queries, i represents the correct classification category of the model, and t represents any other classification except category i. $\delta = tanh([m]) + 1 - x_0$ is the perturbation vector, inspired by the C&W attack, the search of $[m]$ is transformed into the search of δ, so that the perturbation gradient is always valid, $Dist(x^*, x_0)$ is the error limitation, and λ is the regularization parameter. First, we input the model and sample into the model interpreter to obtain the pixels with the greatest contribution to model prediction. These pixels are initialized as the perturbation area, and the original sample is taken as the input. By observing $Loss = minDist(x^*, x_0) + \lambda \cdot f(x^*, t)$, Adam optimization algorithm is used to solve the optimal solution $[m]$, and $\delta = tanh([m]) + 1 - x_0$ is obtained as the optimal perturbation.

4 Experimental Design and Implementation

4.1 The Experimental Setting

Dataset

Cifar10 Dataset. Size 32*32*3 color images, a total of 10 categories, each category 6000 pictures. There were 50,000 training pictures and 10,000 test pictures. White box attack randomly selects 1000 of the 10000 images in the test set and attacks the images that are predicted to be successful. Black box attack randomly selects 100 images from the correct images predicted in the test set for attack.

MNIST Dataset. Handwritten digital data set, gray scale images with a size of 28*28. Including training set has 50000 pictures, test set has 10000 pictures, there are 0 to 9 categories. The white-box attack experiment uses the predicted correct image from the test set of 1000 random images. Black box attack randomly selects 100 images from the correct images predicted in the test set for attack.

Target Model. Convolutional neural networks with different parameters were selected in the experiment of this paper. After training the model, we selected correctly classified images from random 1000 data in the data test set as the attack data set. ResNetV2 network model is tested in white box attack and neural network structure similar to C&W attack is tested in black box attack.

Experimental Environment. PyCharm 2020.2, Python 3.6, AMD Ryzen 7 4800U with Radeon Graphics @1.80 GHz This operation is performed in Windows 10 with 16 GB of memory. The black box attack experiment was conducted on the NVIDIA GeForce RTX 3090GPU server.

Experimental Parameters

LIME Explanatory Tool. We use the integrated LIME interpretation package. In this interpretation package, when we set parameters, we chose the "silc" sharding method according to the test, so that it can be divided more carefully on the smaller dataset of MNIST and CIFAR10. In experiments, due to the special nature of the LIME interpreter, we can obtain the interpreter's interpretation of each category of the classifier's output.

SHAP Value Explanatory Tool. Based on the Shap Value interpreter, set the interpreter to obtain the prediction category of the current highest confidence, and the favorable and unfavorable features in the sample for this decision. According to the understanding of SHAP, favorable features are called positive features and harmful features are called negative features in the experiment. We divide the at-tack scope into positive interpretation region, negative interpretation region, interpretation region, and non-interpretation region (i.e., the region where $value = 0$).

4.2 Experimental Results and Analysis

We tested the attack results based on LIME interpreter and the attack effects based on Shap Value interpreter on Cifar10 and MNIST datasets respectively, as shown in Table 1, 2, 3 and 4. In the adversarial attack based on explanation information, we implement different explanation attacks according to the explanation results of different interpreters.

Table 1. LIME-Guided minimum white-box of adversarial attack.

Dataset	Explanatory information	Success rate	Disturbed pixel ratio	Distortion rate
Cifar 10	i	**99.88%**	**5.58%**	0.6990
	t	29.12%	11.28%	0.7724
	All_explanation	100%	38.71%	0.321
	!All_explanation	100%	60.30%	0.3106
	C&W	100%	98.92%	0.2988
MNIST	i	**81.33%**	**5.30%**	3.1157
	t	33.20%	4.73%	3.0527
	All_explanation	100%	39.60%	3.0645
	!All_explanation	100%	50.55%	3.1584
	C&W	100%	95.03%	2.6828

LIME-Guided Minimum Adversarial Attack. Because the LIME interpreter will provide the characteristics of sample prediction as a favorable feature of the fore-casting process according to the user's requirements. In this context, it is natural to have the intuition that an adversarial attack on these very important features might work better. Our experiment results proof our speculation.

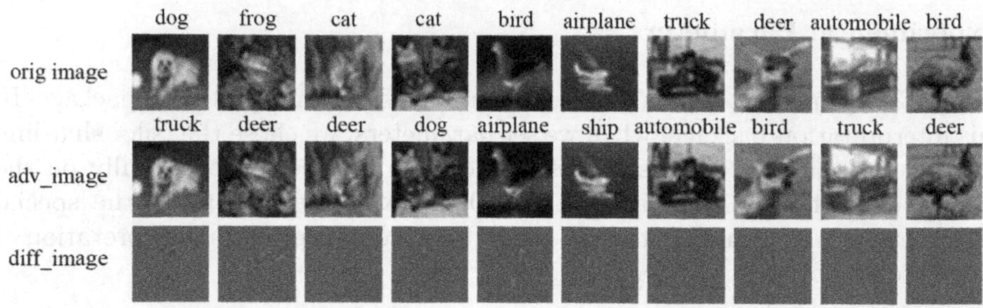

Fig. 2. Successful example of LIME-guided minimum white-box of adversarial attack on Cifar10 dataset.

We separate each category, as well as some other combination interpretation attack range, according to the results of the two kinds of data of attack statistics can be seen (see Table 1). It is good enough to predict the attack success rate of the highest class interpretation region. Only 5.58% pixels are modified, the success rate reaches 99.88%, and the distortion rate is the lowest for other classification interpretation. Some successful sample attacks are shown in Fig. 2. In more complex color images, the effect is more prominent. We attack the comprehensive interpretation information of each category, and the perturbation range increases to 38.71%. Without weakening the success rate of the attack, the distortion rate is similar to the C&W attack effect, but our attack range is reduced by about 60%.

Table 2. Shap-Guided minimum white-box of adversarial attack.

Dataset	Explanatory in-formation	Success rate	Disturbed pixel ratio	Distortion rate
Cifar 10	Value > 0	**100%**	**71.24%**	0.3049
	Value < 0	28.56%	29.96%	0.4958
	Value != 0	100%	76.34%	0.2989
	Value = 0	**99.63%**	**22.93%**	0.6410
	C&W	100%	99.13%	0.2977
MNIST	Value > 0	**91.84%**	**57.65%**	3.0149
	Value < 0	12.99%	19.98%	3.5041
	Value != 0	93.35%	61.33%	2.9511
	Value = 0	**97.58%**	**33.68%**	3.3700
	C&W	100%	95.02%	2.6750

Shap-Guided Minimum Adversarial Attack. Due to the nature of the interpreter, we set up a forward explanation region, a negative explanation region, and a non-explanation region. According to the comparison of results in Table 2, it is found that a good attack success rate has been achieved by hostile attacks based only on the forward explanation region, while the disturbance range is smaller. For for-ward explanation, our attack reduces the number of features by nearly 30% com-pared to C&W attack, achieving a 100% success rate and a distortion rate similar to C&W attack. Some examples of successful attacks are shown in Fig. 3. To our surprise, we found that we still got very good attack success rate for those feature regions with no contribution, but poor attack effect for negative explanation regions. We provide an explanation for this phenomenon, where features that are harmful to current predictions are beneficial to other predictions, and features that are useless to current predictions are useful to other kinds of predictions.

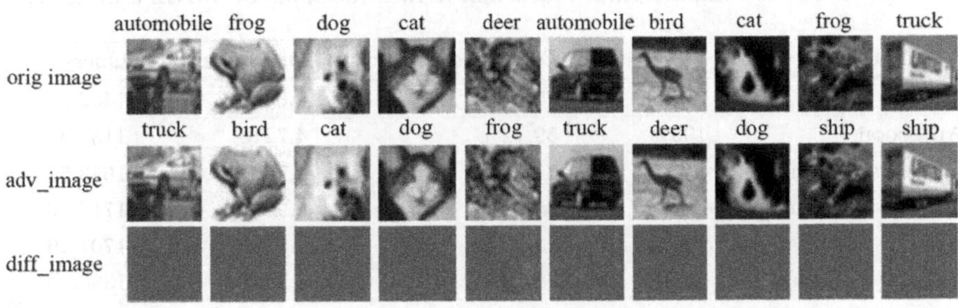

Fig. 3. Successful example of Shap-guided minimum white-box of adversarial attack on Cifar10 dataset.

Black Box Attack. We compared Cifar10 data set and MNIST data set respectively for black box attack, and the results are shown in Table 3 and 4. Compared with ZOO attack, our method has obvious advantages in success rate, disturbed pixel ratio and query cost. Compared with the AutoZoom attack method, the modified pixel ratio of our method decreased by about 93%, but the success rate did not decrease significantly. Although our method achieves similar distortion rates with a very good success rate with only a small amount of pixel perturbation, it increases the query cost compared to the AutoZoom attack. Through compared with other regions in the white box attack, we find that even no contribution area, attack the success rate is still considerable, this shows that for the opponent, Each pixel can provide some convenience for the adversary, and we choose the most important pixel to attack. Although the pixel range is reduced, the removal of pixels also reduces the information entropy, which makes it more difficult for DNNs to extract the information required for classification samples. Therefore, the increase of query cost is very reasonable. In order to balance the query cost with the perturbation range, we appropriately increased the perturbation range and attacked all the interpretation regions of the LIME interpreter. The results showed that the attack cost was reduced nearly three times by only increasing the pixel ratio by about 30%.

Table 3. Effect comparison of black box attack methods on Cifar10 dataset.

Attack model		Success rate	Disturbed pixel ratio	Distortion rate	Query cost
ZOO		91%	93.88%	0.7125	102294.51
Autozoom		100%	98.66%	1.7458	156.64
Our attack	Lime_i	**100%**	**5.70%**	1.0728	792.34
	Lime_all	100%	**36.5%**	1.2818	245.44
	Shap+	100%	66.36%	1.5552	212.50
	Shap_all	100%	75.68%	1.6156	180.74

Table 4. Effect comparison of black box attack methods on MNIST dataset.

Attack model		Success rate	Disturbed pixel ratio	Distortion rate	Query cost
ZOO		87%	25.68%	2.0351	145287.36
Autozoom		100%	59.12%	4.7213	1137.34
Our attack	Lime_i	**96%**	**4.30%**	2.7861	1633.52
	Lime_all	99%	25.41%	3.9032	1717.16
	Shap+	100%	33.05%	4.5585	1707.16
	Shap_all	100%	38.79%	4.2727	1386.90

5 Conclusion

Current developments in the model explanations increasingly diverse, bringing trust but also increasing the risk of attack. In the adversarial example attack algorithm, global perturbation is often used and small perturbation is added to each feature to obtain the adversarial example attack sample, which usually has certain randomness and is easy to detect. In this paper, LIME and Shap Value interpreters are used to design an adversarial example attack algorithm based on interpretation information. The sensitive features provided by the interpreters are used to counter perturbation. We use interpretation information to achieve the effect of JSMA attack, and only modify about 5% of the features to achieve an excellent attack success rate, with better visual effect. To weigh the query efficiency, the distortion rate and the visual effects, to explain in LIME interpreter for all categories, the characteristics of information, only around 38% of perturbation obtained characteristics similar to C&W attack effectiveness, and on the displayed shapes, we also confirmed the positive information only for the characteristics of the attack, the effect can also be similar to the C&W attack. In addition, our method can still maintain good attack success rate and distortion rate in the case of black box. Our attack proves that the interpretive information provided by the model interpreter can provide sensitive points for the adversary to some extent, enabling the adversary to modify very few features to succeed in the attack. Although the perturbation range is reduced, and it has some advantages in the attack success rate and perturbation range, making it difficult to be detected, but for black box attack, it does not reduce the query cost. This is our next research direction, how to use interpretation information to reduce the query budget of attack.

Acknowledgements. This work is supported by This work is supported by the National Natural Science Foundation of China (Grant No. 61966011), Hainan University Education and Teaching Reform Research Project (Grant No. HDJWJG01).

References

1. Molnar, C.: Interpretable Machine Learning (2020). https://www.lulu.com/
2. Tu, C.C., Ting, P., Chen, P.Y., et al.: Autozoom: autoencoder-based zeroth order optimization method for attacking black-box neural networks. In: Proceedings of the AAAI Conference on Artificial Intelligence, vol. 33(01), pp. 742–749 (2019)
3. Aïvodji, U., Bolot, A., Gambs, S.: Model extraction from counterfactual explanations. arXiv preprint arXiv:2009.01884 (2020)
4. Amich, A., Eshete, B.: EG-Booster: explanation-guided booster of ML evasion attacks. arXiv preprint arXiv:2108.13930 (2021)
5. Carlini, N., Wagner, D.: Towards evaluating the robustness of neural networks. In: 2017 IEEE Symposium on Security and Privacy (SP). IEEE, pp. 39–57 (2017)
6. Elshawi, R., Al-Mallah, M.H., Sakr, S.: On the interpretability of machine learning-based model for predicting hypertension. BMC Med. Inform. Decis. Making **19**(1), 1–32 (2019)
7. Shokri, R., Strobel, M., Zick, Y.: On the privacy risks of model explanations. In: AIES 2021: AAAI/ACM Conference on AI, Ethics, and Society. ACM (2021)
8. Garcia, W., Choi, J.I., Adari, S.K., et al.: Explainable black-box attacks against model-based authentication. arXiv preprint arXiv:1810.00024 (2018)
9. Moosavi-Dezfooli, S.M., Fawzi, A., Frossard, P.: DeepFool: a simple and accurate method to fool deep neural networks. In: Proceedings of the IEEE Conference on Computer Vision and Pattern Recognition, pp. 2574–2582 (2016)
10. Milli, S., Schmidt, L., Dragan, A.D., et al.: Model reconstruction from model explanations. In: Proceedings of the Conference on Fairness, Accountability, and Transparency, pp. 1–9 (2019)
11. Ovadia, Y., Fertig, E., et al.: Can you trust your model's uncertainty? evaluating predictive uncertainty under dataset shift (2019)
12. Papernot, N., McDaniel, P., Jha, S., et al.: The limitations of deep learning in adversarial settings. In: 2016 IEEE European Symposium on Security and Privacy (EuroS&P), pp. 372–387 IEEE (2016)
13. Ribeiro, MT., Singh, S., Guestrin, C.: Why should I trust you?: explaining the predictions of any classifier. In: The 22nd ACM SIGKDD International Conference. ACM (2016)
14. Su, J., Vargas, D.V., Sakurai, K.: One pixel attack for fooling deep neural networks. IEEE Trans. Evol. Comput. **23**(5), 828–841 (2019)
15. Severi, G., Meyer, J., Coull, S., et al.: Explanation-guided backdoor poisoning attacks against malware classifiers. In: 30th USENIX Security Symposium (USENIX Security 21), pp. 1487–1504 (2021)
16. Zhao, X., Zhang, W., Xiao, X., et al.: Exploiting explanations for model inversion attacks. In: Proceedings of the IEEE/CVF International Conference on Computer Vision, pp. 682–692 (2021)

17. Chen, P.Y., et al.: Zoo: zeroth order optimization based black-box attacks to deep neural networks without training substitute models. In: Proceedings of the 10th ACM Workshop on Artificial Intelligence and Security, pp. 15–26 (2017)
18. Andriushchenko, M., Croce, F., Flammarion, N., Hein, M.: Square attack: a query-efficient black-box adversarial attack via random search. In: Vedaldi, A., Bischof, H., Brox, T., Frahm, J.-M. (eds.) ECCV 2020. LNCS, vol. 12368, pp. 484–501. Springer, Cham (2020). https://doi.org/10.1007/978-3-030-58592-1_29
19. Du, Z., Liu, F., Yan, X.: Minimum adversarial examples. Entropy **24**(3), 396 (2022)
20. Selvaraju, R.R., Cogswell, M., Das, A., et al.: Grad-CAM: visual explanations from deep networks via gradient-based localization. Int. J. Comput. Vis. **128**(2), 336–359 (2020)
21. Wang, H., Wang, Z., Du, M., et al.: Score-CAM: score-weighted visual explanations for convolutional neural networks (2019)
22. Mothilal, R.K., Sharma, A., Tan, C.: Explaining machine learning classifiers through diverse counterfactual explanations. In: Proceedings of the 2020 Conference on Fairness, Accountability, and Transparency, pp. 607–617 (2020)
23. Ilyas, A., Engstrom, L., Athalye, A., et al.: Query-efficient black-box adversarial examples (superceded). arXiv preprint arXiv:1712.07113 (2017)
24. Lee, H., Kim, S.T., Ro, Y.M.: Generation of multimodal justification using visual word constraint model for explainable computer-aided diagnosis. In: Suzuki, K., et al. (eds.) ML-CDS/IMIMIC -2019. LNCS, vol. 11797, pp. 21–29. Springer, Cham (2019). https://doi.org/10.1007/978-3-030-33850-3_3
25. Meyes, R., de Puiseau, C.W., Posada-Moreno, A., Meisen, T.: Under the hood of neural networks: characterizing learned representations by functional neuron populations and network ablations. arXiv preprint arXiv:2004.01254 (2020)
26. Van Molle, P., De Strooper, M., Verbelen, T., Vankeirsbilck, B., Simoens, P., Dhoedt, B.: Visualizing convolutional neural networks to improve decision support for skin lesion classification. In: Stoyanov, D., et al. (eds.) MLCN/DLF/IMIMIC -2018. LNCS, vol. 11038, pp. 115–123. Springer, Cham (2018). https://doi.org/10.1007/978-3-030-02628-8_13

CIFD: A Distance for Complex Intuitionistic Fuzzy Set

Yangyang Zhao[1,2] and Fuyuan Xiao[2(✉)]

[1] School of Computer and Information Science, Southwest University, Chongqing 400715, China
[2] School of Big Data and Software Engineering, Chongqing University, Chongqing 401331, China
xiaofuyuan@cqu.edu.cn, doctorxiaofy@hotmail.com

Abstract. Intuitionistic fuzzy set (IFS) has attracted much attention because it can deal with fuzziness and uncertainty more flexibly than traditional fuzzy set. Complex intuitionistic fuzzy set (CIFS) extends intuitionistic fuzzy to the complex plane, which can better express and process uncertain information. In this paper, a novel distance measure complex intuitionistic fuzzy distance (CIFD) is proposed for CIFSs. Firstly, inspired by Tanimoto coefficient, a new similarity measure between CIFSs is proposed. Then, based on the similarity measure, the CIFD is proposed and its non-negativity, non-degeneracy, and symmetry are analyzed. Moreover, when CIFS degenerates into classical IFS, CIFD is also applicable to measure the differences between IFSs. Finally, to illustrate the effectiveness of CIFD, an example is given at the end.

Keywords: Complex intuitionistic fuzzy set · Similarity measure · Complex intuitionistic fuzzy distance

1 Introduction

In information fusion, it is inevitable to deal with uncertain information [1–3]. Therefore, many methods are proposed to deal with uncertain information, including Dempster-Shafer (D-S) evidence theory [4–6], evidential reasoning [7–9], entropy-based [10], and fuzzy sets [11]. These methods have been widely used in numerous fields, including clustering [12], classification [13–15], complex network [16–18], uncertainty-based multidisciplinary design optimization [19], parrondo effect [20,21], and decision-making [22,23].

As is well known, fuzzy sets can handle fuzzy and uncertain information well. Therefore, fuzzy sets have been widely studied and extended [24–26]. As one of the extensions of fuzzy sets, intuitionistic fuzzy set (IFS) contains membership

This research is supported by the National Natural Science Foundation of China (No. 62003280), Chongqing Talents: Exceptional Young Talents Project (No. cstc2022ycjh-bgzxm0070), Natural Science Foundation of Chongqing, China (No. CSTB2022NSCQ-MSX0531), and Chongqing Overseas Scholars Innovation Program (No. cx2022024).

Y. Xu et al. (Eds.): ML4CS 2022, LNCS 13655, pp. 271–280, 2023.
https://doi.org/10.1007/978-3-031-20096-0_21

function, non-membership function and hesitation function, which can better express uncertainty [27–29].

In a recent work, a novel complex intuitionistic fuzzy set (CIFS) was proposed, which extends IFS to the complex plane [30]. In CIFS, membership function, non-membership function, and hesitation function are all represented by complex numbers, including amplitude term and phase term. Due to the potentially beneficial property of complex numbers in expressing uncertain information, complex-valued models have been extensively studied [31]. Xiao [32] extended the D-S evidence theory to the complex plane, and proposed complex evidence theory (CET), which has been applied to target recognition, classification, decision-making, and other fields. In addition, since both CET and quantum mechanics are based on complex numbers [33,34], CET can be combined with quantum mechanics to deal with uncertain information [35]. As an extension of IFS, CIFS will degenerate into IFS when the membership function, non-membership function, and hesitation function degenerate from complex numbers to real numbers. Therefore, CIFS provides a more promising framework for dealing with uncertain information.

In IFS, there exist a host of distances that measure the difference between IFSs [36]. However, no existing method can measure the difference between CIFSs in [30]. Therefore, inspired by the Tanimoto coefficient, this paper proposes a novel distance measure complex intuitionistic fuzzy distance (CIFD) for CIFS. When CIFS degenerates into classical IFS, CIFD is also applicable to measure the differences between IFSs. Before proposing CIFD, a novel method to measure the similarity between CIFSs was proposed and its properties were analyzed, including non-negativity, non-degeneracy, and symmetry. Then, based on the novel similarity measure, we propose the complex intuitionistic fuzzy distance, which can measure the differences between CIFSs. CIFD is proved to satisfy non-negativity, non-degeneracy and symmetry. Specifically, to illustrate the effectiveness of CIFD, an example is given at the end.

In Sect. 2, the definition of CIFS is introduced. In Sect. 3, a novel similarity measure is proposed, and then CIFD between CIFS is proposed based on the similarity measure. In Sect. 4, an example is given to show the effectiveness of CIFD. Section 5 gives a conclusion of this paper.

2 Complex Intuitionistic Fuzzy Set

As an extension of fuzzy sets, IFS takes into account the information of membership, non-membership and hesitation. It can better express and process uncertain information. Therefore, IFS is widely studied and extended. A recent work extended IFS to the complex plane and proposed a novel CIFS [30]. The specific definition is below.

Definition 1. *(Complex Intuitionistic Fuzzy Set): Let a non-empty set X be a universe of discourse. A complex intuitionistic fuzzy set (CIFS) $\mathbb{A} \in X$ is defined as:*

$$\mathbb{A} = \{\langle x, \mu^c_{\mathbb{A}}(x), \nu^c_{\mathbb{A}}(x)\rangle | x \in X\}, \tag{1}$$

in which

$$\mu^c_{\mathbb{A}}(x) = \mu_{\mathbb{A}}(x)e^{i\theta_{\mu_{\mathbb{A}}}(x)} : X \to \{\mu^c_{\mathbb{A}}(x)|\mu^c_{\mathbb{A}}(x) \in C, |\mu^c_{\mathbb{A}}(x)| \leqslant 1\}, \tag{2}$$

$$\nu^c_{\mathbb{A}}(x) = \nu_{\mathbb{A}}(x)e^{i\theta_{\nu_{\mathbb{A}}}(x)} : X \to \{\nu^c_{\mathbb{A}}(x)|\nu^c_{\mathbb{A}}(x) \in C, |\nu^c_{\mathbb{A}}(x)| \leqslant 1\}, \tag{3}$$

where $i = \sqrt{-1}$, $\mu_{\mathbb{A}}(x) \in [0,1]$ *and* $\nu_{\mathbb{A}}(x) \in [0,1]$ *represent the magnitude of* $\mu^c_{\mathbb{A}}(x)$ *and* $\nu^c_{\mathbb{A}}$. $\theta_{\mu\mathbb{A}}(x) \in [-\pi,\pi]$ *and* $\theta_{\nu\mathbb{A}}(x) \in [-\pi,\pi]$ *are the phase term. The functions* $\mu^c_{\mathbb{A}}(x)$ *and* $\nu^c_{\mathbb{A}}(x)$ *are the degree of membership and degree of non-membership of the element* $x \in X$ *to the set* X*, respectively.*

In addition to the membership function and the non-membership function, the remaining uncertain membership is assigned to the hesitation function $\pi^c_{\mathbb{A}}(x)$*:*

$$\pi^c_{\mathbb{A}}(x) = 1 - \mu^c_{\mathbb{A}}(x) - \nu^c_{\mathbb{A}}(x). \tag{4}$$

A CIFS can also be written in the Cartesian form, denoted by:

$$\mu^c_{\mathbb{A}}(x) = a_\mu(x) + b_\mu(x)i, \tag{5}$$

$$\nu^c_{\mathbb{A}}(x) = a_\nu(x) + b_\nu(x)i, \tag{6}$$

$$\pi^c_{\mathbb{A}}(x) = a_\pi(x) + b_\pi(x)i, \tag{7}$$

with

$$0 \leqslant \sqrt{a_\mu(x)^2 + b_\mu(x)^2}, \sqrt{a_\nu(x)^2 + b_\nu(x)^2}, \sqrt{a_\pi(x)^2 + b_\pi(x)^2} \leqslant 1. \tag{8}$$

Through Euler's formula, Eq.(2) and Eq.(5) have the following relationship:

$$\mu_{\mathbb{A}}(x) = \sqrt{a_\mu(x)^2 + b_\mu(x)^2}, \tag{9}$$

$$\theta_{\mu_{\mathbb{A}}}(x) = arctan\frac{b_\mu(x)}{a_\mu(x)}, \tag{10}$$

where $a_\mu(x) = \mu_{\mathbb{A}}(x)cos(\theta_{\mu_{\mathbb{A}}}(x))$ and $b_\mu(x) = \mu_{\mathbb{A}}(x)sin(\theta_{\mu_{\mathbb{A}}}(x))$. The absolute value of $\mu^c_{\mathbb{A}}(x)$ is calculated by:

$$|\mu^c_{\mathbb{A}}(x)| = \sqrt{\mu^c_{\mathbb{A}}(x)\bar{\mu}^c_{\mathbb{A}}(x)} = \sqrt{a_\mu(x)^2 + b_\mu(x)^2}, \tag{11}$$

where $\bar{\mu}^c_{\mathbb{A}}(x)$ is the complex conjugate of $\mu^c_{\mathbb{A}}(x)$ denoted by $\bar{\mu}^c_{\mathbb{A}}(x) = a_\mu(x) - b_\mu(x)i$. From the above relationship, we can get:

$$\mu_{\mathbb{A}}(x) = |\mu^c_{\mathbb{A}}(x)|, \tag{12}$$

$$\theta_{\mu_{\mathbb{A}}}(x) = \angle\mu^c_{\mathbb{A}}(x). \tag{13}$$

In addition, non-membership function $\nu_{\mathbb{A}}(x)$ and hesitation function $\pi_{\mathbb{A}}(x)$ also have the above corresponding transformation formula.

CIFS extends the intuitionistic fuzzy set to the complex plane, when $\theta_{\mu\mathbb{A}}(x) = \theta_{\nu\mathbb{A}}(x) = \theta_{\pi\mathbb{A}}(x) = 0$, CIFS degenerates into intuitionistic fuzzy set, so it can better express and deal with the uncertainty in the process of the information fusion. However, there is no existing method to measure the differences between CIFSs. Therefore, inspired by the Tanimoto coefficient, a novel distance is proposed in the next section.

3 New Distance for Complex Intuitionistic Fuzzy Sets

In this section, we first propose a novel similarity measure between CIFSs. Then, based on the novel similarity measure, the complex intuitionistic fuzzy distance (CIFD) is proposed for CIFS. In addition, the properties of CIFD are analyzed and proved.

3.1 Similarity Measure Between CIFSs

Tanimoto coefficient is widely used in many fields for similarity measurement [37]. The specific definition of the Tanimoto coefficient is as follows.

Definition 2. *Let $R = \{r_1, r_2, ..., r_n\}$ and $S = \{s_1, s_2, ..., s_n\}$ be two probability distribution. The Tanimoto coefficient between R and S is defined as follows [37]:*

$$T(R,S) = \frac{\sum_{i=1}^{n} r_i s_i}{\sum_{i=1}^{n} r_i^2 + \sum_{i=1}^{n} s_i^2 - \sum_{i=1}^{n} r_i s_i}. \tag{14}$$

Inspired by the Tanimoto coefficient, we extend it to the complex plane and propose a novel similarity measure between CIFSs.

Definition 3. *(Similarity Measure Between CIFSs): Let $\mathbb{A}$ and $\mathbb{B}$ be two CIFSs on a universe of discourse $X = \{x_1, x_2, ..., x_n\}$ denoted by:*

$$\mathbb{A} = \{\langle x, \mu_{\mathbb{A}}^c(x), \nu_{\mathbb{A}}^c(x), \pi_{\mathbb{A}}^c(x)\rangle | x \in X\},$$

$$\mathbb{B} = \{\langle x, \mu_{\mathbb{B}}^c(x), \nu_{\mathbb{B}}^c(x), \pi_{\mathbb{B}}^c(x)\rangle | x \in X\}.$$

The similarity between CIFSs $\mathbb{A}$ and $\mathbb{B}$ is defined as:

$$Sim(\mathbb{A},\mathbb{B}) = \frac{1}{n}\sum_{i=1}^{n} \frac{|\sum_{j=1}^{3} \mathbb{A}_j(x_i)\bar{\mathbb{B}}_j(x_i)|}{|\sum_{j=1}^{3} |\mathbb{A}_j(x_i)|^2 + |\mathbb{B}_j(x_i)|^2 - \mathbb{A}_j(x_i)\bar{\mathbb{B}}_j(x_i)|}, \tag{15}$$

in which $\mathbb{A}_1(x)$, $\mathbb{A}_2(x)$ and $\mathbb{A}_3(x)$ represent $\mu_{\mathbb{A}}^c(x)$, $\nu_{\mathbb{A}}^c(x)$ and $\pi_{\mathbb{A}}^c(x)$, respectively. $\bar{\mathbb{B}}_j(x)$ is the complex conjugate of $\mathbb{B}_j(x)$, and $|\cdot|$ represents the absolute value operation.

For the denominator in Eq. (15), the following equation can be obtained.

$$\begin{aligned}
&|\mathbb{A}_1\bar{\mathbb{A}}_1 + \mathbb{A}_2\bar{\mathbb{A}}_2 + \mathbb{A}_3\bar{\mathbb{A}}_3 + \mathbb{B}_1\bar{\mathbb{B}}_1 + \mathbb{B}_2\bar{\mathbb{B}}_2 + \mathbb{B}_3\bar{\mathbb{B}}_3 - \mathbb{A}_1\bar{\mathbb{B}}_1 - \mathbb{A}_2\bar{\mathbb{B}}_2 - \mathbb{A}_2\bar{\mathbb{B}}_2| \\
&= |(\mathbb{A}_1 - \mathbb{B}_1)(\bar{\mathbb{A}}_1 - \bar{\mathbb{B}}_1) + (\mathbb{A}_2 - \mathbb{B}_2)(\bar{\mathbb{A}}_2 - \bar{\mathbb{B}}_2) + (\mathbb{A}_3 - \mathbb{B}_3)(\bar{\mathbb{A}}_3 - \bar{\mathbb{B}}_3) \\
&\quad + \mathbb{B}_1\bar{\mathbb{A}}_1 + \mathbb{B}_2\bar{\mathbb{A}}_2 + \mathbb{B}_3\bar{\mathbb{A}}_3| \\
&= |(\mathbb{A}_1 - \mathbb{B}_1)(\bar{\mathbb{A}}_1 - \bar{\mathbb{B}}_1) + (\mathbb{A}_2 - \mathbb{B}_2)(\bar{\mathbb{A}}_2 - \bar{\mathbb{B}}_2) + (\mathbb{A}_3 - \mathbb{B}_3)(\bar{\mathbb{A}}_3 - \bar{\mathbb{B}}_3) \\
&\quad + \mathbb{A}_1\bar{\mathbb{B}}_1 + \mathbb{A}_2\bar{\mathbb{B}}_2 + \mathbb{A}_3\bar{\mathbb{B}}_3|
\end{aligned} \tag{16}$$

Therefore, Eq. (15) can also be written as:

$$Sim(\mathbb{A},\mathbb{B}) = \frac{1}{n}\sum_{i=1}^{n} \frac{|\sum_{j=1}^{3} \mathbb{A}_j(x_i)\bar{\mathbb{B}}_j(x_i)|}{|\sum_{j=1}^{3} |\mathbb{A}_j(x_i) - \mathbb{B}_j(x_i)|^2 + \mathbb{A}_j(x_i)\bar{\mathbb{B}}_j(x_i)|}. \tag{17}$$

The similarity measure between two CIFSs, $Sim(\mathbb{A},\mathbb{B})$, has the following properties.

Property 1. Suppose $\mathbb{A}$ and $\mathbb{B}$ are two CIFSs on a universe of discourse X. The properties of $Sim(\mathbb{A}, \mathbb{B})$ are given as follows:

$P1.1 : 0 \leqslant Sim(\mathbb{A}, \mathbb{B}) \leqslant 1$.
$P1.2 : Sim(\mathbb{A}, \mathbb{B}) = 1$ if and only if $\mathbb{A} = \mathbb{B}$.
$P1.3 : Sim(\mathbb{A}, \mathbb{B}) = Sim(\mathbb{B}, \mathbb{A})$.

For the above properties, the specific proof is as below.

Proof. (1) Through Eq. (17), since $|\cdot|$ represents the absolute value operation, $Sim(\mathbb{A}, \mathbb{B}) \geqslant 0$. $|\mathbb{A}_j(x) - \mathbb{B}_j(x)|$ is a real number greater that 0 and is equal to 0 when $\mathbb{A}_j(x) = \mathbb{B}_j(x)$, therefore, $|\sum_{j=1}^{3} |\mathbb{A}_j(x_i) - \mathbb{B}_j(x_i)|^2 + \mathbb{A}_j(x_i)\bar{\mathbb{B}}_j(x_i)| \geqslant |\sum_{j=1}^{3} \mathbb{A}_j(x_i)\bar{\mathbb{B}}_j(x_i)|$ indicating that $Sim(\mathbb{A}, \mathbb{B}) \leqslant 1$. As a consequence, $P1.1$ and $P1.2$ have been proved.

(2) For two complex number C and $\bar{C}$ that are conjugate to each other, $|C| = |\bar{C}|$. $\mathbb{A}_j(x)\bar{\mathbb{B}}_j(x)$ and $\mathbb{B}_j(x)\bar{\mathbb{A}}_j(x)$ are conjugate to each other, therefore,

$$\begin{aligned} Sim(\mathbb{A}, \mathbb{B}) &= \frac{1}{n} \sum_{i=1}^{n} \frac{|\sum_{j=1}^{3} \mathbb{A}_j(x_i)\bar{\mathbb{B}}_j(x_i)|}{|\sum_{j=1}^{3} |\mathbb{A}_j(x_i)|^2 + |\mathbb{B}_j(x_i)|^2 - \mathbb{A}_j(x_i)\bar{\mathbb{B}}_j(x_i)|} \\ &= \frac{1}{n} \sum_{i=1}^{n} \frac{|\sum_{j=1}^{3} \mathbb{B}_j(x_i)\bar{\mathbb{A}}_j(x_i)|}{|\sum_{j=1}^{3} |\mathbb{B}_j(x_i)|^2 + |\mathbb{A}_j(x_i)|^2 - \mathbb{B}_j(x_i)\bar{\mathbb{A}}_j(x_i)|} \\ &= Sim(\mathbb{B}, \mathbb{A}). \end{aligned} \quad (18)$$

The similarity measure $Sim(\mathbb{A}, \mathbb{B})$ can effectively measure the similarity between CIFSs. The range of $Sim(\mathbb{A}, \mathbb{B})$ is 0 to 1. The larger the value of $Sim(\mathbb{A}, \mathbb{B})$, the more similar the two CIFSs are. In addition, when CIFS degenerates into classical IFS, $Sim(\mathbb{A}, \mathbb{B})$ can also measure the similarity between IFSs.

3.2 The Novel Distance Between CIFSs

Based on the similarity measure between CIFSs proposed above, the novel distance between CIFSs is defined below.

Definition 4. *(Complex Intuitionistic Fuzzy Distance): Let $\mathbb{A}$ and $\mathbb{B}$ be two CIFSs on a universe of discourse X. The CIFD between $\mathbb{A}$ and $\mathbb{B}$ is defined as:*

$$d_{CIFS}(\mathbb{A}, \mathbb{B}) = \sqrt{1 - Sim(\mathbb{A}, \mathbb{B})}. \quad (19)$$

CIFD can measure the differences between CIFSs and has the following properties. The smaller the value of CIFD, the smaller the difference between CIFSs.

Property 2. Let $\mathbb{A}$ and $\mathbb{B}$ be two CIFSs on a universe of discourse X. The CIFD holds the following properties.

$P2.1$ $(Nonnegativity) : 0 \leqslant d_{CIFS}(\mathbb{A}, \mathbb{B}) \leqslant 1$.
$P2.2$ $(Nondegeneracy) : d_{CIFS}(\mathbb{A}, \mathbb{B}) = 0$ if and only if $\mathbb{A} = \mathbb{B}$.
$P2.3$ $(Symmetry) : d_{CIFS}(\mathbb{A}, \mathbb{B}) = d_{CIFS}(\mathbb{B}, \mathbb{A})$.

As previously proved by the similarity measure $Sim(\mathbb{A}, \mathbb{B})$, the above properties of CIFD can be easily proved. Moreover, when CIFS degenerates into classical IFS, CIFD is still applicable to measure the distance between IFSs.

4 Numerical Example

In this section, an example is given to verify the effectiveness and properties of CIFD, including non-negativity, non-degeneracy and symmetry.

Example 1. Let $\mathbb{A}$ and $\mathbb{B}$ be two CIFSs on a universe of discourse X given by:

$$\mathbb{A} = \{\langle x + yi, 1 - x - yi \rangle\},$$

$$\mathbb{B} = \{\langle 1 - x + yi, x - yi \rangle\}.$$

First, we set $y = 0$, and x changes from 0 to 1. In this case, CIFSs $\mathbb{A}$ and $\mathbb{B}$ degenerate to classical IFSs. From Fig. 1, CIFD is also applicable to classical IFS. When $x = 0.5$, in this case $\mathbb{A} = \mathbb{B}$, the distance between them is 0. When x is 0 or 1, the maximum distance of 1 is obtained. As x increases from 0 to 1, the distance decreases from 1 to 0 and then increases from 0 to 1.

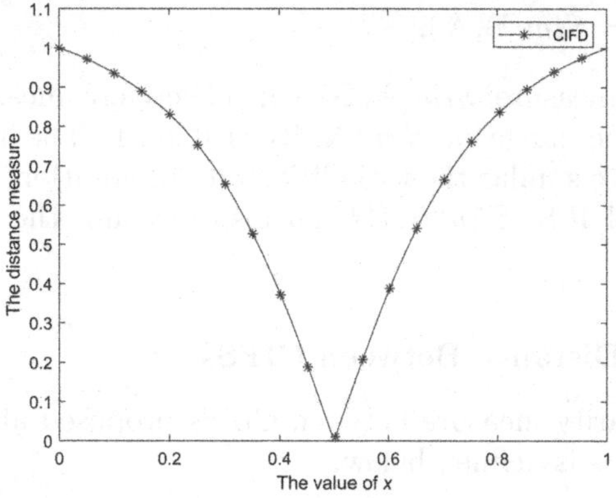

Fig. 1. The result of CIFD in Example 1 under variations in x

Then, to study the relationship between the variation of CIFD and the real and imaginary parts of CIFS, we set $x \in [0, 1]$ and $y \in [-1, 1]$, satisfying $(x^2 + y^2)^{1/2} \leqslant 1$ and $((1 - x)^2 + y^2)^{1/2} \leqslant 1$. Under these conditions, the values of CIFD between $\mathbb{A}$ and $\mathbb{B}$ are shown in Fig. 2.

From Fig. 2(a), when $x = 0.5$, no matter what the value of y is, CIFD always takes the minimum value of 0. This is reasonable since $\mathbb{A} = \mathbb{B}$ in this case. The variation of CIFD between $\mathbb{A}$ and $\mathbb{B}$ with variables x and y is shown in Fig. 2(b). When $x = 1$ and $y = 0$, we have $\mathbb{A} = \{\langle 1, 0 \rangle\}$ and $\mathbb{B} = \{\langle 0, 1 \rangle\}$, and when $x = 0$ and $y = 0$, we have $\mathbb{A} = \{\langle 0, 1 \rangle\}$ and $\mathbb{B} = \{\langle 1, 0 \rangle\}$. In both two cases, $\mathbb{A}$ and

$\mathbb{B}$ are completely different, so CIFD between $\mathbb{A}$ and $\mathbb{B}$ gets the maximum value of 1.

Figures 2(c) and (d) show the CIFD under variables x and y, respectively. CIFD decreases when x changes from 0 to 0.5 and increases when x changes from 0.5 to 1. This is because when $x = 0.5$, in this case $\mathbb{A} = \mathbb{B}$, and as it moves away from 0.5, the distance between them becomes larger and larger. Furthermore, as y varies from -1 to 1, the CIFD value gradually increases form 0 to 1 and then decreases from 1 to 0.

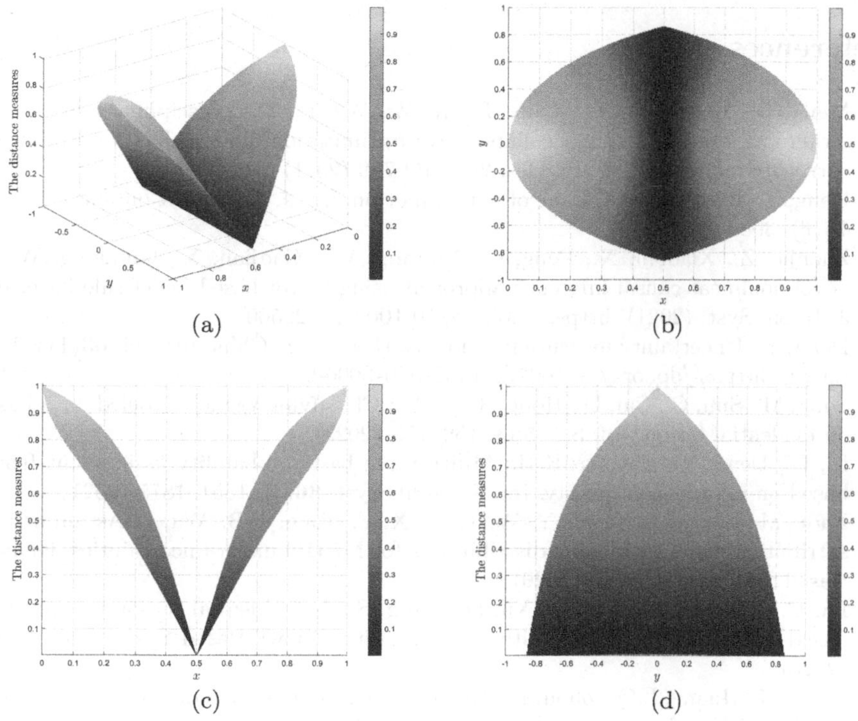

Fig. 2. The value of CIFD varies with the real and imaginary parts of the CIFSs in Example 1. (a) CIFD values. (b) Variations in x and y. (c) CIFD under x variations. (d) CIFD under y variations.

As can be seen from the above analysis, this example also verifies the non-negativity, non-degeneracy and symmetry of CIFD.

5 Conclusion

In this paper, we proposed a novel distance measure CIFD for CIFS. Before giving the definition of CIFD, inspired by Tanimoto coefficient, we proposed a novel similarity measure between CIFS. Then CIFD was proposed based on the novel similarity measure. Moreover, CIFD has been verified to be non-negative, non-degeneracy and symmetry. When CIFS degenerates into IFS, CIFD is also applicable to measuring the distance between IFSs. Specifically, to illustrate the effectiveness of CIFD, an example was given at the end.

References

1. Meng, D., Li, Y., He, C., Guo, J., Lv, Z., Wu, P.: Multidisciplinary design for structural integrity using a collaborative optimization method based on adaptive surrogate modelling. Mater. Des. **206**, 109789 (2021)
2. Deng, Y.: Information volume of mass function. Int. J. Comput. Commun. Control **15**(6), 3983 (2020)
3. Zhenjie, Z., Xiaobin, X., Peng, C., Xudong, W., Xiaojian, X., Guodong, W.: A novel nonlinear causal inference approach using vector-based belief rule base. Int. J. Intell. Syst. (2021). https://doi.org/10.1002/int.22500
4. Deng, Y.: Uncertainty measure in evidence theory. Sci. China Inf. Sci. **63**(11), 1–19 (2020). https://doi.org/10.1007/s11432-020-3006-9
5. Song, M., Sun, C., Cai, D., Hong, S., Li, H.: Classifying vaguely labeled data based on evidential fusion. Inf. Sci. **583**, 159–173 (2022)
6. Li, D., Deng, Y., Cheong, K.H.: Multisource basic probability assignment fusion based on information quality. Int. J. Intell. Syst. **36**(4), 1851–1875 (2021)
7. Zhou, M., Liu, X.-B., Chen, Y.-W., Qian, X.-F., Yang, J.-B., Wu, J.: Assignment of attribute weights with belief distributions for MADM under uncertainties. Knowl.-Based Syst. **189**, 105110 (2020)
8. Fu, C., Xue, M., Chang, W., Xu, D., Yang, S.: An evidential reasoning approach based on risk attitude and criterion reliability. Knowl.-Based Syst. **199**, 105947 (2020)
9. Liu, Z.G., Huang, L.Q., Zhou, K., Denoeux, T.: Combination of transferable classification with multisource domain adaptation based on evidential reasoning. IEEE Trans. Neural Netw. Learn. Syst. **32**, 2015–2029 (2020)
10. Babajanyan, S., Allahverdyan, A., Cheong, K.H.: Energy and entropy: Path from game theory to statistical mechanics. Phys. Rev. Res. **2**(4), 043055 (2020)
11. Pan, L., Gao, X., Deng, Y., Cheong, K.H.: The constrained Pythagorean fuzzy sets and its similarity measure. IEEE Trans. Fuzzy Syst. **30**, 1102–1113 (2021)
12. Wang, Z., Li, Z., Wang, R., Nie, F., Li, X.: Large graph clustering with simultaneous spectral embedding and discretization. IEEE Trans. Pattern Anal. Mach. Intell. **43**(12), 4426–4440 (2021). https://doi.org/10.1109/TPAMI.2020.3002587
13. Xu, X., Zheng, J., Yang, J.-B., Xu, D.-L., Chen, Y.-W.: Data classification using evidence reasoning rule. Knowl.-Based Syst. **116**, 144–151 (2017)
14. Xiao, F., Wen, J., Pedrycz, W.: Generalized divergence-based decision making method with an application to pattern classification. IEEE Trans. Knowl. Data Eng. (2022). https://doi.org/10.1109/TKDE.2022.3177896

15. Zhang, L., Xiao, F.: A novel belief $\chi 2$ divergence for multisource information fusion and its application in pattern classification. Int. J. Intell. Syst. **37**, 7968–7991 (2022). https://doi.org/10.1002/int.22912
16. Zhao, J., Deng, Y.: Complex network modeling of evidence theory. IEEE Trans. Fuzzy Syst. **29**, 3470–3480 (2020)
17. Xiong, L., Su, X., Qian, H.: Conflicting evidence combination from the perspective of networks. Inf. Sci. **580**, 408–418 (2021). https://doi.org/10.1016/j.ins.2021.08.088
18. Jiang, W., Cao, Y., Deng, X.: A novel Z-network model based on Bayesian network and Z-number. IEEE Trans. Fuzzy Syst. **28**(8), 1585–1599 (2020)
19. Meng, D., Xie, T., Wu, P., He, C., Hu, Z., Lv, Z.: An uncertainty-based design optimization strategy with random and interval variables for multidisciplinary engineering systems. In: Structures, vol. 32, pp. 997–1004. Elsevier (2021)
20. Cheong, K.H., Koh, J.M., Jones, M.C.: Paradoxical survival: examining the parrondo effect across biology. BioEssays **41**(6), 1900027 (2019)
21. Lai, J.W., Cheong, K.H.: Parrondo effect in quantum coin-toss simulations. Phys. Rev. E **101**, 052212 (2020)
22. Liu, P., Zhang, X., Pedrycz, W.: A consensus model for hesitant fuzzy linguistic group decision-making in the framework of Dempster-Shafer evidence theory. Knowl.-Based Syst. **212**, 106559 (2021)
23. Wu, Z., Liao, H.: A consensus reaching process for large-scale group decision making with heterogeneous preference information. Int. J. Intell. Syst. **36**, 4560–4591 (2021). https://doi.org/10.1002/int.22469
24. Deng, J., Deng, Y.: Information volume of fuzzy membership function. Int. J. Comput. Commun. Control **16**(1), 1–14 (2021). https://doi.org/10.15837/ijccc.2021.1.4106
25. Deng, Y.: Random permutation set. Int. J. Comput. Commun. Control **17**(1), 1–16 (2022). https://doi.org/10.15837/ijccc.2022.1.4542
26. Garg, H.: A new possibility degree measure for interval-valued q-rung orthopair fuzzy sets in decision-making. Int. J. Intell. Syst. **36**(1), 526–557 (2021)
27. Fei, L., Feng, Y.: Intuitionistic fuzzy decision-making in the framework of Dempster-Shafer structures. Int. J. Intell. Syst. **36**(10), 5419–5448 (2021)
28. Wang, Z., Xiao, F., Ding, W.: Interval-valued intuitionistic fuzzy jenson-shannon divergence and its application in multi-attribute decision making. Appl. Intel. **52**, 1–17 (2022). https://doi.org/10.1007/s10489-022-03347-0
29. Song, Y., Fu, Q., Wang, Y.-F., Wang, X.: Divergence-based cross entropy and uncertainty measures of Atanassov's intuitionistic fuzzy sets with their application in decision making. Appl. Soft Comput. **84**, 105703 (2019)
30. Zhao, Y., Xiao, F.: A novel complex intuitionistic fuzzy set. https://vixra.org/abs/2205.0122
31. Li, Y., Zhu, R., Mi, X., Kang, B.: An intelligent quality-based fusion method for complex-valued distributions using POWA operator. Eng. Appl. Artif. Intell. **109**, 104618 (2022)
32. Xiao, F.: Generalized belief function in complex evidence theory. J. Intell. Fuzzy Syst. **38**(4), 3665–3673 (2020)
33. Deng, X., Jiang, W.: Quantum representation of basic probability assignments based on mixed quantum states. In: 2021 IEEE 24th International Conference on Information Fusion (FUSION), pp. 1–6. IEEE (2021)
34. Ding, W., Lin, C.-T., Cao, Z.: Deep neuro-cognitive co-evolution for fuzzy attribute reduction by quantum leaping PSO with nearest-neighbor memeplexes. IEEE Trans. Cybern. **49**(7), 2744–2757 (2018)

35. Xiao, F., Pedrycz, W.: Negation of the quantum mass function for multisource quantum information fusion with its application to pattern classification. IEEE Trans. Pattern Anal. Mach. Intel. (2022)
36. Szmidt, E., Kacprzyk, J.: Distances between intuitionistic fuzzy sets. Fuzzy Sets Syst. **114**(3), 505–518 (2000)
37. Rogers, D.J., Tanimoto, T.T.: A computer program for classifying plants. Science **132**(3434), 1115–1118 (1960)

Security Evaluation Method of Distance Education Network Nodes Based on Machine Learning

Jiajuan Fang(✉)

Department of Software Engineering, Zhengzhou Technical College, Zhengzhou 450121, China
fangjj75@126.com

Abstract. In the distance education network, the node security problem is often not guaranteed. Therefore, a machine learning based distance education network node security evaluation method is designed to ensure the node security problem through the node security evaluation, and extract the attack characteristic attributes of the distance education network from the traffic and log information. According to this characteristic attribute, a network wide attack model of distance education network nodes is constructed based on hierarchical expansion. This paper uses AHP method to build a distance education network node security evaluation model based on machine learning, and tests the performance of this method. The test results show that this method has high accuracy and low error rate of network node security evaluation, which proves the evaluation performance of this method.

Keywords: Machine learning · Distance education network · Attack characteristic attribute · Node safety assessment

1 Introduction

In formal school education, the traditional teaching method is "Teacher centered, classroom centered and textbook centered" indoctrination teaching. This teaching method is not conducive to students' active learning, nor to cultivating students' learning and working ability, nor to teaching students in accordance with their aptitude. Therefore, the majority of educators continue to explore new ways of educational technology to gradually copy or replace the original teaching model. Practice has proved that CAI, especially distance teaching system, embodies a new teaching idea. It provides an advanced teaching means and modern management tool for changing the traditional educational concept and realizing high-level basic education and multi-level and multi-form education and training [1]. Therefore, education reform needs distance education.

The distance teaching programs broadcast through audio and video television signals not only have sound, it can also transmit TV signals containing images and words through frequency division multiplexing, which brings about the wide popularization and application of distance teaching, and forms a radio and television distance teaching network with radio and television universities and school independent TV teaching

Y. Xu et al. (Eds.): ML4CS 2022, LNCS 13655, pp. 281–295, 2023.
https://doi.org/10.1007/978-3-031-20096-0_22

systems as the main body; After the emergence and wide application of the satellite communication technology, it is combined with the television transmission system on the ground. Using the characteristics of long transmission distance and wide coverage of the satellite communication network, it is used as the backbone transmission network, and the television transmission system is used as the regional or local transmission network. In this way, the teaching information is directly or indirectly sent to the teaching points, and the coverage of the education information is wide, The transmission distance is long, and it has the characteristics of immediacy, flexibility and convenience, so it is widely used, especially for popularizing and developing education in remote areas [2]. However, these long-distance teaching methods, which are composed of radio and television and satellite communication technology, belong to the model of radio and television teaching. The biggest disadvantage of this method is the unidirectional transmission of teaching information, the lack of interaction, and the inability of direct communication between students and teachers [3]. Moreover, this kind of teaching method basically follows the teaching thought and teaching mode of traditional teaching. It is still a blackboard classroom teaching form that "teachers are the center, textbooks are the center, and classrooms are the center".

Based on this background, this paper studies the security evaluation of distance education network nodes, and designs a security evaluation method of distance education network nodes based on machine learning. Extract the characteristic attributes of distance education network attack from the traffic and log information, build the whole network attack model of distance education network nodes, and use the analytic hierarchy process to test the performance of this method. Experimental research shows that this method has high accuracy of network node security evaluation, low error rate, and good evaluation performance.

2 Security Evaluation of Distance Education Network Nodes

2.1 Attack Feature Attribute Extraction

The characteristic data of network attack in distance education is hidden in the traffic and log information. It can effectively fuse the two, extract the key influencing factors driving the attack, reduce the sparsity caused by irrelevant attributes, and avoid affecting the detection results. Traffic and log data sources reflect complementary characteristics in the contribution of attacks [4]. Usually, for traffic analysis, only the information of each layer of packet header can be obtained, so that the characteristics hidden in the packet header can be captured. However, the most important behavior characteristic of a packet is hidden in the load. However, in order to ensure the security of information transmission, the load information is generally encrypted and cannot analyze the data characteristics in the load, which is also the main reason why the detection accuracy of each penetration type attack is very low and the overall detection accuracy is difficult to improve. Therefore, the network attack event identification method based on traffic and log correlation analysis is studied, the association rules between traffic and log are formulated, and the attack characteristic attributes are extracted more comprehensively.

Whether traffic and logs occur in a normal application or an abnormal attack event, they should belong to the same application before they can have a certain correlation.

Moreover, traffic and logs must be on the same device before they can come from the same device. Moreover, traffic and logs usually have a chronological relationship. Traffic is usually used as a request operation to trigger an application, and then a log is generated during the execution of the request operation. In order to maintain the original data characteristics, association is performed from the original data. Based on the above characteristics, association rules are defined as follows:

(1) Storage consistency: the network LAN traffic and the log information of each network node are sent to the unified data management server for storage.
(2) Consistency of data format of the same kind: the format of all traffic data shall be consistent after being structured, and the log information of different network nodes shall also be consistent after being formatted.
(3) Target consistency: the target address of traffic data is consistent with the source address of log information, which is the bridge of association.
(4) Internal consistency of time causality: traffic exists as the cause of attack, and logs exist as the result of attack. The up and down floating time ΔC_T generated by the two relationships is defined as the following formula:

$$\Delta C_T = E_{TTL} + 2E_L \tag{1}$$

In formula (1), E_{TTL} refers to the average network delay; E_L is the average log generation time.

According to the above association rules, the feature extraction steps are as follows:

(1) The characteristic attribute entry related to traffic entered in the current detection is RFOW one, which contains five tuples associated with the log (dstservice, clientip, clientmac, starttime, endcontime), which are the target total address, target IP address, target MAC address, connection start time and connection end time respectively.
(2) In the log information record, the key fields associated with traffic include slogsrc, deviceip, devicemac, and recordtime, which are the event source, host IP address, host MAC address, and logging time [5]. According to the five tuple information in RFOW one, extract the log data set according to the following rules.

   Let R represent the rule set, including:

$$R = (R_1 \cap R_2, R_2 \cap R_3) \tag{2}$$

   In Eq. (2), AA refers to Client IP = Device IP; BB refers to client MAC = Device MAC; CC refers to DST Service = SLog Src.
(3) Perform statistical calculation on the log record set, such as login attempts, login failures, access to sensitive files, audit failures, warnings, etc. as RLog One, that is, log characteristics.
(4) Get the characteristic attribute data of the final input attack detection model. To sum up, the characteristic attributes based on nodes can be obtained.

2.2 Build a Network Wide Attack Model

The whole network attack model of distance education network nodes is constructed based on hierarchical expansion. Hierarchical extended SPN is very suitable for large-scale complex network modeling. Compared with attack graph and other models, this model has the following advantages:

(1) It has a stronger ability to describe the attack process and network status. It can model the distributed system cooperative attack, and clearly express the logic and timing relationship of vulnerability utilization between hosts in complex attacks.
(2) The definition of random transition in SPN is extended, so that the model can reflect the comprehensive impact of attack cost and attack benefit on the attacker's decision-making.
(3) The problem that the state of attack graph increases exponentially is fundamentally solved. The design of network object and hierarchy can effectively control the scale of network state under the condition that the host vulnerability state is fully described.
(4) The model generation method is more convenient. When generating a network attack path, you do not need to search the network state, but only need to add an attack transition in the known state universe space according to the attack rule base.
(5) The model generation algorithm has better performance in simulating the time and space complexity of multi-target attacks. It can generate an integrated Petri net model for multi-target attacks, and save the total time for each target to search and match the attack rule base. The proposed network wide attack modeling method aims to help defenders fully grasp various attack behaviors, and propose defense measures for some key attack paths and vulnerable nodes.

The hierarchical extension of Petri net describing complex network attack system can effectively reduce the number of nodes on each layer of the network. At the same time, the creation of objects makes it possible to reuse subgraphs. The network attack model is abstracted into two aspects: macro attack and micro attack: from the macro point of view, the attack relationship between nodes in the domain network is studied, and the utilization path of network vulnerability is mined; From the microscopic point of view, this paper studies the vulnerability attack methods and the dangerous evolution process on a node. The combination of network attack and host attack can effectively grasp which nodes in the whole network are vulnerable points and which key settings and services on these vulnerable points are noteworthy, so as to lay a foundation for network defense. The hierarchical structure of Petri net can well solve the problem of macro and micro attacks. This chapter adopts the top-down modeling method to make the top-level Petri net describe the attack relationship between the nodes in the domain network, ignoring the attack details on the nodes, and focusing on the vulnerability utilization and risk propagation in the network remote attack. In the lower Petri net, the local attacks on each host are modeled separately, and the state evolution process of the host under attack is described in detail. Finally, the macro network and micro subnet are integrated to realize the whole network attack description modeling of complex network system.

The transition in Petri net represents the attack behavior, and the attacker should have a certain probability to choose the transition. For example, there are many public attack tools and source codes that have been released on the network. These simple attack methods that can be directly obtained are easier to be taken by hackers. At the same time, those attack methods that are destructive and can bring huge benefits are often favored by attackers [6]. Therefore, several assumptions are put forward before modeling:

Hypothesis 1: The attacker is a rational and intelligent decision-maker, who can consider the attack cost and benefit according to the current network situation and state, and will choose a lower cost attack method when the benefits are the same.
Hypothesis 2: The attacker constantly pursues benefits in the process of attack, trying to maximize the benefits. When the attack cost is similar, the attacker is more inclined to take the attack method that has the greatest damage to the target node (resource).
Hypothesis 3: The attacker considers the attack cost and benefit comprehensively, and is more willing to take the attack method with large benefit and low cost.
Hypothesis 4: When the benefit of one attack mode is far greater than that of other attacks, and its cost is also higher than that of others, then compared with those low-cost and low-income attacks, the former is more able to satisfy the attackers.

Based on the above four assumptions, the concept of attack effectiveness is proposed. That is, each attacker will judge the efficiency and attack ability of various feasible attack schemes according to the collected information before taking the attack behavior, and find one or several attack strategies with the highest efficiency to carry out the attack. Under the condition that the attacker is rational, this selection method is consistent with the actual situation.

The attack effectiveness AEP is introduced into each transition to replace the concept of time delay in the traditional stochastic Petri net as the judgment basis of attack decision. Different attackers have different amounts of resources, different knowledge and experience, and the defense performance and resource provision of the attacked node are also very different. Therefore, the cost and benefit of each attack are random, so the attack cost performance is a random variable. If the cost performance of an attack is higher, the probability of the attack behavior is greater. The distribution function that the attack cost performance ratio obeys is determined by the attack cost and the attack income, and these two random variables also obey their respective distribution laws.

The whole network combined attack model is defined as an extended stochastic Petri net with hierarchical structure, where the hierarchical structure is expressed in the form of object net [7]. Object nets express Petri nets in the form of object-oriented technology. The repository node in the top-level network is regarded as an object. The subnet is sealed in the object. Some positions in the subnet are specified to represent the connection between the object and the outside world. These positions are called interface repositories. The outside world sends the topology to the interface library through transition to call the corresponding methods of the object and transfer the operands. The token is extracted from these locations within the subnet to represent the response of the object. In order to reflect the hierarchy, objects arc also allowed to be included inside objects. Every transition in the hierarchical Petri net is associated with a random variable of attack effectiveness.

The construction idea of the whole network attack Petri net is a top-down, step-by-step fine process. The top-level network is used to describe the attack relationship between hosts on the network. The host nodes are regarded as objects, and the top-level network is composed of host objects and attack transitions between objects. The objects in the top-level network can be expanded into subnets (lower level networks) according to the host attack rule set hars. Each host object presents different states after being attacked. These states are divided into two types: one is interface states (is), which can directly interact with external objects. Is the main attack target of the attacker or an important resource to be used to achieve the attack target, and the other is the Middle States (MS) inside the object. Corresponding to the network state information base and attack rule base, the whole network combined attack Petri net can be established. The initial node corresponds to the initial state set ISS. It is a special object that only contains the interface library, and is composed of the service and vulnerability information of all hosts in the network. Host, webserver, ftpserver, DBServer and smtpserver are node types in the network. Each class contains multiple instances. Each instance is initialized in the top-level network as an object, and the six states in vs are its interface library. The known connections and trust relationships among nodes are transformed into access transitions in the network. The attack relationship between network nodes can be inferred from the initial object and NARS. Each object can extend the subnet to describe the migration relationship between host interface states. As shown in host a node, other nodes can also be extended.

Usually, there is more than one important node to be concerned in the network. Due to the limitations of state space and structure, the existing network attack models can only be described and generated for a single attack target. The object-based top-level Petri net has the ability to describe the whole network attack. All hosts on the network can be regarded as victim nodes. The possible attack transitions among all hosts can be generated through the top-level net construction algorithm to form an attack path network.

A rough attack path mining method is proposed by specifying the key objects as the attack targets, which can quickly find the object nodes that contribute to the attack targets in the above complex path network, eliminate irrelevant and isolated nodes, and generate a set of possible attack paths. These paths include not only the exact paths that can be derived directly under the current knowledge level, but also the possible paths with potential attack relationships. Rough path mining can quickly filter the involved surfaces of objects, facilitate convergence as soon as possible when searching for accurate paths, reduce the number of extended objects, and save storage space. At the same time, rough path lays the foundation for network risk assessment.

2.3 Construction of Network Node Security Evaluation Model for Distance Education

The security evaluation model of distance education network nodes based on machine learning is constructed, and the machine learning method used is AHP.

AHP is a qualitative and quantitative analysis method based on multi criteria factors. In the research of index system, AHP hierarchizes the problem, decomposes the problem from the nature of the problem, with direct expression and simple calculation, which reduces the subjectivity of the evaluation process. Therefore, it is widely used to determine the index weight in the field of network security [50,108,109]. AHP decomposes the qualitative elements related to the decision objectives into criteria, schemes and other levels. The scheme level is the candidate set of the decision objectives, and the criteria level is the influencing factor on the scheme level [8].

In order to reduce the subjectivity of attribute assignment, AHP is used to determine the value of attribute of evaluation factors in the process of quantification of evaluation factors.

Quantitative Method Design of Evaluation Factors

Establish Hierarchy

The indicator sources of the network domain are divided into network node static configuration information, device information, access information, traffic information, alarm information and vulnerability information, and then the indicator source information is described as source = {configuration, element, access, netflow, thread, vulnerability}. The attribute vector of the evaluation factor is:

$$f = (f_c, f_e, f_a, f_n, f_t, f_v)^T \tag{3}$$

In formula (3), f_c, f_e, f_a, f_n, f_t and f_v refer to the corresponding attribute vector of each indicator source information; T is the attribute vector threshold.

Before using AHP, it is necessary to determine the hierarchical structure of decision objectives and decision criteria, take the evaluation factors as the decision objectives of the upper level (objective level), and the source information as the decision criteria of the lower level (criterion level), so as to build the hierarchical structure.

Build Judgment Matrix

The relationship between the source information in the criteria layer and the evaluation factors, that is, the possibility that the evaluation factors belong to a certain type of source information. According to these possible relationships, a judgment matrix belonging to the evaluation factors is formed.

The maximum eigenvalue of the judgment matrix and its corresponding eigenvector are obtained by hierarchical single ranking and consistency test. After normalization of the eigenvector, the weight vector f_k is obtained, which represents the source possibility of the k-th evaluation factor. The normalization formula of the eigenvector is:

$$f_k = \frac{2\mu_k}{\sum_{k=1}^{6} \mu_k} \tag{4}$$

In Eq. (4), μ_k refers to the corresponding eigenvector.

The judgment matrix is constructed based on human experience, and there may be unreasonable values, so it is necessary to carry out consistency test.

Implementation of Quantitative Method for Evaluation Factors

Quantitative Results of Evaluation Factors

The result obtained by the evaluation factor quantification method is the evaluation factor attribute vector set F.

Index clustering is the clustering of network security evaluation factors, that is, the evaluation factors with the same effect are gathered together, the clustering results correspond to the criteria level indicators and form hierarchical relationships, and then use these hierarchical relationships to build an index system. At present, many researches have applied hierarchical clustering algorithm to image classification, wireless sensing technology and traffic classification. Hierarchical clustering effectively uses the hierarchical characteristics of data and achieves good results in the accuracy of clustering results. Hierarchical clustering algorithm is divided into split hierarchical clustering and agglomerative hierarchical clustering. Agglomerative hierarchical clustering initially regards each sample as a class and iterates to the end of all samples. Split hierarchical clustering is opposite to agglomerative clustering. In the research, the agglomerative hierarchical clustering, which is more in line with the hierarchical characteristics of the index system, is selected as the implementation method of index clustering. Agglomerative hierarchical clustering combines two clusters according to the distance between clusters, and the result is to build a clustering hierarchy similar to the tree structure. The result of hierarchical clustering is a tree like hierarchical structure, which exactly corresponds to the hierarchical structure of the index system; Hierarchical clustering can get the difference between different clusters, which exactly corresponds to the independence relationship between indicators [9]. Therefore, using hierarchical clustering can intuitively select the appropriate index hierarchy.

Design of index clustering method.

1) Calculate the distance of evaluation factors
   The distance between evaluation factors can be regarded as the difference between evaluation factors, which is reflected in the distance between two points on the two-dimensional plane. The Euclidean distance is used to calculate the distance.
2) Calculate the distance between clusters
   There may be multiple evaluation factors in the cluster, and the distance between clusters is calculated by means of average connection.
3) Initialize class cluster
   Assuming that there are k evaluation factors in the initial stage, C represents the set of hierarchical clustering results, K' represents the number of clusters in the clustering process, and |C| represents the number of cluster centers formed by hierarchical clustering, then the initial state satisfies $|C| = K$, that is, each evaluation factor is taken as a separate initial cluster, and the attribute distance between the initial clusters is calculated.
4) Merge update
   In the iterative process of hierarchical clustering, the nearest two clusters are selected each time, and the two clusters are merged to form a new cluster. In order to merge next time, you need to calculate the distance between the new cluster and other clusters. The process of "merge update" is iterated continuously until the clustering

status meets |C| = 1, that is, all nodes are clustered in one class, and the hierarchical clustering is ended after the complete tree structure is formed.

Implementation of Index Clustering Method
The specific method is shown in Fig. 1.

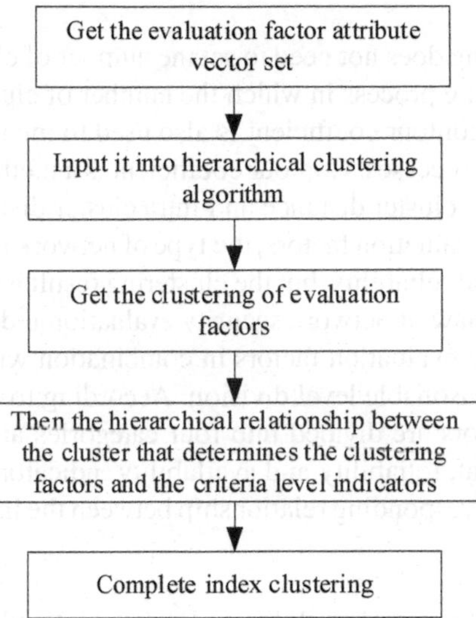

Fig. 1. Index clustering method

Analysis of Index Clustering Results
There is no unified standard for the end condition of hierarchical clustering algorithm. According to the tree structure of hierarchical clustering, this paper mainly considers the following two points when selecting the number of clustering centers:

1) Intra cluster distance. When selecting the number of cluster centers, we should ensure that the nodes in the cluster are close, that is, the distance between the nodes in the cluster is as large as possible, which is reflected in the fact that the tree view of hierarchical clustering is non leaf nodes as low as possible.
2) Distance between clusters. When selecting the number of cluster centers, we should also consider that the clusters are not similar as much as possible, otherwise the clustering effect cannot be achieved. The distance between clusters is reflected in the graph as the distance between adjacent non leaf nodes. The greater the distance, the more dissimilar the two clusters are.

The ideal clustering effect should have the characteristics of the minimum intra cluster distance and the maximum inter cluster distance, that is, the maximum intra cluster distance and the minimum inter cluster distance. Therefore, it is necessary to find a certain threshold. The non leaf nodes below the threshold are dense, and the non leaf nodes above the threshold are sparse. According to the hierarchical structure of index clustering results based on hierarchical clustering, the evaluation factors with dissimilarity between clusters less than 0.23 are closely related, and further subdividing the categories will lead to too many categories and destroy the relationship between nodes in the cluster; The distance between adjacent nodes above 0.23 suddenly increases, which means that the degree of dissimilarity between clusters increases sharply, and the cost of merging clusters up is too high. Therefore, it is appropriate to set the clustering threshold to about 0.23.

Hierarchical clustering does not need to set the number of cluster centers in advance, and can obtain the merging process in which the number of cluster centers iterates from $|C| = K$ to $|C| = 1$. The contour coefficient is also used to measure the clustering effect of these K intermediate processes. Contour coefficient is a method to evaluate clustering effect by combining inter cluster distance and intra cluster distance.

Among the selected evaluation factors, the type of network node equipment is related to vulnerability, threat and reliability, but the clustering result is unique [10, 11]. This situation is in line with the law of network security evaluation index system, so sometimes it is necessary to allocate evaluation factors in combination with network management experience to avoid unreasonable level division. According to the hierarchical relationship, the evaluation factors are divided into four categories at 0.23, which correspond to the vulnerability, threat, reliability and availability indicators in the network domain indicator system. The corresponding relationship between the indicator clustering results is as follows:

(1) The clustering results of vulnerability indicators are: vulnerability severity level; Vulnerability detection reliability; Vulnerability handling strategy; Patch quality; The transport layer protocol of the vulnerability; Time of vulnerability attack; Vulnerability type; Number of vulnerabilities.
(2) The clustering results of threat indicators are: the number of threat attacks; Attack frequency; Time of threat occurrence; Possibility of safety events; The transport layer protocol of the threat; Threat type; The type of device being attacked.
(3) The index clustering results of reliability are: data backup and recovery ability; Network prevention capability; Network topology; Network packet loss rate; Number of safety equipment; Equipment update time; Open ports of equipment; Equipment operating system type; Equipment collapse; The number of threads that the device can parallel.
(4) The index clustering results of availability are: network bandwidth usage; Change rate of network traffic; Number of request response packages; Request response stream size; Frequency of safety incidents; Session access start time; Packet protocol distribution; Network service provision; Packet ip address distribution; Session access duration.

There are too many evaluation factors involved in the process of network security evaluation, which makes the calculation complexity of network security situation high. AHP is used to calculate the relatively important weight of evaluation factors, and select important evaluation factors from many factors, so as to optimize the index system, simplify the calculation of security evaluation, and improve the performance of security situation evaluation.

(1) Index optimization method design

1) Establish hierarchy
According to the established sub domain security evaluation index system model, the network domain evaluation index is composed of vulnerability, threat, reliability and availability indicators. These four indicators are taken as the decision-making objectives, the evaluation factors of the index clustering results in the previous section are taken as the criteria layer, and AHP is used to further optimize the index system.
2) Build judgment matrix
3) Conformance test

(2) Realization of index optimization method
Vulnerability, threat, availability and reliability indicators screen the evaluation factors according to the "least and most important" strategy, that is, a group of evaluation factors with the least number and the most important weight. Rank the evaluation factors according to the importance weight, and select the weight and N evaluation factors greater than 80% for the first time.
(3) Index optimization results
Finally, the rationality of the security situation assessment index system constructed in the network domain is analyzed.

1) Conciseness analysis
First, define the indicators, clarify the specific role of indicators, avoid selecting redundant evaluation factors, and there will be no complex hierarchy. On the other hand, an index optimization strategy is proposed to select representative evaluation factors under the corresponding indexes, which reduces the computational complexity.
2) Availability analysis
This paper points out the information sources of network security situation assessment factors. Combined with domestic and foreign security standards and expert experience, it gives a specific index measurement method. According to the basic assessment data, the measurement data can be calculated, and then the assessment situation value can be obtained.
3) Integrity analysis
At present, the evaluation factors of the network environment are dynamic and changeable. The designed index system is based on the idea of domain and multi-layer division. The situation evaluation indicators are analyzed from the perspective of network domain and behavior domain. In the network domain, it is not limited to the security situation assessment factors of network nodes in specific scenarios, but considers the security situation assessment factors of nodes in the whole network; The evaluation factors of user behavior are included in the evaluation index, and the security situation evaluation index of

behavior domain is added to ensure the integrity of the network node security situation evaluation index system.

4) Independence analysis
The idea of index clustering is to gather the evaluation factors with similar characteristics and divide them into different criteria level indicators according to their role in the index system. The clustering algorithm reduces the subjectivity of artificially dividing the index levels. Hierarchical clustering can be used to mine the hierarchical relationship between evaluation factors in complex and changeable network data. The correlation degree between clustered index clusters is very small, and it can exist independently without relying on other indicators.

5) Accuracy analysis
Comprehensively consider the relevance of indicators, give full play to the role of the indicator system, use analytic hierarchy process to screen indicators, select representative evaluation factors in each indicator cluster, reduce the misleading of unimportant and repeated indicators to the evaluation results, and then improve the accuracy of the evaluation results.
According to the above analysis, the proposed security evaluation model of distance education network nodes is scientific and effective in theory.

3 Case Evaluation Test

The performance of the designed distance education network node security evaluation method based on machine learning is tested, and the method is used to evaluate the security of a distance education network node.

In the construction of the experimental distance education network, all the equipment used are Cisco products. Cisco's routing products and catalyst switching products are at the forefront of network routing switching products in terms of technology and performance, and have high support for IPv6. Their products have been favored by schools in the domestic campus network backbone and have been highly praised by many university network managers. More importantly, the above products' support for IPv6 is in place. Coupled with the continuous updating of IOS, they can better ensure their cutting-edge support for IPv6 technical features.

Select two Cisco catalyst 6500 series switches as core layer devices and back up each other redundantly.

The Cisco catalyst 6500 series has 3, 6, 9, and 13 slot enclosures that provide scalable performance and port density on their interfaces, and has integrated service modules ranging from multi gigabit network security, content switching, telephony, and network analysis modules. Cisco catalyst 6500 series adopts the supervisor failover technology. With the launch of catalyst os5.4 (1), the catalyst 6500 series switch with dual supervisors can support the high availability mode because the switch can synchronize the configuration, operating system, stateful protocol redundancy, etc. of the two supervisors.

Select Cisco Calyt 4500 series switches.

Cisco catalyst 4500 series switches are selected by many systems because they can integrate various network infrastructures, solve many business problems, and provide extended intelligent network services to realize operation in the shortest time and control all types of traffic.

The system features of the experimental distance education network are as follows:

(1) Large capacity switching processing of core switch;
(2) High reliability;
(3) Perfect QoS guarantee;
(4) Network wide DVPN support;
(5) Network wide multicast support.

Test the accuracy and error rate of network node security evaluation of the design method. The test results of network node security assessment accuracy of the design method are shown in Table 1.

Table 1. Test results of network node security assessment accuracy

Number of nodes (pieces)	The highest security assessment accuracy rate (%)	Minimum security assessment accuracy (%)	Average security assessment accuracy (%)
50	95.623	92.326	95.265
60	95.258	91.245	94.265
70	96.452	93.235	95.260
80	95.021	94.201	93.325
90	94.985	91.326	93.201
100	95.458	92.320	93.001
110	95.541	91.547	92.368
120	95.325	91.689	92.025
130	96.257	91.332	92.014
140	96.254	90.214	91.269
150	94.895	90.236	91.654

According to the test results of network node security assessment accuracy in Table 1, the design method has a high accuracy of network node security assessment, indicating that the design method has good node security assessment performance.

The test results of network node security evaluation error rate of the design method are shown in Fig. 2.

The test results of the error rate of the network node security assessment in Fig. 2 show that the error rate of the network node security assessment of the design method is generally low and has a good effect.

To sum up, the network node security evaluation method of distance education network node based on machine learning has higher accuracy, lower error rate and better performance.

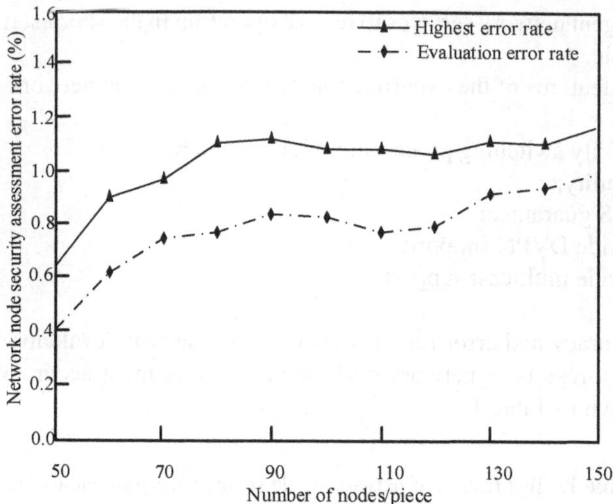

Fig. 2. Test results of network node security assessment error rate

4 Conclusion

In many aspects, the current teaching mode is dominated by teachers. From primary school, junior high school, senior high school to university, including undergraduate education, the cultivation of students' self-study ability is not enough. It only requires that students follow teachers step by step. The purpose of education should be to enable learners to carry out selective and autonomous learning according to their own interests and abilities, expand knowledge, develop personality and cultivate innovation ability. Distance education is a fundamental change and development of traditional education. In the research of distance education, a security evaluation method of distance education network nodes based on machine learning is designed, and good evaluation results are achieved.

With the in-depth development of modern distance education, network node security evaluation is being paid more and more attention and studied, and various application systems are gradually entering the development and application stage. The next step is to analyze the characteristics and differences between academic education and non academic education in distance education; The specific learning objectives of academic education are the same, that is, learners complete all courses and pass the examination; Although non academic education takes obtaining certificates and improving knowledge level as the overall learning objectives, the specific objectives of learners are more personalized and diversified. The network management and learning systems of various non academic projects differ greatly in structure and function. From the perspective of technology application, using big data technology can obtain data that cannot be collected by manpower, quickly analyze the learning process, and summarize all aspects of learners' information or status, so as to fully improve learning ability, improve learning effectiveness, and meet learning needs. In the future, we can conduct in-depth research on this.

References

1. Zhou, Q., Xie, J.: Mobile client data security storage protocol based on multifactor node evaluation. J. Supercomput. **76**(2), 1144–1158 (2020). https://doi.org/10.1007/s11227-018-2521-4
2. Sun, Q., Yang, G., Zhou, A.: An entropy-based self-adaptive node importance evaluation method for complex networks. Complexity **2020**(10), 1–13 (2020)
3. Li, Y., Li, X.: Research on multi-target network security assessment with attack graph expert system model. Sci. Program. **2021**(3), 1–11 (2021)
4. Liu, S.: Human memory update strategy: a multi-layer template update mechanism for remote visual monitoring. IEEE Trans. Multimedia **23**, 2188–2198 (2021)
5. Yi, B., Cao, Y.P., Song, Y.: Network security risk assessment model based on fuzzy theory. J. Intell. Fuzzy Syst. **38**(4), 3921–3928 (2020)
6. Lee, Y., Woo, S., Song, Y., et al.: Practical vulnerability-information-sharing architecture for automotive security-risk analysis. IEEE Access **8**(6), 9–18 (2020)
7. Shuai, L., Shuai, W., Xinyu, L., et al.: Fuzzy detection aided real-time and robust visual tracking under complex environments. IEEE Trans. Fuzzy Syst. **29**(1), 90–102 (2021)
8. Chen, L., Yue, D., Dou, C., et al.: Evaluation of cyber-physical power systems in cascading failure: node vulnerability and systems connectivity. IET Gener. Transm. Distrib. **14**(7), 1197–1206 (2020)
9. Wang, L., Abbas, R., Almansour, F.M., et al.: An empirical study on vulnerability assessment and penetration detection for highly sensitive networks. J. Intell. Syst. **30**(1), 592–603 (2021)
10. Yue, S.B., Wang, Q.H., Wang, X.C., et al.: Simulation of network node correlation risk assessment based on cloud technology. Comput. Simul. **37**(8), 247–251 (2020)
11. Liu, S., Liu, D., Muhammad, K., Ding, W.: Effective template update mechanism in visual tracking with background clutter. Neurocomputing **458**, 615–625 (2021)

MUEBA: A Multi-model System for Insider Threat Detection

Jing Liu(✉), Jingci Zhang, Changcun Du, and Dianxin Wang

School of Computer Science and Technology, Beijing Institute of Technology, Beijing 100081, China
{3120201045,dianxinw}@bit.edu.cn

Abstract. In the current era of digital communications, cyber security and data protection have always been a top priority. More and more organizations are starting to take insider threat security seriously. Traditional rule-based anomaly detection solutions generate a large number of alerts and are difficult to adapt to particular scenarios. UEBA (User and Entity Behavior Analysis), which correlates entities, events, and users, has become an emerging organizational solution by combining all-around contextual analysis through statistical and machine learning methods. In this paper, we propose MUEBA, a multi-model UEBA system for spatiotemporal analysis, combining user individual historical analysis and group analysis to detect insider threats. The individual historical analysis module uses the attention-based LSTM to improve the model's sensitivity to abnormal operations and help security analysts improve their efficiency in responding to threat events. In the group analysis module, we have extended the iForest algorithm in attribute selection and iTree construction, which increased the algorithm's stability. Finally, we comprehensively decide on the above two aspects and propose a full-time user and entity behavior analysis system. Experimental evaluations on the public CERT-4.2 dataset show that our system outperforms either single model in both stability and precision.

Keywords: UEBA · Abnormal detection · LSTM · Attention · iForest · Insider threat

1 Introduction

With the increasingly complex information application scenarios, more and more attention has been paid to the internal security of enterprises in recent years, and one of the most critical risk factors comes from people inside the organization. To some extent, they are trusted and have the corresponding permissions of the organization, so they have access to confidential data and servers. Nevertheless, these people are not entirely reliable [1]. Some utilize their authorized identities to steal confidential information and deliberately destroy the internal system; others may abuse their identity information-all the non-compliance will result in considerable losses or potential threats to the corporation. An Insider Threat

Y. Xu et al. (Eds.): ML4CS 2022, LNCS 13655, pp. 296–310, 2023.
https://doi.org/10.1007/978-3-031-20096-0_23

Report [2] states that the most destructive security threat facing businesses and organizations is the insider threat. Enterprises are accelerating the implementation of user behavior analysis systems, which monitor access to sensitive data and analyze the behavior of employees, including malicious and negligent employees.

Some existing conventional systems are not optimal solutions for insider threats but are more of a management and analysis tool for "security incidents," such as SOC (Security Operations Center) [3], which focuses on assets and models asset risk analysis, and SIEM (Security Information Event Management) [4], which serves as a log management tool by collecting and analyzing various security events and contextual analysis. The rule-based anomaly detection methods [5] generate many meaningless alerts and cannot automatically adapt to particular customer scenarios and the threat type. Also, they are complicated to operate, costly, and time-consuming to upgrade strategies. It requires more personnel and much time to solve abnormal security events.

In 2015, Gartner [6] proposed User and Entity Behavior Analytics (UEBA). UEBA interconnects user activities with entities such as terminals, applications, and networks [7]. Instead of analyzing each event individually, UEBA combines rich contexts and uses statistical and machine learning techniques to analyze the behavior of endpoints, networks, human entities, and non-human entities from multiple sources of heterogeneous data in a multi-dimensional manner. A typical UEBA architecture contains three modules: data processing, algorithm analysis, and scenario application. While the data processing module is responsible for collecting, correlating, and parsing various types of monitoring log data. The analysis module automatically detects and identifies abnormal behavior patterns. The application module provides feedback on the indicators of the algorithm result according to the specific scenario.

UEBA provides a unique perspective on security, and some research has been carried out. There are still some shortcomings with the existing UEBA systems. The main three limitations will be as follows.

- Since users and entities are generating quantities of logs every moment, it is necessary to select the correct size window for analysis. A small window may split specific cases, while a wide window will miss some anomalous scenarios.
- The existing methods only focus on the behavior of users at the temporal level and detect abnormal events based on the historical behavior of individuals. They neglect group behavior at the spatial level, resulting in poor model generalization.
- The existing detection models use deep learning technology methods, and it is not sufficiently interpretable for security personnel to analyze the causes of alerts.

We propose a comprehensive framework of UEBA, analyzing and detecting from temporal and spatial levels. The main work of this paper is as follows.

- Individual Historical Comparison. Anomaly detection of user behavior in the time dimension. We use an attention-based LSTM model that assigns different weights to different features. We train the model to learn the user's behavior patterns and improve the model's sensitivity to some suspicious operations. It overcomes the limitation of the model's lack of interpretation of detection results and helps security analysts improve efficiency in responding to threat events.
- Group Comparison. Outlier analysis of user behavior in the spatial dimension. Considering that users in the same group tend to exhibit similar behavior patterns, we propose an improved Isolation Forest algorithm to extract user behavior features of the same group at specific periods and detect those who deviate from group behavior.
- We synthesize the individual historical comparison results and the group comparison results and propose a spatiotemporal user and entity behavior analysis framework. Experimental results on standard CERT datasets show that the framework we proposed in this paper outperforms other models in threat detection.

2 Related Work

Researchers have used various machine learning methods for abnormal detection on user behavior logs and have proposed a series of insider threat detection models discussed below.

The anomaly detection algorithms used in user and entity behavior analysis include Principal Component Analysis (PCA) [8], One-Class Support Vector Machine (OCSVM) [9], Isolation Forest (iForest) [10], and Local Outlier Factor (LOF) [11]. Some researchers also ensemble several of these methods for analysis and detection. Madhu [12] extended the User and Entity Behavior Analysis (UEBA) module based on the Niara Security Analytics Platform. This module uses the SVD algorithm to implement anomaly detection in user access to servers within an enterprise. Haidar [13] adopted OCSVM training data to produce base classifiers and captured single-class behavioral sequences of users in chronological order. Then they divided sequences into data blocks using a fixed time window and continuously replaced the model based on a time-baseline model update method. Yilin [14] proposed a two-stage anomaly detection algorithm combining LOF and iForest and ultimately calculating a score for each user.

To learn the dependencies between the sequences of user actions, the researchers performed the log analysis of the Long Short Term Memory (LSTM) [15]network, a powerful variant of the Recurrent Neural Network. Lu [16] used LSTM to learn the first few sequences of a user's behaviors and predict the following possible action behavior of the user. If the predicted result does not exceed a set threshold with the actual user behavior, the user is considered to follow a regular behavior pattern. However, this approach requires great caution in selecting the threshold and is prone to a high false alarm rate. Sharma [17]used an LSTM autoencoder to model the user's behavior. They calculated the reconstruction error of the autoencoder on the data of normal behavior and defined the threshold for abnormal behavior based on the reconstruction error. Xiangyu [18] proposed a user behavior analysis (UBA) platform that integrates three unsupervised anomaly detection algorithms, OCSVM, iForest, and LSTM, to detect abnormal user behavior patterns. However, none of them takes the user's group into account.

The interpretability of anomaly detection results helps improve the analysts' speed and accuracy of analysis, thus reducing the anomaly response time. D. Sun [19]initially obtained the causes of abnormal user behavior by calculating the maximum likelihood logarithm and decomposing each count variable into the sum of individual feature terms. Moreover, attention mechanism has become an active area of research due to their intuitiveness. LSTM models based on the attention mechanism have been used to improve the performance of complex sequence modeling tasks [20]. Identifying the most influential features is essential based on anomaly detection results [21]. The attention mechanism provides a dynamic weighted average in processing high-dimensional serial data and provides more discriminative information for subsequent predictions. Xia L. [22] transformed the abnormal behavior detection problem into a time series prediction model by combining the attention mechanism with an LSTM to form a decoding network capable of capturing dynamic changes in behavior. Inspired by previous work, we apply the same concept and use attention-based LSTM to explore which factors the model focuses on during anomaly analysis.

3 Methodology

Our MUEBA framework is shown in Fig. 1, containing three primary modules: data processing, behavior analysis, and assessment.

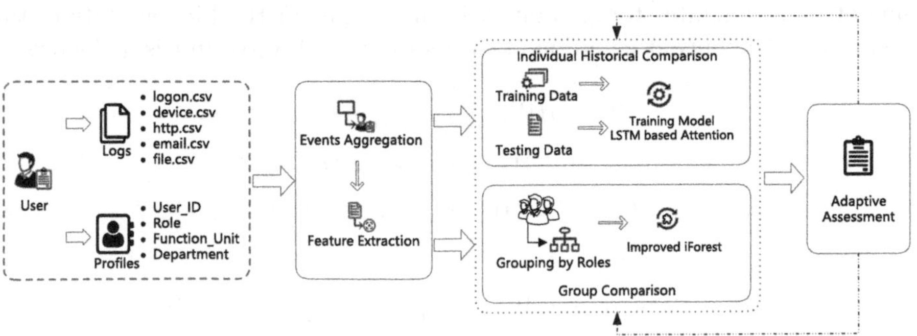

Fig. 1. The framework of our MUEBA system, containing three primary modules: data processing, behavior analysis, and assessment.

- The data processing module interconnects the data of users, entities, and events. It merges various types of source data of each user in chronological order, aggregates multiple types of events to obtain the event sequence of each user, and then performs feature extraction on the user behavior sequence.

- The behavior analysis module consists of two parts: individual historical analysis and group analysis, which compares the current behavior of users with the historical behavior of users and the behavior of people in the same group, respectively.
- The assessment module makes a comprehensive decision based on space and time results. It updates training models based on feedback and performs continuous adaptive risk and trust evaluation for users.

3.1 Individual Historical Analysis

This section analyzes the user's behavior, referring to his past behavior. The first step is to train a model representing a user's behavior pattern. We use an attention-based LSTM to learn the user's historical behaviors. A user's chronological behavior sequence is fed to the model to learn the user's regular behavior patterns. Next, the series of current behaviors to be detected is given to the trained model. The output of the model is the classification result of anomaly detection.

LSTM adds a memory unit to RNN to store information to help propagate the information learned at time t to $t+1$, $t+2$. There are three essential gates to update information between the hidden state and the unit's state. It selectively forgets the irrelevant part of the previous state while selectively updating the state and then outputs the relevant part to the future stage. Figure 2 shows the structure of an LSTM unit, where x_t represents the user's action vector at time t. f_t, i_t, and o_t represent the values of the forgetting gate, input gate, and output gate, respectively. W and b represent the weight matrix and the bias corresponding to the gate. $\tilde{C}$ is the sigmoid activation function. C represents the value of the candidate storage unit. h is the output of the hidden state of the LSTM unit. The output equation of each gate in an LSTM unit is as follows.

$$f_t = \sigma(W_f \cdot [h_{t-1}, x_t] + bf) \tag{1}$$

$$i_t = \sigma(W_i \cdot [h_{t-1}, x_t] + bi) \tag{2}$$

$$\tilde{C} = \tanh(W_c \cdot [h_{t-1}, x_t] + b_c) \tag{3}$$

$$C_t = \sigma(f_t \times C_{t-1} + i_t \times \tilde{C}_t) \tag{4}$$

$$o_t = \sigma(W_o \cdot [h_{t-1}, x_t] + b_o) \tag{5}$$

$$h_t = o_t \times \tanh(C_t) \tag{6}$$

We improved the LSTM model by introducing the attention mechanism according to the labels of users' action sequences, assigning extra attention to the information output from the LSTM hidden layer so that the model can notice the user's behaviors contribute more to the classification decision. Figure 3 shows the structure of our improved attention-based LSTM model. It consists of the input, LSTM, attention, and output layers. We first make a preliminary analysis

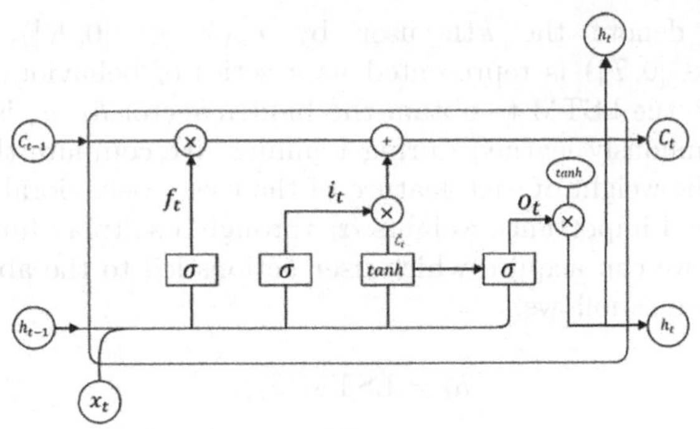

Fig. 2. Structure of an LSTM cell.

of possible anomalous scenarios and use a small number of labeled behavioral vectors for training. For a particular target, the input is weighted and summed by a weight coefficient to identify which features in the input are essential and which are not. That is the essence of the attention mechanism.

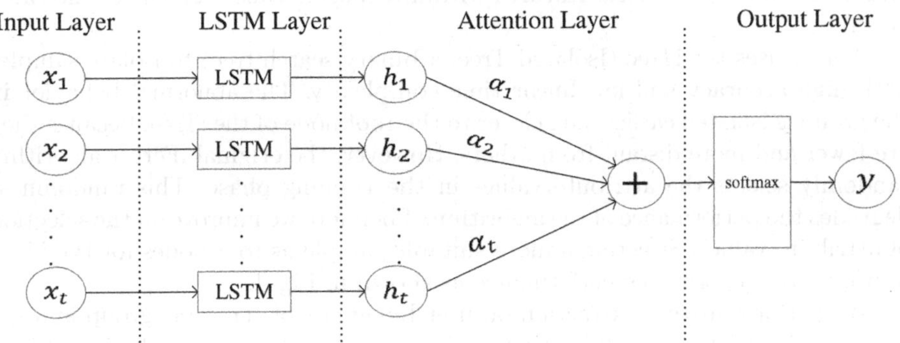

Fig. 3. The structure of our improved attention-based LSTM model, consisting of input, LSTM, attention, and output layers.

The LSTM captures the sequential dependencies between sequences of successive user behaviors, and the output is obtained as the output vector of the hidden layer. Then the output of the hidden layer is fed to the attention layer to get the representation of user behavior on each feature. The attention mechanism selects the vital information in the LSTM storage unit to assign higher weights. When abnormal results are detected, we can see the user behaviors that are most relevant to the abnormal results.

Specifically, denote the kth user by $u_k(k \in [0, K])$, then $S_{u_k} = x_0, x_1, \ldots, x_t(t \in [0, T])$ is represented as a series of behavioral states of user u_k. Input x_t into the LSTM to obtain the hidden vector h_t. u_a is a context vector that is continuously learned during training. We compute the similarity to u_a to measure the weight of each feature of the user's behavioral state. Then we get the normalized importance weights α_t through a softmax function. By visualizing α_t then, we can acquire which user actions led to the abnormal results. The equations are as follows.

$$h_t = \text{LSTM}(x_t) \tag{7}$$

$$u_t = \tanh(W_a h_t + b_a) \tag{8}$$

$$\alpha_t = softmax(u_t, u_a) \tag{9}$$

3.2 Group Analysis

Generally, users and entities in the same department have similar behaviors, while those in different departments do not. Based on the above assumptions, we divide all users into groups based on their roles and departments. We extract and detect uses' behavioral features within a specific time segment of the same group.

iForest uses the iTree (Isolated Tree, a binary search tree) to isolate samples with high accuracy and low linear time complexity. The abnormal behavior in the group is isolated earlier, i.e., closer to the root node of the iTree, because they are fewer and more distant from others. However, the original iForest algorithm randomly selects the attribute values in the training phase. This randomness degrades the performance of the algorithm. Therefore we improve on the selection of attribute values. Selecting a more suitable sample as root nodes for the iTree improves the algorithm's performance as shown in Fig. 4.

We perform feature extraction on user behaviors of the same group and get the behavior vectors of different users as a sample subset. Instead of randomly selecting attributes for division, we improve this by selecting specific attribute values as root nodes. Assuming that the data conform to a normal distribution, the probability that the regression error e in $(\mu - 3\sigma, \mu + 3\sigma)$ is 0.9973 according to the "3σ rule" (where μ, σ are the mean value and standard deviation of e). The parameters μ and σ are calculated using maximum likelihood estimation as follows.

n is the number of the subsamples and the number of candidate root nodes. If a sample falls outside the interval, there is a higher probability of outliers in the sample set, and we chose such a sample set to build an iTree. The improved iForest method selects sample sets that are more likely to have outliers to build iTrees. Next, we divide the current data space into two subspaces using the hyperplane generated by the golden point of the chosen attribute. We then recursively perform the above process, sliding different data dimensions until only one node (no other slices are possible) or the iTree has reached a specific height.

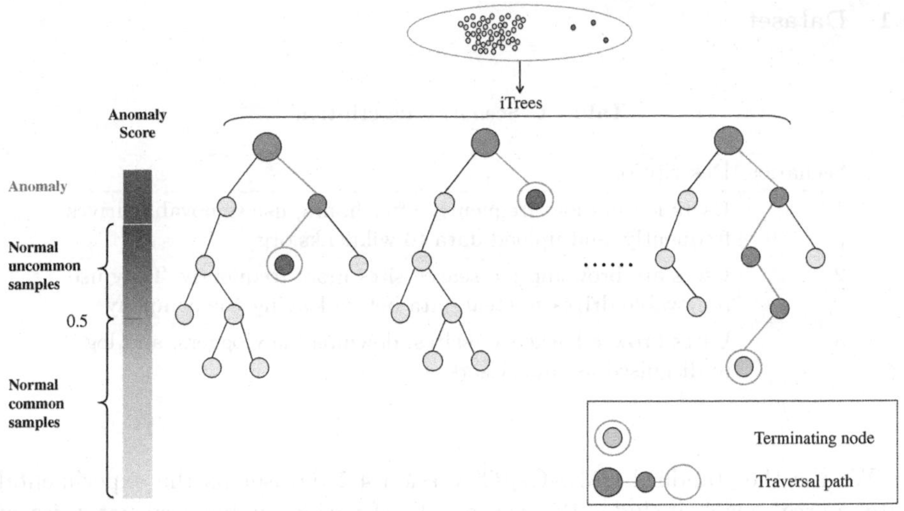

Fig. 4. The specific workflow of iForest and we improved it on the selection of attribute values.

We carry each sample point into iTrees and calculate the height of the sample in each isolated tree. The average height of each vector is normalized to get the score for users' behavior. The formula for calculating the outlier score is below.

$$s(x,n) = 2^{-\frac{E(h(x))}{c(n)}} \tag{10}$$

where $h(x)$ denotes the path length from the root node to node x, $E(h(x))$ is the average of $h(x)$, and $c(n)$ is the normalization function.

3.3 Comprehensive Assessment

By analyzing the Individual Historical Analysis and Group Analysis in sections and Sect. 3.2, we next make a comprehensive decision and output the final classification results. For example, when a user's behavior differs a lot from his historical behavior and not much from the group's behavior, it may be that a change in the joint work task causes this contradiction. Therefore, we specify that the final result is judged as abnormal only when both individual historical analysis and group analysis are abnormal to reduce the false alarm rate.

4 Experiment and Analysis

This section evaluates the effectiveness of our MUEBA system. We first introduce the dataset and data preprocessing, and feature extraction. Then we describe parameter settings. Finally, we demonstrate the validity with specific user examples and compare our system with other state-of-the-art methods.

4.1 Dataset

Table 1. Scenarios description

Scenarios	Description
1	Users log in more frequently after hours, use removable drives frequently, and upload data to wikileaks.org
2	Users are browsing job search sites more frequently. They use removable drives to steal data before leaving the company
3	Users browse hacked websites, download keyloggers, and log in disguised as supervisors

We use the standard CMU-CERT version 4.2 dataset as the experimental data source, which includes the raw events of various behavioral activities of users and the profile information. The user's activity logs consist of five files, namely login.csv, device.csv, email.csv, http.csv, and file.csv. Each event record has a timestamp, user ID, device ID, and activity type. The profile files provide the user's information, including role and department. Moreover, the dataset contains three abnormal scenarios. Table 1 summarizes the scenario description. We evaluate the performance of our proposed system by referring to the marked files, which mark the sequence of abnormal users. It is worth noting that the user's behavior is directly related to the session record. A session contains the logical coherence of all events in the user's activity. Therefore, this paper performs an analysis based on user sessions to extract the feature vectors of user behavior sequences.

4.2 Experimental Settings

Data Processing. The dataset contains 502 days of behavior data for 1000 users, including 70 abnormal, and 32770227 behavior records, including 7323 abnormal. We aggregate various heterogeneous types of events for the same user in chronological order. We consider a login-logout activity as a single session of the user. We finally generated 341,794 sessions, of which 340,801 sessions belong to normal behavior, and 993 sessions contain abnormal behavior and marked the sessions containing abnormal behavior as abnormal sessions.

Feature Extraction. The user ID, device, log-in and log-out timestamp, and session duration are essential features. For HTTP activities, we list keywords, domains, and strings for some hacker sites and job search sites. Usually, users do not visit these sites. If there is an HTTP request for a domain containing these substrings, it is considered abnormal. For email activities, we extract the domain name of each user's mailbox and consider frequent external email exchanges to be abnormal. For device activities and file activities, we calculate their frequencies as features separately. In addition, the user's department is a vital feature to facilitate the group comparison. We finally extract the following feature vectors for each session, as shown in Table 2.

Table 2. Feature extraction

Features	Description
role	User's role
login	User login timestamp
logoff	User logoff timestamp
log_duration	Session duration
logon_PC	On which machine the user logged in
n_http	The number of web visits during a session
job_search	The number of job sites visits during a session
hacking_sites	The number of hacking sites visits during a session
n_email	The number of emails during a session
n_ex_email	The number of extern emails during a session
n_device	The number of devices during a session
n_file	The number of files during a session

Parameters. We divided the dataset into training and testing sets: the first 210 days logs for training and tuning, and the next 292 days logs are for testing and assessing performance. We develop experiments with the Keras framework for the individual historical analysis module. In order to accurately describe the behavior patterns of users over time, we need to pick a suitable step size for the LSTM model. Logically, the weekly behavior of users in the enterprise will form a relatively fixed pattern. We calculated the average number of user sessions per week to be ten and set the step length to 10. For the group analysis module, the dataset contains a total of 46 roles, and the list of users for each type of role is counted monthly. It can be found that the role type of users changes over time. So we dynamically define which group a user belongs to based on the user's role in that month.

4.3 Results Analysis

Comparison with Baselines. We usually use confusion matrices to evaluate the model's effectiveness in anomaly detection, where TP is true positive, FP is false positive, and FN is false negative. We analyze the performance of our system by Precision, Recall and F-measure. Precision and Recall are widely used in the field of information processing to measure the performance of a model. $Precision = \frac{TP}{TP+FP}$ is concerned with the model's ability to detect relevant information, while $Recall = \frac{TP}{TP+FN}$ is concerned with the model's ability to reject non-relevant information. The F-measure calculates the harmonic mean of Precision and Recall and is used to reflect the model's overall performance comprehensively. The higher the F-measure, the better the classification model is. Since our system incorporates and improves both algorithms, LSTM and iForest. The original solution of each algorithm is compared as baselines. They are both the most representative and popular algorithms in the anomaly detection field. Figure 5 shows the results of our system and comparison with baselines. Clearly, our method shows the best performance with an accuracy of 0.94, a recall of 0.96, and an F-measure of 0.95. Our system outperforms each of the methods considered separately. Furthermore, we found that the performance of iForest is sensitive to the change of parameters. The figure shows the mean value of the multiple results. The LSTM is relatively stable and also achieves excellent precision values, indicating that it learns dependencies between sequences of actions. However, the recall rate of LSTM is low, indicating it does not learn all abnormal scenarios, resulting in false negatives. Our proposed method improves both methods, maintaining high precision while learning the full range of abnormal scenarios.

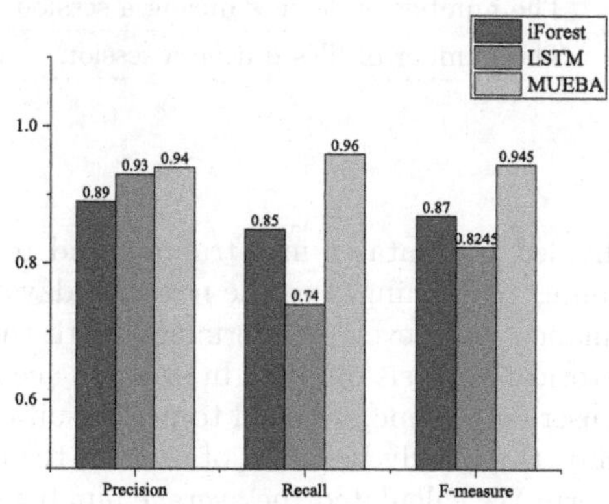

Fig. 5. The results of our MUEBA and comparison with baselines.

Individual Historical. Our approach achieves optimal performance overall. To illustrate our specific individual history analysis and group analysis results, we give examples to compare and analyze the two parts separately. In the individual history analysis module, we train and test the attention-based LSTM model regarding the labels of the anomalous users given in the dataset. According to scenario descriptions provided by the dataset, we output the weights of the attention mechanism on each dimension to verify its effectiveness by taking three scenarios corresponding to three abnormal users as examples during the testing phase, as shown in Fig. 6. The User_ID is EHB0824, HXL0968, and CCA0046, which correspond to the three abnormal scenarios given in the dataset. Apparently, the model noticed more attention to the frequency of USB use and log-in time of user EHB0824; more attention to the number of job website searches and USB use of user HXL0968; and more attention to the number of hacker website visits of user CCA0046. We can conclude that the attention-based LSTM model discovers features with more vital relevance to the results and improves security analysts' efficiency in responding to threat events.

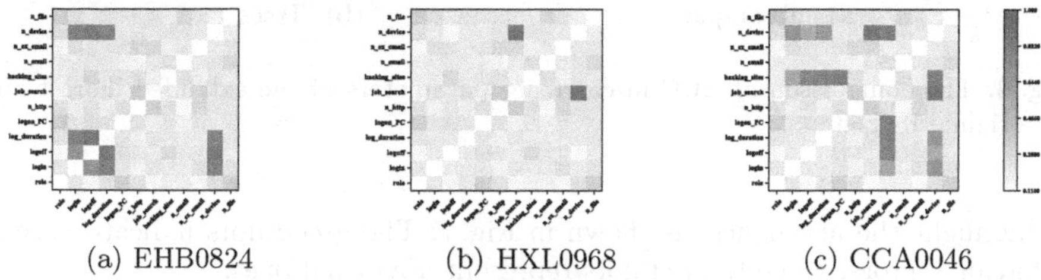
(a) EHB0824 (b) HXL0968 (c) CCA0046

Fig. 6. Distribution of users' attention weights in different scenarios.

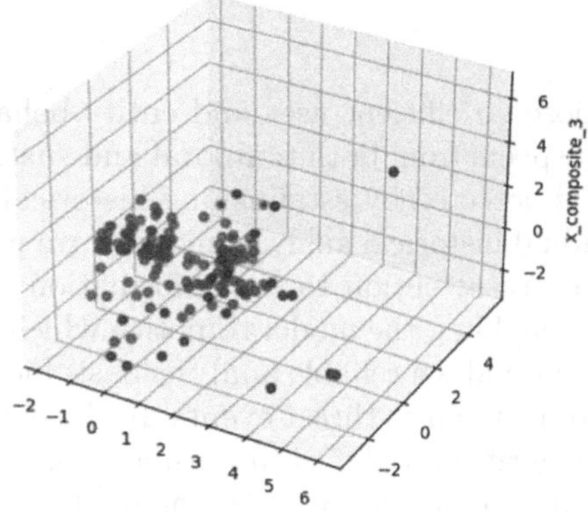

Fig. 7. Visualization of detection results for Group analysis.

Group Analysis. In the group analysis module, since a user's role changes over time, the behavior of all users in this role during this period is extracted when calculating the group baseline. Taking the role of technicians as an example, according to the method introduced above, we extract the behavioral features of all technicians from day 270 to day 300 for anomaly detection. To visualize the group analysis detection results, we normalize the user features, use principal component analysis to reduce the number of dimensions, and plot them in 3D

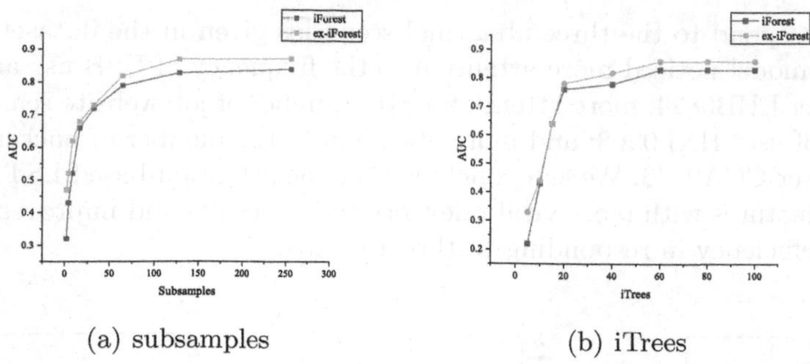

(a) subsamples (b) iTrees

Fig. 8. The comparison of AUC in changing parameters of the extended iForest and the original iForest

to highlight the anomalies, as shown in Fig. 7. The green dots indicate normal behavior vectors, while the red dots represent abnormal ones.

We compare the stability of the extended iForest with the original iForest by changing parameters. Figure 8 show the AUC for subsamples and iTrees, respectively. We can see that the area of the extended iForest is larger than the original one, which proves the effectiveness of our improved method.

5 Conclusion

In this paper, we propose an efficient user and entity behavior analysis system to analyze users in all aspects from both temporal and spatial levels. The abnormal behavior of users is detected by establishing historical baselines and group baselines. In the individual historical analysis module, we use an attention-based LSTM model to give extra attention to the information output from the hidden layer of the LSTM, enabling the model to notice which behavior contributes more to the decision. It provides a reliable analysis basis for security analysts and improves their ability to respond to threat events. In the cluster baseline module, we extend the iForest algorithm to detect abnormal behavior of the same group, which improves the stable performance of the algorithm. Our proposed framework achieves high accuracy and low false alarm rate on the standard CERT dataset.

UEBA focuses on users and entities with behavioral analysis as the guide. "Human" is the core object of insider threat detection within organizations. The personality characteristics of users also largely determine their behavior. Therefore, future work can explore user psychology and create a portrait of the user's characteristics to improve understanding of the user's motivations for performing malicious operations. In addition, user access logs come in a variety of forms. Besides the events and operations mentioned in this paper, users also have other terminal records and traffic data. User and entity logs from various sources should be fully considered in the actual deployment to provide efficient and accurate data and decision support for security personnel to predict the probability of abnormal behavior.

References

1. Daniel C., Michael A., Matthew C., Samuel P., George S., Derrick S.: An Insider Threat Indicator Ontology. Technical Report CMU/SEI-2016-TR-007. Software Engineering Institute, Carnegie Mellon University, Pittsburgh (2016)
2. CSO, CERT Division of SRI-CMU, and Force Point. 2018 U.S. State of Cybercrime. Technical Report (2018)
3. Shuhan, Y.: Deep learning for insider threat detection: review, challenges and opportunities. Comput. Secur. **104**, 102221 (2021). https://doi.org/10.1016/j.cose.2021.102221
4. Sun, X., Zhang, X., Xia, Z., Bertino, E. (eds.): ICAIS 2021. LNCS, vol. 12737. Springer, Cham (2021). https://doi.org/10.1007/978-3-030-78612-0
5. Lavanya, P., Shankar Sriram, V.S.: Detection of insider threats using deep learning: a review. In: Nayak, J., Behera, H., Naik, B., Vimal, S., Pelusi, D. (eds.) Computational Intelligence in Data Mining. Smart Innovation, Systems and Technologies, Vol 281. Springer, Singapore (2022). https://doi.org/10.1007/978-981-16-9447-9_4
6. Gorka S., Avivah L., Toby B., Tricia P.: Market guide for user and entity behavior analytics, Gartner inc. (2018)
7. Kim, J., Park, M., Kim, H., Cho, S., Kang, P.: Insider threat detection based on user behavior modeling and anomaly detection algorithms. Appl. Sci. **9**(19), 4018 (2019). https://doi.org/10.3390/app9194018
8. Emmanuel CandÃĺs, J., Li, X., Ma, Y., John W.: Robust principal component analysis? J. ACM **58**(3), 37 (2011). https://doi.org/10.1145/1970392.1970395
9. Heller, K., Svore, K., Keromytis, A., Stolfo S.: One class support vector machines for detecting anomalous windows registry accesses. In: ICDM Workshop on Data Mining for Computer Security, Melbourne, FL, (2003). https://doi.org/10.7916/D84B39Q0
10. Fei, T.L., Kai, M.T., Zhihua, Z.: Isolation Forest. In: Eighth IEEE International Conference Data Mining, vol. 2008, pp. 413–422 (2008). https://doi.org/10.1109/ICDM.2008.17
11. Breunig, M.M., Kriegel, H.P., Ng, R.T., Sander, J.: 2000. LOF: identifying density-based local outliers. In: Proceedings of the 2000 ACM SIGMOD International Conference on Management of Data. Association for Computing Machinery, New York, NY, USA, pp. 93–104. https://doi.org/10.1145/335191.335388
12. Madhu, S., Minyi, S., Jisheng, W.: User and entity behavior analytics for enterprise security. In: IEEE International Conference on Big Data (Big Data), pp. 1867–1874 (2016). https://doi.org/10.1109/BigData.2016.7840805
13. Haidar, D., Gaber, M. M.: Adaptive one-class ensemble-based anomaly detection: an application to insider threats. In: 2018 International Joint Conference on Neural Networks (IJCNN), pp. 1–9 (2018). https://doi.org/10.1109/IJCNN.2018.8489107
14. Yilin, W., Yun, Z., Cheng, Z., Xianqiang, Z., Weiming, Z.: Abnormal behavior analysis in office automation system within organizations. Int. J. Comput. Commun. Eng. **6**, 212–220 (2017). https://doi.org/10.17706/IJCCE.2017.6.3.212-220
15. Pankaj, M., Lovekesh, V., Gautam, S., Puneet A.: Long short term memory networks for anomaly detection in time series. In: ESANN (2015)

16. Bontemps, L., Cao, V.L., McDermott, J., Le-Khac, N.-A.: Collective anomaly detection based on long short-term memory recurrent neural networks. In: Dang, T.K., Wagner, R., Küng, J., Thoai, N., Takizawa, M., Neuhold, E. (eds.) FDSE 2016. LNCS, vol. 10018, pp. 141–152. Springer, Cham (2016). https://doi.org/10.1007/978-3-319-48057-2_9
17. Sharma, B., Pokharel, P., Joshi, B.: User behavior analytics for anomaly detection using LSTM autoencoder - Insider Threat Detection. In: Porkaew, K., Chignell, M.H., Fong, S., Watanapa, B. (eds.) IAIT, pp. 5:1–5:9. ACM. https://doi.org/10.1145/3406601.3406610
18. Xiangyu, X., et al.: An ensemble approach for detecting anomalous user behaviors. Int. J. Softw. Eng. Knowl. Eng. **28**(11–12), 1637–1656 (2018). https://doi.org/10.1142/S0218194018400211
19. Sun, D., Liu, M., Li, M., Shi, Z., Liu, P., Wang, X.: DeepMIT: a novel malicious insider threat detection framework based on recurrent neural network. In: 2021 IEEE 24th International Conference on Computer Supported Cooperative Work in Design (CSCWD), pp. 335–341 (2021). https://doi.org/10.1109/CSCWD49262.2021.9437887
20. Brown, A., Tuor, A., Hutchinson, B., Nichols, N.: Recurrent neural network attention mechanisms for interpretable system log anomaly detection. CoRR, abs/1803.04967 (2018). https://doi.org/10.1145/3217871.3217872
21. Benchaji, I., Douzi, S., El Ouahidi, B., Jaafari, J.: Enhanced credit card fraud detection based on attention mechanism and LSTM deep model. J. Big Data **8**(1), 1–21 (2021). https://doi.org/10.1186/s40537-021-00541-8
22. Xia, L., Li, Z.: A new method of abnormal behavior detection using LSTM network with temporal attention mechanism. J. Supercomput. **77**(4), 3223–3241 (2020). https://doi.org/10.1007/s11227-020-03391-y

Bayesian Based Security Detection Method for Vehicle CAN Bus Network

Shen Jiang[1(✉)] and Hailan Zhang[2]

[1] School of Mechanical Electrical Engineering, Guangdong University of Science and Technology, Dongguan 523000, China
gggsdf9@163.com

[2] School of Mechanical Electronic and Information Engineering, China University of Mining and Technology (Beijing), Beijing 100083, China

Abstract. The existing on-board can bus network security detection methods have low accuracy in detecting the number of abnormal messages and long detection time. Therefore, combined with Bayesian algorithm, this paper designs a on-board can bus network security detection method. For data preprocessing, establish a classification model, classify network attacks, calculate the information entropy of CAN bus, establish a Bayesian model, learn Bayesian network, continue to reason, and realize the security detection of vehicle can bus network based on Bayesian. The experimental results show that the proposed security detection method has high detection accuracy and short detection time, and can find internal security vulnerabilities in time, providing technical support for the safe operation of vehicles.

Keywords: Bayes · CAN bus · Network security · Clear · Classification · Judgment

1 Introduction

With the development of computer and network technology, automotive technology is gradually developing towards intelligence and networking. The message of can network is broadcast, which can realize reliable communication between ECUs in the car. However, the on-board can bus is vulnerable to external threats, which seriously affects the vehicle driving safety, so it is necessary to carry out intrusion detection on the on-board can bus network security. The traditional CAN bus network security detection method is easy to be affected by other factors. In practical application, it reduces the detection accuracy of the number of abnormal messages, takes a long time to detect, and reduces the detection efficiency. Bayesian classification method has a strong statistical theory as the guiding basis. In the process of classifying, detecting and screening a large number of data, it can reflect the characteristics of high accuracy, low false positive rate, low false negative rate and high real-time. Therefore, based on the advantages of Bayesian algorithm, this paper designs a detection method for vehicle can bus network security.

Y. Xu et al. (Eds.): ML4CS 2022, LNCS 13655, pp. 311–325, 2023.
https://doi.org/10.1007/978-3-031-20096-0_24

2 Data Preprocessing

Data cleaning is to use certain rules and strategies to process the "dirty" data in the database to form data that meets the requirements. Its principle is shown in the following Fig. 1:

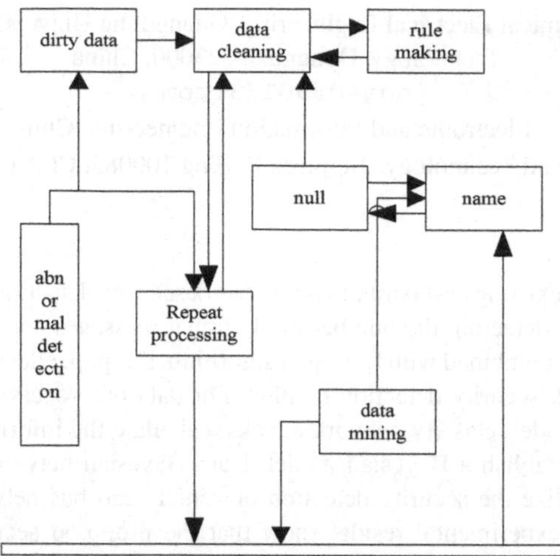

Fig. 1. Principle of data cleaning

During the formation of the database, redundant data will increase the computational complexity [1], which requires cleaning to remove duplicate records. In addition, some records in the database may have errors in format, spelling, naming, etc., which also need to be cleaned. Data cleaning needs to check the value range and mutual relationship of data, and adopt different processing methods for different types of non-conforming data:

Duplicate record [2]. Sort the data in the database, and then judge whether the adjacent data are equal. If they are equal, merge the data, otherwise keep the original data.

Missing data. Relevant statistical methods (mean value, maximum value, minimum value, etc.) are used to replace the missing data.

Wrong data. Use the simple rule base to check, delete it or correct it with the average value.

Inconsistent data. Obtain the connection between data through consistency check and analysis; Or formulate data cleaning rules.

The value difference of data between different characteristic attributes may be large, and the analysis results of data may be affected during data analysis. Therefore, it is necessary to adopt corresponding rules to scale the data to a certain extent to make it meet the corresponding data format and realize the standardized processing of data [3]. Assuming that the input data is $X = \{x_1, x_2, \cdots, x_n\}$, the normalization process is as follows:

$$\dot{x} = \frac{x_i - \overline{x}}{\sigma_y} \tag{1}$$

In the above formula, x_i and $\bar{x}$ respectively represent data processing parameters, and σ_y represents data specification processing parameters.

Most data sets have a large number of characteristic attributes, and the amount of data is also very large. In practical applications, if the model analysis data is directly built on the massive data, it will take a lot of time and is not feasible. Therefore, in the case of maintaining the original characteristics of the data as much as possible, the data can be treated by specification to reduce the computational complexity. The data after the protocol is much smaller than the original data, and the efficiency of data analysis will be higher than the original data. The results of data analysis are basically the same as the original data.

The distance measure of the data in the feature space, the Euclidean distance function is applied to the measure, for two data samples $x_1 = (x_1, x_2, \ldots, x_\text{n})$ and $c_1 = (c_1, c_2, \ldots, c_n)$, their Euclidean distance is recorded as $dis(x_1, c_1)$, and the calculation formula is expressed as:

$$dis(x_1, c_1) = \sqrt{(x_1 - c_1)^2 + \cdots + (x_n - c_n)^2} \tag{2}$$

Step3: similarity measurement. Because the intrusion data has discrete characteristics, some information cannot be processed directly. Therefore, the data needs to be processed. For the continuous numerical similarity, the following formula is used to calculate:

$$d_c(i, j) = |x_{i1} - x_1| + |x_i - x_2| + \cdots + |x_{ip} - x_p| \tag{3}$$

In formula (3), x_{i1}, x_{i2}, x_{ip}, and x_p represent data objects respectively.

On this basis, the discrete data attribute value is calculated, and the following formula is used to calculate the discrete attribute value:

$$\text{sim}(i_k, j_k) = \begin{cases} 0 & \text{if } y_{ik} = y_{jk} \\ 1 & \text{if } y_z \neq y_{jk} \end{cases} \tag{4}$$

In formula (4), y_{ik} and y_{jk} represent the k discrete attribute parameter of object i and object j respectively, and y_z represents the similarity measurement parameter.

Data conversion refers to the reduction of the number of effective variables [4] and the search for invariant forms by means of characteristic expression of data, dimension conversion, etc. Standardization refers to the standardization processing according to the scale of attribute value. According to the attribute characteristics of data, it can be divided into numerical continuous and numerical discrete standardization problems. The process of data fusion is based on semantic hierarchy. Standardization and protocol processing can greatly reduce the number of data sets and improve the efficiency of operations. Data transformation can be further abstracted, organized or transformed to provide more effective and accurate analysis data for the detection system and improve the detection efficiency.

3 Classification of Network Attacks

Present, the attack classification is mainly based on the possible security loopholes in the computer system, the technical means used by the attacker and the detection technology of the attack by the defender. This section classifies network attacks as follows based on technical techniques and means.

(1) Password theft. Password theft has always been a key problem in network security. Password leakage often means that the protection of the whole system has been broken.
(2) Loopholes and Backdoors. Any seemingly perfect code has certain loopholes. Once the loopholes and back doors are found by criminals, they will pose a great threat to the formal safety of cars [5].
(3) Information disclosure. Most protocols have information leakage. As long as you scan the address space and port electronically, you can find the masked host and invade the server.
(4) Viruses and Trojans. Computer viruses and Trojans have great potential damage and are becoming a new attack weapon in information warfare layer by layer.
(5) Deception attack. The main forms are: IP spoofing, ARP spoofing, DNS spoofing, web spoofing, e-mail spoofing, source routing spoofing, address spoofing, non-technical spoofing, etc.
(6) Denial of service. DOS attack is also called denial of service attack. It is the attacker who occupies too much system resources until the system cannot be empty or overloaded and has no way to deal with normal office work, or even causes the disintegration of the attacked host system.

Attacks on security can also be divided into two categories: non active attacks and active attacks. Do not actively attack the information intended to obtain or use the system, but will not cause damage to the system resources, such as eavesdropping and surveillance detection; Active attacks are intended to damage the resources of the system and affect the normal work of the system, such as not receiving services.

The requirement at this stage is that the extraction function should be able to capture enough features from the original information to distinguish alarms belonging to different categories. At the same time, it must also be highly efficient in the case of specific resources.

AFE receives the alarm from the intrusion detection system, processes the traffic, extracts the characteristic information, and outputs the attack characteristic information. The feature information is then transmitted to uacc, which uses various attack feature information for training to establish a classification model composed of multiple classifiers. AIC can automatically identify the type of attack traffic according to the generated classifier. The attack type information in ACC can be provided in several ways, such as manually generated by the administrator or automatically generated by extracting attachment information from the original alarm (when the alarm is generated by SBS). In addition, the type judgment generated by AIC can also be fed back to ACC as known attack type information. The attack classification model is shown in the following Fig. 2:

Extracting feature information from alarm information is a key step, because attack feature is the basis of attack classification. The requirement at this stage is that the extraction function should be able to capture enough features from the original information to distinguish alarms belonging to different categories. At the same time, it must also have high efficiency under specific resource conditions (such as memory space or processing

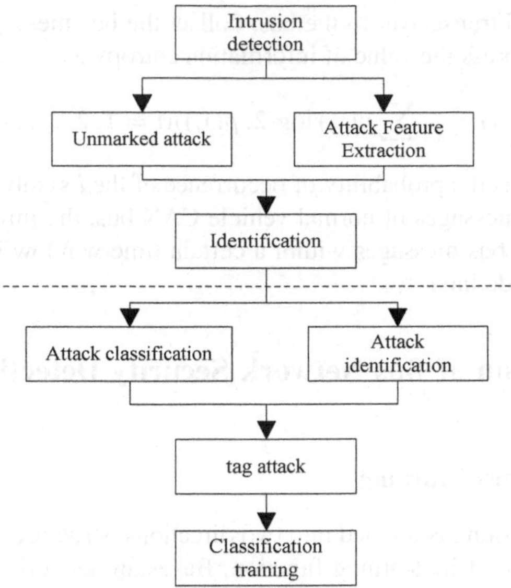

Fig. 2. Attack classification model

capacity) [6]. The formula for classifying attacks is as follows:

$$t = NB(x) \tag{5}$$

In the above formula, t is the classification set of attack types, and $B(x)$ is the Bayesian function.

Based on the above process, the network attack is classified, which provides the basis for the subsequent vehicle CAN bus network security detection.

4 CAN Bus Information Entropy Calculation

For a typical vehicle network protocol, the types of data packets in the vehicle network are limited, and the data packets are sent to the bus according to strict timing and frequency. The CAN bus message cycle is determined, the message type is determined, and the number of messages is stable. The sending of CAN messages is controlled by the CAN bus communication matrix, including ID, signal mapping, and sending method. The randomness of data packets in a standard computer network is much higher than that of the CAN bus. In a strictly regulated vehicle network, the system should be ordered. The information entropy value within a period of time should be stable, generally relatively low, and approaching a range. Most attacks can be monitored by detecting the information entropy value in the vehicle network over a period of time, such as injection of new data packets, man-in-the-middle attacks, flooding attacks, replay attacks, etc. Each attack behavior changes the data in the vehicle network The randomness of the packet leads to the increase or decrease of the information entropy of the system, and the change of the information entropy value is used as a sign of intrusion detection [7].

Connect the CAN transceiver to the bus, collect the bus messages within a certain time window, and express the value of information entropy as:

$$H_1(x) = -\sum p(x_i)\log(2, p(x_i))(i = 1, 2, \ldots, n) \tag{6}$$

where, $p(x_i)$ represents the probability of occurrence of the i symbol.

By counting the messages of normal vehicle CAN bus, the information entropy of normal vehicle CAN bus messages within a certain time window is obtained, and the threshold standard is defined.

5 Implementation of Bus Network Security Detection Based on Bayesian

5.1 Bayesian Network Learning

Bayesian network learning is divided into two directions: structure learning and parameter learning. Because of its learning function, Bayesian network combines with data mining in the era of big data, uses fault samples for learning, and constructs a more realistic Bayesian network model based on data driving.

Structural learning, Bayesian network structural learning is mainly divided into two structural learning methods: Based on dependency testing and given bisection. The structure learning method based on pre dependence test analyzes the interrelation of node variables through statistics and information theory, so as to obtain the optimal network structure. The dependence of nodes is usually determined by the mutual information or conditional mutual information of two points.

Hill Climbing Algorithm, Hill Climbing Algorithm is a scoring search algorithm that uses a local search strategy. The ultimate goal of the hill-climbing algorithm is to find the locally optimal model. It starts from an initial boundless model and changes the local structure of the current model by adding edges, subtracting edges or reversing the direction of edges at each step of the search. Compare the scores of these models with local structural changes with the current model, and find the best solution with the highest score as the current model in the next step. Conversely, if there is no candidate model with a score greater than the current model, stop the search and return the current model as the optimal solution. Since the hill-climbing algorithm selects nodes by heuristic method, it avoids traversal and improves the computational efficiency, but it has three problems: local optimum, highland, and ridge. The local optimum can be understood as the score of a structure is higher than any structure in the current series, but it is not the highest value of the whole, and the algorithm will stop when it thinks it is the optimal solution. The problem of highlands and ridges can be understood as random oscillations when the next search direction cannot be determined, and the forward pace is small, which affects the search efficiency.

Parameter learning of Bayesian network refers to learning the conditional probability table (CPT) of each node according to the data after the Bayesian network has been established, which is generally divided into parameter learning when the data is complete and parameter learning when the data is missing [8].

Parameter learning in the case of whole data. Parameter learning in the case of complete data is mainly divided into two methods: maximum likelihood estimation and Bayesian estimation. The basic principle of maximum likelihood estimation method is to obtain the parameter value when the likelihood function value is maximized as the estimation value. In the maximum likelihood estimation method, the values of the set of parent nodes are given, and the occurrence frequency of various values of each child node is calculated as the conditional probability parameter of the node.

$$L(\theta, X) = P(X|\theta) = \prod_{x \in X} P(X = |x\theta) \tag{7}$$

In the above formula, the conditional probability parameters of X network node set and θ node in this state.

Bayesian estimation is also a method of Bayesian network parameter estimation. Compared with maximum likelihood estimation, Bayesian estimation is more advantageous when dealing with small samples. The difference between the Bayesian estimation method and the traditional statistical method is that compared with the traditional method, the uncertainty is regarded as the infinite approach of the frequency. The size is determined by the original subjective knowledge and the observed phenomenon, so the Bayesian estimation takes the parameter to be determined as a random variable in the learning process, and fully considers the influence of prior knowledge in the learning process, so the obtained results are often better than Maximum likelihood estimation is more reasonable. The basic idea of Bayesian estimation is to use prior knowledge to search for the maximum posterior probability given the above conditions, given the unknown parameters t, topology D and all possible values of the parameters in this case. Parameter value. From the Bayesian formula, it can be known that:

$$P(\theta|D, S) = \frac{P(D|\theta, S)P(\theta|S)}{P(D|S)} \tag{8}$$

In the above formula, $P(\theta|D, S)$ represents the prior probability of parameter θ in the case of S.

Parameter learning in the case of missing data, when the data is missing, because the sample set is incomplete, the maximum likelihood estimation of the sample set cannot be performed. At this time, the expectation maximization algorithm (referred to as the EM algorithm) can be used for network parameter learning. The EM algorithm was originally proposed by Rubin et al. in 1977 and was used for the calculation of maximum likelihood estimation in the case of incomplete data. Lauriten has proved that when the sample set is missing, the expectation maximization algorithm can perform Bayesian network parameters. Learning [9], the algorithm is named because each iteration of the expectation maximization algorithm includes two steps, finding the expected value and finding the maximum value. The solution process is as follows:

$$F = \sum_{l=1}^{n} p\left(x_i^k, \pi_i^j \middle| y_l, \overline{\theta}_s, S^h\right) \tag{9}$$

In the above formula, x_i^k, π_i^j, y_l and S^h respectively represent the learning sample set.

5.2 Inference of Bayesian Networks

Bayesian network reasoning, also known as Bayesian network computing, refers to the use of the conditional probability table and structure of Bayesian network to calculate the probabilities of various states of a node or the edge probabilities and maximum probability states of all variables after given certain evidence. The traditional statistical inference method generally infers the likelihood function of the past and future possible occurrence of an event through the correlation and correlation of variables. The inference method of Bayesian network provides a consistent representation model for the complex dependency and causality among multiple variables, which is a big step forward compared with the traditional correlation representation model. The joint tree algorithm is a Bayesian network precise reasoning method which is the most widely used and the fastest computing speed at present. It converts the Bayesian network into an undirected tree. The nodes of each tree are composed of the largest complete subgraph of the undirected graph, and then gives the message passing rules on the joint tree to calculate the probability. The basic algorithm process is as follows:

1) Moral Graphization of Bayesian Networks. The moral graph of Bayesian network is created by removing the pointing of all edges in the directed graph of Bayesian network and connecting every two parent nodes with common child nodes with undirected edges [10];
2) Moral map three coking. Make a copy of the moral graph obtained in the previous step, select the node x with the smallest weight in the copy, connect the nodes directly connected to x in the original graph and the copy in turn, and then delete the node x and the edges connected to it in the copy, loop until all nodes in the replica are deleted;
3) Determine the group. The non-repetitive node set selected in the triangulation step is considered to be a group;
4) Establish a group association tree. Concatenate the determined cliques as separate sets into a joint tree that satisfies the specificity of cliques;
5) Initialization and messaging. The probability distribution of variables in Bayesian network is added to the joint tree, and the conditional probability and marginal probability are calculated by introducing evidence and global transfer. Message passing is divided into evidence collection stage and evidence diffusion stage. First, any group node x is selected as the root node. Starting from the node R farthest away from it, messages are delivered to the adjacent nodes from far to near in the direction close to x, and evidence is collected. The circle node that receives the message delivered by the neighbor node updates its distribution function and continues to deliver to the upper level until the root node obtains all the messages; Evidence diffusion starts from node x and spreads from near to far south to every node of the joint tree.

5.3 Detection Implementation

The Bayesian network inference mainly starts with the prior probability, and calculates the conditional probability distribution process according to the Bayesian rule. On this basis, the complete combined probability of a set of arbitrary variables is given, and the combined probability of all frontiers and lower-order probabilities is obtained. There is a lot of conditional independence in the Bayesian network in the computation, and we get:

$$P(V_1, V_2 \ldots, V_k) = \prod_{i=1}^{n} p\Big(V_i | \prod(V_i)\Big) \tag{10}$$

In the above formula, V_i represents the direct parent node of the i data, and p represents the conditional probability.

The above process simplifies probabilistic reasoning, but as the evidence spreads in the network graph, each node will receive relevant information from its child node's parent node [11], at this time, $\lambda_x(U)$ is defined as the information transmitted by node X to parent node U. Evidence information, πU is the evidence information passed to U by the parent node of node π [12], which is expressed as:

$$\begin{cases} \lambda_x(U) = P\left(e_e^- | x\right) \\ \pi U = PU\left(e|_x^+\right) \end{cases} \tag{11}$$

where, e represents the partition parameter of child node evidence information.

In this way, the specific reasoning process of Bayesian network is expressed as:

Step1: self node information update. When a node in the data triggers the update, the information from the degree calculation and the information from the child nodes will be used to update the self node information. The update is expressed by the following formula:

$$\varepsilon(x) = ax * \alpha\lambda(x) \tag{12}$$

Among them, $\lambda(x)$ represents the information sent by the child node, and ax is the information sent by the parent node.

Step2: Update from bottom to top, use the received information to calculate the information sent to the parent node U, the formula is as follows:

$$\lambda_X(U) = \sum_x \lambda(x) P(x|u) \tag{13}$$

In the above formula, $\lambda_X(U)$ is the diagnostic information passed from node X to parent node U.

Step3: update from top to bottom to calculate the information sent to child nodes:

$$\pi x_j(x) = \alpha(x) \prod_{k \neq j} \lambda_Y \tag{14}$$

Among them, λ_Y represents the initial information in the child node.

Since the amount of information contained in the identification feature is different, the information obtained when identifying the feature is not the same [13]. Therefore, different weights are assigned to different data, thereby determining the influence of the identification result corresponding to the identification feature. In the algorithm, the decision matrix is constructed by the AHP method, and the largest eigenvalue and the corresponding eigenvector are obtained. Expressed as:

$$A = \lambda_{\varpi} * d(g) \tag{15}$$

Among them, λ_{ϖ} represents the eigenvector corresponding to the largest eigenvalue, and $d(g)$ represents the criterion corresponding to the criterion g.

In the pairwise comparison of each factor, a completely consistent measurement cannot be achieved, so there is a certain error. In order to improve the reliability of the analysis, a consistency test is carried out. The formula is expressed as:

$$\sigma_{c} = \frac{\lambda_{\max} - n}{n - 1} \tag{16}$$

where, n represents the dimension of the matrix, and $\lambda_{\max}$ represents the maximum eigenvalue decision matrix.

After the above processing, the weight of each feature data is added to the Bayesian network, and the weight W_t corresponding to the i attribute is defined as:

$$W = \frac{1}{T}\sum_{DT=1}^{T}\frac{1}{\sqrt{d_{i,DT}}} \tag{17}$$

In the above formula, T represents the number of decision trees established during the weight learning process, and $d_{i,DT}$ represents the minimum depth value corresponding to the i attribute in the decision tree.

Through the above process, each data is weighted to obtain the conditional feature value of each data, and finally the data is fused, as shown in the following Fig. 3:

Based on the above process, data fusion and bus network security detection are completed.

6 Experimental Comparison

In order to verify the effectiveness of the Bayes based CAN bus network security detection method, experiments are carried out, and the traditional detection method is compared with the proposed method, and the detection effects of the two detection methods are compared.

The environment of the simulation experiment system is Windows7, the CANoe (Version8.lSP) of Vector company is used to simulate the vehicle CAN bus network environment, and the Zhou Ligong USB-CAN-II is used to simulate an invaded ECU node to attack the bus network. Connect with laptop via USB, send and receive CAN bus messages through CANTest1.5 software, connect CANO port of USB-CAN-II II to CANH and CANL corresponding to COM3 of CANoe VN164O, and set it as external physical interface of CAN bus in CANoe. CANoe VN1640 is a four-way CAN/LIN bus simulation tool from Vector.

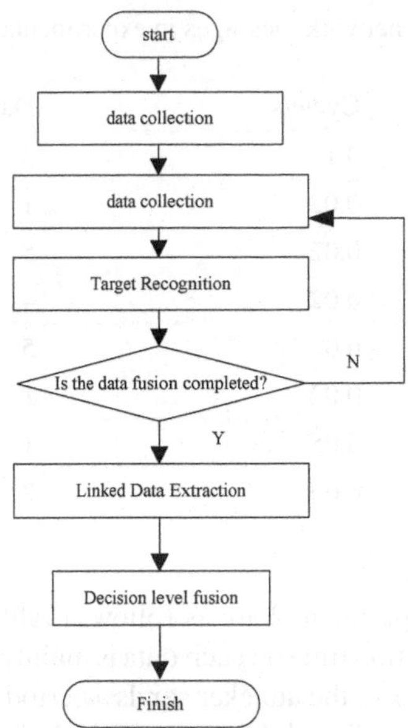

Fig. 3. New energy transaction data fusion process

Since the attack node needs to be set up in the bus network, it is necessary to connect the simulated network of CANo to the external physical interface. VN1640 can provide two-way CAN network physical interface. It can set canpiggy in hardware configuration, assign physical interface to analog bus, and configure the channel used by CANoe in application options. The simulated in-vehicle network uses CANoe's System Demo, which simulates the driving of the car. The working status of each part of the ECU in the CAN network and the situation of message sending. There are two CAN bus networks in the Dmo, namely Power_.train and Comfort. The Power_.train network simulates the power CAN bus of the car, including the main control units such as engine, gear, and brake. The Comfort network simulates the body CAN bus, mainly for functions such as lights and instrument display.

6.1 Experiment Preparation

The basic contents of Experiment 1 are as follows: the experimental data comes from a brand car in China, the data collection environment is in the underground garage, the normal operation during driving, the maximum speed reaches 45 km/h, the collection time is 2 min, and the number of message collection is 26000. Each message of on-board CAN bus uses a unique message identifier ID, and each CAN bus message with different identifier ID carries the data information of specific functions or control commands. The CAN bus message identifier can be regarded as the message ID of the message. Each message ID is trained separately. The sample contains 15 bus messages with different IDs. These messages contain different numbers of abnormal messages, which are detected by the proposed method and the traditional method respectively.

Table 1. CAN network messages in experimental environment

Describe	Cycle/s	Data size/byte
Gateway 1	0.1	3
In the control	0.02	1
Ignition	0.02	5
Engine	0.02	4
Gateway 2	0.02	5
Transmission	0.02	1
Drive Gateway	0.05	1
Car door	0.05	2

The basic contents of Experiment 2 are as follows (Table 1):

In experiment 2, the detection time on each data is mainly detected. In the experimental environment described above, the attacker sends a period of 0.05 s to the power_train subnet in a whole time interval T, and the frame ID is 0×00, Attack packet with a data field length of 8 bytes.

6.2 Analysis of Experimental Results

The detection results on the number of abnormal messages are shown in the following (Table 2):

Table 2. Detection of the number of abnormal packets

Actual number of abnormal packets/piece	Test results of the proposed method/piece	Test results of traditional methods/piece
2450	2441	2252
2312	2318	2032
2152	2149	2011
2562	2556	2301
2595	2589	2354
1625	1631	1765
1345	1356	1032
1455	1452	1165
1525	1523	1689
1502	1509	1301

(continued)

Table 2. (*continued*)

Actual number of abnormal packets/piece	Test results of the proposed method/piece	Test results of traditional methods/piece
1406	1412	1202
1411	1416	1131
1609	1613	1254
1456	1462	1195
1571	1568	1321

Based on the above table, it can be found that the detection accuracy of the proposed detection method is higher than that of the traditional detection method, which is basically consistent with the actual number of abnormal messages.

In the second part of the experiment, the experimental results are as follows Fig. 4:

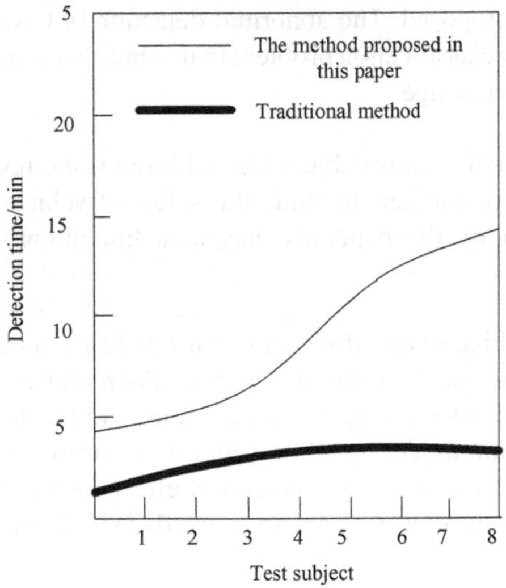

Fig. 4. Comparison of detection time

Based on the above figure, it can be found that the proposed detection method takes less time to detect different types of messages, which is far less than the traditional detection method, and has strong practical significance.

7 Conclusion

An anomaly detection technology model for on-board CAN bus is proposed. An anomaly detection system is installed on the on-board bus to judge whether the bus is invaded by detecting the bus message information, so as to timely and effectively ensure the safety of the on-board bus. Based on the research of a large number of relevant literature at home and abroad, and on the basis of summarizing and drawing lessons from the previous research results, the main innovative work can be summarized as follows:

1) By analyzing the vehicle CAN network communication protocol and monitoring the actual vehicle network, an attack method using CAN network security vulnerabilities is designed.
2) An anomaly detection model based on features and information entropy is proposed for the identification bit of the message. By detecting the probability distribution of different ID messages of the CAN bus, the information entropy of the vehicle CAN bus is calculated, and the information entropy value of the normal CAN bus is used as the abnormality. The detection threshold standard and combined with the whitelist strategy, perform feature value detection on the special CAN ID of the CAN bus. The experimental results show that the model can effectively prevent flooding attacks, a large number of replay attacks and packet attacks that do not appear in the bus.
3) For the data bits of the message, an anomaly detection model based on support vector machine is proposed. The abnormal detection of CAN message data can be regarded as a binary classification problem in machine learning, normal data message and abnormal data message.

Although the research on this subject has achieved some results, it provides many supports and ideas for researchers to study the safety of vehicle bus. However, due to my limited time and ability, this paper also has some limitations. The following aspects deserve further study:

1) The detection model based on information entropy has a good detection effect for a large number of flooding attacks and replay attacks. For replay attacks with small traffic, the change of bus information entropy is not obvious, and the detection effect is poor;
2) The anomaly detection model based on support vector machine has good detection accuracy for most bus packets, but the detection effect for bus packets with changing data bits is not ideal, so the detection accuracy needs to be further improved.

References

1. Duan, Z., Wang, L., Sun, M.: Efficient heuristics for learning bayesian network from labeled and unlabeled data. Intell. Data Anal. **24**(2), 385–408 (2020)
2. Wang, L., Chen, P., Chen, S., Sun, M.: A novel approach to fully representing the diversity in conditional dependencies for learning bayesian network classifier. Intell. Data Anal. **25**(1), 35–55 (2021)
3. Ding, Y., Dong, J., Yang, T., Zhou, S., Wei, Y.: Failure evaluation of bridge deck based on parallel connection bayesian network: analytical model. Materials **14**(6), 1411 (2021)
4. Gupta, K., Sahoo, S., Panigrahi, B.K., Blaabjerg, F., Popovski, P.: On the assessment of cyber risks and attack surfaces in a real-time co-simulation cybersecurity testbed for inverter-based microgrids. Energies **14**(16), 4941 (2021)

5. Rathore, S., Park, J.H.: A blockchain-based deep learning approach for cyber security in next generation industrial cyber-physical systems. IEEE Trans. Industr. Inf. **17**(8), 5522–5532 (2021)
6. Fernández-Caramés, T.M., Fraga-Lamas, P.: Teaching and learning iot cybersecurity and vulnerability assessment with shodan through practical use cases. Sensors **20**(11), 3048 (2020)
7. Kang, Y.L., Feng, L.L., Zhang, J.A.: Research on subregional anomaly data mining based on naive bayes. Comput. Simul. **37**(10), 303–306+316 (2020)
8. Nikoloudakis, Y., Kefaloukos, I., Klados, S., Panagiotakis, S., Markakis, E.K.: Towards a machine learning based situational awareness framework for cybersecurity: an SDN implementation. Sensors **21**(14), 4939 (2021)
9. Dankwa, S., Yang, L.: An efficient and accurate depth-wise separable convolutional neural network for cybersecurity vulnerability assessment based on captcha breaking. Electronics **10**(4), 480 (2021)
10. Liu, S., et al.: Human memory update strategy: a multi-layer template update mechanism for remote visual monitoring. IEEE Trans. Multimedia **23**, 2188–2198 (2021)
11. Liu, S., Liu, D., Muhammad, K., Ding, W.: Effective template update mechanism in visual tracking with background clutter. Neurocomputing **458**, 615–625 (2021)
12. Pascale, F., Adinolfi, E.A., Coppola, S., Santonicola, E.: Cybersecurity in automotive: an intrusion detection system in connected vehicles. Electronics **10**(15), 1765 (2021)
13. Shuai, L., Shuai, W., Xinyu, L., et al.: Fuzzy detection aided real-time and robust visual tracking under complex environments. IEEE Trans. Fuzzy Syst. **29**(1), 90–102 (2021)

Discrete Wavelet Transform-Based CNN for Breast Cancer Classification from Histopathology Images

Yuan Qi[1], Xiaozhang Liu[1(✉)], Hua Li[2], Mingting Liu[2], and Wei Li[1]

[1] School of Computer Science and Technology, Hainan University, Haikou 570228, China
yishulianyi@163.com, lxzh@hainanu.edu.cn
[2] School of Cyberspace Security (School of Cryptology), Hainan University, Haikou 570228, China

Abstract. Breast cancer has the highest mortality rate among cancers in women, but its diagnosis is limited. In recent years, there have been many works applying deep learning to computer-aided diagnosis of breast cancer histopathology images. However, the existing methods focus only on the spatial domain approach and the extracted feature information is not comprehensive enough. Furthermore, to reduce the computational burden, they usually crop images into smaller-sized patches resulting in the loss of a large amount of feature information. To address the above issues, we propose a frequency domain learning method based on discrete wavelet transform and convolutional neural network (CNN) for the classification task of breast cancer histopathology images. The method first extracts the feature information in the time and frequency domains using the wavelet transform, while taking into account the different information contained in the three color components of RGB images. Then, the low-frequency information from the decomposition of different color components is then fused and inputs to the CNN for training, meanwhile, other non-critical information is filtered out to improve the computational efficiency. The accuracy of our method is 99.50%, 99.20%, 99.00% and 99.08% for the binary classification task and 95.79%, 92.91%, 90.83% and 93.37% for the multi-classification task, respectively, on the BreakHis dataset.

Keywords: Image classification · Wavelet transform · CNN · Breast cancer · Transfer learning

1 Introduction

Cancer is the second leading cause for death, and breast cancer has now replaced lung cancer as the world's leading cancer [1]. Therefore, the study of benign and malignant classification of breast cancer and specific types of cancer can assist doctors to observe lesions and structures from various angles more conveniently

Y. Xu et al. (Eds.): ML4CS 2022, LNCS 13655, pp. 326–340, 2023.
https://doi.org/10.1007/978-3-031-20096-0_25

and accurately, which has important practical significance. Breast cancer is a heterogeneous disease, consisting of many entities with different biological, histological and clinical features [2]. An important technique used to detect breast cancer reliably is microscopic examination after biopsy [3]. The resulting information of a breast biopsy is used to perform prognostic assessments [4]. To enhance visibility, these tissues are stained in the laboratory, and the staining process usually uses hematoxylin and eosin (H&E) [5]. In histological and cytological staining, it is highly unlikely that an area is stained with only one color, so slides stained with multiple stains can be used to show the location and status of different markers [6]. At the same time, this means that the currently available feature extraction techniques may lead to a large amount of information loss.

Deep learning algorithms already have excellent work results on image classification and object detection tasks, and convolutional neural networks are the most widely used deep learning framework for learning complex features between image classes [7]. Due to the limitation of computational resources and memory, most CNN models only accept low-resolution (e.g., 224×224) RGB images, so a large portion of the task images are significantly reduced to 224×224 in order to fit the input of the classification network. However, image reduction inevitably leads to information loss and accuracy degradation [8]. Previous works aimed to reduce information loss by learning task-aware refinement networks [9,10]. However, these networks are used for specific tasks, so they have less practical application. Histopathology images of breast cancer intricately connect texture and color information, and these features can be defined in terms of individual color components or pairs of related color components [11].

Therefore, we propose a method that combines convolutional neural networks with frequency domain learning for breast cancer pathology images, the main contributions of this paper are:

- Our method combine multi-color spatial domain features. Considering the different information contained in the three color components of pathological and normal tissue after staining, the original spatial domain features are separated according to RGB color components, and then the multi-dimensional features are fully integrated to improve the model accuracy.
- In our method, the fused multi-dimensional spatial domain features are input into the existing CNN model for training, and the transfer learning idea is used to maximize the advantages of the existing neural network and improve the training efficiency of the model.
- Our method can deal with large input size, use lossless wavelet transform to decompose and downsample the input image, and filter out non-critical information, so as to improve the computational efficiency and reduce the loss of detail information.

The rest of this paper is shown below. Section 2 describes the related work. Section 3 shows the dataset and methods used to conduct this study. Section 4 explains the experiments and analyses of the results. Finally, Sect. 5 highlights the conclusion of this study.

2 Related Work

The diagnosis of histopathological sections requires a pathologist with extensive experience, yet the results are susceptible to personal influence of the specialist [12]. Currently, the most common method of breast cancer diagnosis is manual examination of breast images; however, due to certain unavoidable reasons during manual examination, the test results may be inaccurate and increase the diagnostic time [13]. Before the deep learning revolution, Huang et al. [14] used two separate datasets of different sizes, one small 11-dimensional dataset containing 699 samples and the other large 117-dimensional dataset containing 102,294 samples, and their experiments were done through support vector machines. Also, other machine learning methods have been used to study breast cancer data, such as principal component analysis (PCA) and random forest (RF).

With the development of deep learning, some further great progress has been made in computer-aided diagnosis of breast cancer. Spanhol et al. [15] trained images from the BreakHis dataset through AlexNet and LeNet and ended up with results that outperformed the classification results using hand-made feature descriptors. Li et al. [16] constructed a multi-task learning framework, and to extract features from pathological images, this method uses some network layers selected from Xception. To obtain better recognition results, the feature attributes with different magnifications were embedded accordingly. Alkassar et al. [17] extracted shallow and deep features for classification by using Xception and DenseNet, respectively. Wang et al. [18] proposed the FE-BkCapsNet method, which uses a capsule network and combines semantic information from CNNs to focus on information such as location in images.

Since the cell nucleus to the whole tissue contains information the information from different relevant scales, Araujo et al. designed a CNN network architecture that extracted all relevant information and finally obtained the classification accuracy of 77.8% in a multi-classification task of breast cancer pathology images [19]. To improve the performance of breast cancer pathology image classification tasks, some researchers have tried to design networks using more advanced residual unit. Among them, the network designed by Zhang et al. takes larger image patches as input and extensively compared the performance of VGGNet and three ResNets on this classification task [20]. K. Jabeen et al. use an optimization algorithm based on RGW and RDE to select the best features, and then fuse the selected features with deep learning to perform breast cancer classification [21]. D.M. Vo et al. [22] used CNN-based methods (e.g., Inception) to handle breast cancer classification challenge dataset. The proposed models both achieved significantly higher results compared to existing methods. A. Alqudah et al. [23] proposed a technique to extract local binary pattern features from breast histopathology images, called sliding window-based technique, which were then fed to an SVM classifier to achieve a binary classification task, and finally the SVM classifier obtained an accuracy of 91.12%.

3 Dataset and Methods

3.1 Dataset

We used the publicly available dataset BreakHis, published by Spanhol et al. [14] in 2016, which has a total of 7909 histopathology images. The images were collected between January 2014 and December 2014 and were all obtained from clinical studies.

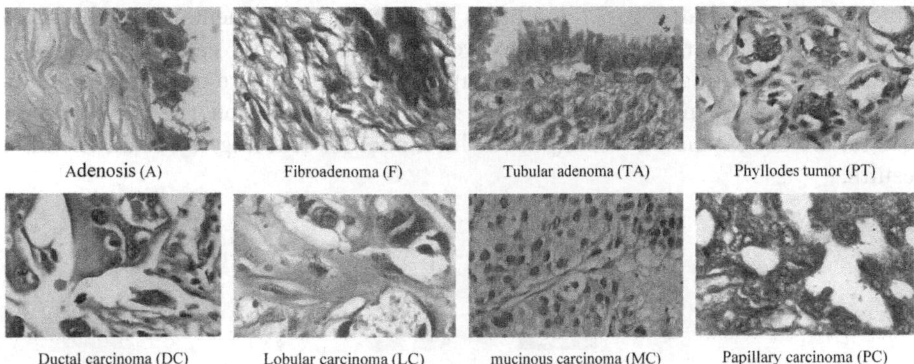

Fig. 1. Some examples from the BreakHis dataset. The first and second rows show four benign tumors and four malignant tumors, respectively. The magnification factor of these mages is 400×.

Table 1. Statistics of the BreakHis dataset for each category of samples.

Classes	Subclasses	Magnification factors				Total	
		40×	100×	200×	400×	Classes	SubClasses
Benign	A	114	113	111	106	2480	444
	F	253	260	264	237		1014
	TA	109	121	108	115		453
	PT	149	150	140	130		569
Malignant	DC	864	903	896	788	5429	3451
	LC	156	170	163	137		626
	MC	205	222	196	169		792
	PC	145	142	135	138		560
Total		1995	2081	2013	1820	7909	

The BreakHis dataset contains both benign and malignant breast cancer histopathology images with different magnifications of 40×, 100×, 200×, and 400×. Figure 1 shows an example image of benign and malignant cancerous lesions at 400×. In turn, each category has four different categories, benign carcinomas are Adenosis (A), Fibroadenoma (F), Tubular Adenoma (TA), Phyllodes Tumor (PT), Ductal Carcinoma (DC), Lobular Carcinoma (LC), Mucinous Carcinoma (MC), Papillary Carcinoma (PC). Table 1 shows the statistics of the BreakHis dataset.

3.2 Overview

The overall architecture of our proposed method is shown in Fig. 2. The original image is separated after resize to obtain three color components, then the three color components are subjected to wavelet transform, and each component is obtained as four different frequency components. The feature matrix of the low-frequency components, which has the greatest influence on the classification results, are concatenated and input to the model for training to obtain the final results.

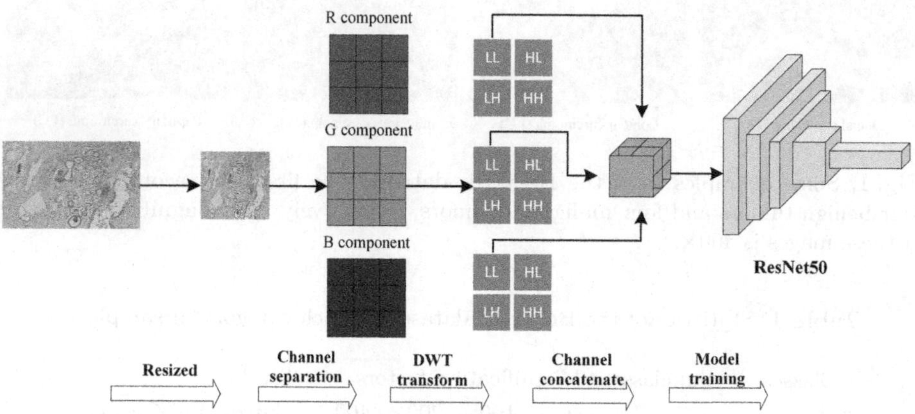

Fig. 2. An overview of the overall architecture.

3.3 Image Processing

In our proposed method, the breast cancer pathology slice dataset images are applied to DWT based on the CNN method. Firstly, the images are resized to a scale of 448 × 448 and the data are expanded by random flipping the images horizontally with a uniform probability distribution function. Initially, before data expansion, the breast cancer pathology section dataset was randomly divided into 70% training set and 30% test set with sizes of 5551 and 2358 images, respectively. In order to prevent overfitting of the model, the dataset was expanded [24]. Finally, the dataset was fed to a modified model of the ResNet50 pre-training variant.

3.4 Discrete Wavelet Transform (DWT)

The deep convolutional neural networks are one of the most powerful of all deep learning methods, but they have a large number of parameters that need to be tuned. Wavelet space in the frequency domain allows for flexible local smoothing filtering with fewer parameters. Our proposed method combines convolutional neural network with wavelet transform, which can return to pixel space after learning parameters in wavelet domain, retains the advantages of CNN while overlaying the advantages of wavelet transform, and makes the feature information input to CNN more comprehensive and effective. In this section, we specifically explain the implementation of the discrete wavelet transform (DWT) that we use.

A wavelet refers to a wave whose energy is very concentrated in the time domain, and wavelet transformation is a mathematical function that essentially projects the signal onto a series of wavelet bases or decomposes the image signal into a set of wavelets after shifting and scaling from the original wavelets [25].

$$\Psi_{m,n}(t) = \frac{1}{\sqrt{|m|}}\Psi(\frac{t-n}{m}), m, n \in R, m \neq 0 \tag{1}$$

For a given input signal, the output of the wavelet transform is related to the wavelet function, m, N. The specific signal transformation process can be defined as Eq. 1, where Ψ is the wavelet function, and m, n are the scale and translation parameters, respectively, represent the computational scale or degree of compression and prompt the temporal location of the wavelet. If the function being expanded is a sequence of numbers, the resulting coefficients are called DWT [26].

Wavelet functions are diverse. Using different wavelet bases to analyze the same problem can produce different results [27]. Haar wavelets are the first applied and simplest orthogonal wavelets, which are single rectangular waves with support domain in the range $t \in [0, 1]$, and allow the simplest decomposition calculations. The Haar wavelet is denoted as [28]:

$$\psi(t) = \begin{cases} 1 & t \in [0, 1/2] \\ -1 & t \in [1/2, 1] \\ 0 & otherwise \end{cases} \tag{2}$$

The two-dimensional discrete wavelet decomposition process of the image can be described as follows: First, one-dimensional wavelet transform is applied to the original image in the row direction to obtain the low-frequency component v_L and high-frequency component v_H. Then, one-dimensional wavelet transform is applied to v_H and v_L in the column direction to obtain the low-frequency component v_{LL} and three high-frequency components v_{HL}, v_{HH}, v_{LH} [29]. The above process can be defined as Eq. (3), (4) and (5).

$$v_L, v_H = 1D^{row} - DWT(Image) \tag{3}$$

$$v_{LL}, v_{LH} = 1D^{colomn} - DWT(v_L) \tag{4}$$

$$v_{HL}, v_{HH} = 1D^{colomn} - DWT(v_H) \tag{5}$$

3.5 Transfer Learning

Training an entire ResNet model from scratch is almost unattainable because of hardware and data set quantity limitations, and migration learning is a technique for retraining a CNN model designed to accomplish similar task scenarios. Therefore, to solve the above problem, pre-trained models that have been trained for other similar tasks are applied to the present work using migration learning techniques [25]. Based on the new training data, a ResNet50 model pre-trained on a similar classification task is put into training with new data by changing a parameter or adjusting the layer weights using migration learning techniques.

4 Experiments and Results

4.1 Training Methodology

We use PyTorch 1.7 with Nvidia GeForce RTX 3090 Graphics Processing Unit (GPU) for all experiments. To prevent the model from overfitting and enhance its robustness, we employ a data augmentation strategy to randomly resize the original image into 448×448 patches. Furthermore, to avoid the influence of special samples on the results, we normalize the data using zero-mean normalization. We trained our network for 300 epochs with an initial learning rate of 0.0001 and optimized the network using the stochastic gradient descent (SGD [30] optimization algorithm with batch size 64, weight decay 5×10^{-4}, and momentum 0.9.

4.2 Evaluation Metrics

We evaluate the overall performance of the proposed method using a confusion matrix, which contains four terms, True Positive (TP), False Positive (FP), True Negative (TN), and False Negative (FN). where TP refers to those images that are correctly classified as benign cancers, FP represents images of benign cancers that are classified as malignant cancers, FN denotes images of malignant carcinomas that are classified as benign carcinomas, and TN represents images that are correctly classified as malignant cancers image. Based on confusion matrix, we used three performance measures on the testing set when evaluating the classification performance of our proposed model. Three performance measures are precision, recall and F1-score. These performance measures can be calculated as follow:

- **Precision:** It refers to the ratio of true Positive data among all data predicted as Positive.

$$Precision = \frac{TP}{TP + FP} \tag{6}$$

- **Recall:** It represents the ability of the model to correctly predict positives from actual positive samples, and is often used as an important measure of correct predictions when the categories are very imbalanced.

$$Recall = \frac{TP}{TP + FN} \tag{7}$$

- **Specificity:** It often refers to as specificity or true negative rate, indicates the ability of the model to correctly predict the picture of malignant carcinoma among all malignant carcinoma predictions.

$$Specificity = \frac{TN}{TN + FP} \tag{8}$$

- **F1-score:** It is the harmonic mean of the precision and recall scores, giving the equal weight to the previous two metrics to measure the accuracy and robustness of the model.

$$F1 - score = \frac{2 \times Precision \times Recall}{Precision + Recall} \tag{9}$$

4.3 Results and Analyses

On the BreakHis dataset, we conduct binary and multi-class breast cancer classification experiments respectively. In this section, we first analyze the results of binary and multi-class breast cancer classification separately, which include accuracy and loss variation plots, confusion matrix, etc. Then, we show the results of our proposed method compared with existing methods and discuss the competitiveness of our proposed model with recently published studies.

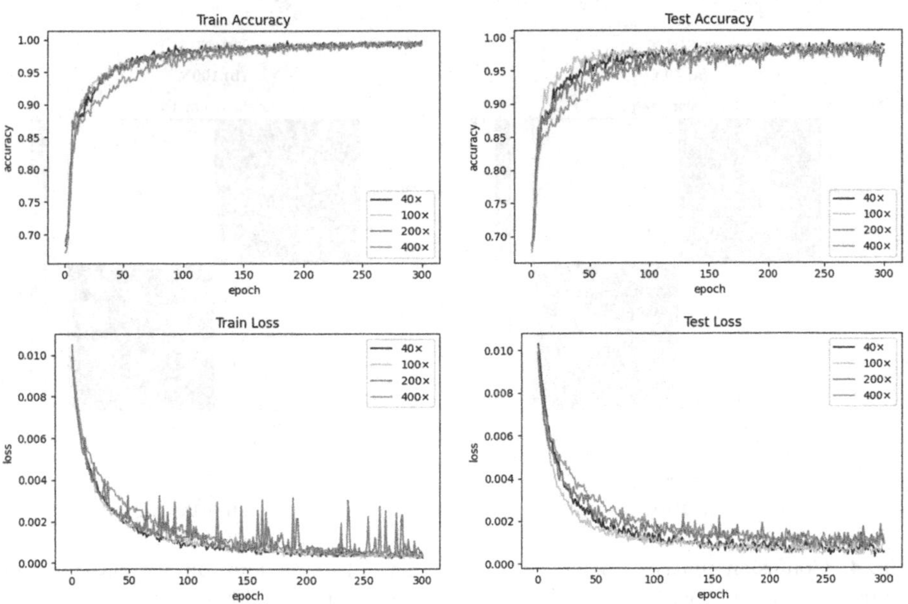

Fig. 3. Results of binary classification of breast cancer at different magnifications, where the first row is the accuracy and the second row is the loss.

Results and Comparison for Binary Classification. The accuracy and loss curve results of the binary classification experiments completed on the BreakHis dataset using our proposed method are shown in Fig. 3, corresponding to 40×, 100×, 200×, and 400× images with different magnification factors. We can see in the figure that the magnification factors of the samples have an impact on the training and testing accuracy. The highest accuracy was obtained from the experiments with 40× magnification images. The optimal verification accuracies were 99.50%, 99.20%, 99.00%, and 99.08%, respectively, all achieving scores above 99. We also evaluated the model using four other typical evaluation metrics (i.e. precision, recall, specificity and F1-score). The results are listed in Table 2.

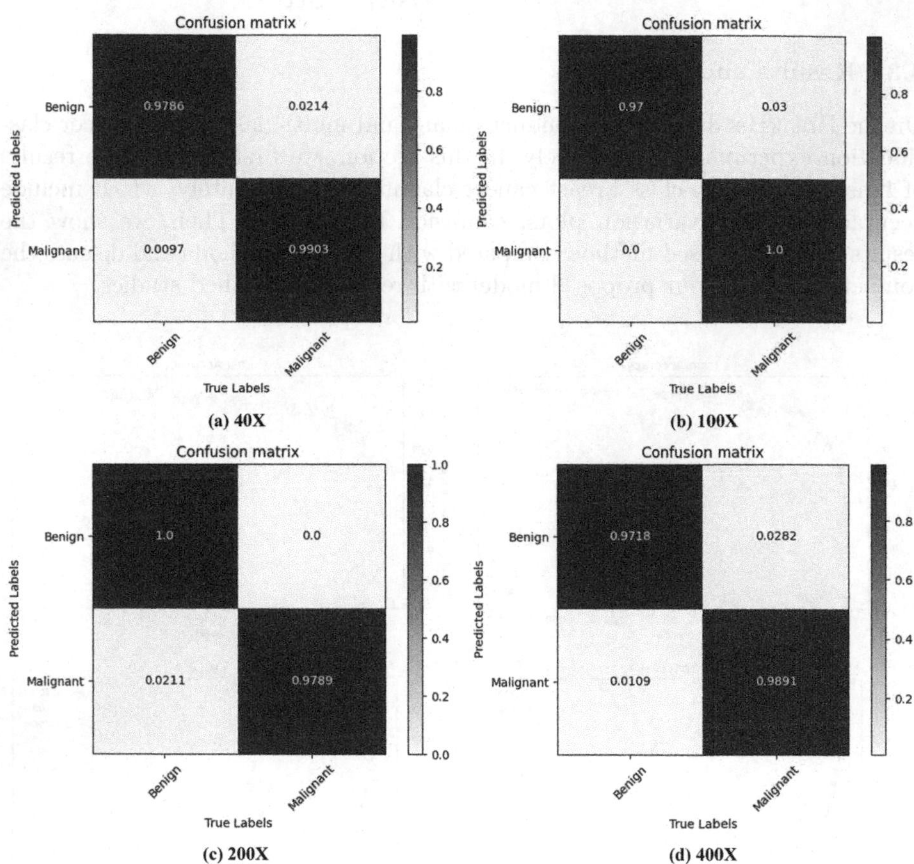

Fig. 4. Confusion matrices achieved by our method of on four binary classification magnifications, that is, (a) 40×, (b) 100×, (c) 200×, and (d) 400×.

Table 2. The evaluation metrics computed from best result of our method in each magnification factor of binary classification.

Performance Evaluation (%)	Magnification factors			
	40×	100×	200×	400×
Precision	98.45	98.65	98.94	98.05
Recall	98.44	99.15	97.58	98.19
Specificity	98.45	99.15	97.58	98.19
F1-score	98.66	98.90	98.26	98.11

In addition, the confusion matrix of the model at different magnifications is given in Fig. 4. It can be seen that the prediction accuracy of the images with the true label Malignant is 100% in the results of 100×, and the prediction accuracy of the images with the true label Benign is 100% in the results of 200×, while the classification error rate of the other magnifications is very low. As shown in Table 2, the image precision of 200X is the highest, but the final accurcy is not the highest. This data indicates that in the process of lesion classification, the probability of misdiagnosing malignant lesions as benign lesions is low, but conversely, the probability of misdiagnosing benign diseases as malignant lesions is high. The reason for this situation is that the image of 200X loses some benign information (the benign lesion area is small, and it is easy to misjudge it as a malignant lesion if only the benign features are reduced). It does not pay full attention to the characteristic area of the lesion as the image of 400X does. However, our model mainly reduces the loss of features. When the identifiable features are reduced, our model does not show obvious advantages.

Table 3. Compared results with the representative CNN-based methods of binary classification on the BreakHis dataset.

Years	Methods	Magnification factors			
		40×	100×	200×	400×
2018	CNN-FNN	90.00	91.00	90.50	90.00
2018	IRRCNN	98.50	98.00	98.00	97.50
2019	BHCNet-3	98.90	99.00	99.50	99.00
2019	VGGNet/ResNet	92.68	90.40	87.30	86.63
2020	VGG-VD16	95.03	90.41	88.48	85.00
2020	22 layers CNN	90.89	90.99	91.00	90.97
2020	BreastNet (CBAM)	97.99	97.84	98.51	95.88
2021	AHoNet	96.53	97.47	99.09	96.52
2022	**Ours**	**99.50**	**99.20**	**99.00**	**99.08**

The results of our method compared with representative methods proposed based on the BreakHis dataset over a 5-year period are shown in Table 3. As shown in this table, the results obtained with our method are significantly better than those proposed in recent years, which is a good indication of the effectiveness of our method for the classification of histopathology images of breast cancer. Our proposed method further shows its performance advantage compared to the new methods proposed in the past two years. Most of the proposed methods in recent years have achieved classification accuracy of 97% or higher, but their accuracy are still lower than our method. Thus, our proposed method achieves excellent performance on the binary classification task.

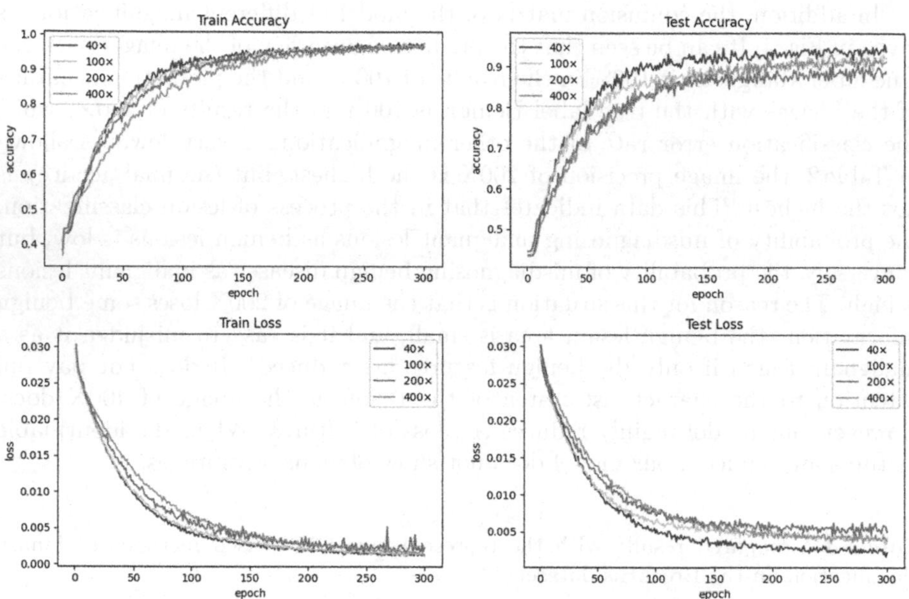

Fig. 5. Results for multi-classification on BreakHis dataset at different magnifications, where the first two represent accuracy and the last two represent loss.

Table 4. The evaluation metrics computed from best result of our method in each magnification factor of multi-classification.

Performance evaluation (%)	Magnification factors			
	40×	100×	200×	400×
Precision	93.47	92.29	89.30	91.36
Recall	93.09	91.58	88.55	90.91
Specificity	99.06	98.83	98.72	98.72
F1-score	93.28	91.94	88.92	91.13

Results and Comparison for Multi-classification. The results of the accuracy and loss curves of the multi-classification experiments completed on the BreakHis dataset using our proposed method are shown in Fig. 5. From the variation of the results in the figure, it can be seen that, unlike the dichotomous classification results, the highest validation accuracy is obtained for the multi-classification experiments with 40× magnification of the image, followed by 400× and the lowest by 200×, with the optimal accuracies of 95.79%, 92.91%, 90.83%, and 93.37%, respectively.

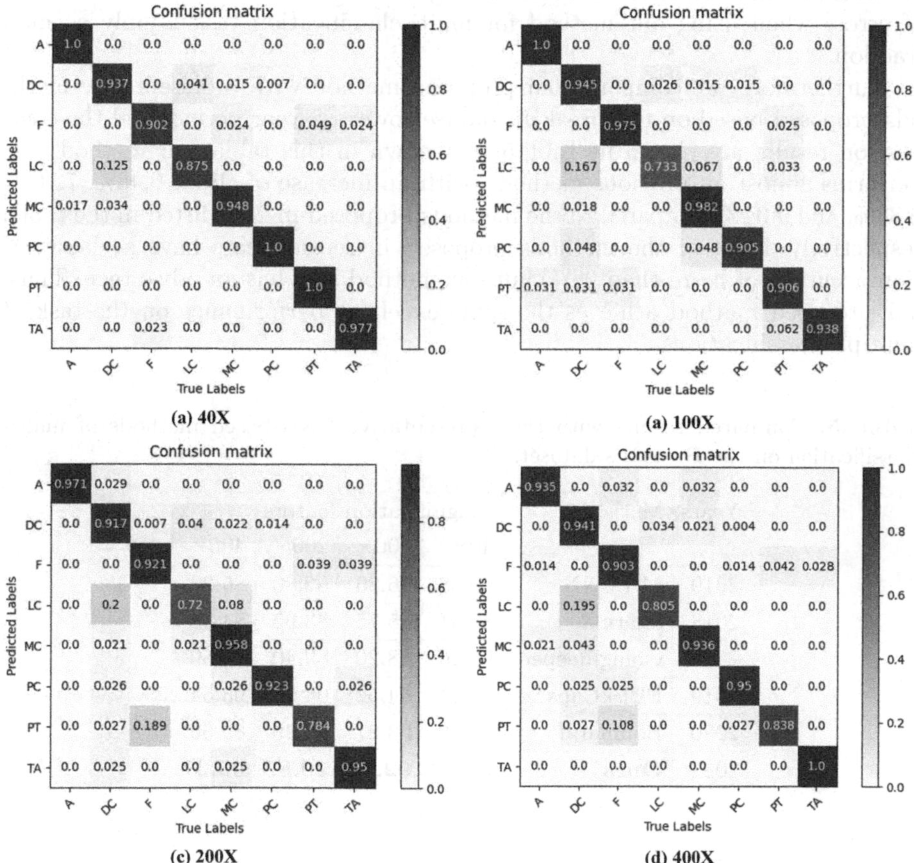

Fig. 6. Confusion matrices achieved by our method of on four binary classification magnifications, that is, (a) 40×, (b) 100×, (c) 200×, and (d) 400×.

As with the binary classification task, the results of the four evaluation metrics used to assess the model performance are listed in Table 4. As can be seen from the table, our proposed method achieves optimal results on the dataset with 40× magnification. Compared with other methods, our method has the highest discrimination accuracy of 40X breast cancer pathological images (and higher than the accuracy of other methods in other magnification). Although there is no obvious advantage in the recognition accuracy of other magnification images, our method mainly focuses on the retention of detailed information, so it performs best on 40X images containing the most information. In practice, the higher the magnification of the image is, the higher requirements equipment and professional operation need. Therefore, if the image can achieve excellent recognition accuracy under the condition of less magnification, it is conducive to saving cost, efficiency and labor. In addition, the confusion matrix of the model at different magnifications is given in Fig. 6. It can be seen that the number of errors when using our method for multi-classification task is only a small fraction.

Furthermore, we compared our proposed method with representative methods proposed based on the BreakHis dataset over a 5-year period, and the comparison results are shown in Table 5. As shown in this table, our method outperforms almost all previous methods, with an increase of about 6.48%, 7.16%, 6.88%, and 9.04% compared to the methods proposed in 2020 listed in the table, respectively. Most of the methods proposed in recent years have a classification accuracy of more than 90%, but our method still has an advantage. Thus, our proposed method achieves the same excellent performance on the task of multiple classifications.

Table 5. Compared results with the representative CNN-based methods of multi-classification on the BreakHis dataset.

Years	Methods	Magnification factors			
		40×	100×	200×	400×
2019	MILCNN	90.38	86.80	82.80	85.20
2018	Sharma	89.31	85.75	83.95	84.33
2019	Going deeper	92.20	88.20	89.40	88.50
2019	FEBkCapsNet	92.71	94.52	94.03	93.54
2020	Boumaraf	94.49	93.27	91.29	89.56
2022	**Ours**	**95.79**	**92.91**	**90.83**	**93.37**

5 Conclusion

We propose a wavelet transform-based binary classification and multi-classification approach for breast cancer identification. The experiments are conducted on the BreakHis dataset and the performance is evaluated using various performance metrics. When the experimental procedure was performed, we considered the difference in the amplification factor. Compared to all results published in scientific reports up to 2016, the results obtained by our proposed method improve the recognition accuracy on the BreakHis dataset by about

3.67% and 2.14%, respectively, both of which are higher than the test accuracy derived by any other CNN-based method for different amplification factors. Thus, the experimental results show advanced test accuracy for breast cancer identification compared to existing methods. In the future, we will further explore the impact of other related methods of frequency domain learning on this medical task.

Acknowledgements. This work is supported by Hainan Province Science and Technology Special Fund (Grant No. ZDYF2022GXJS011).

References

1. de Andrade, K.C., et al.: The tp53 database: transition from the international agency for research on cancer to the us national cancer institute. Cell Death Differ. **29**(5), 1071–1073 (2022)
2. Weigelt, B., Geyer, F.C., Reis-Filho, J.S.: Histological types of breast cancer: how special are they? Mol. Oncol. **4**(3), 192–208 (2010)
3. Loukas, C.G., Kostopoulos, S., Tanoglidi, A., Glotsos, D., Sfikas, K., Cavouras, D.A.: Breast cancer characterization based on image classification of tissue sections visualized under low magnification. Comput. Math. Methods Med. **2013**, 829461:1–829461:7 (2013)
4. Elston, C.W., Ellis, I.O.: Pathological prognostic factors in breast cancer. i. the value of histological grade in breast cancer: experience from a large study with long-term follow-up. Histopathology **19**(5), 403–410 (1991)
5. Wang, Y., Liu, Z.P.: Identifying biomarkers for breast cancer by gene regulatory network rewiring. BMC Bioinformatics **22**(12), 1–15 (2022). https://doi.org/10.1186/s12859-021-04225-1
6. Ruifrok, A.C., Johnston, D.A., et al.: Quantification of histochemical staining by color deconvolution. Anal. Quant. Cytol. Histol. **23**(4), 291–299 (2001)
7. Eroğlu, Y., Yildirim, M., Çinar, A.: Convolutional neural networks based classification of breast ultrasonography images by hybrid method with respect to benign, malignant, and normal using mRmR. Comput. Biol. Med. **133**, 104407 (2021)
8. Pei, Y., Huang, Y., Zou, Q., Zhang, X., Wang, S.: Effects of image degradation and degradation removal to CNN-based image classification. IEEE Trans. Pattern Anal. Mach. Intell. **43**(4), 1239–1253 (2019)
9. Kim, H., Choi, M., Lim, B., Lee, K.M.: Task-aware image downscaling. In: Proceedings of the European Conference on Computer Vision (ECCV), pp. 399–414 (2018)
10. Saeedan, F., Weber, N., Goesele, M., Roth, S.: Detail-preserving pooling in deep networks. In: Proceedings of the IEEE Conference on Computer Vision and Pattern Recognition, pp. 9108–9116 (2018)
11. Gupta, V., Bhavsar, A.: Breast cancer histopathological image classification: is magnification important? In: Proceedings of the IEEE Conference on Computer Vision and Pattern Recognition Workshops, pp. 769–776. IEEE Computer Society (2017)
12. Magesh, G., Swarnalatha, P.: Analysis of breast cancer prediction and visualisation using machine learning models. Int. J. Cloud Comput. **11**(1), 43–60 (2022)
13. Shah, S.M., Khan, R.A., Arif, S., Sajid, U.: Artificial intelligence for breast cancer analysis: trends & directions. Comput. Biol. Med. **142**, 105221 (2022)

14. Huang, M.W., Chen, C.W., Lin, W.C., Ke, S.W., Tsai, C.F.: SVM and SVM ensembles in breast cancer prediction. PLoS ONE **12**(1), e0161501 (2017)
15. Spanhol, F.A., Oliveira, L.S., Petitjean, C., Heutte, L.: Breast cancer histopathological image classification using convolutional neural networks. In: 2016 International Joint Conference on Neural Networks (IJCNN), pp. 2560–2567. IEEE (2016)
16. Li, L., et al.: Multi-task deep learning for fine-grained classification and grading in breast cancer histopathological images. Multimed. Tools Appl. **79**(21), 14509–14528 (2020). https://doi.org/10.1007/s11042-018-6970-9
17. Alkassar, S., Jebur, B.A., Abdullah, M.A., Al-Khalidy, J.H., Chambers, J.: Going deeper: magnification-invariant approach for breast cancer classification using histopathological images. IET Comput. Vis. **15**(2), 151–164 (2021)
18. Wang, P., Wang, J., Li, Y., Li, P., Li, L., Jiang, M.: Automatic classification of breast cancer histopathological images based on deep feature fusion and enhanced routing. Biomed. Signal Process. Control **65**, 102341 (2021)
19. Araújo, T., et al.: Classification of breast cancer histology images using convolutional neural networks. PLoS ONE **12**(6), e0177544 (2017)
20. Zhang, J., Wei, X., Che, C., Zhang, Q., Wei, X.: Breast cancer histopathological image classification based on convolutional neural networks. J. Med. Imaging Health Inform. **9**(4), 735–743 (2019)
21. Jabeen, K., et al.: Breast cancer classification from ultrasound images using probability-based optimal deep learning feature fusion. Sensors **22**(3), 807 (2022)
22. Vo, D.M., Nguyen, N.Q., Lee, S.W.: Classification of breast cancer histology images using incremental boosting convolution networks. Inf. Sci. **482**, 123–138 (2019)
23. Khan, S., Islam, N., Jan, Z., Din, I.U., Rodrigues, J.J.C.: A novel deep learning based framework for the detection and classification of breast cancer using transfer learning. Pattern Recogn. Lett. **125**, 1–6 (2019)
24. Zhuang, F., et al.: A comprehensive survey on transfer learning. Proc. IEEE **109**(1), 43–76 (2020)
25. Ramya, J., Vijaylakshmi, H., Saifuddin, H.M.: Segmentation of skin lesion images using discrete wavelet transform. Biomed. Signal Process. Control **69**, 102839 (2021)
26. Barbhuiya, A.J.I., Hemachandran, K.: Wavelet tranformations & its major applications in digital image processing. Int. J. Eng. Res. Technol. (IJERT) ISSN, 2278–0181 (2013)
27. Zhao, M., Fu, X., Zhang, Y., Meng, L., Tang, B.: Highly imbalanced fault diagnosis of mechanical systems based on wavelet packet distortion and convolutional neural networks. Adv. Eng. Inform. **51**, 101535 (2022)
28. Addison, P.S.: The Illustrated Wavelet Transform Handbook: Introductory Theory and Applications in Science, Engineering, Medicine and Finance. CRC Press, Boca Raton (2017)
29. Yasmeen, F., Uddin, M.S.: A novel watermarking scheme based on discrete wavelet transform-singular value decomposition. Secur. Priv. **5**(3), e216 (2022)
30. Haji, S.H., Abdulazeez, A.M.: Comparison of optimization techniques based on gradient descent algorithm: a review. PalArch's J. Archaeol. Egypt/Egyptol. **18**(4), 2715–2743 (2021)

Machine Learning Based Security Situation Awareness Method for Network Data Transmission Process

Hui Du(✉)

Beijing Polytechnic, Beijing 100016, China
du_hui@tom.com

Abstract. With the popularization and development of computer technology, network has become an essential element in people's daily production and life. Due to the openness of the network and the large number of users, the network data transmission process is vulnerable to attacks, resulting in data loss, tampering and other phenomena. Therefore, this research designs a security situation awareness method for network data transmission process based on machine learning. Firstly, a three-level model of security situation awareness is built, based on which security situation data are collected. Then the sparse self encoder is used to reduce the dimension of security situation data and extract its features. Based on this, the security situation is evaluated based on machine learning support vector machine, and the hierarchical genetic algorithm is used to predict the security situation of data transmission process. The experimental results show that the delay and error of security situational awareness are less than the given maximum limit, and the security situational awareness results are consistent with the actual results, which fully proves that the application effect of this method is good.

Keywords: Machine learning · Network data · Data transmission · Security situational awareness · Support vector machine · Situation prediction

1 Introduction

With the rapid progress of science and technology and the continuous development of society, the impact of science and technology and the Internet on people's work and life is becoming more and more obvious, people's dependence on the network is also gradually deepening, and the continuous changes of the network and technology have also brought a long-term impact on human beings and society [1].

In recent years, there are many attacks using the network, so the security of data transmission in the network system has also received more and more attention. In recent years, there have been an endless stream of attacks and intrusions in the network. However, the network security protection means with limited functions, such as network intrusion detection system, firewall, anti-virus software, cannot help the network security managers to respond to new attacks in a timely and effective manner and protect the network system. Under the condition that the network system often suffers from various

Y. Xu et al. (Eds.): ML4CS 2022, LNCS 13655, pp. 341–355, 2023.
https://doi.org/10.1007/978-3-031-20096-0_26

hazardous events, the concept of network data transmission process security situation is put forward after continuous research by various industries, trying to help the network system resist complex network attacks on the basis of monitoring the network system in all aspects. When the application of network data transmission process security situation has been widely effective, its role has become increasingly significant, and its research has also received more attention.

The security situation of the network data transmission process has accurate results in network monitoring and situation prediction, and the display method is intuitive and very convenient to use. Based on the network data transmission process security situation, the network data transmission process security situation awareness is researched. The difference between the two is that the former contains two parts, namely network data transmission process security situation awareness and network data transmission process security situation prediction.

Machine learning is a discipline that can understand learning, understand the principles and mechanisms of learning, and develop the ability to acquire knowledge and improve oneself through self-learning [2]. In today's quite developed science and technology, machine learning has attracted more and more attention and has many applications in many other fields besides neural computing. It is constantly developing and becoming the basic knowledge of a variety of technologies, providing favorable conditions for all kinds of research.

Therefore, in order to avoid in the process of network data transmission, data loss resulting from the attack, been tampered with, this study based on machine learning to design a method of network data transmission security situational awareness, and according to the results of the situational awareness system history situational conditions to predict the future trend of values, to network data transmission trend conditions have a good grasp of the process. The design idea of this method is as follows:

Firstly, a three-level security situation awareness model is constructed, and in the subsequent process, the model is used to realize the fusion, mining and data analysis based on artificial intelligence of massive data.

Then, based on the collected security situation data, the sparse autoencoder is used to reduce the dimension of the security situation data and extract data features.

Finally, THE security situation of the data transmission process is evaluated based on machine learning-support vector machine, and hierarchical genetic algorithm is used to predict the security situation of the data transmission process.

2 Design of Security Situational Awareness Method in Network Data Transmission Process

2.1 Building a Security Situational Awareness Model

Regarding what is specific security situational awareness, the academic community has not yet given a unified definition. The earliest concept of situational awareness was put forward by Endsley in 1988. The definition of situational awareness in his opinion is: "The acquisition, understanding and short-term prediction of environmental factors in a certain time and space". In order to intuitively express the significance of the overall security situation awareness, it is divided into three-level models, as shown in Fig. 1.

Security situational awareness during network data transmission was first proposed by Tim Bass in 1999 [3]. He pointed out that "the next-generation network intrusion detection system should integrate data collected from a large number of heterogeneous distributed network sensors to achieve situational awareness in cyberspace". Security situation awareness in the network data transmission process is to extract the security factors that may affect the security situation changes in the network data transmission process in a specific network environment, and to understand and visualize the extracted security factor information to predict the possible development trend.

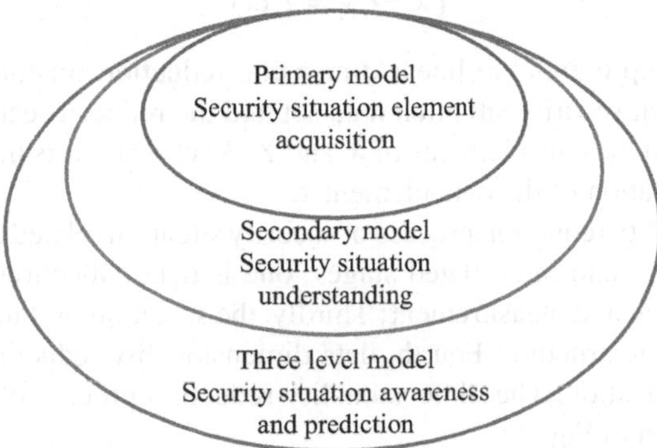

Fig. 1. Schematic diagram of the three-level model of security situational awareness

In fact, security situational awareness in the process of network data transmission is to directly provide network security personnel with a visual real-time security status of the network environment, perceive the possible threats and risks in the network state, and provide a reliable and timely guarantee for the security of network data transmission by using the technology of multi-element data fusion, massive data mining, data analysis based on artificial intelligence and data visualization. By using the network data transmission process security situational awareness technology, network security personnel can understand the current network status, types of attacks, attack time, attack source, which network devices are vulnerable to attacks and other attacks in real time. In this way, network security personnel can clearly guard against existing network attacks and possible network attacks [4].

2.2 Extracting Data Features Related to Security Situation

Based on the security situation awareness model constructed above, the data related to the security situation in the network data transmission process is collected, and the dimensionality reduction processing is performed on it, and the characteristics of the data related to the security situation are extracted to provide support for the subsequent security situation assessment.

Data dimensionality reduction methods are often used in the analysis and visualization of multidimensional data, and are effective methods to solve the dimensionality disaster of high-dimensional data. Therefore, data dimensionality reduction has also become an important research content in security situational awareness in the big data environment [5].

In order to reduce the computational complexity of security situation awareness, the high-dimensional security situation data is transformed into a low-dimensional or higher-dimensional space or even an infinite-dimensional space by a linear or nonlinear method. The dimensionality reduction model of security situation data is (X, F), and the dimensionality reduction expression is

$$\begin{cases} F : X \to Y \\ x \to y = F(x) \end{cases} \tag{1}$$

In formula (1), F represents the linear dimension reduction function of X; X and Y represent the original security situation data set and the reduced security situation data set; x and y represent the data elements of X and Y; $F(x)$ represents the linear dimension reduction transformation of the data element x.

The dimensionality reduction process of security situation related data can be divided into five independent and interrelated stages: one is data collection; Second, data set structure construction and measurement; Thirdly, the selection of dimensionality reduction criteria based on structure; Fourth, data dimensionality reduction; Fifth, machine learning and classification. The dimensionality reduction process of security situation related data is shown in Fig. 2.

As shown in Fig. 2, the data collection process is mainly that each sensor in the big data environment monitors network security objects such as host nodes, network nodes, software, and services, and passes vulnerability detectors, traffic monitoring analyzers, intrusion detectors, etc. Realize the extraction of source data; the process of data set structure construction and measurement is mainly to perform feature analysis, selection and measurement on the extracted data, and obtain business network traffic feature data, vulnerability feature data or attack feature data to form a network security feature database. And acquire empirical knowledge to label the data.

Security situation elements in the big data environment mainly include business applications and services, vulnerable points, attacks and other data. These data are generally used to monitor the host nodes, network nodes, software, business applications, services and other network security objects through various sensors, and extract the source data through vulnerability detectors, traffic monitoring analyzers, intrusion detectors and so on.

The traditional self coder usually directly copies the input layer to the hidden layer in the feature extraction process, which cannot accurately describe the internal characteristics of the data in the big data environment. Sparse autoencoder is an unsupervised machine learning algorithm that adds a sparse penalty term to the traditional autoencoder network to better extract sparse data features. Improve the efficiency and accuracy of feature extraction. The sparse autoencoder avoids the disadvantage that the traditional autoencoder directly copies the input layer to the hidden layer and cannot effectively extract features, and improves the performance of the traditional autoencoder [6].

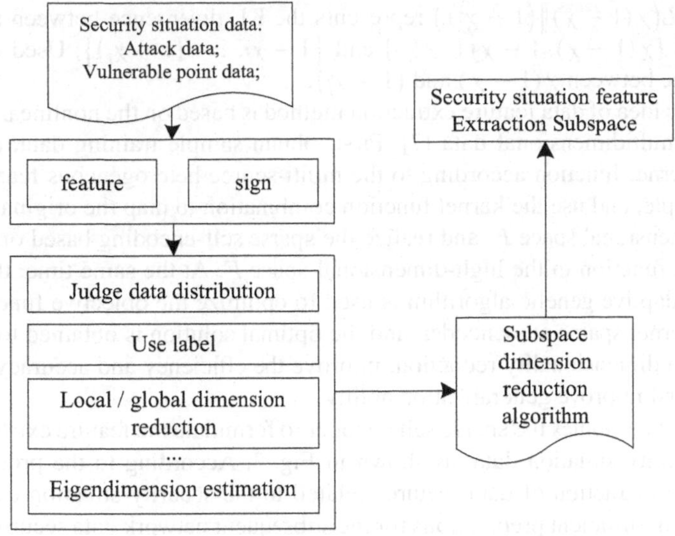

Fig. 2. Schematic diagram of the dimensionality reduction process for data related to security situation

The input of the sparse autoencoder is the dimensionality-reduced security situation data set $Y = \{y_1, y_2, \cdots, y_n\}$, and the output is $Z = \{z_1, z_2, \cdots, z_m\}$, and its objective function is as follows:

$$\begin{cases} J_{SAE}(\theta) = L(y, z) + \alpha\beta_s \\ L(y, z) = \sum_{i=1}^{m} \|y - z\|^2 \end{cases} \quad (2)$$

In formula (2), $J_{SAE}(\theta)$ represents the objective function of the sparse autoencoder; $L(y, z)$ represents the loss function; α represents the penalty factor, which is the weight coefficient of the sparse penalty term; β_s represents the sparse penalty term.

A penalty term is added to the objective function to constrain and suppress the average activation value output by neurons in the hidden layer. The average activation χ_j of the j neuron in the hidden layer of the sparse autoencoder is expressed as:

$$\chi_j = \frac{1}{n}\sum_{i=1}^{n} \left(h_j(y_i)\right) \quad (3)$$

In formula (3), $h_j(y_i)$ represents the activation value of the hidden layer neuron j. The formula for calculating the sparse penalty term β_s is:

$$\beta_s = \sum_{j=1}^{h} KL(\chi \,\|\, \chi_j) + KL\big(\chi(1-\chi)\,\|\,(1-\chi_j)\big) \quad (4)$$

In formula (4), $KL(\chi \,\|\, \chi_j)$ represents the KL divergence between the general distributions $\{\chi, 1-\chi\}$ and $\{\chi_j, 1-\chi_j\}$, which is used to measure the difference between

χ and χ_j; $KL(\chi(1-\chi)\|(1-\chi_j))$ represents the KL divergence between the general distributions $\{\chi(1-\chi), 1-\chi(1-\chi)\}$ and $\{1-\chi_j, 1-(1-\chi_j)\}$, Used to measure the difference between $\chi(1-\chi)$ and $(1-\chi_j)$.

The basic idea of data feature extraction method is based on the nonlinear and sparse features of multidimensional data [7]. First, obtain sample training data, construct a combined kernel function according to the multi-source heterogeneous features of the training sample, and use the kernel function combination to map the original sample to the high-dimensional space F, and realize the sparse self-encoding based on the kernel combination function in the high-dimensional space F. At the same time, the iterative method of adaptive genetic algorithm is used to optimize the objective function of the combined kernel sparse autoencoder, and the optimal solution is obtained to obtain the effect of data dimensionality reduction, improve the efficiency and accuracy of feature extraction, and improve generalization ability.

This paper combines the sparse self encoder to formulate the feature extraction algorithm of security situation data, as shown in Fig. 3. According to the process shown in Fig. 3, the extraction of data features related to the security situation can be completed, making sufficient preparations for the subsequent network data security situation assessment.

2.3 Network Data Security Situation Assessment

On the basis of extracting relevant data features of security situation, machine learning support vector machine is applied to realize accurate assessment of security situation during network data transmission, as shown below:

Security situation indicators generally refer to the elements that can describe the security attributes that affect the network data transmission process. To establish an indicator system that can comprehensively and objectively reflect the security situation, only twoorthree indicators are not enough, because the selected indicators need to cover the main factors in the security situation system. However, it is not feasible to select too many indicators, because as the number of indicators increases, it will be more difficult to determine the priority of indicators. At the same time, the established indicator system will be too complex, and the amount of calculation will also increase significantly [8]. Therefore, the selection of security situation indicators should follow the following principles:

a) Principle of independence: Due to the complexity of the network data transmission process, the network security attributes referred to by an indicator may often contain multiple situational factors. Situation assessment has an impact, so selecting relatively independent indicators and reducing the correlation between indicators can better reflect the security situation;
b) The principle of operability: the selected indicators should be easy to obtain, and the selection of data indicators that are difficult to collect and count in the process of network data transmission should be avoided, and the data of the indicators must be reliable and accurate;
c) Principle of principal component: When the data set is too large and there are too many features, the features that can better reflect the changes in the security state of

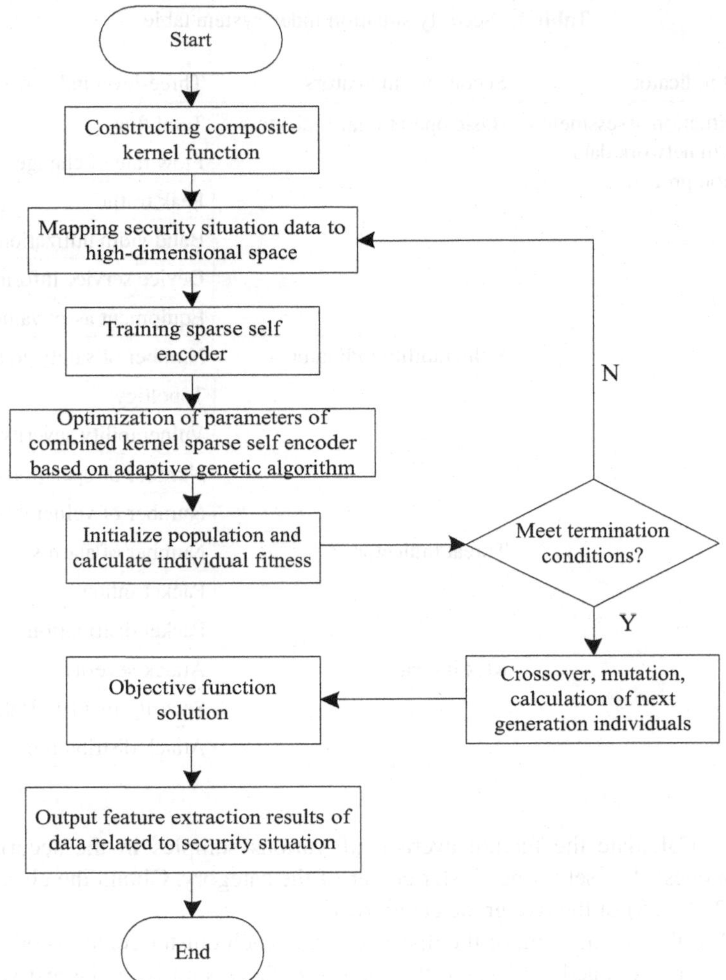

Fig. 3. Flow chart of data extraction related to security situation

the network data transmission process should be selected as indicators. Reduce the number of security posture indicators.

After selecting the security situation indicators, the security situation indicator system can be established, as shown in Table 1.

In order to facilitate the research, the security situation indicators are quantified. Due to space limitations, the quantification process is not displayed.

The steps of security situational awareness assessment of network data transmission process based on support vector machine are as follows:

Table 1. Security situation index system table

First-level indicator	Secondary indicators	Three-level indicator
Security situation assessment indicators in network data transmission process	Basic operational indicators	Total flow
		Flow rate of change
		Peak traffic
		Bandwidth utilization
		Device service information
		Equipment asset value
	Vulnerability indicator	Number of safety equipment
		Topology
		Vulnerability severity
		Number of open ports
		Number of vulnerabilities
	Threat indicator	Number of alarms
		Packet inflow
		Packet distribution
	Risk indicator	Attack severity
		Security Incident Rate
		Attack distribution

Step 1: Calculate the feature average of various samples in the security situational awareness data set as the cluster center of the category. Obtain the cluster center $o_i(i = 1, 2, 3, 4, 5)$ of the five grade categories;

Step 2: Calculate the sum of the distances from each cluster center to other cluster centers, sort the obtained values, put the category whose sum is the largest value first, and record its cluster center as O_1, at this time there are 4 categories remaining, repeat the previous steps, calculate the sum of the distances from each cluster center to the remaining cluster centers, take the maximum value after sorting and denote it as O_2, and so on, until all 5 reordering are obtained It ends after the cluster center of, and its order is denoted as O_1, O_2, O_3, O_4, O_5;

Step 3: The samples corresponding to the center O_1 in the cluster are marked as $+1$ category, and the samples corresponding to the O_2, O_3, O_4, O_5 cluster center are marked as -1 category. The classification model is trained by the support vector machine algorithm, and the classifier of the root node is obtained. The same operation is used for the remaining categories, and the classifiers of the binary tree sub-nodes are continuously constructed in the order of O_i, until all the classifiers are constructed, and the output result is the security situation assessment result of the network data transmission process.

The above process has completed the security situation assessment of the network data transmission process, and laid a solid foundation for the prediction of the security situation of the subsequent network data transmission process.

2.4 Prediction of Network Data Security Situation

Based on machine learning hierarchical genetic algorithm, the security situation of network data transmission process is predicted, which provides a certain guarantee for the security of network data transmission process.

The parameters of hierarchical genetic algorithm are the key factors affecting the security situation prediction. Therefore, this section focuses on the parameter design of hierarchical genetic algorithm, as shown below:

(A) Encoding and initialization

In the hierarchical genetic algorithm, the control gene is composed of binary code, and each bit in the binary code corresponds to the hidden layer node one by one. When a bit is "0", the corresponding node is invalid; otherwise, when it is "1", the corresponding node is valid [9]. In order to improve the efficiency of genetic algorithm, the parameter genes are encoded by floating-point numbers and directly expressed by the value of the basis function center and expansion constant of the hidden layer node.

Assuming that the population size in the genetic process is Q, the population size has a greater impact on the performance of the algorithm. If the value of Q is too small, the result will be difficult to achieve the predicted goal. If the valuc of Q is too large, the calculation will be complicated and the efficiency will be reduced. According to experience, the population size is preferably 20 ~ 160. Let the maximum evolutionary algebra be G;

(B) Fitness function design

The fitness function is an important basis for judging whether an individual's solution satisfies the optimization objective. For the hierarchical genetic algorithm, the optimization goal is to minimize the error function SSE between the expected output p' and the actual output p. The error function is expressed as

$$SSE = \sum_{i=1}^{N} \left(p_i' - p_i\right)^2 \tag{5}$$

In formula (5), p_i' and p_i respectively represent the i expected output and actual output.

However, in order to make the training algorithm meet the requirements of small error and less number of hidden layer nodes, the network structure is simplified. Therefore, the minimum information criterion fitness function is used to comprehensively evaluate the performance of the network model. The fitness function expression is

$$f = \left\{ N \log\left[\frac{1}{N}\sum_{i=1}^{N}\left(p_i' - p_i\right)^2\right] + 4M \right\} + \delta \tag{6}$$

In formula (6), f represents the fitness function; N represents the number of samples; M represents the number of hidden layer nodes in the individual; δ represents a sufficiently large value. It can be obtained from this formula that the smaller the error function value is, the smaller the number of hidden layer nodes, and the larger the value of the fitness function.

(C) Genetic manipulation

a) Selection and replication

Selection operation is the use of selection operators to simulate the phenomenon of "natural selection, survival of the fittest" in the biological world. According to the fitness value of an individual, whether the individual can enter the next generation can be determined. Roulette gambling can generally be used. Individuals with high fitness have a high probability of "survival" and those with low fitness have a low probability of "survival". However, roulette may cause individuals with higher fitness values not to be selected, resulting in "premature" and falling into local optimization [10]. Therefore, this paper adopts the best individual preservation mechanism. The best individuals in this generation population are directly retained to the next generation, skipping crossover and mutation operations, and the remaining individuals are selected by roulette.

b) Crossover operation

Crossover operations generate new populations by simulating genetic recombination during the genetic process. In the Hierarchical Genetic Algorithm, due to the different coding methods of the control gene and the parameter gene, and their roles are also different, the two genes are crossed respectively. For control genes using binary coding, single-point crossover can be used. Select an identical point in the two control genes respectively, and use this point as a dividing point to combine the front part and the back part of the first control gene with the back part and the front part of the second control gene respectively. For parametric genes encoded by floating-point numbers, a new crossover operator needs to be designed. The method of simulating binary crossover can be used to cross the parameter genes of the two selected bodies g_1 and g_2 to generate new offspring.

c) Mutation operation

The mutation operation randomly changes the value of a gene in the chromosome with a small probability, so as to improve the chromosome diversity in the population and reduce the possibility of falling into a local optimum.

For the binary-coded control gene, a certain gene can be randomly reversed. For parameter genes encoded by real numbers, uniform variation can generally be used. By randomly selecting an individual in the population, setting its parameter gene as $g_i = \left(c_{i,1}, c_{i,2}, \cdots, c_{i,M}\right)$, and M as the dimension of the sample input vector, randomly select one of the components, assuming that the variation element is $c_{i,k}$, then randomly select a value in the defined interval of the element.

d) Algorithm stop condition

The stop condition of the algorithm is set to stop the evolution of the population. The general stop condition can be set as:

- stop when the fitness of the best individual in the group is less than a certain threshold.
- stop when the maximum evolution algebra is exceeded.

Input the above determined parameters into the hierarchical genetic algorithm, and input the relevant data of the historical network data transmission process into the algorithm. The output result is the security situation prediction result, which provides a guarantee for the security of network data.

The above process realizes the awareness of the security situation in the process of network data transmission, and provides help for the development and application of the network.

3 Experiment and Result Analysis

3.1 Experiment Preparation Stage

In order to verify the application performance of network data transmission process security situational awareness method based on machine learning, the following experiments are designed. The applicability and effectiveness of the method are important.

The experiment takes a local area network as the object for verification. The structure of the local area network is shown in Fig. 4.

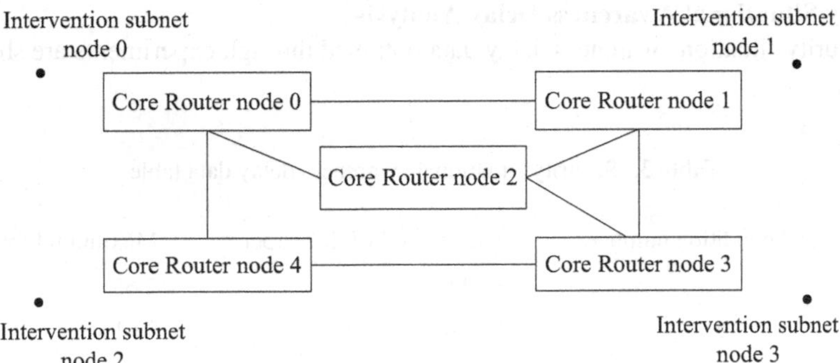

Fig. 4. Experimental network structure

Based on this network, it detects the security situation during information transmission between core router node 3 and core router node 4. Ten experimental conditions with obvious differences were set, as shown in Table 2.

The above has completed the setting of a variety of experimental conditions, which provides convenience for the smooth progress of the subsequent network data transmission process security situational awareness experiment.

3.2 Analysis of Experimental Results

In order to visually display the application performance of the proposed method, security situational awareness delay, security situational awareness numerical error and security

Table 2. Description of experimental conditions

Experimental condition number	Amount of data to be transmitted	Number of vulnerable nodes/individual
1	10.23 MB	1
2	23.45 MB	3
3	30.12 MB	5
4	45.16 MB	8
5	50.19 MB	9
6	62.10 MB	10
7	69.58 MB	12
8	70.14 MB	13
9	75.40 MB	16
10	80.25 MB	20

situational awareness results are selected as evaluation indicators. The specific analysis process of experimental results is as follows:

Security Situational Awareness Delay Analysis

The security situation awareness delay data obtained through experiments are shown in Table 3.

Table 3. Security situational awareness delay data table

Experimental condition number	The method of this paper	Maximum limit
1	1.02 s	2.65 s
2	1.60 s	3.01 s
3	2.01 s	4.59 s
4	2.64 s	5.48 s
5	2.98 s	6.50 s
6	3.54 s	7.01 s
7	3.90 s	8.02 s
8	4.56 s	9.25 s
9	5.09 s	10.20 s
10	6.52 s	11.45 s

As shown in Table 3, the security situation awareness delay obtained by using this method is less than the given maximum limit, indicating that this method can perceive the security situation faster.

Numerical Error Analysis of Security Situational Awareness
Figure 5 shows the numerical error data of security situational awareness obtained through experiments. As shown in Fig. 5, the numerical errors of security situational awareness obtained by using this method are less than the given maximum limit, indicating that the security situational awareness accuracy of this method is higher.

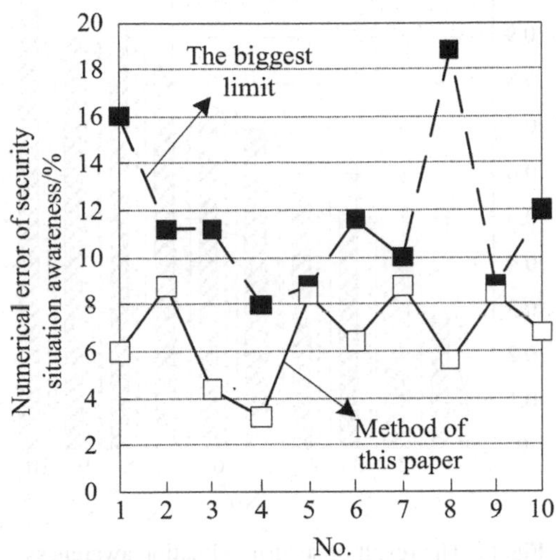

Fig. 5. Numerical error data graph of security situational awareness

Analysis of Security Situational Awareness Results
The classification standard of security situation awareness is shown in Table 4.

Table 4. Classification standard of security situation awareness level

Grade	Situation Description	Value range
Level one	Safety	0.00 –0.20
Level two	Mild danger	0.21–0.40
Level three	General hazard	0.41– 0.60
Level four	Moderate risk	0.61–0.80
Level five	High risk	0.81–1.00

The security situation awareness results obtained through experiments are shown in Fig. 6. As shown in Fig. 6, the security situation awareness results obtained by applying this method are consistent with the actual results, indicating that the security situation awareness accuracy of this method is high. The above experimental data show that the security situation awareness delay and the security situation awareness numerical error obtained by using this method are less than the given maximum value, and the security situation awareness results are consistent with the actual results, which fully confirms the effectiveness and availability of this method.

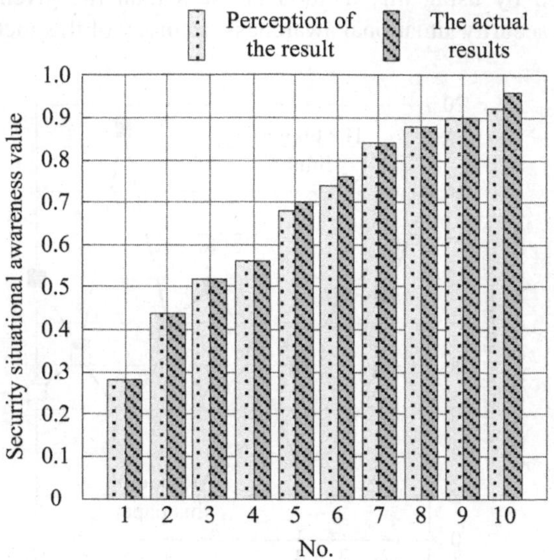

Fig. 6. The result of security situation awareness

4 Conclusion

In this paper, the introduction of machine learning, support vector machine (SVM) as a result, we design a network security situational awareness methods, data transmission process after the application of this method, the security situational awareness time delay and the maximum error is less than the given threshold, shows that the method reduces the security situational awareness numerical error of time delay and security situational awareness, enhanced security situational awareness results consistent with the actual result. This method can provide a more effective method support for the security of network data transmission, and also provide a certain reference for the research of security situation awareness.

References

1. Nikoloudakis, Y., et al.: Towards a machine learning based situational awareness framework for cybersecurity: an SDN implementation. Sensors **21**(14), 4939–4946 (2021)

2. Liu, S., Liu, D., Muhammad, K., et al.: Effective Template Update Mechanism in Visual Tracking with Background Clutter. Neurocomputing **458**(1), 615–625 (2021)
3. Ran, Z., et al.: Prediction algorithm for network security situation based on BP neural network optimized by SA-SOA. Int. J. Performabil. Eng. **16**(8), 1171–1182 (2020)
4. Qing, L., Ming, Z.: Network security situation detection of internet of things for smart city based on fuzzy neural network. Int. J. Reason. Based Intell. Syst. **12**(3), 222–227 (2020)
5. Haofang, Z., Chunying, K., Yao, X.: Research on network security situation awareness based on the LSTM-DT model. Sensors **21**(14), 4788–4795 (2021)
6. Shuai, L., et al.: Human memory update strategy: a multi-layer template update mechanism for remote visual monitoring. IEEE Trans. Multimed. **23**(1), 2188–2198 (2021)
7. Junjun, R.: Network security situation assessment model based on information quality control. Int. J. Performabil. Eng. **16**(4), 673–680 (2020)
8. Lv, G., et al.: Simulation of quantitative assessment method for data security situation of wireless network communication. Comput. Simul. **37**(7), 337–340+372 (2020)
9. Haitao, L., Ying, L.: Integrated monitoring algorithms for software data security situation on private cloud computing platform. Int. J. Internet Protoc. Technol. **14**(1), 1–8 (2021)
10. Shuai, L., et al.: Fuzzy detection aided real-time and robust visual tracking under complex environments. IEEE Trans. Fuzzy Syst. **29**(1), 90–102 (2021)

Multi-objective Hydrologic Cycle Optimization for Integrated Container Terminal Scheduling Problem

Ben Niu[1], Yuda Wang[1,2], Jia Liu[1], and Qianying Liu[3](✉)

[1] College of Management, Shenzhen University, Shenzhen 518060, China
[2] Greater Bay Area International Institute for Innovation, Shenzhen University, Shenzhen 518060, China
[3] School of Computing Science, University of Glasgow, Glasgow G12 8QN, UK
2665227L@student.gla.ac.uk

Abstract. This paper uses the multi-objective rep-guided hydrological cycle optimization (MORHCO) algorithm to solve the Integrated Container Terminal Scheduling (ICTS) Problem. To enhance the global search capability of the algorithm and improve the quality of the Pareto front, MORHCO algorithm employs both elite flow operators and merit-based evaporation as well as precipitation operators to enhance its performance. Two test functions and the ICTS problem are used to validate the performance of the proposed algorithm. The results show that MORHCO algorithm significantly outperforms the original MOHCO algorithm and the four selected algorithms on the test functions as well as the ICTS problem. This is the first time that HCO algorithm has been applied to the solution of the NP-hard problem.

Keywords: Hydrological cycle optimization · Integrated container terminal scheduling · Multi-objective optimization

1 Introduction

In recent years, maritime transport has played an increasingly important role in world trade, accounting for more than 80% of the total, and with a trend of increasing year on year. As a key link in maritime transport, the scheduling of container terminals plays an extremely important role [1]. Container terminal scheduling problems can usually be divided into three aspects: berth allocation, crane scheduling and yard truck scheduling [2]. Current researchers usually concentrate on one of the three areas of research, with fewer examining ICTS problem. Damla Kizilay [3] points out that the ICTS problem is an ongoing and immature area of research, and therefore this paper examines the ICTS problem. The objective of this paper is to minimise service time as well as minimise operating costs.

The ICTS problem is an NP-hard puzzle. In this paper, we use the MORHCO algorithm to solve the ICTS problem. Inspired by the flow of water bodies, Niu [4, 5] proposed the hydrological cycle optimization (HCO) algorithm in 2018. The researcher achieved

Y. Xu et al. (Eds.): ML4CS 2022, LNCS 13655, pp. 356–365, 2023.
https://doi.org/10.1007/978-3-031-20096-0_27

promising results on the test function and then applied the HCO algorithm to the solution of the nurse scheduling problem (NSP) [6], but the NSP is a single-objective problem. A multi-objective hydrological cycle optimization algorithm (MOHCO) has been developed and applied to the feature selection problem [7]. Applying the original MOHCO to the ICTS problem, it is difficult to obtain excellent Pareto fronts. As a promising algorithm, the hydrological cycle algorithm is expected to solve the integrated container terminal scheduling problem. Specifically, we enhance the performance of the hydrological cycle algorithm by improving the flow operator, evaporation operator and apply it to the solution of the ICTS problem. In order to verify the performance of MORHCO algorithm, we will adopt some other heuristic algorithms to solve ICTS problem, such as novel multi-objective particle swarm optimization (NMPSO) [8], NSGA-II with adaptive rotation based simulated binary crossover (NSGA-II + ARSBX) [9], adaptive geometry estimation-based many-objective evolutionary algorithm (AGE-MOEA) [10], direction guided evolutionary algorithm (DGEA) [11] and etc.

The framework for writing the rest of the paper is described below. In Sect. 2, the basic principles of HCO and MORHCO are presented. Then Sect. 3, the objective function and notations of the ICTS problem are introduced. Section 4 are experiments and discussions. Finally, conclusions are given in the last section.

2 HCO

2.1 The Basic Hydrologic Cycle Optimization Algorithm

The HCO algorithm [4] is inspired by the phenomenon of the hydrological cycle in nature and can be described by three important operators -- flow, infiltration, evaporation and precipitation. Their specific meanings are described below.

Flow. The flow operator, which is the core algorithm of the original HCO method, converges the population towards a better region. Each individual X_i moves to the better individual X_j. If the fitness of X_{new} is better than X_i, the ith individual continues to flow to the new position until the fitness becomes worse or the maximum flow FlowMax is reached. However, if X_{new} is not as fit as X_i, X_i retains its original position.

$$X_{new} = X_i + \left(X_j - X_i\right). * rand(1, N) \tag{1}$$

Infiltration. The Infiltration operator is designed to avoid local optima, and it performs a neighbourhood search. During this operation, the dimension SD is determined randomly and the position of the ith individual $X_{i,SD}$ is given by the following equation:

$$X_{i,SD} = X_{i,SD} + \left(X_{i,SD} - X_{j,SD}\right). * \ (rand(1, SD) - 0.5) \tag{2}$$

Evaporation and Precipitation. The evaporation and precipitation operator facilitates the maintenance of the diversity of the population and the escape from local optima. Each individual has a P_{eva} probability of being evaporated. If an individual is evaporated, it will be precipitated to another position with two selection rules, (1) it will be precipitated to a random position in the search space, and (2) it will be precipitated to a neighbouring position of the best position so far generated by a Gaussian variation.

2.2 Modified Hydrologic Cycle Optimization Algorithm

In order to enhance the performance of the initial MOHCO algorithm, two strategies are used in this paper, as detailed below:

The pseudo codes of MORHCO are described in Algorithm, which are described as follows:

Algorithm MORHCO

```
Initialization
Initialize maximum number of function evaluations (maxFE), parameters such as the
  maximum sizes of POP, number of decision variables and REP (nPOP, nVar, nREP).
Randomly initialize the positions of POP
Evaluate POP, sort out the non-dominated solutions in POP and put them into the REP
Search procedure
while (the maxFE is not reached) do
  POP performs the flow operation described in 2.2
  If accept the new position
    Update REP
  End If
  POP performs the infiltration operation described in 2.1
  POP performs the evaporation and precipitation operation described in 2.2
  If rand() < P_eva(i)
    If rand() < 0.1
      Pop sink to a random location in the search space
    End If
    Else
      Pop precipitates to the hitherto best position of a neighbouring position generated
      by Gaussian variation
    End Else
  End If
  Update REP
  maxFE = maxFE + 1
End while
```

Elite Flow Operator: According to this strategy, an individual X_i no longer randomly chooses a better individual X_j in the population than it, but flows to each non-dominated solution in the external repository (REP), aiming to find the optimal flow direction from it. Compared to the flow operator in Sect. 2.1, the FlowMax parameter is not needed because the number of elite flow operator flows is the same as the number of non-dominated solutions in the REP. If X_{new} is less fit than X_i, then X_i retains its original position.

Evaporation and Precipitation Based on Superiority and Inferiority: According to this strategy, the average distance between each individual in the population and the Rep non-dominant solution should be calculated, and the evaporation probability

Peva can be calculated by formula (3). According to the formula, the dominant individual whose average distance is closer to the non-dominant solution of REP has a higher probability of evaporation. Meanwhile, in order to enhance the global search ability of evaporation and precipitation operators, the dynamic compensation strategy is adopted for the evaporation probability of disadvantaged individuals, and the formula (4) can be described as follows:

$$P_{eva}(\mathrm{i}) = exp(-(dis(i)/Dis_{average})^3) \tag{3}$$

$$P_{eva}(i) = P_{eva}(i) + rand() * 0.5 \tag{4}$$

3 HCO for Integrated Container Terminal Scheduling

3.1 Integrated Container Terminal Scheduling Model

In this section a bi-objective integrated port scheduling model is presented, with the first objective being to reduce vessel service times and the second objective being to minimise costs. The model's assumptions and constraints are specified in the Problem formulation of this article [2], which was provided by our previous work, and can be described as follows:

$$\begin{aligned} minf_1 = &\sum_{i\in V}\sum_{j\in B}\sum_{k\in O}\frac{n_i^{Load}+n_i^{UnLoad}}{vq_i}x_{i,j,k} \\ &+\sum_{i\in V}\sum_{j\in B}\sum_{k\in O}(s_i-a_i)x_{i,j,k}+\sum_{i\in V}\sum_{j\in B}\sum_{k\in O}\left(s_i+\frac{n_i^{Load}+n_i^{UnLoad}}{vq_i}-d_i\right)x_{i,j,k} \end{aligned} \tag{5}$$

$$\begin{aligned} minf_2 = &\sum_{i\in V}\sum_{j\in B}\sum_{k\in O}D_{i,j}^{Unload}n_i^{Unload}c^{vehicle}x_{i,j,k} \\ &+\sum_{i\in V}\sum_{j\in B}\sum_{k\in O}D_{i,j}^{Load}n_i^{Load}c^{vehicle}x_{i,j,k}+c^{crane}\sum_{i\in V}(n_i^{Load}+n_i^{UnLoad}) \end{aligned} \tag{6}$$

The objective of function (1) aims to minimise service times, including loading and unloading times for all containers, waiting times and delays for all vessels. The objective of function (2) is to minimise total operating costs, including trucking costs for import and export containers and operating costs for quay cranes.In addition, the meaning of the notations in the formula is explained as follows:

Indices

$i \in V$, V is a group of vessels, and $i = 1, 2,\ldots, n$.
$j \in B$, B is a group of berths, and $j = 1, 2,\ldots, m$.
$k \in O$, O is a group of service orders, and $k = 1, 2,\ldots, o$.

Parameters

W_i: subset of V for any vessel p with $s_p > a_i$.
v : efficiency of operations of quay cranes, TEU/h.
q_{max}: the maximum number of quay cranes that can serve a vessel.
Q : total number of quay cranes available.
a_i: the scheduled arrival time of vessel i.
d_i: the estimated departure time of vessel i.
$c^{vehicle}$: the cost of transporting one metre of container. It is fixed and a constant.
c^{crane}: costs incurred by quay crane for unloading or loading a container. It is fixed and a constant.
$D_{i,j}^{Load}$: the distance between berth j where vessel i is docked and the initial location (box area) of the container to be delivered to vessel i.
$D_{i,j}^{Unload}$: the distance between berth j where vessel i calls and the destination (box area) where the containers unloaded by vessel i are to be transported.
n_i^{load}: the number of containers will be loaded into vessel i.
n_i^{Unload}: the number of containers will be unloaded from vessel i.

Decision Variables

s_i: start time when the vessel begins loading and unloading containers i.
q_i: refers to the number of quay cranes allocated to vessel i.

3.2 Encoding

Each individual position vector represents a feasible solution, and the decision vector solution set dimension is 3*nships. The first nShips dimension represents the priority of each ship, and the search range for this part is set to (0, nShips). The second nShips dimension represents the berth location of each ship and is set to (0, nBerths). The third nShips dimension represents the number of cranes assigned to each ship and the search range is set to (0, nCranes). The model used in this case is set with a number of ships of 15, berths of 5 and cranes of 17. The final result is a Pareto frontier with respect to the minimisation time and cost fitness functions.

4 Experiments and Discussions

4.1 Parameter Settings

In all experiments, we used the parameter Settings suggested by the original paper of other comparison algorithms. The maximum number of function evaluations is 40,000, and the population number is 200. Perform 10 separate runs for each problem.

The Generational Distance (GD) [12] is a metric to evaluate the Pareto optimal frontier (PF), which measures the convergence of the PF. For GD, a smaller value means better performance of the algorithm, as it measures the distance between the true PF and the PF obtained by the algorithm. The GD is calculated as follows:

$$GD = \frac{\sqrt{\sum_{i=1}^{n} d_i^2}}{n} \quad (7)$$

where n denotes the number of vectors in the Pareto solution and di is the Euclidean distance between the i-th vector and the nearest vector of the true PF in the target space. If GD = 0, it means that the PFs obtained by the algorithm are all true PFs. MORHCO parameters are set as above.

4.2 Benchmark Test Function Experimental Results

NMPSO, NSGA-II + ARSBX, AGE-MOEA, DGEA, MOHCO and MORHCO run on test problem ZDTs with the following results.

Table 1. Results of GD (Mean/Std) for ZDTs with 30 dimensions.

Test Problems	D = 30						
	GD	NMPSO	NSGA-II	MOEA	DGEA	MOHCO	MORHCO
ZDT1	Mean	1.48E − 05	4.99E − 05	**1.25E − 05**	2.44E − 02	1.83E − 03	1.02E − 02
	Std	1.77E − 05	9.10E − 06	**7.13E − 06**	1.49E − 02	5.79E − 03	3.22E − 02
ZDT4	Mean	5.98E + 01	4.82E + 00	2.45E − 01	1.23E + 01	7.40E − 03	**2.26E − 03**
	Std	1.50E + 01	1.85E + 00	1.50E−01	5.86E + 00	2.34E − 02	**7.15E − 03**
Best times				2			2

Table 2. Results of GD (Mean/Std) for ZDTs with 35 dimensions.

Test Problems	D = 35						
	GD	NMPSO	NSGA-II	MOEA	DGEA	MOHCO	MORHCO
ZDT1	Mean	**6.34E − 06**	6.49E − 05	1.42E − 05	4.43E − 02	1.41E − 03	1.24E − 02
	Std	**4.17E − 06**	8.64E − 06	4.63E − 06	3.35E − 02	4.45E − 03	3.93E − 02
ZDT4	Mean	8.56E + 01	9.45E + 00	5.98E − 01	1.87E + 01	3.51E − 02	**7.08E − 03**
	Std	4.38E + 01	3.58E + 00	2.52E − 01	1.37E + 01	1.11E − 01	**2.24E − 02**
Best times		2					2

Table 3. Results of GD (Mean/Std) for ZDTs with 40 dimensions.

Test Problems	D = 40						
	GD	NMPSO	NSGA-II	MOEA	DGEA	MOHCO	MORHCO
ZDT1	Mean	**1.18E − 05**	6.84E − 05	1.64E − 05	7.06E − 02	1.77E − 02	1.68E − 02
	Std	1.12E − 05	1.13E − 05	**6.93E − 06**	1.52E − 02	5.59E − 02	5.33E − 02
ZDT4	Mean	9.50E + 01	1.20E + 01	1.19E + 00	2.61E + 01	3.51E − 03	**1.14E − 03**
	Std	4.66E + 01	4.19E + 00	4.62E − 01	1.22E + 01	1.11E − 02	**3.59E − 03**
Best times		1		1			2

Table 4. Results of GD (Mean/Std) for ZDTs with 45 dimensions.

Test Problems	D = 45						
	GD	NMPSO	NSGA-II	MOEA	DGEA	MOHCO	MORHCO
ZDT1	Mean	**1.03E − 05**	8.23E − 05	1.80E − 05	7.42E − 02	7.35E − 03	8.30E − 03
	Std	6.95E − 06	1.22E − 05	**3.60E − 06**	2.18E − 02	2.33E − 02	2.62E − 02
ZDT4	Mean	1.64E + 02	1.56E + 01	2.16E + 00	3.29E + 01	6.18E − 03	**3.38E − 03**
	Std	4.06E + 01	1.05E + 01	9.48E − 01	1.30E + 01	1.95E − 02	**1.07E − 02**
Best times		1		1			2

4.3 ICTS Problem Experimental Results

NMPSO, NSGA-II + ARSBX, AGE-MOEA, DGEA, MOHCO and MORHCO run on ICTS problem with the following results.

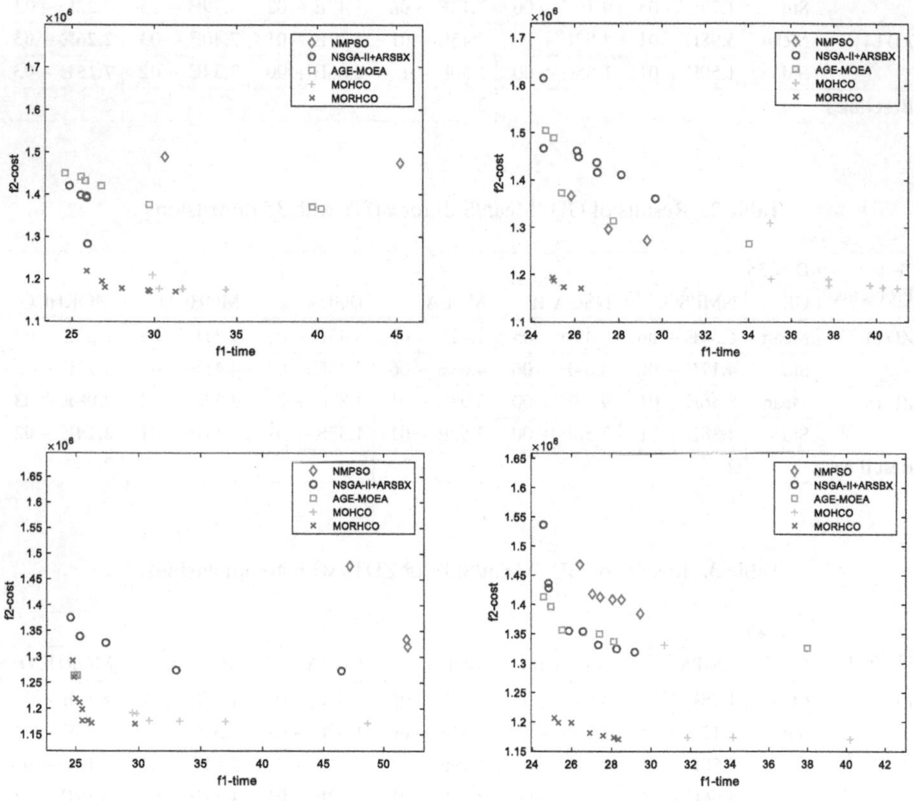

Fig. 1. Pareto solution sets obtained by each algorithm for ICST in 10 runs

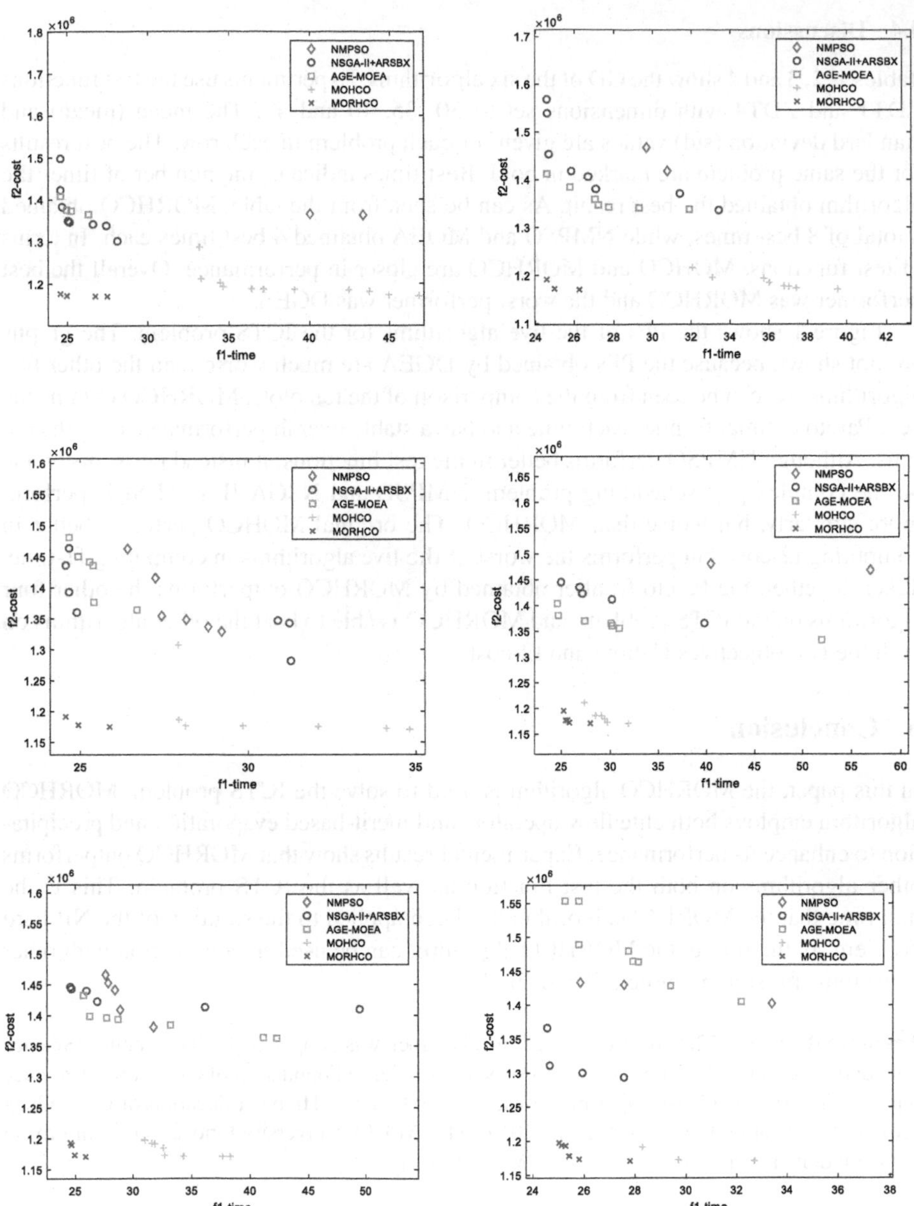

Fig. 1. *(continued)*

4.4 Discussions

Tables 1, 2, 3 and 4 show the GD of the six algorithms. Experiments use the test functions ZDT1 and ZDT4 with dimensions set to 30, 35, 40 and 45. The mean (mean) and standard deviation (std) values are given for each problem in each row. The best results for the same problem are marked in bold. Best times indicates the number of times the algorithm obtained the best result. As can be seen from the table, MORHCO obtained a total of 8 best times, while NMPSO and MOEA obtained 4 best times each. In terms of test functions, MOHCO and MORHCO are closer in performance. Overall the best performer was MORHCO and the worst performer was DGEA.

Figure 1 shows the PFs of the five algorithms for the ICTS problem. The graphs are not shown because the PFs obtained by DGEA are much worse than the other five algorithms. As can be seen from the comparison of the ten plots, MORHCO obtains the best Pareto optimal frontier each time and has a stable overall performance over the ten runs. Although NMPSO performs better in the test functions, it instead performs worse on the complex port scheduling problem. NMPSO and NSGA-II + ARSBX perform more similarly, but worse than MORHCO. The original MOHCO performs better in computing f2-cost, but performs the worst of the five algorithms in computing f1-time. Taken together, the Pareto frontier obtained by MORHCO outperforms the other four algorithms on the ICTS problem, and MORHCO is able to beat the other algorithms on both the two objectives f1-time and f2-cost.

5 Conclusion

In this paper, the MORHCO algorithm is used to solve the ICTS problem. MORHCO algorithm employs both elite flow operators and merit-based evaporation and precipitation to enhance its performance. Experimental results show that MORHCO outperforms other algorithms on both the test function as well as the ICTS problem. This is the first time that the MORHCO algorithm has been applied to the solution of the NP-hard problem. In the future, the MORHCO algorithm can be used in conjunction with other algorithms for solving more complex problems.

Acknowledgement. The work described in this paper was supported by The Natural Science Foundation of China (Grant No. 71971143), Natural Science Foundation of Guangdong Province (Grant No. 2020A1515010749), Key Research Foundation of Higher Education of Guangdong Provincial Education Bureau (Grant No. 2019KZDXM030), University Innovation Team Project of Guangdong Province (Grant No. 2021WCXTD002).

References

1. Cheimanoff N, Fontane F, Kitri MN, Tchernev N.: Exact and heuristic methods for the integrated berth allocation and specific time-invariant quay crane assignment problems. Comput. Oper. Res. **141**, 105695 (2022)
2. Niu, B., Liu, Q., Wang, Z., Tan, L., Li, L.: Multi-objective bacterial colony optimization algorithm for integrated container terminal scheduling problem. Nat. Comput. **20**(1), 89–104 (2020). https://doi.org/10.1007/s11047-019-09781-3

3. Kizilay, D., Eliiyi, D.T.: A comprehensive review of quay crane scheduling, yard operations and integrations thereof in container terminals. Flex. Serv. Manuf. J. **33**(1), 1–42 (2020). https://doi.org/10.1007/s10696-020-09385-5
4. Yan, X., Niu, B.: Hydrologic cycle optimization part i: background and theory. In: Tan, Y., Shi, Y., Tang, Q. (eds.) Advances in Swarm Intelligence. LNCS, vol. 10941, pp. 341–349. Springer, Cham (2018). https://doi.org/10.1007/978-3-319-93815-8_33
5. Niu, B., Liu, H., Yan, X.: Hydrologic cycle optimization part ii: experiments and real-world application. In: Tan, Y., Shi, Y., Tang, Q. (eds.) Advances in Swarm Intelligence. LNCS, vol. 10941, pp. 350–358. Springer, Cham (2018). https://doi.org/10.1007/978-3-319-93815-8_34
6. Liu, Q., Niu, B., Wang, J., Wang, H., Li, L.: Nurse scheduling problem based on hydrologic cycle optimization. In: CEC, pp 1398–1405. IEEE (2019)
7. Song, X., Liu, M.T., Liu, Q., Niu, B.: Hydrological cycling optimization-based multiobjective feature-selection method for customer segmentation. Int. J. Intell. Syst. **36**(5), 2347–2366 (2021)
8. Lin, Q., et al.: Particle swarm optimization with a balanceable fitness estimation for many-objective optimization problems. IEEE T. Evolut. Comput. **22**(1), 32–46 (2018)
9. Pan, L., Xu, W., Li, L., He, C., Cheng, R.: Adaptive simulated binary crossover for rotated multi-objective optimization. Swarm Evol. Comput. **60**, 100759 (2021)
10. Panichella, A.: An adaptive evolutionary algorithm based on non-Euclidean geometry for many-objective optimization. In: The Genetic and Evolutionary Computation Conference, pp 108–120 (2019)
11. He, C., Cheng, R., Yazdani, D.: Adaptive offspring generation for evolutionary large-scale multiobjective optimization. IEEE Trans. Syst. Man Cybern. Syst. **99**, 1–13 (2020)
12. Veldhuizen, D.V.: Multiobjective Evolutionary Algorithms: Classifications, Analyses, and New Innovations (1999)

High Voltage Power Communication Network Security Early Warning and Monitoring System Based on HMAC Algorithm

Zhengjian Duan(✉)

School of Management, Hefei University of Technology, Hefei 230009, China
duanzhengjian46896@163.com

Abstract. Aiming at the problems of long time consuming and low accuracy of the current high voltage power communication network security early warning and monitoring system, a high voltage power communication network security early warning and monitoring system based on HMAC algorithm is proposed and designed. The system hardware adopts Siemens S7–1200 CPU, PT120 platinum thermal resistance and temperature transmitter, two-wire access method and three-wire access method to realize port access. Wrnb-230 sensor is selected as the core sensing equipment, and information monitoring is realized through YHJCQ's photosensitive electronic monitoring device. Information monitoring is realized by the light sensing electronic monitoring device of YHJCQ. The characters of early warning information are numerically processed by Bagging-SVM coding, and the support vector machine model is constructed to integrate the early warning parameters. According to the redundancy matrix of early warning parameters, the accommodating space parameters of the early warning platform are allocated to realize the network security early warning. The experimental results show that the designed HMAC algorithm based high-voltage power communication network security warning monitoring system can detect the abnormal state of intrusion signals well, and the warning accuracy is higher.

Keywords: HMAC algorithm · High voltage power · Power communication · Communication network · Safety warning · Early warning monitoring

1 Introduction

In recent years, the scale of power grid business has been increasing, and the degree of power grid informatization has become higher and higher. Although it has brought great convenience to people's life, it has also brought a series of security challenges [1]. However, under the influence of complex external environmental factors, some power communication equipment accidents often occur in high-voltage internal power communication equipment, which seriously affects the operation of power grid and communication network [2].

Information and communication technology plays an important role in ensuring the normal operation of the power network. In order to optimize energy resources in a wide

Y. Xu et al. (Eds.): ML4CS 2022, LNCS 13655, pp. 366–379, 2023.
https://doi.org/10.1007/978-3-031-20096-0_28

range, my country has put in a large number of UHV power grids, which also puts forward higher requirements for power communication security [3, 4]. The existing research methods mainly achieve secrecy through various cryptographic algorithms. Although they have certain confidentiality effects, the traditional methods have certain limitations in the face of increasing high hacker attacks.

In order to determine the fault type, fault range and other information within the shortest time of the fault of high-voltage power communication equipment, At present, a high-voltage power communication equipment fault system based on optical fiber technology is also designed. In this system, optical fiber temperature sensing technology, dynamic ampacity calculation method and a variety of environmental sensor principles are used to monitor all levels of faults of high-voltage power communication equipment. Although the above methods can pre-warning and identify the faults of high-voltage power communication equipment, the design of the connection point between the communication equipment and the data port is complex, and the maintenance of the system needs a lot of time and cost. Therefore, this paper proposes and designs a high voltage power communication network security warning and monitoring system based on HMAC algorithm.

2 Hardware Design of High-Voltage Power Communication Network Security Early Warning Monitoring System Based on HMAC Algorithm

2.1 HMAC-Based Logic Controller

The logic controller shell designed in this paper has high strength and corrosion resistance, and can protect the internal hardware structure in the environment of large dust density, large temperature change and strong electromagnetic interference [5, 6]. The following is the basic structure diagram of the logic controller designed in this paper:

Looking at Fig. 1, it can be seen that the main component of the logic controller is the control processor, so this paper will use two Siemens S7–1200 CPUs to process the information of the control program in the logic controller, and then use the arithmetic unit in the controller to process the two. The workload of each CPU is calculated, and more data to be processed is input from the input unit to the CPU with less workload [7]. The peripheral interface in the logic controller is of I/O expansion type, so that the external fault signal can be directly entered into the interface and stored to avoid the loss of parameters during CPU processing. The storage elements in the logic controller are bidirectional expansion, which can store and extract data at the same time. The applied storage types are EPROM and RAM respectively.

2.2 HMAC-Based Fault Sensor

The fault sensor based on HMAC mainly provides stable operating parameters for empirical mode decomposition. The main parameters of empirical mode decomposition include high-voltage temperature, electric power communication equipment current, high-voltage internal water level, relevant gas concentration, illumination and other

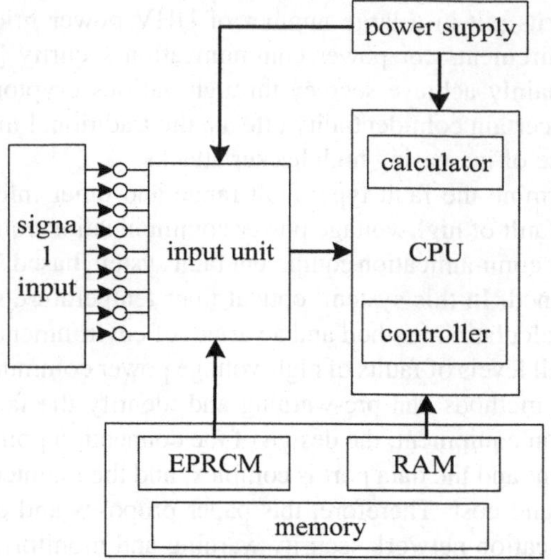

Fig. 1. Schematic diagram of the basic structure of the logic controller

parameters. Therefore, the sensor designed in this paper needs to meet the requirements of completing parameter acquisition [8]. The circuit diagram of the fault sensor is shown in Fig. 2 below:

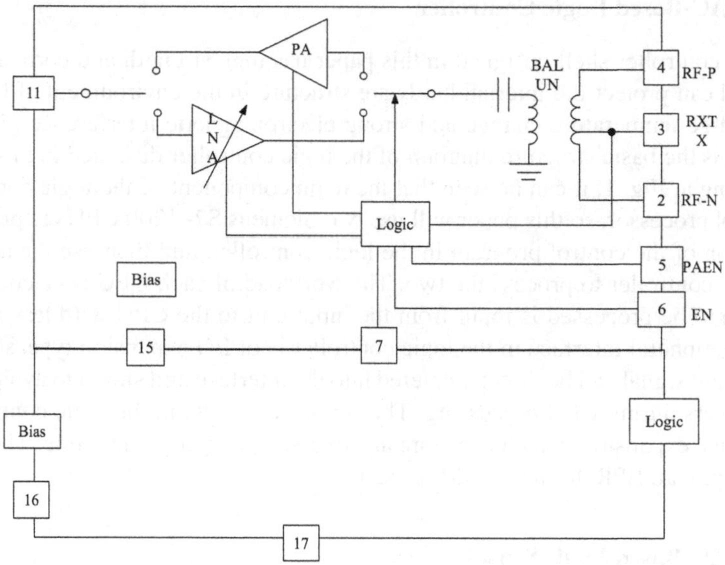

Fig. 2. Fault sensor circuit diagram

According to Fig. 2, it can be seen that the fault sensor circuit propagates to the three capacitors after three current transmissions. For the sensing of temperature parameters, this paper selects pt120 platinum thermal resistance and temperature transmitter as the core components of parameter sensing for high-voltage internal temperature. When the current inside the device and cable is greater than 4mA, the pt120 platinum thermal resistance and temperature transmitter can send temperature analog signals to the outside, and the sensor's sensing temperature range is −40 °C–450 °C [9].

2.3 HMAC-Based Signal Receiving Port

Empirical mode decomposition (EMD) requires a stable signal receiving port as the hardware foundation on the basis of known data.

The signal receiving port designed in this paper is shown in the following figure:

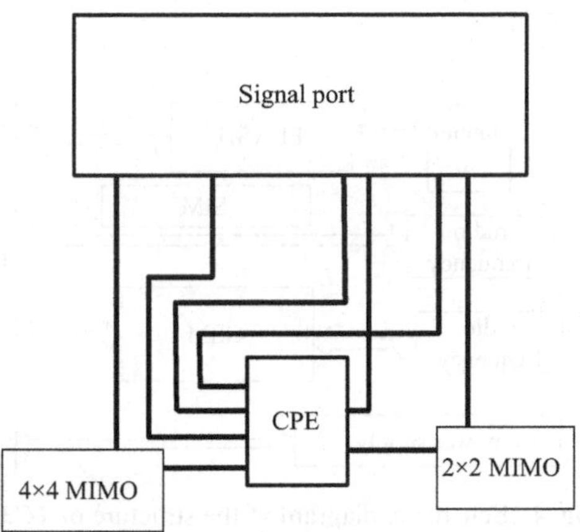

Fig. 3. Signal receiving port

As shown in Fig. 3, the signal receiving port is mainly realized by the two-wire access method and the four wire access method. The signal receiving port under the two-wire access method is mainly used to connect with the sensor. This port is a passive port, which reduces the interference of external power supply to the sensing data. The port is set with 8 interfaces to connect the temperature sensor, current sensor, water level sensor, gas sensor, switch and other structures. The signal receiving port under the three wire system access method can be divided into positive and negative poles. The active port can provide a more stable data decomposition channel for empirical mode decomposition technology [10].

There is also a S7–1000 type CPU microprocessor at the signal receiving port. The internal port of the processor is connected to the PROFINET communication interface, which helps the empirical modal decomposition to establish the physical connection port of the data, and realizes the hardware configuration without using the switch. Data association [11].

2.4 Design of Fault Early Warning Equipment Based on HMAC

The design of fault early warning equipment based on HMAC includes the structure of fault monitoring terminal, GSM network interface and data control module. The fault monitoring terminal directly transmits fault data to the empirical mode decomposition model [12], which requires strong processing performance, so the GSM wireless communication monitoring terminal module of Siemens is selected. The module adopts the TC35 structure, which can accommodate the GSM network baseband at the same time. Components such as processors, radios, memory cards, batteries, ZIF connectors, etc., meet the data requirements of empirical mode decomposition. The structure of TC35 is as follows:

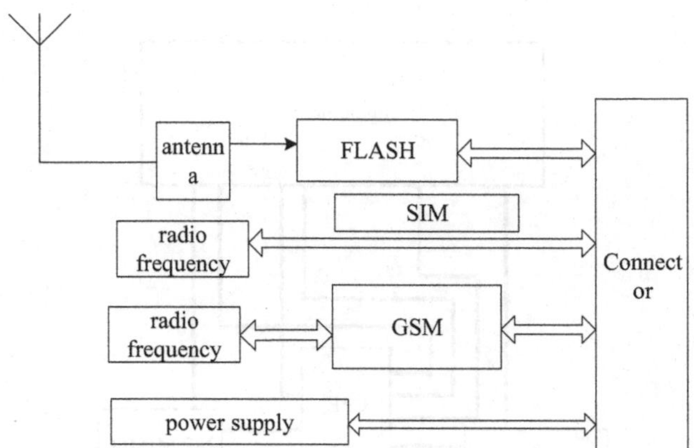

Fig. 4. Schematic diagram of the structure of TC35

According to Fig. 4, the network interface outside the TC35 structure is connected to the RS232 serial port, and a SIM card slot is set at the serial port to facilitate the fault maintenance personnel to directly obtain the fault data.

2.5 Data Sensing Module

In the initial stage of designing the system hardware, in order to effectively detect the validity of the early warning data, a data sensing module is set up to sense the grating light wave characteristics of different structures. In this paper, the data sensing module selects the WRNB-230 type sensor, which is usually used in conjunction with display instruments, recording instruments, electronic computers, etc. The two-wire output is 4–20 mA, and the anti-interference ability is strong. The bridge of the transmitter generates an unbalanced signal, which is converted into a 4–20 mA DC signal after amplification and sent to the working instrument, and the working instrument displays the corresponding parameter value. The basic error of the instrument shall not exceed the combined error of the basic error of the thermocouple and temperature transmitter. While ensuring data sensing, the storage structure of early warning information shall be managed to realize efficient and safe data sensing operation.

2.6 Monitoring Module

The data monitor of the monitoring module in this paper selects a photosensitive electronic monitoring device with model YHJCQ. The discharge counter has a waveform of 8/20 us and an amplitude of 50A to 100 kA. It can operate accurately and reliably, with low residual voltage and great current capacity. The input signal range is 0.1 mA to 200A, with RS485 communication interface, which can realize multi-computer communication or communication with the host computer, effectively ensuring the transmission and monitoring of data. The monitor uses wavelet transform to measure and analyze the harmonics of non-stationary time-varying signals. It can regularly record and store the change trend of power parameters such as voltage, current, active power, reactive power, frequency and phase, realize the effective transformation of internal data, and obtain the light sensing characteristic parameters of unit grating according to the relevant characteristics of power parameters to complete the data monitoring operation.

2.7 Early Warning Module

The early warning instrument of the early warning module in this paper is the data early warning demodulator of FBG-Scan 800. The early warning device has 8 independent optical channels, and each optical channel has up to 40 sensors, which can completely collect the wavelength stability parameters of light sensing data with a sampling rate below 1pm, and can maintain wavelength accuracy without time-of-flight correction. It has the function of depolarized light source to reduce the noise effect caused by birefringence. Its high dynamic range is above 30 dB, it can be externally triggered, and it has the characteristics of detecting sensors belonging to the same optical channel at the same time. When the wavelength linearity is 10pm, the operating temperature is between 0 and 45 °C, and the operating humidity is within 0% to 80%RH without condensation, it can effectively warn the light sensing information data in different stages, and make corresponding transmission response to the light sensing signal inside the grating, and convert the collected warning information into the warning signal mode through the optical channel, so as to realize the design of the warning module.

3 Software Design of High-Voltage Power Communication Network Security Early Warning Monitoring System Based on HMAC Algorithm

As an iterative algorithm, HMAC algorithm can effectively improve the performance of integrated learning, build a good data structure analysis model based on the theory of statistical learning, and completely analyze the hidden information of early warning data. Classify the sample training set into different data types, enhance the classification ability of the system, and then obtain more reliable early warning information.

The principal component analysis is used to transform the high-dimensional structure data of the external early warning system into low-dimensional structure data to obtain new orthogonal characteristic parameters. According to the characteristics of high-voltage power communication network, the structural adjustment of early warning parameters is carried out according to the wavelength parameters of the sensing platform. Quickly demodulate the wavelength signal, output the intrusion motive data according to the eigenvalue data of the early warning control platform, remove the interference of external factors on the system platform operation, transmit the user information of relevant units through the platform sensing system, and set the corresponding data transmission formula:

$$T + C = 2\cos\frac{1}{2}(S + z)\cos\frac{1}{2}(S - z) \tag{1}$$

In the above formula, T represents the transmission parameter; C represents the transmission command; S represents the platform sensing principle; z represents the intrusion motivation parameter.

Adjust the early warning data input behavior, and process the early warning sampling data corresponding to the output wavelength of different sensing platforms. In the early warning platform, the data with long wavelength resolution is transmitted to the communication optical cable channel to strengthen the internal supervision and management of the channel. Increase the warning frequency of dynamic warning information, control the data frequency component in time-varying signals, and analyze the correlation of warning parameters.

The transition sensing data, according to the form of high-voltage power communication network, respectively processes the intrusion information around the high-voltage power communication network to realize the full coverage operation of high-voltage power communication network protection. Conduct early warning structural parameters in the early warning platform and identify early warning incentive signals with different attributes. Set the alert calculation formula according to the characteristics of the platform algorithm space with strong alert performance:

$$Q = \sum_{k=0}^{n} a^{n-k} - P \tag{2}$$

In the above formula, Q represents the eigenvalue parameter; n represents the platform algorithm data; k represents the intrusion information collection index; a represents the early warning information of different attributes; P represents the excitation signal wavelength.

Consider the intrusion data information in the platform, measure the early warning interval, and establish the early warning metric formula, where L represents the early warning metric parameter; M represents the platform intrusion parameter; E represents the result eigenvalue of the redundancy matrix; I represents the platform accommodation space parameter.

$$L = \iiint_E (\nabla \cdot M)\mathrm{d}E = \oint\!\!\!\oint_I M \cdot \mathrm{d}I \tag{3}$$

After determining the control performance indicators, load forecasting technology is introduced to carry out distributed control of the high-voltage power communication network. The load forecasting technology used in this paper is short-term load forecasting. The influence of load changes, after setting the accuracy threshold, determine the power load value.

The HMAC algorithm is introduced to forecast the load of high-voltage power communication network and calculate the load value. The calculation formula is shown in formula (4):

$$A(x;\gamma,\beta)=B(x;\gamma,\beta) \tag{4}$$

Among them, $A(x;\gamma,\beta)$ represents the load demand value of the high-voltage power communication network; x represents the eigenvector inside the input of the high-voltage power communication network, which records the load value of the database, the weather conditions and other characteristics of the communication process in detail. B represents the parameter function to be used, and the least squares support vector is introduced to set the regression function; γ,β represents the distribution parameter, which is optimized through model training.

In the power communication machine room, complete parameter optimization, determine a single learning model, and combine the single learning model to form multiple models, so as to improve the control accuracy. The prediction results are shown in formula (5):

$$\hat{y}_m=f(A_1,\cdots A_i),\, i=1,2,\cdots N \tag{5}$$

Among them, $\hat{y}_m$ represents the predicted load results completed by multiple models; A_i represents the prediction results of each model of the high-voltage power communication network; f represents the generalized function during prediction, and this function can determine the average value.

The high-voltage power communication network is a smart grid, so more types of data can be obtained, and the amount of data is more abundant. When setting the single prediction model, we should improve the data set and accuracy, and use linear fusion to realize linear weighting.

The gradient boosting regression tree is introduced to determine the data set. After determining multiple basis functions, there are k total of basis functions to realize approximate numerical calculation. The calculation formula is shown in formula (6):

$$F(x;\gamma,\beta)=\sum_{K}^{i=1}B(x;\gamma_k,\beta_k) \tag{6}$$

where, $B(x;\gamma_k,\beta_k)$ represents the internal parameter function of the high-voltage power communication network, and this function is set as the basis function to determine the decision tree through the basis function; γ,β in the decision tree is a valid parameter.

Update the data to get a new data model, as shown in formula (7):

$$F_k(x)=F_{k-1}(x)+vH(x;\gamma,\beta) \tag{7}$$

Among them, $F_k(x)$ represents the updated data model; v represents the reduced data parameters, and the reduced parameters are used to prevent the simulation from overfitting, thereby preventing the loss function from rapidly decreasing.

Adding the cyclic network to the high-voltage power communication network, because it has a fixed weight, external input and internal state of the neural network, it can be regarded as the behavior dynamics of the internal state with the weight and external input as parameters. The model is established through the cyclic neural network, and the neurons are used for self feedback. The memory function of neurons is used to process sequences of different lengths. According to the output results of sequence length correlation, the memory information is obtained and the output calculation is realized. In the recurrent neural network, all nodes exist in the hidden layer, and the nodes of the hidden layer are related to each other. The structure of the recurrent neural network is shown in Fig. 5 below:

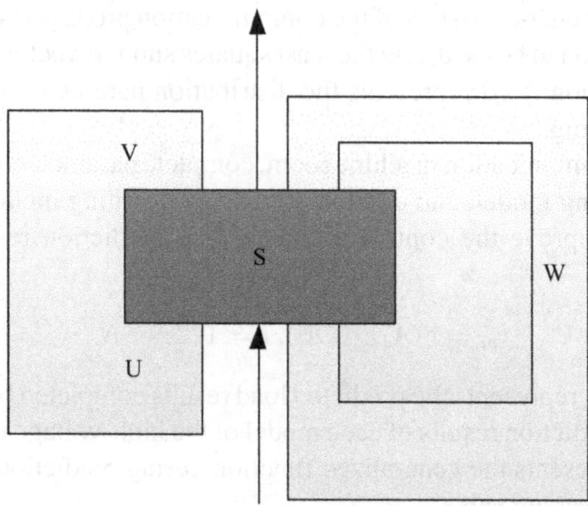

Fig. 5. Recurrent neural network structure

Observing Fig. 6, we can see that in the recurrent neural network designed in this paper, it consists of three basic structures: input layer, output layer and hidden layer. X represents the vector input from the input layer, and S represents the state vector in the hidden layer; O represents the vector output in the output layer. Calculate the weight from the input layer to the hidden layer and denote it by U, and the weight from the hidden layer to the output layer is denoted by V. After analyzing the values inside the input layer and the previous state hidden layer at the same time, determine the hidden vector inside the recurrent neural network.

The circular neural network is used to realize the circular processing of information inside the power communication room, determine the data set $\{(x_i, y_i)\}$, obtain the short-term prediction model according to the determined data set, and analyze the regression function of information inside the power communication room using the prediction model, as shown in formula (8):

$$F(x) = \kappa^T \cdot \varphi(x) + \sigma \tag{8}$$

Among them, $F(x)$ represents the obtained regression function; κ represents the internal weight of the regression function; $\varphi(x)$ represents the nonlinear transformation value generated by the feedback of the obtained power communication room into the high-dimensional space; σ represents the paranoia generated in the process of establishing the regression function quantity.

After determining the regression function, the least squares support vector machine is introduced to expand the traditional vector machine into a support vector machine to obtain the regression function under the minimum support vector machine:

$$Z = \sum_{n}^{i=1} \alpha_i k(x, x_i) + b \tag{9}$$

Among them, Z represents the regression function under the obtained minimum support vector machine, α_i represents the input value of the recurrent neural network; k represents the number of input neurons; b represents the output error factor.

Since this paper introduces the nonlinear regression function $\varphi(x)$ generated by the feedback of the power communication room to the high-dimensional space, it is necessary to map all the data to the high-dimensional space, and realize the calculation in the high-dimensional space to ensure better performance of the calculation results.

4 Experimental Studies

In order to verify the effectiveness of the high-voltage power communication network security early warning monitoring system based on the HMAC algorithm designed in this paper, an experiment is set up.

Set the experimental parameters, adjust through the MOIsm130 device, set the signal sampling rate to 650 Hz, and debug through the working device with a wavelength of 1450–1700 nm to ensure that different channels can pass more than 80 test units smoothly, so that each different The information of the test unit, so that the monitoring range can be maintained at 3–15 m. The early warning system set up in this paper is used to compare the intrusion signal and the external temperature rise signal, and the early warning effect of the early warning system proposed in this paper is analyzed under different signals.

The equipment used in the experiment is shown in Table 1 below:

Table 1. Experimental equipment

Device name	Device model
QKD Terminal A	QKDM-POL40A-24U4
QKD Terminal B	QKDM-POL40B-24U4
Key Management Service System	NF-5270 M3
Video telephony server	Espace U1910
Switch	S5700

(continued)

Table 1. (*continued*)

Device name	Device model
Video call	Espace 8950
Average key rate	2 Kbps
Channel attenuation	13 dB

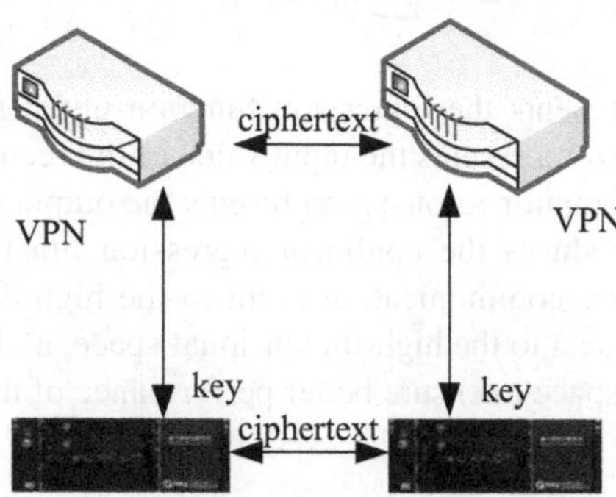

Fig. 6. Test structure

Set the test structure as shown in Fig. 6 below:

Set the operation parameters, set the network test parameters, including the frame length and quantum VPN. Record the data obtained after the test. If the detection process is not completed, retest, analyze the data, and evaluate again.

The obtained intrusion signal experiment results are shown in the following figure (Fig. 7):

It can be seen from the above figure that the temperature rise signal detected by the early warning system in this paper is very different from the intrusion signal. Comparing the intrusion signal with the normal signal, the vibration characteristics of the intrusion signal are very obvious. The curve adopts the rising mode, and the maximum and minimum values cannot be detected locally. According to the characteristics of amplitude distribution, although the intrusion curve is distributed on the maximum and minimum values, the number of points distributed is relatively small, which can prove that the distribution of intrusion actions is extremely uneven, while the distribution mode adopted by normal monitoring is uniform. According to the frequency domain, the intrusion signal adopts the vibration mode, and the spectrum distribution is not centralized. It vibrates in the frequency range of 3–5 Hz, and the signal with temperature rise will not have 0 frequency point. It can be seen that the early warning system designed in this paper can accurately complete the early warning judgment.

In order to further verify the effectiveness of the system, the system proposed in this paper is selected for experimental comparison with the optical fiber-based high-voltage power communication network security early-warning monitoring system and the weak grating array-based high-voltage power communication network security early-warning

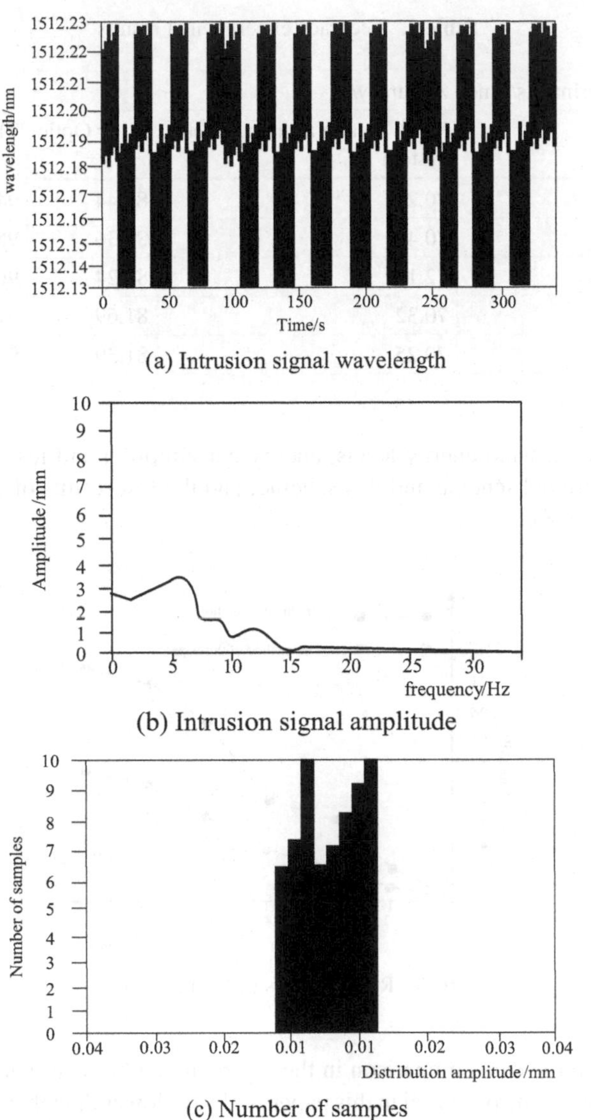

(a) Intrusion signal wavelength

(b) Intrusion signal amplitude

(c) Number of samples

Fig. 7. The experimental results of the presence of intrusion signals

monitoring system, and the accuracy is analyzed. The experimental results are shown in Table 2 below:

According to the above table, the early warning accuracy of the early warning system designed in this paper is higher than that of the traditional system. The system designed in this paper does not rely on the classifier for data analysis during early warning analysis. However, the traditional early warning system relies too much on the classifier, resulting in unbalanced information and a variety of misclassification states in the analysis process.

Table 2. Accuracy experimental results

Number of experiments/time	Accuracy/%		
	Weak grating array perimeter system	Fiber Optic	This article system
1	70.25	80.44	94.25
2	70.44	81.36	95.36
3	72.15	81.24	96.78
4	70.32	81.69	97.58
5	70.25	81.39	97.26

Under different wind energy levels, energy consumption and loss tests are carried out for the traditional scheme and this scheme, and the test results of the two schemes are recorded (Fig. 8).

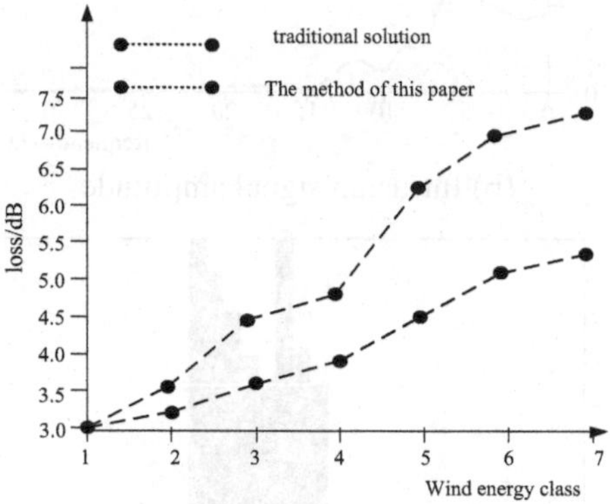

Fig. 8. Result of loss test experiment

According to the data comparison in the figure, it can be seen that the energy consumption of the scheme proposed in this paper is always lower than that of the traditional scheme. As the wind energy level increases, this gap becomes more and more obvious. The splicing loss of the traditional power communication ring network security protection scheme is affected by the number of spliced fiber connections and spliced nodes at the same time. As the wind energy level increases, the number of connection nodes also increases, so the connection loss increases accordingly. Even if the line of the high-voltage power communication network security early warning monitoring system based on the HMAC algorithm studied in this paper is disturbed by the wind, the quantum key can be encoded again at the terminal, thereby reducing the loss.

5 Conclusion

Based on the design of the traditional high-voltage power communication network security early warning and monitoring system, this paper designs a new high-voltage power communication network security early warning and monitoring system based on HMAC algorithm. The system takes the internal sensor as the early warning basis, extracts the early warning signal through the sensing characteristics of the demodulation device, makes corresponding early warning instructions according to different signal frequencies, improves the accuracy of early warning, and can analyze a large amount of intrusion data, With strong data reliability, it can timely respond to the early warning information, reduce the error rate of the early warning system, and better meet the needs of users. However, the system is easy to be affected by the transmission distance in the actual application process, so the next step is to enhance the long-distance warning performance of the overall early warning system as the research subject to analyze the effectiveness of the early warning system.

References

1. Wu, Y., Chen, J., Ru, Y., et al.: Research on power communication network planning based on information transmission reachability against cyber-attacks. IEEE Syst. J. **6**(99), 1–12 (2020)
2. Chen, G., Sun, P., Zhang, J.: Repair strategy of military communication network based on discrete artificial bee colony algorithm. IEEE Access **3**(09), 2–9 (2020)
3. Wang, S., Liu, X., Liu, S., et al.: Human short-long term cognitive memory mechanism for visual monitoring in IoT-assisted smart cities. IEEE Internet Things J. https://doi.org/10.1109/JIOT.2021.3077600
4. Liu, W., Wu, H., Yu, F., et al.: Design of information security access system in the power grid based on improved Bayesian algorithm. Wireless Pers. Commun. **5**(10), 1–17 (2021)
5. Liu, W., Wu, H., Yu, F., et al.: Design of information security access system in the power grid based on improved Bayesian algorithm. Wireless Pers. Commun. **58**(10), 1–17 (2021)
6. Li, L.L., Shen, Q., Tseng, M.L., et al.: Power system hybrid dynamic economic emission dispatch with wind energy based on improved sailfish algorithm. J. Clean. Prod. **14**(18), 128318–128322 (2021)
7. Liu, S., He, T., Dai, J.: A survey of CRF algorithm based knowledge extraction of elementary mathematics in Chinese. Mobile Networks Appl. **26**(5), 1891–1903 (2021). https://doi.org/10.1007/s11036-020-01725-x
8. Shen, B., Gui, Y., Chen, B., et al.: Application of spindle power signals in tool condition monitoring based on HHT algorithm. Int. J. Adv. Manuf. Technol. **106**(4), 5–11 (2020)
9. Shuai, L., Shuai, W., Xinyu, L., et al.: Fuzzy detection aided real-time and robust visual tracking under complex environments. IEEE Trans. Fuzzy Syst. **29**(1), 90–102 (2021)
10. PanYiming, Y., Lanfeng, Z.Z., et al.: Research on lightweight design of mobile car machine based on response surface method. Comput. Simul. **37**(5), 91–95 (2020)
11. Peng, W., Hongbing, J., Long, L., et al.: AOA measurement data association based on multi-way order Association. Acta Electron. Sin. **49**(3), 454–460 (2021)
12. Songhua, L., Bingbing, H., Xun, L., et al.: Empirical mode decomposition of median complementary sets. Acta Automatica Sinica **47**, 1–13 (2021)

Large Scale Network Intrusion Detection Model Based on FS Feature Selection

Mei Hong, Yingyong Zou, and Chun Ai(✉)

Office of Academic Research, Changchun University, Changchun 130022, China
hongmei12315@163.com

Abstract. Intrusion detection is one of the important means to ensure network security, aiming at the problem that the current network intrusion detection model cannot obtain the ideal network intrusion detection effect, a large-scale network intrusion detection model based on FS feature selection is designed. This study takes the NSL-KDD dataset as an example, and performs numerical and normalization processing on it. The main features are selected using the grey wolf optimization algorithm fused with cuckoo search. Taking the feature as input, the C4.5 algorithm is used to realize network intrusion detection. The results show that under the application of the constructed model, the accuracy rate (A), detection rate (D), and precision rate (P) are all greater than 90%, and the F1 score is greater than 1, indicating that the model has a good performance in network intrusion detection.

Keywords: Feature selection · Pretreatment · Network intrusion · C4.5 algorithm

1 Introduction

With the continuous development of network technology and scale, network information security has become the common focus of all countries in the world. Practice has proved that only relying on security measures such as firewalls and user identity authentication systems cannot fully guarantee the security of networks and computer systems. How to quickly and effectively discover all kinds of new intrusion behaviors is very important to ensure network security. Intrusion detection (intrusion detection) is a proactive security protection technology, which is a technology that detects intrusions by collecting and analyzing the information of the protected system. It has always been favored by researchers as the second security line of defense after the firewall [1–3].

As a reasonable supplement to the firewall, intrusion detection technology makes up for the deficiency of the firewall. It is a dynamic security mechanism, which can monitor, prevent and resist the intrusion behavior. It combines real-time collection and system analysis with network monitoring to deal with network intrusion, so as to improve the integrity of information security structure, and expand the administrator's ability to manage network security. Intrusion detection technology can monitor the network in real time without affecting the performance of the network, so it has good real-time

Y. Xu et al. (Eds.): ML4CS 2022, LNCS 13655, pp. 380–393, 2023.
https://doi.org/10.1007/978-3-031-20096-0_29

performance [4, 5]. Because intrusion detection system plays an important role in the field of network security, and it has some imperfections in technology, it is necessary to conduct in-depth research on intrusion detection.

At present, there are many intrusion detection systems based on machine learning methods such as neural networks, support vector machines, naive Bayes, and decision trees. The main function of these detection systems is to monitor the network and computer systems in real time, find and identify intrusion behaviors or attempts in the system, and give out intrusion alarms [6]. However, the current network data contains a large number of redundant and noisy variables (features), which leads to a decrease in the accuracy of the detection model and a long training time for the detection model. If the value is too large, the final classification result will be biased, and the convergence of the parameters will also be affected, resulting in an increase in the training time of the classifier. Therefore, the purpose of feature selection is to remove these irrelevant and redundant features that will interfere with the detection effect, so as to retain the most important features in the data and remove the noise, greatly reduce the computational time overhead of the algorithm, improve the data processing speed, and even improve the accuracy of the algorithm. Therefore, the intrusion detection method based on feature selection is very necessary.

Therefore, in order to improve the effect of network intrusion detection, a large-scale network intrusion detection model based on FS feature selection is designed. A grey wolf optimization algorithm combined with cuckoo search is applied to the feature selection of network intrusion detection, and its update mechanism is implemented, which enhances the global search ability of the algorithm in the feature selection of network intrusion detection. It is expected that the method in this paper can provide reliable technical support for network information security management.

2 Network Intrusion Detection Model Design

Today, with the rapid development of computer technology, the development of network has become an important guarantee for social development, most of the development of technology relies on the support of network development, the security of network directly affects the security of social development, For example, viruses, worms, Trojans and so on lead to information leakage, system paralysis and so on. This indicates that network security is becoming more and more important, and the requirements for network security are also getting higher and higher. The worm virus led to the destruction of the computer, and the computer security problem began to be concerned by people [7]. However, the network security problem did not become less and less because more and more people studied it. On the contrary, with the rapid expansion of the network scale, the complexity of the structure and the rapid expansion of the application domain, many information security problems have emerged, and people begin to pay attention to these information security problems, more and more information security defense technologies are used to defend and ensure the stability of the system. The intrusion detection model shows good scalability and superior detection effect.

Intrusion detection helps the system to deal with network attacks by collecting information from several key points in a computer network or system, and then analyzing the information to find out whether there are behaviors that violate security policies and signs of being attacked in the network or system. At present, the threats to communication on the computer network mainly include the following:

(1) Interception: The intruder eavesdrops on the communication content of others on the network.
(2) Interruption: Communication on the network is intentionally interrupted by an intruder.
(3) Tampering: The intruder intentionally tampered with the message transmitted on the network.
(4) Forgery: The intruder transmits the forged information through the network.

Intrusion detection is mainly realized by performing the following tasks: monitoring and analyzing users and system activities; Audit system architecture and weaknesses; Identify and reflect known attacks and respond to relevant personnel; Statistics and analysis of abnormal behavior patterns; Evaluate the integrity of key systems and data files; Audit tracks and manages the operating system to identify violations of security policies.

Intrusion Detection System (IDS for short) is a real-time network traffic monitoring system, which takes different security measures according to the monitoring results to minimize the harm.

2.1 Intrusion Detection Dataset

KDD CUP99 data set has laid the foundation for the research of network security intrusion detection, it is the benchmark data set in the field of intrusion detection [8]. It contains two parts: the identified test set and the unidentified training set, and some new attack types have been added to the test set. Therefore, KDD CUP99 is the most widely used classic data set in the field of intrusion detection. However, KDD CUP99 still has some problems. Its training set has a lot of redundant data, and its test set also has a lot of duplicate records. In order to improve these problems, researchers proposed a new data set based on KDD CUP99 data set, nsl-kdd data set, this data set is a 20% subset extracted from the KDD CUP99 data set, and improved it, the final classification accuracy will be higher and the test accuracy will also be improved. In addition, the various types of training samples selected in the new data set are the same as the original KDD CUP99 data. The percentage of concentrated samples is inversely proportional, which makes the classification rates of different detection methods vary widely, the scope of use is wider, and the evaluation is more effective; at the same time, the size of the NSL-KDD dataset is also much smaller than the original KDD CUP99 dataset., there is no need to randomly select a small part of the original data set, which saves a lot of time and cost in the intrusion detection experiment while ensuring the accuracy. The NSL-KDD dataset mainly includes four categories: DOS is a denial of service, probe is a port attack, r2l (remote to local) is a remote user attack, and u2l (user to root) is a privilege escalation attack.

2.2 Intrusion Detection Data Preprocessing

Numerical Value

The features of each sample in the data set can be divided into three categories according to the data type: continuous numerical, discrete numerical and non numerical features. The first two categories can be directly used in the algorithm, and the non numerical features must be processed. In the experiment, numerical values are used to replace non numerical attributes in features. Table 1 shows the corresponding relationship between non numerical features and numerical values in the sample data.

Table 1. Numerical correspondence

Tcp-1	udp-2	http-3
Icmp-6	smtp-7	ftp-8
other-11	ecr_i-12	eco i-13
urp_ i-16	SO-17	pop_3–18
telnet-21	RSTO-22	sunrpc-23
REJ-26	pm_dump-27	netstat-28
pop_ 2–31	Z39 _50–32	uucp_path-33
csnet ns-36	domain _u-9	ftp_ data-10

The last item of all samples in the data set represents the category of the sample, such as normal, snmpgetattack, etc. In this experiment, only four types of attacks and one normal state are analyzed, so the attack types in the category labels are first classified, and finally Get five items of normal, DOS, R2L, U2R and PROBING, and then digitize these five items.

Data Normalization

Normalization or standardization is a very important stage of data preprocessing, which will make data processing more efficient, improve the expressiveness of the data, and improve the convergence speed of the model.

Data standardization can eliminate the noise of the data to a certain extent, reduce the influence of outliers or extreme values, and stabilize the data. The most commonly used data normalization method is z-score, It handles data falling in the range from negative infinity to positive infinity, there is no definite extreme value, and it is decentralized. In dealing with both continuous variables and When there are intrusion detection datasets with discrete variables, it is not as good as Min-Max normalization. In general, Min-Max normalization is one of the most common methods for processing data features in machine learning, and it is also often used in intrusion detection processes, which can be regarded as a linear normalization method. Linear Min-Max normalization is expressed as:

$$s_i' = \frac{s_i - \min(s_i)}{\max(s_i) - \min(s_i)} \in [0, 1] \tag{1}$$

where, s_i and s_i' represent the data before and after normalization; $\min(s_i)$. $\max(s_i)$ represents the minimum and maximum values in the data sample.

2.3 FS Feature Selection

In the past intrusion detection methods, the focus of research is basically on feature recognition and classification algorithms, but feature selection is often ignored. However, the original data set without feature selection contains a large amount of redundant feature information. These features with redundant information will interfere with the classifier's correct identification of targets, the purpose of feature selection is to remove these irrelevant and redundant features that will interfere with the detection effect, so as to keep the most important features of the data and remove the noise, and can greatly reduce the calculation time cost of the algorithm, improve the speed of data processing and even improve the accuracy of the algorithm, therefore the intrusion detection method based on feature selection is very necessary. Combined with the feature dimension of the network intrusion detection data set, a gray wolf optimization algorithm combined with cuckoo search is applied to the feature selection of network intrusion detection. In the iterative process, the algorithm integrates Levi's flight mechanism to update the position of the population, so that the algorithm can avoid falling into local optimization.

Grey Wolf Optimization Algorithm Integrating Cuckoo Search

Generally, the population of gray wolves is controlled between 5 and 12, and they have a strict hierarchy. In the gray wolf population, the main division is $\alpha, \beta, \delta, \varepsilon$, these 4 grades. Among them, the α gray wolf is the leadership class, responsible for leading the actions of other gray wolves in the population. β gray wolf is the second class, responsible for helping the gray wolf in the leadership class to make various decisions and activities. The δ gray wolves are the third stratum, they obey the orders of the α, β gray wolves and manage the lower gray wolves. ε gray wolf is the bottom of the population. In practical problems, α, β, δ corresponds to the three solutions with the best fitness. In the iterative process, the GWO algorithm always follows the gray wolf α, β, δ to update the position of the wolf pack, resulting in its weak global search ability and easy to fall into local optimum. In particular, when applied to the field of network intrusion detection, the GWO algorithm is more prone to local optimal problems due to the high dimensionality of the dataset. The CS algorithm combines the Levi flight mode to find the bird's nest and randomly updates the position of the bird's nest according to the predetermined probability Pa, which makes it easy to jump from the current area to other areas, and has a strong global search ability. Therefore, on the basis of the existing work, this paper attempts to further deepen the fusion idea of GWO algorithm and CS algorithm, and integrates the two disturbance processes that appear in CS algorithm in the way of updating the position of GWO algorithm, and combines the Levi flight of CS algorithm. Finally, the improved grey wolf optimization (CS-GWO) algorithm fused with cuckoo search is applied to the feature selection of network intrusion detection. The specific process is shown in Fig. 1 below.

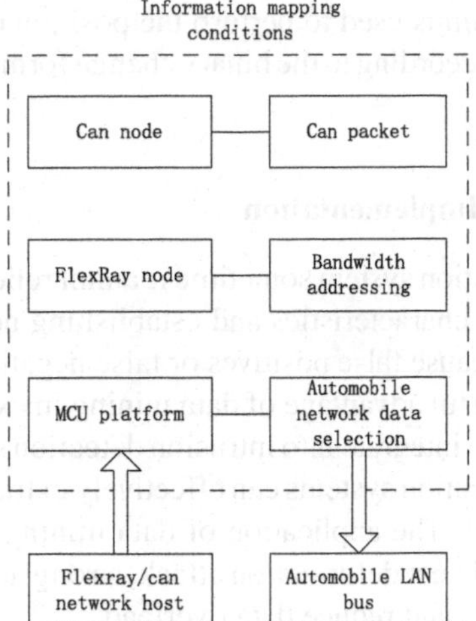

Fig. 1. Flow of grey wolf optimization algorithm with cuckoo search

The update mechanism of CS-GWO algorithm is mainly divided into three steps:

In the first step, the Levi flight mechanism is used to disturb the positions of the three gray wolves with the best fitness values.

The second step is to use the update mechanism of GWO algorithm to update the gray wolf location information, so that the wolves gather towards the prey.

The third step is to randomly update the position of gray wolf population according to the preset probability value Pa.

In the first step and the third step, the positions of the three gray wolves with the best fitness value and the whole gray wolf population are disturbed respectively, forcing the wolf population to jump out of the local optimization randomly in the process of approaching the prey, and enhancing the global search ability of GWO algorithm in the feature selection of network intrusion detection. For the continuous problem transformed into the discrete problem of feature selection, in this paper, the GWO algorithm is transformed into binary by using the transformation function to transform the update mechanism [9]. According to the conversion function, firstly, the wolf pack location is updated as shown in Eq. (2).

$$L(n+1) = round\left[\frac{L_{\alpha}(n) + L_{\beta}(n) + L_{\delta}(n)}{3}\right] \tag{2}$$

where, $L(n+1)$ represents the wolf pack position of the $n+1$ iteration; $L_{\alpha}(n)$. $L_{\beta}(n)$ and $L_{\delta}(n)$ represent the positions of gray wolves in the n wolf pack iteration α, β, δ.

Update the wolf pack position between 0 and 1 according to the following formula.

$$L_i(n) = \begin{cases} 0, rand < \dfrac{1}{1+\exp[|L_i(n)|]} \\ 1, \text{otherwise} \end{cases} \tag{3}$$

In the formula, $i = \alpha, \beta, \delta$ is a gray wolf; *rand* represents a random number in the interval [0,1].

Finally, the CS algorithm is used to perturb the position of the optimal α, β, δ gray wolf, and it is transformed according to the binary change formula proposed by Rodrigues et al.

2.4 Intrusion Detection Implementation

The existing intrusion detection system sometimes cannot reflect the actual situation well in extracting user behavior characteristics and establishing normal or abnormal pattern database, which is easy to cause false positives or false negatives and cause losses to the network system. The powerful advantage of data mining in extracting features and rules from data makes it a trend to integrate into intrusion detection systems, using data mining technology in intrusion detection systems can effectively extract useful information from a large amount of data [10]. The application of data mining to intrusion detection has the following advantages: detect deformation attack, strong adaptability, low false alarm rate, low false negative rate, and reduce data overload.

The classification methods in data mining mainly include support vector machine method, rough set method and decision tree method. Each method is suitable for different situations, and different methods can be selected to solve different problems. Decision tree is an important data mining classification method, which can classify and predict data, extract features describing important data classes from massive data, and predict future data trends. It has the advantages of high speed, high precision, and simple generated patterns, and has received extensive attention in data mining.

Its main function is to reveal the structured information in data. By applying simple decision rules, large record sets can be divided into interconnected small record sets. With each successive segmentation, the members in the result set become more and more similar to each other. Decision tree is one of the most widely used inductive reasoning algorithms. It is a method to approximate the value of discrete function. It has the advantages of high classification accuracy, simple operation and good robustness to noisy data. Therefore, it has become a practical and popular data mining algorithm. The decision tree is constructed from the root node, the appropriate attributes are selected to divide the sample set into several subsets to establish the branches of the tree, and then the lower nodes and branches of the tree are repeatedly established in each branch subset until the end conditions are met. Test the category of new sample data with the trained decision tree. By using decision tree, data rules can be visualized, the time required to construct decision tree is relatively short, and the output results are easy to understand and have high precision. Its biggest advantage is that it does not require a lot of background knowledge. As long as the training sample set can be written in the expression of "attribute value", the decision tree learning algorithm can be used to classify. Common decision tree methods include ID3, C4.5, CART, et al. Here, C4.5 algorithm is used for intrusion detection. The specific process is shown in Fig. 2 below.

(1) Information gain rate

The information gain criterion has a preference for attributes with a large number of possible values. In order to reduce the possible adverse effects of this preference, the C4.5 algorithm uses the information gain rate to select the optimal division

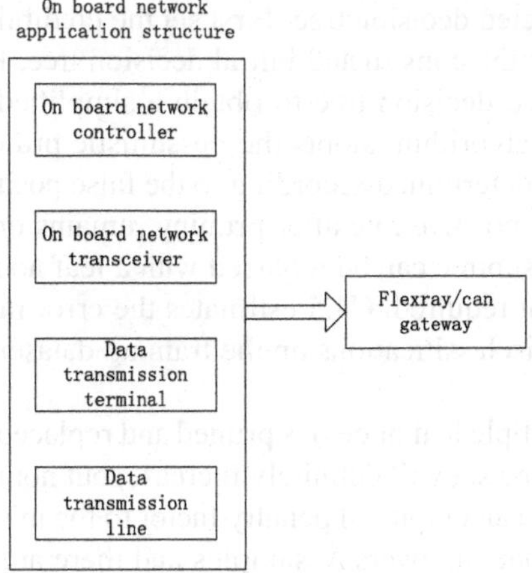

Fig. 2. Intrusion Detection Based on C4.5 Algorithm

attribute. Gain rate $G(D|A)$ formula:

$$G(D|A) = \frac{I(D|A)}{V(A)} \tag{4}$$

In,

$$V(A) = -\sum_{k=1}^{K} \frac{|D_k|}{|D|} \cdot \log_2 \frac{|D_k|}{|D|} \tag{5}$$

In the formula, $V(A)$ is the information entropy; $I(D|A)$ is the information gain; $A = \{a_1, a_2, ..., a_k\}$, k values. If A is used to divide the sample set D, k branch nodes will be generated, of which the k node contains all samples in D whose value is a_k on the attribute A, denoted as D_k. In general, the more possible values of attribute A (that is, the larger k is), the larger the value of $V(A)$ will usually be.

The information gain rate criterion has a preference for attributes with a small number of values. Therefore, C4.5 algorithm does not directly select the candidate partition attribute with the largest information gain rate, but first finds the attribute with higher information gain than the average level from the candidate partition attributes, and then selects the attribute with the highest information gain rate.

The implementation steps are as follows:

(1) Collect intrusion information and select certain data to form a unified intrusion sample set.
(2) The sample set is preprocessed to remove the attributes irrelevant to the decision, reduce the dimension of the data set, and form the training set of the decision tree.
(3) The training set is trained, and the relevant rule information is established through certain calculation.

(4) Pruning the constructed decision tree. First set the credibility, and then use the IF-THEN rule to prune the constructed initial decision tree. Pruning is performed on the already generated decision tree to obtain a simplified version of the pruning decision. The C4.5 algorithm adopts the pessimistic pruning method, whether to prune the subtree is determined according to the false positive rate before and after pruning. If the false positive rate after pruning remains or decreases compared to before pruning, the subtree can be replaced with a leaf node. Therefore, a separate pruned dataset is not required. C4.5 estimates the error rate on unknown samples by the number of misclassifications on the training dataset.

If a subtree (with multiple leaf nodes) is pruned and replaced by a leaf node, the false positive rate on the training set will definitely increase, but not necessarily on new data. Therefore, we need to add an empirical penalty factor to the misjudgment calculation of the subtree. For a leaf node, it covers N samples and there are E errors, then the error rate of the leaf node is $\frac{E+0.5}{N}$. This 0.5 is the penalty factor, then a subtree has L leaf nodes, then the misjudgment rate of the subtree is estimated as:

$$R = \frac{\sum E_i + L \cdot 0.5}{\sum N_i} \tag{6}$$

where, E_i represents the number of misjudged samples of each leaf node of the subtree; L is the number of leaf nodes of the subtree; N_i is the sample number of each leaf node.

Then the number of false positives of the tree is Bernoulli distribution. We can estimate the mean B and standard deviation C of the number of false positives of the tree:

$$B = N \cdot R \tag{7}$$

$$C = \sqrt{N \cdot R \cdot (1 - R)} \tag{8}$$

After replacing the subtree with a leaf node, the number of misjudgments of the leaf is also a Bernoulli distribution, because the subtree is merged into a leaf node, so $L = 1$, substituting it into the formula for calculating the misjudgment rate above, you can get the leaf The false positive rate R' of the node is

$$R' = \frac{E + 0.5}{N} \tag{9}$$

Therefore, the mean value F of the number of misjudgments of leaf nodes is

$$F = NR' \tag{10}$$

Here, a conservative splitting scheme is adopted, that is, only when there is enough confidence to ensure that the accuracy rate after splitting is higher than that without splitting, otherwise it will not split -- that is, it should be pruned. If you want to split (i.e. do not prune), at least ensure that the sum of B and C after splitting is less than F, and in order to ensure a sufficiently high confidence, adding a standard deviation can have a

95% confidence. Therefore, to split (i.e. do not prune), you need to meet the following inequality

$$B + C < F \tag{11}$$

On the contrary, it is not split, that is, the condition of pruning:

$$B + C \geq F \tag{12}$$

(5) Classify the type of intrusion to determine whether it is an attack or what kind of attack.

3 Model Application Test

3.1 Model Application Test Tool

Weka is the abbreviation of Waikato knowledge analysis environment. It is an open source data processing tool based on Java. Weka provides all functions required for data mining, including data filtering, feature selection, data conversion, various mining models, result evaluation and graphic display. It can implement its own mining algorithm on Weka and integrate it into Weka.

The data format required by Weka is extremely simple, it is essentially a two-dimensional table. A row in this two-dimensional table can be regarded as a record in a relational database or a statistical sample. The vertical row is regarded as an attribute, which is equivalent to a field in a relational database or a variable in statistics. Such a table is the data set we want to process, and in Weka, it represents a certain relationship (Relation) between attributes. The format in which Weka stores data is an ARFF file, which is a type of ASCLL file. The ARFF file is essentially a two-dimensional table, and Weka also supports files in CSV and Excel formats, and can convert it to each other data format. Support local and remote data connections, read data in the database as a data source for data mining and analysis. Supported databases include oracle, Mysql, Sqlserver, Access, et al.

3.2 Training Set and Test Set Samples

7680 pieces of data were extracted from the NSL-KDD dataset. The sample data of training set and test set are shown in Table 2.

3.3 Feature Selection Results

The grey wolf optimization algorithm combined with cuckoo search finally selected 11 of the 68 features, as shown in Table 3.

Table 2. Training set and test set samples

Intrusion type	Attack means	Training set	Test set
DoS	PingofDeath	256	351
	TearDrop	653	358
	UDPflood	462	369
Probe	Port scan	362	247
	IP scan	247	361
R2L	Spy	325	351
	FtpWrite	554	350
	MultihopAttack	422	433
U2L	qlAttack	687	215
	Perl	254	423
normal	/	345	341

Table 3. Feature selection results

Serial number	Features	Fitness
1	Destination Port	1.4482
2	Total Length of Bwd Packets	1.3245
3	Fwd Packet Length Min	0.6452
4	Bwd Packet Length Mean	0..8912
5	Bwd Packet Length Std	1.3287
6	Flow Bytes/s	1.0246
7	Fwd IAT Min	0.9214
8	Packet Length Mean	1.4233
9	Init_Win_ Bytes_ forward	2.5844
10	Init_Win_ Bytes_ backward	1.689

3.4 Evaluation Indicators

This time, the accuracy (A), detection rate (D), accuracy (P) and F1 score are used as indicators to evaluate the performance of the model. The accuracy rate shows the overall performance of the intrusion detection model and represents the ratio of the number of correctly predicted samples to the total number of predicted samples. Detection rate to show the detection performance of intrusion detection model for abnormal behavior, which is called recall rate in the deep learning index; Accuracy rate refers to the ratio of the number of positive samples correctly predicted to the number of positive samples predicted. F1 is the harmonic average of accuracy rate and recall rate to express the classification effect of the model. The index used this time is also a commonly used performance evaluation index in the field of network intrusion detection and in-depth learning model. The calculation formula is as follows:

$$A = \frac{TP + TN}{TP + FP + FN + TN} \tag{13}$$

$$D = \frac{TP}{TP + FN} \tag{14}$$

$$P = \frac{TP}{TP + FP} \tag{15}$$

$$F1 = 2 \cdot \frac{P \cdot D}{P + D} \tag{16}$$

where, *TP* represents the correctly identified target traffic, *TN* represents the correctly identified other traffic, *FP* represents the incorrectly identified target traffic, and *FN* represents the unrecognized target traffic.

3.5 Model Application Performance

Comparing the methods in this paper with the naive Bayesian method, the intrusion detection performance of the two methods in four types of attacks and one normal state is shown in Table 4.

It can be seen from Table 4 that under the application of the constructed model, the accuracy rate (A), detection rate (D), and precision rate (P) are all greater than 90%, and the F1 score is greater than 1, indicating that the model has good network intrusion detection performance.However, the accuracy (a), detection rate (d) and accuracy (P) of naive Bayes method are all around 80%, or even lower, which is far lower than the method in this paper.

In order to further reflect the efficiency of the methods in this paper, the detection time of the two methods is compared, and the results are shown in Table 5.

Table 4. Model intrusion detection performance

Type	Method	Accuracy (A)%	Detection rate (D) %	Precision (P) %	F1 score
DoS	Method in this paper	94.561	92.322	95.452	97.564
	Naive Bayes	83.211	81.315	83.154	80.615
Probe	Method in this paper	95.426	93.565	94.485	97.355
	Naive Bayes	84.245	80.915	86.470	86.914
R2L	Method in this paper	93.657	92.227	92.555	95.482
	Naive Bayes	80.547	80.332	81.647	80.614
U2L	Method in this paper	93.874	90.144	93.687	96.782
	Naive Bayes	78.472	79.364	79.614	80.155
normal	Method in this paper	95.627	93.688	94.568	97.475
	Naive Bayes	74.982	80.694	75.941	82.647

Table 5. Test time result

Type	Method	Test time(s)
DoS	Method in this paper	4.12
	Naive Bayes	11.23
Probe	Method in this paper	4.52
	Naive Bayes	11.11
R2L	Method in this paper	4.36
	Naive Bayes	10.89
U2L	Method in this paper	4.68
	Naive Bayes	10.87
normal	Method in this paper	3.21
	Naive Bayes	11.54

4 Conclusion

Nowadays, with the rapid development of computer network, it is particularly important to ensure the security of network information. Intrusion detection technology, which can actively protect information security, has attracted much attention as a safeguard measure. Therefore, a large-scale network intrusion detection model based on FS feature selection is constructed. The model is tested and proved to be effective. However, this study still has some shortcomings: in the future work, we plan to use this feature selection method to train more classifiers. In the multi classification problem, because some categories in NSL-KDD data set appear very few times, how to train models with high accuracy and strong generalization ability from these labels with very few training numbers is also the focus of future research work. In addition, the data source is the standard NSL-KDD data set, but the real-time network data can not be fully represented by this data set. If conditions permit in the future, this work should be strengthened and tested through real real real-time network data.

Aknowledgement. 1. General project of Jilin Provincial Department of Education: Detection Model of Network Intrusion Based on FS Feature Selection and Extreme Learning Machine (jjkh20210615kj).

2. General project of Jilin Provincial Department of Education: Building Intelligent Data Analysis Platforms to Help the Operation and Management of Insurance Enterprises (jjkh20220598kj).

3. General project of Jilin Provincial Department of Education: Research on Robot Bending Personalized Orthodontic Arch Wire Forming (jjkh20200561kj).

References

1. Dong, R.H., Yan, H.H., Zhang, Q.Y.: An intrusion detection model for wireless sensor network based on information gain ratio and bagging algorithm. Int. J. Network Secur. **22**(2), 218–230 (2020)
2. Zhou, J., He, P., Qiu, R., Chen, G., Wu, W.: Research on intrusion detection based on random forest and gradient lifting tree. J. Software **32**(10), 3254–3265 (2021)
3. Song, W., Beshley, M., Przystupa, K., et al.: A software deep packet inspection system for network traffic analysis and anomaly detection. Sensors **20**(6), 1637 (2020)
4. Asad, H., Gashi, I.: Dynamical analysis of diversity in rule-based open source network intrusion detection systems. Empir. Softw. Eng. **27**(1), 1–30 (2022)
5. Dong, R.H., Li, X.Y., Zhang, Q.Y., et al.: Network intrusion detection model based on multivariate correlation analysis – long short-time memory network. IET Inf. Secur. **14**(2), 166–174 (2020)
6. Liu, S., Liu, D., Muhammad, K., Ding, W.: Effective template update mechanism in visual tracking with background clutter. Neurocomputing **458**, 615–625 (2021)
7. Zhang, Z., Ding, J., Song, Z.: Worm virus propagation model in a predator-prey time-delay wireless sensor network. Control Eng. **28**(12), 2343–2350 (2021)
8. Lijian, Z., Jinpeng, C.: Optimization and detection simulation of anomaly detection algorithm based on extended Jarvis Patrick clustering. Electron. Des. Eng. **30**(13), 100–104 (2022)
9. Wang, Z., He, Y., Li, H., Zhang, F.: Binary particle swarm optimization algorithm based on novel S-type transformation function for solving knapsack problem with single continuous variable. Comput. Appl. **41**(2), 461–469 (2021)
10. Daihua, Z., Yong, S., Xiangfei, Z., Bing, W.: Simulation of network intrusion data autonomous defense based on data mining. Comput. Simul. **37**(10), 263–267 (2020)

Research on Intelligent Detection Method of Automotive Network Data Security Based on FlexRay/CAN Gateway

Jiatong Wei[1(✉)], Kai Ma[2], and Chunhua Kong[1]

[1] College of Automotive Engineering, Jilin Communications Polytechnic, Changchun 130012, China
ouyangmeixue100@163.com

[2] Jilin Communications Polytechnic, Changchun 130012, China

Abstract. In order to improve the transfer rate of data information parameters by the car network host and avoid the occurrence of information false detection, this paper carries out research on the intelligent detection method of data security of the Internet of vehicles based on FlexRay/CAN gateway. According to the connection form of the FlexRay/CAN gateway, the EDF scheduling algorithm is solved, and the calculation expression of the known queue forwarding efficiency is combined to complete the vehicle network data forwarding processing based on the FlexRay/CAN gateway. According to the definition form of the vehicle network, the accurate data domain analysis results are obtained, and then the design of the vehicle network data security intelligent detection method based on the FlexRay/CAN gateway is completed by calculating the traffic detection coefficient. The experimental results show that compared with the traditional detection method, the FlexRay/CAN gateway can greatly improve the transfer rate of the data information parameters of the car network host, and has strong practical value in solving the problem of false detection of data information.

Keywords: FlexRay/CAN Gateway · Automobile network data · Safety intelligent detection · Queue forwarding efficiency · On board network · Data field

1 Introduction

In the modern automotive industry, many traditional mechanical control elements have been replaced by electronic control units (ECUs). Some cars are equipped with more than 20 or even more than 40 ECUs, and there is an increasing trend as the performance of the vehicle improves. This has caused the electronic circuits connecting these devices to expand rapidly, wiring harnesses have become more complex, and wiring has become more difficult, placing a huge burden on system design, assembly, inspection, and maintenance. The traditional wiring harness connection and point-to-point communication bring great difficulties to the installation, inspection and maintenance of the system. Therefore, the complex automotive network technology develops rapidly, and different

Y. Xu et al. (Eds.): ML4CS 2022, LNCS 13655, pp. 394–408, 2023.
https://doi.org/10.1007/978-3-031-20096-0_30

types of fieldbuses are rapidly applied in the automotive industry. As a hub for information exchange between different networks, automotive gateways have been widely studied at home and abroad, and have been used in automotive in-vehicle networks and industrial production. Especially as the most popular CAN network at present, it has been widely used in other network protocol gateways.

There are many bus protocols currently available for automotive networking, each with its own advantages and disadvantages. One protocol cannot meet the needs of all automotive applications. In order to realize the data interaction between different buses, it is necessary to use the network integration technology gateway to realize the network interconnection and process the data from the vehicle embedded network. The gateway needs to be able to parse the different network protocols connected, and encapsulate the message into a format that conforms to the network protocol, so as to realize the upload and release of data. A typical gateway consists of multiple automotive network interfaces (FlexRay/CAN) with embedded microcontrollers and peripheral functions. CAN is the abbreviation of CAN (Controller Area Network). CAN transmission speed is fast, fault tolerance is strong, and cost-effective. The maximum transfer rate is 1Mbps. It is the mainstream protocol for automotive networking and is widely used in modern cars. For electronic control systems and communication systems. Many researchers also conduct research on automotive network data based on this, and propose related data communication technologies and data security detection technologies. For example, Ren et al. proposed a data security communication model for the Internet of Vehicles nodes based on blockchain technology, aiming at the problems of excessive load and high data security risks in the central entity of the Internet of Vehicles communication architecture [1]. Although this method can effectively ensure the transmission security of IoV data, its data transmission rate is not high. For example, Besseghier M et al. proposed a joint channel estimation and data detection method based on OFDM cooperative system in order to ensure the security of data transmission and improve the data transmission rate [2]. This method mainly uses the Alamouti space-time block coding based orthogonal frequency division multiplexing cooperative system in the relay node to improve the stability of its data connection and the rate of channel data transmission, and then uses the maximum likelihood (ML) algorithm to use equal intervals The pilot symbols are used to derive the channel estimator, calculate the equalizer and apply it to improve receiver data detection. Although this method effectively improves the security of data transmission, its data transmission rate is still poor. Based on this, this paper proposes an intelligent detection method for vehicle network data security based on FlexRay/CAN gateway. The next-generation automotive bus protocol FlexRay supports synchronous and asynchronous data transmission at rates of approximately 10Mbps, ensuring stable data transmission, fault tolerance and message response time, and provides redundancy measures in dual-channel mode. The FlexRay bus also replaces multiple high-speed CAN buses, reducing complexity and cost. The higher reliability and safety of FlexRay will replace CAN as a critical safety component in the car. It is hoped that through the research in this paper, the security and communication rate of the Internet of Vehicles data communication will be improved.

2 Data Forwarding Based on FlexRay/CAN Gateway

For the forwarding processing of automotive network data, it is necessary to solve the specific value of queue forwarding efficiency index based on FlexRay/CAN gateway and under the application principle of EDF scheduling algorithm. This chapter will carry out in-depth research on the above contents.

2.1 FlexRay/CAN Gateway Settings

The automobile gateway is located in the center of the automobile network and is responsible for the interaction and sharing of vehicle information. The several networks it connects are different protocols [3]. Their payload, data rate and real-time processing requirements are different. The gateway must be able to effectively process all the import and export data from these interfaces. Many problems need to be considered in the design of automobile network gateway.

One of the important issues is payload and latency. CAN nodes transmit information in 8-bit packets, while FlexRay nodes can transmit up to 254 bytes of data, with overhead per transmission [4]. Addressing and encoding cycles consume the maximum available bandwidth. In extreme cases, the system transfer capacity depends on the maximum effective bandwidth of the bus. Data buffering needs to fill enough CAN data packets into the system data packets. For system packets at an input CAN rate of 1 Mb/s into a FlexRay network with 10 Mb/s, buffering enough data may incur significant delays in CAN data. The other extreme is to configure the transfer capacity of the system to transfer extremely low payloads of 1 to 4 bytes. Here, excessive bandwidth will waste the overhead cycle for addressing and coding. FlexRay bus is for important real-time applications. For example, it is used in safety critical systems with high real-time requirements such as steering system and chassis. The system bus must ensure that messages from these systems are sent to the destination node before the deadline [5]. The reason for the delay is that the system has too much buffered data and does not schedule according to priority.

The MCU model of the FlexRay/CAN gateway system in this paper is MC9S12XF512. FlexRay technology provides the high-speed communication bandwidth required by current active driving systems and future self-driving cars with drive-by-wire capabilities [6]. The S12XF family expands the range of FlexRay solutions that automotive system designers can choose from. The small size of the S12XF MCU is ideal for space-constrained applications such as distributed actuator and sensor control modules communicating with a 32-bit central controller on a FlexRay network. The 16-bit S12XF device serves as the end node for a variety of advanced safety and active driving applications including: suspension control, active rollover prevention, active braking, lane departure warning systems, parking dispatch collaboration and electronic parking systems.

The physical layer channel has an independent receiving and transmitting channel, with a maximum speed of 10Mbps. In the working state, the host can access the receiving module and transmitter of TJA1080, and send and receive physical layer data through its operation [7]. All data frames on the bus will reach all TJA1080 on the bus. Each TJA1080 will pass through the receiving filter after receiving the bus data frame; The filter filters out data frames that do not belong to its own address, and only stores its own data frames and broadcast frames in the receive FIFO. The temperature detection module of TJA1080 is used to detect the equipment temperature. If the temperature exceeds a certain value, the bus transceiver will be automatically closed.

The complete FlexRay/CAN gateway structure is shown in Fig. 1.

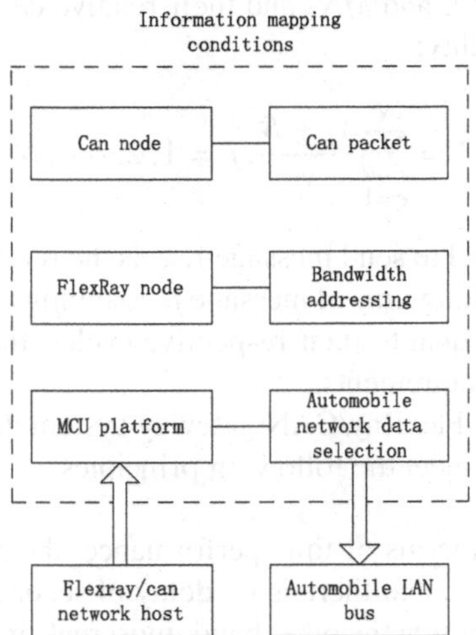

Fig. 1. FlexRay/CAN gateway connection structure

Using appropriate data frame conversion method and scheduling algorithm to manage the data in the gateway buffer can effectively improve the system payload, reduce the delay time of data in the gateway, and ensure the real-time transmission of real-time data. This problem will directly affect the performance of the gateway and the whole body network.

2.2 EDF Scheduling Algorithm

EDF scheduling algorithm is a priority-based dynamic scheduling algorithm. The EDF algorithm assigns the task priority according to the length of the task from the deadline [8]. The task that is closer to the deadline gets the higher priority, and the priority of the task changes with time. Since the message in the FlexRay/CAN gateway system cannot be interrupted once it starts to transmit, the scheduling of the CAN bus network is a non-preemptive scheduling. The non-preemptive EDF algorithm for CAN bus network can be described as follows:

- Assign task priority according to the length of the task from the deadline. The task closer to the deadline gets higher priority;
- The priority of the task is not fixed, but changes with time, and the priority of the task is uncertain relative to time;

- The task cannot be preempted. The current transmission task will not be interrupted by the newly arrived task with higher priority. The high priority transmission task waiting in the queue can not be executed until the task is completed [9].

Whether a group of tasks can be scheduled can usually be determined by using the decision theorem of the EDF scheduling algorithm: Assume N periodic message transmission tasks, $M1$, $M2$, $M3$, and MN, and their relative deadlines gradually increase, if the The following inequality:

$$Z = \sum_{c=1}^{N} \frac{v_j + B}{x_j}, j = 1, 2, \cdots, N \tag{1}$$

where, v_j is the time required to send message j, x_j is the relative deadline of message j, and B is the maximum blocking time of message j. assuming that their respective relative deadlines are less than or equal to their respective cycles, these N messages can meet their respective deadline requirements.

Under the action of the FlexRay/CAN gateway system, the application of the EDF scheduling algorithm must meet the following principles:

(1) Real time message: in terms of time performance, the requirements for real-time messages are very strict, and there is no delay of seconds or even milliseconds in safety critical occasions. On the other hand, most real-time messages have a certain time limit, and only the latest messages are desirable. If the message is not received within the specified time within a certain period of time, a new real-time message will be generated at this time and the timeout message will be discarded. Therefore, the general real-time message does not need to be sent again. In the whole message composition, the data proportion of real-time messages is relatively low, and the occupancy of bandwidth is also low;
(2) Hard real-time message: This type of message has very strict real-time requirements and is mostly used in safety-critical parts. If the node message cannot reach the destination node within the specified time, it will cause damage to the performance of the entire system, and may even bring catastrophic consequences [10];
(3) Soft real-time message: This type of message has stricter real-time requirements. Such messages allow for occasional loss. If the node message does not reach the destination node within the specified time, the performance of the entire control system may decrease linearly, and may even reach zero;
(4) Non real time messages: these messages do not require very strict real-time performance, and may have a relatively long time delay, mostly including user programming data, configuration data, some system status monitoring data, etc. This kind of data has a relatively large amount of data in the system and occupies a large amount of bandwidth. The data it transmits is generally not allowed to be lost, and error control or retransmission mechanisms need to be adopted to ensure the integrity and accuracy of the data;
(5) Periodic message: this type of message is sampled periodically by the sensor and sent. The characteristics of periodic messages are as follows: 1) messages occur periodically, generally for fixed end-to-end message transmission. 2) Such messages

are generally real-time messages. 3) It accounts for a small proportion in data communication and occupies a fixed bandwidth;

(6) Aperiodic messages: Aperiodic messages are mostly time departure messages, asynchronous messages, and random messages without periodicity. Its characteristics are: 1) messages occur randomly, and most of them conform to the negative exponential distribution; 2) the proportion of non-real-time data in the transmitted data is relatively large; 3) the data traffic is relatively large;

(7) Burst news: This kind of data is generated suddenly, such as alarm information. Most of them are real-time data, and the traffic is generally less;

(8) Deadline: the maximum delay that a message can accept from its generation to the destination acceptance point. It should be less than or equal to the period of the periodic message;

(9) Message response time: refers to the time interval between the sending node sending the message and the receiving node receiving the message completely. It consists of four parts: the waiting time of the message at the sending node, the transmission delay of the message, the transmission delay on the link, and the delay of the message waiting to be processed at the receiving node. In order to complete the time constraint of message transmission, the response time must be less than the deadline.

2.3 Queue Forwarding Efficiency

The arbitration field part of the CAN message frame is divided into two segments, the former segment is the inter-queue priority of the message frame, and the latter segment is the queue internal priority. The inter-queue priority of the CAN message frame is set to the primary priority, and the internal priority of the queue is the secondary priority. It is assumed that there are N information frames to be sent in the queue, and the priority identifier of these information frames may be set to $1, 2, \cdots, N$. Identifier 1 has the highest priority in descending order. For the information frame priority comparison, the primary priority is first compared, and if the primary priority is the same, then the secondary priority is compared. According to the mechanism of sending messages on the CAN bus, it is assumed that the arrival behavior of the information frame sent to FlexRay conforms to the Poisson distribution, so that the forwarding process can be regarded as a customer queuing process for N priority classes. If the information frame is arbitrated, It will always transmit all the data bits of the group, and will not be interrupted by the information frame group of higher priority in the process of transmitting non-arbitration domain data, so the queuing process is non-preemptive. If K data is packaged at one time, the transmission process of the CAN information frame in the buffer can be regarded as an M/G/K queue.

λi represents the arrival rate of information frames with priority i, here is the number of information frames arriving in a unit time. $i = 1, 2, \cdots, N$;

μi represents the service rate of the information frame with priority i, and here is the number of information frames that are successfully packaged and sent per unit time. $i = 1, 2, \cdots, N$;

ρi represents the utilization rate of the information frame with priority i. when this information frame is served here, the probability that the gateway is occupied is equal to $\frac{\lambda}{k\mu i}$, $i = 1, 2, \cdots, N$;

Wi represents the waiting time of the information frame with priority i in the gateway, $i = 1, 2, \cdots, N$;

Xi indicates the time that the information frame with priority i occupies the service desk. Here, it is the time that the information frame is packaged and sent to the FlexRay/CAN bus.

The queuing time for an information frame with priority i is divided into 3 parts:

(1) The service time of the information frame that arrives before i but has not yet been served;
(2) The service time of the information frame group that arrives after i but is served before it;
(3) The remaining transmission time of the information frame being transmitted, that is, the blocking time;

In this way, the average waiting time of information frame i can be obtained:

$$\overline{W}i = Z \cdot \sum_{j=1}^{i-1} \lambda i \mu i X i \rho i \tag{2}$$

FlexRay/CAN has two formats of time period: static and dynamic. The sending time of the static period is fixed. The transmission delay in this situation can be ignored, and the delay of the dynamic period is mainly considered.

FlexRay/CAN is a professional tool for network and ECU development, testing and analysis, supporting the entire system development process from requirements analysis to system implementation. CANoe's rich functionality and configuration options are widely used by OEM and supplier network design engineers, development engineers and test engineers. In the early stages of development, CANoe can be used to build a simulation model on which to perform a functional evaluation of the ECU. After completing the development of the ECU, the simulation model can be used for functional analysis, testing of the entire system, and the integration of the bus system and the ECU. In the process of developing a distributed communication system using CANoe, the network node model is established on the basis of the database. Communication between these nodes can be fully simulated and analyzed. In the following development process, a real ECU can be used instead of a single simulation node.

3 Design of Intelligent Detection Method for Vehicle Network Data Security

Based on the FlexRay/CAN gateway system, the design and application of a new intelligent detection method for automotive network data security are realized according to the processing flow of on-board network definition, data domain analysis and flow detection coefficient calculation.

3.1 Definition of In-Vehicle Network

In-vehicle network refers to a network that connects some smart devices with the help of network communication protocols, and can send signals from related sensors to the system. On this basis, a data communication protocol is developed, which can realize the conversion between the data and information of the vehicle, thereby building a vehicle network system, also known as the CAN-BUS bus. The short-frame data structure, lossless bus arbitration technology and flexible communication scheme meet the real-time and reliability requirements of automobiles. In-vehicle network technology is relatively mature, and all have certain anti-interference ability and high reliability. The multi-master bus communication system is supported and controlled by the in-vehicle network. The communication medium can be optical fiber and cable. It is mainly used in automobile engine system, sensor system, etc. The bit rate of the bus is as high as 1mb/s. The in-vehicle network data bus mainly transmits data in each system, so that each control unit forms a whole, all information is transmitted along two lines, the number of control units and the amount of interrelated information increase with the increase of the number, In this way, the problem of increasing the number of plugs and the corresponding wiring required for each message can be solved.

The on-board network controller receives the data sent by the control unit and processes these data to the on-board network transceiver. At the same time, the data transmitted by the on-board network transceiver is received by the on-board network controller, processed and finally processed to the control unit. The ultimate purpose of the on-board network transceiver is to convert the transmitted data information into electrical signals, and send the electrical signals to the transmission route in the process of receiving and transmitting data. A resistor will be installed at the data transmission terminal to prevent the reflection of system data in the transmission terminal, and then return to the original path. If so, the system data transmission will be directly affected. The complete on-board network structure is shown below (Fig. 2).

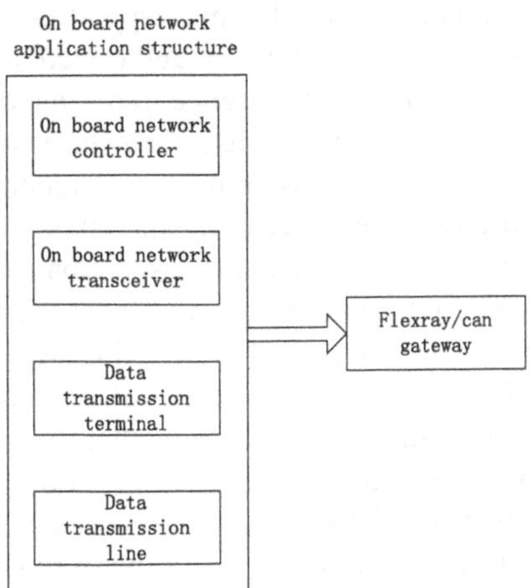

Fig. 2. In-vehicle network structure

When transmitting data, it needs to be transmitted back and forth in both directions. These two lines are called CAN-H line and CAN-L line respectively. The in-vehicle network bus is twisted together by two wires, the main purpose is to prevent external electromagnetic interference and external radiation, if the potentials of the two wires are opposite, one wire is at high level (5V) and the other is at low level (0), the sum of the voltages remains the same and remains a constant. Through this method, the in-vehicle network data bus can be protected from external electromagnetic field interference, and the external radiation of the in-vehicle network data bus is also neutral, and there is no radiation.

3.2 Data Domain Analysis

The HTM data prediction model directly processes the bit sequence from a single ID data field, and takes the data field bits in each packet as input. Therefore, the input to the predictor model is shape (number of groups) × Binary matrix of (bits). In the actual detection system, it is necessary to design a method to send the data into the predictor in a continuous or discontinuous time window.

First of all, it is necessary to establish a car inspection database, which stores a large amount of car inspection data. According to different authorizations, it has different data retrieval and query rights, and different vehicle inspection data query rights can query different ranges of car inspection data. The overall structure of the automobile network based on FlexRay/CAN gateway is divided into three layers. The first layer is the user login system, the second layer is the data query system, and the third layer is the detection data statistics system.

The main task of the first layer is to receive and collect the basic information of users, conduct identity authentication, give corresponding permissions according to different identity authentication, and transfer the corresponding information to the second layer.

The main task of the second layer is to receive the information of the first layer, determine the range of vehicle inspection data that users can query, accept the information transmitted by the first layer and lock it in the corresponding query condition box, and clear and lock the query condition box that is not authorized to use, so as to prevent the leakage of vehicle inspection data and interference to normal queries. Query according to the query criteria, display the query results, view the test data, and print out the automobile test data report. When an external inspection report is selected, the external inspection report can be printed. When selecting the chassis report, print the chassis report. The external inspection data and chassis inspection results are reflected in the vehicle inspection report. The information received from the first layer and the query conditions of this layer should also be passed to the third layer.

The main task of the third layer is to accept the relevant information of the second layer, determine the range of vehicle inspection data that the user can count, accept the information transmitted by the second layer and lock it in the corresponding statistical condition box, and the statistical condition box that is not authorized to be used. Clear and lock to prevent car detection data leakage and interference with normal statistics. According to the statistical conditions, it can make statistics and display the statistical results, check the statistical results, and print out the statistical result sheet of the vehicle inspection data.

Database design is the core technology in the development and construction of information system. It is the technology to establish database and its application system. Database design is to construct the best database mode in the specified application environment, establish the database and its application system, realize effective data storage, and meet various application needs of users. Database represents an important research topic of database in application field. The first stage of database design is database requirement analysis. The main work of this stage is to collect basic data and lay a solid foundation for the next design according to the basic data processing process.

Standardization of data helps eliminate data redundancy in the database. ThirdNormal Form is generally considered to be the optimal balance of performance, scalability and data integrity. Use as many fields as possible when choosing numeric and text types. Be very careful when using smaUint and tinyint types in SQL, if the data is too long, the operation calculation cannot be performed. The information of the unit user stored in the unit user identity authentication table. Among them, the unit number is the identity authentication number by linking the unit name with the vehicle basic information table, and the different query and statistics authority of the unit is distinguished by the different number segments of the unit number.

Let ω represent the initial query assignment of the vehicle network data information, $\overline{D}$ represent the unit accumulation of the vehicle network data, f represent the vehicle network information query coefficient, and μ represent the operation characteristics of the established detection instructions. With the support of the above physical quantities, the formula (2) can define the automobile network data domain expression based on FlexRay/CAN gateway as:

$$K = \sum_{\omega=1}^{+\infty} \left(\overline{W} i \frac{f\overline{D}}{|\mu|^2} \right) \tag{3}$$

From the perspective of the time domain, anomalies in which packets are added or removed are treated as a flow sequence frequency detection problem. To detect these anomalies, the time information of all captured IDs is first converted into a feature vector, and then the ID features containing normal behaviors are trained by the traffic anomaly detection method, and behaviors that deviate from the normal features are defined as anomalies and alerts are issued.

3.3 Flow Detection Coefficient

In the vehicle network, CAN bus flow detection does not capture all the information in any two time points, but captures the data in a fixed length of time window interval to measure. Select to set the capture window length to l_κ seconds, where κ represents the traffic information definition coefficient, and count the following parameters for each packet ID:

- p: Packet ID number;
- a: The total number of single IDs in the unit time window;
- η_p: The average time interval of the corresponding ID packets, that is, the ID data packet cycle;

- σ_p^2: The time interval variance value of the corresponding ID packet;

The FlexRay/CAN gateway is an efficient traffic anomaly detection method suitable for solving point anomalies in in-vehicle networks, with wide availability and high-quality software implementation. By finding the optimal hypersphere, the method divides it into two types: normal packets and abnormal packets, which can effectively resist attacks of unknown intrusion types.

Let h_1 and h_2 represent two randomly selected vehicle network data information flow calibration values, and the inequality condition of $h_1 \neq h_2$ is always true. In combination with the above physical quantities, the flow detection coefficient expression can be defined as:

$$E = \frac{\sqrt{\frac{l_k}{a} p\left(\eta_p \cdot \sigma_p^2\right)}}{(h_1 - h_2)^2} \tag{4}$$

On the high-speed CAN bus, Impreza and Explorer transmit fewer data packets. The data rate of the low-speed bus is one-fourth of that of the high-speed bus, and it has a considerably lower packet transfer rate. The total number of IDs in Impreza is slightly more than half that of Explorer. While Impreza transfers slightly less than the Explorer bus, the packet rate variation per bus remains largely unchanged. The size of the window can affect the performance of the model, so the flow model is evaluated as a separate method under different time window lengths. Longer windows yield more reliable detections, but shorter windows yield faster results, so it's worth exploring the relationship between window length and performance.

4 Case Analysis

In order to highlight the practical application value of the intelligent detection method for vehicle network data security based on FlexRay/CAN gateway, the following comparative experiments are designed. Taking the intelligent detection method of automotive network data security based on FlexRay/CAN gateway as the application technology of the experimental group, and the traditional detection method as the application technology of the control group, the Cortex-A9 processor was selected as the experimental equipment, and the experimental group and the control group were used respectively to analyze all the data. Select the host device for control, and record the specific numerical changes of the relevant experimental indicators.

First, the experimental values are screened according to the process shown in Fig. 3; Then, the numerical level of variable indexes in the experimental group and the control group were recorded; Finally, the change of experimental data is analyzed and the experimental rules are summarized.

The transfer rate of data information parameters by the automobile network host can reflect the probability of information false detection events. Without considering other interference conditions, the faster the transfer rate of the automobile network host for the data information parameters, the lower the probability of information false detection events, that is, the security level of the detection method is relatively high; On the

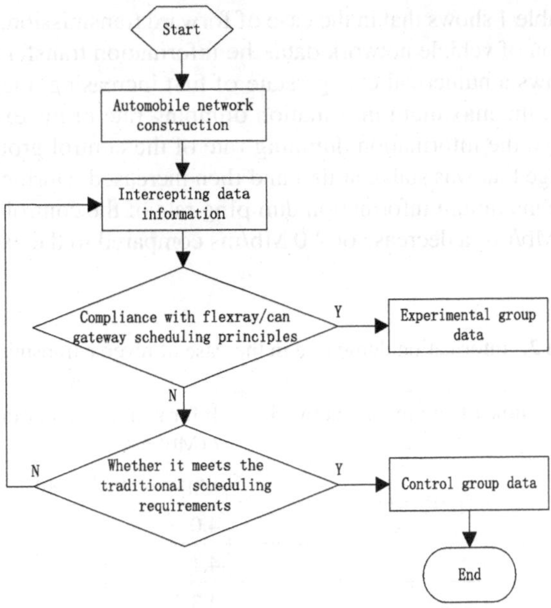

Fig. 3. Screening of experimental data

contrary, if the automobile network host has a slow transfer rate for data information parameters, it means that the probability of information false detection events is high, that is, the security level of the detection method is relatively low.

The following table records the specific experimental values of data information parameter transfer rate under two different transmission conditions.

Table 1. Information transfer rate in the case of forward transmission

Data transmission volume of automobile network/(Gb)	Information transfer rate/(Mb/ms)	
	Experimental group	Control group
1.0	5.3	3.5
2.0	5.5	3.5
3.0	5.7	3.5
4.0	5.8	3.6
5.0	5.8	3.7
6.0	5.8	3.8
7.0	5.8	3.9
8.0	5.9	4.0
9.0	6.1	4.1

Analysis of Table 1 shows that in the case of forward transmission, with the increase of the accumulation of vehicle network data, the information transfer rate of the experimental group shows a numerical change state of first increasing, then stabilizing, and finally increasing., the maximum information dumping rate of the experimental group reached 6.1 Mb/ms; the information dumping rate of the control group showed a state of numerical change that was stable at first and then increased. During the whole experiment process, the maximum information dumping rate of the control group could only be It reached 4.1 Mb/ms, a decrease of 2.0 Mb/ms compared to the experimental group maximum.

Table 2. Information dump rate in the case of reverse transmission

Data transmission volume of automobile network / (Gb)	Information transfer rate / (Mb/ms)	
	Experimental group	Control group
1.0	4.0	3.1
2.0	4.1	3.2
3.0	4.3	3.3
4.0	4.4	3.4
5.0	4.5	3.4
6.0	4.6	3.2
7.0	4.7	3.2
8.0	4.8	3.0
9.0	4.8	3.0

Analysis of Table 2 shows that in the case of reverse transmission, with the increase of the accumulation of vehicle network data, the information transfer rate of the experimental group shows a state of numerical change that first increases and then stabilizes. The maximum rate reached 4.8 Mb/ms; the information dumping rate of the control group showed a numerical change state of first increasing, then stabilizing, and finally decreasing. During the entire experiment, the maximum information dumping rate of the control group could only reach 3.4 Mb /ms, a decrease of 1.4 Mb/ms compared to the experimental group maximum.

To sum up, the experimental rule is:

- The traditional detection method can not effectively control the transfer rate of automobile network data information under the forward transmission and reverse transmission, which indicates that the application ability of this method in solving the problem of information error detection is relatively limited;
- The intelligent detection method based on FlexRay/CAN gateway can effectively control the transfer rate of vehicle network data information in the case of forward

transmission and reverse transmission, indicating that this method can better solve the problem of information false detection.

To sum up, the FlexRay/CAN gateway has a decisive influence on the performance of the automotive electronic system, and is a key component in the automotive electronic system, and its related technologies will become an important factor in determining the development level of the automotive electronic system.

5 Conclusion

With the help of various network communication technologies, people have realized more control over vehicles, such as navigation and positioning, and three-way communication of "vehicle, person, and road". However, the information security of intelligent networked vehicles is also a part that cannot be ignored. Mobile phone applications used to control vehicles, complex internal sensor control systems and software vulnerabilities may become new risk points, and automotive information security has become one of the four major security issues in the automotive field. Therefore, the research on anomaly detection in the Internet of Vehicles is of great significance. In the study of this paper, when the input stream data changes, the memory of the model is also updated; when the input pattern changes due to firmware upgrade or component replacement, the detection system also continuously learns new patterns in the CAN network. The binary data stream before CAN bus decoding is classified and input into each data sequence predictor for training, identification and prediction. The follow-up judgment mechanism of vehicle network data abnormality is explored, and a complete abnormality judgment process is proposed. Experiments show that the intelligent detection method based on FlexRay/CAN gateway can effectively control the transmission rate of vehicle network data and information, and has the ability to better solve the problem of information misdetection. This method has certain research value.

Aknowledgement. Innovation team of automobile service engineering in cold area, Fund number: 2019–5.

References

1. Tiaojuan, R., Jiaying, Z., Yourong, C., et al.: Research on data security communication model for iovs nodes based on blockchain. Autom. Technol. **05**, 30–35 (2021)
2. Besseghier, M., Bouzidi, D.A., Abdelhak, Z., et al.: Joint channel estimation and data detection for OFDM based cooperative system. Telecommun. Syst. **73**(4), 545–556 (2020)
3. Liu, L., Peng, Y., Wang, L., Li, A., Yu, P.A., Lwb, C., et al.: Improving EGT sensing data anomaly detection of aircraft auxiliary power unit. Chin. J. Aeronaut. **33**(2), 448–455 (2020)
4. Zhang, L., Leach, M.: Evaluate the impact of sensor accuracy on model performance in data-driven building fault detection and diagnostics using Monte Carlo simulation. Build. Simul. **15**(5), 769–778 (2021)
5. Liu, S., He, T., Dai, J.: A survey of CRF algorithm based knowledge extraction of elementary mathematics in Chinese. Mob. Networks Appl. **26**(5), 1891–1903 (2021). https://doi.org/10.1007/s11036-020-01725-x

6. Wenxiu, Z., Xinyin, W., Wei, Y., et al.: Stochastic resonance weak signal detection based on hybrid intelligent algorithm. Comput. Simul. **38**(06), 469–474 (2021)
7. Marques, R.S., Epiphaniou, G., AlKhateeb, H., et al.: A Flow-based multi-agent data exfiltration detection architecture for ultra-low latency networks. ACM Trans. Internet Technol. **21**(4), 1–30 (2021)
8. Gao, P., Li, J., Liu, S.: An introduction to key technology in artificial intelligence and big data driven e-learning and e-education. Mobile Networks Appl. (2021)
9. Zhang, R., Venkitasubramaniam, P.: False data injection and detection in LQG systems: a game theoretic approach. IEEE Trans. Control Network Syst. **7**(1), 338–348 (2020)
10. Lynda, B., Zhang, G., Bouzefrane, S., et al.: An outlier ensemble for unsupervised anomaly detection in honeypots data. Intell. Data Anal. **24**(4), 743–758 (2020)
11. Liu, S., Wang, S., Liu, X., Gandomi, A.H., Daneshmand, M., Muhammad, K., De Albuquerque, V.H.C.: Human memory update strategy: a multi-layer template update mechanism for remote visual monitoring. IEEE Trans. Multimedia **23**, 2188–2198 (2021)

Adversarial Attack and Defense on Natural Language Processing in Deep Learning: A Survey and Perspective

Huoyuan Dong[1], Jialiang Dong[1], Shuai Yuan[2], and Zhitao Guan[1(✉)]

[1] School of Control and Computer Engineering, North China Electric Power University, Beijing 102206, China
guan@ncepu.edu.cn
[2] Department of Finance, Operations, and Information Systems (FOIS), Brock University, St. Catharines, ON, Canada

Abstract. Natural language processing (NLP) presently has become a new paradigm and enables a variety of applications such as text classification, information retrieval, and natural language generation by leveraging deep learning techniques. However, recent studies have shown that the NLP models based on deep neural network are susceptible to maliciously designed adversarial examples. Therefore, the main challenges lie in improving the robustness and ensuring the security of the system. In this paper, we first introduce common NLP tasks and quality measures on adversarial example. Next, we present a comprehensive review on literature in terms of both adversarial attack and defense methods, based upon the granularity and type. Our work is also the first of its kind to provide a brief overview of the adversarial examples on Chinese texts as a result of the language difference. Finally, we summarize this study by providing directions for future research.

Keywords: Adversarial attack · Adversarial defense · Natural language processing · Deep neural network

1 Introduction

As part of the emerging artificial intelligence technologies, deep neural network models have become an established paradigm in natural language processing (NLP) and enabled a variety of applications such as news classification, text entailment, machine translation, sentiment analysis, and question and answer systems [1]. Meanwhile, these models may become vulnerable to the security threats from adversarial examples due to the underlying nature of high-dimensional input space, local linearity, weak robustness, and difficulty of interpretability [2]. An adversarial example is a designed instance that confuses a neural network model to output incorrect results with high confidence by applying small indistinguishable perturbations to the original examples. In NLP context, adversarial attacks and defenses are usually studied with sequential textual data. Because of the major challenges from lexical, syntactic, grammatical, semantic constraints, as

Y. Xu et al. (Eds.): ML4CS 2022, LNCS 13655, pp. 409–424, 2023.
https://doi.org/10.1007/978-3-031-20096-0_31

well as discrete and non-differentiable text input spaces, greater risks are incurred in NLP compared to traditional image processing domain. Consequently, these adversarial examples can be applied to attack NLP systems thus resulting in significant security issues to stakeholders. On the other hand, adversarial examples can also serve as input to test the vulnerability and adversarial robustness of NLP models such that they can be improved before implementation and deployment. Since adversarial examples play an important role in evaluating the robustness of NLP models and ensuring system security, substantial amount of research has focused on it.

In order to summarize the research progress in the field and provide directions for future exploration, this paper systematically reviews the literature in the domain of textual adversarial attack and defense. Compared with existing review articles [3, 4], this work contributes to the body of knowledge by:

1) including the most recent studies especially in the last one or two years;
2) incorporating studies and models on NLP in both Chinese and English to ensure the completeness of the review;
3) providing analysis on both similarities and differences from various attack and defense methods.

2 Preliminary

2.1 Definition of Adversarial Example

Without loss of generality, a neural network model can be represented by $F : X \to Y$ where X denotes an N-dimensional example space and Y denotes the set of example labels. Suppose F is a classifier, and for a given testing example $x \in X$, the adversarial example x^* can be expressed as:

$$x^* = x + \delta_x \ and \ \|\delta_x\|_p < \varepsilon \tag{1}$$

$$F(x^*) \neq F(x) \ or \ F(x^*) = t \tag{2}$$

$$\|\delta_x\|_p = \sqrt[p]{\sum_{n=1}^{N} |x_n^* - x_n|^p} \tag{3}$$

In Eq. (1), δ_x denotes the perturbation and ε is an upper bound of its size. And t in Eq. (2) denotes a category other than the ground truth y, x_n in Eq. (3) refers to the *n-th* dimensional component of x, and $\| \cdot \|_p$ is the "length" of the vector parametrization l_p, where the common values of p are 1, 2, and ∞.

2.2 Common Tasks and Datasets

Natural language processing involves numerous tasks, which can be divided into four categories according to the task level: resource construction, basic tasks, application tasks, and application systems. The current textual adversarial tasks are mainly focused on the application tasks level and Table 1 lists the common tasks of adversarial attack and defense, the datasets, and the evaluation metrics. It is worth noting that input completeness is a key property of the task, determining whether the input information provides complete information semantically, and in turn is directly related to the model creativity and task difficulty.

Table 1. Common tasks and datasets for textual adversary.

Tasks	Type	Input property	Common datasets	Metrics
Text classification (TC)	Text to label	Complete	AG News, DBpedia	ACC
Sentiment analysis (SA)	Text to label	Complete	IMDB, SST, Yelp	ACC
Neural machine translation (NMT)	Text to text	Complete	WMT	BLEU
Dialogue system	Text to text	Incomplete	SQuAD, WebQA	BLEU, ROUGE
Summary generation	Text to text	Complete	LCSTS	ROUGE
Natural language inference (NLI)	Text to label	Complete	SNLI	ACC
Named entity recognition (NER)	Text to label	Complete	CLUENER	F value

2.3 Adversarial Example Quality Assessment

To evaluate the textual adversarial tasks, the metrics consider not only the accuracy of the target prediction, but also the semantic similarity between the adversarial examples and the normal ones. Since the textual data space is discrete, the current similarity measures are based on the word embedding space. Consequently, the similarity measures mainly include:

Cosine Similarity: For textual data, the correlation between two words can be measured by the cosine of the angle between their word embedding vectors A and B. As shown in Eq. (4), A_i and B_i represent the components of vectors A and B, respectively.

$$\cos\theta = \frac{\sum_{i=1}^{n} A_i \times B_i}{\sqrt{\sum_{i=1}^{n} (A_i)^2} \times \sqrt{\sum_{i=1}^{n} (B_i)^2}} \tag{4}$$

Euclidean Distance: The Euclidean distance is the linear distance between the word vectors.

Word Movers Distance (WMD): The Word Movers Distance [5] is defined as the minimum distance required to move all words p_i in document P to all words q_j in document Q. This is shown in Eq. (5) below, where T denotes the distance weight between words and d denotes the Euclidean distance between words p_i and q_j.

$$WMD(P, Q) = \sum_{i,j=0}^{M,N} T_{i,j} \times d(p_i, q_j) \tag{5}$$

In addition to the automatic evaluation metrics above, manual assessment is also supplementary tool that can measure the quality of the adversarial examples in terms of its fluency, coherence, consistency, and logic.

2.4 Textual Adversarial Example Classification

As shown in Fig. 1, textual adversarial examples can be classified into character-level, word-level, sentence-level and combined multi-level according to the granularity of the perturbation applied to the textual data. Particularly, an example involving multiple word substitutions can be considered as a phrase-level example.

In the meantime, the type of attacks can be categorized as white-box, grey-box, and black-box depending on the adversary's level of knowledge on the target model, and targeted or untargeted with regard to whether or not the output is designed.

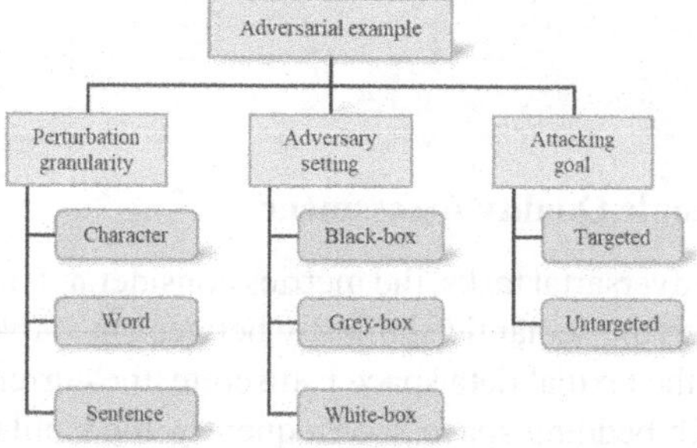

Fig. 1. Categorization on adversarial examples generating methods.

3 Textual Adversarial Attack

3.1 Character Level

Character-level textual adversarial attacks are relatively simple theoretically and can be performed efficiently, thus they are quite common to be applied in application tasks such as text sentiment classification. Gao et al. [6] propose the DeepWordBug attack method in the scenario of black-box such that it defines a scoring function to determine the "important words" that may be manipulated in the text. Then these "important words" are perturbed constrained by a given Levenshtein distance. Experimental results on the IMDB movie review dataset have demonstrated that the classification accuracy of the model is reduced by approximately 70%.

In recent years, pre-trained models, e.g. BERT with fine-tuning operations have emerged as a new paradigm for natural language processing tasks. He et al. [7] point out that pre-trained models in the black-box setting are also subject to adversarial example attacks. As shown in Fig. 2, the approach proposed by He et al. has two phases: firstly, the adversary obtains the query-prediction pair from the target model by producing an input query example. Then, a replica of the target model is locally reconstructed based on the query-prediction pair as an "extracted model". Second, the adversary develops adversarial examples on the local white-box "extracted model" by 1) identifying the token with the largest gradient in the original example input sequence and considering it as the token with the largest information, 2) generating natural adversarial examples through characters misspelling. Because of the transferability property, the adversarial examples from the "extracted model" are capable of attacking the original target model.

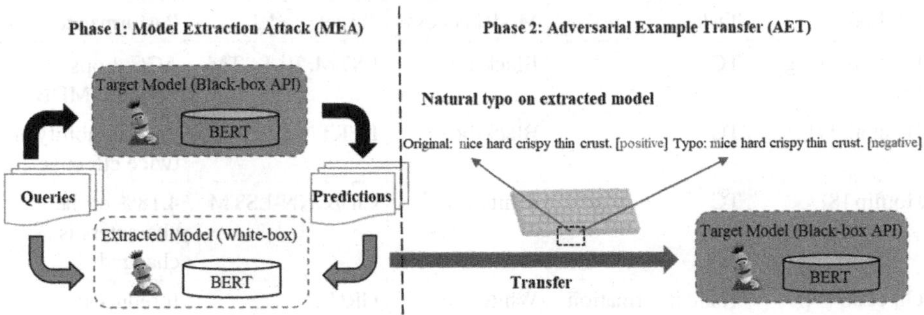

Fig. 2. The overview of black-box attack on BERT model.

In the settings of white-box, Ebrahimi et al. [8] propose a gradient-based HotFlip attack method that applies a unique thermal representation of text and transfers operations such as insertion and deletion of characters as vectors in the input space. Thus, the loss can be estimated by directional derivatives, using a bundle-based search algorithm to find the optimal perturbation operation. Gil et al. [9] develop a new distillation model with knowledge from the optimization on white-box models, and generate adversarial examples 19–39 times faster by applying HotFlip on it.

Neural machine translation tasks are also considered as one of the primary targets for textual adversarial attacks. Ebrahimi et al. [10] design the FIDS-W white-box attack model where four operators on characters including alteration, deletion, insertion, and swapping are performed to generate adversarial examples. Furthermore, various types of adversarial examples are also combined based on the proportion of each operation in the natural noise.

3.2 Word Level

Black-Box. To ensure the lexical and syntactic correctness with semantic similarity of the generated adversarial examples, Ren et al. [11] develop a probability weighted word saliency (PWWS) attack method based on synonym substitution. This method is designed specifically for text classification tasks, and the alternative dataset is constructed by WordNet synonym network. Similarly, Jin et al. [12] successfully attacked models such as BERT by using the TextFooler method on text classification and entailment tasks. It ranks the words by calculating word importance scores I_{w_i}, as shown in Eq. (6). Furthermore, the cosine similarity between each word and the candidate in embedding space is calculated, and the top n synonyms are chosen to replace the original one sequentially, until the model classification becomes incorrect. Emmery et al. [13] also use BERT as a masked language model to generate words for replacement purpose and apply the dropout technique in order to avoid semantic bias.

Table 2. Summary of the attributes from various attack methods.

Method	Task	Model access	Target model	Performance
DeepWordbug [6]	TC	Black-box	LSTM, Bi-LSTM	ACC drops to 26% on IMDB
He et al. [7]	TC	Black-box	BERT	Transferability is twice effective
Hotflip [8]	TC	White-box	CharCNN-LSTM	4.18% of the characters is changed
Gil et al. [9]	Toxic information detection	White-box	GRU	It reduces generation time by 19x-39x
FIDS-W [10]	NMT	White-box	CNN	Change one word in a translation
PWWS [11]	TC	Black-box	CNN, Bi-LSTM	ACC is down by 81.1%, 82.9%, respectively on IMDB
TEXTFOOLER [12]	TC, NLI	Black-box	WordCNN, WordLSTM, BERT	ACC is down by 90%, 87.5%, 81.7% respectively on AG
Lexical replacement [13]	Gender prediction	Black-box	Logistic Regression, N-Gram	The accuracy drops to 0

(continued)

Table 2. (*continued*)

Method	Task	Model access	Target model	Performance
Attention and local sensitivity hash [14]	TC	Black-box	BERT, LSTM	75% reduction in queries
WSLS [15]	NMT	Black-box	RNN, Transformer	BELU drops to 36.71%, 41.55%, respectively
Language and position related attack [16]	NMT	Black-box	Transformer	BELU drops to 17.4%
For word sense disambiguation [17]	NMT	Black-box	Transformer, LSTM, ConvS2S	Grammar error rate is 1.04%
AdvGen [18]	NMT	White-box	Transformer	BLEU is improved by 2.8 on Chinese-English translation
Iterative approximation [19]	TC	White-box	CNN, RNN	The attack success rate on IMDB is 96.12%, 99.09%

Typically, to search for the optimal solution in a huge space while maintaining the semantic consistency or similarity is a NP-hard problem. Maheshwary et al. [14] adopt both attention mechanism and locality sensitive hashing (LSH) technique to reduce the number of queries in the black-box scenario where LSH is designed to find the nearest neighbors in high-dimensional space. In this paper, for a given input vector ***m***, its hash *h*(***m***) is computed based on a random projection approach, and similar vectors are able to obtain the same hash with high probability. Thus the nearest candidate can be found in a timely fashion.

$$I_{w_i} = \begin{cases} p(y_{true}\,|\,x) - p(y_{true}\,|\,x_{\backslash w_i}) \quad if\ F(x) = F(x_{\backslash w_i}) = y_{true} \\ (p(y_{true}\,|\,x) - p(y_{true}\,|\,x_{\backslash w_i})) + p(\bar{y}\,|\,x_{\backslash w_i}) - (p(\bar{y}\,|\,x) \\ if\ F(x) = y_{true}, F(x_{\backslash w_i}) = \bar{y}\ and\ y_{true} \neq \bar{y} \end{cases} \tag{6}$$

Zhang et al. [15] propose a black-box attack method called Word Saliency speedup Local Search (WSLS) for neural machine translation tasks. It is based on the word saliency to facilitate the filtering and searching process on local words replacement, and is able to skip the locations leading to ineffectiveness of the attack. The experimental results demonstrate that the NMT models have been attacked offline successfully, as well as the online translators such as Baidu and Bing. In addition, Zeng et al. [16] observe that it is more efficient to focus on the source language than the target language, and also the front positions of target sentences or their counterparts in source sentences than other positions. Since Word Sense Disambiguation (WSD) is a common source of translation errors in NMT, attacks can be implemented by modifying and/or inserting adjectives before polysemous words in sentences [17].

White-Box. Under the white-box condition, Cheng et al. [18] study the gradient-based adversarial example generation method AdvGen for the NMT tasks specifically. The adversarial example $x*$ is obtained from the following Eq. (7), and the optimal solution can be determined by a greedy strategy such that the adversarial examples are evaluated through the translation loss of the benign inputs.

$$\{x^* \mid R(x^*, x) \leq \varepsilon, \arg\max J(x^*, y_{true}; \theta)\} \tag{7}$$

Meng et al. [19] adopt an iterative approach to estimate the decision boundary of a deep neural network model. Inspired by geometry, this method performs word replacement in the original text example in the direction of the line between the current text vector and the nearest point on the decision boundary.

3.3 Sentence Level

For the Machine Reading Comprehension (MRC) tasks, Lin et al. [20] observe that due to the general statistical bias on MRC models, novel language models such as BERT, ALBERT, and RoBERTa can be successfully attacked on the RACE dataset by simply replacing one of the incorrect alternative options with a "magnet option". The "magnet option" is the irrelevant option with high interference score in the RACE dataset. Wang et al. [21] propose a Controlled Adversarial Text Generation (CAT-Gen) model based on attribute loss where the attributes in the original example are replaced by controlled attributes with unrelated labels. Jia et al. [22] develop the ADDSENT adversarial sentence generation method, as illustrated in Fig. 3, with four steps.

For targeted attacks, Wang et al. [23] study the adversarial attack method T3 on general NLP tasks. T3 converts the discrete text data into a continuous space by using a tree-structure-based autoencoder to optimize perturbations, and then applies a tree-structure-based decoder to normalize the correctness of the grammar. This approach achieves almost 100% attack success rate on the BERT model in a white-box setting from their experiments.

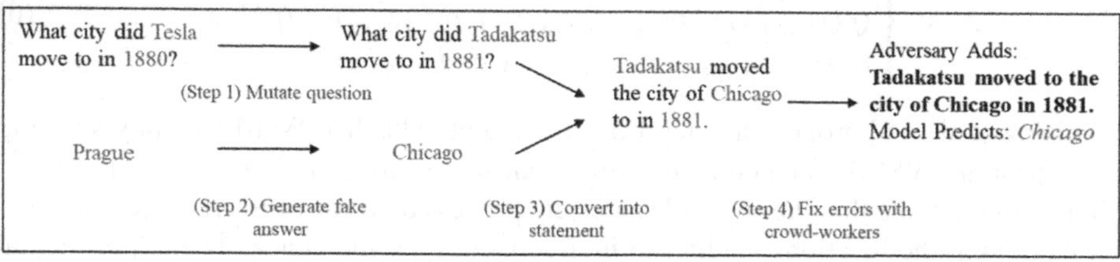

Fig. 3. An illustration of adversarial examples generation.

3.4 Multi-level Combinations

Multi-level combined attacks generally refer to the simultaneous adversarial attacks with various granularities on the target model, which are more common in cross-model and multilingual scenarios. Tan et al. [24] develop two adversarial example generation methods for word-level and phrase-level attacks on multilingual models, respectively. Both methods adopt translations from bilingual dictionaries as replacement schemes and combine two adversarial examples as training examples. The specific information of different attack methods is listed in Table 2.

4 Textual Adversarial Defense

4.1 Robust Encoding

To protect from character-level adversarial example attacks, Belinkov et al. [25] propose a word representation method where the average embedding of all characters of a given word is considered as its embedding vector. For NMT tasks, this method provides significant immunity to perturbations from character disorder. However, it fails to defend against attacks with unknown characters, e.g., spelling errors from adjacent keys on the keyboard. Wang et al. [26] design a word-level defense model SEM (Synonym Encoding Method) for synonym substitution-based attacks. The method inserts an encoder before the input layer of the target model such that each synonym family is mapped onto a unique vector. Experimental results in this study demonstrate its effectiveness against synonym substitution and other associated transferable attacks.

4.2 Randomization

Randomization is another common dimension for adversarial defense. Zhou et al. [27] develop a randomized defense method based upon Dirichlet Neighborhood Ensemble (DNE). During the training, the DNE generates embedding vectors for each word from a convex hull of every single word and its synonyms. Consequently, the virtual sentences can be constructed and expanded further by the training data. It has been observed that the model's performance against adversarial attacks by synonym substitution is significantly improved after training. Bao et al. [28] propose the Anomaly Detection with Frequency-Aware Randomization (ADFAR) defense method particularly for the pre-trained language model by randomized replacing the examples based on word frequency. Furthermore, an anomaly detector is also trained before the randomization process such that only anomalous examples determined by the detector are randomized during inference phase. Experimental outcomes show that the robustness of the pre-trained language model is improved without incurring longer inference time and weaker generalization performance.

4.3 Adversarial Training

Adversarial training is the process during which a neural network model is trained by combining specific adversarial examples with the original benign inputs as an augmented dataset. After the adversarial training, the robustness of the model is significantly

Table 3. Summary of the attributes from various defense methods.

Category	Method	Task	Granularity
Robust encoding	Average Embedding [25]	NML	Character
	SEM [26]	TC	Word
Randomization	DNE-based randomization [27]	TC, NLI	Word
	ADFAR [28]	TC, NLI	Word
Adversarial training	AMDA [29]	TC	Word
	Gradient projection Adversarial training [30]	TC	Word
Adversarial detection	FGWS-based detection [31]	TC	Word, phrase
	BERT-Defense [32]	Sentence recovery	Character, word
	InfoBERT [33]	NLI, QA	Word
	DARCY [34]	TC	Word, phrase
Verifiable Defense	WordDP [35]	TC	Word, phrase
	Based on random smoothing [36]	TC	Word, phrase
	Based on LiRPA [37]	N/A	N/A

enhanced while the generalization performance over benign inputs is maintained. Therefore, adversarial training becomes one of the most common means of defense and the focus of pertinent work in the literature.

Adversarial data augmentation (ADA) is widely used in the adversarial training process. Si et al. [29] design the Adversarial and Mixup Data Augmentation (AMDA) method, where the training example pairs are linearly interpolated to develop the new virtual samples, i.e., the adversarial samples. When the mix-up is performed, it combined the hidden representations on the upper layers of BERT model. The results show that the robustness of the pre-trained language model is improved under strong adversarial attacks.

In order to enhance the efficiency of adversarial example generation during the training process, Wang et al. [30] develop a fast gradient projection approach such that the optimal substitution word is determined by the projected size of each candidate for replacement in the gradient direction. Experiments show that the generation is about 20 times faster compared to other methods.

4.4 Adversarial Detection

Mozes et al. [31] propose an adversarial example detection method based on word frequency variation by calculating the frequencies of both original words and candidates in the training set. Then a Bayesian hypothesis testing is carried out to compare them statistically. When anomalies are detected, pre-trained masked language models are used to recover the normal examples depending on the contextual information [32, 33]. Le et al. [34] develop the DARCY, a generic trigger detection-based and active defense model, to capture potential attacks by searching and injecting multiple trapdoors in the target model. The classification accuracy has reached 99% from the experiments.

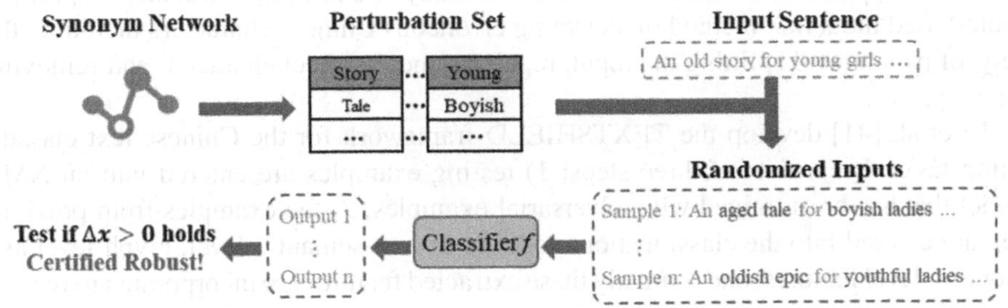

Fig. 4. A pipeline of the robustness certification approach.

4.5 Certified Defense

Certified defense indicates that the robustness of the target model can be proved theoretically under particular constraints. Given certain input perturbations, to limit the neural network outputs has become an important philosophy for certified defense models. Wang et al. [35] develop the WordDP framework from the exponential mechanism such that the robustness can be proved by using the randomness of differential privacy during inference. Ye et al. [36] establish a random set based on stochastic smoothing techniques, where a new classifier is trained by replacing input sentences with random words. Figure 4 illustrates the steps on the robustness certification. Xu et al. [37] propose an automatic framework for perturbation analysis on a given neural network structure based on the linear relaxation-based perturbation analysis (LiRPA) technique. The details of different defense methods are listed in Table 3.

5 Adversarial Examples on Chinese Texts

5.1 Adversarial Attack on Chinese Text

As a result of the unique sparsity, multiple meanings of a given word, and homophones in Chinese language, the techniques in terms of processing textual data such as word segmentation and semantic understanding will be different from English. Wang et al. [38] propose the WordHanding method to obtain the importance score of each word and replace it with homophones accordingly. Cheng et al. [39] develop the WordChange attack method, which splits the keywords and inserts extra words simultaneously. Moreover, this work also explores perturbation methods such as the substitution between the words pronounced with different tongue positions, and homophones. Under the black-box setting, the WordChange approach reduces the classification accuracy of the LSTM model by 48%.

5.2 Adversarial Defense on Chinese Text

Similar to the defense on English textual adversarial examples, detection-based methods can also be applied on Chinese text. As the first study of this kind, Yeh et al. [40] propose a rule-based induction method on detecting erroneous Chinese characters including the steps of parsing and splitting the input, repairing the incorrect character, and removing the copy.

Li et al. [41] develop the TEXTSHIELD framework for the Chinese text classification tasks. It consists of three steps: 1) testing examples are entered into an NMT model that has been trained with adversarial examples, 2) the examples from previous step are entered into the classification model to extract semantic-level, glyph-level and phonetic-level features, and 3) finally these extracted features are incorporated to regular categories.

6 Discussion

6.1 Reason of Adversarial Vulnerability

The study on theories and practices pertaining to adversarial example attacks is still a primary concern among IT professionals and researchers. Szegedy et al. [2] provide possible explanations that each individual neuron in a neural network does not contain semantic information and a discontinuity may exist on the mapping between inputs and outputs. Goodfellow et al. [42] argue that the local linearity of a neural network leads to its vulnerability, and the adversarial example can be considered as a characteristic of the high dimensional dot product. Alternatively, Ilyas et al. [43] consider the adversarial example as a natural feature, while such features are less robust regarding the chosen similarity measures.

It is widely accepted that the adversarial examples take advantage of the vulnerabilities in the models or algorithms, thus may result in incorrect decisions. Therefore, the exploration on the decision boundaries and the interpretability of AI algorithms is a possible direction for future research.

6.2 Generality of Methods

Despite the transferability capability of adversarial examples, the majority of the attack and defense methods cannot be applied everywhere on any model. For example, the sentence-level attacks may not be carried out effectively at word-level and the attacks against LSTM models may work on BERT models with lower performance. Although certified defense methods are capable of achieving high generality to a certain extent, high-quality input examples are required while satisfying the model assumptions, resulting in the limit of applicability. Therefore, another direction worth exploring is the existence of a generalized framework and the way to design it.

6.3 Adversarial Examples in Real-World Scenarios

In real-world adversarial scenarios, examples are not only one single modality, but include image, speech etc. Furthermore, effectiveness and efficiency will also become extremely critical in real-time online systems. The methods and models in the current literature are mostly based on ideal conditions or testing on offline datasets without taking feedbacks from the real-world systems. Hence, to implement adversarial attacks and defenses in real-world scenarios becomes a promising avenue to pursue.

7 Conclusion

The study on textual adversarial attack and defense is an emerging area that spans the domains of NLP and artificial intelligence security. In this paper, we systematically review the relevant literature and discuss the challenges for future research. Since a complete theory to explain the existence of adversarial examples and the relationships with deep neural networks has not been fully developed, the security issues on NLP systems incur high complexity. The stakeholders would benefit from this future avenue of research with the explosive growth and availability of massive datasets, the ongoing optimization on the pre-trained model, and the improvement on both computational resources and AI theory development.

Acknowledgements. The work is supported by the National Natural Science Foundation of China under Grant 61972148.

References

1. LeCun, Y., Bengio, Y., Hinton, G.: Deep learning. Nature **521**(7553), 436–444 (2015)
2. Szegedy, C., Zaremba, W., Sutskever, I., et al.: Intriguing properties of neural networks. In: Proceedings of the 2nd International Conference on Learning Representations, pp. 1–10 (2014)
3. Wenqi, W., Lina, W., Benxiao, T., et al.: Towards a robust deep neural network in text domain: a survey. arXiv preprint arXiv:1902.07285 (2019)
4. Zhang, W., Sheng, Q., Alhazmi, A., et al.: Adversarial attacks on deep-learning models in natural language processing: a survey. ACM Trans. Intell. Syst. Technol. **11**(3), 24:1–24:41 (2020)
5. Kusner, M., Sun, Y., Kolkin, N., et al.: From word embeddings to document distances. In: Proceedings of the International Conference on Machine Learning, Lille, pp. 957–966. ACM (2015)
6. Gao, J., Lanchantin, J., Soffa, M.L., et al.: Black-box generation of adversarial text sequences to evade deep learning classifiers. In: Proceedings of the 2018 IEEE Security and Privacy Workshops, San Francisco, pp. 50–56. IEEE (2018)
7. He, X., Lyu, L., Xu, Q., et al.: Model extraction and adversarial transferability, your BERT is vulnerable!. In: Proceedings of the 2021 Conference of the North American Chapter of the Association for Computational Linguistics: Human Language Technologies, pp. 2006–2012. NAACL (2021)

8. Ebrahimi, J., Rao, A., Lowd, D., et al.: HotFlip: white-box adversarial examples for text classification. In: Proceedings of the 56th Annual Meeting of the Association for Computational Linguistics, Melbourne, pp. 31–36. ACL (2018)
9. Gil, Y., Chai, Y., Gorodissky, O., et al.: White-to black: efficient distillation of black-box adversarial attacks. In: Proceedings of the 2019 Conference of the North American Chapter of the Association for Computational Linguistics: Human Language Technologies, Minneapolis, pp. 1373–1379. NAACL (2019)
10. Ebrahimi, J., Lowd, D., Dou, D.: On adversarial examples for character-level neural machine translation. In: Proceedings of the 27th International Conference on Computational Linguistics, Santa Fe, pp. 653–663. ACM (2018)
11. Ren, S., Deng, Y., He, K., et al.: Generating natural language adversarial examples through probability weighted word saliency. In: Proceedings of the 57th Conference of the Association for Computational Linguistics, Florence, pp. 1085–1097. ACL (2019)
12. Jin, D., Jin, Z., Zhou, J.T., et al.: Is BERT really robust? A strong baseline for natural language attack on text classification and entailment. In: Proceedings of the Thirty-Fourth AAAI Conference on Artificial Intelligence, New York, pp. 8018–8025. AAAI (2020)
13. Emmery, C., Kadar, A., Chrupala, G.: Adversarial stylometry in the wild: transferable lexical substitution attacks on author profiling. In: Proceedings of the 16th Conference of the European Chapter of the Association for Computational Linguistics: Main Volume, pp. 2388–2402. ACL (2021)
14. Maheshwary, R., Maheshwary, S., Pudi, V.: A strong baseline for query efficient attacks in a black box setting. In: Proceedings of the 2021 Conference on Empirical Methods in Natural Language Processing, Punta Cana, pp. 8396–8409. ACL (2021)
15. Zhang, X., Zhang, J., Chen, Z., et al.: Crafting adversarial examples for neural machine translation. In: Proceedings of the 59th Annual Meeting of the Association for Computational Linguistics, pp. 1967–1977. ACL (2021)
16. Zeng, Z., Xiong, D.: An empirical study on adversarial attack on NMT: languages and positions matter. In: Proceedings of the 59th Annual Meeting of the Association for Computational Linguistics, pp. 454–460. ACL (2021)
17. Emelin, D., Titov, I., Sennrich, R.: Detecting word sense disambiguation biases in machine translation for model-agnostic adversarial attacks. In: Proceedings of the 2020 Conference on Empirical Methods in Natural Language Processing, pp. 7635–7653. ACL (2020)
18. Cheng, Y., Jiang, L., Macherey, W.: Robust neural machine translation with doubly adversarial inputs. In: Proceedings of the 57th Conference of the Association for Computational Linguistics, Florence, pp. 4324–4333. ACL (2019)
19. Meng, Z., Wattenhofer, R.: A geometry-inspired attack for generating natural language adversarial examples. In: Proceedings of the 28th International Conference on Computational Linguistics, Barcelona, pp. 6679–6689. ACM (2020)
20. Lin, J., Zou, J., Ding, N.: Using adversarial attacks to reveal the statistical bias in machine reading comprehension models. In: Proceedings of the 59th Annual Meeting of the Association for Computational Linguistics and the 11th International Joint Conference on Natural Language Processing, pp. 333–342. ACL (2021)
21. Wang, T., Wang, X., Qin, Y., et al.: CAT-Gen: improving robustness in NLP models via controlled adversarial text generation. In: Proceedings of the 2020 Conference on Empirical Methods in Natural Language Processing, pp. 5141–5146. ACL (2020)
22. Jia, R., Liang, P.: Adversarial examples for evaluating reading comprehension systems. In: Proceedings of the 2017 Conference on Empirical Methods in Natural Language Processing, Copenhagen, pp. 2021–2031. ACL (2017)
23. Wang, B., Pei, H., Pan, B., et al.: T3: tree autoencoder constrained adversarial text generation for targeted attack. In: Proceedings of the 2020 Conference on Empirical Methods in Natural Language Processing, pp. 6134–6150. ACL (2020)

24. Tan, S., Joty, S.R.: Code-mixing on sesame street: dawn of the adversarial polyglots. In: Proceedings of the 2021 Conference of the North American Chapter of the Association for Computational Linguistics: Human Language Technologies, pp. 3596–3616. NAACL (2021)
25. Belinkov, Y., Bisk, Y.: Synthetic and natural noise both break neural machine translation. In: Proceedings of the 6th International Conference on Learning Representations, Vancouver, pp. 1–13. ACM (2018)
26. Wang, X., Jin, H., Yang, Y., et al.: Natural language adversarial defense through synonym encoding. In: Proceedings of the Thirty-Senventh Conference on Uncertainty in Artificial Intelligence. AUAI (2021)
27. Zhou, Y., Zheng, X., Hsieh, C.J., et al.: Defense against synonym substitution-based adversarial attacks via Dirichlet neighborhood ensemble. In: Proceedings of the 59th Annual Meeting of the Association for Computational Linguistics and the 11th International Joint Conference on Natural Language Processing, pp. 5482–5492. ACL (2021)
28. Bao, R., Wang, J., Zhao, H.: Defending pre-trained language models from adversarial word substitution without performance sacrifice. In: Proceedings of the Findings of the Association for Computational Linguistics: ACL/IJCNLP 2021, pp. 3248–3258. ACL (2021)
29. Si, C., Zhang, Z., Qi, F., et al.: Better robustness by more coverage: adversarial and mixup data augmentation for robust finetuning. In: Proceedings of the Findings of the Association for Computational Linguistics: ACL/IJCNLP 2021, pp. 1569–1576. ACL (2021)
30. Wang, X., Yang, Y., Deng, Y., et al.: Adversarial training with fast gradient projection method against synonym substitution based text attacks. In: Proceedings of the Thirty-Fifth AAAI Conference on Artificial Intelligence, pp. 13997–14005. AAAI (2021)
31. Mozes, M., Stenetorp, P., Kleinberg, B., et al.: Frequency-guided word substitutions for detecting textual adversarial examples. In: Proceedings of the 16th Conference of the European Chapter of the Association for Computational Linguistics: Main Volume, pp. 171–186. EACL (2021)
32. Keller, Y., Mackensen, J., Eger, S.: BERT-defense: a probabilistic model based on BERT to combat cognitively inspired orthographic adversarial attacks. In: Proceedings of the Findings of the Association for Computational Linguistics: ACL/IJCNLP 2021, pp. 1616–1629. ACL (2021)
33. Wang, B., Wang, S., Cheng, Y., et al.: InfoBERT: improving robustness of language models from an information theoretic perspective. In: Proceedings of the 9th International Conference on Learning Representation (2021)
34. Le, T., Park, N., Lee, D.: A sweet rabbit hole by DARCY: using honeypots to detect universal trigger's adversarial attacks. In: Proceedings of the 59th Annual Meeting of the Association for Computational Linguistics and the 11th International Joint Conference on Natural Language Processing, pp. 3831–3844. ACL (2021)
35. Wang, W., Tang, P., Lou, J., et al.: Certified robustness to word substitution attack with differential privacy. In: Proceedings of the 2021 Conference of the North American Chapter of the Association for Computational Linguistics: Human Language Technologies, pp. 1102–1112. NAACL (2021)
36. Ye, M., Gong, C., Liu, Q.: SAFER: a structure-free approach for certified robustness to adversarial word substitution. In: Proceedings of the 58th Annual Meeting of the Association for Computational Linguistics, pp. 3465–3475. ACL (2020)
37. Xu, K., Shi, Z., Zhang, H., et al.: Automatic perturbation analysis for scalable certified robustness and beyond. In: Proceedings of the Advances in Neural Information Processing Systems 33: Annual Conference on Neural Information Processing Systems 2020. MIT Press (2020)
38. Wang, W., Wang, R., Wang, L., Tang, B.: Adversarial examples generation approach for tendency classification on Chinese texts. Ruan Jian Xue Bao/J. Softw. **30**(8), 2415–2427 (2019)

39. Cheng, N., Chang, G., Gao, H., et al.: WordChange: adversarial examples generation approach for Chinese text classification. IEEE Access **8**, 79561–79572 (2020)
40. Yeh, J.F., Lu, Y.Y., Lee, C.H., et al.: Chinese word spelling correction based on rule induction. In: Proceedings of the Third CIPS-SIGHAN Joint Conference on Chinese Language Processing, Wuhan, pp. 139–145. ACL (2014)
41. Li, J., Du, T., Ji, S., et al.: TextShield: robust text classification based on multimodal embedding and neural machine translation. In: Proceedings of the 29th USENIX Security Symposium, pp. 1381–1398. USENIX Association (2020)
42. Ian, J.G., Jonathon, S., Christian, S.: Expaining and harnessing adversarial examples. In 3rd International Conference on Learning Representations, San Diego. ICLR (2015)
43. Ilyas, A., Santurkar, S., Tsipras, D., et al.: Adversarial examples are not bugs, they are features. In: Proceedings of the Advances in Neural Information Processing Systems 32: Annual Conference on Neural Information Processing Systems 2019, Vancouver, pp. 125–136. MIT Press (2019)

A Novel Security Scheme for Mobile Healthcare in Digital Twin

Nansen Wang, Wenbao Han, and Wei Ou(✉)

School of Cyberspace Security, Hainan University, Haikou, China
ouwei@hainanu.edu.cn

Abstract. The rapid development of mobile devices and 5G networks has promoted the widespread use of mobile healthcare, allowing us to check our health status at any time and from any location, as well as facilitating doctors' analysis of the condition through timely analysis of these data. However, the convenience provided by mobile healthcare has also exposed data security issues. Medical data, for example, is easily leaked, and the collection of patient treatment data lacks standardized management. To address these issues, we designed a mobile medical data security scheme based on Federated Learning and Digital Twin to guarantee medical data security. The scheme consists of a state-aware module and a digital twin module. The state-aware module collects medical data and stores it encrypted to the blockchain, ensuring the security, trustworthiness, and traceability of medical data. The digital twin module uses horizontal federated learning and digital twin to combine data from multiple medical institutions to build a federated model and a patient digital twin model in an iterative process, which solves the problem of "data silos" while ensuring privacy and security, and aids in the improvement of medical solutions and helps improve medical care. We have conducted experiments and evaluations of the techniques adopted in this scheme, verifying the effectiveness and feasibility.

Keywords: Mobile healthcare · Data security · Horizontal federated learning · Digital twin · Blockchain · ShangMi Cryptographic Algorithms (SM)

1 Introduction

Mobile healthcare is a technology that provides medical services and information through mobile communication technology. With the rapid development of mobile devices and related technologies, we can collect, share, transmit, process and access remote healthcare data generated in medical services and interact with users through these data. Mobile healthcare realizes comprehensive monitoring of personal health through the integration and sharing of basic medical information, as well as the perfect application of mobile networks, artificial intelligence, big data, and other technologies [1].

Y. Xu et al. (Eds.): ML4CS 2022, LNCS 13655, pp. 425–441, 2023.
https://doi.org/10.1007/978-3-031-20096-0_32

However, mobile healthcare also faces great challenges. One of the most critical issues is ensuring users' privacy and security in mobile healthcare activities and the security of mobile healthcare data. Currently, there are four major problems with mobile healthcare. First is the problem of medical data leakage. Medical institutions do not take sufficient security protection in the transmission, anti-tampering, storage, and use of medical data [2]. Secondly, there is a lack of regulation on medical and patient information collection and use. Medical institutions have not established uniform norms for collecting and storing patients' personal information. Third, the system itself is highlighted by security issues. Fourth, the risk of mobile terminal applications has increased, posing a significant threat to medical data security.

To address the above issues, we designed a mobile healthcare data security scheme based on Federated Learning and Digital Twin. We combined the federated learning with digital twin technology to extend the twin model to a vast domain, federate multiple parties' data, and keep entities in sync with the model in a dynamic, iterative process. The Digital Twin provides a more efficient method of information collection and processing for the medical process and improves the medical staff's degree of control over the information [3]. We have introduced Blockchain technology into the system to ensure the tamper-proof modification and correctness of medical data and realize credibility and traceability. We introduced data encryption in the system to ensure the security of medical information by encrypting medical data and authenticating users through cryptographic algorithms.

2 Related Works

Our proposed security scheme is a framework based on several emerging technologies and algorithms, such as the combination of federated learning and digital twin. Therefore, this section reviews the current work on 1) traditional AI techniques' application in healthcare, 2) federated learning's application in healthcare, and 3) digital twin and related techniques' application in healthcare.

2.1 Application of Traditional AI Technologies in the Medical Field

In recent years, traditional artificial intelligence techniques, such as convolutional neural networks, have made great strides in the medical field. For example, Lijing Wang et al. [4] proposed DEFSI (Deep Learning-Based Epidemic Forecasting with Synthetic Information), an epidemic forecasting framework that integrates the strengths of artificial neural networks and causal methods. Benyun Shi et al. [5] proposed EpiRep, a novel embedding method, to learn node representations of a network by maximizing the likelihood of preserving groups of infected nodes due to the epidemics starting from every single node on the network. Bin Zou et al. [6] investigate the utility of multi-task learning to disease surveillance using Web search data. Fred S. Lu et al. [7] proposed a methodological framework that dynamically combines two distinct influenza tracking techniques, using an ensemble machine learning approach, to achieve improved state-level influenza activity estimates in the United States. Zhonglin Ye et al. [8] modeled the future network evolution results of the networks based on the link prediction algorithm, introducing the future link probabilities between vertices without edges into the network representation learning tasks. Liang Zhao et al. [9] proposed a novel semi-supervised deep learning framework that integrates the strengths of computational epidemiology and social media mining techniques.

2.2 Federated Learning in the Medical Field

Although traditional artificial intelligence technology is widely used in the medical field, with the development of technology and industry, medical institutions are increasingly not satisfied with the application of data from individual institutions. Thus "data silos" problem gradually emerged. At this time, federated learning technology is an excellent solution to this problem. For example, Olivia Choudhury et al. [10] proposed a federated learning framework to learn a global model from distributed health data held locally at different sites. Moreover, it uses a differential privacy mechanism to protect the model from potential privacy attacks further. Hai Jin et al. [11] proposed that the large cluster should be divided into multiple smaller clusters in its geographical area and organized with a BFL. They further proposed CFL, a cross-cluster FL system facilitated by the cross-chain technique. CFL connects multiple BFL clusters, where only a few aggregated updates are transmitted over long distances across clusters, thus improving the system efficiency. Qian Yang et al. [12] proposed a simple yet effective algorithm named Federated Learning on Medical Datasets using Partial Networks (FLOP) that shares only a partial model between the server and clients. Mathieu Andreux et al. [13] proposed a novel federated learning approach for deep learning architectures via the introduction of local-statistic batch normalization (BN) layers, resulting in collaboratively-trained yet center-specific models. Rajesh Kumar et al. [14] proposed a data normalization technique that dealt with data heterogeneity and designed a method to collaboratively train a global model using blockchain technology with federated learning while preserving privacy.

2.3 Digital Twin and Related Technologies in Healthcare and Other Fields

In recent years, the digital twin has also shown excellent adaptability to the healthcare field. The digital twin has been used in many fields, such as healthcare and industrial IoT. For example, Chao Fan et al. [15] present the Disaster City Digital Twin as a unifying paradigm. The four main components of the proposed Digital Twin paradigm include multi-data sensing for data collection, data integration and analytics, multi-actor game-theoretic decision making, and dynamic network analysis. Zhipeng Cai et al. [16] proposed a novel framework for privacy-preserved traffic sharing among taxi companies, which jointly considers participants' privacy, profits, and fairness.

In addition, technologies that are closely related to the digital twin are worth discussing. For example, Huan Yang et al. [17] mainly focuses on the data storage reliability problem in heterogeneous wireless sensor networks. They design an algorithm to jointly optimize data routing and storage node deployment to minimize data delivery and data storage costs. Xu Zheng et al. [18] proposed a privacy-preserved data sharing framework for IIoTs (Industrial Internet of Things). The framework allows data contributors to share their contents upon requests. The uploaded contents will be perturbed to preserve the sensitive status of contributors. The differential privacy is adopted in the perturbation to guarantee privacy preservation.

3 Structure

This system is a scheme designed to solve the security problem of mobile healthcare data. The system collects patients' healthcare data through the data-aware layer and stores them on the blockchain network; the interactive layer analyzes the data, performs horizontal federated learning, and constructs patients' digital twin; the application layer provides healthcare services based on the data and digital twin to predict patients' physical conditions and assist and guide the treatment process. The system is divided into five layers from the bottom up, including the foundation layer, the perception layer, the blockchain management layer, the interaction layer, and the application layer. The architecture of the system is shown in Fig. 1.

Foundation Layer. This layer includes system hardware facilities and operating environment, which are the underlying facilities of the system. Hardware facilities mainly refer to the sensors, computer systems, etc.; operating environment mainly refers to the computer's operating system, etc.

Perception Layer. This layer is mainly responsible for collecting sensor monitoring data and medical data. It is divided into two parts: medical institutions and mobile monitoring. According to the function classification, it mainly includes scene monitoring interface and human health data interface. The perception layer also cleans and pre-processes the collected data.

Blockchain Layer. This layer mainly includes distributed ledger, consensus mechanism, smart contract, etc. The data uploaded by the perception layer is mainly uploaded and stored in the distributed ledger by calling intelligent contracts on the chain through the interface.

Interaction Layer. This layer mainly includes local models, Horizontal Federated Learning, data modeling and model evolution, etc. Trusted medical data from the blockchain layer are trained by horizontal federated learning and used to optimize and adapt digital twin models. This is an iterative process to continuously optimize the federation learning model and the digital twin model with new data.

Application Layer. This layer provides smart applications for users. It includes warning threshold setting, warning and alarm, and access control. Patients can

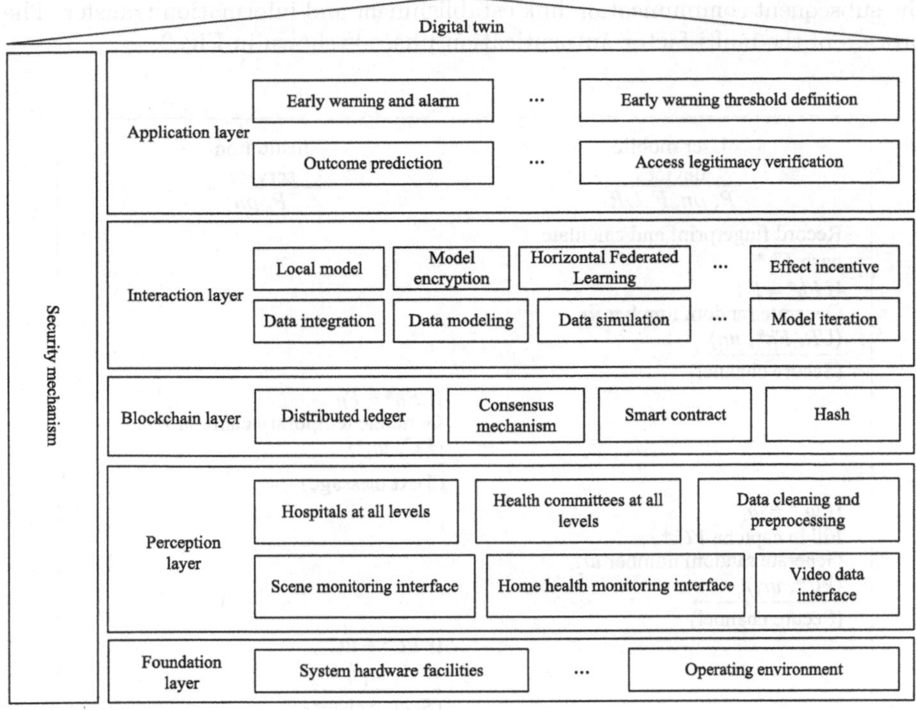

Fig. 1. System structure

view their healthcare data and scientific assessments, and doctors can keep abreast of patients' physical conditions to achieve fine-grained patient safety and health management. The system can set early warning thresholds and will alert when the data reaches the threshold, making predictions about the patient's health so that the doctor can choose the appropriate treatment plan.

4 Module

4.1 Multi-factor Authentication Module

Access control to the medical system is significant because of the high degree of privacy of medical industry-related operations and medical data. To ensure the authenticity and security of their access, users must undergo a rigorous authentication process before gaining access to the system. This system uses multi-factor authentication technology based on user passwords, SMS verification codes, and user fingerprint identification as access control.

In the multi-factor authentication phase, the system mainly identifies the user's fingerprint information and password, as well as verifies the user's phone number by SMS verification code, and ensures the timeliness and continuity of the login phase by utilizing random numbers to lay a good foundation for the subsequent communication link establishment and information transfer. The process of the multi-factor authentication phase is shown in Fig. 2.

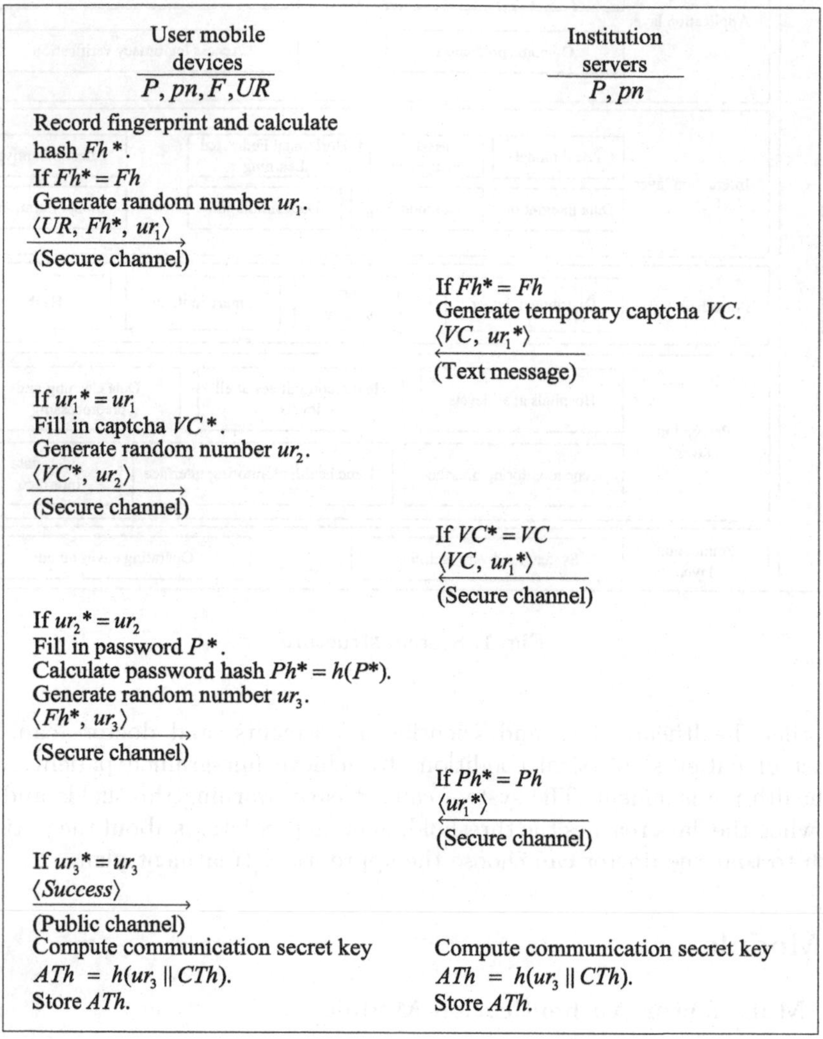

User mobile devices: P, pn, F, UR

Institution servers: P, pn

Record fingerprint and calculate hash Fh^*.
If $Fh^* = Fh$
Generate random number ur_1.
$\langle UR, Fh^*, ur_1 \rangle$ →
(Secure channel)

If $Fh^* = Fh$
Generate temporary captcha VC.
← $\langle VC, ur_1^* \rangle$
(Text message)

If $ur_1^* = ur_1$
Fill in captcha VC^*.
Generate random number ur_2.
$\langle VC^*, ur_2 \rangle$ →
(Secure channel)

If $VC^* = VC$
← $\langle VC, ur_1^* \rangle$
(Secure channel)

If $ur_2^* = ur_2$
Fill in password P^*.
Calculate password hash $Ph^* = h(P^*)$.
Generate random number ur_3.
$\langle Fh^*, ur_3 \rangle$ →
(Secure channel)

If $Ph^* = Ph$
← $\langle ur_1^* \rangle$
(Secure channel)

If $ur_3^* = ur_3$
$\langle Success \rangle$ →
(Public channel)
Compute communication secret key $ATh = h(ur_3 \| CTh)$.
Store ATh.

Compute communication secret key $ATh = h(ur_3 \| CTh)$.
Store ATh.

Fig. 2. Multi-factor authentication phase process

Step 1. After the user's local device UMD receives the user login request, it reminds the user to enter the fingerprint and calculates the extracted fingerprint hash Fh^*. The UMD then calls the fingerprint hash Fh of the registered user from the local trusted execution environment and compares whether Fh^* is equal to Fh. An error message is returned to the user if they are not equal, and the login process is terminated. If equal, a random number ur_1 is generated. The user identifier UR, the extracted fingerprint hash Fh^*, the random number ur_1 and the confirmation message are sent to the institution server IS.

Step 2. After the institution server IS receives the information, it queries the user information by the user identity UR. It compares the fingerprint hash Fh stored on the server with the extracted fingerprint hash Fh^*. If Fh^* is the same as Fh, the server will obtain the user's registered cell phone number pn. The system generates a temporary verification code VC and sends the verification code VC and the random number ur_1^* to the user device UMD via SMS.

Step 3. The user device UMD receives the SMS and extracts the random number ur_1^* and compares it with the locally generated random number ur_1. If ur_1^* is the same as ur_1, the user is reminded to fill in the verification code VC^*. Subsequently, the user device generates a random number ur_2 and sends the verification code VC^* and the random number ur_2 to the institution server IS via a secure channel.

Step 4. After receiving the message, the institution server IS compares the temporary verification code VC with the verification code VC^* input by the user. If it is the same, it returns the random number ur_2^* with the confirmation message to the user device UMD.

Step 5. The user device UMD receives the message, extracts the random number ur_2^*, and compares it with the random number ur_2 generated locally. If it is the same, it reminds the user to enter the private key password P^* and calculates the private key password hash $Ph^* = h(P^*)$. The user device generates the random number ur_3 and sends the private key passphrase hash Ph^* and the random number ur_3 to the institution server IS through a secure channel.

Step 6. After the institutional server IS receives the message, it compares the user password hash Ph stored on the server with the received user password hash Ph^*. If it is the same, the calculation returns the confirmation message with the random number ur_3^* to the user device.

Step 7. The user device UMD receives the message, extracts the random number ur_3^* and compares it with the locally generated random number ur_3. If it is the same, the user is prompted for successful authentication and returns a confirmation message to the server. Subsequently, the user device UMD and the institution server IS use $ATH = h(ur_3 \parallel CTh)$ as the secret communication key in this post-authentication communication and establish the communication link.

4.2 Cryptographic Module

Medical Data Encryption. There has been much concern about the security of medical data. Medical data contains many private user information and must be encrypted at all stages. In terms of encryption algorithms, this system uses SM4 and SM2 algorithms. When the medical system uploads medical data, the data encryption process is as follows: The system initially uses the SM4 algorithm to generate a symmetric key to ensure the security of the previously produced key and store the encrypted medical data in the blockchain. The SM2 algorithm is used. Suppose doctors or patients wish to examine medical data. In that case, they must gain user authorization first, then extract and decrypt the encrypted SM4 key, which they will use to decrypt the medical data and convert it to plaintext for display. The medical data encryption process is shown in Fig. 3.

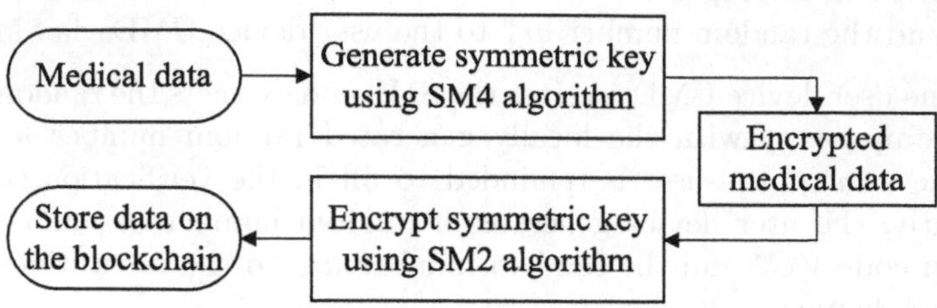

Fig. 3. Encryption process in the Blockchain

Signature of Treatment Results. The doctor needs to treat the patient according to the treatment plan, so it is essential to ensure the accuracy and integrity of the treatment results, which requires the digital signature of the treatment results. The system uses the SM2 elliptic curve algorithm for the digital signature and the SM3 hash algorithm for the message digest. Each doctor in this system holds a private key to identify themselves and a system key generator for signing message digests. Firstly, the results are signed using the SM2 algorithm, and then the message digest is generated using the SM3 algorithm after the doctor proposes a diagnosis. The SM4 algorithm is then used to encrypt the bundled signature and message digest, and the encrypted data are stored on the blockchain. In order for patients to see the feedback, firstly, the system decrypts the SM4 encrypted data with a shared symmetric key to obtain the signed message digest with the message body, then decrypts the digital signature with the corresponding doctor's public key to obtain the message digest, and finally derives the message hash to compare with the known message digest. The digital signature flow is shown in Fig. 4.

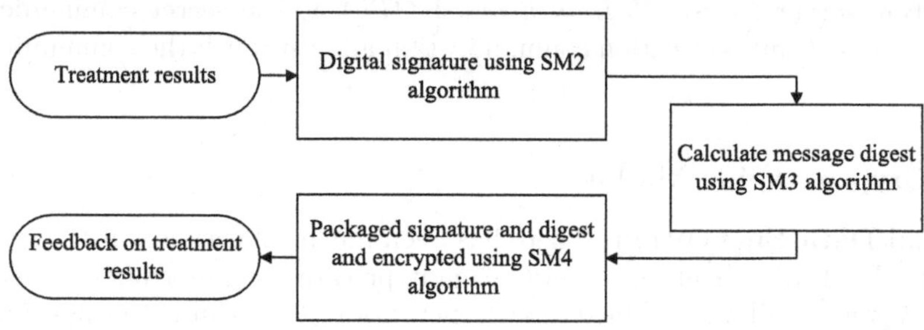

Fig. 4. Signature process

4.3 Blockchain Module

Blockchain is a distributed shared database that uses distributed ledgers, consensus mechanisms, and other technologies. It is built with features like tamper-proofing, traceability, and decentralization and is built using smart contracts, hash encryption, and other technical algorithms. We will use Fisco Bcos as an example to demonstrate the blockchain workflow.

Step 1. The client constructs a transaction containing the sending and receiving addresses, transaction-related data, and transaction signature. The client then sends the transaction to the node via a Channel or RPC Channel.

Step 2. The node determines whether a transaction is legitimate by signature verification upon receipt. If the transaction is legitimate and the first time it is sent, it will be placed in the transaction pool, and if not, it will be discarded. At the same time, the node broadcasts the transaction to all nodes in the network.

Step 3. The nodes will sort the transactions by timestamp order, assemble them into blocks to be consensus, and send them to each node for processing.

Step 4. The node fetches out the transaction from the block upon receipt and invokes the block validator to execute them one by one. The result and status of the transaction execution are returned encapsulated in a transaction receipt.

Step 5. FISCO BCOS generally uses the PBFT algorithm to ensure the consistency of the whole system. After the consensus is reached, the node writes the block and the execution result to the persistent storage and starts a new process round.

The blockchain module flow is shown in Fig. 5.

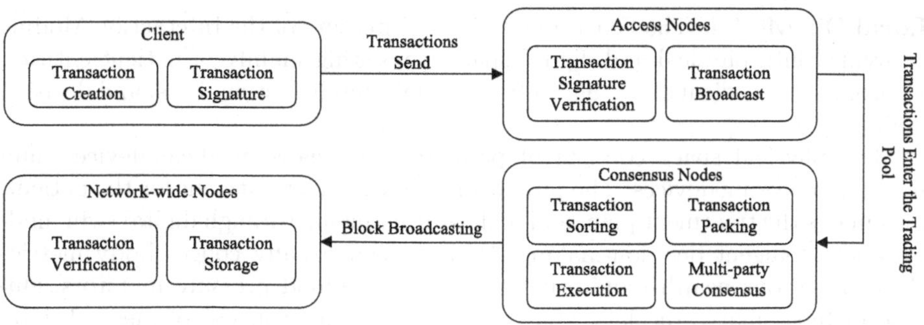

Fig. 5. Blockchain module

4.4 Interaction Module

Modern hospitals and public healthcare institutions use digital twin technology to establish digital twin at the patient and institutional levels and synchronize digital models with the real environment through medical data generated from daily operations, which is an excellent contribution to patient care and treatment. However, for some technical and individual privacy reasons, medical data is often not well communicated between the healthcare institutions, resulting in "data silos". Therefore, this section extends the digital twin from the institution level to the city and even provincial level through the combination of federated learning and digital twin. This allows digital twin to be built and function at the municipal and even provincial level, and protects the privacy of individuals in medical data. The federated twin architecture is shown in Fig. 6.

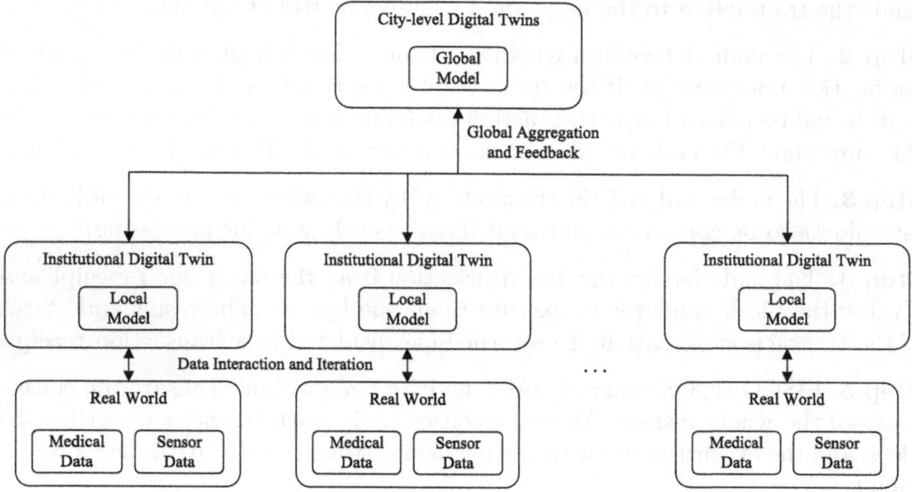

Fig. 6. Federated Twin Model Architecture

Local DT Model. The Federated Twin Architecture of the Interaction Module is divided into physical and digital space, consisting mainly of patient entities, environment, medical data, digital twin models, intelligent analysis, and decision making.

The physical space consists of patients, physicians, medical devices, and health monitoring devices. The physician performs the treatment for the patient, formulates the treatment plan, and makes adjustments through digital twin models and intelligent decision-making. Patients can usually collect body metrics through various health monitoring devices (e.g., blood pressure monitors, glucose meters, smart bracelets, etc.). The digital space consists of medical data, iterative digital twin models, synchronous aggregation and iteration of federated twin, and intelligent analysis components.

The system pre-processes medical data, builds local digital twin models (individual and institutional level) by convolutional neural networks, and uses subsequent medical data and feedback from federated learning for continuous optimization to synchronize physical space mapping to digital space. The system encrypts and uploads the digital twin parameters to the federated learning server for global aggregation and iterative processes.

Global DT Model Aggregation. The federated twin global aggregation process is shown in Fig. 7.

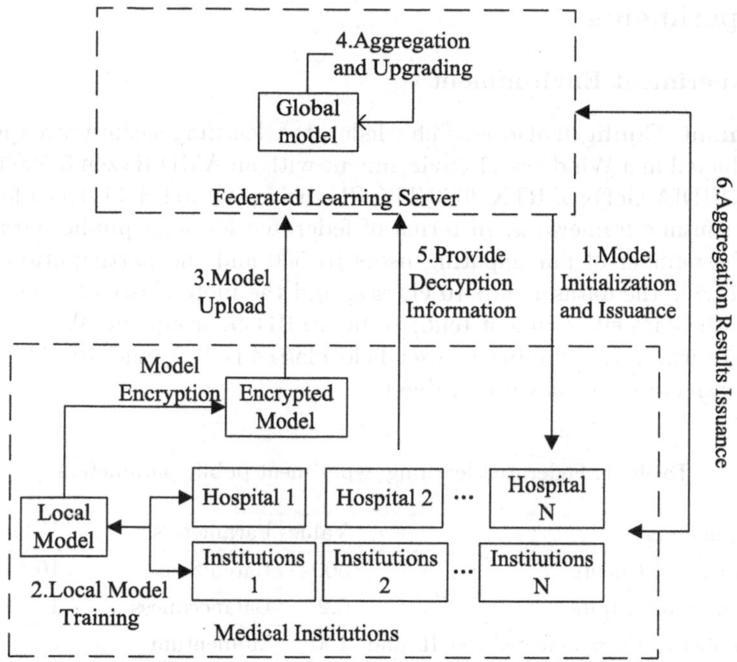

Fig. 7. Federated Twin Global Aggregation

At the beginning of an aggregation round, the Federated Learning Server builds an initial model through pre-training using a public dataset stored on the server. The server then selects a subset of all registered local healthcare institutions to participate in the aggregation and distributes the initial model and other required information [19]. The selected institutions begin model training using local medical data, generating model parameters and encrypting them.

At the same time, the institution uses the local data to train and maintain a local digital twin model (at the individual and institutional levels) via a convolutional neural network. This step does not affect each other with local training. Subsequently, the institution uploads the encrypted model parameters to the server for secure aggregation. After receiving enough model parameters, the server starts the secure aggregation. After successful aggregation, the local institution participating in the aggregation provides the server with enough encrypted information to obtain the aggregation results to optimize and tune the digital twin model maintained locally. The next round of aggregation will begin, an iterative process.

It is worth mentioning that the public dataset used to initialize the model does not contain private information and characteristics of individual citizens.

5 Experiments

5.1 Experiment Environment

Experiment Configurations. The federated learning accuracy experiment was conducted in a Windows 11 environment with an AMD Ryzen 5 5600X CPU and an NVIDIA GeForce RTX 3070 Ti GPU, using Pytorch 1.11.0 as a federated learning runtime framework. In terms of federated learning public parameters, we set the number of participating users to 500 and the participation rate to 0.2. We divide the dataset into 10 classes, and the more classes the user holds, the more the data environment tends to be an IID environment. We mainly test three cases where the number of user-held classes is 1, 5, and 10. The specific public parameters are shown in Table 1.

Table 1. Federated learning experiment public parameters

Parameters	Value	Parameters	Value
Number of Clients	500	Batch Size	10
Participation Rate	0.2	Balancedness	1
Number of Users Selected Per Round	100	Momentum	0
Iterations	5000	Classes Per Client	1, 5, 10

The Blockchain throughput and latency experiments were conducted in an Ubuntu 18.04 environment. We used the Fisco Bcos framework and set up 16 nodes to simulate the blockchain environment. Because the federated chain, such as the Fisco Bcos framework, is suitable for the public social environment such as a hospital, which invests it the traceability and admission control, we tested three consensus algorithms adopted by Fisco Bcos in a federated chain environment, namely PBFT, RAFR, and RPBFT. The specific parameters are shown in Table 2.

Table 2. Blockchain experiment public parameters

Parameters	Value	Parameters	Value
Nodes	16	Max transactions of block	1000
Number of transactions	10000	Consensus & working nodes	4:1
Max speed	5000	Consensus type	PBFT, RAFT, RPBFT

Datasets, Networks and Aggregation Algorithms. The federated learning experiment uses the MNIST dataset, a public set of handwritten digital images containing 60,000 training data and 10,000 test data. In terms of neural networks, we compare the performance of three networks: CNN, Logistic, and LSTM. Where CNN is a four-layer network, the LSTM network is 128 in size and has two hidden layers. In terms of federated learning aggregation algorithms, we tested three aggregation algorithms, which are FedAvg, signSGD, and STC, respectively. STC is a compression algorithm proposed by Felix Sattler et al. [20] that can significantly compress the number of iterations and communications during aggregation while ensuring model accuracy and convergence speed.

5.2 Results

Accuracy Comparison. We start out by investigating the three networks' accuracy and loss curves for different IID cases. Figure 8 shows the accuracy and loss curves of the model with three different networks.

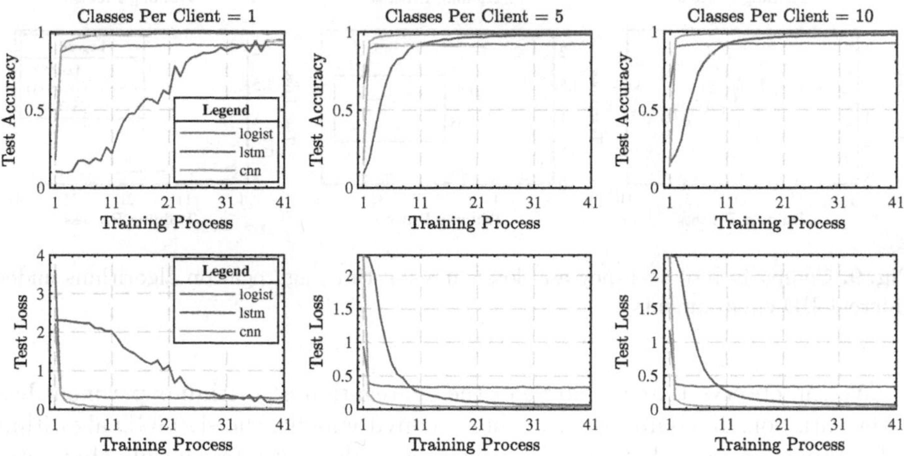

Fig. 8. Comparison of accuracy and loss curves of three networks under different IID environments

This graph enables us to compare the model's accuracy, convergence speed, and other information. We can see that in the non-IID environment (Classes Per Client = 1), the LSTM converges very hard and only converges to a similar accuracy as the CNN and Logist almost by the end of the experiment. Moreover, as the data environment tends to IID, the LSTM can normally converge, but the convergence rate is slower than the other two networks. Regarding final accuracy, LSTM is close to CNN and higher than Logist.

It is worth mentioning that in the cases of IID (Classes Per Client = 5,10), the Logist model starts relatively high at the very beginning of training, which may favor model building at the very beginning of public health emergencies such as COVID-19. However, the data structure from multiple medical institutions in a real medical environment may be different, which corresponds to a non-IID situation, so this feature may not be fully utilized. Therefore, it can be concluded that CNN networks with features such as fast convergence and high accuracy may be more suitable for the medical environment.

We then tested the accuracy and loss curves of three aggregation algorithms in different IID cases. Figure 9 shows the accuracy and loss curves of the model with three different aggregation algorithms.

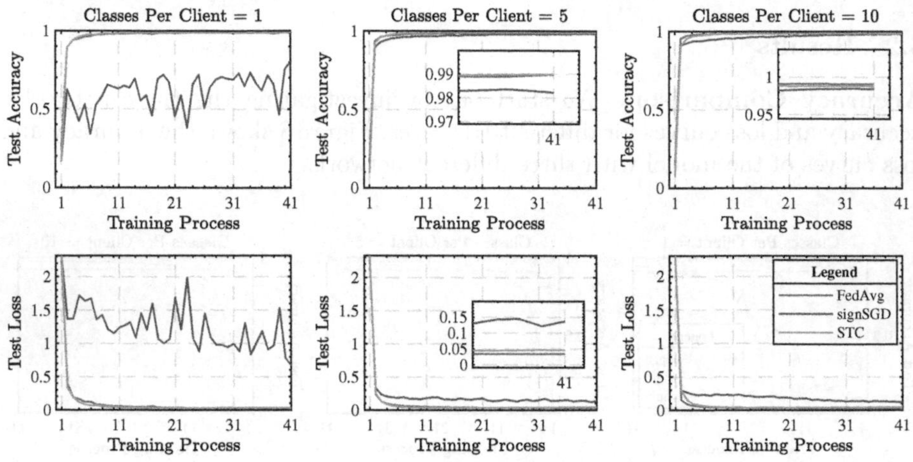

Fig. 9. Comparison of accuracy and loss curves of three aggregation algorithms under different IID environments

We can observe that the curve of the aggregation algorithm experiment has fewer variations in comparison. In the IID environment, the signSGD algorithm fails to converge, and the accuracy curve constantly fluctuates sharply above and below 0.6, while the loss curve constantly fluctuates sharply around 1.

Finally, we can conclude that considering the complexity and heterogeneity of the real operating environment, as well as the compression effect of the STC algorithm on the amount of communication and iteration, the STC algorithm is more suitable for the actual medical environment.

Throughput and Latency Comparison. Finally, the blockchain system's performance (i.e., throughput and latency) was tested to see if it could be applied in a federated healthcare system. This experiment compares three consensus algorithms used by the Fisco Bcos framework: PBFT, RAFT, and RPBFT. We selected the two most representative features of the healthcare system for testing: patient case construction and medical data upload. Figure 10 and 11 show the throughput and latency data for the two functions.

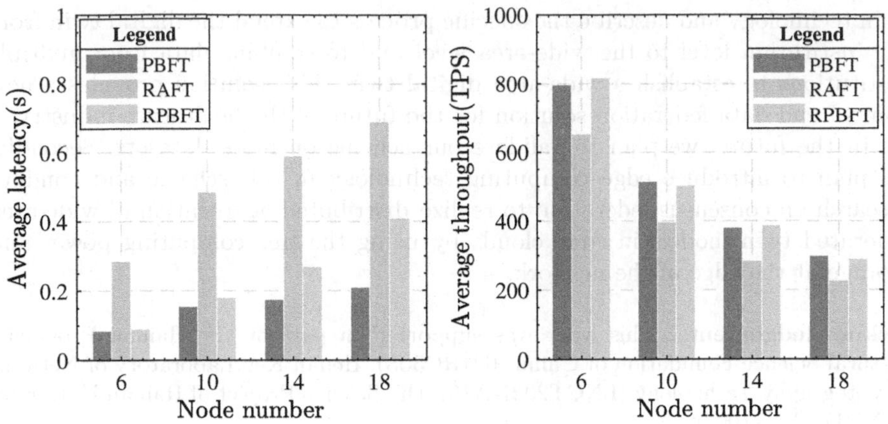

Fig. 10. Throughput and latency data for patient case construction function

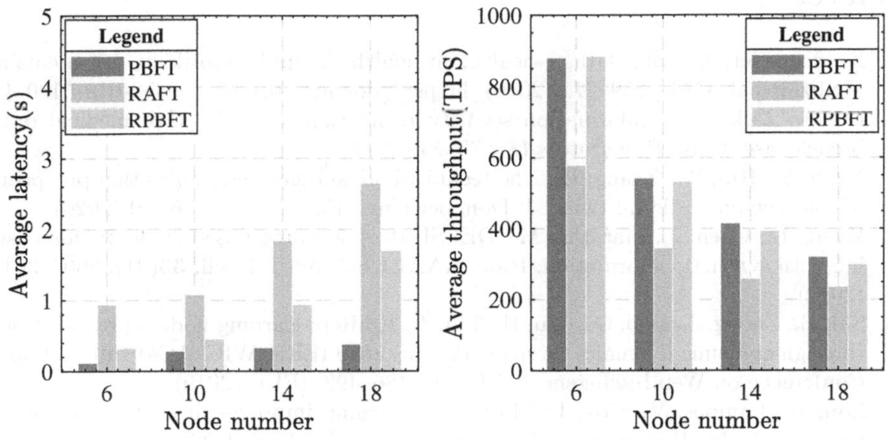

Fig. 11. Throughput and latency data for medical data upload function

The PBFT algorithm has the lowest latency among the three algorithms, followed by the RPBFT algorithm. Moreover, the throughputs of the PBFT algorithm and RPBFT algorithm are nearly equal. Therefore, compared to RAFT and RPBFT, the PBFT algorithm is more suitable for federated chains in the medical environment.

6 Conclusion

This paper proposes a mobile health data security scheme based on horizontal joint learning and digital twin. The federated chain Fisco Bcos framework ensures the trustworthiness of mHealth user data. On the premise of reliable medical data, we propose a scheme combining horizontal federated learning with digital twin technology and describe the specific process to extend the digital twin from the institution level to the wide-area level and to combine data from multiple institutions to establish a wide-area digital twin. This solution provides a new control and data federation solution for the future of the healthcare industry.

In the future, we plan to validate our scheme on more datasets. Secondly, we plan to introduce edge computing technology in this scheme and conduct research on consensus federation to realize distributed aggregation of wide-area federated twin models in edge clouds by using the free computing power and storage at the edge of the network.

Acknowledgements. This work was supported in part by the Hainan Provincial Natural Science Foundation of China (621RC508), Henan Key Laboratory of Network Cryptography Technology (LNCT2021-A16), the Science Project of Hainan University (KYQD(ZR)-21075).

References

1. Katzenmeier, C.: Big data, e-health, m-health, ki und robotik in der medizin. Medizinrecht **37**(4), 259–271 (2019). https://doi.org/10.1007/s00350-019-5180-4
2. Li, M.: Talk about information security protection from the U.S. medical data breach case. Chin. Procurators (8), 72–75 (2017)
3. Yuan, Y., Rui, W., Zhang, H.: The technical advantages and application prospects of "blockchain + digital twin". J. Dongbei Univ. Finance Econ. **6**, 10 (2020)
4. Wang, L., Chen, J., Marathe, M.: DEFSI: deep learning based epidemic forecasting with synthetic information. Proc. AAAI Conf. Artif. Intell. **33**(01), 9607–9612 (2019)
5. Shi, B., Zhong, J., Bao, Q., Qiu, H., Liu, J.: EpiRep: learning node representations through epidemic dynamics on networks. In: 2019 IEEE/WIC/ACM International Conference on Web Intelligence (WI), pp. 486–492. IEEE (2019)
6. Zou, B., Lampos, V., Cox, I.: Multi-task learning improves disease models from web search. In: Proceedings of the 2018 World Wide Web Conference, pp. 87–96. WWW 2018, International World Wide Web Conferences Steering Committee, Republic and Canton of Geneva, CHE (2018). https://doi.org/10.1145/3178876.3186050
7. Lu, F.S., Hattab, M.W., Clemente, C.L., Biggerstaff, M., Santillana, M.: Improved state-level influenza nowcasting in the United States leveraging Internet-based data and network approaches. Nat. Commun. **10**(1), 1–10 (2019)
8. Ye, Z., Zhao, H., Zhang, K., Wang, Z., Zhu, Y.: Network representation based on the joint learning of three feature views. Big Data Min. Analytics **2**(4), 248–260 (2019). https://doi.org/10.26599/BDMA.2019.9020009
9. Zhao, L., Chen, J., Chen, F., Wang, W., Lu, C.T., Ramakrishnan, N.: SimNest: social media nested epidemic simulation via online semi-supervised deep learning. In: 2015 IEEE International Conference on Data Mining, pp. 639–648 (2015). https://doi.org/10.1109/ICDM.2015.39
10. Choudhury, O., et al.: Differential privacy-enabled federated learning for sensitive health data (2019). https://doi.org/10.48550/ARXIV.1910.02578, https://arxiv.org/abs/1910.02578

11. Jin, H., Dai, X., Xiao, J., Li, B., Li, H., Zhang, Y.: Cross-cluster federated learning and blockchain for internet of medical things. IEEE Internet Things J. **8**(21), 15776–15784 (2021). https://doi.org/10.1109/JIOT.2021.3081578
12. Yang, Q., Zhang, J., Hao, W., Spell, G.P., Carin, L.: FLOP: Federated Learning on Medical Datasets using Partial Networks. In: Proceedings of the 27th ACM SIGKDD Conference on Knowledge Discovery & Data Mining, pp. 3845–3853. KDD 2021, Association for Computing Machinery, New York, NY, USA (2021). https://doi.org/10.1145/3447548.3467185
13. Andreux, M., du Terrail, J.O., Beguier, C., Tramel, E.W.: Siloed federated learning for multi-centric histopathology datasets. In: Albarqouni, S., et al. (eds.) DART/DCL -2020. LNCS, vol. 12444, pp. 129–139. Springer, Cham (2020). https://doi.org/10.1007/978-3-030-60548-3_13
14. Kumar, R., et al.: Blockchain-federated-learning and deep learning models for COVID-19 detection using CT imaging. IEEE Sensors J. **21**(14), 16301–16314 (2021). https://doi.org/10.1109/JSEN.2021.3076767
15. Fan, C., Zhang, C., Yahja, A., Mostafavi, A.: Disaster city digital twin: a vision for integrating artificial and human intelligence for disaster management. Int. J. Inf. Manage. **56**, 102049 (2021). https://doi.org/10.1016/j.ijinfomgt.2019.102049, https://www.sciencedirect.com/science/article/pii/S0268401219302956
16. Cai, Z., Zheng, X., Yu, J.: A differential-private framework for urban traffic flows estimation via taxi companies. IEEE Trans. Ind. Inform. **15**(12), 6492–6499 (2019). https://doi.org/10.1109/TII.2019.2911697
17. Yang, H., Li, F., Yu, D., Zou, Y., Yu, J.: Reliable data storage in heterogeneous wireless sensor networks by jointly optimizing routing and storage node deployment. Tsinghua Sci. Technol. **26**(2), 230–238 (2021). https://doi.org/10.26599/TST.2019.9010061
18. Zheng, X., Cai, Z.: Privacy-preserved data sharing towards multiple parties in industrial IoTs. IEEE J. Sel. Areas Commun. **38**(5), 968–979 (2020). https://doi.org/10.1109/JSAC.2020.2980802
19. Bonawitz, K., et al.: Towards federated learning at scale: system design. Proc. Mach. Learn. Syst. **1**, 374–388 (2019)
20. Sattler, F., Wiedemann, S., Müller, K.R., Samek, W.: Robust and communication-efficient federated learning from non-iid data. IEEE Trans. Neural Netw. Learn. Syst. **31**(9), 3400–3413 (2020). https://doi.org/10.1109/TNNLS.2019.2944481

Construction of Security Risk Prediction Model for Wireless Transmission of Multi Axis NC Machining Data

Guoqiang Zhao[1(✉)], Meitao Zhang[2], and Yingying Wu[3]

[1] Shandong Vocational College of Science and Technology, Weifang 261053, China
pxy201201@126.com
[2] Weichai Heavy Machinery Co., Ltd., Weifang 261108, China
[3] Weichai Power Co., Ltd., Weifang 261061, China

Abstract. In multi axis NC machining, there is a certain security risk in wireless data transmission. A security risk prediction model for wireless data transmission in multi axis NC machining is designed. Through frequent pattern mining, multi axis NC machining data wireless transmission security risk data mining is implemented. Based on machine learning, the security risk prediction model of data wireless transmission is constructed. The model is mainly divided into four parts: data collection and processing module, grey synthesis and Markov prediction module, Bayesian network and evidence theory module and risk quantification calculation module. AHP method is used to analyze the weight of model indexes. Test the prediction performance of the model. The test results show that the accuracy of risk prediction of the model in different scenarios is high, higher than 88%, and the prediction time is short, less than 6 s, which proves the prediction performance of the model.

Keywords: Multi axis NC machining · Frequent pattern mining · Wireless data transmission · Safety risk prediction model

1 Introduction

Multi axis machine tool refers to a CNC machine tool with at least 1–2 rotating coordinate axes, i.e. 4–5 axes, in addition to the three moving coordinate axes of X, y and Z. As a kind of machine tool equipment used for drilling and tapping in the mechanical field, multi axis machine tools first appeared in Japan, and then were introduced to the mainland through Taiwan. It has a history of 20 years. An ordinary multi axis machine tool can process several or even dozens of holes or threads at a time. If equipped with air (liquid) pressure device, it can automatically carry out fast forward, work in (work out), fast backward and stop. Multi hole machine tool, also known as group drilling, can be used for drilling or tapping. For general models, 2–16 holes can be drilled at the same time to improve efficiency. The number of fixed machine types is not limited. The form and size of drilling shafts can be designed and processed according to the needs of customers. Multi axis machine tools are widely used in drilling and tapping of porous

Y. Xu et al. (Eds.): ML4CS 2022, LNCS 13655, pp. 442–456, 2023.
https://doi.org/10.1007/978-3-031-20096-0_33

parts in the machinery industry [1]. Such as automobile and motorcycle porous parts: engine box, aluminum casting shell, brake drum, brake disc, steering gear, wheel hub, differential housing, axle head, half shaft, axle, pumps, valves, hydraulic components, solar accessories, etc. Multi axis machine tools can be divided into two specifications: adjustable and fixed. Within the processing range of adjustable multi axis machine tools, the number of spindles and the distance between spindles can be adjusted at will. A single feed can process several holes at the same time. When it works with the hydraulic machine tool, it can automatically carry out fast forward, work advance (work exit), fast backward and stop Compared with single axis drilling (tapping), the workpiece has high machining precision and fast work efficiency, which can effectively save the human, material and financial resources of the investor. In particular, the automation of machine tools greatly reduces the labor intensity of operators. The fixed multi axis machine tool adopts the design scheme of single piece (workpiece) special machine. According to the reasons of high machining frequency and large quantity of machined parts, the equipment of one machine is specially customized, so there is no need to worry about the size deviation in its work. In addition to conventional products, special design can also be carried out according to the special requirements of customers. Multi axis machine tools can be divided into two types according to the axis activity range: adjustable and fixed.

With the development of numerical control machining technology, multi axis machine tools have gradually developed into multi axis numerical control machining machines. Numerical control machining technology is an automatic machining technology developed in the 1940s to adapt to the machining of complex shape parts. Its research originated from the aircraft manufacturing industry. In 1952, the world's first CNC machine tool, the three coordinate vertical milling machine, came out. It can control the milling cutter to process the continuous space curved surface, which opened the prelude of the CNC machining technology. With the rapid development of computer technology, the traditional manufacturing industry has started a fundamental change. The industrial developed countries have invested a lot of money in the research and development of modern manufacturing technology and put forward a new manufacturing mode. Numerical control technology is a high-tech mechatronics technology deeply integrating microelectronics technology, computer technology, information technology, monitoring technology and machining technology. It has the characteristics of high precision, high efficiency and flexible automation. It plays an important role in realizing flexible automation, integration and intelligence in the manufacturing industry. The application of this technology can improve the function, efficiency and flexibility of machining equipment to a new level, Western developed countries treat numerical control technology as strategic materials, and invest a huge amount of money to ensure to occupy the leading position in this industry [2]. After the development of NC (numerical control), CNC (computer numerical control), FMC (flexible manufacturing unit), FMS (flexible manufacturing system), FA (factory automation), CIM (Computer Integrated Manufacturing), NC technology has become an important symbol to measure the level of a country's machinery manufacturing industry. The research, mastering and application of numerical control technology are the driving force for the sustainable development of modern manufacturing industry, and also the means to deal with the global economic integration in the 21st century.

In order to improve the utilization rate of multi axis NC machine tools and ensure the quality of data transmission such as NC program, control parameters and tool compensation, the security of wireless transmission of multi axis NC machining data is studied, and a risk prediction model of wireless transmission of multi axis NC machining data is constructed based on machine learning.

2 Security Risk Prediction Model for Wireless Transmission of Multi Axis NC Machining Data

2.1 Wireless Data Transmission Security Risk Data Mining

Through frequent pattern mining, multi axis NC machining data wireless transmission security risk data mining is implemented. Frequent pattern mining is an important subject in data mining research. Its purpose is to find patterns (such as itemsets, subsequences or substructures) that frequently appear in data sets. It is the basis of association rules, correlation analysis, classification, clustering and other data mining tasks. With the continuous collection and storage of a large amount of data, frequent pattern mining can help many applications such as recommendation system, personalized website and customer purchase habit analysis [3]. However, both the content of frequent patterns and the counting information may reveal the user's privacy information or disclose the user's real identity. Frequent pattern mining is to find a set of patterns whose frequency exceeds the minimum threshold. In static data sets, the candidate set based frequent pattern mining method represented by Apriori algorithm has been widely studied and many related algorithms have been extended. According to different mining methods, mining algorithms can be divided into three categories: candidate set based mining algorithm, pattern growth based mining algorithm and bitmap based mining algorithm.

The problem of frequent pattern mining can be regarded as a search problem, which aims to search frequent patterns in database space with the highest efficiency. Because the scale of database is usually large, frequent pattern mining algorithm needs to search in a huge space, so how to improve the efficiency of the algorithm is the main problem to solve the frequent pattern mining algorithm. The search space of frequent pattern mining is not equal to the database space. In some hierarchical mining algorithms, because the database is scanned repeatedly, and the search algorithm space exceeds the database space, and some algorithms use the strategy of sampling and pruning, the search algorithm may only search a part of the data in the database, and the search space may be smaller than the database space [4].

The frequent pattern mining methods used are as follows: combining the advantages of Apriori algorithm and FP growth algorithm, an Apriori frequent pattern mining algorithm ICP tree based on improved compact pattern tree is proposed. The algorithm is based on pattern growth and uses compact tree structure to represent data. In the first step, through a database scan, all transaction item sets in the database are inserted into the compact mode tree one by one, and then a compact mode tree containing only frequent items is constructed by using the tree reconstruction operation; The second step is to establish the conditional subtrees of each 1-frequent term by using the divide and conquer strategy; The third step is to mine the condition subtree to generate candidate itemsets by using the generation test method in Apriori algorithm, and scan the corresponding condition subtree to calculate the support of candidate itemsets to obtain all the frequent patterns that meet the conditions.

Apriori algorithm and FP growth algorithm are the most representative algorithms in the field of frequent pattern mining, but they inevitably have their own advantages and disadvantages in pattern mining. For Apriori algorithm, the main shortcomings are as follows: first, the original database needs to be scanned repeatedly when counting the support of itemsets, resulting in a large amount of time and memory being consumed at this stage; Second, before the join step, a lot of time will be spent to judge whether the itemset meets the join conditions, and a large number of redundant candidate sets will be generated, making the subsequent pruning step and support counting step difficult to implement. For FP growth algorithm, although the mining speed is fast and the database does not need to be scanned repeatedly. However, when the database is very large, it is almost impossible to build conditional frequent pattern tree based on main memory, which is the biggest drawback of FP growth algorithm. At the same time, the establishment of frequent pattern bases and conditional FP trees by recursive methods for frequent pattern mining will occupy a lot of memory resources. This problem is particularly prominent when dealing with large and dense data sets. In addition, when constructing FP Tree, the database needs to be traversed twice, and the constructed tree structure does not support interactive mining and incremental mining, so it can not effectively deal with data flow problems. Apriori algorithm is simple and easy to understand and implement. When the number of candidate sets is effectively reduced, the efficiency of mining frequent patterns will be greatly improved; FP growth algorithm avoids candidate generation and is based on divide and conquer strategy, so it has better scalability and effectiveness [5]. In order to effectively improve the efficiency of frequent pattern mining, the two algorithms are combined to give full play to their respective advantages and avoid their own shortcomings.

The proposed algorithm combines the improved compact pattern tree with the candidate generation test mechanism of Apriori algorithm in order to quickly search the frequent patterns in the database. Although Apriori algorithm is one of the most classical algorithms in frequent pattern mining, it requires a large number of comparison steps before the connection step, and will generate a large number of redundant candidate sets. Therefore, the time cost of subsequent pruning steps and support counting steps is increased. Therefore, the proposed algorithm first adds the connection preprocessing operation before the connection step of Apriori algorithm, and the main purpose is to reduce the number of comparisons and reduce the number of candidate sets. In addition, although FP Tree is the first tree structure in the pattern growth algorithm, it does not support interactive mining and incremental mining, and needs to scan the database twice. Therefore, compact pattern tree is selected to replace the traditional frequent pattern tree. The proposed algorithm extends the compact pattern tree and constructs a new tree structure ECP tree. The new tree structure only uses the frequent items in the transaction item set, not all the items in the transaction item set. The new tree structure only scans the database once, and the constructed tree structure supports not only interactive mining but also incremental mining, so it can effectively deal with data flow problems. Finally, the improved points are combined with APFT algorithm to mine frequent patterns.

Algorithm improvement scheme:

Optimize Connection Steps

Before putting forward the idea of optimization, we first understand two properties about sets.

Property 1: k-itemsets containing K different terms have k different subsets of (k − 1) - terms;

Property 2: suppose I is an item in the k-term set. According to property 1, there must be (k − 1) subset in the k-term set containing item I.

In the connection step of Apriori algorithm, the previous (k-1) items need to be compared many times, which greatly increases the time cost of the algorithm. It is found that the following properties exist:

Property 3: suppose I is an item in the frequent K - itemset FK. If the frequent K - itemset containing item I can continue to generate frequent (k + 1) - itemsets, the sum of the number of frequent itemsets containing item I in the frequent K - itemset FK must be greater than or equal to K. If it is not greater than or equal to K, FK will be deleted from the non participating connection.

According to property 3, the connection step can be optimized, the frequent itemsets can be preprocessed before connection, and the non-conforming frequent k-itemsets fk [6] can be deleted.

The pre-processing operations before the connection step are as follows:

Step 1: count the support count of each item;
Step 2: implement pruning.

Expand Compact Tree

Because CP tree contains all items in the process of tree construction, both frequent items and infrequent items participate in the construction of the tree. Therefore, the compact pattern tree is extended, and a new tree structure ECP tree is proposed. The new tree structure only uses the frequent items in the transaction item set, not all items in the transaction item set, and deletes the infrequent items.

The construction of new trees also includes two stages:

(1) Insertion phase;
(2) Refactoring phase. In the insertion phase, the transaction records in the transaction database are scanned one by one, and the items are inserted into the ECP tree according to the order in which they appear in the transaction item set, instead of the dictionary order. In the reconstruction phase, the items are rearranged in descending order according to the support count of the items, and only the frequent items are retained, and the tree is reconstructed by using the sorted frequent items. In the tree reconstruction, the branch sorting method (BSM) is improved, and a new branch sorting method IBSM is proposed, which can effectively reconstruct the newly proposed tree structure. In the improved method, if the path is not sorted according to the new sorting order, remove the path, delete the infrequent items, arrange the remaining frequent items into a temporary array according to the sorting

order, and finally insert them into the tree in order. Repeat this process to finally get a compact pattern tree.

In the improved branch sorting method, according to the basic principle of IBSM, given t and I, iSORT containing only frequent items is constructed in descending order according to the support count of items in I; Then, check all branches of t one by one to find all unsorted paths containing only frequent items. If found, sort the paths and insert them into t; Finally, when there are no branches to be processed, the reconstruction of T is completed. Tsort is a new reconstruction tree containing only frequent items.

When reconstructing the tree, if any sorted path containing only frequent items is found, this paper will not only skip the sorting operation of the path, but also pass the sorting information of the path to all branch nodes of the same path of the entire branch, indicating that the path from the branch node to the root node has been sorted. If you encounter the same item sorting in subsequent paths, you no longer need to sort the paths from the root node to the branch node. Therefore, when sorting other remaining paths in the same branch, only the sub path is checked to determine whether the rank of all items in the sub path is less than that of the branch node [7]. If such an item is not found, this article retains the sub path from the root node to the branch node, that is, the common prefix path, and only deals with the sub path from the branch node to the leaf node. Otherwise, the entire path from the leaf node to the root node is sorted. After processing all the child paths from the branch node, this article will process the next available branch node.

The newly proposed tree structure can construct a highly compact schema tree by scanning the database only once. The new tree structure supports interactive mining, in which users can change the specified minimum support threshold for the same database. In this case, this article can save the tree after inserting all transaction item sets, and then reconstruct the tree according to the minimum support threshold specified by the user. The total support count of all items is saved in the i-list. Only frequent items can be retained according to different minimum support thresholds without rescanning the database. Therefore, the new tree structure does not need to rescan the database like FP Tree to realize interactive mining. The new tree structure supports incremental mining, in which transaction item sets in the original database can be added and / or deleted. In this case, this article can insert all transaction itemsets into the original database and save the tree. When adding a new transaction itemset or deleting some old transaction itemsets, you can add branches of the new transaction itemset to the tree and delete those deleted transaction itemset branches. The reconstruction tree does not need to scan the original database again like FP Tree [8].

2.2 Build a Data Wireless Transmission Security Risk Prediction Model

A data wireless transmission security risk prediction model is built based on machine learning. The model is mainly divided into four parts: the first part is data collection and processing. The collected data and the data summarized according to expert knowledge are analyzed and processed and stored in the database; The second part is the grey synthesis and Markov prediction model. According to the established risk evaluation index system, the impact value of data chain security risk is calculated through this model; The third part is the Bayesian network and evidence theory model. The Bayesian network is established through data analysis and expert knowledge to deduce the probability of risk occurrence; The fourth part is the risk quantitative calculation model, which calculates the final value of the risk according to the calculated impact value of the risk and the probability of the risk.

In the second part, during the risk assessment, it is difficult to quantify accurately because of incomplete data information, uncertain operation mechanism and unclear decision-making. The grey system theory is a theory to deal with the problem of less data and uncertainty. It studies the grey system theory and risk security assessment technology, and puts forward the grey assessment method of data chain risk security, Based on the risk grey evaluation method and the analytic hierarchy process, a grey comprehensive evaluation model of data link system risk is established, and the specific steps of evaluation are described in detail. According to the calculated data link risk impact value, according to the Markov prediction model, combined with historical data, the prediction of future risk impact value is given.

When calculating the impact value of risk occurrence, the grey number exists in the data link index system, so it is necessary to use the whitening weight function to concretize the grey number. The calculation model of the impact value of risk occurrence is shown in Fig. 1.

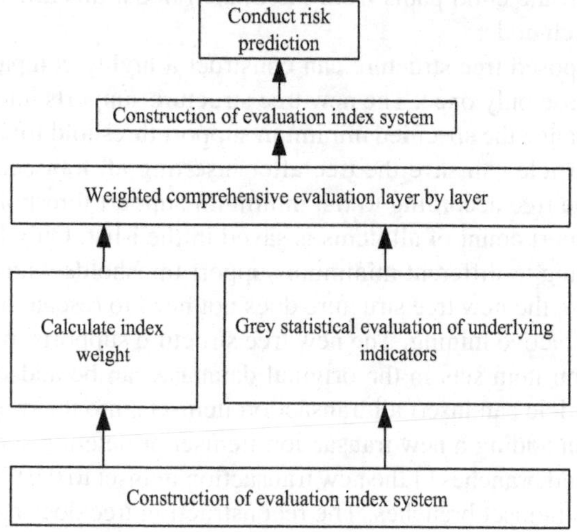

Fig. 1. Calculation model of risk occurrence impact value

When calculating the impact value of risk occurrence, the index system of the risk assessment system should be established first as the basis for calculating the index weight, expert scoring, dividing the risk grade and determining the assessment grey class. Then it divides the risk grade, experts' score, determines the evaluation grey class, and calculates the index weight; Then the bottom indicators are statistically evaluated, and finally the risk level of the whole system is evaluated by the method of weighted comprehensive evaluation layer by layer.

The comprehensive evaluation index system is a set of indicators that can comprehensively reflect the security characteristics of information systems, and have internal relations and complementary functions. The establishment of the evaluation index system is the basis for comprehensive evaluation. Whether the selection of evaluation indexes is appropriate and whether each evaluation index describes the measurement of a certain feature size of the system from different aspects is related to whether the evaluation can play its role and function and directly affect the evaluation results [9].

After the establishment of the risk assessment index system, in order to control and manage the risk, the results of the risk assessment can be graded. The evaluator shall calculate the risk value of each evaluation index according to the adopted risk calculation method, set the risk value range for each grade according to the distribution of risk value, and then grade all risk calculation results. Each grade represents the severity of the corresponding risk. Generally speaking, the higher the grade, the higher the risk. Based on the classification of security protection level and the classification practice of international crisis management, and referring to the example of risk classification table in the code for information security risk assessment of information security technology, the risk classification is shown in Table 1.

Table 1. Risk classification

Serial number	Grade	Identification	Describe
1	One	Very low	Once it happens, the impact is almost non-existent
2	Two	Low	Once it happens, the impact is low, which is generally limited to the machine tool, and can be solved quickly through certain means
3	Three	In	Once it happens, it will cause certain impact on plant operation, but the impact area and medium degree are not large
4	Four	High	Once it happens, it will have a great impact on plant operation
5	Five	Very high	Once it happens, it will have a serious impact on plant operation

Whether the index value determination standard is scientific and reasonable has a great impact on the evaluation results. Therefore, pay attention to the following points when determining the grade and standard of indicators:

(1) Objective rationality. The number of evaluation standard grades and the scope of each grade should be scientific, reasonable and in line with people's logical thinking habits of judgment. At the same time, the evaluation standards should not be divorced from reality.
(2) Dynamic. The index evaluation standards formulated shall be in line with the actual situation of the whole process.

(3) Quantitative. When determining the index standards, the standards of each grade shall be quantified as much as possible, and the range of each grade shall be scaled with specific numerical values to facilitate judgment and evaluation.

In the process of risk assessment, the risk levels of different assessment indicators can be compared intuitively, so as to determine the security strategy of the information system. The security strategy should comprehensively consider the cost of risk control and the impact of risk, and propose an acceptable risk range. For the risk of some assets, if the calculated risk value is within the acceptable range, the risk is acceptable, and the existing safety measures shall be maintained; If the risk assessment value is outside the acceptable range, that is, the risk value is higher than the upper limit of the acceptable range, the risk is unacceptable, and new safety measures need to be taken to control and reduce the risk.

When evaluating and scoring evaluation indicators, certain standards must be followed. However, most of the indicators cannot be directly assessed quantitatively only through some specific values. These indicators can only be quantified by consulting the personnel with professional experience, according to the characteristics of each sub indicator and referring to expert experience, and then the scoring sample matrix of the evaluation indicators can be generated.

In the third part, D-S evidence theory is used to fuse various information data, and Bayesian network is used to give more accurate risk probability assessment results.

The calculation steps of risk occurrence probability are as follows: firstly, construct the Bayesian network structure according to historical data and expert knowledge, then carry out parameter learning, carry out probability reasoning according to the parameter learning results to obtain the posterior probability, and finally use D-S evidence theory to fuse different posterior probabilities to obtain the final probability.

2.3 Determination of Evaluation Index Weight

As each indicator has different impact on the whole, in order to reflect the importance of each indicator, it is necessary to assign different weights to each indicator to reflect the rationality of the comprehensive evaluation. The weight reflects the relative importance of each indicator. In the multi indicator evaluation system, the importance of each indicator to the goal is different. When measuring the importance of each indicator to the goal, different weights should be given. In the evaluation process, the determination of weight is an important basic step. AHP, principal component analysis, entropy method and other methods can be used to determine the weight of evaluation indicators. In the research, AHP method is mainly used to analyze the weight of indicators.

Analytic hierarchy process (AHP) is a multi criteria decision-making method that can effectively deal with variables that are not easy to quantify. Using AHP to solve problems can be divided into four steps: first, establish the hierarchical structure of the problem; Second, construct pairwise comparison judgment matrix; Thirdly, the relative weights of the elements to be compared are calculated from the judgment matrix; Fourth, calculate the combination weight of each layer of elements.

Construct Hierarchical Structure

The construction of hierarchical structure is actually the process of analyzing things. The top layer of the hierarchical structure is the focus of the goal, and only contains one element. The lower layer can contain several elements. The corresponding elements of the adjacent two layers are arranged according to certain rules, and all the elements in the same layer have the same level of magnitude. If they are too different, they belong to different levels. The general hierarchy model is divided into three layers.

Construct Pairwise Comparison Judgment Matrix

The judgment matrix indicates the relative superiority between the elements of the current layer and its associated elements for a certain element of the previous layer.

For example, scheme layer $P_1, P_2, \cdots, P_n$ is associated with upper layer criterion C_K. The judgment matrix of these schemes on criterion C_K is established as follows:

$$B = \begin{bmatrix} B_{11} & \cdots & B_{1N} \\ B_{21} & \cdots & B_{2N} \\ \vdots & \vdots & \vdots \\ B_{M1} & \cdots & B_{MN} \end{bmatrix}^T \tag{1}$$

In formula (1), B_{MN} refers to the relative importance or superiority of scheme P_M compared with scheme P_N for criterion C_K. The value of B_{MN} is determined according to the data, statistical data, expert opinions and the experience of system analysts; T is the matrix threshold [10].

The analytic hierarchy process uses the 1–9 scale method to quantitatively describe the comparison of the two elements, as follows:

The value of B_{MN} is 1, indicating that P_M and P_N are equally important;
The value of B_{MN} is 3, indicating that P_M is slightly more important than P_N;
The value of B_{MN} is 5, indicating that P_M is significantly more important than P_N;
The value of B_{MN} is 7, indicating that P_M is much more important than P_N;
The value of B_{MN} is 9, indicating that P_M is more important than P_N;
The values of B_{MN} are 2, 4, 6 and 8, indicating that it is in the middle of the above two adjacent judgments.

The judgment matrix shall have the following characteristics:

$$B_{MN} = 1 \tag{2}$$

$$B_{MN} = \frac{T}{B_{NM}} \tag{3}$$

Consistency test shall also be conducted for the given judgment matrix. The test steps are as follows:

Table 2. 1–10 order average random consistency index RI

Serial number	Order	RI
1	One	0
2	Two	0.32
3	Three	0.62
4	Four	0.98
5	Five	1.28
6	Six	1.58
7	Seven	1.85
8	Eight	2.18
9	Nine	2.53
10	Ten	2.85

Step 1. Calculate the consistency index CI;
Step 2. Find the corresponding average random consistency index RI, as shown in Table 2.
Step 3. Calculate the consistency ratio cr. When its value is less than 0.1, it is considered that the judgment matrix meets the consistency requirements, otherwise it should be adjusted.

3 Model Test

3.1 Experimental Data

For the multi axis NC machining data wireless transmission security risk prediction model, its performance is tested by experiments.

The experimental multi axis NC machining machine tool is a four axis linkage machine tool, that is, there are at least four motion coordinates on a machine tool, which are three linear motion coordinates and one rotary motion coordinate respectively. It can enable the workpiece to complete the machining of the other four surfaces except the mounting surface and the top surface after one clamping. Four axis linkage CNC machine tools can be divided into vertical and horizontal types in terms of structural configuration, both of which are equipped with a rotary workbench. In addition to the three linear moving axes x, y and Z, a rotation axis should be added to the motion coordinates of the four axis linkage NC machine tool. This rotation axis can be axis a rotating around the X axis, axis B rotating around the Y axis, or axis C rotating around the Z axis. Since the spindle of the machine tool is usually set as axis Z, if the workbench rotates around axis Z, the purpose of changing the spindle movement direction cannot be achieved. In fact, the configuration of the movement axis of the four axis linkage NC machine tool can only be (x, y, z, a) or (x, y, z, b).

The multi axis NC machining data used in the experiment came from the NC software of a multi axis NC machining machine tool.

The NC programming method based on master model is recommended in UG system, and the NC machining model is established by assembly method in UG system. The master model is a three-dimensional model from the design. While the design department carries out product design, assembly design, structural analysis, simulation design, NC machining design and other work can be carried out synchronously. The product design gives the design master model, and other departments can reference the data of the master model at the same time. When the master model is updated, other models will change accordingly. In the machining module, the design model can be referenced into the machining assembly model by using the assembly method, and the NC machining process design and tooling design can be carried out at the same time of product design. When the main model, that is, the design model, changes, the machining model will change accordingly. The method of using master model is beneficial to realize concurrent design of product design and manufacturing process, improve product design efficiency and greatly shorten product development cycle.

3.2 Analysis of Test Results

Using the experimental data to test the risk prediction performance of the design model, mainly testing its risk prediction accuracy in two scenarios.

The first test scenario is a scenario with large amount of wireless transmission data of multi axis NC machining data. The test results are shown in Fig. 2.

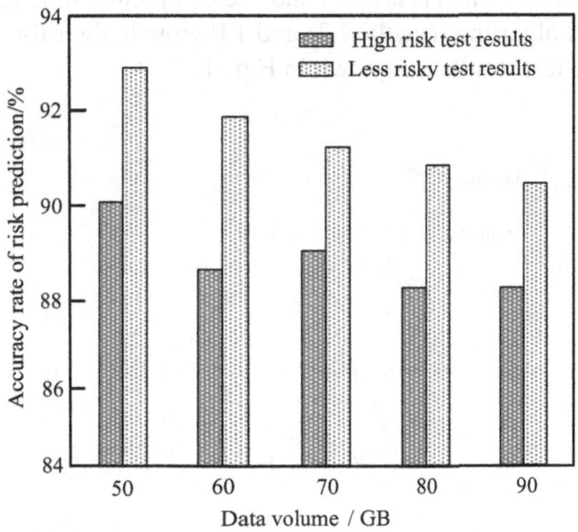

Fig. 2. Test results in scenarios with large amount of data

According to the test results in the scenario with large amount of data in Fig. 2, the overall risk prediction accuracy of the design method is higher than 88% in the scenario with large amount of data.

The second test scenario is the scenario where the wireless transmission of multi axis NC machining data is small. The test results of risk prediction accuracy are shown in Fig. 3.

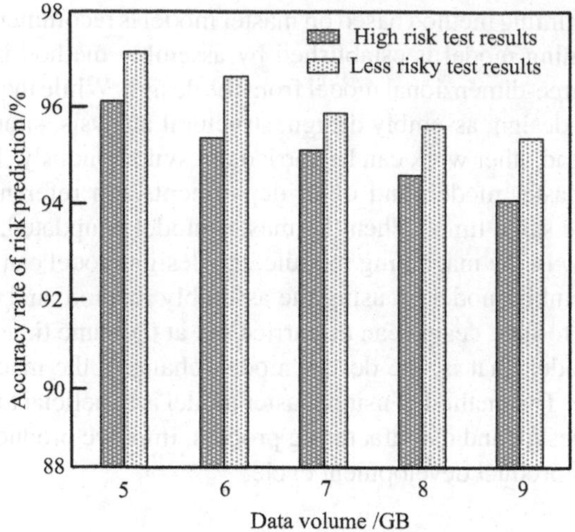

Fig. 3. Test results in a scenario with a small amount of data

According to the test results in Fig. 3, in the scenario with a small amount of data, the overall risk prediction accuracy of the design method is higher than 94%.

The prediction time experiment is completed through the number of multi axis NC machining data labels, 500 labels are set, and the completion time of the single method (method 1), Apriori algorithm (method 2) and FP growth algorithm (method 3) in this paper is tested. The test results are shown in Fig. 4.

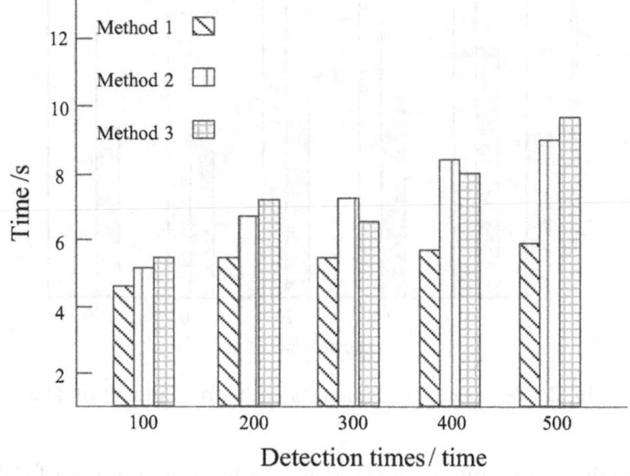

Fig. 4. Test results of prediction time of different methods

According to the analysis of Fig. 4, with the increasing number of tests, the test time detected shows an upward trend in varying degrees. When the number of detection is small, the difference between the prediction time of this method and methods 2 and 3 is small. However, with the increase of detection times, the prediction time gap of the three methods gradually increases. On the whole, the prediction time of this method is less, and the maximum time is only 6 s, while method 2 needs 11 s and method 3 needs 12 s.

4 Conclusion

Modern advanced manufacturing technology is developing towards digitalization, automation, intelligence, integration and networking. Multi axis NC machine tools, especially four axis and five axis NC machining centers, are more and more widely used in the process of advanced manufacturing. Especially for some polyhedral hole series parts with various spatial structures and mechanical parts with complex spatial surfaces, multi axis machining centers show great machining advantages. The use of multi axis CNC machine tools has greatly promoted the development of modern manufacturing integration technology and management information modernization technology, and promoted its popularization and application in modern advanced manufacturing industry. In the research of multi axis NC machine tool, a security risk prediction model of wireless transmission of multi axis NC machining data is designed. In the research process, this paper realizes the wireless transmission security risk prediction of multi axis NC machining data from three aspects: Data Mining of wireless transmission security risk, construction of data wireless transmission security risk prediction model based on machine learning, and determination of evaluation index weight using AHP method. The experimental results show that the risk prediction accuracy of the constructed model is high. Here we need to thank Weifang Science and technology development planning project for its support to this article.

Acknowledgement. Weifang Science and Technology Development Plan Project (2021GX037).

References

1. Elhoseny, M., Shankar, K.: Reliable data transmission model for mobile ad hoc network using signcryption technique. IEEE Trans. Reliab. **69**(3), 1077–1086 (2020)
2. Fan, Y., Zhao, G., Lei, X., et al.: SBBS: a secure blockchain-based scheme for IoT data credibility in fog environment. IEEE Internet Things J. **8**(11), 9268–9277 (2021)
3. Nguyen, N.P., Long, D.N., Hong, T.N., et al.: Performance analysis and optimization of ergodic secrecy rates for downlink data transmission in massive MIMO-NOMA networks. Wirel. Netw. **28**(1), 355–365 (2022)
4. Mamaghani, M.T., Hong, Y.: Improving PHY-security of UAV-enabled transmission with wireless energy harvesting: robust trajectory design and communications resource allocation. IEEE Trans. Veh. Technol. **69**(8), 8586–8600 (2020)
5. Liu, S., Wang, S., Liu, X., et al.: Human memory update strategy: a multi-layer template update mechanism for remote visual monitoring. IEEE Trans. Multimed. **23**, 2188–2198 (2021)
6. Yang, H.C., Xu, F., Alouini, M.S.: Statistical energy efficiency characterization for wireless transmission over fading channels. IEEE Trans. Veh. Technol. **69**(11), 13947–13951 (2020)

7. Gao, P., Li, J., Liu, S.: An introduction to key technology in artificial intelligence and big data driven e-Learning and e-Education. Mob. Netw. Appl. **26**, 2123–2126 (2021)
8. Ji, W., Zhu, W.: Profit maximization for sponsored data in wireless video transmission systems. IEEE Trans. Mob. Comput. **19**(8), 1928–1942 (2020)
9. Liu, S., Wang, S., Liu, X., et al.: Fuzzy detection aided real-time and robust visual tracking under complex environments. IEEE Trans. Fuzzy Syst. **29**(1), 90–102 (2021)
10. Li, L., Liang, J.: Research on early warning model of information disclosure risk in third-party payment system. Comput. Simul. **38**(2), 394–398 (2021)

Spiking Neural Networks Subject to Adversarial Attacks in Spiking Domain

Xuanwei Lin[1], Chen Dong[1,2], Ximeng Liu[1,3(✉)], and Dong Cheng[1]

[1] College of Computer and Data Science, Fuzhou University, Fuzhou 350108, China
dongchen@fzu.edu.cn, snbnix@gmail.com, chengdong2021@foxmail.com
[2] Fujian Key Laboratory of Network Computing and Intelligent Information Processing (Fuzhou University), Fuzhou 350108, China
[3] Key Lab of Information Security of Network Systems (Fuzhou University), Fuzhou 350108, Fujian Province, China

Abstract. Spiking neural networks are widely deployed in neuromorphic devices to simulate brain function. In this situation, SNN security becomes significant while lacking in-depth research. Nowadays, most existing work generate adversarial sample by adding perturbations to the pixel domain, which may be appropriate for fooling spiking neural networks on the static datasets than neuromorphic ones. Therefore, this work proposes a spike perturbation superimposed attack algorithm, named SPS, which generates adversarial samples using the accumulation of multiple perturbation spike trains to generate more general adversarial sample. Our work aims to the adversarial attack again SNNs and design the adversarial sample from a different perspective than the pixel domain, but rather the spike trains domain. Firstly, the SPS algorithm uses the surrogate gradient to calculate the spike trains' gradient and perturbs the spike trains according to the gradient direction. Then, the method of spike trains superposition accumulates multiple perturbation spike trains and generates adversarial spike trains. Finally, the adversarial spike trains are mapped to the adversarial sample. The experimental results show that the attack success rate of SPS is better than state-of-the-art works, and the mean values are 95.42%. Experiments are also conducted on neuromorphic and static datasets to investigate the SPS performance under different conditions further. The results show that the SPS attack works perfect on both image and neuromorphic datasets.

Keywords: Adversarial sample · Spiking neural networks · SNNs · Spike trains · Neuromorphic dataset

1 Introduction

Spiking neural networks (SNNs) are regarded as the third generation of neural network models, which are closer to the working mechanism of the human brain [1]. This promise of SNNs comes from the favorable properties they exhibit in

Y. Xu et al. (Eds.): ML4CS 2022, LNCS 13655, pp. 457–471, 2023.
https://doi.org/10.1007/978-3-031-20096-0_34

real neural circuits, such as high biological plausibility, energy-efficient, and temporal information processing capability [2]. In recent years, this line of research has coincided with an increased interest in efficient hardware implementations for traditional deep neural networks (DNNs), as the huge demand for computational resources has become a hindrance as deep learning moves toward real-world scenarios such as automated driving, robotics, or the Internet of Things (IoT). Meanwhile, SNNs hold great promise for reducing computational resources due to their low power consumption and fast inference demonstrated on neuromorphic devices. For example, IBM TrueNorth [3], Intel Loihi [4], SNNs can be efficiently deployed on specialized neuromorphic hardware.

With the application of SNNs on neuromorphic devices in the real world, it is fundamental to ensure the secure operation of these devices. Nevertheless, the vulnerability of SNNs to potentially malicious adversarial attacks has attracted little attention so far. Therefore, it is essential to investigate the potential of adversarial attacks on spike neural network (SNN) models for computer-aware tasks. Its novel attack methods can also confuse the SNN, causing misjudgments or resulting in a system run-down. Especially in areas where data is important, adversarial attacks pose SNN-based systems at serious risk, such as in data-critical domains like face and voice recognition [5]. Thus, the research on adversarial attacks is imminent.

However, potential security risks in spike trains generated by the original samples are not identified. From this perspective, our work targets the spike trains of the original example to generate an adversarial sample, and we propose a new class of attack method Spike Perturbation Superimposed (SPS) attack. This algorithm can generate adversarial spike trains by the original spike trains and then map adversarial spike trains to adversarial samples. The SPS is evaluated on the Static MNIST, CIFAR10, and Neuromorphic N-MNIST datasets, the most common benchmark datasets within the static and neuromorphic community. The main contributions of this paper are as follows:

- A new ideology is proposed to attack SNNs, called the SPS attack, which starts from the novel perspective of corrupting spike trains to generate adversarial samples. SPS attack adds perturbation to spike trains using the potential attack capability of surrogate gradient functions, which can reduce the potential search space and improve the probability of successful attacks.
- An idea of cumulative attack is introduced, using simulation steps T to superimpose adversarial spike trains. The SPS algorithm takes the spike trains' superposition to accumulate multiple perturbation spike trains and generate adversarial spike trains. This method uses multiple perturbation spike trains to generate more robust adversarial spike trains and makes adversarial spike trains generate adversarial samples that are indistinguishable from the original samples.
- To further analyze the performance of the SPS algorithm under different experimental settings and to verify the reasonableness of our experimental settings, a large number of experiments are set up in this paper to analyze the SPS algorithm to generate better adversarial samples under the set parameters.

The rest of the paper starts with illustrations of the SNNs and adversarial attack for SNNs in Sect. 2. Moreover, Sect. 3 presents the design of adversarial perturbation. Finally, Sect. 4 contains our experiments and analysis results, followed by a conclusion in Sect. 5.

2 Preliminary and Related Work

Considering the many essential components involved in this paper, we will provide the necessary preliminary knowledge and related work in this section. First, the background of spiking neural networks (SNNs) is introduced. Then the existing research about adversarial attacks on SNNs is present.

2.1 Spiking Neural Networks

Unlike previous generations of neurons that used continuous values for their output signals, SNNs use spike trains to encode the input information. Thus, SNNs use binary operation (0-Silence, 1-Fire) and lend themselves well to fast and energy-efficient implementation on hardware devices [3,4]. There are many types of spike neuron models to build, e.g., Hodgkin-Huxley (HH) model [6], Leaky Integrate and Fire (LIF) model [7]. LIF model is the most commonly adopted spiking neuron model, and it can make each input spike contributes to increasing the neuron membrane potential V over time. LIF model is also used in our work, and the subthreshold dynamics of the LIF neuron are defined as:

$$\tau \frac{\mathrm{d}V(t)}{\mathrm{d}t} = -(V(t) - V_{\text{rest}}) + X(t), \tag{1}$$

$$\begin{cases} o(t) = 1 \& V(t) = V_{\text{rest}}, & \text{if } V(t) \geq V_{th} \\ o(t) = 0, & \text{if } V(t) < V_{th} \end{cases} \tag{2}$$

where $V(t)$ represents the membrane potential of the neuron at time t, $X(t)$ represents the input to neuron at time t, τ is the membrane time constant, $o(t)$ represents the resulting output spike, and V_{rest} is the resting potential.

2.2 Adversarial Attack for SNNs

Adversarial attacks attracted widespread interest when they were first found for deep convolutional networks [8]. Generally speaking, traditional attacks generate perturbations for the input image in the pixel domain. There are various adversarial attacks [9–11] have been proposed to generate adversarial samples, which have almost imperceptible perturbation to the original sample but still manage to fool the trained models.

However, the application scenario of the above-proposed attack methods is more suitable for DNNs than SNNs. We can find why this happens in the differences between DNNs and SNNs. DNNs usually have a fully connected structure, receive continuous values, and output continuous values. SNNs, on the other hand, use spike signals which are a series of discrete signals that occur at points in time, rather than continuous values [12]. Therefore, SNNs are not directly available to many of the adversarial attack methods used in DNNs; further research on adversarial attacks in SNNs becomes necessary.

Recently, several adversarial attack methodologies for SNNs have been proposed. Marchisio et al. [13] presented a set of DVS-Attacks for SNNs, which is the first to generate adversarial attacks on DVS signals. Still, DVS-Attacks did not give the magnitudes of the resulting perturbations. Sharmin et al. [14] proposed a method to attack DNNs, and then the adversarial samples fool the equivalent converted SNNs. The attacker must attack the trained DNNs model that approximates the SNNs to carry out the attack. Liang et al. [15] proposed a G2S/RSF attack for SNNs, and their method is generated adversarial samples but is more perceptible. Venceslai et al. [16] presented a methodology to attack SNNs through bit-flips triggered by adversarial perturbations, but it also faces the challenge of perceptible. Büchel et al. [17] proposed a set of PGD-based attack algorithms, which target neuromorphic datasets but do not attack static datasets. There is some work [18,19] demonstrates that the inherent robustness of SNNs results in attacks such as FGSM, PGD, etc., not being as effective in SNNs as they are in DNNs.

3 Spike Perturbation Superimposed Attack Method

Most of the existing adversarial attack methods are concerned with adding perturbations to the original sample in the pixel domain. In contrast, our approach is different in that we craft the adversarial perturbation based on the properties of SNNs, by adding perturbations to the spike trains and thus achieving the attack. This section presents the details of the proposed Spike Perturbation Superimposed (SPS) attack method. SPS method is a new class of attacks that perturb spike trains to affect spike values, with the eventual goal of producing an imperceptible sample X^{adv} and fooling the SNN classifier f.

3.1 Problem Description and Solutions

In adversarial attacks, the attack methods usually can be of two types: one does not require the computation of gradients, and the other is computing gradients to generate perturbations, e.g., the model's rule is gradient-free unsupervised or gradient-based supervised learning. We focus on the gradient-based attack due to the potential for a high attack success rate and then find efficient spike perturbations to disturb the classifier. But the adversarial attacks in SNNs face some challenges, the following key questions need to be investigated:

- (1). Can a non-linear spike trains gradient be efficiently calculated while reducing the search space for adversarial samples?
- (2). Can an adversarial sample be generated in the spike trains domain instead of the SOTA work where a perturbation is added to the pixel domain to generate an adversarial sample?

Further research has been done to address the above-mentioned challenges.

Surrogate Gradient. The first challenge concerns the non-differentiability of the spiking nonlinearity. Several approaches have been devised to overcome this challenge with varying degrees of success. The more general approach is defining the surrogate gradient as a continuous relaxation of the actual gradient. Surrogate gradient enables a good performance of SNN training and can significantly reduce the potential complexity and computational cost [20]. Thus, we use a surrogate gradient as an alternative approach to overcoming the difficulties with the spiking nonlinearity in this work. The output of the spike function $g(x)$ is only 0 or 1, so we can use the following definition to represent the process of issuing a spike:

$$\Phi(x) = \begin{cases} 1, x \geq 0 \\ 0, x < 0. \end{cases} \tag{3}$$

where $g(x) = \Phi(x)$, it is obvious that the spike function is not differentiable, so its gradient cannot be calculated. The core idea of surrogate gradient is that in forward propagation, the output of the neuron is discrete 0 and 1 using $g(x) = \Phi(x)$, while in backward propagation, the gradient of the surrogate gradient function $g'(x) = \sigma'(x)$ is used instead of the gradient of the spike function. We use the most common sigmoid function $\sigma(\alpha x)$ as surrogate gradient function:

$$\sigma(\alpha x) = \frac{1}{1 + \exp(-\alpha x)}. \tag{4}$$

where $\alpha \in (0, \infty)$ can control the smoothness of the function.

Finding Imperceptible Spike Perturbations. Many existing works are to transfer the attacks in DNN to SNN [14,17,21], but they do not fully use the characteristics of SNN to attack. Therefore, a further understanding of the SNN operation mechanism is needed. The original sample exists as discrete spike trains in the SNN, so being able to add noise to the spike trains to affect the final output is what we most expect to do. Since the production of the spike trains are binary, the direct use of a single run for classification results is highly susceptible to interference. Therefore, the output of the SNNs is generally considered the frequency of issue (or issue rate) of the output layer over a period T, and the level of issue rate indicates the response size of the class.

Previous research [22] has shown that robustness to an adversarial sample of SNNs trained on rate-coded inputs improves with the reduction in training time step. Thus, how to find an efficient adversarial perturbation is a complex problem. We add noise to the spike trains, which is different from the conventional method of adding noise to the image. Although we disturb the single spike and cause the output to be biased towards the wrong category, the SNN classifier f is still correctly classified when it goes through the large enough time step T. Therefore, this underlines the need for an improved method that generates an efficient adversarial sample, as proposed in the following subsections.

3.2 Problem Formulation

The following general form step obtains spike adversarial perturbations based on the above discussion. First, the goal of the attacker is to fool the SNN with imperceptible perturbation, so this problem can formulate as follow:

$$\begin{aligned} &\hat{f}(\boldsymbol{x}+\boldsymbol{\delta}) \neq \hat{f}(\boldsymbol{x}) \\ \text{subject to } &\boldsymbol{l} \preccurlyeq \boldsymbol{x}+\boldsymbol{\delta} \preccurlyeq \boldsymbol{u}, \end{aligned} \tag{5}$$

where δ is the perturbation magnitude, $\boldsymbol{l}$, $\boldsymbol{u} \in \mathbb{R}^n$ denote the lower and upper bounds of the values of $\boldsymbol{x}+\boldsymbol{\delta}$, and $\hat{f}$ is the source model. Second, the Eq. (5) is a form for finding the adversarial perturbation generalization. Further, to find a more suitable adversarial sample for SNN, we focus on adding noise on spike trains. Hence, the Eq. (5) can be converted into the following problem:

$$\begin{aligned} &\hat{f}(\mathcal{R}^T+\boldsymbol{\delta}') \neq \hat{f}(\mathcal{R}) \\ \text{subject to } &\boldsymbol{l}^{\mathcal{R}^T} \preccurlyeq \mathcal{R}^T+\boldsymbol{\delta}' \preccurlyeq \boldsymbol{u}^{\mathcal{R}^T}. \end{aligned} \tag{6}$$

where $\mathcal{R}^T = \left(r^1, r^2, \cdots, r^T\right)$ is the spike trains of $\boldsymbol{x}$ with the Poisson encoding in the time step T. We exploit the property of SNN to produce perturbation, so it can generate the adversarial samples that fit SNNs more closely.

The following subsection provides a method for solving the problem formulated in Eq. (6) and introduces the SPS attack method, a compatible yet efficient algorithm for generating perturbations and carving adversarial samples.

3.3 Spike Perturbation Superimposed Attack on Static and Neuromorphic Datasets

In solving the above problem, only adding a signal spike train can't affect the model's prediction, so we propose an SPS attack algorithm, a cumulative procedure. The attack strength is continuously increased during each addition of perturbation to the spike trains but not long after reaching a certain time T to converge. Then, we reconstruct the adversarial sample by superimposing the generated spike perturbations trains at the moment T. The overview of the proposed algorithm is illustrated in Fig. 1.

The SPS algorithm can be a powerful attack method based on the application of surrogate gradient and perturbation superimposed. The overall attack algorithm of SPS is also provided in the Algorithm 1. The SPS algorithm first initializes the input. Since the spike matrix generated by Poisson coding can be very close to the original image, it has good performance superiority in practical application scenarios [23]. Therefore, we use Poisson coding to process the input data, converting the input image into spike trains $\mathcal{R}$ with simulation step T, where $\mathcal{R} = (r_1, r_2, \ldots, r_T)$ (Step 2), $\mathcal{R}$ is a tensor of shape (T, w, h), w and h are the width and height of the image respectively. Next, we use the surrogate gradient method to calculate the gradient of the spike trains and perturb the original spike trains (Step 6). Therefore, the Eq. (1)–(2) can further convert into an explicitly iterative version to ensure computational feasibility. To this end,

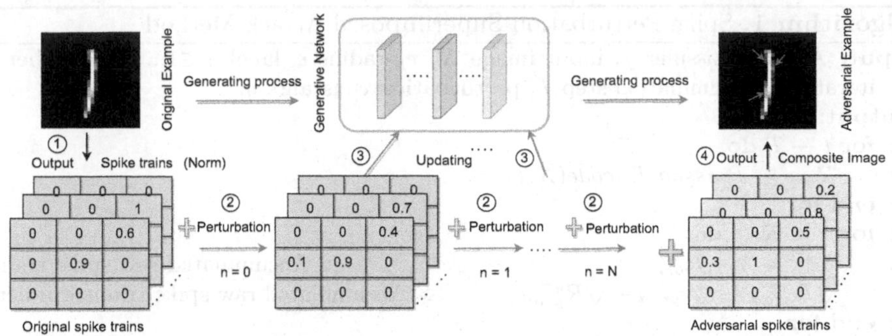

Fig. 1. Overview of the adversarial attack flow for SNNs. The attack flow consists of four part: ① is to generate spike trains with simulation step size T from the original samples by Poisson coding and normalize it; ② is to add perturbations to spike trains and iterate N times; ③ is the adversarial spike trains generated at each iteration to update the generative network; ④ is to generate adversarial samples from the accumulated adversarial spike trains by spike mapping.

the Euler's method is used to solve the conversion of the Eq. (1)–(2) and obtain an iterative expression:

$$V_t = V_{t-1} + \frac{1}{\tau}\left(-\left(V_{t-1} - V_{\text{reset}}\right) + X(t)\right), \tag{7}$$

$$o_t = f\left(V_t - V_{th}\right). \tag{8}$$

where V_t represents the membrane potential after neuronal dynamics at time-step t. S_t denotes the output spike at time t, which equals 1 if there is a spike and 0 otherwise. Equation (8) describe the spike generative process, where $f(x)$ is the step function, which satisfies $f(x) = 0$ when $x < 0$, otherwise $f(x) = 1$. Due to the the step function is non-differentiable, Eq. (4) is used instead in this paper.

For a given input X with label y, the spatio-temporal spike pattern of the output layer is converted into spike rate vector, the loss function is defined by mean squared error (MSE):

$$L = MSE(\boldsymbol{X}, \boldsymbol{Y}) = \frac{1}{T}\sum_{t=0}^{T-1} L_t = \frac{1}{T}\sum_{t=0}^{T-1}\frac{1}{C}\sum_{i=0}^{C-1}\left(o_{t,i} - y_{t,i}\right)^2 \tag{9}$$

Based on the iterative LIF neuron model Eq. (7)–(8) and a given loss function Eq. (9), the gradient propagation can be governed by:

$$\begin{cases} \frac{\partial L}{\partial V_i^{t,n}} = \frac{\partial L}{\partial o_i^{t,n}}\frac{\partial o_i^{t,n}}{\partial V_i^{t,n}} + \frac{\partial L}{\partial V_i^{t+1,n}}\frac{\partial V_i^{t+1,n}}{\partial V_i^{t,n}} \\ \frac{\partial L}{\partial o_i^{t,n}} = \sum_j \frac{\partial L}{\partial V_j^{t,n+1}}\frac{\partial V_j^{t,n+1}}{\partial o_i^{t,n}} + \frac{\partial L}{\partial V_i^{t+1,n}}\frac{\partial V_i^{t+1,n}}{\partial o_i^{t,n}} \end{cases} \tag{10}$$

At this point, we accumulate multiple spike trains with simulation step T to generate the final adversarial spike trains, which are mapped to an image by the

Algorithm 1. Spike Perturbation Superimposed Attack Method

Input: A SNN classifier f, input image X, r_p-radius ϵ, label $y \in 1,...,K$, number of iterations N, simulation step T, perturbation constants η;
Output: X_{adv}

for $t \leftarrow T$ **do**
 $\mathcal{R}_{ori} \leftarrow Poisson\_Encode(X, t)$;
end for
for $r \leftarrow \mathcal{R}_{ori}$ **do**
 $\mathcal{R}_{ori}^{acc} \leftarrow r + \mathcal{R}_{ori}^{acc}$ ▷ Accumulated raw spike trains.
 $\nabla\mathcal{R}_{grad}^{acc} \leftarrow \nabla r_{grad} + \nabla\mathcal{R}_{grad}^{acc}$ ▷ Accumulated raw spike trains gradient.
end for
$\mathcal{R}_{norm}^{ori} \leftarrow spike\_norm\left(\mathcal{R}_{ori}^{acc}\right)$ ▷ Norm operation.
for $n \leftarrow N$ **do**
 for $t \leftarrow T$ and $r \leftarrow \mathcal{R}_{ori}$ **do**
 ▷ Iterative generation of accumulated adversarial spike trains.
  if $t == 0$ **then**
   $\mathcal{R}_{adv}^{t} \leftarrow \mathcal{R}_{norm}^{ori} + \eta \cdot sign\left(\nabla\mathcal{R}_{grad}^{acc}\right)$
   $\mathcal{R}_{adv}^{t} \leftarrow clip\left(\mathcal{R}_{adv}^{t}, \mathcal{R}_{norm}^{ori} - \epsilon, \mathcal{R}_{norm}^{ori} + \epsilon\right)$
  else
   $\mathcal{R}_{adv}^{t} \leftarrow \mathcal{R}_{adv}^{t-1} + \eta \cdot sign\left(\nabla r_{grad}\right)$
   $\mathcal{R}_{adv}^{t} \leftarrow clip\left(\mathcal{R}_{adv}^{t}, \mathcal{R}_{adv}^{t-1} - \epsilon, \mathcal{R}_{adv}^{t-1} + \epsilon\right)$
  end if
 end for
 Updating.
end for
$X_{adv} \leftarrow spike\_map\left(R_{adv}^{T}, T\right)$ ▷ Spike trains convert to X_{adv}
Return X_{adv}

spike to generate the adversarial sample. The next step is to check if the new iterate $\boldsymbol{X}_{adv}$ can fool the target classifier f.

Finally, the SPS attack is an untargeted attack, and it can be processed according to different data forms. Limiting the size of the noise can make the spike mapped adversarial samples maintain high attack performance while also being human-imperceptible. Even though it can be easily transformed to a targeted method, by simply computing the distance between the original sample and the target category, the gradient is calculated based on the loss to achieve the attack.

4 Experiments

In this section, the experimental setup and results are presented, and the effectiveness of the proposed SPS attack is also evaluated.

4.1 Experimental Setup

Datasets. The experiments are evaluated on both static and neuromorphic datasets. The static datasets include MNIST [24] and CIFAR10 [25]. The neuromorphic datasets include N-MNIST [26], captured by dynamic vision sensors. Unlike frame-based data, neuromorphic datasets are composed of event-based data. Each event is encoded with four components (x, y, p, t), representing the x-coordinate, the y-coordinate, the polarity, and the timestamp, respectively.

Network Information. The detailed network structure setting during training and trained accuracy is shown in Table 1. Where N_{down} is the down-sample modules, each of which contain N_{conv} (Conv2d_Spiking Neurons) repeated and a max-pooling layer, and the networks also consist of N_{fc} (Fully Collected Layer) repeated; $V_{threshold}$ is the threshold voltage of the neuron, v_{reset} is the reset voltage of the neuron and the MSE as the default loss function.

Table 1. Network hyper-parameters and accuracy

Datasets	*Input_Size*	N_{conv}	N_{down}	N_{fc}	$V_{threshold}$	v_{reset}	*batch_size*	$Acc(MSE)$
MNIST	28×28×1	1	2	2	1	0	64	97.72%
CIFAR10	32×32×3	3	2	2	1	0	16	93.50%
N-MNIST	34×34×2	1	2	2	1	0	16	99.61%

Evaluation metric. To evaluate our algorithm, the Attack Success Rate (ASR) is computed by us. It can be computed as follow:

$$ASR = \left| \boldsymbol{X} \in \mathfrak{D} : f(\boldsymbol{X}) \neq f(\boldsymbol{X}^{adv}) \right| / |\mathfrak{D}|, \tag{11}$$

where $\mathfrak{D}$ is a dataset, this equation can measure the efficiency of the algorithm.

4.2 Experimental Results

In this subsection, we evaluate the effectiveness of the proposed algorithm using more experiments with state-of-the-art (SOTA) methods. More specifically, to better investigate the results of our approach in different datasets, extensive experiments are conducted on multiple types of datasets (traditional static dataset MNIST, CIFAR10; and neuromorphic dataset N-MNIST). We also conducted experiments on the CIFAR10-DVS dataset, and although our proposed method is able to cause high attack success rates, the experimental results for this data are not presented in the paper due to the low prediction accuracy of its trained model (CIFAR10-DVS (*Acc*): 64.80%, ASR: 99.92 ± 0.08%).

Before the SPS algorithm generates the adversarial samples, we set several hyper-parameters. The η is used to control the size of the added perturbation; usually, the enormous value, the more significant the effect will be. However, the larger the η, the worse the invisibility of the adversarial samples, so ϵ is used to constrain the range of the spike perturbation to make the generated adversarial samples invisible to the human eye, the smaller the value of ϵ, the better.

Then we also analyze the reasons for the selected parameter values. Most existing works are compared for a more comprehensive analysis of the SPS attack algorithm, and the experiment results are shown in Table 2. The experimental results show that our method has a significant performance on both static and neuromorphic datasets, with 4.73% improvement on the MNIST dataset and 0.04% improvement on the N-MNIST datasets. Although the PGD method has caused a high attack effect than the SPS method, it did not produce a superior effect on the neuromorphic datasets. Our proposed SPS method applies to static datasets and is capable of causing high ASR on neuromorphic datasets.

Intuitively, the superiority of the SPS algorithm consists of two main aspects: Firstly, the introduction of alternative gradients potentially improves attack performance, reducing the search space overhead when searching the decision boundaries of the SNNs model. Secondly, adding perturbations to the spike trains and generating adversarial samples can make full use of the properties of SNNs. In the simulation step T, noise and information from the original sample are accumulated in the spike trains. When setting a reasonable T value, the SPS algorithm can generate adversarial samples invisible to humans and cause misclassification of the model with high confidence.

Table 2. The performance of SPS attack algorithm, High-latency attack [22], Low-latency attack [18], [17], G2S/RSF [27] on the MNIST, CIFAR10 and N-MNIST datasets.

Type	Static				Neuromorphic
Dataset	MNIST			CIFAR10	N-MNIST
Acc(%)	97.72			93.50	99.61
	Existing works				
ASR(%)	High-latency [22]	FGSM	–	85	–
		PGD	–	**96.2**	–
	Low-latency [18]	FGSM	–	64.5	–
		PGD	–	94.7	–
	[17]	PGD	–	–	48.63
		Probabilistic PGD	–	–	54.46
		SparseFool	–	–	**99.76**
	[15]	G2S/RSF	**91.31**	76.86	97.38
	Ours	**SPS**	**96.04**	**90.46**	**99.80**
Enhancement			**+4.73**	–	**+0.04**

Moreover, to further investigate the effect of the SPS attack method on the simulation time step T, hyperparameter settings, etc., extensive experimental analyses are performed in the next subsection.

4.3 Further Analysis

In this section, three aspects are studied: the simulation time steps T, the setting of hyper-parameters, and the optimizer selection. A large number of experiments will be done to perform a reasonable analysis.

Analysis of the SPS Method at Different Simulation Steps T. Intuitively, the SPS attack is affected at different simulation steps T, and assume that the larger T is obtained, the better the adversarial sample will be.

However, experimental results show that this is not the case, as the attack capability of SPS will reach its peak when T reaches a certain value, and the performance of SPS will be reduced when T is increased again. In the Fig. 2, the multiples sets of T values for the experiments are set, as the T value increases, the ASR value increases with it, and when it reaches a specific value (MNIST: $T = 35$, CIFAR10: $T = 25$, N-MNIST: $T = 15$), the peak is reached the ASR value will keep decreasing as T increases.

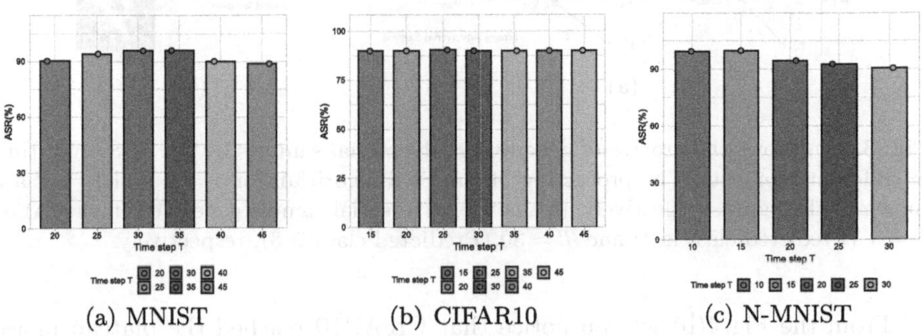

Fig. 2. Multiple simulation time steps T were set, and by observing the changes of the ASR values of the SPS attack at different time steps T, it can be found that there is an increasing and then decreasing trend with the increase of time steps T.

The possible reasons for such a phenomenon are: (1). T is small, the added noise can only have a limited effect, and the adversarial samples generated using adversarial spike trains are not enough to cause a significant impact on the SNNs; (2). T reaches a specific value, the SPS attack allows the added noise to maximize the impact on the decision boundary of the SNNs model, making the generated adversarial samples fool the source model; (3). T exceeds a specific value, it also means that more information is added to the original sample, and then the impact of the added noise is limited by the inherent robustness of SNNs [19].

The adversarial samples generated by experimenting with different T are shown in Fig. 3. When $T = 1$, the generated adversarial samples are significantly different from the original images, but the SNNs still classify them correctly; when $T = 30$, the adversarial samples are almost indistinguishable from the original samples and make the SNNs misclassify them.

Analysis of the SPS Method Under Different Hyper-parameter Settings. To investigate different hyperparameter settings in the SPS algorithm, we set multiple sets of hyper-parameter values for the experiments. The results are shown in Fig. 4. As the η value increases, the ASR value increases with it, and when it reaches a specific value, the ASR increases very slowly even if the η value increases. Thus, we need to set the optimal parameter value so that the SPS algorithm can obtain the optimal solution, and here the parameter is set to the value at the inflection point.

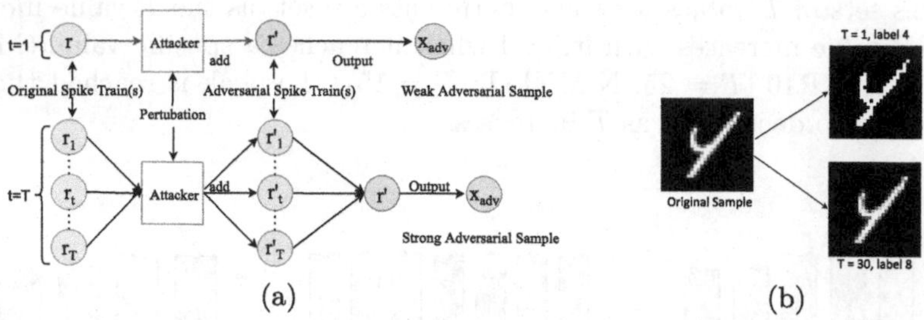

Fig. 3. (a). shows the process of generating adversarial samples by the SPS algorithm at different moments. The processing of the SPS algorithm for $t = 1$ and $t = T$ are shown in the figure, respectively. (b). is the adversarial sample generated in the (a) at $T = 1$ (Predicted class is 4) and $T = 30$ (Predicted class is 8), respectively.

From the Fig. 4(b) we can notice that CIFAR10 reached the plateau phase much earlier ($\eta = 0.1$). By further investigation, the original network trained with CIFAR10 has a larger T', while our generative network is set up with T smaller than T'. In the SPS algorithm, we want to know the simulation step T is how it affects the results of ASR. Thus, we fix the values of η and ϵ, then increase or decrease the T of the SPS algorithm. The results are shown in Fig. 2(b), which further confirms that the value of ASR can also be influenced by adjusting the value of T, but large or small T plays an inverse role for the SPS algorithm, so we need to set the optimal T.

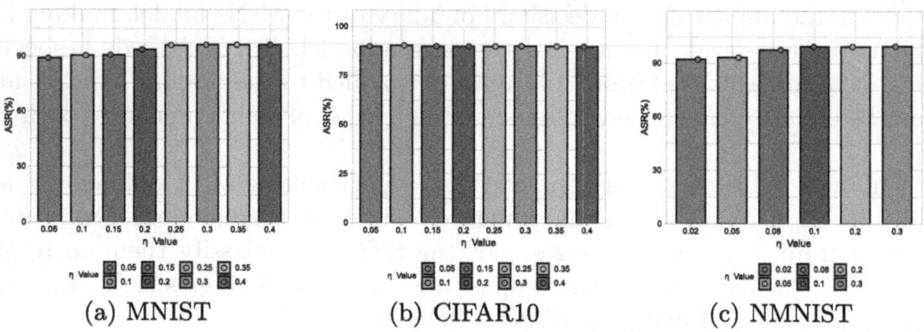

Fig. 4. Setting different η for the MNIST, CIFAR10 and N-MNIST, respectively. As the value of η increases, the value of ASR also increases, and when a specific value is reached, η has merely an effect on ASR. The $\eta = 0.25$, $\eta = 0.1$ and $\eta = 0.1$ are the inflection point for the the MNIST, CIFAR10, N-MNIST, respectively.

To demonstrate the effect of SPS on the neuromorphic dataset, the SPS algorithm perturbs the spike trains and maps the adversarial spike trains to the adversarial sample. Then the generated adversarial sample is misclassified by the classifier. We can see from the results (in Table 2) that the SPS algorithm is suitable for static datasets and neuromorphic datasets. In other words, it shows that the SPS algorithm is a general attack algorithm.

Analysis of SPS Method on Optimizer Selection. In this experiment, two optimizers are chosen, namely Adam and SGD with momentum. By analyzing the performance of these two optimizers on different datasets, the best optimizer is selected as the optimizer for the SPS algorithm.

Towards this end, Adam and SGD with momentum (momentum = 0.9) are used as the optimizer of the SPS algorithm, and the parameter settings are the same for the experiment. The final experimental results are shown in Fig. 5(a), the Adam's ASR is significantly higher than SGD on the MNIST and N-MNIST datasets, besides Adam and SGD perform similarly on the CIFAR10 dataset. From the results, using Adam as the optimizer is better than SGD, so the SPS algorithm uses Adam as its optimizer.

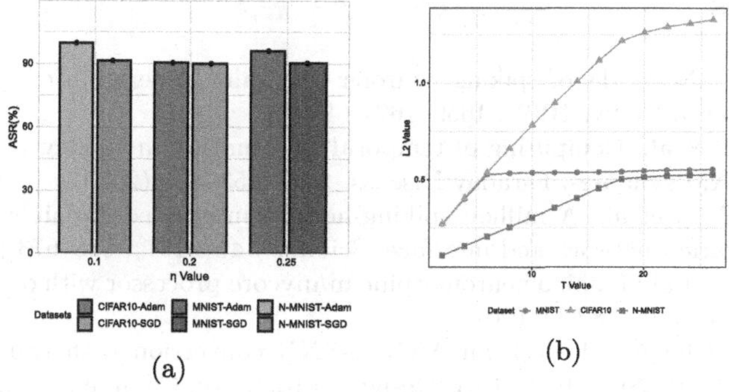

Fig. 5. (a). Effectiveness of the SPS algorithm for attacks with different optimizers (SGD, Adam). (b). Variation of L2 values with T moments under optimizer Adam.

Remark: The SPS algorithm causes a significant decrease in the model's accuracy on both static and neuromorphic datasets. At the same time, the average value of ASR can also reach 95.42%. The above discussion shows that SPS performs better on neuromorphic and static datasets. A slight modification of the spike trains may cause vital damage to the static and neuromorphic dataset. Therefore, the generated adversarial samples have an attack success rate and are indistinguishable from the original ones. Besides, the L2 values are calculated for each data set at the optimal setting. The calculation results are shown in Fig. 5(b), where the L2 values will also converge as T converges to a specific value. Experimental results further validate our previous conjecture that the perturbative impact of the generated adversarial samples will converge when the value of T reaches a particular value. As the value of T continues to increase, the SPS algorithm will introduce more information about the original sample on the one hand. Still, on the other hand, it will reduce the effect of the perturbation on the adversarial sample.

5 Conclusion

This paper proposes a novel adversarial algorithm (SPS) that exploits original spike trains to generate an adversarial sample. SPS generates adversarial samples by perturbing spike trains. However, due to the inherent robustness of SNNs, we need to do further manipulations. Thus, the SPS algorithm generates the final adversarial spike trains by accumulating the multiple perturbed spike trains and mapping them to the adversarial samples. Experimental results show that the SPS algorithm outperforms SOTA work on static and neuromorphic datasets.

Acknowledgement. This work received support from the National Natural Science Foundation of China (No. 62072109, No. U1804263); Natural Science Foundation of Fujian Province (No. 2021J06013, No. 2020J01500).

References

1. Maass, W.: Networks of spiking neurons: the third generation of neural network models. Neural Netw. **10**(9), 1659–1671 (1997)
2. Wang, W., et al.: Computing of temporal information in spiking neural networks with ReRAM synapses. Faraday Discuss. **213**, 453–469 (2019)
3. Merolla, P.A., et al.: A million spiking-neuron integrated circuit with a scalable communication network and interface. Science **345**(6197), 668–673 (2014)
4. Davies, M., et al.: Loihi: a neuromorphic manycore processor with on-chip learning. IEEE Micro **38**(1), 82–99 (2018)
5. Ho, N.D., Chang, I.J.: Tcl: an ANN-to-SNN conversion with trainable clipping layers. In: 2021 58th ACM/IEEE Design Automation Conference (DAC), pp. 793–798. IEEE (2021)
6. Noble, D.: A modification of the Hodgkin-Huxley equations applicable to Purkinje fibre action and pacemaker potentials. J. Physiol. **160**(2), 317 (1962)
7. Gerstner, W., Kistler, W.M., Naud, R., Paninski, L.: Neuronal Dynamics: From Single Neurons to Networks and Models of Cognition. Cambridge University Press, Cambridge (2014)
8. Szegedy, C., et a.: Intriguing properties of neural networks. arXiv preprint arXiv:1312.6199 (2013)
9. Goodfellow, I.J., Shlens, J., Szegedy, C.: Explaining and harnessing adversarial examples. arXiv preprint arXiv:1412.6572 (2014)
10. Carlini, N., Wagner, D.: Towards evaluating the robustness of neural networks. In: 2017 IEEE Symposium on Security and Privacy (sp), pp. 39–57. IEEE (2017)
11. Mo, K., Tang, W., Li, J., Yuan, X.: Attacking deep reinforcement learning with decoupled adversarial policy. IEEE Trans. Dependable Secure Comput. (2022)
12. Tavanaei, A., Ghodrati, M., Kheradpisheh, S.R., Masquelier, T., Maida, A.: Deep learning in spiking neural networks. Neural Netw. **111**, 47–63 (2019)

13. Marchisio, A., Pira, G., Martina, M., Masera, G., Shafique, M.: Dvs-attacks: adversarial attacks on dynamic vision sensors for spiking neural networks. In: 2021 International Joint Conference on Neural Networks (IJCNN), pp. 1–9. IEEE (2021)
14. Sharmin, S., Panda, P., Sarwar, S. S., Lee, C., Ponghiran, W., Roy, K.: A comprehensive analysis on adversarial robustness of spiking neural networks. In: 2019 International Joint Conference on Neural Networks (IJCNN), pp. 1–8. IEEE (2019)
15. Liang, L., et al.: Exploring adversarial attack in spiking neural networks with spike-compatible gradient. IEEE Trans. Neural Netw. Learn. Syst. (2021)
16. Venceslai, V., Marchisio, A., Alouani, I., Martina, M., Shafique, M.: Neuroattack: undermining spiking neural networks security through externally triggered bit-flips. In: 2020 International Joint Conference on Neural Networks (IJCNN), pp. 1–8. IEEE (2020)
17. Büchel, J., Lenz, G., Hu, Y., Sheik, S., Sorbaro, M.: Adversarial attacks on spiking convolutional networks for event-based vision. arXiv preprint arXiv:2110.02929 (2021)
18. Kundu, S., Pedram, M., Beerel, P.A.: Hire-SNN: harnessing the inherent robustness of energy-efficient deep spiking neural networks by training with crafted input noise. In: Proceedings of the IEEE/CVF International Conference on Computer Vision, pp. 5209–5218 (2021)
19. El-Allami, R., Marchisio, A., Shafique, M., Alouani, I.: Securing deep spiking neural networks against adversarial attacks through inherent structural parameters. In: 2021 Design, Automation & Test in Europe Conference & Exhibition (DATE), pp. 774–779. IEEE (2021)
20. Lillicrap, T.P., Cownden, D., Tweed, D.B., Akerman, C.J.: Random synaptic feedback weights support error backpropagation for deep learning. Nature Commun. **7**(1), 1–10 (2016)
21. El-Allami, R., Marchisio, A., Shafique, M., Alouani, I.: Securing deep spiking neural networks against adversarial attacks through inherent structural parameters. arXiv preprint arXiv:2012.05321 (2020)
22. Sharmin, S., Rathi, N., Panda, P., Roy, K.: Inherent adversarial robustness of deep spiking neural networks: effects of discrete input encoding and non-linear activations. In: Vedaldi, A., Bischof, H., Brox, T., Frahm, J.-M. (eds.) ECCV 2020. LNCS, vol. 12374, pp. 399–414. Springer, Cham (2020). https://doi.org/10.1007/978-3-030-58526-6_24
23. Diehl, P.U., Pedroni, B.U., Cassidy, A., Merolla, P., Neftci, E., Zarrella, G.: Truehappiness: neuromorphic emotion recognition on truenorth. In: 2016 International Joint Conference on Neural Networks (IJCNN), pp. 4278–4285. IEEE (2016)
24. LeCun, Y., Cortes, C., Burges, C.: Mnist handwritten digit database (2010)
25. Krizhevsky, A., Hinton, G., et al.: Learning multiple layers of features from tiny images (2009)
26. Orchard, G., Jayawant, A., Cohen, G.K., Thakor, N.: Converting static image datasets to spiking neuromorphic datasets using saccades. Front. Neurosci. **9**, 437 (2015)
27. Liang, L., et al.: Exploring adversarial attack in spiking neural networks with spike-compatible gradient. arXiv preprint arXiv:2001.01587 (2020)

Diverse Web APIs Recommendation with Privacy-preservation for Mashup Development

Shengqi Wu[1](✉), Lianyong Qi[1], Yuwen Liu[2], Yihong Yang[3], Ying Miao[1], and Fei Dai[4]

[1] School of Computer Science, Qufu Normal University, Jining, China
wuwenshanjun@gmail.com, lianyongqi@qfnu.edu.cn

[2] College of Computer Science and Technolog, China University of Petroleum, Beijing, China

[3] School of Information Engineering, China University of Geosciences, Wuhan, China

[4] College of Big Data and Intelligent Engineering, Southwest Forestry University, Kunming, China
daifei@swfu.edu.cn

Abstract. The increasing number of web APIs in various APIs sharing communities makes it possible for mashup developers to create their interested mashups efficiently and conveniently. However, the large number of web APIs with similar functions bring a problem that it is hard for developers to choose the appropriate APIs. Otherwise, APIs with similar functions always cause the redundancy of recommendation and this may limit developers' options, which further leads to the dissatisfaction of developers. To address these problems, we first construct a web APIs correlation graph according to Mashup-Api interaction records. Based on the graph, we then propose a MinHash-based and diverse web APIs recommendation method named Min-Div, which can recommend the Top-K optimal results with best diversity and achieve privacy protection. Finally, we conduct a series of experiments and evaluation results prove the effectiveness and usefulness of the proposed Min-Div method.

Keywords: API recommendation · Diversity · MinHash · Privacy · Correlation graph

1 Introduction

With the rapid development of intelligent network and the popularity of Service-Oriented Architecture (SOA), a large number of web Application Programming Interfaces (APIs) which can be accessed remotely and can achieve plentiful functions have been developed. Meanwhile, some APIs sharing communities (i.e., programmableweb.com, PW) which gather various web APIs have been emerged [3,15]. According to the development requirements and the commercial value, mashup developers can choose several interested APIs to compose them together and conveniently create an expected mashup.

Y. Xu et al. (Eds.): ML4CS 2022, LNCS 13655, pp. 472–485, 2023.
https://doi.org/10.1007/978-3-031-20096-0_35

However, massive web APIs make it difficult for mashup developers to select the suitable web APIs because of the compatibility uncertainty among different APIs. Thus, it is essential to design an effective and compatible web API recommendation method for the mashup development. Currently, the number of web API recommendation methods grow vigorously and most of them take the compatibility among different APIs into consideration. To satisfy the mashup developers' functional needs, these methods normally recommend a group of APIs with better compatibility which also represents a better cooperation among different APIs. And the effectiveness can be achieved by integrating these APIs together, which is also important to promote the mashup development. However, these existing methods and researches often have the following disadvantages.

(1) The existing methods often ignore the diversity of web APIs. Because of API numbers' sharply increasing, the functions achieved by different web APIs always have some similarity. Therefore, it may cause the redundancy of recommendation and bring some needless job if we ignore the diversity. Otherwise, recommending web APIs with similar functions may constrict the choice space of developers, which makes it possible that developers' expectations cannot be met if they are dissatisfied with the recommended result.
(2) The existing methods often ignore the privacy protection of mashup developers. Protecting enterprises or mashup developers' sensitive information is often at an even higher priority. When the developers input their requirements to the recommender system, it is possible to lead to the information leakage. And some mashup developers do not want their search information are recorded in the network, so privacy protection is regarded as an important business.

To address these challenges, a MinHash-based and diverse web APIs recommendation method named Min-Div is proposed in this paper. This novel recommendation method not only considers the compatibility among different APIs, but also takes the diversity into consideration. And it also protects the privacy of developers' information in the recommendation process. Therefore, Min-Div can achieve diversity of recommendation and protect privacy in the same time.

The major contributions of this paper are three folds and they are as follows.

(1) According to the mashup-api usage records, we model the compatibility between any two APIs as the times they have ever been composed together. And we construct a web APIs correlation graph which provides the compatibility information and the functional information of APIs.
(2) Based on the web APIs correlation graph and the developers' expectations, we get the candidate sets of APIs and we utilize the MinHash algorithm to select the Top-K groups of APIs with the optimal diversity. In the process of utilizing MinHash algorithm, we achieve the privacy protection in the same time.
(3) Large-scale experiments are conducted in the real dataset crawled from PW. And the effectiveness of our method can be proved by comparing it with other state-of-the-art methods.

The remainder of this paper is organized as follows. In Sect. 2, the API recommendation methods in recent years are investigated and introduced. Section 3 illustrates the details of our proposed method. And in Sect. 4, we conduct massive experiments on the PW dataset and we prove the effectiveness of our method. In the last, we conclude our paper and discuss the future work in Sect. 5.

2 Related Work

In recent years, all kinds of web APIs recommendation methods continuously appear. And we will introduce these researches in this Section.

The methods based on collaborative filtering (CF) and matrix factorization (MF) are very popular in these years. Gao et al. [5] utilize collaborative learning techniques to study the implicit knowledge in IIoT, which can deeply exploit the valuable relationships between APIs and users. After that, they enhance the matrix factorization model based on the mined implicit knowledge. Considering the geographic location information in mashup-API interaction records, Botangen K A et al. [2] propose an API recommendation method based on probabilistic matrix factorization and it has been proved that this method can increase the precision of recommendation. Meissa M et al. [10] construct a recommendation model named PWR (Personalized Web API Recommendation), which recommends APIs and provides personalized suggestions to users without decreasing the accuracy. Lian et al. [8] utilize the neural graph collaborative filtering technique to propose a novel APIs recommendation method which exploits the high-order connectivity between APIs and users. And this proposal can further improve the accuracy of recommendation. However, these methods based on CF and MF may cause the lack of diversity and produce redundancy.

Considering the shortcomings of the above methods, some novel models are proposed to address them. Yao et al. [17] enhance the recommendation diversity by developing a latent variable model to uncover the latent correlations between APIs and analyzing their co-invocation patterns. By exploring the reusable composition context, their proposal can help to identify the most appropriate APIs for developers' composition tasks. In order to facilitate automatic mashup composition, a novel automated method called SerFinder is proposed in [1]. This method mainly addresses the issue that some methods mostly focus on recommending individual APIs but ignore the diversity. By optimizing those methods, it achieves collectively recommending APIs to developers. Due to the existence of recommendation redundancy and the negligence of cooperation relations among APIs, a novel APIs recommendation framework is proposed by Gao et al. [6], which focuses on recommending API sets instead of APIs. And the diversity of this method has been proved by experiments. Cheng et al. [4] propose ATD and PAD method to achieve diverse API recommendation based on a similarity graph and their proposal can effectively reduce the unnecessary computation overheads. However, all these methods ignore the close correlation between APIs. Thus, the introduce of graph which can reflect APIs' correlation is very important.

The introduce of graph brings a new research direction to APIs recommendation. Based on Mashup-API co-invocation patterns, Wang et al. [14] construct a refined knowledge graph, based on which they propose an unsupervised API recommendation method. This method utilizes deep random walks to learn implicit low-dimensional embedding representations of entities and it is proved that it performs well on the accuracy and efficiency. Ling et al. [9] propose a novel graph embedding method named GeAPI, which can deeply explore the connection among different APIs. In order to utilize the close correlation among APIs, Qi et al. construct a web APIs correlation graph which contains all the APIs and their functional descriptions. In [12], they model the APIs recommendation problem as a minimum group Steiner tree method which focuses on searching the optimal result with the least node numbers. In [11], they regard the times that two APIs have been composed together as the compatibility degree and they expect to get the optimal result with the best compatibility. In [13], they consider both the compatibility and node number, based on which they further increase the precision and recall of recommendation.

The common shortcoming of the above methods is that they cannot achieve the multi-objective optimization of compatibility, diversity and privacy protection. To address these issues, we propose a MinHash-based and diverse web APIs recommendation method (i.e., Min-Div) which can increase the diversity of recommendation and protect the privacy of developers' information with the compatibility guarantee. The details of Min-Div is illustrated in the next Section.

3 Our Approach: Min-Div

Figure 1 introduces the major framework of our proposed Min-Div. Min-Div mainly consists of three steps. Step 1 is to construct the web APIs correlation graph and it is conducted in the offline phase. Step 2 is to utilize Steiner tree search algorithm to search for the candidate API sets based on mashup developers' input keywords. And Step 3 selects the optimal Top-K API sets with the best diversity which is calculated by MinHash algorithm. The details from Step 1 to Step 3 are described in the following three subsections.

3.1 Step 1: Construct Web APIs Correlation Graph

In order to sufficiently explore the connection degree between APIs, we extract the compatibility information from the Mashup-Api interaction records as well as the historical usages. If two APIs have ever been composed together to develop a common mashup, then we regard the two APIs are compatible. And we take the times they are integrated together as the degree of their compatibility. Otherwise, we can also get the information about APIs' corresponding functions which represent the functions they can achieve from the Mashup-Api interaction records.

After extracting the information about APIs, we construct the web APIs correlation graph G (i.e., Fig. 2). And we use the example in Fig. 2 to illustrate the process of building web APIs correlation graph. For each API which is in the Mashup-Api interaction records, we set a corresponding node v in the correlation

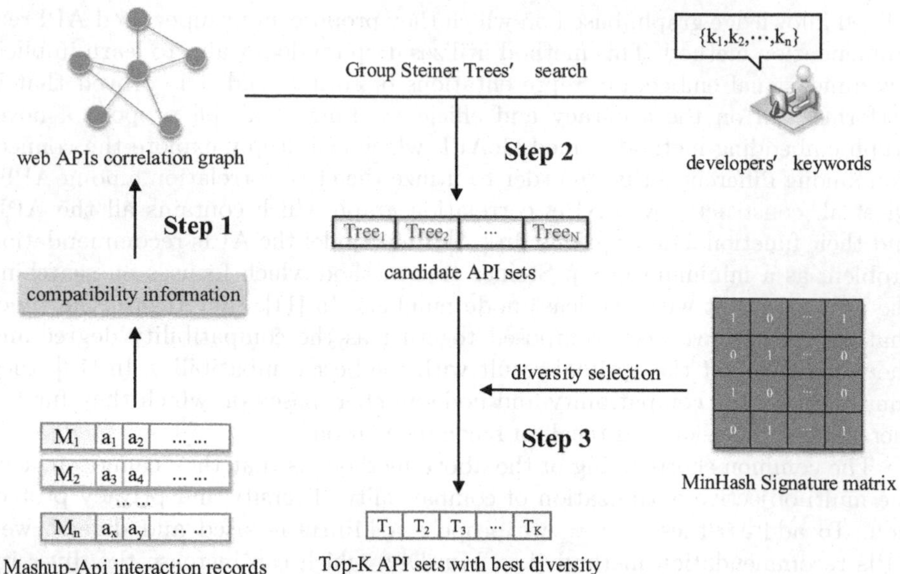

Fig. 1. The framework of Min-Div

graph and all the nodes (i.e., v_1, v_2, ..., v_5 in Fig. 2) form a node set V. Otherwise, each node contains its functional keyword set that represents the functions its corresponding API can achieve. For example, in Fig. 2, the functional keyword set of v_4 is $\{k_2, k_4, k_5\}$. To indicate the compatibility between APIs, there is an edge e linking two nodes if the two corresponding APIs have ever been composed together to develop a common mashup and all the edges form an edge set E. We regard the times that two APIs have been integrated together as the weight value w of edge and all the weight values form a weight set W. For example, there is an edge between v_1 and v_5 in Fig. 2, which represents the two corresponding APIs are compatible. And the weight value of the edge is 2, which means they have ever been integrated together for 2 times.

After repeating the above process, we can build a web APIs correlation graph $G(V, E, W)$. For the obtained graph G (i.e., Fig. 2), we adopt normalization to all the weight values by replacing them with their reciprocal (i.e., we obtain Fig. 3 from Fig. 2). Then, we will use Steiner tree algorithm to search the candidate API sets with better compatibility as well as smaller weight values in the next subsection.

3.2 Step 2: Search for the Candidate API Sets

According to the expectations of mashup developers, we need to confirm the compatibility of our recommendation result that can meet developers' requirements. Thus, we need to search for the candidate API sets with good compatibility based on the obtained web APIs correlation graph. Here, we will introduce some definitions as follows.

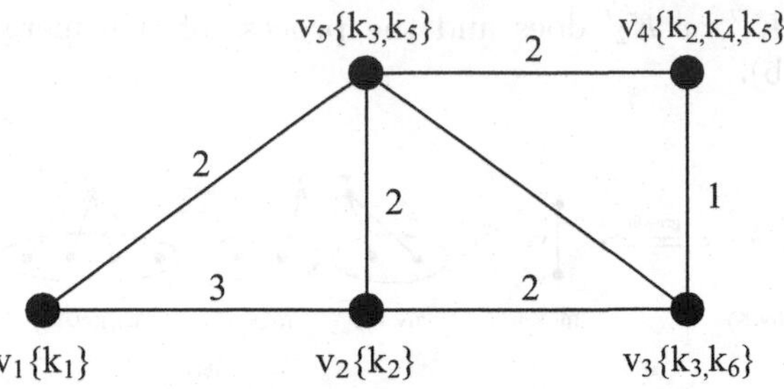

Fig. 2. An example: web APIs correlation graph

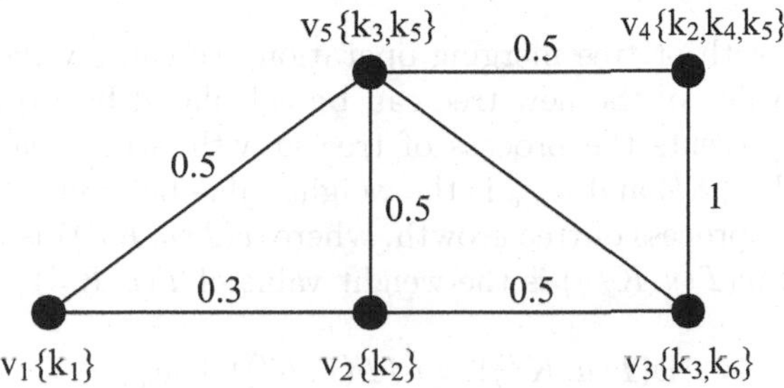

Fig. 3. Normalized web APIs correlation graph

Steiner Tree. Given a web APIs correlation graph $G(V, E, W)$ and a node set $V' \subseteq V$. Then, T is a Steiner Tree if T is a connected tree which contains all the nodes in V'.

Group Steiner Tree. Given a web APIs correlation graph $G(V, E, W)$ and a group of node sets V_1, V_2, ..., $V_l \subseteq V(V_i \cap V_j = \emptyset, 1 \leq i, j \leq l, i \neq j)$. Then, T is a Group Steiner Tree if T is a connected tree which contains only one node from each node set $V_r (1 \leq r \leq l)$.

In order to get the candidate web API sets with better compatibility, we need to search for the group Steiner trees with smaller weight values in the web APIs correlation graph. We first select the nodes whose keywords contain one required keyword as an initial root node. Then, we conduct tree growth and tree merging operation.

Tree growth. We assume the required keyword set that is input by a mashup developer is K. For a tree $T(v, K')$ where v is its root node and K' is its containing keyword set, if $K' \neq K$, then this tree need to conduct tree growth operation. The process of tree growth operation is described in Fig. 4(a). Tree $T(v, K')$ searches for a neighbor node u and takes u as the new root node of the new tree $T(u, K'')$ to finish the operation of tree growth ($K' \subseteq K''$).

Tree merging. For two trees $T(v, {K_1}')$ and $T(v, {K_2}')$, they will be merged to be a new tree $T(v, {K_1}' \cup {K_2}')$ if ${K_1}' \cap {K_2}' = \emptyset$ and ${K_1}' \cup {K_2}'$ contains more required keywords than $K_1{}'$ or $K_2{}'$ does and the process of tree merging operation is shown in Fig. 4(b).

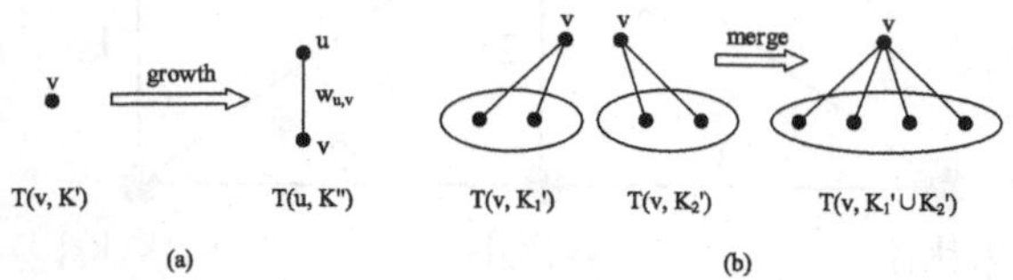

Fig. 4. Tree growth and tree merging operation

After tree growth or tree merging operation, we can always get a new tree and the weight value of the new tree can be calculated by Eq. (1) and Eq. (2). Equation (1) represents the process of tree growth, where $w(T(v, K'))$ is the weight value of $T(v, K')$ and $w_{u,v}$ is the weight value between u and v. Equation (2) represents the process of tree growth, where $w(T(v, K_1{}'))$ is the weight value of $T(v, K_1{}')$ and $w(T(v, K_2{}'))$ is the weight value of $T(v, K_2{}')$.

$$w(T(u, K'')) = w(T(v, K')) + w_{u,v} \tag{1}$$

$$w(T(v, K_1{}' \cup K_2{}')) = w(T(v, K_1{}')) + w(T(v, K_2{}')) \tag{2}$$

We repeat the operation of tree growth and tree merging until we have searched the whole web APIs correlation graph. Then, we can find several group Steiner trees that cover the keywords in required keyword set K, from which we select the candidate trees (i.e., API sets) with smaller weight values as well as better compatibility.

3.3 Step 3: Select Optimal API Sets with Best Diversity

After we get the candidate API sets, we need to select the optimal ones with the best diversity from them. It is well known that diversity need to be measured by calculating the similarity. However, when there are many sets need to compare diversity, it is very time-consuming for traditional methods to judge the similarity between each pair of them. Thus, we need a method that can reduce the calculation dimension, i.e., MinHash. MinHash is an efficient algorithm which can measure the similarity by reflecting the feature vectors to a signature matrix and it can achieve privacy protection by transforming the information to hash values [7,16]. Now, we will use an example to illustrate the details of MinHash algorithm.

We assume there are one item set $U = \{a, b, c, d, e\}$ and four feature sets $S_1 = \{a, d\}$, $S_2 = \{c\}$, $S_3 = \{b, d, e\}$, $S_4 = \{a, c, d\}$. Feature vectors can reflect feature sets. For example, the feature vector of S_1 is $\{1, 0, 0, 1, 0\}$. Then, we can utilize feature vectors and row numbers to mark them, and build an initial matrix for them in Table 1.

Table 1. The initial matrix built for the feature sets

Row	Item	S_1	S_2	S_3	S_4
0	a	1	0	0	1
1	b	0	0	1	0
2	c	0	1	0	1
3	d	1	0	1	1
4	e	0	0	1	0

In the MinHash technique, it is need to use a hash function to map elements of the sets to integers. And hash function should be in the form of : $h(x) = (ax + b) \bmod m$, where x is the row number of original characteristic matrix i.e., $x \in \{0, 1, 2, 3, 4\}$. And a and b are any random numbers smaller or equal to the largest row number and both must be unique for each hash function. Otherwise, m is a prime number larger than the largest row number (i.e., m=5). Additionally, m and a must be coprime number. Considering these conditions, we set two hash functions $h1 : (x + 1) \bmod 5$ and $h2 : (3x + 1) \bmod 5$. Then, we can get the new table in Table 2.

Table 2. Updated permutation numbers using hash functions

Row	S_1	S_2	S_3	S_4	$h1$	$h2$
0	1	0	0	1	1	1
1	0	0	1	0	2	4
2	0	1	0	1	3	2
3	1	0	1	1	4	0
4	0	0	1	0	0	3

Then, we can get the signature matrix from Table 2. For the feature vector of each set S, when the vector value is 1, we need to compare all the corresponding hash values and select the smallest one as the signature value. For example, when the vector value of S_1 is 1, its corresponding hash values for hash function $h1$ are 1 and 4. Then, we take 1 as its signature value for $h1$. The process need to be repeated for every feature set and every hash function. After that, the signature matrix can be achieved and it is shown in Table 3.

Finally, we utilize *Jac-Similarity* to calculate the similarity between every two feature sets based on the signature matrix. And the equation of *Jac-Similarity* is shown in Eq. (3). In Eq. (3), the denominator represents the total number of items in set A and set B, and the numerator represents the total number of common items in set A and set B.

Table 3. The signature matrix

	S_1	S_2	S_3	S_4
$h1$	1	3	0	1
$h2$	0	2	0	0

$$Jac - Similarity = \frac{|A \cap B|}{|A \cup B|} \tag{3}$$

Based on the similarity equation, we calculate the similarity between every two feature sets. For example, the similarity between S_1 and S_3 is 1/2. By this way, we can select the optimal API sets with the best diversity from the candidate ones and we recommend the optimal results to mashup developers.

4 Experiment

In this section, we will measure the performance of Min-Div by conducting experiments on the PW dataset which is crawled from APIs sharing platform PW.com. The dataset provides the interaction records about 18478 APIs and 6146 mashups, as well as the functional descriptions of these APIs. According to the information provided by PW dataset, we construct a web APIs correlation graph. And based on the graph, we conduct our experiments.

4.1 Evaluation Metrics and Compared Methods

Our proposal is a MinHash-based APIs recommendation method which performs well in diversity and privacy protection. And our goal is to achieve diverse APIs recommendation. As a result, we mainly focus on the comparison of diversity with other methods to prove the effectiveness of Min-Div. In this paper, our evaluation metrics include:

• **coverage.** It is the ratio of the number of recommended function categories to the total number of functions. And it is the larger the better. The metric coverage is described in Eq. (4), where the denominator represents the total number of functions, and the numerator represents the number of recommended function categories.

$$\text{coverage} = \frac{|set(category_r)|}{|set(category_t)|} \tag{4}$$

• **diversity.** It is used to represent the dissimilarity of the recommendation result. And it is the larger the better. The metric diversity is described in equation (5), where the denominator represents the total number of all items in an API set and the numerator represents the total similarity values between each pair of APIs in an API set.

$$diversity = 1 - \frac{\sum_{i,j \in item} Sim(i,j)}{\frac{1}{2}|item|(|item|-1)} \tag{5}$$

• **redundancy.** It is the ratio of surplus function categories that are recommended. And it is the smaller the better. The metric redundancy is described in equation (6), where the denominator represents the number of all recommended functions, and the numerator represents the number of all surplus functions.

$$redundancy = \frac{|list(category_s)|}{|list(category_r)|} \tag{6}$$

The two methods that are compared with Min-Div are as follows.

(1) K-CAR [14]. It is a web APIs recommendation method which models the problem as a minimum Steiner tree search process. It mainly focuses on searching the optimal APIs with the best compatibility according to the keywords that are input by mashup developers.
(2) WAR_{text} [15]. It is a web APIs recommendation method which is based on the web APIs correlation graph, and it also models the recommendation as a minimum Steiner tree search problem. It contributes to searching the optimal result with the best compatibility and least API numbers based on the input keywords.

4.2 Experiment Comparison

In order to prove the effectiveness of our method, we compare our method with K-CAR and WAR_{text} based on the three metrics. We assume the number of keywords input by mashup developers is from 2 to 6 and it is represented by L. Otherwise, we assume the number of hash functions is 40 and the value of K in final Top-K recommendation result is 3. With this hypothesis, we conduct our experiment and compare it with other methods. The comparison results are shown as follows.

(1) *coverage.* The comparison result of coverage is shown in Fig. 5, where the coverage of Min-Div is always higher than K-CAR and WAR_{text} when the number of input keywords L varies from 2 to 6. The reason is that Min-Div can explore more categories of APIs' functions and recommends them to developers. Thus, the coverage of Min-Div is the highest.
(2) *diversity.* The comparison result of diversity is shown in Fig. 6, where the diversity of Min-Div is always higher than K-CAR and WAR_{text} when the number of input keywords L varies from 2 to 6. The reason is that Min-Div utilizes MinHash to get the similarity between different APIs and further calculates the dissimilarity between different API sets. Thus, the optimal API sets with the best diversity can be recommended to developers, which causes the higher diversity of Min-Div.

(3) *redundancy.* The comparison result of redundancy is shown in Fig. 7, where the redundancy of Min-Div is always lower than K-CAR and $\mathrm{WAR}_{\mathrm{text}}$ when the number of input keywords L varies from 2 to 6. The reason is that Min-Div mainly focuses on promoting the diversity of recommendation and the recommended APIs' functions are the most diverse ones. Thus, the redundancy of the recommendation is more lower than the other two methods.

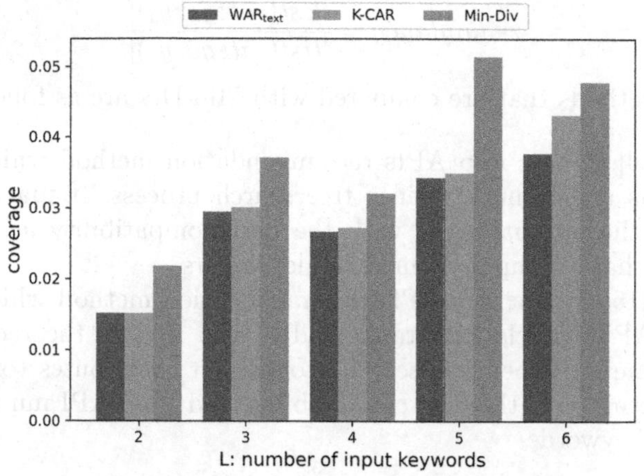

Fig. 5. Coverage comparisons of three methods

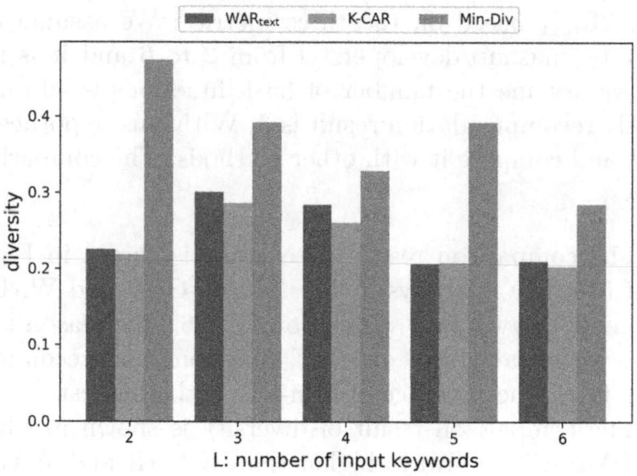

Fig. 6. Diversity comparisons of three methods

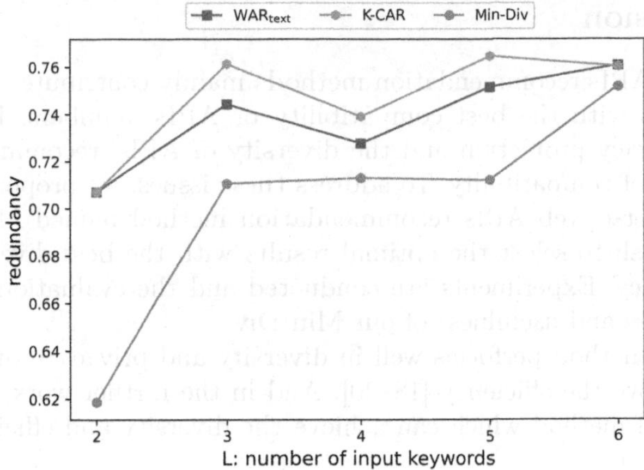

Fig. 7. Redundancy comparisons of three methods

(4) *parameter.* When utilizing MinHash to achieve the diversity of recommendation, we set the number of hash functions as 40. It is proved that 40 is the most appropriate parameter in Table 4, where L is the number of input keywords and F is the number of hash functions. For every number of input keywords, we record the experiment result in coverage, diversity and redundancy when F varies from 30 to 70 and we mark the optimal results with bold font. As shown in Table 4, when F is 40 or 70, the number of bold fonts is the most. Considering the time and space cost, we finally select 40 as the number of hash functions.

Table 4. The experiment results with different function numbers

		F=30	F=40	F=50	F=60	F=70
Coverage	L=2	**0.0219**	**0.0219**	**0.0219**	**0.0219**	**0.0219**
	L=3	0.0373	0.0371	**0.0375**	**0.0375**	0.0374
	L=4	0.0318	**0.0321**	**0.0321**	**0.0321**	0.0316
	L=5	0.0513	**0.0514**	0.0513	0.0505	**0.0514**
	L=6	0.0475	**0.0478**	**0.0478**	**0.0478**	0.0476
diversity	L=2	0.3933	**0.4749**	0.3689	0.3981	0.2972
	L=3	**0.4038**	0.3926	0.3952	0.3952	0.4026
	L=4	0.2994	**0.3285**	0.2957	0.3231	0.2545
	L=5	0.3487	**0.3925**	0.3627	0.3388	0.3542
	L=6	0.2779	0.2849	0.2908	0.2886	**0.3117**
redundancy	L=2	0.6186	0.6186	0.6176	**0.6175**	0.6194
	L=3	0.7113	0.7105	0.7092	**0.7075**	0.7107
	L=4	0.7147	0.7129	0.7134	**0.7124**	0.7183
	L=5	**0.695**	0.7119	0.696	0.7076	0.6952
	L=6	0.7504	0.7517	**0.7502**	0.7509	0.7511

5 Conclusion

Previous web APIs recommendation methods mainly contribute to recommending the results with the best compatibility or APIs' numbers. However, they ignore the privacy protection and the diversity of APIs' recommendation with the guarantee of compatibility. To address these issues, we propose a MinHash-based and diverse web APIs recommendation method named Min-Div, which utilizes MinHash to select the optimal results with the best diversity and protects the privacy. Experiments are conducted and the evaluation results prove the effectiveness and usefulness of our Min-Div.

While our method performs well in diversity and privacy protection, it still needs to improve the efficiency [18–20]. And in the further work, our goal is to explore a novel method which can achieve the diversity and efficiency of APIs' recommendation.

Acknowledgments. This work was supported in part by the Dou Wanchun Expert Workstation of Yunnan Province No.202105AF150013.

References

1. Almarimi, N., Ouni, A., Bouktif, S., Mkaouer, M.W., Kula, R.G., Saied, M.A.: Web service API recommendation for automated mashup creation using multi-objective evolutionary search. Appl. Soft Comput. **85**, 105830 (2019). https://doi.org/10.1016/j.asoc.2019.105830
2. Botangen, K.A., Yu, J., Sheng, Q.Z., Han, Y., Yongchareon, S.: Geographic-aware collaborative filtering for web service recommendation. Expert Syst. Appl. **151**, 113347 (2020). https://doi.org/10.1016/j.eswa.2020.113347
3. Chen, C., et al.: "More Than Deep Learning": post-processing for API sequence recommendation. Empirical Softw. Eng. **27**(1), 1–32 (2022). https://doi.org/10.1007/s10664-021-10040-2
4. Cheng, H., Zhong, M., Wang, J.: Diversified keyword search based web service composition. J. Syst. Softw. **163**, 110540 (2020). https://doi.org/10.1016/j.jss.2020.110540
5. Gao, H., Qin, X., Barroso, R.J.D., Hussain, W., Xu, Y., Yin, Y.: Collaborative learning-based industrial IoT API recommendation for software-defined devices: the implicit knowledge discovery perspective. IEEE Trans. Emerg. Topics Comput. Intell. (2020). https://doi.org/10.1109/TETCI.2020.3023155
6. Gao, W., Wu, J.: A novel framework for service set recommendation in mashup creation. In: 2017 IEEE International Conference on Web Services (ICWS), pp. 65–72. IEEE (2017). https://doi.org/10.1109/ICWS.2017.17
7. Kumar, C., Chowdary, C.R., Shukla, D.: Automatically detecting groups using locality-sensitive hashing in group recommendations. Inf. Sci. **601**, 207–223 (2022). https://doi.org/10.1016/j.ins.2022.04.028
8. Lian, S., Tang, M.: API recommendation for mashup creation based on neural graph collaborative filtering. Connect. Sci. **34**(1), 124–138 (2022). https://doi.org/10.1080/09540091.2021.1974819
9. Ling, C.-Y., Zou, Y.-Z., Lin, Z.-Q., Xie, B.: Graph embedding based API graph search and recommendation. J. Comput. Sci. Technol. **34**(5), 993–1006 (2019). https://doi.org/10.1007/s11390-019-1956-2

10. Meissa, M., Benharzallah, S., Kahloul, L., Kazar, O.: A personalized recommendation for web API discovery in social web of things. Int. Arab J. Inf. Technol. **18**(3A), 438–445 (2021)
11. Qi, L., et al.: Finding all you need: web APIs recommendation in web of things through keywords search. IEEE Trans. Comput. Soc. Syst. **6**(5), 1063–1072 (2019). https://doi.org/10.1109/TCSS.2019.2906925
12. Qi, L., He, Q., Chen, F., Zhang, X., Dou, W., Ni, Q.: Data-driven web APIs recommendation for building web applications. IEEE Trans. Big Data (2020). https://doi.org/10.1109/TBDATA.2020.2975587
13. Qi, L., Song, H., Zhang, X., Srivastava, G., Xu, X., Yu, S.: Compatibility-aware web API recommendation for mashup creation via textual description mining. ACM Trans. Multimidia Comput. Commun. Appl. **17**(1s), 1–19 (2021). https://doi.org/10.1145/3417293
14. Wang, X., Liu, X., Liu, J., Chen, X., Wu, H.: A novel knowledge graph embedding based API recommendation method for Mashup development. World Wide Web **24**(3), 869–894 (2021). https://doi.org/10.1007/s11280-021-00894-3
15. Wu, s, et al.: Popularity-aware and diverse web APIs recommendation based on correlation graph. IEEE Trans. Comput. Soc. Syst. (2022). https://doi.org/10.1109/TCSS.2022.3168595
16. Wu, W., Li, B., Chen, L., Gao, J., Zhang, C.: A review for weighted MinHash algorithms. IEEE Trans. Knowl. Data Eng. (2020). https://doi.org/10.1109/TKDE.2020.3021067
17. Yao, L., Wang, X., Sheng, Q.Z., Benatallah, B., Huang, C.: Mashup recommendation by regularizing matrix factorization with API co-invocations. IEEE Trans. Serv. Comput. **14**(2), 502–515 (2018). https://doi.org/10.1109/TSC.2018.2803171
18. Zhou, X., Liang, W., Luo, Z., Pan, Y.: Periodic-aware intelligent prediction model for information diffusion in social networks. IEEE Trans. Netw. Sci. Eng. **8**(2), 894–904 (2021)
19. Zhou, X., Liang, W., Ma, J., Yan, Z., Kevin, I., Wang, K.: 2D federated learning for personalized human activity recognition in cyber-physical-social systems. IEEE Trans. Netw. Sci. Eng. **9**, 3934–3944 (2022)
20. Zhou, X., Liang, W., She, J., Yan, Z., Kevin, I., Wang, K.: Two-layer federated learning with heterogeneous model aggregation for 6G supported internet of vehicles. IEEE Trans. Veh. Technol. **70**(6), 5308–5317 (2021)

Network Security Evaluation Method of College Freshmen Career Counseling Service Based on Machine Learning

Shuilan Song(✉) and Xinjiu Liang

Nanning University, Nanning 530200, China
ssh1120@126.com

Abstract. Because the career guidance service network for college freshmen is vulnerable to malicious attacks, network security is difficult to be guaranteed, therefore, a network security evaluation method based on machine learning is proposed for college freshmen career counseling services. According to the principle of index system, 3 primary indexes and 15 secondary evaluation indexes are selected. Three collectors are used to collect index data and implement pretreatment. Using the entropy weight method to calculate the index weights, taking this as input, the evaluation method based on BP neural network is used to obtain the network security trend. The experimental results show that, the average relative error, mean square error and root mean square error of the proposed method are low, which proves that the network security evaluation effect of the proposed method is better.

Keywords: Machine learning · College freshman career counseling service · Evaluation index · BP neural network · Network security evaluation

1 Introduction

With the development of Internet technology and its increasingly wide application in real life, the traditional security technology can no longer solve the security threats faced by the current network. Security has become one of the key factors restricting its development, and various network defense methods have emerged. For example, firewall, intrusion detection, encryption, etc. [1]. Firewall technology has a certain effect on the protection of external network attacks, but it has no effect on the attacks within the firewall. Intrusion detection technology is a relatively mature security defense technology at present, but the accuracy of the current detection results is not high, and there are widespread phenomena of false detection and missed detection. Encryption technology is mainly used in digital signature, identity authentication, security protocols and other aspects to provide security for information transmission. However, the current attacks such as brute force cracking and weak password guessing make encryption technology unable to absolutely ensure information security. Therefore, there is an urgent need for a new security technology that can deal with the daily data of large-scale networks and form targeted protection strategies to improve network security performance.

Y. Xu et al. (Eds.): ML4CS 2022, LNCS 13655, pp. 486–500, 2023.
https://doi.org/10.1007/978-3-031-20096-0_36

In order to solve the above problems, experts at home and abroad have carried out in-depth research. Reference [2] proposes a smart campus network security evaluation based on neural network. Using the powerful nonlinear fitting ability of neural network, a group of evaluation results with strong generalization ability are obtained through simulation training of quantitative evaluation indexes, and finally a group of evaluation models with strong applicability are obtained to evaluate the security of campus network. This method can effectively improve the security of campus network, but the average relative error is large. Reference [3] proposes a hesitant fuzzy language envelope analysis model based on analytic hierarchy process and its application in the network security evaluation of edge nodes. By solving the goal programming model, the optimal network security criteria weight information is obtained, and the analytic hierarchy process constraint cone corresponding to the network security criteria weight information is further constructed as the constraint condition of the hesitant fuzzy language envelope analysis model to obtain the ranking result of mobile user security evaluation The average relative error of this method is small, but its safety is low. Reference [4] by building a network system model under information threat and applying semi Markov devices to detect unauthorized activities in the data transmission process under network scanning attacks, network security can be improved, but the mean square error is large.

The network security evaluation method is an independent security defense mechanism. According to the network security evaluation index, the security situation elements that affect the normal operation of the network can be effectively obtained from the massive security data, and the network security status can be quantitatively analyzed to provide a strong basis for the administrator to implement targeted security defense strategies. Therefore, this paper puts forward a method of network security evaluation of college freshman career counseling service based on machine learning. According to the principles of systematization, approximation, hierarchy and operability, the network security situation of college freshman career counseling service is divided into three sub situations, and the network security evaluation index system is constructed; Use syslog data collector, SNMP data collector and Nessus data collector to collect and preprocess data, and improve processing efficiency; The network security evaluation model of BP neural network is established, and the index weight is determined by entropy weight method to improve the reliability of the model, so as to complete the network security evaluation based on machine learning.

2 Research on Network Security Evaluation Based on Machine Learning

Network security assessment is an active security defense mechanism. It will standardize and integrate multi-source heterogeneous data adopted in security equipment through data fusion technology, and then obtain the security situation factors affecting the normal operation of the network from the merged data, adopt reasonable and accurate assessment methods to assess the security situation obtained, obtain the current cyber security status, and predict the future cyber security trend according to the current security situation [5]. Network security assessment helps network managers to understand the network security threats more intuitively and implement response strategies accordingly. Simultaneously grasps the network security tendency and the possible network attack behavior, provides the reliable basis for the administrator to formulate the effective prevention strategy.

2.1 Construction of Network Security Evaluation Index System

Constructing a reasonable network security evaluation index system of college freshmen career counseling service is the basis of comprehensive and accurate evaluation of network security situation. If the index system is too large, it will increase the computational complexity and reduce the performance and real-time of the evaluation [6]. Conversely, if too few indicators are established, the indicators that can participate in the assessment are not complete enough to accurately and comprehensively reflect the current state of the network, resulting in the loss of guidance for cybersecurity posture assessment [7, 8]. So we must choose a reasonable network security situation evaluation index system, so that we can get accurate and comprehensive evaluation results when we apply it to the evaluation. At present, there is no unified network security situation assessment index system. But the construction of index system should be based on certain theoretical knowledge, and then according to the specific needs of evaluation, establish a relatively comprehensive and perfect index system. This article has carried on the research and the study to the target system's construction principle, now summarizes it as follows. The construction principles of the indicator system are as follows:

(1) Systematic principle. Network security situational awareness is an overall and macroscopic concept. Therefore, in order to reflect the current network security situation comprehensively, systematically and accurately, we should select some representative indicators which can reflect the current network operation status from different aspects.
(2) Principle of similarity. There are many factors related to network security in the whole network system, some of which are similar or related. This should be fully considered when constructing the index system.
(3) The principle of hierarchy. Because of the complexity of network structure and the difference between network devices and information transmission, the index system should consider all levels of the system as much as possible.
(4) Principle of easy operation. This principle mainly manifests in two aspects. For the index system constructed, on the one hand, it should be convenient to obtain it directly or indirectly in the network system. On the other hand should be convenient for follow-up.

Referring to the GB/T 20984-2007 Specification of Network Information Security Risk Assessment and in combination with the Network Security Situation Assessment System established by predecessors, this study divides the Network Security Situation of College Freshmen Career Counseling Service into three sub-situations according to the principle of index selection and comprehensive analysis from different perspectives and levels (Table 1).

Table 1. Index system of network security situation

Primary index	Secondary indicators
Threat sub situation	Attack severity
	Number of alerts
	Frequency of security incidents
	Distribution of various data packets
Fragile sub situation	Vulnerability severity
	Number of safety equipment
	Number of open ports
	Network topology
	Operating system security
Basic operation sub situation	Total network traffic
	Intra network peak traffic
	Intra network traffic change rate
	Bandwidth utilization
	Equipment service status
	Asset value

(1) Threat subsituation: The threat to the university freshman career guidance service network is an assessment of the security situation of the network itself from various external threats. Often the behavior that most affects network security is an external threat that causes a network service outage or data loss. External threats are usually composed of various network attacks and triggered network security events, and the distribution of data packets can provide the corresponding threat distribution trend. Therefore, the attack severity, the number of alarms, the frequency of security events and the distribution of each kind of packets are chosen as the secondary indicators.
(2) Vulnerable sub-situation: The vulnerability of the university freshman career counseling service network focuses on describing the security defects existing in the network itself, so its main carrier is the configuration of each device in the network topology environment, and the vulnerability of vulnerabilities and topology structure is usually the breach of network attacks, and exploiting the vulnerabilities needs to open ports, so the relevant vulnerabilities, the number of security devices, the number of open ports, the network topology structure and the security of the operating system can well reflect the vulnerable sub-situation.
(3) Basic Operation Sub-trend: The basic operation sub-trend of the college freshmen career guidance service network reflects the operation state of the current network, and the change trend of the index shows a continuous network operation state. When the basic operation sub-trend fluctuates violently, it shows that the operation state of the previous moment has changed greatly from the current state. Therefore, the basic operation of the network is closely related to the time. At the same time, the

property of the host computer in the network system determines the safe operation of the network to some extent.

2.2 Data Collection and Pretreatment of Evaluation Index

Original data collection is the first step of network security situation assessment, which is the basis of subsequent assessment. There are various network devices in the complex network environment, such as common hosts, servers, routers, switches, firewalls and IDS (Intrusion Detection Systems). Most of these network devices are structurally distinct and run different network protocols and services, and even though some acquisition techniques provide a uniform format, some data may be cross-cutting, such as system log data that may contain some traffic data [9]. Therefore, it is necessary to unify the format of the four kinds of original data, and then give them to the original situation index extraction module for subsequent processing. At the same time, a timing scheduler is added to the module, which is mainly used to dynamically collect the data in a certain period of time.

College freshmen career guidance service network will produce a large number of data in the process of operation, these data sources are different, the need for different means of collection. The data collection process of evaluation indicators is shown in Fig. 1.

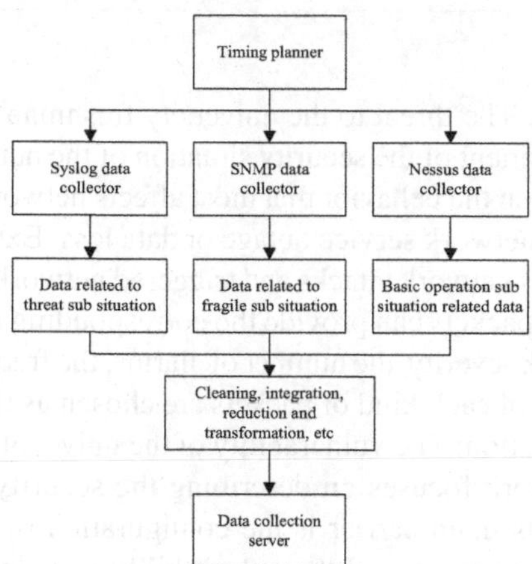

Fig. 1. Data collection process for assessment indicators

First, the three kinds of data are collected by different methods, then these data are pre-processed in real time to form a unified data format, and finally handed over to the data acquisition server. The timer is also set in the logic structure, whose main task is to trigger the data collector in different time periods.

(1) Syslog data collector

The log system records all kinds of events in the network system of college freshmen career counseling service, which plays a key role in evaluating the network security level. There are a large number of network devices in the network, and different protocols run on various devices, the data format is diverse, and the links in the network are also complicated. In addition, because security devices in the network use a first-in, first-out (FIFO) approach to logging, the new log information overwrites the old log information, resulting in the overwriting of some of the old log information that was of critical importance [10]. Therefore, this article uses Syslog to collect system logs.

Syslog uses the Syslog protocol, which was developed in the TCP/IP (Transmission Control Protocol/Internet Protocol) system of the Berkeley Software Distribution Research Center (BSD) at the University of California, and is currently available for logging. The Syslog Data Collector collects the system log data of the device through the Syslog protocol. It has a uniform and standard data format. Therefore, the collected log data is more readable, and can be easily post-processed. When collecting data through Syslog, there are mainly two steps: first, because different devices support Syslog in different ways, it is necessary to turn on the corresponding Syslog protocol support in each device and configure it accordingly; second, because of the number of devices being collected, it is necessary to introduce multi-threading technology to complete the simultaneous collection of log information of different devices. The dynamic configuration function of syslog supports dynamic collection very well. Only need to modify the configuration file, the new network device will be recognized and can collect system log data.

(2) SNMP data collector

College freshmen career guidance service network will produce a large number of traffic information, traffic data as a key component of network security situation assessment availability indicators. SNMP (Simple Network Management Protocol) is an application layer protocol of TCP/IP protocol cluster. SNMP system includes MIB (Management Information Base), SMI (structure of management information) and SNMP. All SNMP-enabled devices maintain an MIF3 (Modeling intermodal fluidity freight flows). In MIB-2, there are seven main variables: system, interface, at, ip, icmp, tcp, udp, and so on. This paper mainly uses SNMP data collector, using SNMP protocol, by setting the device OID (Object Identifier), to achieve the goal of traffic data acquisition. The specific process is as follows:

Step 1: Initialize. During development, the DefaultUdpTransportMapping interface object is typically instantiated using UDP (User Datagram Protocol) and then instantiated as a parameter in the constructor of the SNMP class.
Step 2: Construct the send destination. For SNMPv2 and SNMPv1, you need to instantiate a CommunityTarget object and set the SNMP version, community name, destination address, retransmission time, and wait time; for SNMPv3, you need to instantiate a User Target object and set the security collection and security name in addition to the SNMP version, community name, destination address, retransmission time, and wait time.
Step 3: Construct the sending message. SNMPv2 and SNMPv1 require PDU (Power Distribution Unit) class objects to be instantiated, and SNMPv3 requires ScopedPDU class objects to be instantiated. In addition, we need to generate an OID object,

bind the OID field we need to query to a PDU or ScopedPDU object, and set the PDU message type (GET, GETNEXT, RESPONSE, TRAP, SET).
Step 4: Construct the appropriate listener and send message. When using asynchronous mode, we need to implement the Response Listener interface object as the listening object of the response message, then send the message through the send function, and finally obtain the collected data through the listening object.

(3) Nessus data collector
There may be a large number of vulnerability data in the host or server of college freshmen career guidance service network. This paper collects vulnerability data through Nessus vulnerability scanning tool. It is a well-known vulnerability scanning tool, using C/S (Client/Server) architecture, supporting remote vulnerability scanning, scanning results stored in the database and provide a visual interface. Program development, Nessus can also be extended to the development of plug-ins, to facilitate the programmer programming according to special needs, hiding the specific internal details [11]. It can also according to different needs, will scan the results stored in the specified database or table file. It mainly includes the following functions:

(1) Scan Options Configuration: Before scanning, it is necessary to first determine the target of the scan, including the IP address or address range of the equipment to be scanned, and the port number of the equipment to be scanned, and then configure which database or data table the scan results are stored in. These configuration information will be written to the XML (Extensible Markup Language) configuration file to complete the specific device vulnerability scanning.
(2) Plug-in function configuration: Absolute or relative path call scan instructions according to different scan tasks, and then customize the scan of specific devices in combination with scan configuration files and store the results in the designated database.

Data acquisition is usually preprocessed to facilitate subsequent operations. Common data preprocessing steps are cleaning, integration, reduction and transformation.

(1) Data cleansing is intended to remove unrelated data from the collected data and outlier data that clearly deviates from normal values, and to treat and clean missing and "dirty" data to supplement missing data [12].
(2) Data integration refers to the integration of scattered data into a unified data set in accordance with certain requirements and purposes, thereby facilitating the sharing and utilization of information by maintaining the overall consistency of data sources.
(3) Data reduction refers to the reduction of data without changing the distribution of the data itself, thereby improving the efficiency of data processing.
(4) Data transformation is the process of transforming data from one form to another in order to facilitate subsequent processing. Through certain data transformation, data is transformed or consolidated into a form suitable for analysis, providing a more effective data form for network security posture understanding [13]. The goal of

data preprocessing is to ensure that the entire process from data collection, storage, analysis to visualization does not introduce too many errors and irrelevant data.

2.3 Implementation of Network Security Assessment Based on Machine Learning

The network security assessment technology of college freshmen career guidance service is the process of processing, understanding and merging the elements related to security in the network, so as to obtain the current network security situation [14]. At present, there are four kinds of methods in network security situation assessment, which are based on mathematical model, knowledge reasoning, pattern recognition and machine learning. The method based on machine learning includes two steps: training and evaluation. The training is mainly to find the relationship between evaluation index set and network security situation. The evaluation is to map the new index input set to the network security situation value by the relation of training steps. The mathematical model is as follows:

$$G = S(x_1, x_2, ..., x_n) \tag{1}$$

In the formula, G represents the network security evaluation value of the university freshman career counseling service, and the value is $[0, 1]$; x_i is the influencing factor of the network operation, namely, the evaluation index, among which the university freshman career counseling service network; S is the specific evaluation method, namely the network security quantitative evaluation model based on the BP (Back Propagation) neural network, and the specific process is shown in Fig. 2.

In the evaluation field of BP neural network, the relationship between evaluation data and effectiveness value is usually difficult to be expressed by function. In the field of evaluation, the key point of BP neural network application is the data set of input layer. First of all, the data set should be objective, so as to ensure that the BP neural network learning process is not disturbed by human factors. The data set should have certain completeness, the more complete the range of data, the better the learning effect of neural network will be. In addition, for the evaluation problem, the selection of evaluation data should accord with the characteristics of the evaluation object, so as to maximize the fitting ability of neural network. In addition, the BP neural network theory knowledge is more perfect, it can solve the problem of nonlinear mapping, higher performance. The BP neural network is composed of a single input layer, an output layer and several hidden layers. Each neural network consists of several neurons, and its computing process is composed of forward computing process and reverse computing process. In the forward calculation process, the input layer receives input vectors, and outputs them from the hidden layer by calculating the parameter matrix and activation function between the input layer and the hidden layer, and outputs the results from the output layer by calculating the parameter matrix and activation function between the hidden layer and the output layer. If the output does not meet expectations, then the back-propagation, that is, the back-calculation process. Taking the sum of squares of output errors as the objective function, the network model adjusts parameter values according to gradient descent method to reduce errors. The model structure is shown in Fig. 3.

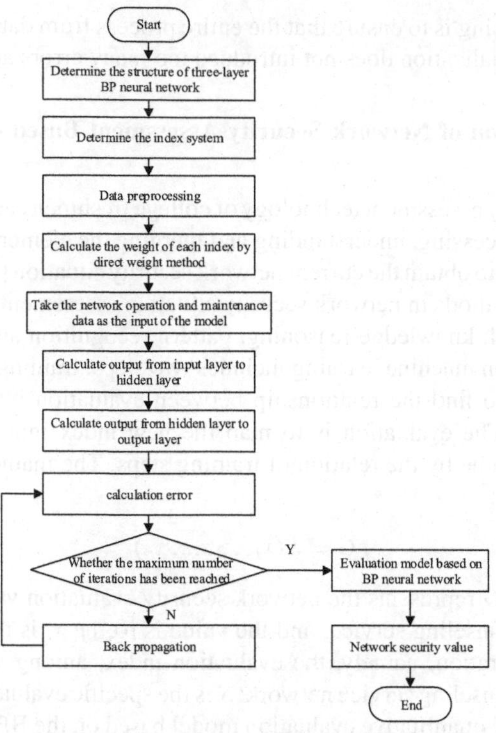

Fig. 2. Network security assessment model based on bp neural network

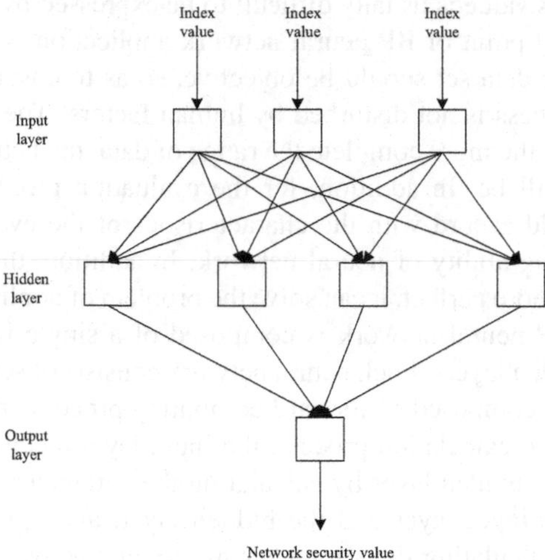

Fig. 3. BP neural network model structure

Take the university freshman career guidance service network security appraisal as the object. Assume that there are n evaluation indicators, as input vectors $X =$

$(x_1, x_2, ..., x_n)$, input layer has n neurons; output layer has m neurons, output vectors $G = (g_1, g_2, ..., g_m)$; hidden layer has only one layer, there are t neurons, hidden layer output vectors $R = (r_1, r_2, ..., r_t)$. The connection weight between the input layer and the hidden layer is $V = \left(v_1, v_2, ..., v_j, ..., v_t\right)$ and the connection weight between the hidden layer and the output layer is $W = (w_1, w_2, ..., w_k, ..., w_m)$; the output threshold of the neurons in the hidden layer is a, and the output threshold of the neurons in the output layer is b. For the j neuron of the hidden layer, its output is:

$$r_j = f\sum_{i=1}^{n} w_k r_j - a_j \tag{2}$$

$$f = \frac{1}{1 + e^{-x}} \tag{3}$$

f is the activation function of choice.

Similarly, for the k neuron in the output layer, the output is:

$$g_k = f\sum_{j=1}^{t} w_k r_j - b_k \tag{4}$$

The cumulative error H_k is calculated as follows:

$$H_k = \frac{\sqrt{\sum_{k=1}^{m} (g_k - p_k)^2}}{2} \tag{5}$$

In the equation, p_k represents the expected output vector of k, $P = (p_1, p_2, ..., p_m)$.

The above is a forward calculation process. If the error does not meet the expected value, the gradient descent method is used to adjust the parameter matrix between input layer and hidden layer, the threshold of hidden layer, the parameter matrix between hidden layer and output layer, and the output layer threshold. This process is called reverse computation. In the reverse calculation process, the partial derivative is obtained for each parameter that needs to be adjusted, the parameter value is changed according to the gradient descent method, and the learning rate q is set to control the parameter change range. BP neural network needs to go through many iterations of forward and backward calculation process, set iteration times or allowable error range as iteration termination conditions, and get the final model.

Entropy weight method is to determine the influence weight of the index on the comprehensive evaluation according to the information entropy of the index. In the network security evaluation method based on BP neural network, the final training effect of BP neural network model is affected by the initial value of model parameters. Proper selection of initial values can greatly improve the training efficiency of the model and avoid falling into the local optimal solution. In this paper, the input of BP neural network model is the index data of network security evaluation, so the index weight optimized by entropy weight method is used as the initialization parameter. The process is shown in Fig. 4.

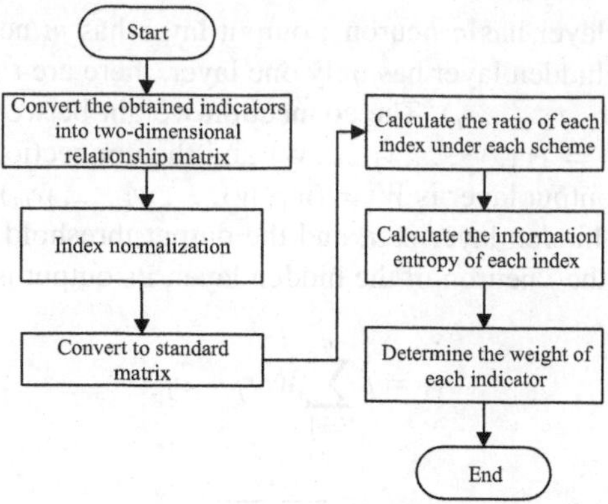

Fig. 4. Process of index weight calculation based on entropy weight method

Entropy weight method can profoundly reflect the differentiation ability of indexes, determine the weight of indexes, and has high reliability and accuracy. In the network situation assessment problem, the index weight calculated by entropy weight method is used as the initial parameter value of the BP neural network model.

Referring to the Cyber Network Awareness Materials of MS-ISAC (Multi-State Information Sharing and Analysis Center) and the Cyber Security Basic Situation Index of the National Internet Emergency Response Centre, the Cyber Security Situation Level of College Freshmen Career Counseling Services is divided into five levels, namely, excellent, good, medium, poor and dangerous, as shown in Table 2 [15].

Table 2. Network security posture security level classification table

Safety level	Network security value
Excellent	0–0.2
Good	0.2–0.4
General degree	0.4–0.75
Poor	0.75–0.9
Dangerous	0.9–1.0

3 Method Application Test

3.1 Attack Environment

In this paper, two data sets are selected: LLDOS1.0 attack scenario in DARPA2000 (Defense Advanced Research Projects Agency) data set provided by Lincoln Laboratory of Massachusetts Institute of technology, and Denial-Of-Service (DOS) attack scenario in UNSW-NB15 (The UNSW-NB15 Dataset Description) data set to better verify the effectiveness of the proposed method.

This experiment uses the LLDOS 1.0 attack scenario in the DARPA2000 (Defense Advanced Research Projects Agency) dataset provided by the Lincoln Laboratory of the Massachusetts Institute of Technology.

3.2 Test Data

In the sample making of situation assessment in this paper, firstly, the situation assessment indexes obtained by mining technology and analysis software are used to obtain the bottom index value. Then, according to the network situation assessment system, the underlying index values are arranged and obtained, and the index values are segmented according to the set time slice. At the same time, it is combined with the real situation value in time sequence, and finally 300 sets of data are obtained, that is, 300 samples, 15 index values of secondary indexes are input into the evaluation model as the characteristics of each sample.

3.3 Index Weight

Based on the entropy weight method, the weights of evaluation indexes are calculated, and the results are shown in Table 3.

Table 3. Weights of evaluation indicators for input samples

Secondary indicators	Sample 1	Sample 2	Sample 3
Attack severity	0.2515	2.4564	1.6872
Number of alerts	1.2663	2.1015	1.2742
Frequency of security incidents	2.3588	1.0152	1.0435
Distribution of various data packets	0.4542	1.0465	1.8944
Vulnerability severity	0.6321	0.2814	1.2165
Number of safety equipment	1.3479	0.7145	2.1887
Number of open ports	1.8461	0.6245	1.4232
Network topology	0.6548	0.7341	2.3454
Operating system security	0.3452	0.3145	0.4652
Total network traffic	1.1146	0.4215	0.0134
Intra network peak traffic	1.5468	0.6481	0.5635
Intra network traffic change rate	1.0145	1.7452	0.7844
Bandwidth utilization	0.5412	2.4485	0.4586
Equipment service status	0.0123	0.5444	1.2468
Asset value	1.1642	0.7481	1.4545

3.4 Evaluation Model Training

In this paper, the model is trained by batch process, and 10 samples are input for each batch. The evaluation results of some samples fit the real value of network security as shown in Fig. 5.

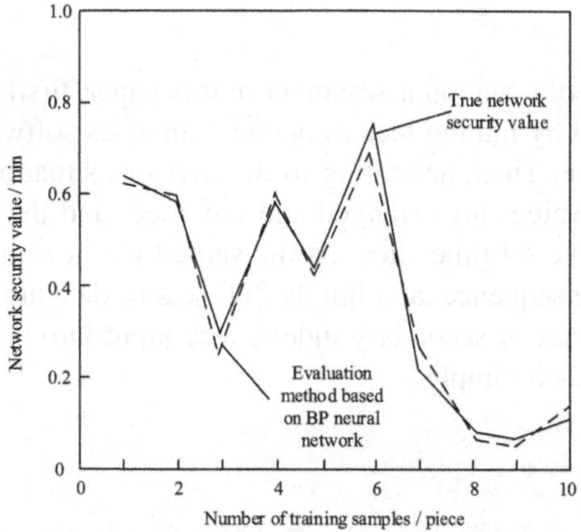

Fig. 5. Assessment model training results

According to Fig. 5, the training process of evaluation model, except for individual samples of network security evaluation value and the actual value of the relatively large gap, the overall fitting degree is high, in line with BP neural network training expectations.

3.5 Network Security Posture

In this paper, the trained BP neural network is compared with the reference evaluation methods: the method of reference [2], the method of reference [3] and the method of reference [4]. Enter 30 test samples into the assessment model for situation assessment, and the network security situation results are shown in Fig. 6.

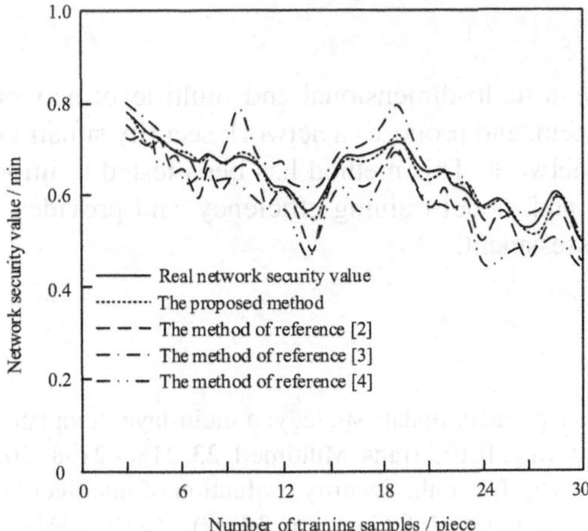

Fig. 6. Network security posture

Note: Higher Situation Values Mean Less Security.

According to Fig. 6, the evaluation results obtained by using the method of reference [2], the method of reference [3] and the method of reference [4] deviate from the true value to a relatively high degree, and the proposed method result is more consistent with the real value curve.

3.6 Method Accuracy Analysis

Referring to the safety grade table of situation value, this paper selects the evaluation results of some samples randomly from the test samples, so as to compare more intuitively the difference between the situation real value and the evaluation results of various methods, and then evaluates the accuracy of the evaluation model by using the three performance indexes of average relative error MAPE, mean square error MSE and mean square root error RMSE, as shown in Table 4.

Table 4. Precision analysis table of four assessment methods

Evaluation method	MAPE	MSE	RMSE
The proposed method	3.5542	0.0545	0.1220
The method of reference [2]	5.4522	0.2451	1.2562
The method of reference [3]	6.5485	0.2955	1.8544
The method of reference [4]	5.8442	0.2688	1.3253

As can be seen from Table 4, compared with the method of reference [2], the method of reference [3] and the method of reference [4], the error of the proposed method is lower and the precision is higher.

4 Conclusions

This paper constructs a multi-dimensional and multi-level network security situation assessment index system, and proposes a network security situation assessment method based on BP neural network. This method has been tested to improve the accuracy of situation assessment and model training efficiency, and provides support for network operation situation assessment.

References

1. Liu, S., et al.: Human memory update strategy: a multi-layer template update mechanism for remote visual monitoring. IEEE Trans. Multimed. **23**, 2188–2198 (2021)
2. Yan, X., Wu, C., Zhang, L., et al.: Security evaluation of intelligent campus network based on neural network. Changjiang Inf. Commun. **34**(09), 16–19 (2021)
3. Chen, Z., Lin, M.: Hesitant fuzzy linguistic envelopment analysis model based on analytic hierarchy process and its application in cybersecurity evaluation of edge nodes. Appl. Res. Comput. **38**(01), 209–214 (2021)
4. Fatkieva, R.R.: Complex of models for network security assessment of industrial automated control systems. Inform. Autom. **19**(3), 621–643 (2020)
5. Liu, S., Liu, D., Muhammad, K., Ding, W.: Effective template update mechanism in visual tracking with background clutter. Neurocomputing **458**, 615–625 (2021)
6. Sengupta, S., Chowdhary, A., Sabur, A., et al.: A survey of moving target defenses for network security. IEEE Commun. Surv. Tutor. **22**(3), 1909–1941 (2020)
7. Liu, S., Wang, S., Liu, X., Lin, C.-T., Lv, Z.: Fuzzy detection aided real-time and robust visual tracking under complex environments. IEEE Trans. Fuzzy Syst. **29**(1), 90–102 (2021). https://doi.org/10.1109/TFUZZ.2020.3006520
8. Wang, H., Liu, Y.: Security situation assessment of power information system based on fuzzy petri net. Electr. Saf. Technol. **22**(08), 5–8 (2020)
9. Li, Y., Zhang, Z.: Network security risk loss assessment method based on queuing model. Comput. Simul. **38**(04), 258–262 (2021)
10. Vajjha, H., Sushma, P.: Techniques and limitations in securing the log files to enhance network security and monitoring. Solid State Technol. **64**(2), 1–8 (2021)
11. Zhang, H., Meng, X., Zhang, X., et al.: CANsec: a practical in-vehicle controller area network security evaluation tool. Sensors **20**(17), 4900 (2020)
12. Han, J., Kim, D.: Security offloading network system for expanded security coverage in IPv6-based resource constrained data service networks. Wireless Netw. **26**(6), 4615–4635 (2020)
13. Ochodek, M., Hebig, R., Meding, W., et al.: Recognizing lines of code violating company-specific coding guidelines using machine learning: a method and its evaluation. Empir. Softw. Eng. **25**(2), 220–265 (2020)
14. Lin, S.S., Shen, S.L., Zhou, A., et al.: Risk assessment and management of excavation system based on fuzzy set theory and machine learning methods. Autom. Constr. **122**(4), 103490 (2021)
15. Zhang, L., Mu, D., Hu, W., et al.: Machine-learning-based side-channel leakage detection in electronic system-level synthesis. IEEE Netw. **34**(3), 44–49 (2020)

FedTD: Efficiently Share Telemedicine Data with Federated Distillation Learning

Ning Li, Nansen Wang, Wei Ou(✉), and Wenbao Han

School of Cyberspace Security (School of Cryptology), Hainan University, Haikou 570228, Hainan, China
ouwei@hainanu.edu.cn

Abstract. With the Internet of Things and medical technology development, patients use wearable telemedicine devices to transmit health data to hospitals. The need for data sharing for public health has become more urgent under the COVID-19 pandemic. Previously, security protection technology was difficult to solve the increasing security risks and challenges of telemedicine. To address the above hindrances, Federated learning (FL) solves the difficulty for companies and institutions to share user data securely. The global server iterative aggregates the model parameters from the local server instead of uploading the user's data directly to the cloud server. We propose a new model of federated distillation learning called FedTD, which allows the different models between local hospital servers and global servers. Unlike traditional federated learning, we combine the knowledge distillation method to solve the non-Independent Identically Distribution (non-IID) problem of patient medical data. It provides a security solution for sharing patients' medical information among hospitals. We tested our approach on the COVID-19 Radiography and COVID-Chestxray datasets to improve the model performance and reduce communication costs. Extensive experiments show that our FedTD significantly outperforms the state-of-the-art.

Keywords: Telemedicine devices · Federated learning · Knowledge distillation · Non-IID

1 Introduction

Currently, the prevention and control of the Novel coronavirus pneumonia epidemic have become a new routine, and telemedicine terminals continue to empower epidemic prevention and control management. Wearable medical terminals are electronic terminals that can be worn directly on the body and have medical functions such as sign monitoring, disease treatment and drug delivery. With the development of artificial intelligence and big data technology, wearable medical terminals can perceive, record, analyze, regulate, intervene and even treat diseases or maintain physical health with software support, overcoming the drawbacks of traditional medical terminals. Wearable medical terminals play a huge role in optimizing the allocation of medical resources, reducing medical costs, and improving the efficiency of medical services.

Y. Xu et al. (Eds.): ML4CS 2022, LNCS 13655, pp. 501–515, 2023.
https://doi.org/10.1007/978-3-031-20096-0_37

Due to the proliferation of telemedicine terminals and the variety of remote operation and maintenance methods of terminal manufacturers, the risk of data leakage has increased. The previous network security technologies were difficult to deal with the above problems, and the security risks and challenges of telemedicine terminals are increasing day by day [1, 2]. In recent years, cyber-attacks and data theft incidents against telemedicine terminals have occurred frequently. The life and health security of telemedicine terminals and users have been seriously threatened. Wearable medical terminals solve the limitations and unattainable functions of traditional medical terminals, which brings a new direction of innovation to the field of telemedicine. According to a report by Constella, the number of personal data leakage in the healthcare industry in 2020 increased 1.5 times compared to 2019. In 2021, the situation did not improve. According to the OCR HHS, the number of victims of medical data leakage increased more than 1.5 times compared to 2020.

Fortunately, Federated Learning (FL) is a distributed computing technique [3] that solves data silos by deploying models on the local hospital serves. The hospital trains the stored encrypted medical data through a local model. Then the trained model parameters are sent to the global server instead of directly transferring the patient's medical data to the cloud server. This way guarantees the privacy of the user's data and solves the data isolation problem, which is data is difficult to share and use effectively.

The global server in Federated Learning aims to improve the general performance of the trained model by aggregating the local model parameters transmitted to the clients. After that, the global server broadcasts the new model to the local server until the model converges. However, it has two major problems to solve. First, the model training process requires a constant exchange of model parameters that leads to high communication delays. Second, it trained the same model between different clients, but the data is heterogeneous. This causes the training results to increase slowly after the client updates the local model.

To address the above issues, federated distillation (FD) is used by extending knowledge distillation techniques to the FL framework [4]. Hinton et al. [5] defined the knowledge of the model as the softened logits, and the student model mimics the knowledge of the teacher model to gain its abilities. Rohan, et al. [6] proposed a distributed online knowledge distillation method where the communication costs size does not depend on the model size but on the output dimension. Federation Augmentation (FAUG), corrects the non-IID training dataset a data augmentation scheme using Generative Adversarial Networks (GAN), which provides suitable training between privacy leakage and data access security. Model outputs (called knowledge) exchange model parameters as they are exchanged between clients and servers [7]. Because the size of the knowledge is smaller than the model architecture, and it can train its special models based on individual clients, it is considered a framework for efficient communication and accurate model training.

In this paper, to solve the problem of heterogeneity of user data in hospitals, we combine federated learning and distillation learning to propose a new algorithm called FedTD. To summarize, our key contributions are as follows:

(1) In the FedTD approach, the exchanged model outputs of local hospital servers are logits instead of model parameters, alleviating privacy risks and reducing communication overhead.
(2) The global server can be fused with the logits from the local servers to prepare for the medical guidance of the local hospital servers.
(3) We experiment with FedTD on COVID-19 Radiography and COVID-Chestxray datasets with different degrees of non- IID. Extensive experiments show that our algorithm achieves higher accuracy compared with the state-of-the-art.

This paper is organized as follows. The second part provides examples of the current state of research on the work of previous generations of medical data sharing and the distillation of federated learning. The third section explains our proposed telemedicine system architecture diagram, and our algorithm explains it in detail. In the fourth section, we compared medical data with the current excellent distillation federated learning experiments. The experimental results show that the accuracy of our training is more accurate, and the communication overhead is low. We summarize the research and future work in the last part.

2 Related Works

2.1 Secure Sharing of Medical Data

Griggs et al. [8] proposed a blockchain-medical remote monitoring system that solves the problem of message storage size in blocks, realizes authorized alliance management and privacy maintenance of anonymous users and guarantees real-time analysis and real-time recording of data records through smart contracts. Musale et al. [9] proposed a gait-based lightweight, seamless security authentication framework capable of authenticating and identifying users on widely used smart health watches, which extracts not only statistical features from collected sensor data but also features related to human behavior to distinguish between different styles more accurately and effectively. Nguyen et al. [10] proposed a medical data sharing scheme that uses mobile cloud computing and blockchain, interacts with the medical sharing system through mobile terminals, collects data, stores patient data addresses in the blockchain, stores data sets in cloud centers, and implements access control mechanisms based on the public keys and data addresses of medical staff to achieve decentralized data storage and data sharing. Vallathan et al. [11] proposed a prediction-based encryption scheme for telemedicine applications to ensure security, which includes the integration of three modules of prediction, padding, and chaotic map encryption, which greatly enhances the security of patient medical data and medical scan images. Lin et al. [12] proposed a signature scheme for healthcare attributes, which can prevent forgery attacks, and inference attacks by malicious nodes can prevent by introducing multiple permissions and pseudo-random seeds, but centralized data management systems are prone to complicit attacks by malicious nodes, leading to problems such as data leakage and single points of failure. Wang et al. [13] proposed a blockchain-based medical key management scheme that uses a network of body sensors to design lightweight backup and efficient recovery schemes for the keys of system nodes, which can effectively protect private information and promote the application of blockchain medical care. Li et al. [14] proposed a half-sensor compression-sensing encryption scheme that uses half-sensors to have multiple signals of different dimensions while also using the measurement matrix generated by the chaotic sequence to reduce the number of data stores and computational overhead and ensure the safe sharing of medical data.

2.2 Knowledge Distillation in Federated Learning

Knowledge distillation in federated learning has recently emerged as an effective method for addressing user heterogeneity. We have conducted extensive research on the current area of combining federation learning with distillation learning.

Li et al. [15] proposed FedMD using migration learning and knowledge distillation. This framework allows different clients to design different network structures based on their computational power and protects the privacy security of the dataset and the privacy security of the model under the condition of jointly training out a model. However, it requires less computation than the sum of individual KL loss between the student model (global model) and each teacher model (client model) in ensemble KD. Chang et al. [16] in Cronus, each client uses the local dataset and the soft-labeled public dataset jointly for local training. Li et al. [17] proposed that Feddane performed ensemble distillation for each client, aiming to learn strong personalized models, but not the global model. Lin et al. [18] proposed FedDF training models. This knowledge distillation technique combined with federation learning reduces privacy risks and costs and allows flexible aggregation of heterogeneous client models without many restrictions on the model's university and data structure. He et al. [19] proposed FedGKT for solving the problem of resource limitations of edge devices, reducing the communication costs of large CNNs, and asynchronous training, maintaining model accuracy comparable to federated learning. Sun et al. [20] proposed a novel framework for federation and distillation learning called FEDMD-NFDP and eliminated the previous cost explosion problem of adding noise to differential privacy. Li et al. [21] proposed a one-shot federated learning algorithm for the cross-silo setting algorithm called FEDKT. By exploiting knowledge transfer techniques, FEDKT can apply to any classification model and can be flexibly obtained with differential privacy guarantees. However, FEDKT is a single-shot algorithm, but it is still suitable for situations where multiple rounds are allowed. FEDKT can be used as an initial step for the first round of learning the global model. Parties can then use the global model to tune the iterative joint learning algorithm. Seo et al. [22] proposed Mix2FLD to apply an inverse hybrid algorithm to MixFLD, which not only ensures local data privacy but also allows for high accuracy. A distributed learning framework for exchanging model outputs rather than joint learning (FL) based on exchanging model parameters. An online version of knowledge refinement that drives efficient communication through a novel method of grouping model outputs. Chen et al. [23] proposed powerful knowledge transfer between its black-box local models controls that FEDBE. It unifies and significantly reduces the size of the information exchanged between parties. It generates a series of global models from the Bayesian perspective using the local models, then summarizes these models into one global model by ensemble knowledge distillation. Sattler et al. [24] proposed that FEDAUX modifies the FD training procedure in two ways: first, a jointly supervised pre-training of auxiliary data is performed to find the model initial for distributed training. Unsupervised pre-training and weighted set distillation using auxiliary data. Zhu et al. [25] proposed a data-free knowledge distillation method to address heterogeneous FL, called FEDGen server, in which a lightweight generator was learned to integrate user information in a data-free manner, which was broadcast to the user and reconciled using that local training. Cheng et al. [26] proposed a framework that can prevent negative and malicious knowledge transfer called FedGems. This framework further improves the robustness of FL against poisoning attacks and reduces the cost of communication between the server and the client, but this framework has some limitations, such as the dependency on marking as public datasets. Gong et al. [27] proposed a single-issue federated learning framework called FedAD that theoretically preserves the efficiency of using only untagged and domain name public data and efficiently available network bandwidth resources, demonstrating the applicability of FedAD to real-world cross-institutional learning through medical image data.

3 Methods

In this section, we introduce our efficient communication model of federated distillation learning called Fed-TD. We will first introduce the present definition of the problem studied in this paper, then introduce the details of our algorithm. Figure 1 visualizes the training procedure for the telemedicine scenarios, and we summarize the corresponding algorithm in Algorithms 1.

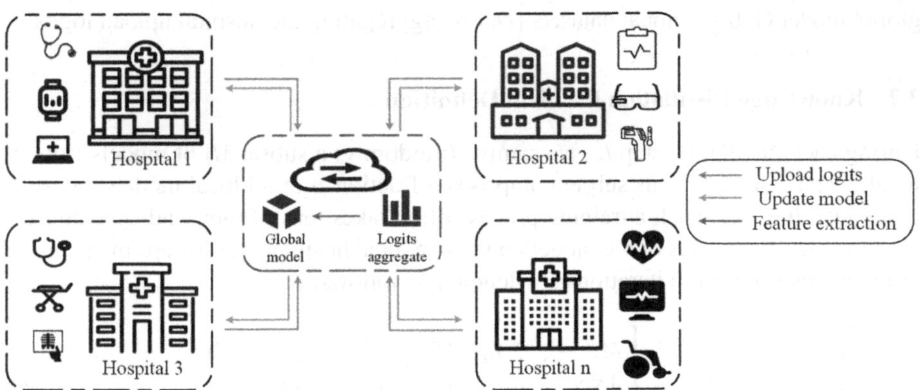

Fig. 1. Overview of the FedTD telemedicine data sharing architecture.

We use federated distillation learning to ensure that patients store telemedicine terminal data in the servers of the local hospital, and it is difficult for attackers to crack medical privacy data through model parameters, reducing the risk of medical data leakage. This ensures that patients can share data quickly and efficiently when using convenient telemedicine technology.

In the telemedicine scenario, common telemedicine devices include wheelchairs, glasses, and watches. They transmit the patient's medical data to the local hospital server using encryption. Then local hospital servers up the logits to a global cloud server. The cloud server then receives the logits uploaded by the hospitals to obtain a global model through feature extraction and transmits the new model to the hospitals through a federated learning process. In this way, the local patient's health data can use effectively without being transferred directly to the global server.

3.1 Problem Definition

In our approach, we assume a set of N hospitals store patients' medical data, whose dataset is stored in local servers denoted as $\{D_n\}n \in \{1, \ldots, N\}$. Let θ be the model parameter in the global server and patients. Where $\mathcal{L}(\theta, x_n, y_n)$ is the loss function of the training medical data sample x_n and its label y_n. The empirical local loss function for local server is to minimize:

$$L_n(\theta) = \frac{1}{D_n}\sum\nolimits_{\{x_n, y_n\} \in \mathcal{D}_n} \mathcal{L}(\theta, x_n, y_n)\# \quad (1)$$

The telemedicine device does not exchange patient's health data directly, but uses cryptographic encryption to transmit data to the local hospital server. Hospitals can use cloud services to access datasets $\{D_c\}$. The goal of our work is to train a collection of N models M^n to adapt to the local hospital dataset. When a doctor is unable to resolve a patient's problem through a local hospital, a solution can be obtained by accessing a global server. To address this issue. Since, our proposed FedTD is agnostic to the type of network architecture, each local neural network can be customized to have its model, helping adapt the model to its local data distribution. We also get a solution from the global model G, train global datasets $\{D_c\}$ by aggregating the hospital upload logits.

3.2 Knowledge Distillation Problem Definition

During each distillation step t, , we sample (randomly) a subset M_t of models from all local hospital servers. This subset comprises a fraction ρ of all local models. Where ξ is the learning rate. Such a training process often takes tens of thousands update steps to converge. Parameters of the model on the t-th local hospital after t steps of stochastic gradient descent (SGD) iterations are denoted as follows:

$$M_t^n = \begin{cases} M_t^n - \xi \tilde{\nabla} L_t\left(M_{t-1}^n\right) & t \mid \tau \neq 0 \\ \frac{1}{n}\sum_{i=1}^n \left[\theta_{t-1}^i - \xi \tilde{\nabla} L_i\left(\theta_{t-1}^i\right)\right] & t \mid \tau = 0 \end{cases} \quad (2)$$

Knowledge Distillation (KD) is the process of distilling knowledge from a large and well-trained teacher model to a small student model. We use the Kullback-Leibler divergence to ensemble all teachers' soft labels. Neural networks typically produce class probabilities by using a "softmax" as

$$Z_t(\theta) = softmax(\theta) = \frac{\exp\left(\frac{\gamma(x_i)^n}{T}\right)}{\sum_{i=1}^n \exp\left(\frac{\gamma(x_i)}{T}\right)} \text{ for } x \in D_{log}\# \quad (3)$$

Let x_i represent as input the logit of i-the health sample. Where γ is the softmax function, which will output the prediction score of teacher model Z_t. To enable the peak probability congruence among hospitals, we require the refined peak probabilities of all hospitals to be a constant value τ. After distillation of local knowledge, hospitals send the soft label Z_t of the updated local models to the global server.

3.3 Global Server Aggregation

The distillation loss of the global dataset is $\{D_c\}$ the cross-entropy loss for the teacher logit and the student logit, which is

$$\ell_g = \sum_{i=1}^{N} \frac{\ell_g(Z_t(D_c), Z_S(D_c)^i)}{N} \tag{4}$$

Algorithm1: FedTD

Input: N: number of hospitals; T: communication round;
$\{D_n\}\, n \in \{1, \ldots, N\}$: the datasets of hospitals;
Initialize: local hospital server model M^n and global server model G
for each communication round $t = 1, \ldots, T$ *do*
$H_t \leftarrow$ random subset(ρ fraction) from N clients
for $n \in H_t$ in parallel do:
Local server update: $M_t^n = M_{t-1}^n - \xi \widetilde{\nabla} L_i(M_{t-1}^n)$
Compute the logits: $Z_t(\theta) =$ softmax(θ) for $\theta \in D_{logit}$
Send the soft label Z_t of the updated client models to the Cloud server
end for
Server calculates the average soft label for each hospital $Z_S^n = \frac{1}{|C_t|} \sum_{i \in S_t}^{i \neq n} Z_t^i$
Cloud Server updates the global model: $G = G_{t-1} - \xi \widetilde{\nabla} \ell_g(G_{t-1})$
end for
Output: global G and N client M^n

On the global server, it trains the larger model with the reference dataset and the outcomes obtained from local hospital servers to extract the generalized knowledge. Afterward, the global server broadcasts its knowledge as the soft target of the updated global model to all hospitals. After the local server finishes distillation, it generates the global server knowledge based on uploaded by hospitals. And it transferred the new model to the corresponding hospitals. This process iterates over multiple communication rounds until convergence. Obviously, different from FedAvg, in our algorithm, we exchange the soft targets instead of the model parameters. Thus, it can significantly reduce the communication costs of the training process.

4 Experiments and Analysis

4.1 Experimental Environment

In this section, we validate the efficacy of the FedTD algorithm with the COVID-19 Radiography [28, 29] and COVID-Chestxray [30] datasets. We implement our experiments via PyTorch on NVIDIA GeForce RTX 3060 Ti GPU and AMD Ryzen 7 5800H. We wrote codes using Python 3.8 and Tensorflow 2.3.

In the federated learning setup, we assume each computer to be a hospital server that stores the telemedicine data. We also have a computer emulated as a global server. During the implementation, we use Dirichlet distribution Dir(α) to simulate the non-IID data distribution among patients, where a smaller α shows a higher data heterogeneity. We set $\alpha = 0.2, 0.5$ and 1. The local hospital datasets are unbalanced and have a few training samples. In all experiments, the neural network model is ResNet [31]. Communication round T = 200. In each communication round, we randomly select 10 hospitals to take part in the learning process. The local update and distillation, the batch size B = 32. We set the local update steps and the distillation steps as 15 epochs in each communication round. The step sizes of the local update and distillation are set to 0.02 and 0.002, respectively. The number of global epochs R = 4.

In this experiment, we use accuracy (ACC) as the indicator for the classification of the results. To do this, we first obtain True Positive (TP), True Negative (TN), False Positive (FP), and False Negative (FN). Second, the ACC can be calculated as follows:

$$ACC = \frac{\mathrm{TP} + \mathrm{TN}}{\mathrm{TP} + \mathrm{TN} + \mathrm{FP} + \mathrm{FN}} \tag{5}$$

4.2 Performance Evaluation

In order to simulate medical scenarios more realistically, the communication resources of various hospital servers differ. In data fusion with global services, only servers from some local hospitals are involved. Therefore, we set the number of local hospital services is N for each round of training to 2, 4, 6, 8, and 10, which means that 20%, 40%, 60%, 80% and 100% of local servers taking part in the federated distillation learning process in each communication round.

We use the COVID-Chestxray dataset as patient data stored in local hospitals, where the data heterogeneity $\alpha = 1$. We use the same color to represent the number of hospitals taking part in the training. It showed the experimental results in Fig. 2. For all values of all N, the test accuracy gradually increases as the number of communication rounds increases. When the training process converges, the test accuracy of the training varies slightly. Although test accuracy is similar, the training time overhead varies widely, as shown in Fig. 3. For example, when 80% of hospitals are involved, the value of communication costs is 16.18. But when 40% of hospitals are involved, the communication costs is 8.25. The more hospitals involved in the training, the greater the medical data that needs to be trained and the longer the time costs.

Federated distillation uses a global distillation model that allows local hospital model output to be exchanged between the central server and the taking part clients. In the

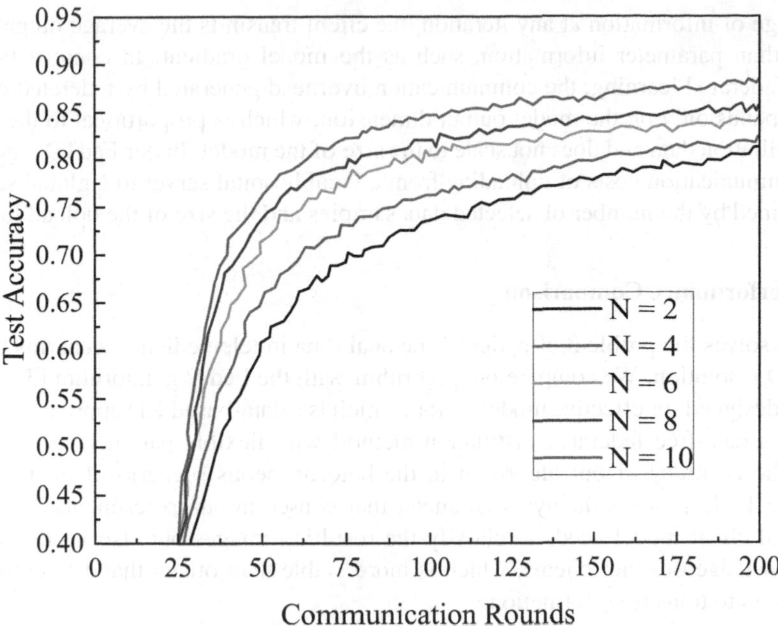

Fig. 2. Test accuracy under different number of local hospitals.

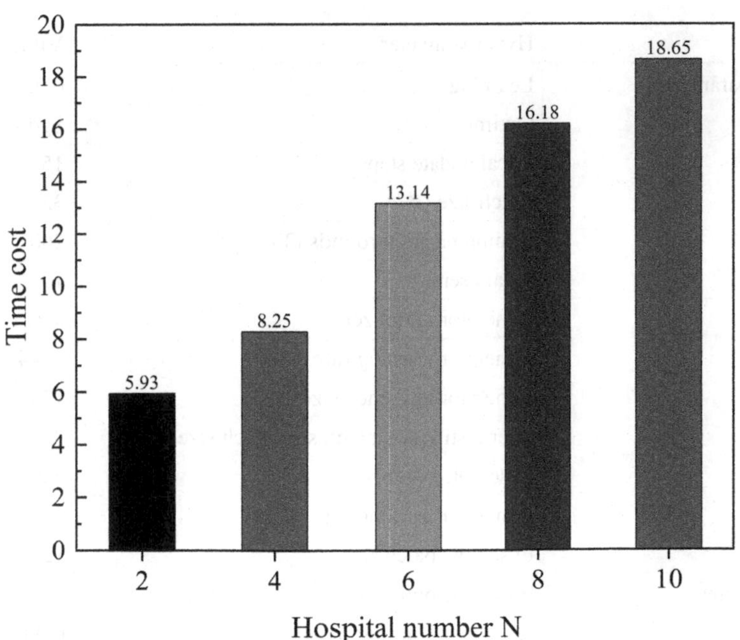

Fig. 3. Time costs under the different number of local hospitals.

exchange of information at any iteration, the client transmits the average output logits rather than parameter information, such as the model gradient. In contrast to traditional federated learning, the communication overhead generated by federated distillation depends only on the model output dimension, which is proportional to the size of the distillation data and does not scale to the size of the model. In our FedTD algorithm, the communication costs of uploading from a local hospital server to a global server is determined by the number of selected data samples and the size of the upload logits.

4.3 Performance Comparison

FedTD solves the problem of patients' medical data in telemedicine scenarios that are non-IID resolution. We compare our algorithm with the FedAvg algorithm [3]. FedDF [18] is designed for effective model fusion, which is a data-based KD approach. FedGen [25] is a data-free federated distillation method with flexible parameter sharing. We show the accuracy of our algorithm in the heterogeneous scenario of medical data. And the Table 1 shows the hyperparameter that is used in our experiments. In FedTD, the local client model needs to classify the resulting images but also needs to distill the knowledge of other clients, which is more stable than others that rely entirely on generators to transmit information.

Table 1. Hyperparameter that are used in our experiments.

	Hyperparameter	Value
Shared parameters	Learning rate	0.02
	Optimizer	Sgd
	Local update steps	15
	Batch size (B)	32
	Communication rounds (T)	200
	Total users	10
FedGen	Generator optimizer	adam
	Generator learning rate	10–4
	Generator inference size	128
	User distillation batch size batch size	32
FedDF	Ensemble optimizer	adam
	Generator learning rate	10–4
	Ensemble batch size	128
FedTD(Our)	Ensemble optimizer	adam
	Generator learning rate	0.002
	Ensemble batch size	32

Table 2. Test accuracy on COVID-Chestxray.

COVID-Chestxray			
	$\alpha = 1$	$\alpha = 0.5$	$\alpha = 0.2$
Global Server	88.36 ± 0.16		
FedAvg	82.69 ± 0.15	81.92 ± 0.56	79.93 ± 0.75
FedDF	83.93 ± 0.34	82.77 ± 0.42	81.67 ± 0.26
FedGen	84.42 ± 0.23	83.83 ± 0.73	82.74 ± 0.59
FedTD	**86.67 ± 0.19**	**84.26 ± 0.31**	**83.65 ± 0.25**

Table 3. Test accuracy on COVID-19 Radiography.

COVID-19 Radiograph			
	$\alpha = 1$	$\alpha = 0.5$	$\alpha = 0.2$
Global Server	72.88 ± 0.32		
FedAvg	56.29 ± 0.32	55.83 ± 0.34	54.21 ± 0.65
FedDF	58.34 ± 0.44	57.16 ± 0.53	56.97 ± 0.46
FedGen	64.73 ± 0.26	63.41 ± 0.29	62.24 ± 0.31
FedTD	**67.86 ± 0.33**	**66.64 ± 0.11**	**65.35 ± 0.34**

Table 2 shows that we use the COVID-Chestxray dataset for experiments, and the first row shows test accuracy of the global server is 91.36%. In the case of $\alpha = 0.2$, which means a high degree of heterogeneity between the data. FedAvg algorithm has an accuracy of 79.93% on the local hospital servers. But FedTD achieves 83.65% accuracy in local hospital servers. We can see that the non-IID of data has a greater impact on the training results of federated learning. It also demonstrates the effectiveness of distillation learning, which should be able to train unique models based on the features of patient data. It shows the effectiveness of distillation federated learning. And our algorithm is also beyond FedDF and FedGen.

Table 3 shows that we use COVID-19 Radiography datasets for experiments, and the first row shows test accuracy of the global server is 72.88%. The table clearly shows that our proposed FedTD is better than the other three algorithms in various cases where medical data is heterogeneous. Obviously, our method is ~11% higher than FedAvg. FedGen also gets a good training results, FedGen has ~6% higher training accuracy than FedDF.

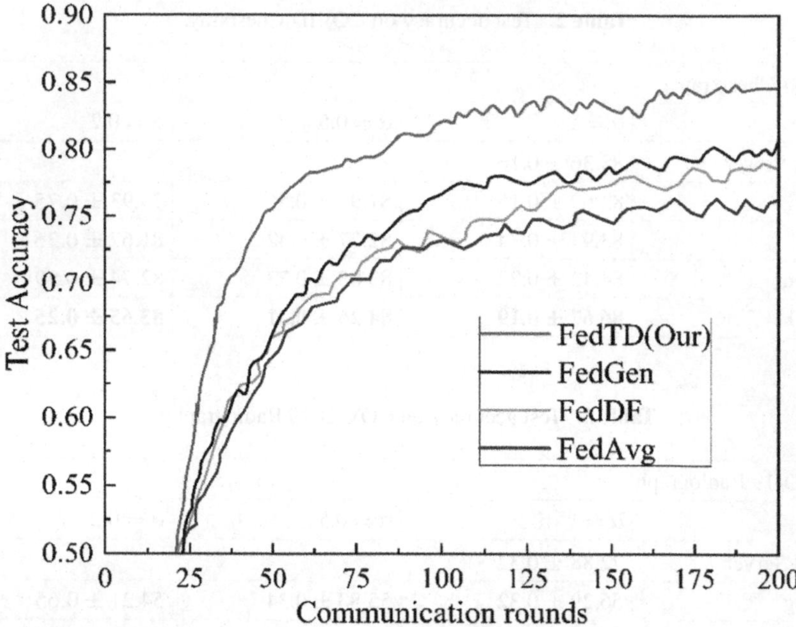

Fig. 4. Test accuracy trends of four methods over COVID-Chestxray dataset.

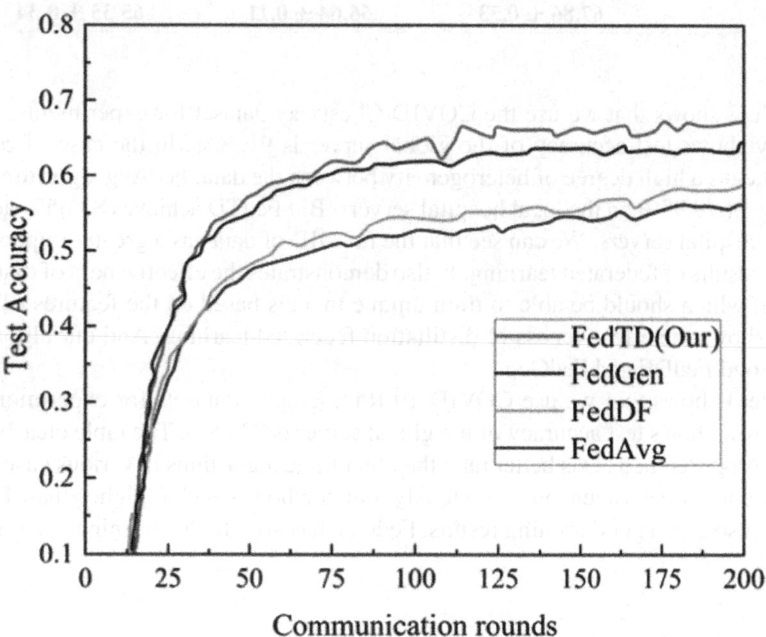

Fig. 5. Test accuracy trends of four methods over COVID-19 Radiography dataset.

For each figure, the X-axis represents the number of train rounds, and the Y-axis represents the accuracy of the model. The four curves with different colors represent a trend in the accuracy of model inference for four methods. Figure 4 shows that 80% of the local hospital servers are involved in the training process. When the accuracy of the model does not improve significantly, we think the model reaches convergence. Our experiment used the COVID-Chestxray dataset and $\alpha = 0.5$. From the figure, we can see that our algorithm model converges faster. The model accuracy of the FedAvg algorithm is only 73.6. We can see that accuracy fluctuates during training and the main reason for the decline is the bias introduced in the global distillation of unbalanced data samples.

Figure 5 shows that 20% of the local hospital servers are involved in the training process. Figure 2 shows our training using the COVID-19 Radiography dataset and $\alpha = 0.2$. We can see that the model accuracy of all methods improves with increasing training rounds. Although our accuracy is similar to FedGen sometimes, our final training results were 3% higher than FedGen. Although the results of FedDF algorithm are lower than FedGen, it is more accurate than the FedAvg.

5 Conclusion

In this paper, we propose a new federated learning algorithm called FedTD. Our solutions solve the problem of heterogeneous data for patients. Hospitals transmit logits information instead of model parameters for knowledge exchange. And the communication overhead is also significantly reduced compared to traditional federated learning. We tested our approach on the COVID-19 Radiography and COVID-Chestxray datasets to improve the model performance and reduce communication costs. Extensive experiments show that FedTD performance is better than the state-of-the-art under heterogeneous data. In the future, we will combine FedTD with blockchain technology to reduce the impact of poisoning attacks during federated learning.

References

1. Research Report on Medical Internet of Things Security. Institute of Security, China Academy of Information and Communications Technology (2021)
2. IoT Endpoint Security White Paper[R]. IoT Security Innovation Lab (2019)
3. McMahan, B., Moore, E., Ramage, D., et al.: Communication-efficient learning of deep networks from decentralized data. In: Artificial Intelligence and Statistics, pp. 1273–1282. PMLR, (2017)
4. Hard, A., Rao, K., Mathews, R., et al.: Federated learning for mobile keyboard prediction (2018). arXiv preprint arXiv:1811.03604
5. Hinton, G., Vinyals, O., Dean, J.: Distilling the knowledge in a neural network, **2**(7) (2015). arXiv preprint arXiv:1503.02531
6. Anil, R., Pereyra, G., Passos, A., et al.: Large scale distributed neural network training through online distillation (2018). arXiv preprint arXiv:1804.03235
7. Jeong, E., Oh, S., Kim, H., et al.: Communication-efficient on-device machine learning: federated distillation and augmentation under non-iid private data (2018). arXiv preprint arXiv:1811.11479

8. Griggs, K.N., Ossipova, O., Kohlios, C.P., et al.: Healthcare blockchain system using smart contracts for secure automated remote patient monitoring. J. Med. Syst. **42**(7), 1–7 (2018)
9. Musale, P., Baek, D., Werellagama, N., et al.: You walk, we authenticate: lightweight seamless authentication based on gait in wearable IoT systems. IEEE Access **7**, 37883–37895 (2019)
10. Nguyen, D.C., Pathirana, P.N., Ding, M., Seneviratne, A.: Blockchain for secure EHRs sharing of mobile cloud based E-health systems. IEEE Access **7**, 66792–66806 (2019)
11. Vallathan, G., Rajani, T., Kumaraswamy, E., et al.: A prediction based encryption approach for telemedicine applications. In: IOP Conference Series: Materials Science and Engineering, vol. 981, no. 3, p. 032008. IOP Publishing (2020)
12. Lin, Q., Yan, H., Huang, Z., et al.: An ID-based linearly homomorphic signature scheme and its application in blockchain. IEEE Access **6**, 20632–20640 (2018)
13. Shuai, W., Jing, W., Xiao, W., et al.: Blockchain-powered parallel healthcare systems based on the ACP approach. IEEE Trans. Comput. Soc. Syst. **5**(4), 942–950 (2018)
14. Li, L., Liu, L., Peng, H., et al.: Flexible and secure data transmission system based on semitensor compressive sensing in wireless body area networks. IEEE Internet Things J. **6**(2), 3212–3227 (2018)
15. Li, D., Wang, J.: Fedmd: heterogenous federated learning via model distillation (2019). arXiv preprint arXiv:1910.03581
16. Chang, H., Shejwalkar, V., Shokri, R., et al.: Cronus: robust and heterogeneous collaborative learning with black-box knowledge transfer (2019). arXiv preprint arXiv:1912.11279
17. Li, T., Sahu, A.K., Zaheer, M., et al.: Feddane: a federated newton-type method. In: 2019 53rd Asilomar Conference on Signals, Systems, and Computers, pp. 1227–1231. IEEE (2019)
18. Lin, T., Kong, L., Stich, S.U., et al.: Ensemble distillation for robust model fusion in federated learning. Adv. Neural. Inf. Process. Syst. **33**, 2351–2363 (2020)
19. He, C., Annavaram, M., Avestimehr, S.: Group knowledge transfer: federated learning of large cnns at the edge. Adv. Neural. Inf. Process. Syst. **33**, 14068–14080 (2020)
20. Sun, L., Lyu, L.: Federated model distillation with noise-free differential privacy (2020). arXiv preprint arXiv:2009.05537
21. Li, Q., He, B., Song, D.: Practical one-shot federated learning for cross-silo setting (2020). arXiv preprint arXiv:2010.01017
22. Seo, H., Park, J., Oh, S., et al.: Federated knowledge distillation (2020). arXiv preprint arXiv: 2011.02367
23. Chen, H.Y., Chao, W.L.: Fedbe: making bayesian model ensemble applicable to federated learning (2020). arXiv preprint arXiv:2009.01974
24. Sattler, F., Korjakow, T., Rischke, R., et al.: Fedaux: leveraging unlabeled auxiliary data in federated learning. IEEE Trans. Neural Netw. Learn. Syst., 1–13 (2021)
25. Zhu, Z., Hong, J., Zhou, J.: Data-free knowledge distillation for heterogeneous federated learning. In: International Conference on Machine Learning, pp. 12878–12889. PMLR (2021)
26. Cheng, S., Wu, J., Xiao, Y., et al.: FedGEMS: federated learning of larger server models via selective knowledge fusion (2021). arXiv preprint arXiv:2110.11027
27. Gong, X., Sharma, A., Karanam, S., et al.: Ensemble attention distillation for privacy-preserving federated learning. In: Proceedings of the IEEE CVF International Conference on Computer Vision, pp. 15076–15086 (2021)
28. Chowdhury, M.E.H., Rahman, T., Khandakar, A., et al.: Can AI help in screening viral and COVID-19 pneumonia? IEEE Access **8**, 132665–132676 (2020)

29. Rahman, T., Khandakar, A., Qiblawey, Y., et al.: Exploring the effect of image enhancement techniques on COVID-19 detection using chest X-ray images. Comput. Biol. Med. **132**, 104319 (2021)
30. Cohen, J.P., Morrison, P., Dao, L.: COVID-19 image data collection (2020). arXiv preprint arXiv:2003.11597
31. He, K., Zhang, X., Ren, S., et al.: Deep residual learning for image recognition. In: Proceedings of the IEEE Conference on Computer Vision and Pattern Recognition, pp. 770–778 (2016)

Increase Channel Attention Based on Unet++ Architecture for Medical Images

Fei Wu[✉], Sikai Liu, Bo Li, and Jinghong Tang

School of Information Engineering, East China Jiaotong University, Nanchang 330013, China
834435610@qq.com

Abstract. At present, image segmentation technology has become increasingly mature. The application of image segmentation technology in the field of medical images is also more and more extensive. However, the growing demand is not enough for current medical image segmentation models. Unet++ is a good basic model in the field of medical image segmentation. On this basis, we add a channel attention module for long skip connections. Solve the problem of serious loss of eigenvalues in the process of long skip connections. This can get better accuracy and better image segmentation. At the same time, our added channel attention module can effectively increase the robustness of the network model. Through our experimental analysis and result judgment, our designed C-Unet++ can play a better role in medical image segmentation.

Keywords: Segmentation · Skip connection · Attention · Deconvolution

1 Introduction

Computers are developing very rapidly in the current era, so computers can have excellent performance in various fields [1]. The application of computers in the field of medical images can better help doctors solve problems and find intractable diseases. Computers can help doctors save a lot of time in image processing. However, in the field of medical images, there are still many problems that need the help of computers to solve [2]. The current computer technology is sufficiently developed, and the computer conditions are mature enough to accurately analyze images [3].

CT scan images of medical images, if deep learning is introduced to assist in treating patients, can effectively help doctors solve problems [4]. Simply looking at the current situation, if there is no auxiliary judgment of deep learning, CT scan images require many years of professional experience to make accurate judgments, which is too high for the professional requirements of talents [5].

In recent times, deep learning has achieved remarkable results in medical image segmentation. Deep convolutional networks can shine even more in medical image segmentation [6].

Since 2012, there have been many excellent deep learning models for medical image segmentation. Such as VGG16 [7] and GoogleNet [8]. These models have achieved very good results. But with the development of the times, the effect of these models is far

Y. Xu et al. (Eds.): ML4CS 2022, LNCS 13655, pp. 516–520, 2023.
https://doi.org/10.1007/978-3-031-20096-0_38

from enough.In 2015, a deep learning network model with a U-shaped structure was proposed. The emergence of Unet [9] has laid an excellent foundation for future medical image segmentation, and many scholars have made continuous improvements on this basis. In 2018, a more complex Unet network model was designed, named Unet++ [10]. Unet++ adds some structures on the original basis and increases the robustness of the network itself [11].

2 Proposed Approach

2.1 Network Architecture

We design a new model named C-Unet++. The network results are shown in Fig. 1. We add a channel attention mechanism based on the Unet++ model. This mechanism can effectively help solve the problem of eigenvalue loss in the process of long skip connections [19].

The network structure we designed is mainly composed of the following parts: Down-sampling, Up-sampling, Conventional Skip connection. Our channel attention module works on the Conventional Skip connection. This module can also greatly increase the robustness of the network structure.

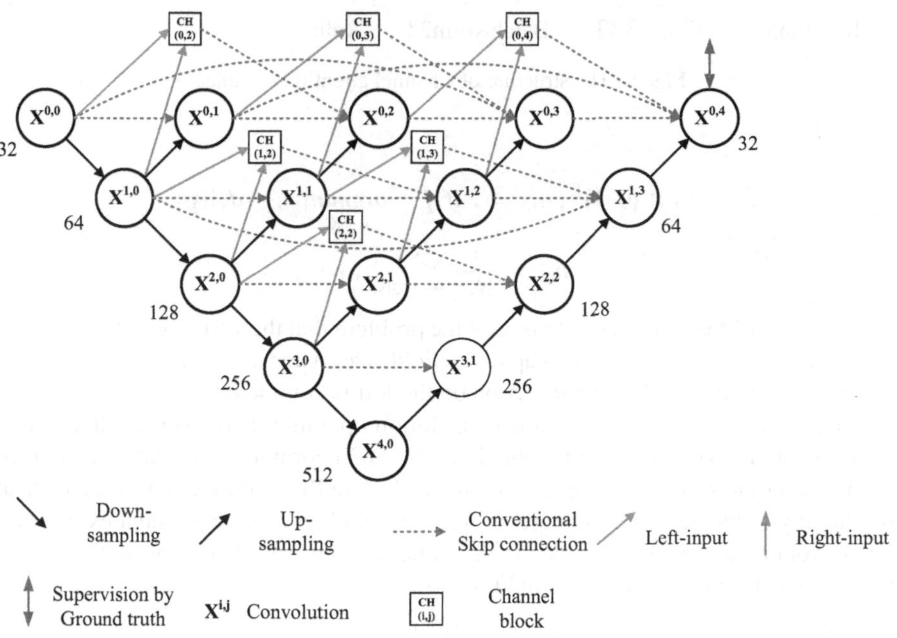

Fig. 1. The C-Unet++ model architecture.

2.2 Channel Attention Module

The channel attention module we designed is shown in Fig. 2. The attention module is divided into left and right parts. After entering the input, first perform the AvgPool2d operation. The AvgPool2d formula is shown in (1) (2). In formula (1) (2), x_i represents the value of each data, d_k represents the average value, and $\underset{\kappa \leq K}{argmin}||x_i - d_k||_2^2$ represents the minimum variance. h_m is the final average value of α_i calculated.

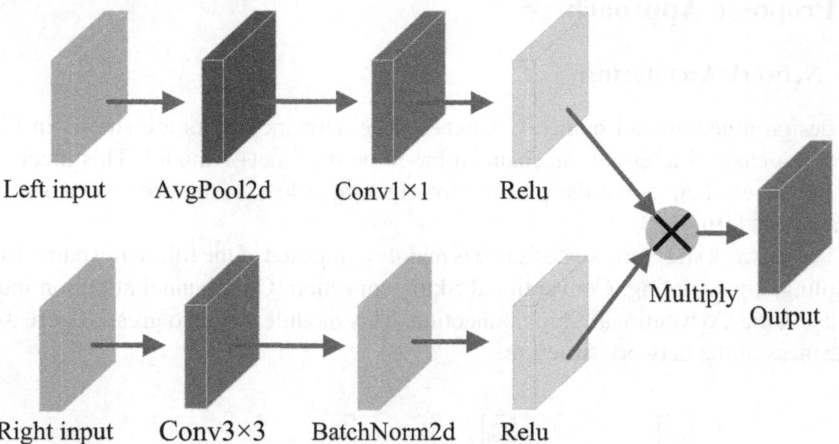

Fig. 2. The structure of Channel attention module.

$$\alpha_i \in \{0, 1\}^K, \alpha_{i,j} = 1 \text{ if } j = \underset{\kappa \leq K}{argmin}||x_i - d_k||_2^2 \tag{1}$$

$$h_m = \frac{1}{|N_m|}\sum\nolimits_{i \in N_m} (\alpha_i) \tag{2}$$

The role of Mean-pooling is to reduce the problem that the variance of the estimated value is too large due to the large gap of the field size. After that, use a 1*1 convolution kernel for convolution. The input section on the left is complete.

After entering the right input, the convolution operation is performed first, using a 3 * 3 convolution kernel. The following BatchNorm2d normalizes the data. The purpose of this operation is to reduce the amount of data before ReLU correction, so as to ensure the stability of the network structure performance and reduce the gradient explosion in the convolutional neural network. At the same time, it can also increase the training process. The formula of BatchNorm2d is shown in (3).

$$y = \frac{X - E[X]}{\sqrt{Var[X] + \epsilon}} * \gamma + \beta \tag{3}$$

The meaning of $E[X]$ in the formula refers to the mean of the input. The meaning of $Var[X]$ in the formula is the variance of the input. ϵ is 1e–5. Initial value is 1. β Initial value is 0. The two values of γ and β are to be learned. The final result is the result from high*low, then perform the ReLU function.

3 Experiments

To validate our approach, we used data sets from the ISBI liTS 2017 Challenge. The number of images in the training set is 400 and the number of test sets is 20.

The number of experiments performed in this experimental process was 200 times. The data being compared are dice, IoU, Hausdorff distance. Other state-of-the-art models involved in the comparison are, Unet, Unet++, ResUnet, attention-Unet, and our own C-Unet++. The results are shown in Table 1.

Table 1. Compare results with other models.

class	Unet[8]	Unet++ [9]	ResUnet	Attention-Unet	C-Unet++
Dice	0.925	0.934	0.936	0.933	**0.952**
Iou	0.861	0.877	0.881	0.875	**0.909**
Hausdorff distance	7.37	6.43	6.82	6.53	**4.10**

4 Conclusion

During experiments, we strive to iteratively validate. At the same time, the method and model are modified, and finally C-Unet++ is improved. The results show that our model has a certain improvement on the basis of the original model. The main improvement is that in the long-hop connection process, the Channel module is added to solve the problem of eigenvalue loss. We can conclude that the Channel module plays an important role in our improved C-Unet++. The reason why the Channel module can achieve such excellent results in the long-hop connection process mainly comes from the AvgPool2d in the left input and the BatchNorm2d function in the right input. Although our work has made great progress, our model is still insufficient. Therefore, we hope to have further improvements in the future. In the future, we will introduce new attention mechanisms to improve our own models.

Acknowledgments. This paper was supported by the National Natural Science Foundation of China Project No. 61863013.

References

1. Jiang, N., Duan, F., Chen, H., Huang, W., Liu, X.: :MAFI: GNN-based Multiple aggregators and feature interactions network for fraud detection over heterogeneous graph. IEEE Trans. Big Data (2021). https://doi.org/10.1109/tbdata.2021.3132672
2. He, H., et al.: A hybrid-attention nested UNet for nuclear segmentation in histopathological images. Front. Molec. Biosci. (2021). https://doi.org/10.3389/fmolb.2021.614174

3. Wang, L., Li, X., Raju, S., Yue, C.P.: Simultaneous magnetic resonance wireless power and high-speed data transfer system with cascaded equalizer for variable channel compensation. IEEE Trans. Power Electron. **34**(12), 11594–11604 (2019). https://doi.org/10.1109/TPEL.2019.2916021
4. Jiang, N., Dong, X., Zhou, J., Yan, H., Wan, T., Zheng, J.: Toward optimal participant decisions with voting-based incentive model for crowd sensing. Inf. Sci. **512**, 1–17 (2020). https://doi.org/10.1016/j.ins.2019.09.068
5. Wu, J., et al.: U-Net combined with multi-scale attention mechanism for liver segmentation in CT images. BMC Med. Inf. Decis. Mak. **21**, 1–12 (2021). https://doi.org/10.1186/s12911-021-01649-w
6. Stankiewicz, A., Marciniak, T., Dabrowski, A., Stopa, M., Marciniak, E., Obara, B.: Segmentation of preretinal space in optical coherence tomography images using deep neural networks. Sensors **21**, 7521 (2021). https://doi.org/10.3390/s21227521
7. Simonyan, K., Zisserman, A.: Very deep convolutional networks for large-scale image recognition. In: Computer Vision and Pattern Recognition (2014). https://arxiv.org/abs/1409.115
8. Szegedy, C., et al.: Going deeper with convolutions. In: 2015 IEEE Conference on Computer Vision and Pattern Recognition (CVPR) (2015). https://doi.org/10.1109/CVPR.2015.7298594
9. Ronneberger, O., Fischer, P., Brox, T.: U-Net: convolutional networks for biomedical image segmentation. IEEE Access (2015). https://arxiv.org/abs/1505.04597
10. Zhou, Z., Siddiquee, M.M.R., Tajbakhsh, N., et al.: A nested U-net architecture for medical image segmentation. In: DLMIA (2018). https://arxiv.org/abs/1807.10165
11. Ren, H., Huang, T., Yan, H.: Adversarial examples: attacks and defenses in the physical world. Int. J. Mach. Learn. Cybern. **12**(11), 3325–3336 (2021). https://doi.org/10.1007/s13042-020-01242-z

Distributed Power Load Missing Value Forecasting with Privacy Protection

Ying Miao[1(✉)], Lianyong Qi[1], Haoyang Wu[1], Yuxin Tian[1], Shengqi Wu[1], Yuqing Wang[1], Fei Dai[2], and Shaoqi Ding[1]

[1] School of Computer Science, Qufu Normal University, RiZhao 276800, China
miaoying5253@gmail.com, {lianyongqi,yuxintian}@qfnu.edu.cn

[2] College of Big Data and Intelligent Engineering, Southwest Forestry University, Kunming 650224, China
daifei@swfu.edu.cn

Abstract. In the era of the Internet of Things (IoT) supporting 5 G technology, the Smart Grid (SG) is an important part of Smart City. Specifically, load forecasting is a key ingredient of the sustainable development of the SG. Similarly, the data collected from the IoT devices (i.g., smart appliances, smart meters) is one of the key factors to improve the accuracy of the prediction results. However, two challenges are present in the process of data collection, where we use multi-source data for load forecasting. First, in the process of collecting data from different platforms, we should protect the users' privacy information. Second, data loss is caused by some reasons (i.g., equipment power failure and communication failure), which affects the accuracy of load forecasting. Considering the above challenges, we propose a new distributed Locality-Sensitive Hashing (LSH) method for load forecasting, named LF_{dLSH}. At last, a case study is put forward to illustrate the feasibility of our approach.

Keywords: Smart grid · Load forecasting · Distributed LSH · Privacy-preservation

1 Introduction

Smart Cities mainly use big data technology to improve the allocation efficiency of power resources, thus making residents' lives more convenient. The SG is the core element of smart city structure. Compared with traditional power grid, smart grid can dynamically adjust users' power demand according to load forecasting.

Load forecasting is highly dependent on data collected from the IoT devices (e.g., smart meters, smart appliances) to predict power consumption accurately and efficiently. However, these data contains a lot of users' privacy information. In addition, data which is obtained from different platforms is generally not centralized. This distributed situation will leads to not only the conflict of interest but also the efficiency issues in the process of data sharing between platforms [1–3].

Y. Xu et al. (Eds.): ML4CS 2022, LNCS 13655, pp. 521–534, 2023.
https://doi.org/10.1007/978-3-031-20096-0_39

In the process of collecting and transferring the data, data loss will inevitably occur. These missing value of power data are caused by equipment failure, communication interruption or other reasons. However, the integrity of data is the key to the success of prediction.

In view of the above challenges, we propose a novel load forecasting method named LF_{dLSH}, which is based on the theory of distributed Locality-Sensitive Hashing (LSH) [4]. In the LF_{dLSH}, we consider prediction efficiency, privacy protection and data integrity. In general, our academic contributions mainly include the following aspects.

(1) According to the data from different IoT devices (i.e., multi-source data), we propose a distributed LSH-based load forecasting method named LF_{dLSH}. This method can protect users' privacy information and improve the efficiency of data integration.
(2) Considering the integrity of electricity data, we proposed method (i.e., LF_{dLSH}) mainly solves the problem of data loss in the process of data collection. In this method, we use LSH technology to improve the speed and efficiency of the operation process of predicting the missing value of power data.

The rest of this paper is structured as follows. In Sect. 2, we summarize the related work. In Sect. 3, we illustrate the research motivation and formalize the load missing value prediction problem. In Sect. 4, we introduce the new method (i.e., LF_{dLSH}) in detail. In Sect. 5, we use a case to analyze the feasibility and effectiveness of our method. Finally, we describe our conclusions of this paper and explain the future work in Sect. 6.

2 Related Work

Next, we briefly describe the research progress of load forecasting from two aspects: privacy protection and missing value forecasting.

2.1 Privacy Protection in Load Forecasting

The SG is one of the promising applications in the 5G IoT. However, privacy protection in data is one of the key factors determining the development of smart grid. In [5], the authors propose a smart grid privacy protection model using k-anonymity algorithm to protect data. They summarized the role of Quasi-Identifier in K-anonymity algorithm, and then analyzed the improved L-diversity algorithm from the aspect of anonymous data privacy. In [6], the authors propose a lightweight anonymous authentication smart grid key agreement scheme, which establishes a shared session key after authentication between smart meters and service providers.

The anonymous algorithm is used to protect the privacy of data, but the accuracy of Short-Term Load Forecast (STLF) is not considered. In [7], the authors analyze the impact of two privacy protection schemes on the accuracy of STLF, which are Model Distributed Predictive Control (MDPC) and load balancing. In [8], the authors integrate differential privacy (DP) [9] into Long-Short Term Memory (LSTM) [10] model for the first time, and propose a differentiated private load forecasting model.

In view of the previous research that anonymous authentication could not identify malicious users, the authors in [11] used the group blind signature structure in the smart grid for the first time. Their scheme realizes anonymous authentication and conditional anonymity, and ensures that private data will not be tampered in the transmission process. In [12], in order to ensure that the smart meter can read the correct reading when attacked, End-User Privacy Protection Scheme (EPPS) is proposed. In [13–17], the authors introduce various hash techniques to balance the relationship between accuracy and privacy protection. Nevertheless, in the above schemes, the accuracy of prediction is often sacrificed when protecting private data.

2.2 Missing Power Data Prediction

Data integrity is one of the key factors for the accuracy of load forecasting. Therefore, the missing value forecasting technology is very important in smart grid. In [18], the authors propose eight different flexible Fuzzy Inductive Reasoning (FIR) prediction strategies to deal with the prediction of missing data in smart grid. With the increasing number of missing values in the training data set, the authors found that the causal correlation strategy performed better in prediction accuracy.

Although intelligent devices have developed well, data loss is inevitable due to equipment failure, accidental power failure or other reasons. Two widely used methods to deal with missing values are Historical Average (HA) and Linear Interpolation (LI). However, the above two methods have little effect on some random and variable data. In [19], a method using the weighted sum of HA and LI as interpolation data is proposed. In [20], the authors apply KNN algorithm to calculate the optimal length of historical data, and propose an adaptive missing value interpolation method based on learning.

The above missing value interpolation methods need iterative application or determine the appropriate number of neighbors. Therefore, in [21], the authors proposed a deep learning framework for missing value interpolation using Denoising Automatic Encoder (DAE). Considering the global and local changes of data variables, in [22], the authors propose an interpolation method based on statistics and machine learning.

Although many aspects have been considered in the above methods, no load forecasting algorithm has been found to deal with distributed data from multiple platforms while considering privacy protection. In view of this situation, we propose a new load power loss prediction method based on distributed LSH, named LF_{dLSH}. Details are as follows.

3 Motivation and Formulation

In this section, we first explain the motivation of the new method (i.e., LF_{dLSH}), and then formulate the problem for the convenience of subsequent work. The symbols used are described in Table 1.

Table 1. Specification of symbols in this paper.

Symbol	Specification
EN	number of power equipment types
TL	size of a time period
DN	number of time periods in a day
TN	number of hash tables
DM	number of days per month
Z	a date variable
n_i	number of record in barrel b_i
EF_k	number of hash function used by equipment E_k
$b_1, ..., b_n$	barrel in hash table
d_x,d_y,p_x,p_y	thresholds recruited in LSH definition
d(ů,ů)	the distance between two electrical data
s(ů)	the LSH function
P(ů)	probability function
S(ů)	the LSH function family

3.1 Motivation

The integrity of data is one of the decisive factors for the success of load forecasting. Due to equipment failure, transmission error and other reasons, power data is missing in the process of collection. On the other hand, the data comes from different intelligent devices, that is, the data required for load forecasting is distributed storage.

With the help of Fig. 1, we briefly describe the scenario of load forecasting. In the figure, there are two different intelligent power generation equipment, power control center, and power users such as homes and factories. As a transfer station, the power control center controls the input and output of power (as shown by the arrow in the figure). In addition, the control center stores power data distributed to the data cloud storage center. The control center is not only responsible for converting power between power providers and users, but also responsible for collecting data information of different equipment for analysis, prediction and corresponding adjustment.

3.2 Formulation

In this section, we formulate the problem of power loss value load forecasting. For ease of understanding and description, we use five-tuple $SG\_LSH(E, ET, TL, Day, day_t)$, where

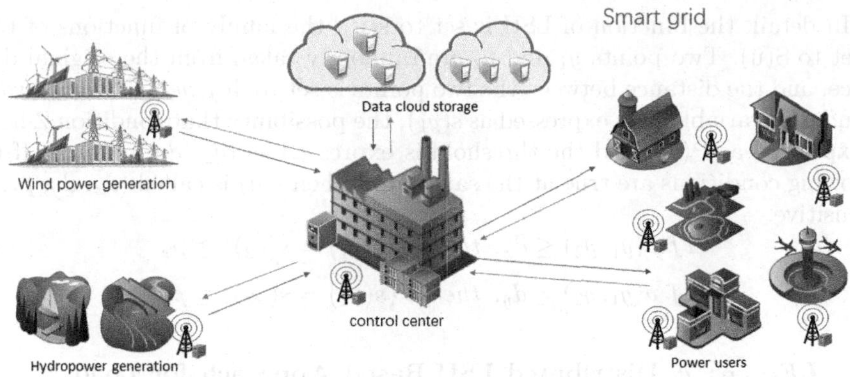

Fig. 1. High level conceptual framework of smart grid.

(1) $E = \{E_1, ..., E_{EN}\}$: $e_n(1 \leq n \leq EN)$ denotes the n-th equipment, which contain the n-th part of the load forecasting data of every day.
(2) $ET = \{ET_1, ..., ET_{EN}\}$: $ET_k(1 \leq k \leq EN)$ denotes the time period data in the power equipment E_k.
(3) TL is the size of a time period, e.g., assuming 30 min as a time period, there are 48 time periods in a day.
(4) $Day = \{day_1, ..., day_{DM}\}$: $day_m(1 \leq m \leq DM)$ means the m-th day of the month. Here, the data set used in load forecasting is the data collected from different power equipment every day.
(5) day_t : a target day to predict the power loss value. Here, $day_t \in Day$ holds.

4 A Novel Load Forecasting Approach: LF_{dLSH}

Our new load power missing value prediction approach is based on distributed LSH. This method can not only deal with the distributed data in different devices, but also protect the privacy. Therefore, we first briefly introduce the principle of LSH. Subsequently, we describe LF_{dLSH} in detail.

4.1 LSH: Locality-Sensitive Hashing

In [4], in order to solve $\in -NNS$ problem, the authors first proposed the LSH method. This method has been proved to be effective in solving the approximate nearest neighbor problem. For example, solve the service recommendation problem based on LSH in [23,24]. In short, LSH algorithm uses hash buckets to store points.

A more vivid description is that (1) two adjacent points in the original setting still have a neighbor relationship after hashing, and (2) two non adjacent points in the original setting still have a non adjacent relationship after hashing. The function with the above conditions is called LSH function.

In detail, the function of LSH is set to s(ů), the family of functions of LSH is set to S(ů). Two points y_1 and y_2 are randomly taken from the original data space, and the distance between the two points is set to d(y_1,y_2). The hash value or index of variable y_1 is expressed as s(y_1), the possibility that condition Z holds is expressed as P(Z), and the threshold is expressed as (d_x, d_y, p_x, p_y). If the following conditions are true at the same time, then s(ů) is called (d_x, d_y, p_x, p_y)-sensitive.

$$If\ d(y_1, y_2) \leq d_x,\ then\ P(s(y_1) = s(y_2)) \geq p_x \tag{1}$$

$$If\ d(y_1, y_2) \geq d_y,\ then\ P(s(y_1) = s(y_2)) \leq p_y \tag{2}$$

4.2 LF_{dLSH}: A Distributed LSH-Based Approach for Load Forecasting

In this subsection, we will introduce our LF_{dLSH} approach in four steps.

Step 1 (Generation Sub-Indices Offline):

Generally, the use of index is an effective method to improve the speed of information retrieval. Therefore, we use time node index to assist in load forecasting.

Concretely, for each power equipment $E_j(1 \leq k \leq EN)$, a family of LSH functions $S_j()$ is matched to found a sub-index offline for $day \in Day$ based on power data read by equipment. Since the degree of linear correlation between the two variables x and y should be judged by pearson correlation coefficient (PCC) [25], we use the LSH function family $S_j()$ corresponding to PCC to establish the date node index.

Firstly, for a day, its time periods $\{ET_{j,1}, ..., ET_{j,DN}\}$ are converted to a ET-dimension vector $\overrightarrow{day(j)} = (ET_{j,1,TL}, ..., ET_{j,DN,TL})$, where TL express a time period, and the missing data in a section of power equipment data set is represented by $ET_{j,i,TL} = 0$. Then, the LSH function $s_j()$ of the above ET-dimension vector is shown by Eq. (3).

$$s_j(day) = \begin{cases} 1 & if\ \overrightarrow{day(j)} \bullet \overrightarrow{p} > 0 \\ 0 & if\ \overrightarrow{day(j)} \bullet \overrightarrow{p} \leq 0 \end{cases} \tag{3}$$

Here, $\overrightarrow{p}$ is an ET-dimension vector $(p_1, .., p_{DN})$ in which the data are random values of [-1,1]; the sign • means the point multiplication. In general, our explanation of Eq. (3) is as follows: vector $\overrightarrow{p}$ is a hyperplane with a cutting function, then we take two vectors $\overrightarrow{y_1}$ and $\overrightarrow{y_2}$ at random. If $\overrightarrow{y_1}$ and $\overrightarrow{y_2}$ are on the same flank of $\overrightarrow{p}$ (i.e., both $\overrightarrow{y_1} \bullet \overrightarrow{p} > 0$ & $\overrightarrow{y_2} \bullet \overrightarrow{p} > 0$ hold, or, both $\overrightarrow{y_1} \bullet \overrightarrow{p} \leq 0$ & $\overrightarrow{y_2} \bullet \overrightarrow{p} \leq 0$ hold), then $\overrightarrow{y_1}$ and $\overrightarrow{y_2}$ are largely similar.

Secondly, since the vector $\overrightarrow{p}$ is composed of random numbers in the interval [-1,1], the above process can be repeated EF_k times with different vector $\overrightarrow{p}$. Then we can obtain the sub-index (i.e., $S_j(day) = (s_j^1(day), ..., s_j^{EF_j}(day))$) of the day data node in the electrical equipment, where $f_k^j(day)(1 \leq j \leq EF_k)$

can be obtained according to Eq. (3). It is worth mentioning that the above sub index (i.e., $S_j(day)$) is the 0–1 vector of the EF_j dimension.

In addition, we can use the following pseudo code to represent the above process(see Algorithm. 1).

Step 2 (Merge Sub-Indices as Date Index Offline):

In step 1, we can get the EN sub-indices $S_1(day), ..., S_{EN}(day)$ according to the data in different power equipment. Next, we merge the EN sub-indices offline into a date node index $S(day) = (S_1(day), ..., S_{EN}(day))$ with dimension $\sum_{j=1}^{EN} D_j$. Subsequently, for each $day \in Day$, Then, we obtain the mapping relationship "$day \rightarrow S(day)$" by repeating the above process. Finally, we put the resulting mapping relationship into hash table H_Tab.

In addition, we can use the following pseudo code to represent the above process(see Algorithm. 2).

Step 3 (Find similar date for day_t online):

In step 1, the selected hash function family $S_i()(1 \leq i \leq EN)$ obtains the sub index offline and in step 2, the sub index is merged offline to obtain the date index, so we can calculate the index $S(day_t)$ of day_t online. Then, we can obtain $S(day_t)$ corresponding barrels from the H_Tab obtained in step 2. If the operation of finding the bucket is successful, all dates in the bucket are considered as similar dates of day_t and put them in data set SD_Set. If the bucket finding operation fails, due to the probability characteristics of LSH, we can not simply think that day_t there is no similar date. This is because this feature of LSH can not guarantee that all similar dates can be found every time, and some qualified results will be ignored.

We can relax the search conditions for similar days by repeating steps 1 and 2 to create TN hash tables $HT_1, ..., HT_TN$. Then, when the condition in Eq. (4) is true, we think that day_t has a similar date. At the same time, the number of similar dates related to day_t in the bucket is equal to $S(day_t)_z$, and then these similar dates are put into the data set DD_Set.

$$\begin{aligned} &\exists\ day(\in Day)\ and\ z(\in 1, ..., TN), \\ &\quad satisfy\ S(day)_z = S(day_t)_z\ in\ HT \end{aligned} \tag{4}$$

In addition, we can use the following pseudo code to represent the above process(see Algorithm. 3).

Step 4 (Top-K Power Missing Value Load Forecasting):

In Step 3, we get a similar date data set DD_Set of day_t. Then we can carry out load forecasting of power loss value according to the data set DD_Set. Specifically, we predict the missing power value in the TL time period according to Eq. (5).

$$ET.S_t = \frac{1}{|SD - Set|} * \sum_{day_i \in SD-Set} ET.S_i \tag{5}$$

Algorithm 1. Generation Sub-Indices Offline

Require: $E = \{E_1, ..., E_{EN}\}$: equipment set
$ET = \{ET_1, ..., ET_{EN}\}$: the time period
$Day = \{day_1, ..., day_{DM}\}$: date set
Ensure: $S_1(day), ..., S_{EN}(day)$
for x=1 to EN **do**
  for y=1 to EF_e **do**
    for z=1 to ET **do**
      $s_{x,y,z}$ = random[-1,1]
    end for
    $\overrightarrow{p_y} = (s_{x,y,1}, ..., s_{x,y,DN})$
    for g=1 to DM **do**
      $\overrightarrow{day_g(x)} = (ET_{x,1,TL}.F_g, ..., ET_{x,DN,TL}.S_g)$
      if $\overrightarrow{day(z)} \bullet \overrightarrow{p} > 0$
        then $s_x^y(day_g) = 1$
        else $s_x^y(day_g) = 0$
      end if
    end for
  end for
  for h = 1 to DM **do**
    $S_x(day_h) = (s_1^x(day), ..., s_{EF_e}^x(day))$
  end for
end for
return the EN sub-indices $S_1(day), ..., S_{EN}(day)$;

Algorithm 2. Merge Sub-Indices as Date Index Offline

Require: $Day = \{day_1, ..., day_{DM}\}$: date set
$S_1(day), ..., S_{EN}(day)$: the EN sub-indices
Ensure: $S(day_1)...S(day_{DM})$
for d = 1 to DM **do**
  $F(day_d) = (F_1(day_d), ..., F_{EN}(day_d))$
end for
creat hash table HT based on $S(day_1)...S(day_{DM})$
return $S(day_1)...S(day_{DM})$;

Here, ET represents the time period in the power equipment, and $ET.S_i$ represents the power value in the corresponding time period in the power equipment E. Finally, we will sort the time periods in the power equipment according to the results obtained by Eq. (5), and take the power values of the first k time periods as the results of load forecasting.

In addition, we can use the following pseudo code to represent the above process(see Algorithm. 4).

Algorithm 3. Find similar date for day_t online

Require: $S_i()(1 \leq i \leq EN)$: the sub index offline
$S(day_1)...S(day_{DM})$: the date index
$Day = \{day_1, ..., day_{DM}\}$: date set
Ensure: DD_Set of day_t
SD-Set $= \phi$
for q = 1 to TN **do**
  duplicate Step 1,2 to obtain HT_q
  match to bucker BK corresponding to $S(day_t)_q$
  if BK $\neq \phi$
    then collect date data from BK into SD-Set
  end if
end for
return a similar date data set DD_Set of day_t;

Algorithm 4. Top-K Power Missing Value Load Forecasting

Require: DD_Set: a similar date data set of day_t
$ET = \{ET_1, ..., ET_{EN}\}$: the time period
$Day = \{day_1, ..., day_{DM}\}$: date set
day_t: a target date
Ensure: R-Set: load forecasting results of day_t
R-Set $= \phi$
for each time quantum ET in E **do**
  if $ET.S_t = 0$
    then count = 0
      for $day_x \in$ SD-Set **do**
        if $ET.S_x \neq 0$
        then count++
          $ET.F_{target} = ET.F_{target} + ET.F_x$
        end if
      end for
      $ET.S_t = ET.S_t/\text{count}$
  end if
end for
take Top-K load forecasting results with $ET.F_{target}$ into R-Set
return R-Set to day_t;

5 Case Study

In order to prove the feasibility of our proposed approach (i.e.,LF_{dLSH}), in this section, we use a case to illustrate the process of this approach. Here we use two different power devices to collect power data. Then we assume that a time period is 60 min, so a day includes 24 time periods. In order to facilitate the display and calculation, we take the data in the electrical equipment for 5 days and take 5 time periods every day.

Step 1 (Generation Sub-Indices Offline):

In this step, We use a hash function group with four hash functions (i.e., $S_k(day) = (s_k^1(day), ..., s_k^4(day))$). the detailed hash function family is shown in (6).

$$S_{10\times4} = \begin{bmatrix} 0.934 & 0.558 & -0.127 & 0.055 \\ 0.094 & -0.604 & 0.897 & 0.875 \\ 0.945 & 0.725 & 0.572 & 0.043 \\ 0.429 & 0.966 & 0.732 & -0.783 \\ 0.395 & -0.672 & -0.653 & -0.683 \end{bmatrix} \tag{6}$$

It can be seen from Eq. (3) that the hash function is multiplied by the data in the electrical equipment. Then repeat the above process four times using different hash functions to obtain the sub index of one of the devices. For ease of observation, we convert the sub index of the 0–1 vector into a decimal number. The sub index of electrical equipment is shown in (7). Here, $s_h(day)$ represents a sub-indice in the h-th device.

$$\begin{aligned} s_1(day) &= [1\ 1\ 0\ 3\ 3] \\ s_2(day) &= [0\ 1\ 0\ 1\ 1] \end{aligned} \tag{7}$$

Step 2 (Merge Sub-Indices as Date Index Offline):

From the previous step, we get two sub indexes of power equipment. Then, we merge the two device sub indexes, as shown in (8). Then, the combined index values are synchronized to each power equipment platform.

$$S_{1,2}(day) = \begin{bmatrix} 1\ 1\ 0\ 3\ 3 \\ 0\ 1\ 0\ 1\ 1 \end{bmatrix} \tag{8}$$

Step 3 (Find similar date for day_t online):

In this step, we repeat step 1 and step 2 four times to obtain four different hash tables. As shown below, (9) and (10) are sub indexes obtained from four different families of hash functions, and (11) is the combined index value. Where $s_k^{TN}(day)$ represents the sub index in the k-th electrical device obtained through the TN-th hash function family.

$$\begin{aligned} s_1^1(day) &= [1\ 1\ 0\ 3\ 3] \\ s_1^2(day) &= [5\ 1\ 4\ 1\ 1] \\ s_1^3(day) &= [2\ 2\ 0\ 2\ 2] \\ s_1^4(day) &= [1\ 1\ 2\ 5\ 5] \end{aligned} \tag{9}$$

$$\begin{aligned} s_2^1(day) &= [0\ 1\ 0\ 1\ 1] \\ s_2^2(day) &= [4\ 4\ 4\ 1\ 1] \\ s_2^3(day) &= [0\ 0\ 0\ 0\ 2] \\ s_2^4(day) &= [1\ 1\ 2\ 5\ 5] \end{aligned} \tag{10}$$

$$
\begin{aligned}
S_{1,2}^{1}(day) &= \begin{bmatrix} 1 & 1 & 0 & 3 & 3 \\ 0 & 1 & 0 & 1 & 1 \end{bmatrix} \\
S_{1,2}^{2}(day) &= \begin{bmatrix} 5 & 1 & 4 & 1 & 1 \\ 4 & 4 & 4 & 1 & 1 \end{bmatrix} \\
S_{1,2}^{3}(day) &= \begin{bmatrix} 2 & 2 & 0 & 2 & 2 \\ 0 & 0 & 0 & 0 & 2 \end{bmatrix} \\
S_{1,2}^{4}(day) &= \begin{bmatrix} 1 & 1 & 2 & 5 & 5 \\ 1 & 1 & 2 & 5 & 5 \end{bmatrix}
\end{aligned} \tag{11}
$$

Then, we can get a similar date matrix according to Eq. (4) and the above values, as shown in (12). In the obtained similarity matrix, its row represents the date in the first electrical equipment, and its column represents the date in the second electrical equipment.

$$
SM_{5\times 5} = \begin{bmatrix} 1 & 1 & 0 & 1 & 0 \\ 1 & 1 & 1 & 0 & 1 \\ 1 & 1 & 1 & 1 & 0 \\ 0 & 0 & 1 & 1 & 1 \\ 0 & 1 & 0 & 1 & 1 \end{bmatrix} \tag{12}
$$

Step 4 (Top-K Power Missing Value Load Forecasting):

We can predict the missing value of electrical equipment by using the similarity matrix obtained in step 3 and Eq. (5). The data in two electrical equipment with missing values can be obtained from the data set, as shown in (13). Finally, the predicted matrices are calculated by Eq. (5) is shown in (14).

$$
\begin{aligned}
FirDevMiss_{5\times 10} &= \begin{bmatrix} 25 & 24 & 0 & 0 & 29 \\ 35 & 31 & 21 & 19 & 25 \\ 31 & 22 & 18 & 15 & 40 \\ 38 & 0 & 28 & 29 & 30 \\ 0 & 29 & 22 & 28 & 22 \end{bmatrix} \\
SecDevMiss_{5\times 10} &= \begin{bmatrix} 148 & 97 & 0 & 0 & 77 \\ 153 & 122 & 75 & 57 & 60 \\ 148 & 87 & 81 & 61 & 59 \\ 245 & 0 & 125 & 90 & 94 \\ 0 & 192 & 118 & 91 & 107 \end{bmatrix}
\end{aligned} \tag{13}
$$

$$
\begin{aligned}
FirDevFore_{5\times 10} &= \begin{bmatrix} 25 & 24 & 19 & 19 & 29 \\ 35 & 31 & 21 & 19 & 25 \\ 31 & 22 & 18 & 15 & 40 \\ 38 & 37 & 28 & 29 & 30 \\ 39 & 29 & 22 & 28 & 22 \end{bmatrix} \\
SecDevFore_{5\times 10} &= \begin{bmatrix} 148 & 97 & 62 & 56 & 77 \\ 153 & 122 & 75 & 57 & 60 \\ 148 & 87 & 81 & 61 & 59 \\ 245 & 197 & 125 & 90 & 94 \\ 248 & 192 & 118 & 91 & 107 \end{bmatrix}
\end{aligned} \tag{14}
$$

6 Conclusions and Future Work

In this paper, considering the collected electrical equipment data with missing values, we propose a new load forecasting method (i.e.,LF_{dLSH}) with encryption function, which can process the distributed stored data. Firstly, LF_{dLSH} method can obtain the data index value in electrical equipment through offline calculation, which greatly improves the calculation efficiency. Secondly, this method introduces distributed LSH, which makes the cooperation between multiple platforms more efficient. Finally, this method mainly predicts the missing values in the electrical equipment data, which protects the integrity of the data and improves the accuracy of the subsequent prediction.

In the future work, we will use multiple sets of real data to verify and improve our method. In addition, we will pay more attention to the study in the privacy protection [26] and distributed data storage [27].

Acknowledgements. This work was supported in part by the Dou Wanchun Expert Workstation of Yunnan Province No.202105AF150013.

References

1. Zhou, X., Liang, W., Ma, J., Yan, Z., Kevin, I., Wang, K.: 2D federated learning for personalized human activity recognition in cyber-physical-social systems. In: IEEE Transactions on Network Science and Engineering (2022)
2. Zhou, X., Liang, W., She, J., Yan, Z., Kevin, I., Wang, K.: Two-layer federated learning with heterogeneous model aggregation for 6G supported internet of vehicles. IEEE Trans. Veh. Technol. **70**(6), 5308–5317 (2021)
3. Zhou, X., Liang, W., Luo, Z., Pan, Y.: Periodic-aware intelligent prediction model for information diffusion in social networks. IEEE Trans. Netw. Sci. Eng. **8**(2), 894–904 (2021)
4. Har-Peled, S., Indyk, P., Motwani, R.: Approximate nearest neighbor: towards removing the curse of dimensionality. Theory of Computing, vol. 8, no. 14, pp. 321–350 (2012). http://www.theoryofcomputing.org/articles/v008a014
5. Shuo, Y., Weimin, W., Zhiwei, K., Hua, F., Yan, Z.: Smart grid data privacy protection algorithm. In: International Symposium on Intelligent Signal Processing and Communication Systems (ISPACS), pp. 242–246 (2017)
6. Zhang, L., Zhao, L., Yin, S., Chi, C.-H., Liu, R., Zhang, Y.: A lightweight authentication scheme with privacy protection for smart grid communications. Future Gener. Comput. Syst. **100**, 770–778 (2019). https://www.sciencedirect.com/science/article/pii/S0167739X19310398
7. Chin, J.-X., Zufferey, T., Shyti, E., Hug, G.: Load forecasting of privacy-aware consumers. In: IEEE Milan PowerTech, 1–6 (2019)
8. Soykan, E.U., Bilgin, Z., Ersoy, M.A., Tomur, E.: Differentially private deep learning for load forecasting on smart grid. In: 2019 IEEE Globecom Workshops (GC Wkshps), pp. 1–6 (2019)
9. Dwork, C.: Differential privacy. In: Bugliesi, M., Preneel, B., Sassone, V., Wegener, I. (eds.) ICALP 2006. LNCS, vol. 4052, pp. 1–12. Springer, Heidelberg (2006). https://doi.org/10.1007/11787006_1

10. Graves, A.: Long short-term memory long short-term memory. In: Supervised Sequence Labelling with Recurrent Neural Networks. Studies in Computational Intelligence, vol. 385, pp. 37–45. Springer, Heidelberg (2012). https://doi.org/10.1007/978-3-642-24797-2_4
11. Kong, W., Shen, J., Vijayakumar, P., Cho, Y., Chang, V.: A practical group blind signature scheme for privacy protection in smart grid. J. Parallel Distrib. Comput. **136**, 29–39 (2020). https://www.sciencedirect.com/science/article/pii/S0743731519301285
12. Singh, N.K., Mahajan, V.: End-user privacy protection scheme from cyber intrusion in smart grid advanced metering infrastructure.: Int. J. Crit. Infrastruct. Prot. **34**, 100410 (2021). https://www.sciencedirect.com/science/article/pii/S1874548221000020
13. Wan, S., Xia, Y., Qi, L., Yang, Y.-H., Atiquzzaman, M.: Automated colorization of a grayscale image with seed points propagation. IEEE Trans. Multimedia **22**(7), 1756–1768 (2020)
14. Xu, X., et al.: A computation offloading method over big data for IoT-enabled cloud-edge computing. Future Gener. Comput. Syst. **95**, 522–533 (2019). https://www.sciencedirect.com/science/article/pii/S0167739X18319770
15. Qi, L., Xiang, H., Dou, W., Yang, C., Qin, Y., Zhang, X.: Privacy-preserving distributed service recommendation based on locality-sensitive hashing. In: IEEE International Conference on Web Services (ICWS), pp. 49–56 (2017)
16. Yan, C., Cui, X., Qi, L., Xu, X., Zhang, X.: Privacy-aware data publishing and integration for collaborative service recommendation. IEEE Access **6**, 43021–43028 (2018)
17. Liu, J., Jin, T., Pan, K., Yang, Y., Wu, Y., Wang, X.: An improved KNN text classification algorithm based on simhash. In: 2017 IEEE 16th International Conference on Cognitive Informatics Cognitive Computing (ICCI*CC), pp. 92–95 (2017)
18. Jurado, S., Nebot, À., Mugica, F., Mihaylov, M.: Fuzzy inductive reasoning forecasting strategies able to cope with missing data: a smart grid application. Appl. Soft Comput. **51**, 225–238 (2017). https://www.sciencedirect.com/science/article/pii/S1568494616306093
19. Peppanen, J., Zhang, X., Grijalva, S., Reno, M.J.: Handling bad or missing smart meter data through advanced data imputation. In: IEEE Power Energy Society Innovative Smart Grid Technologies Conference (ISGT), pp. 1–5 (2016)
20. Kim, M., Park, S., Lee, J., Joo, Y., Choi, J.K.: Learning-based adaptive imputation methodwith KNN algorithm for missing power data. Energies **10**(10), 1668 (2017). https://www.mdpi.com/1996-1073/10/10/1668
21. Ryu, S., Kim, M., Kim, H.: Denoising autoencoder-based missing value imputation for smart meters. IEEE Access **8**, 40656–40666 (2020)
22. Su, T., Shi, Y., Yu, J., Yue, C., Zhou, F.: Nonlinear compensation algorithm for multidimensional temporal data: a missing value imputation for the power grid applications. Knowl.-Based Syst. **215**, 106743 (2021). https://www.sciencedirect.com/science/article/pii/S095070512100006X
23. Qi, L., Zhang, X., Dou, W., Ni, Q.: A distributed locality-sensitive hashing-based approach for cloud service recommendation from multi-source data. IEEE J. Sel. Areas Commun. **35**(11), 2616–2624 (2017)
24. Qi, L., Wang, R., Hu, C., Li, S., He, Q., Xu, X.: Time-aware distributed service recommendation with privacy-preservation. Inf. Sci. **480**, 354–364 (2019)
25. Benesty, J., Chen, J., Huang, Y., Cohen, I.: Pearson correlation coefficient. In: Noise Reduction in Speech Processing. Springer Topics in Signal Processing, pp. 1–4. Springer, Heidelberg (2009). https://doi.org/10.1007/978-3-642-00296-0_5

26. Xia, Y., Wu, L., Zheng, X., Yu, T., Jin, J.: Data dissemination with trajectory privacy protection for 6G-oriented vehicular networks. IEEE Internet Things J. **9**, 21469–21480 (2022)
27. Kou, G., Yi, K., Xiao, H., Peng, R.: Reliability of a distributed data storage system considering the external impacts. IEEE Trans. Reliab., 1–10 (2022)

Differentially Private Generative Model with Ratio-Based Gradient Clipping

Jianchen Lin[1,4] and Yanqing Yao[1,2,3](✉)

[1] State Key Laboratory of Software Development Environment, Beihang University, Beijing 100191, China
{sy1939206,yaoyq}@buaa.edu.cn

[2] State Key Laboratory of Cryptology, Beijing 100878, China

[3] Key Laboratory of Aerospace Network Security, Ministry of Industry and Information Technology, School of Cyber Science and Technology, Beihang University, Beijing 100191, China

[4] State Grid Fujian, Fuzhou 350100, China

Abstract. As a branch of deep learning, conditional Generative Adversarial Net (cGAN) has achieved remarkable results in target-oriented image generation, but the process of training the model lacks privacy guarantee. Differential Privacy (DP) is a privacy-preserving mechanism that could be utilized in the Stochastic Gradient Descent (SGD) of deep learning to maintain the confidentiality of training data. However, the quality and diversity of differentially private conditional image synthesis remain large room for improvement because traditional mechanisms with thick granularities and rigid clipping bounds in Differentially Private SGD (DPSGD) could lead to huge performance loss. To tackle this, we propose three algorithms with different clipping granularities and clipping bound distributions, and investigate the effects on enhancing conditional image generation under Differentially Private Projection cGAN (DP-PcGAN). We compare and analyze the performance of our strategies with methods concerned in terms of seven metrics, finding ratio-based gradient clipping highly effective and robust in training DP-PcGAN for generating visually promising images. Specifically, the Per-layer RGC surpasses previous methods under all evaluation metrics utilizing the second least privacy expense for MNIST dataset, while Per-unit RGC attains encouraging outcomes with a moderate converging speed under FashionMNIST dataset.

Keywords: Differential Privacy (DP) · Ratio-baed Gradient Clipping (RGC) · Generative Adversarial Net (GAN)

This work is supported by the National Key Research and Development Program of China (No. 2021YFB3100400), the National Natural Science Foundation of China (grant no. 62072023), Beijing Municipal Natural Science Foundation (grant no. 4202035), the Open Project Fund of the State Key Laboratory of Cryptology (grant no. MMKFKT202120), the Exploratory Optional Project Fund of the State Key Laboratory of Software Development Environment, and the Fundamental Research Funds of Beihang University.

Y. Xu et al. (Eds.): ML4CS 2022, LNCS 13655, pp. 535–549, 2023.
https://doi.org/10.1007/978-3-031-20096-0_40

1 Introduction

One of the most common structures of deep learning is Convolutional Neural Network (CNN) [14]. Generative Adversarial Net (GAN) [11] is a branch of deep learning targeting data synthesis. With the help of CNN, GAN has shown its prominence in many data generation practices. However, huge steps taken by artificial intelligence raise the concern that how individual privacy could be well preserved in deep learning. A common way to protect a model against the attackers is to preserve the privacy of its gradients so that the confidentiality of model weights could also be maintained. Many techniques were addressed to deal with this issue.

1.1 An Overview of Differential Privacy

Algorithms have been proposed to protect data secrecy like K-Anonymity [27], L-Diversity [17] and T-Closeness [16], but none of the three methods provide exact definitions on how much privacy they can quantitatively preserve. ϵ-Differential Privacy (DP) [8] offers a strong confidentiality guarantee with systematical and mathematical proof, laying the theoretical foundation for future privacy protection studies. However, the algorithm is incapable of maintaining utility while preserving secrecy. Therefore, a relaxed version (ϵ, δ)-DP [9] is addressed.

Studies considering (ϵ, δ)-DP in composition for reducing privacy expenses under iterative procedures are widely investigated like Basic Composition Theorem [8], Advanced Composition Theorem [9], Rényi Differential Privacy (RDP) [20], zero-Concentrated Differential Privacy (zCDP) [7], etc. To conclude, these accountants are designed for decreasing the privacy expenses in iterative processes like Differentially Private Stochastic Gradient Descent (DPSGD).

1.2 An Overview of DPSGD and Gradient Clipping

The two main differences between DPSGD and SGD lie in gradient clipping and noise adding. The techniques mentioned above are introduced in the thesis [1], and we name the clipping strategy in [1] as Per-item Gradient Clipping (Per-item GC, a.k.a. Per-example GC) because the granularity of clipping is item-wise. Since most noise-adding processes inherit the same granularity of clipping, we would ignore the address of Per-item Gradient Perturbation for the rest of our manuscript except for introduction. However, model utility trained under DPSGD would ultimately drop because of the reduction and perturbation on gradients compared to the noise-free training under SGD. Therefore, introduced below are previous solutions to the utility drop problem in DPSGD.

G. Acs et al. [2] address Private Approximation of Average Norm, which establishes a histogram of clipping bounds to calculate the maximum value of noisy norm counts within a batch in order to preserve utility by clipping the least gradients. Andrew et al. [3] creatively treat clipping bound as a learnable parameter whose learning rate is determined by a quantile γ, which denotes the probability of gradient norms of batch items less than the optimal clipping bound. Pichapati et al. [25] propose AdaCliP that decomposes gradients as $w_i^t = \frac{g_i^t - a_i^t}{b_i^t}$, and noise addition would be carried out on g_i^t instead of w_i^t. Lee et al. [15] accelerate gradient clipping process by computing per-item gradient norm layer-wise.

However, studies mentioned above mainly utilize Per-item GC [1] considering gradients with respect to training samples in a batch, but model gradients vary between layers, even filters (units). Per-layer Gradient Clipping (GC) [18] dives into the granularity of clipping by having gradients clipped according to the layer-wise clipping bound $\frac{C}{\sqrt{m}}$ where m denotes the count of layers. Per-unit Adaptive Gradient Clipping (AGC) [6] steps further into the granularity by having gradients clipped adaptively according to the norms of weights in feature maps. With room for improvement, the target of our manuscript is to address algorithms that could achieve better performance utilizing finer granularities of clipping and noising while maintaining high efficiency.

1.3 An Overview of Differentially Private GANs

Most noise-adding procedures of training differentially private GANs focus on gradient and loss function perturbation [10]. X. Zhang et al. [32] creatively apply Functional Mechanism [30] to the loss function, where Laplace noise is added to the polynomial coefficients of its Taylor Expansion. X. Zhang et al. [31] propose three strategies in GAN training: adaptive clipping, parameter grouping, and warm starting, greatly improving the convergence of the model. However, these strategies require access to a small number of public data for utility improvement, which is a strong precondition when there is a lack of training items concerning individual privacy. L. Xie et al. [29] choose Wasserstein Distance [4] to measure the difference between the distribution of generated data and training data instead of Jensen-Shannon divergence (JS divergence). And there are more advanced ways for satisfying the condition like Spectral Normalization [22]. J. Jordon et al. [13] employ PATE structure in constructing the discriminator of GAN, which only requires generated data for the training of student discriminators. R. Torkzadehmahani et al. [28] apply conditional GAN (cGAN) [21] with RDP [20], enabling the model to generate images under certain conditions with privacy protection, which remains large room for enhancement in terms of quality and diversity.

1.4 Our Contributions

Our contributions and techniques are as follows.

1. We creatively propose one averaging gradient clipping strategy Per-unit GC and two ratio-based algorithms, i.e., Per-layer RGC and Per-unit RGC with smart clipping bound distributions. We apply them to a Projection cGAN (PcGAN) [23] for investigating the effect of finer-grained clipping mechanisms and smart clipping bound distributions on improving target-oriented image synthesis under DP constrain.

2. We carry out thorough evaluations on the effects on improving conditional image generation under DP-PcGAN by making comprehensive comparisons between our algorithms and previous studies utilizing Inception Score (IS) [26], Fréchet Inception Distance (FID) [12], their enhanced versions with class-wise settings (i.e., Between Class IS (BCIS), Within Class IS (WCIS), Between Class FID (BCFID), Within Class FID (WCFID) [5]), Area under ROC Curve (AuROC) under MNIST and FashionMNIST datasets.
3. Our RGCs achieve promising results in both quality and diversity of generated images under most evaluation scores for both datasets while costing moderate privacy expenses. Additionally, the Per-layer RGC utilizes approximately $\frac{1}{3}$ privacy expense for generating images of much higher quality under MNIST dataset with AuROC (MLP) of 96.46% for macro-average and 96.69% for micro-average, AuROC (LR) of 96.43% for macro-average and 96.59% for micro-average, in comparison with the best results 88.16%(MLP) and 87.57%(LR) in the only study [28] targeting differentially private conditional image generation, demonstrating better robustness and effectiveness in training DP-PcGAN for generating visually promising images.

2 Preliminaries

2.1 Differential Privacy

Definition 1. *(ϵ, δ)-DP [9] defines a randomized mechanism $\mathcal{A}$: $\mathcal{D} \mapsto \mathcal{R}$ over adjacent datasets $\mathcal{D}$, $\mathcal{D}'$ where $\|\mathcal{D} - \mathcal{D}'\|_1 \leq 1$, which means the datasets differ in only one element. For any $\mathcal{O} \subset \mathcal{R}$, $\epsilon > 0$ and $\delta > 0$, the mathematical definition is as follows.*

$$\Pr[\mathcal{A}(\mathcal{D}) \subset \mathcal{O}] \leq e^{\epsilon} \Pr\left[\mathcal{A}\left(\mathcal{D}'\right) \subset \mathcal{O}\right] + \delta \tag{1}$$

Definition 2. *A randomized mechanism $\mathcal{A}$: $\mathcal{D} \mapsto \mathcal{R}$ is said to satisfy (α, ϵ)-RDP [20] for any adjacent datasets $\mathcal{D}$, $\mathcal{D}'$ if*

$$\frac{1}{\alpha - 1} \log \mathrm{E}_{x \sim \mathcal{A}(\mathcal{D}')} \left(\frac{\Pr[\mathcal{A}(\mathcal{D}) \subset \mathcal{O}]}{\Pr[\mathcal{A}(\mathcal{D}') \subset \mathcal{O}]} \right)^{\alpha} \leq \epsilon \tag{2}$$

Theorem 1. *A function satisfying (α, ϵ)-RDP is $\left(\epsilon + \frac{\log 1/\delta}{\alpha - 1}, \delta\right)$-DP for $\forall \delta \in (0, 1)$ [20].*

The above theorem enables us to transfer any (α, ϵ)-RDP to (ϵ, δ)-DP that represents a common standard for privacy expense comparison.

2.2 Differentially Private Stochastic Gradient Descent

Algorithm 1 illustrates the details of DPSGD [1]. For all clipping choices, given a minibatch of training samples (X_t, Y_t), gradients for every item $g(x_i)$ in the minibatch are firstly computed through the loss function $\mathcal{L}(x_i, y_i)$, secondly clipped

Algorithm 1: DPSGD[1]

Input: Minibatch size bs, training pairs (X_t, Y_t) composed of (x_i, y_i) drawn from data$\{(x_1, y_1), ..., (x_N, y_N)\}$ with probability $\frac{bs}{N}$ in iteration t, loss function $\mathcal{L}$, model weights w, Gradient Clipping Mechanism GCM, total clipping bound C, *Clipping Choice*(i.e., Per-item GC [1], Per-layer GC [18], Per-layer RGC, Per-unit GC, and Per-unit RGC), Gradient Perturbation Mechanism GPM, noise multiplier σ

Output: Perturbed gradients $\tilde{g}(X_t)$ of of training batch X_t

for (x_i, y_i) *in* (X_t, Y_t) **do**

  $g(x_i) \leftarrow \nabla_{w(x_i)} \mathcal{L}(x_i, y_i)$

  $\bar{g}(x_i) \leftarrow GCM(g(x_i), C, Clipping\ Choice)$

end

$\tilde{g}(X_t) \leftarrow GPM(\sum_{x_i \in X_t} \bar{g}(x_i), GCM, \sigma)$

return $\tilde{g}(X_t)$

with Gradient Clipping Mechanism (GCM), and finally processed by clipped gradients averaging and noise addition in Gradient Perturbing Mechanism (GPM). Additionally, we would like to note the granularity of GCM is the same with GPM once the former is determined in our thesis. For example, the address of Per-layer GC [18] indicates both layer-wise granularities of clipping and noise adding [1], which has a slight difference with the algorithm in the manuscript [18].

3 Gradient Clipping and Perturbation Mechanism

3.1 Per-unit Gradient Clipping and Perturbation

Inspired by Per-unit AGC [6] and Per-layer GC [18], we are interested in the effect of the two methods combined. Per-unit GC possesses a rigid bound $\frac{C}{\sqrt{n}}$ with a finer-grained clipping granularity. Demonstrated by line 8 of Algorithm 2, the $unit\_bound_j^l$ representing the distribution of total clipping bound C for unit j in layer l is given as the ratio between C and $\sqrt{n}$, the square root of the number of units, so that the total norm of clipped gradients would be maintained in C.

The noise for each gradient in every unit would be much less because of the smaller clipping bound as shown by line 10 in Algorithm 3. The unit-level differential privacy for unit gradients from different training items x_1 and x_2 is depicted by the green rectangles in Fig. 1. Moreover, the computational time of Per-unit GC is much less than Per-unit AGC because unit count is a deterministic value that could be calculated before training.

3.2 Per-unit Ratio Gradient Clipping and Perturbation

As shown by line 8 of Algorithm 2, we could replace the $unit\_bound_j^l$ in Per-unit GC as $\sqrt{\frac{p_j^l}{q}} \cdot C$ where p_j^l represents the number of gradients in the specific unit j in layer l while q stands for the total number of gradients in the model. The

Algorithm 2: Gradient Clipping Mechanism

Input: *Clipping Choice* (i.e., Per-layer RGC, Per-unit GC, and Per-unit RGC), gradient number r^l in layer l, gradient number p_j^l in unit j layer l, total gradient number q, total unit number n, total clipping bound C, gradients of a model $g(x_i)$ whose input is a training item x_i,

Output: Clipped gradients $\bar{g}(x_i)$ of training item x_i

if *Clipping Choice is Per-layer RGC* **then**
  $layer\_bound^l \leftarrow \sqrt{\frac{r^l}{q}} \cdot C$
  for $g^l(x_i)$ *in* $g(x_i)$ **do**
    $\bar{g^l}(x_i) \leftarrow \min(1, \frac{layer\_bound^l}{\|g^l(x_i)\|_2}) \cdot g^l(x_i)$
  end
end
if *Clipping Choice is Per-unit GC or Per-unit RGC* **then**
  $unit\_bound_j^l \leftarrow \frac{C}{\sqrt{n}} or \sqrt{\frac{p_j^l}{q}} \cdot C$
  for $g_j^l(x_i)$ *in* $g(x_i)$ **do**
    $\bar{g}_j^l(x_i) \leftarrow \min(1, \frac{unit\_bound_j^l}{\|g_j^l(x_i)\|_2}) \cdot g_j^l(x_i)$
  end
end
return $\bar{g}(x_i)$

Algorithm 3: Gradient Perturbation Mechanism

Input: Gradient Clipping Mechanism GCM, $layer\_bound^l$ in layer l, $unit\_bound_j^l$ in unit j layer l, Averaged clipped gradients $\sum_{x_i \in X_t} \bar{g}(x_i)$ whose inputs are training items $x_i \in X_t$ in minibatch t, the number of training items $|X_t|$ in minibatch t, Gaussian noise $N(0, \cdot)$ with zero means, noise multiplier σ

Output: Perturbed gradients $\tilde{g}(X_t)$ of training batch X_t

if *GCM is layer-wise* **then**
  $S^l \leftarrow layer\_bound^l$
  for $\sum_{x_i \in X_t} \bar{g}^l(x_i)$ *in* $\sum_{x_i \in X_t} \bar{g}(x_i)$ **do**
    $\tilde{g}^l(X_t) \leftarrow \frac{1}{|X_t|}(\sum_{x_i \in X_t} \bar{g}^l(x_i) + N(0, (\sigma \cdot S^l)^2))$
  end
end
if *GCM is unit-wise* **then**
  $S_j^l \leftarrow unit\_bound_j^l$
  for $\sum_{x_i \in X_t} \bar{g}_j^l(x_i)$ *in* $\sum_{x_i \in X_t} \bar{g}(x_i)$ **do**
    $\tilde{g}_j^l(X_t) \leftarrow \frac{1}{|X_t|}(\sum_{x_i \in X_t} \bar{g}_j^l(x_i) + N(0, (\sigma \cdot S_j^l)^2))$
  end
end
return $\tilde{g}(X_t)$

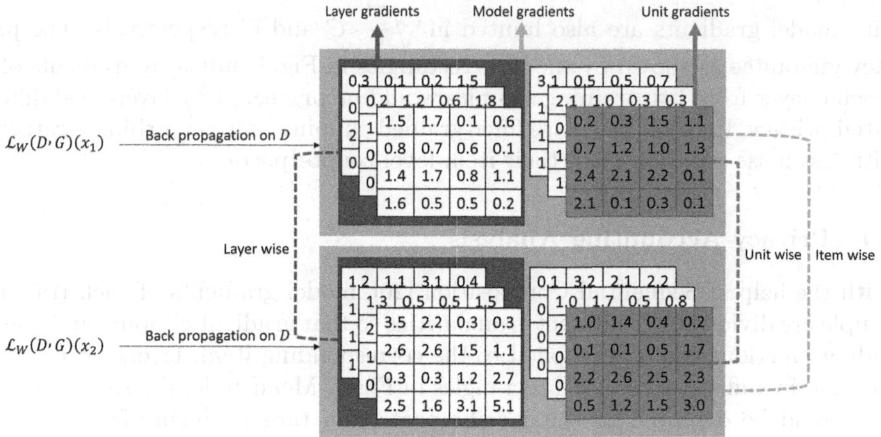

Fig. 1. Demonstration of item, layer and unit granularities

distribution of total clipping bound is controlled by the ratio between the number of unit gradients p_j^l and the number of model gradients q where $\sum_l \sum_j p_j^l = q$. This ratio appears to be more reasonable than the rigid one $\frac{1}{\sqrt{n}}$ in Per-unit GC because units with more gradients should be provided with larger bounds without prior knowledge to their values that are going to be computed in later backpropagation. When every unit norm is deliberately limited under $\sqrt{\frac{p_j^l}{q}} \cdot C$, the total norm of clipped gradients is consequently constrained in C.

The noise added to every gradient in the unit would be relatively less as demonstrated by line 10 in Algorithm 3 while the clipping is not so aggressive as those rigid bounds in Per-item GC [1], Per-layer GC [18], and Per-unit GC, providing a finer granularity of differential privacy with less perturbation. Meanwhile, since the ratio $\frac{p_j^l}{q}$ is deterministic and pre-computable, the time expense should be identical with Per-unit GC and much smaller than Per-unit AGC [6].

3.3 Per-layer Ratio Gradient Clipping and Perturbation

The *layer_bound*^{l} in Per-layer GC [18] is substituted as $\sqrt{\frac{r^l}{q}} \cdot C$ manifested by line 2 of Algorithm 2. r^l indicates the number of gradients in the particular layer l while q demonstrates the total number of gradients in the model where $\sum_l r^l = q$. And the noise distribution becomes $N(0, (\sigma \cdot S^l)^2)$ as illustrated by line 4 of Algorithm 3 where S^l is the bound we mentioned above, and the added noise should be less than Per-item Gradient Perturbation because smaller clipping bounds for layers would result in smaller noise variance.

Though the added noise under this granularity is larger than Per-unit GC and Per-unit RGC, Per-layer RGC offers larger bounds for every layer than the two strategies. Similarly, the training time would not be affected due to reasons illustrated in the former two algorithms, and the norms of layer gradients together with model gradients are also limited in $\sqrt{\frac{r^l}{q}} \cdot C$ and C respectively. The privacy guarantee as shown by the blue rectangles in Fig. 1 indicates gradients of a specific layer from two training samples would be protected by layer-level differential privacy. In brief, these are finer-grained clipping and perturbing strategies with less noise addition than their item-level counterparts.

3.4 Privacy Accounting Analysis

With the help of Sequential Composition [20], model gradients of each training sample are divided into different granularities so that gradient clipping and noise-adding functions could be applied to the corresponding item, layers, or units as pictured by differently colored rectangles in Fig. 1. Meanwhile, the same accountant could be deployed to the specific protection target varying from item to finer-grained levels (e.g., layer, unit), and the privacy expense would accumulate with the increase of the number of layers or units.

4 Differentially Private Projection cGAN

We employ PcGAN [23] instead of cGAN [21] and ACGAN [24] whose discriminators concatenate one-hot label vectors with input images. In other words, PcGAN greatly outperforms former practices in conditional image generation under privacy protection.

Algorithm 4 outlines the training process of Differentially Private Projection cGAN (DP-PcGAN). At the beginning of each iteration, T minibatches of real data (X_t, Y_t) will be chosen from training pairs $\{(x_1, y_1), ..., (x_N, y_N)\}$ with probability $\frac{bs}{N}$ where bs represents minibatch size while N stands for the number of training samples, and T minibatches of vector Z_t are selected from random distribution $p_z(z)$ the same length with X_t or Y_t.

When training the Projection Discriminator [23], the loss for every element in a minibatch $D\_loss(x_i, y_i, z_i)$ is calculated for DPSGD. We utilize Wasserstein Distance [4] as our loss function for MNIST dataset and Hinge loss [23] for FashionMNIST dataset. The computed gradients would be clipped with the strategy chosen in Gradient Clipping Mechanism GCM as shown by line 6 of Algorithm 4. After having gradients clipped, $\tilde{g}_D(X_t)$ the perturbed gradients of minibatch t is calculated as the sum of the minibatch clipped gradients $\sum_{x_i \in X_t} \bar{g}_D(x_i)$ and Gaussian noise in function GPM, then the weights of discriminator w_D could be updated with the optimizer taking a step toward the direction offered by $\tilde{g}_D(X_t)$. Before discriminator training ends the consumed RDP would be collected.

In the training process of the generator, the computation in G_loss is parallel between data samples as can be seen in line 12 of Algorithm 4, which is distinct from that of the differentially private Projection Discriminator because the generator could be trained without noise addition owing to the Post-processing property [20]. After its gradients are calculated, new weights w_G would be updated through $g_G(Z_t)$.

At the end of the training, the cumulated RDP would be transformed into (ϵ, δ)-DP so that the privacy cost could be evaluated under the same benchmark.

Algorithm 4: DP-PcGAN

Input: Minibatch size bs, training pairs$\{(x_1, y_1), ..., (x_N, y_N)\}$, random distribution $p_z(z)$, total training step T, discriminator updates per generator update T_D, weights w_D of discriminator D, weights w_G of generator G, loss of discriminator $D\_loss(\cdot)$, Gradient Clipping Mechanism GCM, *Clipping Choice* (i.e., Per-item GC [1], Per-layer GC [18], Per-layer RGC, Per-unit GC, and Per-unit RGC), total clipping bound C, Gradient Perturbation Mechanism GPM, noise multiplier σ, *Optimizer*(i.e., Adam, RMSProp), learning rate lr,

Output: Differentially Private Conditional Generator G

```
step = 0;
while step ≤ T do
    -Randomly sample T minibatches (X_t, Y_t) in training data
     {(x_1, y_1), ..., (x_N, y_N)} with probability bs/N, T minibatches Z_t from p_z(z)
     the same length with X_t or Y_t
    for (x_i, y_i) and z_i in (X_t, Y_t) and Z_t do
        g_D(x_i) ← ∇_{w_D(x_i)} D_loss(x_i, y_i, z_i)
        ḡ_D(x_i) ← GCM(g_D(x_i), C, Clipping Choice)
    end
    g̃_D(X_t) ← GPM(Σ_{x_i ∈ X_t} ḡ_D(x_i), σ, GCM)
    w_D ← Optimizer(w_D, g̃_D(X_t), lr)
    Accumulate RDP for the iterative process
    if T/T_D is an integer then
        g_G(Z_t) ← ∇_{w_G(Z_t)} − D(G(Z_t, Y_t), Y_t)
        w_G ← Optimizer(w_G, g_G(Z_t), lr)
    end
end
Convert cumulated RDP to (ε, δ)-DP
```

5 Experimental Results

5.1 Experimental Settings

Configurations and Datasets. The training datasets we use are the MNIST hand-written digits dataset containing 60,000 training images and 10,000 test images of figures from 0 to 9, and FashionMNIST dataset with 60,000 training items and 10,000 test items of 10 classes of wearings. Our backbone is a PcGAN with six residual blocks for up-sampling and down-sampling [22], and we replace the BatchNorm layers with InstanceNorm in case of privacy violation [19], but this might lead to a decrease in model performance.

Evaluation Metrics. The evaluation metrics include Inception Score (IS) [26], class-wise Inception Score [5] (i.e., Within Class IS (WCIS) and Between Class IS (BCIS)), Fréchet Inception Distance (FID) [12], class-wise Fréchet Inception Distance (i.e. Within Class FID (WCFID) and Between Class FID (BCFID)), and Area under ROC curve (AuROC).

Class-wise Inception Score and Fréchet Inception Distance are the advanced versions of Inception Score and Fréchet Inception Distance because the class-wise metrics take image quality and diversity both within classes and between classes into consideration. AuROC metric evaluates generator by testing the performance of classifiers pre-trained on images generated by different algorithms. In brief, the higher the IS, BCIS scores, and the lower the WCIS, FID, BCFID, WCFID scores, the better the generation. For AuROC metric, its value varies between 0 and 1, and a classifier with a larger AuROC away from 0.5 indicates better generator performance in our experiments.

Comparisons are made between the algorithms we propose, i.e., Per-unit GC, Per-unit RGC, Per-layer RGC and methods that are addressed in previous studies, i.e., Per-item GC [1], Per-layer GC [18]. For the unit-level granularity, we only divide the fully connected layer of Projection Discriminator into smaller units while keeping the remaining units as layers to reduce privacy expense.

Training Settings. We set batch size bs as 128, noise multiplier σ as 1.0, and δ as 10^{-5}. The remaining hyper-parameters for tuning are learning rate lr, discriminator updates per generator update T_D, clipping bound C.

We run 4,000 iterations on MNIST dataset, 300,000 iterations on FashionMNIST dataset, and save the trained generators every 10 iterations for the former 100 iterations for the latter. Considering AuROC metric, for both datasets we train classifiers using 60,000 images 6,000 per class synthesized by the best-score generator of each algorithm and test on 10,000 validation set images.

5.2 Comparison and Analysis

Scores Comparison and Analysis. As can be seen in Table 1, our algorithm Per-layer RGC achieves promising results among all strategies under MNIST dataset while costing the second least privacy expense $(3.24, 10^{-5})$-DP. Under FashionMNIST dataset, Per-unit RGC attains good outcomes for most evaluation metrics. Moreover, the training iterations for Per-unit RGC are less than $\frac{1}{4}$ that of Per-item GC [1] and close to that of Per-layer GC [18].

To be more specific, Per-layer RGC outperforms previous methods with much higher IS, BCIS scores, lower WCIS, FID, class-wise FID scores than Per-item GC [1] and Per-layer GC [18] while spending the second least ϵ under MNIST dataset. Per-unit RGC undertakes the first and second places under most evaluation methods for FashionMNIST dataset.

The reason why Per-layer RGC performs well under MNIST dataset is the ratio-based gradient clipping would bring less clipping for gradients than Per-layer GC [18] and less noise addition than Per-item GC [1]. The mediocre performance of Per-unit RGC under MNIST dataset is caused by the frequent clipping

Table 1. Scores for GCMs under MNIST and FashionMNIST datasets

Dataset	GCM	IS↑	BCIS↑	WCIS↓	FID↓	BCFID↓	WCFID↓	ϵ ↓	Iterations↓
MNIST	Real Data	9.93	9.86	1.00	0.12	0.18	0.54	–	–
	Per-item GC [1]	8.71	4.99	1.74	5.87	6.17	**12.30**	**1.27**	3440
	Per-layer GC [18]	**8.88**	**6.09**	**1.45**	10.88	9.52	19.01	4.35	**1930**
	Per-layer RGC	**9.33**	**6.75**	**1.38**	**5.42**	**5.26**	**11.99**	**3.24**	**1100**
	Per-unit GC	8.66	5.23	1.65	**4.82**	**4.66**	12.58	5.92	2850
	Per-unit RGC	8.82	5.41	1.63	6.03	6.16	13.29	5.15	2200
FMNIST	Real Data	9.93	9.72	1.02	0.02	0.04	0.08	–	–
	Per-item GC [1]	7.77	3.36	2.31	6.99	6.57	8.19	**8.18**	276000
	Per-layer GC [18]	8.36	**4.02**	**2.07**	5.58	4.87	6.10	**27.43**	**56000**
	Per-layer RGC	**8.44**	3.54	2.38	**3.93**	**3.56**	**4.73**	36.93	88000
	Per-unit GC	**8.42**	3.70	2.27	5.84	5.14	6.44	33.89	**53000**
	Per-unit RGC	8.05	**3.99**	**2.01**	**4.85**	**4.21**	**5.59**	36.81	60000

↑ indicates the higher the better and ↓ means vice versa

of smaller units in the fully connected layers of Projection Discriminator, which probably misleads the discriminator into making wrong classifications. However, the drawback of Per-unit RGC under MNIST dataset turns to be its advantage under FashionMNIST dataset since the latter training items are more likely to cause gradient explosion that needs dense clipping.

However, the results of FashionMNIST dataset also indicate gradient explosion might help average clipping strategies like Per-layer GC to converge faster than its ratio-based counterpart because of the aggressive way of gradient clipping. Therefore, the scores of Per-unit GC behave alike Per-layer GC while converging faster because of smaller noise addition. Though reaching convergence slower, ratio-based algorithms always attain better results under FashionMNIST dataset than their counterparts, which means smarter clipping strategies would take longer to reach better local minimums that are impossible for the averaging algorithms to arrive at no matter how many iterations are given to train.

AuROCs Comparison and Analysis. The AuROCs of the two RGCs for both datasets constantly rank in the first and second places regardless of the averaging strategies as depicted by Fig. 2 and Fig. 3. To take CNN classifier as an example, the black curves representing Per-unit RGC achieve 97.43% on macro-average and 97.17% on micro-average for MNIST dataset, 88.32% on macro-average and 88.49% on micro-average for FashionMNIST dataset, which exceeds the proposed algorithms by reaching the closest performance to real data, namely 99.95% on both macro-average and micro-average for MNIST, 99.40% on macro-average and 99.59% on micro-average for FashionMNIST. While the green curves on behalf of Per-layer RGC undertake similar encouraging results, with 97.21% on macro-average and 97.59% on micro-average for MNIST dataset, 88.40% on macro-average and 88.23% on micro-average for FashionMNIST dataset, which still outperforms the former-proposed clipping methods. The results of other classifiers also demonstrate the efficacy of ratio-based algorithms.

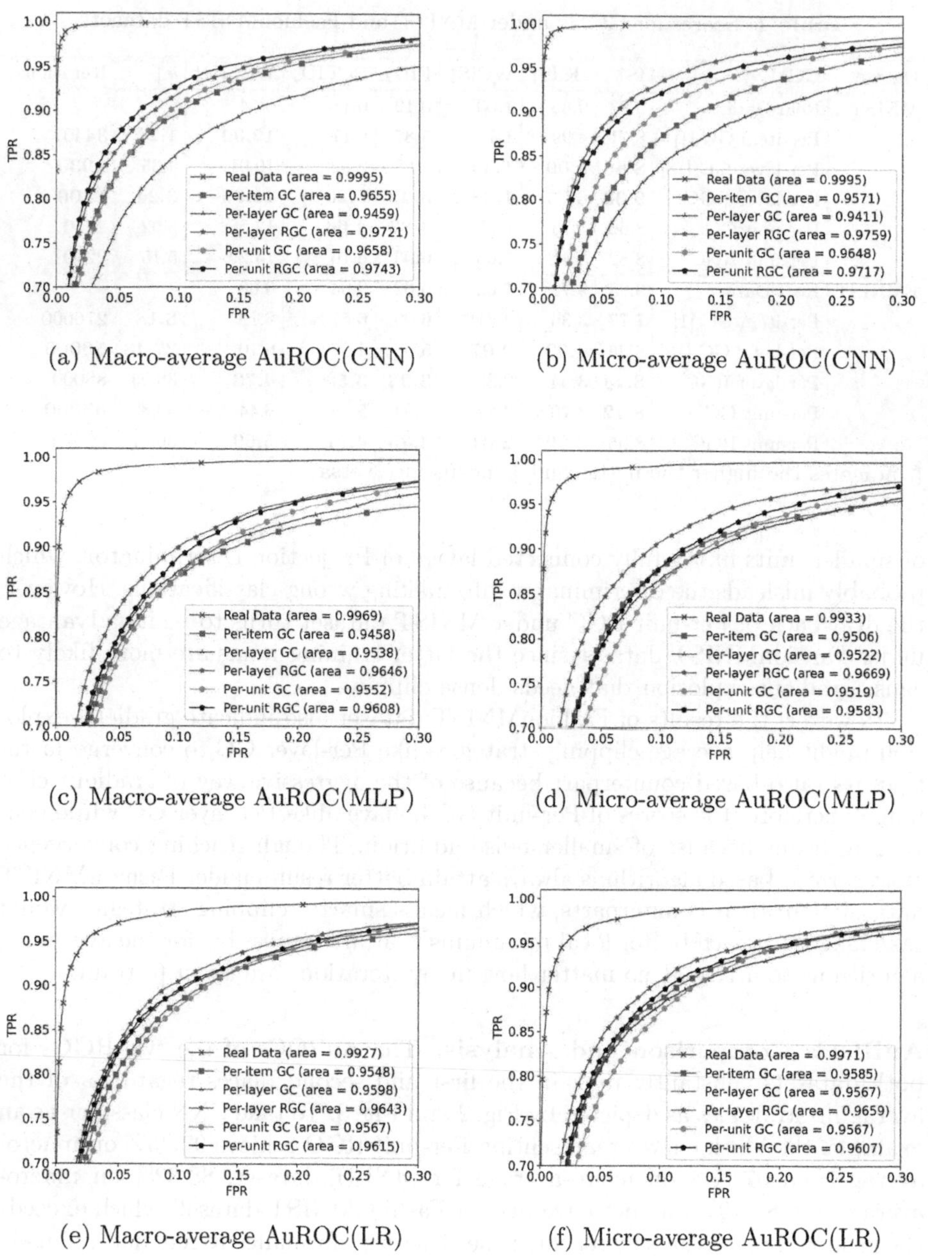

(a) Macro-average AuROC(CNN) (b) Micro-average AuROC(CNN)

(c) Macro-average AuROC(MLP) (d) Micro-average AuROC(MLP)

(e) Macro-average AuROC(LR) (f) Micro-average AuROC(LR)

Fig. 2. AuROCs on macro-average and micro-average for MNIST dataset

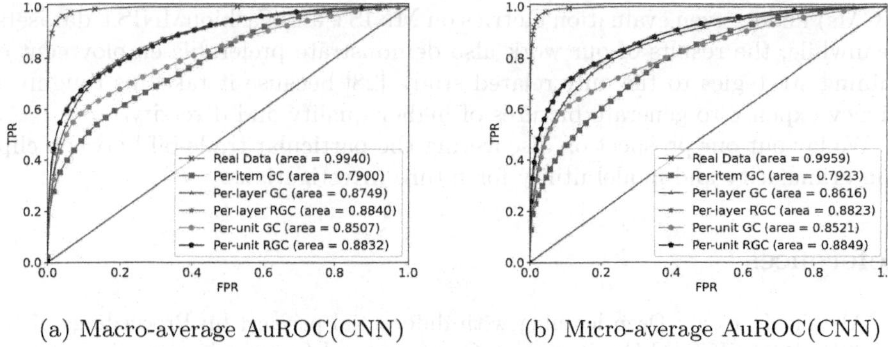

(a) Macro-average AuROC(CNN) (b) Micro-average AuROC(CNN)

Fig. 3. AuROCs on macro-average and micro-average for FashionMNIST dataset

Moreover, though some of the scores of the RGCs fall behind the proposed algorithms, the AuROCs under all classifiers and averaging strategies manifest the effectiveness and robustness of our ratio-based clipping algorithms to generate real-looking pictures for classification under privacy protection. Besides, the AuROCs of Per-unit RGC under MNIST dataset also highlight the importance of various evaluation strategies because the algorithm does not perform well under score assessment while its AuROCs show a different picture.

In addition, our Per-layer RGC could generate more visually satisfying images under MNIST dataset with AuROC (MLP) of 96.46% for macro-average and 96.69% for micro-average, AuROC (LR) of 96.43% for macro-average and 96.59% for micro-average, in comparison with the best results 88.16%(MLP) and 87.57%(LR) [28] that consume roughly three times of our privacy budget.

5.3 Summary

In conclusion, a clipping strategy with a reasonable granularity and a smart clipping bound distribution would result in appropriate gradient norms reduction and small noise addition simultaneously. The performance rankings among the remaining algorithms vary with training sets and evaluation methods, indicating less noise addition alone sometimes won't bring about better utility because the corresponding clipping might be aggressive. Therefore, it is the combination of these merits that ultimately enable the ratio-based algorithms to generate visually promising images while costing moderate privacy expenses.

6 Conclusion

In this paper, we investigate the impacts of different gradient clipping granularities and clipping bound distributions in DPSGD. Specifically, our Ratio Gradient Clipping (RGC) algorithms achieve promising results in differentially private conditional image generation among five Gradient Clipping Mechanisms

(GCMs) under seven evaluation metrics on MNIST and FashionMNIST datasets. Meanwhile, the results of our work also demonstrate preferable employment of training strategies to the only related study [28] because it takes us roughly $\frac{1}{3}$ privacy expense to generate pictures of higher quality and diversity.

We lay out our prospect on discovering the particular trade-off between clipping granularity and model utility for future investigations.

References

1. Abadi, M., et al.: Deep learning with differential privacy. In: Proceedings of the 2016 ACM SIGSAC Conference on Computer and Communications Security, pp. 308–318 (2016)
2. Acs, G., Melis, L., Castelluccia, C., De Cristofaro, E.: Differentially private mixture of generative neural networks. IEEE Trans. Knowl. Data Eng. **31**(6), 1109–1121 (2018)
3. Andrew, G., Thakkar, O., McMahan, H.B., Ramaswamy, S.: Differentially private learning with adaptive clipping. arXiv preprint arXiv:1905.03871 (2019)
4. Arjovsky, M., Chintala, S., Bottou, L.: Wasserstein generative adversarial networks. In: Proceedings of the 34th International Conference on Machine Learning, Vol. 70, pp. 214–223 (2017)
5. Benny, Y., Galanti, T., Benaim, S., Wolf, L.: Evaluation metrics for conditional image generation. Int. J. Comput. Vis. **129**(5), 1712–1731 (2021)
6. Brock, A., De, S., Smith, S.L., Simonyan, K.: High-performance large-scale image recognition without normalization. arXiv preprint arXiv:2102.06171 (2021)
7. Bun, M., Steinke, T.: Concentrated differential privacy: simplifications, extensions, and lower bounds. In: Hirt, M., Smith, A. (eds.) TCC 2016. LNCS, vol. 9985, pp. 635–658. Springer, Heidelberg (2016). https://doi.org/10.1007/978-3-662-53641-4_24
8. Dwork, C.: Differential privacy: a survey of results. In: Agrawal, M., Du, D., Duan, Z., Li, A. (eds.) TAMC 2008. LNCS, vol. 4978, pp. 1–19. Springer, Heidelberg (2008). https://doi.org/10.1007/978-3-540-79228-4_1
9. Dwork, C., Roth, A., et al.: The algorithmic foundations of differential privacy. Found. Trends Theor. Comput. Sci. **9**(3–4), 211–407 (2014)
10. Fan, L.: A survey of differentially private generative adversarial networks. In: The AAAI Workshop on Privacy-Preserving Artificial Intelligence (2020)
11. Goodfellow, I.J., et al.: Generative adversarial nets. In: Proceedings of the 27th International Conference on Neural Information Processing Systems, Vol. 2, pp. 2672–2680 (2014)
12. Heusel, M., Ramsauer, H., Unterthiner, T., Nessler, B., Hochreiter, S.: GANs trained by a two time-scale update rule converge to a local Nash equilibrium. arXiv preprint arXiv:1706.08500 (2017)
13. Jordon, J., Yoon, J., Van Der Schaar, M.: PATE-GAN: generating synthetic data with differential privacy guarantees. In: International Conference on Learning Representations, pp. 1–21 (2018)
14. LeCun, Y., et al.: Backpropagation applied to handwritten zip code recognition. Neural Comput. **1**(4), 541–551 (1989)
15. Lee, J., Kifer, D.: Scaling up differentially private deep learning with fast per-example gradient clipping. Proc. Priv. Enhancing Technol. **2021**(1) (2021)

16. Li, N., Li, T., Venkatasubramanian, S.: t-closeness: Privacy beyond k-anonymity and l-diversity. In: 2007 IEEE 23rd International Conference on Data Engineering, pp. 106–115. IEEE (2007)
17. Machanavajjhala, A., Kifer, D., Gehrke, J., Venkitasubramaniam, M.: l-diversity: privacy beyond k-anonymity. ACM Trans. Knowl. Discov. Data (TKDD) **1**(1), 3-es (2007)
18. McMahan, H.B., Ramage, D., Talwar, K., Zhang, L.: Learning differentially private recurrent language models. arXiv preprint arXiv:1710.06963 (2017)
19. Meta: Building image classifier with differential privacy. https://opacus.ai/tutorials/building_image_classifier
20. Mironov, I.: Rényi differential privacy. In: 2017 IEEE 30th Computer Security Foundations Symposium (CSF), pp. 263–275. IEEE (2017)
21. Mirza, M., Osindero, S.: Conditional generative adversarial nets. arXiv preprint arXiv:1411.1784 (2014)
22. Miyato, T., Kataoka, T., Koyama, M., Yoshida, Y.: Spectral normalization for generative adversarial networks. arXiv preprint arXiv:1802.05957 (2018)
23. Miyato, T., Koyama, M.: cGANs with projection discriminator. In: International Conference on Learning Representations, pp. 1–21 (2018)
24. Odena, A., Olah, C., Shlens, J.: Conditional image synthesis with auxiliary classifier GANs. In: International Conference on Machine Learning, pp. 2642–2651. PMLR (2017)
25. Pichapati, V., Suresh, A.T., Yu, F.X., Reddi, S.J., Kumar, S.: Adaclip: Adaptive clipping for private sgd. arXiv preprint arXiv:1908.07643 (2019)
26. Salimans, T., Goodfellow, I., Zaremba, W., Cheung, V., Radford, A., Chen, X.: Improved techniques for training GANs. Adv. Neural. Inf. Process. Syst. **29**, 2234–2242 (2016)
27. Sweeney, L.: k-anonymity: a model for protecting privacy. Int. J. Uncertainty, Fuzziness Knowl.-Based Syst. **10**(05), 557–570 (2002)
28. Torkzadehmahani, R., Kairouz, P., Paten, B.: DP-CGAN: differentially private synthetic data and label generation. In: Proceedings of the IEEE/CVF Conference on Computer Vision and Pattern Recognition Workshops (2019)
29. Xie, L., Lin, K., Wang, S., Wang, F., Zhou, J.: Differentially private generative adversarial network. arXiv preprint arXiv:1802.06739 (2018)
30. Zhang, J., Zhang, Z., Xiao, X., Yang, Y., Winslett, M.: Functional mechanism: regression analysis under differential privacy. arXiv preprint arXiv:1208.0219 (2012)
31. Zhang, X., Ji, S., Wang, T.: Differentially private releasing via deep generative model (technical report). arXiv preprint arXiv:1801.01594 (2018)
32. Zhang, X., Ding, J., Errapotu, S.M., Huang, X., Li, P., Pan, M.: Differentially private functional mechanism for generative adversarial networks. In: 2019 IEEE Global Communications Conference (GLOBECOM), pp. 1–6. IEEE (2019)

Differential Privacy Protection Algorithm for Data Clustering Center

Mingyang Ma, Hongyong Yang(✉), and Fei Liu

Ludong University, Yantai 264025, Shandong, China
hyyang@yeah.net

Abstract. With the rapid development of the information era, data mining is widely used in various fields as a technique that can discover the interrelationship between data, but it also inevitably brings some privacy leakage problems. Differential privacy as an emerging privacy protection technology, because of its strict provability it has received great attention and been widely studied. By analyzing the privacy leakage problem in the traditional K-means algorithm, this paper proposes an improved differential privacy K-means algorithm to improve and protect for the selection of data clustering centers. When improvement, the degree of privacy protection and the availability of the clustering algorithm are analyzed. The initial centroids are selected by using the within-cluster sum of squared errors, and the different privacy intensity assigned to each cluster is calculated by using the silhouette coefficient. Finally, the experimental results demonstrate the feasibility of the differential privacy protection algorithm for data clustering center proposed in this paper.

Keywords: Differential privacy · K-means algorithm · Clustering

1 Introduction

When people surf the Internet, there will be a lot of activity data left in the database. After analyzing and processing these data, people hope to get the potential value behind them, so as to make better decisions and even predict the future development [1]. The current big data analysis is to mine the hidden and meaningful information in a large number of data with diverse characteristics, and create the value of utilization in different scenarios to form the data support for making relevant decisions [2]. However, these data generally contain users' privacy, so privacy security has become a very important part.

For this reason, domestic and international researchers have done a lot of effective work in clustering algorithm and differential privacy, aiming at protecting data security and improving availability and operation efficiency. The K-means algorithm was first proposed by Macqueen [3]. Because it is easy to understand and faster than other algorithms, it has been widely concerned and applied. However, K-means algorithm also has many disadvantages, for example, it is sensitive to the selection of initial center point, and is greatly affected

Y. Xu et al. (Eds.): ML4CS 2022, LNCS 13655, pp. 550–559, 2023.
https://doi.org/10.1007/978-3-031-20096-0_41

by outliers. Therefore, many scholars have proposed a series of ideas, for example, in 2017, Oliveira et al. [4] used the idea of species evolution to determine the number of K. Ultimatey, the accuracy of clustering results can be improved while ensuring the operation efficiency of the algorithm. Junchuang Yang et al. [5] made a detailed overview of K-means algorithm, and summarized and prospected its future in two aspects. In 2005, Blum et al. [6] proposed the differential privacy k-means algorithm, but this method has some problems such as poor clustering effect. In terms of improving the initial center point, Nissim [7] and others optimized it based on the differential privacy k-means algorithm, which improved the clustering effect to a certain extent. For the aspect of adding noise, the existing differential privacy K-means research methods mostly use the mean square method and the equal difference decreasing sequence.

By studying differential privacy and K-means clustering algorithm, this paper proposes an improved K-means clustering privacy protection algorithm. By improving the initial center point selection and the privacy budget allocation scheme, the clustering effect is improved and the data security is protected.

2 Differential Privacy

In 2006, Dwork put forward the idea of differential privacy. The main idea is that the query result is not sensitive to the change of a specific data in the data set. In the process of protection, the data may be destroyed to some extent, making the data unavailable. Paradoxically, the higher the distortion, the higher the intensity of privacy protection. Therefore, these two aspects need to be weighed [8].

2.1 Basic Definition

Definition 1. *Suppose there is a random algorithm M, for any two adjacent data sets D and D', if algorithm M satisfies*

$$Pr[M(D) \in S] \leq e^{\epsilon} \times Pr[M(D') \in S] \tag{1}$$

It is said that algorithm M provides ϵ- differential privacy protection and provides privacy protection by randomizing the output results.

The parameter ϵ represents the privacy protection budget. It is used to ensure the probability that the output results of random algorithm M are consistent when a record is added or reduced in the data set. When ϵ is closer to 0, the closer the distribution of data output by M on D and D', the higher the degree of privacy protection. When $\epsilon = 0$, the output distribution coincides, but the availability of the original data is lost. Therefore, a trade-off needs to be made between the degree of privacy protection and availability.

2.2 The Laplace Mechanism

The differential privacy mechanism is usually realized by adding noise. This paper mainly introduces the Laplace mechanism.

Definition 2. *The Laplace Mechanism. Given the data set D, there is a query function f, and its global sensitivity is Δf, then the random algorithm $M(D)$*

$$M(D) = f(D) + Lap(\frac{\Delta f}{\epsilon}) \tag{2}$$

provides differential privacy protection.

The definition formula of global sensitivity is shown in (3), which aims to measure the difference of individuals in the response of the data set.

$$\Delta f = \max_{D,D'} \|f(D) - f(D')\|_1 \tag{3}$$

The noise added according to the Laplace mechanism follows the Laplace distribution, and its probability density formula is shown in (4).

$$p(x|\mu, b) = \frac{1}{2b} exp(-\frac{|x-\mu|}{b}) \tag{4}$$

where μ is the position parameter and b is the scale parameter, and the distribution can be recorded as Lap(b).

3 Differential Privacy K-Means Clustering Algorithm

The traditional K-means algorithm is prone to privacy leakage problem, the main reasons are as follows: During the iteration process, privacy may be leaked when calculating the distance between the data point and the cluster centroid; The attacker can infer the attribute value according to the centroid of the final clustering. Based on this, we can use the way of adding noise to protect data.

The differential privacy k-means (DPK-means) algorithm protects the privacy of data by adding the random noise of Laplace distribution to the sum of data points and the number of points in each cluster. In d-dimensional space, the addition or deletion of data points will affect each dimension and the number of data points, so the total global sensitivity is $\Delta f = d + 1$. Then the noise introduced into the DPK-means algorithm is $Lap = (\frac{d+1}{\epsilon})$. The process of DPK-means algorithm is as follows:

(1) Firstly, K random centers are selected for a given data set. The random center point must be within the limits of all data sets, so the generation of random numbers needs to be realized by using the minimum and maximum values of each dimension of the data set.
(2) Traverse all data, find the center point closest to each point and record it, that is, assign each point to a cluster. The distance uses the Euclidean distance

$$d(x, y) = \sqrt{\sum_{i=1}^{n} (x_i - y_i)^2} \tag{5}$$

(3) Update the center point. Calculate the sum and number of data points in each cluster, add Laplace random noise respectively, and update the cluster center point to $C' = \frac{sum'}{num'}$.
(4) Recalculate the cluster allocation result of each data point. If there is any change, return to step (3). Otherwise, the algorithm ends and outputs the divided cluster set.

DPK-means algorithm can effectively strengthen privacy protection, but there are also problems. In addition to the limitations of K-means algorithm itself, the allocation of privacy budget has not been considered and adding noise will affect the accuracy and availability of clustering.

4 Improved Differential Privacy K-Means Algorithm

4.1 Centroid Improvement Design

Sum of Squares of Error. SSE is used to estimate the degree of dispersion of data. Its formula is shown in (6),

$$SSE_i = \sum_{x_j \in C(i)} \|x_j - c_i\|^2 \tag{6}$$

where c_i is the central point and x_j is the data point in cluster C(i). SSE is used as part of the evaluation index to select the cluster centroid, so as to ensure that the initial centroids are distributed in data intensive areas as much as possible.

Improved Clustering Center Algorithm. In order to optimize the instability of cluster classification caused by randomly selecting the initial centroid in the traditional K-means clustering algorithm. The idea of the improved algorithm of the initial clustering centroid is as follows:

(1) Assuming that each data point is the centroid, select the m/k data points closest to the current centroid with the Euclidean distance (m is the total number of data points), so as to form m clusters, and calculate SSE_i in each cluster.
(2) The centroid of the cluster with the smallest SSE is stored in the set C, and the rest of the points are stored in set D.
(3) Set the scoring method to score all the points in D to select the next center point. The purpose of this scoring is to select the point that is as far as possible from the center point of C and has a smaller sum of squared errors within the cluster, with the scoring formula as in (7). Select the point with the largest score from D as the next initial centroid, store it in C, and delete it from D.

$$Score(i) = \alpha(\frac{mindist_i}{dist_{max}}) + (1 - \alpha)(1 - \frac{SSE_i}{SSE_{max}}) \tag{7}$$

where α represents the weight of the two scoring parts, and dist is the farthest distance from the point of D to the initial centroid. This method can help the initial centroid fall in the data intensive area and make the distribution of the initial centroid more uniform.

(4) Repeat step (3) until k initial centroids are selected and stored in C.

4.2 Improved Design of Privacy Protection

Silhouette Coefficient. Silhouette Coefficient is generally used to evaluate the clustering results. The formula is shown in (8). The value range of silhouette coefficient is [−1, 1]. The closer the value is to 1, the better the clustering performance.

$$S(x_i) = \frac{b - a}{max(a, b)} \tag{8}$$

Intra-cluster similarity a is the distance from each record to the cluster center in the same cluster. Inter-cluster dissimilarity b is the minimum of all cluster center distances of clusters that different from this record. The average silhouette coefficient of each cluster is calculated as formula (9), where num_k refers to the total number of data of the k-th cluster.

$$S_k = \sum_{i=1}^{num_k} \frac{S(x_i)}{num_k} \tag{9}$$

Cluster Center Design with Privacy Protection. The focus of this paper is to study the algorithm with high degree of privacy protection and stable availability of clustering results. It uses the silhouette coefficient to improve. At the end of each clustering, it calculates the silhouette coefficient for different clusters and allocates different privacy budgets.

(1) Firstly, according to the improved centroid method mentioned in Sect. 4.1, k initial centroids are obtained. The center and distance of each data point are recorded.
(2) For each cluster, obtain the sum of its attribute vectors $clustersum_k^0$ and the total number of data points $clusternum_k^0$, add random noise to them respectively, get a new $clustersum_{k'}^0$ and $clusternum_{k'}^0$, and calculate a new initial centroid according to the formula $C_k^0 = \frac{clustersum_{k'}^0}{clusternum_{k'}^0}$.
(3) If the initial centroid changes, the data set needs to be divided again. For each data, the nearest center point is selected to form a cluster and recorded.
(4) Calculate the sum of attribute vectors of each cluster and the total number of data points.
(5) Calculate the average silhouette coefficient of each cluster S_k, finding out the minimum value of the silhouette coefficient of all clusters. Set the privacy budget size of the k-th cluster in the t-th iteration as ϵ_k^t. Random noise is $N_k^t = Lap(\frac{\Delta f}{\epsilon_k^t})$. The calculation of the privacy budget is shown in Eq. (10).

Since the range of silhouette coefficient is $[-1, 1]$, the processing method of $\frac{1+S_{min}}{1+S_k}$ makes its value range in $[0, 1]$. Different privacy budgets are given to different clusters.

$$\epsilon_k^t = \frac{\epsilon}{2^t}\frac{1+S_{min}}{1+S_k} \tag{10}$$

(6) New clustering centers are calculated according to random noise,

$$C_k^t = \frac{clustersum_k^t + N_k^t}{clusternum_k^t + N_k^t} \tag{11}$$

(7) The termination condition is set to the end of ten iterations or when the distance between the new cluster center and the previous iteration center is less than 0.1. If the above conditions are met, the algorithm ends and outputs the cluster set, otherwise return to step (3).

The above algorithm uses silhouette coefficient to evaluate clusters. If the clustering effect is good, relatively small random noise will be added, and poor clusters will add large random noise. Privacy budgets of different sizes will be allocated for different clusters in each iteration, which can effectively reduce the number of iterations and improve the availability of clustering results.

4.3 Privacy Protection Analysis

Let a pair of adjacent data sets be recorded as D_1 and D_2, and the output results of the improved algorithm on these two data sets are recorded $M(D_1)$ and $M(D_2)$. The real clustering query results are recorded as $f(D_1, x)$ and $f(D_2, x)$, the query results with noise are recorded as $\varphi(x)$, and the global sensitivity is Δf. The privacy analysis of the algorithm is as follows:

It can be seen from the definition of differential privacy and the probability density function of Laplace distribution

$$\begin{aligned} Pr[M(D) \in S] &= Pr[Lap(b) = \varphi(x) - f(D_1, x)] \\ &= \frac{1}{2b}exp(-\frac{|\varphi(x) - f(D_1, x)|}{b}) \end{aligned} \tag{12}$$

$b = \frac{\Delta f}{\epsilon'}$, where ϵ' represents the differential privacy budget in this algorithm. According to the global sensitivity formula

$$\|f(D_1, x) - f(D_2, x)\|_1 \leq \Delta f \tag{13}$$

Then

$$\begin{aligned} \frac{Pr[M(D_1) \in S]}{Pr[M(D_2) \in S]} &= \frac{\frac{1}{2b}exp(-\frac{\epsilon'|\varphi(x)-f(D_1,x)|}{\Delta f})}{\frac{1}{2b}exp(-\frac{\epsilon'|\varphi(x)-f(D_2,x)|}{\Delta f})} \\ &= exp(\frac{\epsilon'(|\varphi(x) - f(D_1, x)| - |\varphi(x) - f(D_2, x)|)}{\Delta f}) \\ &\leq exp(\frac{\epsilon'(|f(D_1, x) - f(D_2, x)|)}{\Delta f}) \\ &\leq exp(\frac{\epsilon'\Delta f}{\Delta f}) \leq exp(\epsilon') \end{aligned} \tag{14}$$

According to the improved method of differential privacy budget proposed in this paper (the range of silhouette coefficient is $[-1, 1]$)

$$\sum \epsilon_{k^t} = \sum \frac{\epsilon}{2^t}[(1 + S_{min})/(1 + S_k)] \leq (\frac{1}{2} + \frac{1}{2^2} + \frac{1}{2^3} + \ldots)\epsilon \leq \epsilon \tag{15}$$

Final reasoning

$$\frac{Pr[M(D_1) \in S]}{Pr[M(D_2) \in S]} \leq exp(\epsilon') \leq exp(\epsilon) \tag{16}$$

it can satisfy the ϵ-differential privacy protection.

5 Experimental Results and Analysis

5.1 Experimental Data Set

The iris data set in UCI database is selected as the data set, which is suitable for cluster analysis. It contains three different sub varieties with 50 samples of each kind. Clustering is carried out according to the differences of calyx length and width, petal length and width of these varieties.

5.2 Evaluation Index of Clustering Results

Clustering results need to be measured from two aspects: privacy and availability. Privacy is described in Sect. 4.3 of this paper, and availability will be analyzed using two evaluating indicators: F-measure and NICV.

F-Measure. F-measure index is often used to evaluate the availability of classification. It is an index that comprehensively considers the accuracy and recall rate. Between zero and one, the closer it is to one, the higher the clustering availability. Taking the cluster as the unit, the accuracy is P_i, and the recall rate is R_i. Then for a data set of size m, the calculation formula of F-measure is as follows:

$$F - measure = \sum_i \frac{M_i}{m} \frac{2R_iP_i}{R_i + P_i} \tag{17}$$

NICV. NICV is short for normalized intra-cluster variance and can be used to assess the performance of clustering, with smaller values representing better results. The formula is:

$$NICV = \frac{1}{N} \sum_{i=1}^{k} \sum_{x_j \in c_i} \|x_j - c_i\|^2 \tag{18}$$

where c_i, x_j represent the centroid and data point of each cluster, N is the total number of data points.

5.3 Experimental Results and Analysis

Graphical Representation of Experimental Results. Iris dataset is divided into three categories, so the value of K is three. The data dimension is four, the global sensitivity $\Delta f = d + 1 = 5$, the initial privacy budget is set to one, then the initial centroid added random noise is Lap (5). Since the number of each cluster is about 50, the added random noise is set from −50 to 50 to avoid large deviation. Due to the singleness of a single experiment, the visual diagram only provides reference, and the specific analysis needs to use the evaluation index.

First, simply explore the data set, use different colors to indicate the three species, and visualize the data, as shown in Fig. 1. According to the differential privacy k-means algorithm mentioned in this paper, the clustering division results are visually displayed by color. In most cases, the clustering results are shown in Fig. 2. But at the same time, there are also cases of poor clustering effect, as shown in Fig. 3. The reason for this situation is that the initial center point is randomly generated, which brings uncertainty of the result and falls into local optimization. Then it is realized according to the improved idea of this paper. The α of the center point improvement part is set to 0.5, and the method will stably select three initial center points. The improved visualization is shown in Fig. 4.

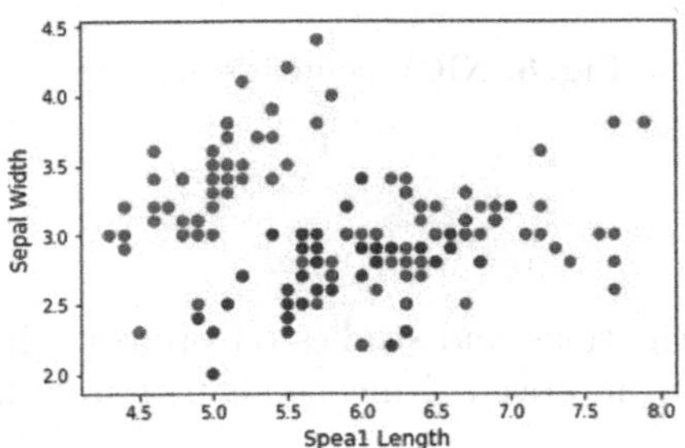

Fig. 1. Calyx length and width scatter

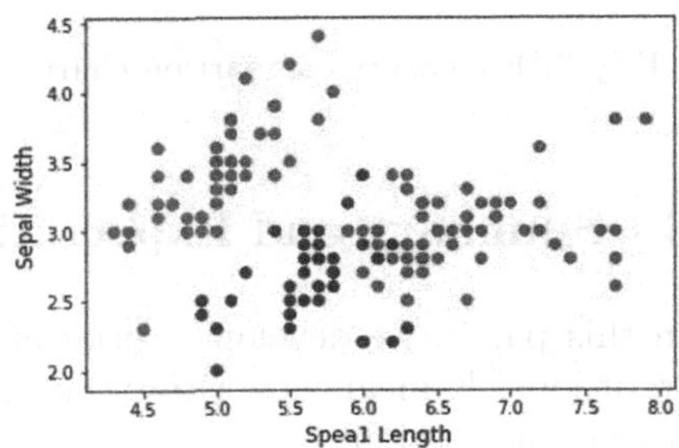

Fig. 2. Better distribution of clustering results under DPK-means

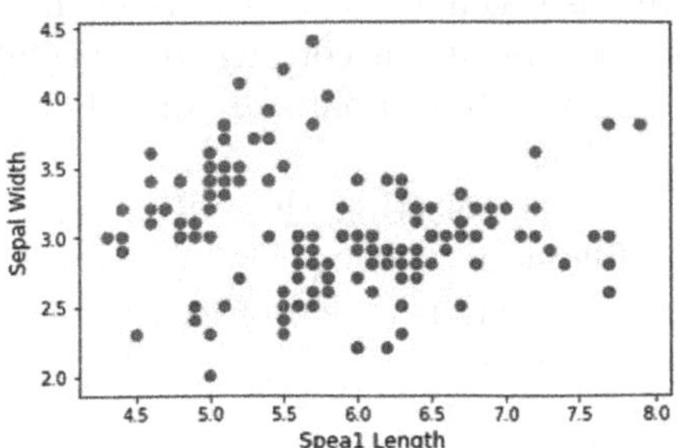

Fig. 3. DPK-means falls into local optimal clustering results

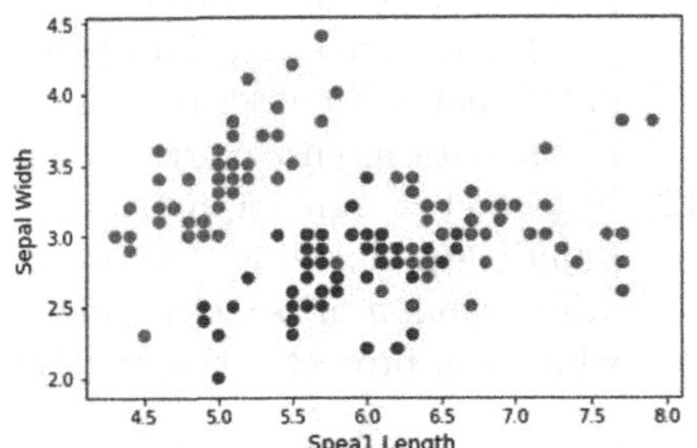

Fig. 4. Improved differential privacy K-means results

Analysis of Evaluation Indicators. Verify the F-measure and NICV of differential privacy K-means and the improved algorithm in this paper on Iris data set, select ten different privacy budgets respectively, and conduct ten experiments on the same privacy budget to obtain the average. The F-measure results are shown in Fig. 5. The improved algorithm in this paper can produce more stable and average higher F-measure values, that is, the clustering results are closer to the original data, and the clustering availability is improved. The NICV results are shown in Fig. 6. Under the same privacy budget, the NICV of the improved algorithm in this paper is less than that of DPK-means algorithm and is relatively stable, indicating that the clustering performance of this algorithm is improved.

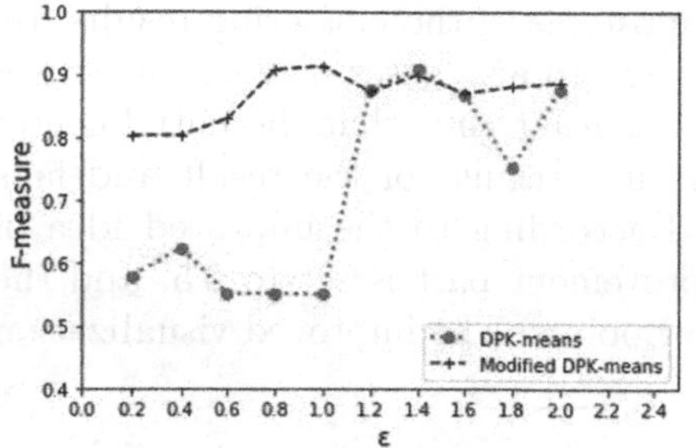

Fig. 5. F-measure comparison chart

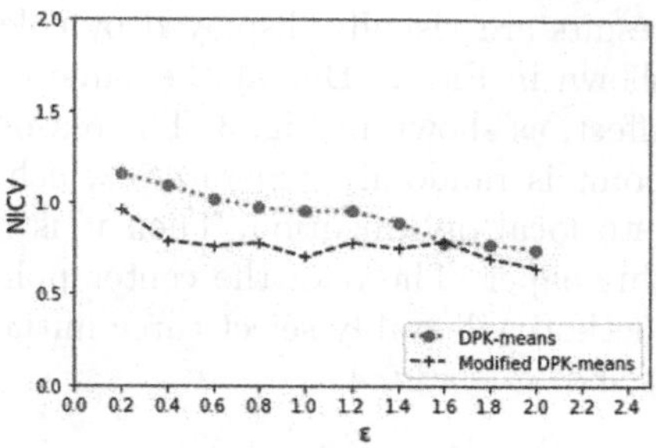

Fig. 6. NICV comparison chart

6 Summary and Expectation

In this paper, we develop a series of investigations and studies on problems in traditional K-means algorithm, and propose improved K-means algorithm with privacy protection.

(1) Improvements to the initial center point. In the implementation, firstly, the sum of squares of the errors of each cluster is calculated, and the center point of the cluster with the smallest value is taken as the first initial center point. The remaining data points are selected in turn according to the rules of this paper, in order to ensure that the initial center points are distributed in the data intensive area as much as possible.
(2) Improved design for privacy protection. After selecting the initial center point, each cluster is evaluated with the Silhouette Coefficient. In each iteration, random noise with different privacy budgets is added to each cluster, which can protect the privacy of the cluster center.

Although this paper optimizes the differential privacy K-means algorithm, it improves the availability of clustering to a certain extent. However, with the application and development of big data, people also need privacy protection more and more. This field is still worthy of in-depth investigation and research. Future research work can be considered from the following aspects, for example, the data set in this paper is numerical data, does not involve non-numerical data, and the scale is small. Secondly, the K value is artificially selected, how to be automatically selected is also worth studying.

References

1. Cheng, Q.: Research on improvement of K-means clustering algorithm based on differential privacy. Guangxi University (2021). https://doi.org/10.27034/d.cnki.ggxiu.2021.000705
2. Ding, Z., Lin, K.: Research on key technologies of privacy protection in the context of big data. Comput. Program. Skills Maint. **02**, 72–74 (2022). https://doi.org/10.16184/j.cnki.comprg.2022.02.048
3. Mac Queen, J.: Some methods for classification and analysis of multivariate observation. In: Proceedings of the Fifth Berkeley Symposium on Mathematical Statistics and Probability, pp. 281–297. University of California Press, Berkeley (1967)
4. Oliveira, G.V., Coutinho, F.P., Campello, R.J.G.B., et al.: Improving K-means through distributed scalable metaheuristics. Neurocomputing **246**, 45–57 (2017)
5. Yang, J., Zhao, C.: Survey on K-means clustering algorithm. Comput. Eng. Appl. **055**(023), 7–14, 63 (2019)
6. Blum, A., Dwork, C., Mc Sherry, F., et al.: Practical privacy: the Su LQ framework. In: Proceedings of the Twenty-Fourth ACM SIGMOD-SIGACT-SIGART Symposium on Principles of Database Systems, pp. 128–138 (2005)
7. Nissim, K., Raskhodnikova, S., Smith, A.: Smooth sensitivity and sampling in private data analysis. In: Proceedings of the Thirty-Ninth Annual ACM Symposium on Theory of Computing, pp. 75–84 (2007)
8. Zhang, K.: Research on data publishing and mining method based on differential privacy. Nanjing University of Posts and Telecommunications (2021). https://doi.org/10.27251/d.cnki.gnjdc.2021.001366

Improved Kmeans Algorithm Based on Privacy Protection

Caixin Wang, Lili Wang[(✉)], and Hongyong Yang

Ludong University, Yantai, Shandong 264025, China
wanglili78@hotmail.com, hyyang@yeah.net

Abstract. Privacy protection is a hot research topic in the field of network security. The traditional Kmeans clustering algorithm realizes the clustering of massive data by selecting the center point of the initial cluster, but privacy disclosure may occur in the clustering process and the publicity of the clustering results. This paper proposes an improved Kmeans algorithm with differential privacy protection, where density measurement is introduced into the original Kmeans to improve the in-class similarity of clusters and ensure that the selected centers are in relatively dense areas. The distance measure is introduced to reduce the similarity between clusters and improve the repellency of different cluster centers. The average maximum similarity between classes is applied to optimize the cluster number K, while the optimal initial intra-class center are dynamically programmed. To solve the problem of privacy disclosure, Laplace noise is introduced to protect information security. Experimental results show that the proposed algorithm has better clustering availability and data reliability than traditional algorithms.

Keywords: Differential privacy · Kmeans clustering · Dynamic programming

1 Introduction

With the large-scale application of the Internet in e-commerce, finance, finance, military and other fields, in recent years, data security and privacy leakage incidents continue to occur, how to ensure data privacy security has become a research hotspot in the field of big data applications. Li [1] et al. proposed a trajectory data privacy protection technology based on data partition; Zhang [2] et al. proposed a network location privacy protection algorithm; Louiseet [3] al. analyzed the communication content of data leakage in recent years; Dwork [4] proposed a differential privacy protection model to solve the problem of database information leakage.

Due to its high efficiency and high speed, Kmeans clustering algorithms are widely used in many fields. However, the Kmeans clustering algorithm still has some flaws, such as using the initial random data as the center of the clustering method, manually determining the number of clusters of classes, and privacy

Y. Xu et al. (Eds.): ML4CS 2022, LNCS 13655, pp. 560–567, 2023.
https://doi.org/10.1007/978-3-031-20096-0_42

leakage problems during the clustering process. Aiming at the above problems, Shiet [5] et al. introduced a small number of labeling algorithms, which solved the problem of randomly selecting the initial cluster center to a certain extent; Lin [6] et al. combined the nearest neighbor algorithm with the Kmean algorithm, which can effectively improve the accuracy of the algorithm; Wang [7] et al. proposed an improved algorithm based on kurtosis test, which improves the adaptability of the algorithm to complex data sets;Zhang [8] et al. combined the density parameters with the Kmeans algorithm to determine the optimal number of class clusters; Zhou [9] et al. proposed an improved algorithm based on weight density, which improved the accuracy of clustering.

Based on the learning of existing optimization algorithms, this paper proposes an improved Kmeans algorithm based on privacy protection, and introduces a density measure on the basis of the original Kmeans to ensure that the intraclass similarity of cluster classes is high; the distance metric is introduced to ensure that the interclass similarity between clusters is low; the average maximum similarity between classes can be introduced, which can dynamically determine the optimal number of clusters of classes and obtain the best initial in-class center; and the differential privacy protection mechanism is introduced to protect the security of information.

2 Relevant Theoretical Basis

2.1 Differential Privacy

Under the differential privacy model, the difference between the final result of a single data in the dataset and the data not in the dataset is very small, and the attacker cannot obtain the real raw data.

Definition 1. *With algorithm Q, for any two sets of adjacent datasets A and A', C is any kind of clustering, ε is defined as a privacy protection budget, if the algorithm Q satisfies:*

$$\Pr[Q(A) \in C] \leq e * \Pr[Q(A') \in C] \tag{1}$$

the algorithm Q provides ε -privacy protection budget.

Differential privacy is mainly achieved by adding Laplace noise interference mechanisms. This article applies Laplace mechanisms for privacy protection.

Theorem 1. *The global sensitivity of the dataset A under query function f is $\triangle f$, if the algorithm $Q(A)$satisfies:*

$$Q(A) = f(A) + Lap(\triangle f/s) \tag{2}$$

the algorithm Q provides differential privacy protection.

2.2 Kmeans

Among the clustering algorithms, the most commonly used algorithm is the Kmeans algorithm. The Kmeans algorithm execution steps are described below:

Algorithm 1. Standard Kmeans algorithm.

Input: Dataset X; Initial Class Cluster Data K; Maximum Number of Iterations;
Output: K clusters; Evaluation function values Dis;

1: Freely select K data from the dataset X as the initial clustering center;
2: Calculates the similarity between the remaining data and each cluster center, and then assigns it to the cluster center that most closely resembles it;
3: Calculate the latest cluster center according to the cluster center update formula;
4: Repeat steps 2 and steps 3 until the evaluation function reaches convergence or the number of iterations reaches the highest frequency;

Where the cluster center update formula is:

$$z_g = \frac{1}{\mid Z_j \mid} \sum_{x_g \in Z_j} x_g \tag{3}$$

where $\mid Z_j \mid$ is the number of data in class Z_j in the dataset; x_g is the data in class Z_j.

The evaluation function uses the sum of squares of the distances within the class:

$$Dis = \sum_{i=1}^{K} \sum_{x_g \in Z_j} \parallel x_g - z_j \parallel^2 \tag{4}$$

where K is the total number of clusters; x_g is the data in class Z_j; and z_j is the class center vector of class Z_j.

3 Improved Kmeans Algorithm Based on Privacy Protection

3.1 Kmeans Algorithm Based on Dynamically Allocating Cluster Centers

This chapter proposes a Kmeans algorithm based on dynamic allocation of cluster centers, which introduces density measurements, selects the N data with the largest point density from the total data as the most alternate center set, and then selects the center point from this set, which can ensure that the similarity within the cluster class is high. At the same time, the distance measurement is introduced, when a new cluster center is selected, the point farther away from the current center is usually selected, which can ensure that the similarity between clusters is low. The algorithm introduces the average maximum similarity between classes, which dynamically determines the optimal number of algorithm cluster classes K and obtains the optimal initial cluster class center.

The Kmeans algorithm based on the dynamic allocation of cluster centers performs the following steps:

Algorithm 2. Standard Kmeans algorithm.

Input: Dataset X; Neighborhood Radius R; Number of High Density Points N; Initial AM Value; Maximum Number of Iterations;

Output: K clusters; Evaluation function values Dis;

1: Calculate the point density of each data in dataset X, select the data with the maximum point density of N, and put it into the alternative set B;

2: The data of the two largest point densities from alternate set B are selected as the initial initial cluster centers, and the two points are removed from alternate set B;

3: Select a piece of data from alternate set B to make it the farthest away from the current initial cluster center, set it to the next initial cluster center point, and remove the point from alternate set B;

4: Iterate all the data in dataset X according to the above cluster centers and divide them into corresponding cluster classes.;

5: Calculate the AM value at this time;

6: If the currently calculated AM value is smaller than the previous AM value, you can proceed with the algorithm, proceed to step 7. Otherwise, the true initial cluster center is selected as the cluster center at the smallest AM value, proceed to step 8;

7: Calculate the latest cluster center according to the cluster update formula, select a data from candidate set B so that the distance from the latest cluster center is the maximum value, set it as the next initial cluster center point, and remove the point from the alternate set B;

8: Calculate the distance from the remaining data of dataset X to the center of each cluster, and allocate them to the corresponding cluster class according to the distance between them and the center of each cluster;

9: Recalculate the cluster centers according to the data class update formula;

10: Repeat steps 8 and steps 9 until the evaluation function reaches convergence or the number of iterations reaches the highest frequency;

3.2 Improved Kmeans Algorithm Based on Privacy Protection

Privacy leakage problems occur during the execution of the Kmeans algorithm, so the differential privacy algorithm is introduced on the basis of the Kmeans algorithm based on the dynamic allocation of cluster centers.

The privacy budget ε' of each iteration is related to the data dimension d, the number of iterations t, the dataset range r and the initial privacy budget value ε:

$$\varepsilon' = \frac{\varepsilon}{(dr+1)t} \tag{5}$$

The introduction of Laplace noise is as follows:

$$f = Lap(b) \tag{6}$$

where $b = \Delta f/s$. The steps to perform the improved Kmeans algorithm based on privacy protection are as follows:

Algorithm 3. Standard Kmeans algorithm.

Input: Dataset X; Neighborhood Radius R; Number of High Density Points N; Initial AM Value; Maximum Number of Iterations;

Output: K clusters; Evaluation function values Dis;

1: Calculate the point density of each data in dataset X, select the data with the maximum point density of N, and put it into the alternative set B;
2: The data of the two largest point densities from alternate set B are selected as the initial cluster centers, and the two points are removed from alternate set B;
3: Select a piece of data from alternate set B to make it the farthest away from the current initial cluster center, set it to the next initial cluster center point, and remove the point from alternate set B;
4: Iterate all the data in dataset X according to the above cluster centers and divide them into corresponding cluster classes.;
5: Calculate the AM value at this time;
6: If the currently calculated AM value is smaller than the previous AM value, you can proceed with the algorithm, proceed to step 7. Otherwise, the true initial cluster center is selected as the cluster center at the smallest AM value, proceed to step 8;
7: Calculate the latest cluster center according to the cluster update formula, select a data from candidate set B so that the distance from the latest cluster center is the maximum value, set it as the next initial cluster center point, and remove the point from the alternate set B;
8: Calculate the distance from the remaining data of dataset X to the center of each cluster, and allocate them to the corresponding cluster class according to the distance between them and the center of each cluster;
9: Recalculate the cluster centers according to the data class update formula, calculates the current Laplace noise and then adds Laplace noise to the current cluster center;
10: Repeat steps 8 and steps 9 until the evaluation function reaches convergence or the number of iterations reaches the highest frequency;

---

4 Experimental Validation

4.1 Experimental Design

Experimental Data. The datasets used in the experiment are the Iris in the UCI database, the Raisin-Dataset in the UCI database, the Wine in the UCI database, and the S-sets dataset in article [10], where the S-sets dataset consists of four sub-datasets S1 to S4, and the specific data of each dataset is shown in the table:

Table 1. Data information table

Datasets	Number of samples	Data dimensions
Iris	150	4
Raisin-Dataset	900	7
Wine	1788	13
S1 S4	5000	2

Due to the large size of the data in the dataset, this paper normalizes the values of the above datasets and normalizes the values of the datasets to between [0, 1].

Evaluation Indicators

Clustering Performance Analysis. In this paper, the sum of squares of the distance within the class (*Dis*) is used to evaluate the performance of the algorithm clustering. The evaluation function values are inversely proportional to the clustering results.

Cluster Availability Analysis. In this paper, the F-measure is used to analyze the cluster availability of the algorithm. F-measure is a measure of cluster availability, which is related to the precision and recall rate of information retrieval. For datasets X, a larger total F-measure means better cluster availability.

4.2 Experimental Results

Clustering Performance Results. In order to evaluate the performance of the improved Kmeans algorithm based on privacy protection, the above datasets were experimented with the algorithm 1 (the standard Kmeans algorithm), the algorithm 2 (the Kmeans algorithm based on dynamically allocating cluster centers), and the algorithm 3 (the improved Kmeans algorithm based on privacy protection). In order to avoid errors in a single experiment, the average of 50 experimental results for the above three algorithms is the most final result. The following table shows the evaluation function values of these three algorithms under each set of datasets:

Table 2. The evaluation function values for three algorithms

Datasets	Algorithm 1	Algorithm 2	Algorithm 3
Iris	0.574615	0.429593	0.425721
Raisin-Dataset	0.241687	0.23744	0.204162
Wine	0.216091	0.215672	0.206860
S1	92.069043	73.767559	71.239381
S2	97.736398	95.647008	94.821958
S3	62.980461	62.140359	52.252677
S4	45.296839	41.372232	41.348386

The evaluation function is used to determine the quality of the clustering results, and the smaller the value of the evaluation function of the same data set, the more concentrated the data objects in the class under the algorithm, and the better the clustering effect of the algorithm. As can be seen from Table 2, under the same data set, the evaluation function value of Algorithm 3 is lower than that of the other two algorithms, so the clustering performance is optimized under certain circumstances.

Cluster Availability Results. In order to evaluate the availability of the improved Kmeans algorithm based on privacy protection, this experiment uses the algorithms 1, 2, and 3 to calculate the F-measure values of each dataset. In order to avoid errors in a single experiment, the average of 50 experimental results for the above three algorithms is the most final result. The following table shows the F-measure values of these three algorithms in each dataset.

Table 3. The F- measure values for the three algorithms

Datasets	Algorithm 1	Algorithm 2	Algorithm 3
Iris	0.818491	0.823502	0.824265
Raisin-Dataset	0.818491	0.737003	0.749616
Wine	0.818491	0.663610	0.669257
S1	0.818491	0.564290	0.545370
S2	0.476839	0.477783	0.473717
S3	0.519322	0.556601	0.532997
S4	0.491677	0.503664	0.499563

The higher the total F-measure, the better the cluster availability. As can be seen from the table, the cluster availability of Algorithm 2 and Algorithm 3 is stronger than the cluster availability of Algorithm 1. And, the clustering availability of algorithm 3 is slightly lower than that of Algorithm 2, which is due to adding noise on the basis of Algorithm 2, which will inevitably lead to a slight decrease in clustering availability. In addition, by observing that the availability of Algorithm 3 and Algorithm 2 is small, it can also be seen that the clustering availability of Algorithm 3 is excellent.

5 Conclusion

In this paper, the improved Kmeans algorithm based on privacy protection is proposed, which introduces density measurement, distance measurement and average maximum similarity between classes on the basis of the original Kmeans, which can dynamically determine the optimal number of clusters K and the best initial center within the class. At the same time, differential privacy protection Laplace noise is introduced, which better protects the privacy of information. Experimental results show that the proposed algorithm has good clustering performance and data reliability. However, the algorithm needs to calculate the point density of all data in the process of dynamic planning, and when the amount of data is too large, there will be a problem of high time complexity. Therefore, further work will be carried out to reduce the time complexity of the algorithm.

References

1. Li, S., Shen, H., Sang, Y., et al.: An efficient method for privacy-preserving trajectory data publishing based on data partitioning. J. Supercomput. **76**(7), 5276–5300 (2020)
2. Zhang, P., Durresi, M., Durresi, A.: Internet network location privacy protection with multi-access edge computing. Computing **103**(3), 473–490 (2020). https://doi.org/10.1007/s00607-020-00860-3
3. Thomas, L., et al.: A framework for data privacy and security accountability in data breach communications. Comput. Secur. **116**, 102657 (2022)
4. Dwork, C.: Differential privacy. In: Bugliesi, M., Preneel, B., Sassone, V., Wegener, I. (eds.) ICALP 2006. LNCS, vol. 4052, pp. 1–12. Springer, Heidelberg (2006). https://doi.org/10.1007/11787006_1
5. Yongge, S., et al.: Hybrid data mining method of telecom customer based on improved Kmeans and XGBoost. J. Phys. Conf. Ser. **2010**(1), 012060 (2021)
6. Lin, T., Zhao, X., Sang, Y.: K-means clustering algorithm for nearest neighbor optimization. Computer Sci. **46**(S5), 216–219 (2019)
7. Wang, T., Gao, J.: An improved k-means algorithm based on kurtosis test. In: Proceedings of 2019 3rd International Conference on Artificial Intelligence, pp. 214–248. Automation and Control Technologies, New York (2019)
8. Zhang, Y., et al.: Improved K-means algorithm combining density parameters and center substitution and new clustering effectiveness index. Computer Sci. **49**(01), 121–132 (2022)
9. Zhou, H.: Number of mixed data clusters and initial class center determination algorithm and implementation. Shanxi University, Shanxi (2020)
10. FrÃnti, P.: K-means properties on six clustering benchmark datasets. Appl. Intell. **116** , 4743–4759 (2018)

Symmetry Structured Analysis Sparse Coding for Key Frame Extraction

Yujie Li[1], Benying Tan[1(✉)], Shuxue Ding[1], Christian Desrosiers[2], and Ahmad Chaddad[1(✉)]

[1] School of Artificial Intelligence, Guilin University of Electronic Technology, Guilin 541004, China
{yujieli,by-tan,sding}@guet.edu.cn, ahmad8chaddad@gmail.com

[2] Ecole de Technology Superieure, Montreal, Canada
christian.desrosiers@etsmtl.ca

Abstract. The efficiency of sparse coding based key frame extraction algorithm is influenced by various sparse regularization and optimization strategies. However, sparse coding with an analytical model for key frame extraction is still a challenging task. In this paper, we present a new analysis sparse coding algorithm for key frame extraction using minimax concave penalty (MCP). Analysis sparse coding has low computation complexity compared to the common synthesis model. Furthermore, analysis sparse coding can automatically lead to symmetry structured for key frame extraction. In this context, the MCP sparse regularization is non-convex that can promote the sparsity of solutions. Unlike conventional non-convex sparse regularization in formulating a non-convex sparse coding cost function, MCP can maintain the convexity that can be used to solve the optimization problem for obtaining the global minimum. The proposed key frame extraction algorithm leads into the following: 1) provides more compressed key frames, 2) decreases the computational complexity and 3) accelerates the process tasks. Our results demonstrate the effectiveness of the proposed symmetry structured with analysis sparse coding algorithm that is validated with both simulations and a number of challenging real-world scenarios, outperforming the state-of-the-art techniques.

Keywords: Key frame extraction · Analysis sparse coding · Minimax Concave Penalty (MCP) · Non-convex

1 Introduction

Key frame extraction [19,22], which consists in representing a video using a small set of the most informative frames, plays an important role in computer vision

This work was supported in part by the National Natural Science Foundation of China (61903090), Guangxi Natural Science Foundation (2022GXNSFBA035644, 2021 GXNSFBA220039), Guangxi Science and Technology Major Project (AA22068057), and the Foreign Young Talent Program (QN2021033002L).

Y. Xu et al. (Eds.): ML4CS 2022, LNCS 13655, pp. 568–585, 2023.
https://doi.org/10.1007/978-3-031-20096-0_43

[11,23]. Sparse coding-based key frame extraction is attracting a remarkable attention due to its appealing advantages, simplicity and mature mathematical analysis [12,16]. Notably, sparse coding [18,39] can extract a few (sparse) frames containing the main information of the original video. Current sparse coding key frame extraction algorithms are based on a synthesis model where a sparse coefficient matrix is required to learn, and the original video can be expressed as the linear combination of a few selected key frames [3,4,10]. Specifically, the few non-zero elements of the sparse coefficient matrix correspond to the most compressed set of key frames to represent the entire video. The effectiveness of sparse coding key frame extraction methods depends on the regularization term used to enforce sparsity, which is commonly based on the l_1 or l_0 norm. As an improvement, we propose a minimax concave penalty (MCP) [36,38] as sparse regularization for key frame extraction. MCP, which belongs to the family non-convex sparse regularization (NSR) approaches, promotes the accuracy of solutions and can obtain nearly unbiased estimators. Moreover, the minimizer of the MCP penalty is easily obtained via a hard threshold that, unlike the soft threshold, does not underestimate large components. Additionally, MCP maintains the convexity of the formulated cost function so that convex optimization methods can be used to optimize this function and obtain the global minimum. In this work, we use the non-convex MCP as sparsity constraint to formulate a key frame extraction problem where a sparse coefficient matrix is learned from the original video frames. The MCP sparse constraint can maintain the convexity of the cost function, thereby avoiding the presence of spurious local minimum in the cost function. Moreover, the forward-backward splitting (FBS) algorithm is used to perform sparse coding efficiently.

The analysis model for sparse coding [27], which differs the synthesis model [1,25,33] in its principle and structure, is a promising improvement for sparse representation learning. In this model, an analysis dictionary (or analysis operator) is sought to transform the signal vector to a high-dimensional space, i.e., $\mathbf{\Omega S} = \mathbf{X}$, where the analysis coefficient vector $\mathbf{X}$, assumed to be sparse [21,37], is the representation of $\mathbf{S}$. Compared to the mature synthesis model, the analysis model usually has a simpler optimization procedure. It can also achieve a symmetrical structure in the representation, a property that we leverage in this work for the extraction of key frames from videos.

We design a novel key frame extraction model based on analysis sparse coding. This model considers sparsity regularization and structure symmetry simultaneously using a non-convex group sparsity penalty, which leads to a coefficient matrix with strong sparsity and a low reconstruction error [34,35]. Furthermore, a decomposition scheme is used to split the sparse coefficient matrix into rows forming separate groups. In addition, the rows and corresponding columns in the sparse coefficient matrix will have a symmetrical sparsity structure, as illustrated in Fig. 1. Thus, the position of selected key frames can be estimated automatically from the non-zero rows/columns in the symmetrical sparse coefficient matrix, without the need for additional operators. The optimization problem resulting from this decomposition scheme can be transformed into a set of subproblems that can be solved efficiently with respect to each row.

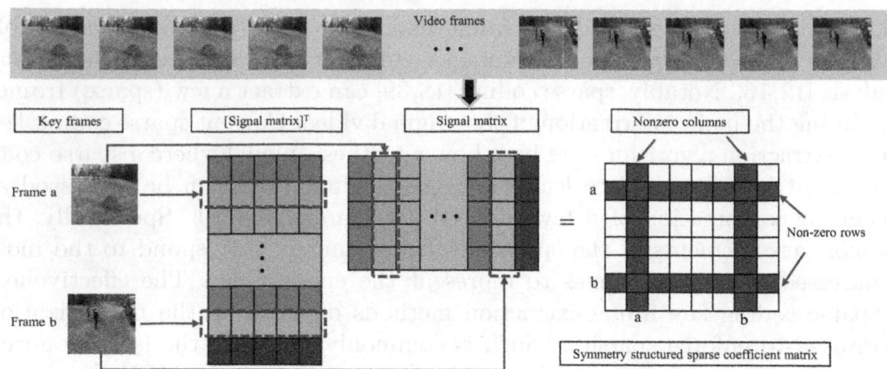

Fig. 1. Model of the proposed key frame extraction.

Our contributions can be summarized as follows:

1) We present a novel sparse coding model based on the minimax concave penalty (MCP) for the problem of key frame extraction. To the best of our knowledge, our key frame extraction approach is the first to consider sparsity structure symmetry while computing the sparse coefficients.
2) We propose a highly-efficient method for symmetry structured sparse coding built on the forward-backward splitting (FBS) algorithm. The proposed alternating update scheme yields a low computational complexity by decomposing the non-convex optimization problem into easy to solve sub-problems.
3) We validate the proposed key frame extraction approach on both synthetic data and real videos, showing our approach to achieve a state-of-the-art accuracy along with a better key frame compression compared to recent methods for this task.

The rest of this paper is organized as follows. Section 2 presents related works on sparse coding and key frame extraction. In Sect. 3, we first formulate the sparse coding model with MCP regularization, and then describe the general alternating update scheme for optimization. Afterwards, Sect. 4 presents the accelerated FBS algorithm proposed to promote efficiency. In Sect. 5, we describe the experiments and performance metrics employed to evaluate the proposed method and to compare it against recent algorithms. Finally, Sect. 6 summarizes the key contributions and results of our work.

1.1 Notation

We start by defining the notations used in this work. Throughout the paper, a boldface uppercase letter (e.g., $\mathbf{A}$) denotes a matrix, a boldface lowercase letter (e.g., $\mathbf{a}$) denotes a vector, and a lowercase letter (e.g., a_{ij}) or boldface uppercase letter (e.g., $\mathbf{A}_{ij}$) denotes the ij-th entry of $\mathbf{A}$. $\|\mathbf{A}\|_\mathrm{F}$ denotes the Frobenius norm, which is defined by $\|\mathbf{A}\|_F^2 = \sum_{i,j} |\mathbf{A}_{ij}|^2$. $\mathbf{A}^T$ denotes the transpose matrix of $\mathbf{A}$.

2 Related Work

Sparse coding approaches for key frame extraction [7,15] have been widely studied in the literature. These approaches do not require segmentation/shot detection or semantic understanding, and can be used in an adaptive manner to extract the most representative elements from images or videos [13,39]. Key frame extraction methods can be roughly categorized as segment-based [30] or shot-based approaches [2,28]. Segment-based algorithms find key segments corresponding to regions around each key frame [14,17]. This provides an additional discriminative information in short time intervals. On the other hand, shot-based algorithms determine key frames by comparing a reference frame with each subsequent frame in the video [9,26]. Recent work related to attention-based video summary (Attn.) proposed a key frame extraction approach with visual attention [5], where key frames are extracted using a deep neural network. In [29], a deep semantic features video summary (DFS) model was presented to select the key frames using deep features of the video frames. Similarly, the VGG-based video summary (VGG) [32] approach obtains key frames using deep semantic features from the VGG network. Despite their improved accuracy, these algorithms are unable to achieve high-performance metrics in terms of data compression.

The various algorithms for sparse coding mainly differ with respect to their sparse regularization and optimization approach [35]. For the sparse coding problem, the choice of sparse regularization is essential since it has a direct impact on the learned representation. Typical sparse regularization terms include the l_0-norm, the l_1-norm and the non-convex determinant measure [35]. Most sparse coding algorithms for key frame extraction are based on these regularization terms. For instance, the sparse modeling representation selection (SMRS) method for video classification and summarization [6] uses the l_1-norm to achieve a sparse representation corresponding to key frames. The key frame extraction method in [20] also considers the l_1-norm to include other types of information, in addition to pure video. In [35], the determinant measure was used as sparse constraint for better key frame extraction results. As mentioned before, existing sparse coding-based algorithms for key frame extraction rely on the traditional synthesis model, which does not consider the structural information of video frames in the sparse coefficient matrix.

3 Formulation

The general analysis sparse coding model was built by considering an additional regularization term $J_{\mathbf{X}}(\mathbf{X})$ on the coefficient matrix $\mathbf{X}$:

$$\hat{\mathbf{X}} = \arg\min_{\mathbf{X}} f(\mathbf{X}) = \|\boldsymbol{\Omega}\mathbf{S} - \mathbf{X}\|_F^2 + \lambda J_{\mathbf{X}}(\mathbf{X}).$$

In this formulation, λ is a positive parameter, while $\boldsymbol{\Omega}$ and $\mathbf{S}$ denote the analysis dictionary and the signals, respectively.

3.1 Analysis Sparse Coding with MCP Sparse Regularization

We now introduce our MCP sparse regularization approach and present some related definitions. We first formulate our sparse coding model as

$$\min_{\mathbf{X}} f(\mathbf{X}) = \|\boldsymbol{\Omega}\mathbf{S} - \mathbf{X}\|_F^2 + \lambda J_{\mathrm{MCP}}(\mathbf{X}), \tag{1}$$

where

$$J_{\mathrm{MCP}}(\mathbf{X}) = \|\mathbf{X}\|_1 - \min_{\mathbf{Z}} \left\{ \|\mathbf{Z}\|_1 + \frac{\rho}{2\lambda}\|\mathbf{X} - \mathbf{Z}\|_F^2 \right\} \tag{2}$$

is the minimax concave penalty sparse regularization imposed on matrix $\mathbf{X}$.

Definition 1. For a given parameter $\rho > 0$, the MCP can be defined as

$$J_{\mathrm{MCP}}(x) = \begin{cases} |x| - \frac{\rho}{2}x^2, & |x| < \frac{1}{\rho} \\ \frac{1}{2\rho}, & |x| \geqslant \frac{1}{\rho}. \end{cases} \tag{3}$$

Definition 2. The Moreau envelope of a proper lower semi-continuous function f is given by

$$f(\mathbf{x}) = \inf_{\mathbf{y}} f(\mathbf{y}) + \frac{1}{2}\|\mathbf{y} - \mathbf{x}\|_2^2. \tag{2}$$

where $\mathbf{x}, \mathbf{y} \in \mathbb{R}$. Vector $\mathbf{x}$ is called the proximal centre and inf is the infinium of the set.

Definition 3. Assume f is a convex function, the proximal operator of f can be defined as

$$\mathbf{prox}_f(\mathbf{x}) = \arg\min_{\mathbf{y}} f(\mathbf{y}) + \frac{1}{2}\|\mathbf{y} - \mathbf{x}\|_2^2. \tag{3}$$

The above MCP formulation is for a single variable. However, we can extend it to the multivariate case by rewriting it as a Moreau envelope:

$$J_{\mathrm{MCP}}(\mathbf{x}) = \|\mathbf{x}\|_1 - \min_{\mathbf{z}} \left\{ \|\mathbf{z}\|_1 + \frac{\rho}{2\lambda}\|\mathbf{x} - \mathbf{z}\|_2^2 \right\}. \tag{4}$$

Here, $J_{\mathrm{MCP}}(\mathbf{x})$ is non-convex, and ρ can control the convexity of the MCP. Using this definition, we can then construct the cost function as follows:

$$(\hat{\mathbf{X}}, \hat{\mathbf{Z}}) = \arg\min_{\boldsymbol{\Omega},\mathbf{X}} \max_{\mathbf{Z}} F(\mathbf{X}, \mathbf{Z}). \tag{5}$$

where

$$\begin{aligned} F(\mathbf{X}, \mathbf{Z}) = &\frac{1}{2}\|\boldsymbol{\Omega}\mathbf{S} - \mathbf{X}\|_F^2. \\ &+ \lambda\|\mathbf{X}\|_1 - \lambda\|\mathbf{Z}\|_1 - \frac{\rho}{2}\|\mathbf{X} - \mathbf{Z}\|_F^2 \end{aligned} \tag{6}$$

Since the combined optimization problem of (5) is intractable, we employ an optimization scheme that updates the dictionary coefficient matrix $\mathbf{X}$ and auxiliary variable $\mathbf{Z}$ in an alternating fashion. The update scheme can be expressed as

$$(\mathbf{X}^{(k+1)}, \mathbf{Z}^{(k+1)}) = \arg\min_{\mathbf{X}} \max_{\mathbf{Z}} F(\mathbf{X}, \mathbf{Z}) \tag{7}$$

where $\mathbf{X}$ and $\mathbf{Z}$ are updated using the following equations:

$$\begin{aligned} \mathbf{X}^{(k+1)} &= \arg\min_{\mathbf{X}} \frac{1}{2}\|\boldsymbol{\Omega}\mathbf{S} - \mathbf{X}\|_F^2 \\ &\qquad + \lambda\|\mathbf{X}\|_1 - \frac{\rho}{2}\|\mathbf{X} - \mathbf{Z}^{(k)}\|_F^2 \end{aligned} \tag{8}$$

$$\mathbf{Z}^{(k+1)} = \arg\min_{\mathbf{Z}} \lambda\|\mathbf{Z}\|_1 + \frac{\rho}{2}\|\mathbf{X}^{(k+1)} - \mathbf{Z}\|_F^2 \tag{9}$$

The first option to solve (8) and (9) is applying an iterative optimization scheme, however this has relatively high computational complexity. Another option is to update both $\mathbf{X}$ and $\mathbf{Z}$ in an iteration. As shown in (7), $F(\mathbf{X}, \mathbf{Z})$ is a saddle-shaped function which is convex in $\mathbf{X}$ and concave in $\mathbf{Z}$. Consequently, we can apply a proximal method, such as the FBS or Douglas-Rachford splitting (DRS) algorithms, to reach a global minima. In this work, we consider the FBS algorithm for solving (7).

4 Algorithm

We consider FBS as an alternating optimization scheme that solves the sparse coding problem in (7). When $0 < \lambda < 1$, the formulated MCP sparse-regularization-based cost function is convex. We can then write it as a saddle-point problem and solve it using FBS, which can be viewed as a proximal gradient method for optimizing the general convex problem. Specifically, FBS solves the following form of the minimization problem:

$$\min_{\mathbf{a}} f_1(\mathbf{a}) + f_2(\mathbf{a}) \tag{10}$$

where $f_1(\mathbf{a})$ should be convex and differentiable and $f_2(\mathbf{a})$ is arbitrarily convex (e.g., not necessarily smooth). Let $P(\mathbf{a}) = \nabla f_1(\mathbf{a})$ and $Q(\mathbf{a}) = \partial f_2(\mathbf{a})$. It can be shown that a vector $\mathbf{a}^*$ is the solution of (10) if and only if $\mathbf{0} \in P(\mathbf{a}^*) + Q(\mathbf{a}^*)$ holds.

This property leads to the following update rule for (10):

$$\boldsymbol{\omega}^{(k)} = \mathbf{a}^{(k)} - \mu P(\mathbf{a}^{(k)}) \tag{11}$$

$$\mathbf{a}^{(k+1)} = (\mathbf{I} + \mu Q)^{-1}(\boldsymbol{\omega}^{(k)}) = \mathrm{prox}_{\mu Q}(\boldsymbol{\omega}^{(k)}) \tag{12}$$

The convergence of this update scheme is guaranteed for $0 < \mu < 2/L(\nabla f)$, where $L(\nabla f)$ is the Lipschitz constant of ∇f [31]. Applying the FBS algorithm to solve the l_1-norm regularized problem for $\mathbf{X}$ in (8), we then get

$$\mathbf{I}^{(k)} = \mathbf{X}^{(k)} - \mu(\mathbf{X}^{(k)} - \mathbf{S}^T\mathbf{S}) + \mu\rho(\mathbf{X}^{(k)} - \mathbf{Z}^{(k)}) \tag{13}$$

$$\mathbf{X}^{(k+1)} = \mathrm{soft}(\mathbf{I}^{(k)}; \lambda\mu). \tag{14}$$

Likewise, solving the l_1-norm regularized problem for $\mathbf{Z}$ (9) is achieved as follows:

$$\mathbf{II}^{(k)} = \mathbf{Z}^{(k)} + \mu\rho(\mathbf{X}^{(k)} - \mathbf{Z}^{(k)}) \tag{15}$$

$$\mathbf{Z}^{(k+1)} = \mathrm{soft}(\mathbf{II}^{(k)}; \lambda\mu). \tag{16}$$

The optimization procedure is summarized in Algorithm 1. Based on the Lipschitz condition mentioned above, the algorithm converges for $0 < \mu < 2/\max(1, \rho/(1-\rho))$.

4.1 Key Frame Extraction Algorithm

In the key frame extraction task, the signal matrix $\mathbf{S}$ is comprised of video frames $\mathbf{Y}$ and the transpose of the signal matrix, $\mathbf{Y}^T$, represents the analysis dictionary $\mathbf{\Omega}$, as illustrated in Fig. 1. The corresponding formulation can be expressed as

$$\hat{\mathbf{X}} = \arg\min_{\mathbf{X}} f(\mathbf{X}) = \|\mathbf{Y}^T\mathbf{Y} - \mathbf{X}\|_F^2 + \lambda J_{\mathbf{X}}(\mathbf{X}). \tag{17}$$

Algorithm 1: Analysis sparse coding using the forward-backward splitting algorithm (ASC-FBS)

Require: Data matrix $\mathbf{S}$, dictionary matrix $\mathbf{\Omega}$, the regularization parameter λ, parameter ρ and μ.

Initialize: matrices $\mathbf{X}^{(0)} \in \mathbb{R}^{n\times N}$, $\mathbf{Z}^{(0)} \in \mathbb{R}^{n\times N}$, the parameter λ and ρ are positive constants; $0 < \mu < 2/\max(1, \rho/(1-\rho))$.

for $k = 0$ to maxIteration **do**

  Compute $\mathbf{X}^{(k+1)}$ with (13)-(14).

  Compute $\mathbf{Z}^{(k+1)}$ with (15)-(16).

end for

return $\mathbf{X}^{(k+1)}$, $\mathbf{Z}^{(k+1)}$

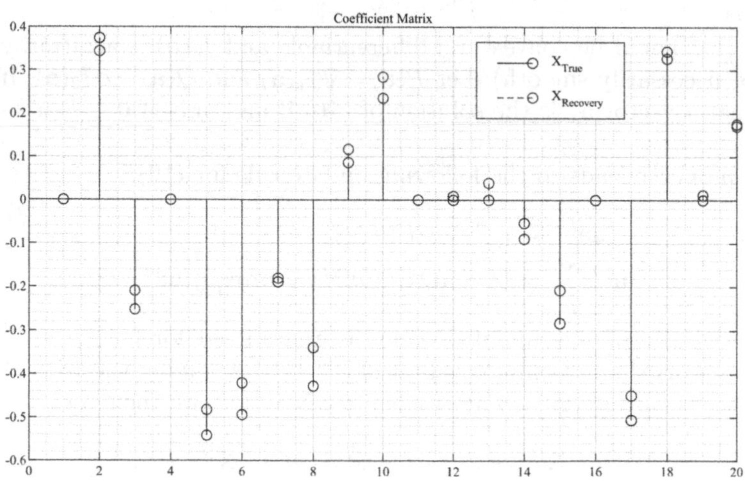

Fig. 2. Sparse coefficient recovery by ASC-MCP.

We note that $\mathbf{X}$ is not a Gram matrix because we used MCP sparse constraint to measure it. We apply the proposed ASC-FBS algorithm to obtain the sparse coefficient matrix. Our overall MCP-regularized sparse coding approach for key frame extraction, called ASC-MCP, is summarized in Algorithm 2.

Algorithm 2: Key frame extraction by analysis sparse coding with the MCP regularizer (ASC-MCP)

Require: Raw video matrix $\mathbf{Y}$, whose N columns correspond to N frames and the regularization parameter λ.

Initialize: matrices $\mathbf{X}^{(0)} \in \mathbb{R}^{N \times N}$, $\mathbf{Z}^{(0)} \in \mathbb{R}^{N \times N}$, the parameter λ and ρ are positive constants; $0 < \mu < 2/\max(1, \rho/(1-\rho))$.
Let $\mathbf{S} = \mathbf{Y}$, $\boldsymbol{\Omega} = \mathbf{Y}^T$.
for $k = 1, 2, ..., N$ **do**
    Compute $\mathbf{X}$ using ASC-FBS.
end for
Output:$\mathbf{X}$.
Find the non-zero rows in the sparse coefficient matrix $\mathbf{X}$, which are the corresponding indices of the key frames for the whole video.

5 Experiments

We evaluate the proposed ASC-FBS and ASC-MCP algorithms using synthetic and SumMe[1] datasets, respectively [8]. To validate our approach's performance, we compare it against 7 other methods: the determinant measure-based sparse coding model in [35] (SC-det), the sparse modeling representation selection (SMRS) algorithm in [6], the attention-based method in [5] (Attn.), the deep semantic features model in [29] (DFS), the VGG-based method in [32] (VGG), the interestingness-based model in [8] (Intr.), and a baseline using uniform sampling (Uni.). We note that SC-det and SMRS are also based on sparse coding.

5.1 Performance on Synthetic Data

As previously mentioned, we evaluate the proposed algorithm 1 (ASC-FBS) by simulating experiments with synthetic data. When the synthetic data was built, we randomly generated a dictionary matrix by sampling from a Gaussian distribution and then normalizing its rows to have a norm of 1. Similarly, we generated a Gaussian-distributed sparse coefficient matrix $\mathbf{H}$ with 13 non-zero elements in each column. For generating the sample signals and assessing the recovered the sparse coefficient, we considered $\mathbf{H}$ as the ground-truth dictionary.

To evaluate the performance of our ASC-FBS algorithm, we compared its recovered sparse coefficient matrix with the ground-truth. Fig. 2 shows that the non-zeros of the recovered matrix are almost the same as those in the ground truth matrix, both in terms of their position and value.

[1] http://www.vision.ee.ethz.ch/~gyglim/vsum/.

The behaviour of our algorithm mainly depends on two parameters: regularization parameter λ, which balances the approximation error and the sparsity regularizer, and parameter ρ affecting the convexity of the MCP. In the next experiment, we select λ and ρ based on the coefficient matrix recovery error. The error values obtained for different values of λ and ρ are shown in Fig. 3. Based on this experiment, we selected $\lambda = 0.005$ and $\rho = 0.5$ for the parameters, and set $\mu = 1.9/\max(1, \rho/(1-\rho)) = 1.9$.

5.2 Key Frame Extraction Performance

The SumMe dataset consist of videos related to events, holidays, and sports. These videos contain many similar frames that are raw or minimally edited. All videos are labeled and summarized by humans. Their length ranges from 1 min to 5 min, and their frame number ranges from 950 to 6,438.

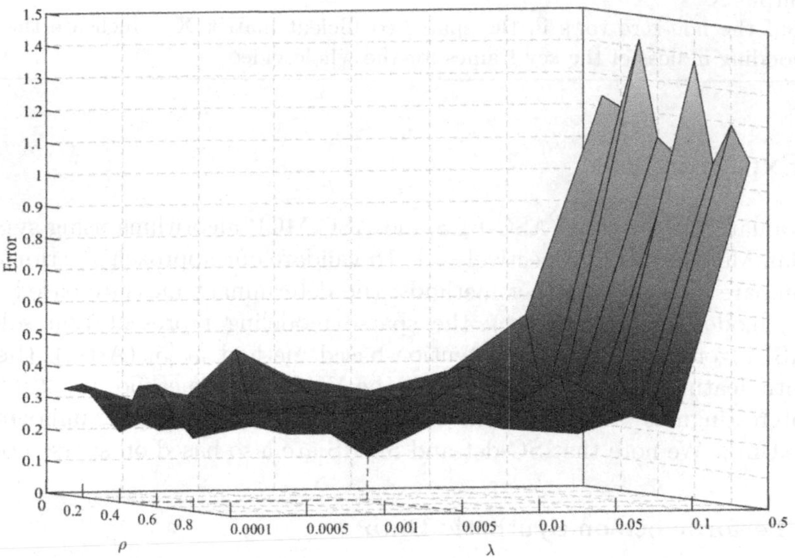

Fig. 3. Coefficient recovery error with various values of λ and ρ.

Performance Metrics. We use summary length [35] to evaluate the compression quality of the extracted key frames. This metric is defined as $S = N_{\text{keyframes}}/N$, where $N_{\text{keyframes}}$ and N are the number of extracted key frames and total number of video frames, respectively. A shorter summary length corresponds to fewer key frames being extracted from the video and, thus, a higher video compression rate. We also consider the F-measure [24] as the second metric for evaluating the key frame extraction accuracy, which corresponds to the harmonic mean between the precision P and recall R:

$$F\text{-measure} = \frac{2P \cdot R}{P + R}, \tag{18}$$

A higher F-measure corresponds to a better result.

Performance of Key Frame Extraction Methods. We adopt a single video of the SumMe dataset, called "Cooking", as a leading example to visualize results. We extract features from all 1,275 frames of the video and then apply our ASC-MCP algorithm to select the key frames among these. Figure 4 shows the 20 key frames extracted by ASC-MCP. We see that the selected frames summarize different stages of cooking a meal. Thus, there are seven main actions in the video that correspond to the red rectangular sections in the figure. For instance, the first action is cutting seafood, the second is cooking meat, the third is grabbing onion, etc. Figure 5 shows the first five key frames (highlighted by a red rectangle) and their neighboring frames. As can be seen, the selected key frames form a compressed version of the video segment, which avoids many redundant frames. Overall, these experimental results indicate that ASC-MCP can effectively find a few key frames to represent the whole video.

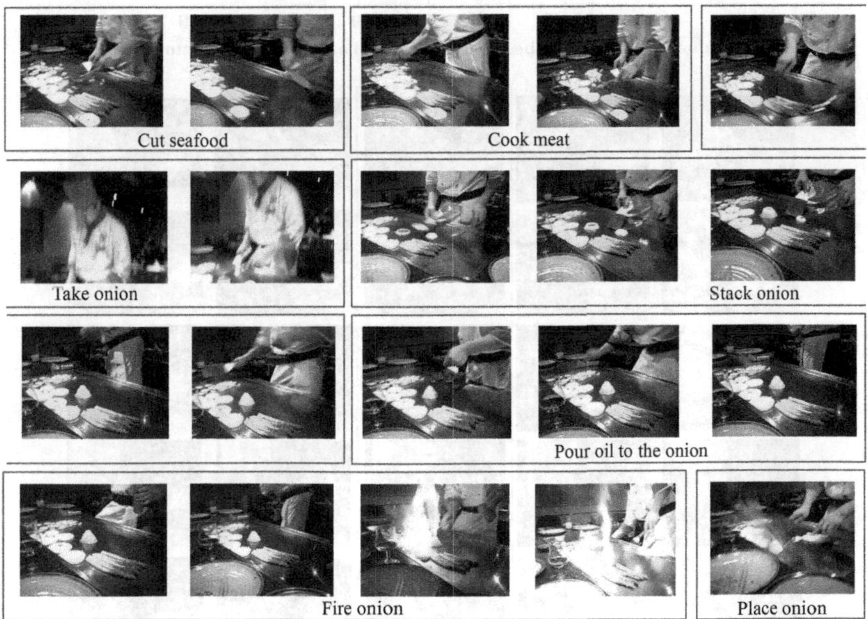

Fig. 4. Key frames obtained from the "Cooking" video by ASC-MCP.

Table 1. Summary length (%) for SC-det, ASC-det, SMRS, ASC-l_1, and ASC-MCP.

Video No.	SC-det	ASC-det	SMRS	ASC-l_1	ASC-MCP (ours)
Base jumping	0.88	0.86	**0.59**	0.75	0.64
Bearpark climbing	1.59	**0.90**	1.98	0.99	1.26
Bike Polo	1.90	1.27	1.54	**1.05**	1.11
Bus in Rock Tunnel	0.64	0.41	0.55	0.43	**0.39**
Car over camera	0.05	0.45	**0.002**	0.38	0.35
Cooking	2.82	1.73	2.20	**1.49**	1.57
Excavators river cross	0.70	0.49	0.77	0.43	**0.39**
Fire Domino	1.26	0.88	1.01	**0.82**	0.88
Jumps	1.89	1.05	2.00	1.05	**0.95**
Kids playing in leaves	1.11	0.72	1.20	0.85	**0.68**
Paintball	0.15	0.26	**0.09**	0.15	0.10
Paluma jump	1.30	0.69	1.18	**0.61**	0.93
Playing ball	1.54	1.22	**1.15**	1.22	1.25
Playing on water slide	1.83	**1.01**	1.79	1.22	1.08
Saving dolphins	–	0.56	1.16	0.56	**0.48**
Scuba	**9.32**	10.05	14.82	10.09	11.62
St Maarten Landing	**1.20**	1.31	1.31	1.37	1.49
Statue of Liberty	1.04	1.06	1.12	**0.75**	0.86
Valparaiso Downhill	**1.62**	2.53	1.64	1.92	2.53
Best/All	3/19	2/19	4/19	**5/19**	**5/19**

Bold front values represent the best performance, i.e., the lowest summary length.

Fig. 5. The first five key frames (in the red rectangle) and the neighboring frames from the 'Cooking' video (Color figure online).

The analysis sparse coding for key frame extraction can lead to symmetry structure, we compared the performances of analysis sparse coding with different sparse constraints. We conduct the comparison experiments with two sparse coding based methods (sparse coding with the determinant measure (SC-det), sparse coding with the l_1-norm (SMRS)) and two analysis sparse coding based methods (analysis sparse coding with the determinant measure (ASC-det), analysis sparse coding with the l_1-norm (ASC-l_1)).

The summary length performances obtained by SC-det, ASC-det, SMRS, ASC-l_1, and ASC-MCP are reported in Table 1. As can be observed, the analysis sparse coding based algorithms (ASC-l_1 and the proposed ASC-MCP) outperform the other methods with respect to this metric. This finding demonstrates that the analysis sparse coding can achieve more compressed results and our proposed algorithm can find a more compressed set of key frames for the video.

Moreover, Table 2 reports the F-measure of all tested sparse coding and analysis sparse coding based methods for videos of the SumMe dataset. We find that sparse coding based algorithms (SC-det and SMRS) can obtain the highest accuracy for 8 videos, which demonstrates that the sparse coding based methods outperform the analysis sparse coding based methods with respect to this F-measure metric. However, as mentioned before, our algorithm provides a much smaller summary length compared to SC-det and SMRS. The proposed ASC-MCP can obtain the highest accuracy for 3 videos, which is the best among the analysis sparse coding methods. Thus the MCP regularizer (ASC-MCP)

Table 2. F-measure for SC-det, ASC-det, SMRS, ASC-l_1 and ASC-MCP.

Video No.	SC-det	ASC-det	SMRS	ASC-l_1	ASC-MCP (ours)
Base jumping	**0.29**	0.25	0.24	0.23	0.25
Bearpark climbing	0.17	0.25	**0.29**	0.23	0.25
Bike Polo	0.21	0.22	0.00	0.21	**0.21**
Bus in Rock Tunnel	0.23	0.23	**0.26**	0.21	0.23
Car over camera	**0.28**	0.21	0.25	0.20	0.20
Cooking	0.19	0.25	**0.28**	0.24	0.27
Excavators river cross	**0.57**	0.25	0.00	0.22	0.22
Fire Domino	0.28	0.25	0.24	0.25	**0.28**
Jumps	**0.31**	0.26	0.30	0.24	0.26
Kids playing in leaves	0.27	0.24	**0.28**	0.23	0.24
Paintball	**0.44**	0.20	0.20	0.19	0.32
Paluma jump	0.14	0.23	**0.26**	0.22	0.23
Playing ball	0.19	0.24	**0.26**	0.23	0.24
Playing on water slide	**0.31**	0.22	0.00	0.21	0.22
Saving dolphins	–	0.25	0.00	0.25	**0.25**
Scuba	0.26	0.23	**0.26**	0.22	0.23
St Maarten Landing	**0.32**	0.25	0.00	0.23	0.25
Statue of Liberty	0.13	0.19	**0.21**	0.18	0.20
Valparaiso Downhill	**0.61**	0.24	0.28	0.22	0.24
Best/All	**8/19**	0/19	**8/19**	0/19	3/19

Bold front values represent the best performance, i.e., the lowest summary length.

can achieve more accurate key frames compared with the determinant measure (ASC-det) and the l_1-norm (ASC-l_1).

Additionally, we see from Table 3 that ASC-MCP has significantly lower runtimes in comparison to other methods. We find that analysis sparse coding based algorithms (ASC-det, ASC-l_1, and the proposed ASC-MCP) have less computation time compared with sparse coding based algorithms (SC-det and SMRS), and the proposed ASC-MCP has the lest computation time for all videos. For example, the running time of Base jumping is 140 by the proposed ASC-MCP, which is 916 times faster than 128234 by SC-det, 7 times faster than 944 by ASC-det, 68 times faster than 9584 by SMRS, and 2 times faster than 271 by ASC-l_1. To sum up, these results show that ASC-MCP achieves a less computation time comparable to the other methods, while providing a more compressed set of key frames. The fast runing time of the proposed ASC-MCP can be used for video real-time processing.

We also conduct comparison experiments with other video summary approaches besides the sparse coding based methods. Table 4 reports the F-measure of 19 videos in the SumMe dataset compared with a random baseline (uniform sampling (Uni.) [29]) and other existing approaches, including the traditional key frame extraction methods (i.e., VGG [32], attentionbased video summary (Attn.) [5], deep semantic features video summary (DFS) [29], and interestingness-based video summary (Intr.) [8]). Table 4 confirms that our

Table 3. Time (s) for SC-det, ASC-det, SMRS, ASC-l_1 and ASC-MCP (ours).

Video No.	SC-det	ASC-det	SMRS	ASC-l_1	ASC-MCP (ours)
Base jumping	28234	944	9584	271	**140**
Bearpark climbing	18180	807	6427	851	**210**
Bike Polo	15368	799	3978	161	**144**
Bus in Rock Tunnel	29345	755	6793	126	**78**
Car over camera	17700	147	7236	120	**93**
Cooking	424	1.9	188	2.4	**1.7**
Excavators river cross	39828	3933	28654	400	**317**
Fire Domino	1262	8.5	539	7.4	**4.9**
Jumps	382	5.5	157	2.1	**1.2**
Kids playing in leaves	14497	637	11931	**173**	272
Paintball	5497	1662	3479	578	**559**
Paluma jump	5271	119	1863	41	**2**
Playing ball	5124	155	1905	30	**13**
Playing on water slide	4748	133	1946	26	**12**
Saving dolphins	–	924	13889	608	**474**
Scuba	7463	138	5181	83	**62**
St Maarten Landing	3945	152	1334	23	**17**
Statue of Liberty	13379	163	5007	99	**88**
Valparaiso Downhill	40841	771	15079	399	**199**
Best/All	0/19	0/19	0/19	1/19	**18/19**

Bold front values represent the best performance, i.e., the lowest summary length.

proposed ASC-MCP performs the best in 11 videos (out of 19 videos) of the SumMe dataset in terms of F-measure. Furthermore, although our proposed method, DSSC-log, is an unsupervised method, it can achieve a higher average F-measure than current existing algorithms.

5.3 Computational Complexity

Next, we analyze the computational complexity of the proposed algorithm. This complexity of each iteration is in $O(Nr)$, where N is the number of frames in the video and r the dimension of a single frame. As shown in Table 3, this low complexity translates into reduced runtimes compared to SC-det and SMRS.

5.4 Discussion

Based on the experimental results, our approaches provide promising metrics that are discussed as follows:

1) The analysis sparse coding can exploit the symmetry structure for key frame extraction. The results in Table 1 shows that the analysis sparse coding based methods (our proposed algorithm and ASC-l_1) perform the best in terms of the summary length for most videos (5/19) in the SumMe dataset, as compared with the sparse coding based methods (SMRS and SC-det). The results demonstrate that the proposed ASC-MCP can extract more compressed frames.
2) The computation time of the analysis sparse coding based methods is much faster than the sparse coding based method, and the proposed ASC-MCP is the fastest among the other analysis sparse coding based methods. The results in Table 3 show that the proposed algorithm perform the best in terms of the running time for all videos (19/19) in the SumMe dataset. The results demonstrate that the proposed ASC-MCP has the lowest computation.
3) Table 4 shows that our proposed ASC-MCP performs better in 11 videos (out of 19 videos) of the SumMe dataset in terms of the F-measure in comparison with the existing approaches besides sparse coding based methods. This demonstrates that the proposed ASC-MCP can obtain accurate key frames from most videos.

Table 4. F-measure of various videos obtained by different video summary approaches. Uni.; VGG; Attn.; Intr.; DFS; the results of these existing methods were taken from Table 4 of [35].

Video name	F-measure					
	Uni.	VGG	Attn.	Intr.	DFS	ASC-MCP (ours)
Base jumping	0.247	0.062	0.194	0.121	0.077	**0.25**
Bearpark climbing	0.225	0.134	0.227	0.118	0.178	**0.25**
Bike Polo	0.190	0.069	0.076	**0.356**	0.235	0.21
Bus in Rock Tunnel	0.114	0.120	0.112	0.135	0.151	**0.23**
Car over camera	0.245	0.048	0.201	**0.372**	0.132	0.20
Cooking	0.076	0.285	0.118	0.321	**0.329**	0.27
Excavators river cross	0.107	0.030	0.041	0.189	0.134	**0.22**
Fire Domino	0.103	0.124	0.252	0.130	0.022	**0.28**
Jumps	0.054	0.000	0.243	**0.427**	0.015	0.26
Kids playing in leaves	0.051	0.243	0.084	0.089	**0.278**	0.24
Paintball	0.071	0.270	0.281	0.320	0.274	**0.32**
Paluma jump	0.058	0.056	0.028	0.181	**0.428**	0.23
Playing ball	0.123	0.127	0.140	0.174	0.194	**0.24**
Playing on water slide	0.075	0.092	0.124	0.200	0.183	**0.22**
Saving dolphins	0.146	0.103	0.154	0.145	0.121	**0.25**
Scuba	0.070	0.160	0.200	0.184	0.154	**0.23**
St Maarten Landing	0.152	0.153	**0.419**	0.313	0.015	0.25
Statue of Liberty	0.184	0.098	0.083	0.192	0.143	**0.20**
Valparaiso Downhill	0.083	0.110	0.231	0.242	**0.258**	0.24
Best/All	0/19	0/19	1/19	3/19	4/19	**11/19**

Bold front values represent the best performance, i.e., the highest F-measure.

6 Conclusion

We proposed a novel key frame extraction approach, based on analysis sparse coding with the MCP regularizer, which the analysis sparse coding exploits the symmetry structure of the sparse coefficient matrix and the MCP regularizer can achieve more compressed key frames. Moreover, we developed an efficient optimization scheme for sparse coding using the forward-backward algorithm. Experimental results show that the proposed approach outperforms recent algorithms for key frame extraction, achieving an accuracy on par with the state-of-the-art in addition to a reduced representation size and lower runtimes. In future work, we plan to extend the proposed ASC-MCP approach to more complex video-processing tasks, such as 3D videos.

References

1. Aharon, M., Elad, M., Bruckstein, A.: K-SVD: an algorithm for designing overcomplete dictionaries for sparse representation. IEEE Trans. Signal Process. **54**(11), 4311–4322 (2006). https://doi.org/10.1109/TSP.2006.881199
2. Antani, S., Kasturi, R., Jain, R.: A survey on the use of pattern recognition methods for abstraction, indexing and retrieval of images and video. Pattern Recogn. **35**(4), 945–965 (2002)
3. Bao, C., Hui, J., Quan, Y., Shen, Z.: Dictionary learning for sparse coding: algorithms and convergence analysis. IEEE Trans. Pattern Anal. Mach. Intell. **38**(7), 1356–1369 (2015)
4. Dang, C., Radha, H.: RPCA-KFE: key frame extraction for video using robust principal component analysis. IEEE Trans. Image Process. **24**(11), 3742–3753 (2015)
5. Ejaz, N., Mehmood, I., Wook Baik, S.: Efficient visual attention based framework for extracting key frames from videos. Sig. Process. Image Commun. **28**(1), 34–44 (2013). https://doi.org/10.1016/j.image.2012.10.002. https://www.sciencedirect.com/science/article/pii/S0923596512001828
6. Elhamifar, E., Sapiro, G., Vidal, R.: See all by looking at a few: sparse modeling for finding representative objects. In: 2012 IEEE Conference on Computer Vision and Pattern Recognition (CVPR), pp. 1600–1607. IEEE (2012)
7. Gu, X., Lu, L., Qiu, S., Zou, Q., Yang, Z.: Sentiment key frame extraction in user-generated micro-videos via low-rank and sparse representation. Neurocomputing **410**, 441–453 (2020)
8. Gygli, M., Grabner, H., Riemenschneider, H., Van Gool, L.: Creating summaries from user videos. In: Fleet, D., Pajdla, T., Schiele, B., Tuytelaars, T. (eds.) ECCV 2014. LNCS, vol. 8695, pp. 505–520. Springer, Cham (2014). https://doi.org/10.1007/978-3-319-10584-0_33
9. Nandini, H.M., Chethana, H.K., Rashmib, B.S.: Shot based keyframe extraction using edge-LBP approach. J. King Saud Univ. - Comput. Inf. Sci. **34**(7), 4537–4545 (2020)
10. Hu, W., et al.: Multi-perspective cost-sensitive context-aware multi-instance sparse coding and its application to sensitive video recognition. IEEE Trans. Multimedia **18**(1), 76–89 (2015)
11. Huang, C., Wang, H.: Novel key-frames selection framework for comprehensive video summarization. IEEE Trans. Circ. Syst. Video Technol. **30**(2), 577-589 (2019)
12. Jeong, D., Yoo, H.J., Cho, N.I.: A static video summarization method based on the sparse coding of features and representativeness of frames. EURASIP J. Image Video Process. **2017**(1), 1–14 (2016). https://doi.org/10.1186/s13640-016-0122-9
13. Ji, Z., Ma, Y., Pang, Y., Li, X.: Query-aware sparse coding for multi-video summarization. Information Sci. **478**, 152–166 (2017)
14. Ju, S.X., Black, M.J., Minneman, S., Kimber, D.: Analysis of gesture and action in technical talks for video indexing. In: IEEE Computer Society Conference on Computer Vision & Pattern Recognition (2002)
15. Kumar, M., Loui, A.C.: Key frame extraction from consumer videos using sparse representation. In: IEEE International Conference on Image Processing (2011)
16. Lee, H., Battle, A., Raina, R., Ng, A.Y.: Efficient sparse coding algorithms. In Adv. NIPS **19**, 801–808 (2007)
17. Li, H., Chen, G.: Segment-based stereo matching using graph cuts. In: Computer Vision and Pattern Recognition (2004)

18. Li, N., Sun, B., Yu, J.: A weighted sparse coding framework for saliency detection. In: Computer Vision & Pattern Recognition (2015)
19. Li, Y., Kanemura, A., Asoh, H., Miyanishi, T., Kawanabe, M.: Extracting key frames from first-person videos in the common space of multiple sensors. In: IEEE International Conference on Image Processing, ICIP, pp. 3993–3997 (2017)
20. Li, Y., Kanemura, A., Asoh, H., Miyanishi, T., Kawanabe, M.: Key frame extraction from first-person video with multi-sensor integration. In: IEEE International Conference on Multimedia and Expo, ICME, pp. 1303–1308 (2017)
21. Li, Y., Tan, B., Kanemura, A., Ding, S., Chen, W.: Analysis sparse representation for nonnegative signals based on determinant measure by DC programming. Complexity **2018**, 1–12 (2018)
22. Li, Y., Shi, J., Lin, D.: Low-latency video semantic segmentation. In: IEEE Conference on Computer Vision and Pattern Recognition, CVPR, pp. 5997–6005 (2018)
23. Mademlis, I., Tefas, A., Pitas, I.: Regularized SVD-based video frame saliency for unsupervised activity video summarization. In: 2018 IEEE International Conference on Acoustics, Speech and Signal Processing (ICASSP), pp. 2691–2695. IEEE (2018)
24. Martin, D., Fowlkes, C., Tal, D., Malik, J.: A database of human segmented natural images and its application to evaluating segmentation algorithms and measuring ecological statistics. In: IEEE International Conference on Computer Vision (2002)
25. Meng, Y., Dai, D., Shen, L., Gool, L.V.: Latent dictionary learning for sparse representation based classification. In: IEEE Conference on Computer Vision & Pattern Recognition (2014)
26. Money, A.G., Agius, H.: Video summarisation: a conceptual framework and survey of the state of the art. J. Vis. Commun. Image Represent. **19**(2), 121–143 (2008)
27. Nam, S., Davies, M.E., Elad, M., Gribonval, R.: The cosparse analysis model and algorithms. Appl. Comput. Harmonic Anal. **34**(1), 30–56 (2013)
28. Nasreen, A., Shobha, G.: Key frame extraction from videos-a survey. Int. J. Comput. Sci. Commun. Netw. **3**(3), 194 (2013)
29. Otani, M., Nakashima, Y., Rahtu, E., Heikkilä, J., Yokoya, N.: Video summarization using deep semantic features. In: Asian Conference on Computer Vision, pp. 361–377 (2016)
30. Phan, S., et al.: Multimedia event detection using segment-based approach for motion feature. J. Sign. Process. Syst. **74**(1), 19–31 (2013). https://doi.org/10.1007/s11265-013-0825-4
31. Selesnick, I.: Sparse regularization via convex analysis. IEEE Trans. Signal Process. **65**(17), 4481–4494 (2017)
32. Simonyan, K., Zisserman, A.: Very deep convolutional networks for large-scale image recognition. Computer Science (2014)
33. Simsek, M., Polat, E.: Performance evaluation of pan-sharpening and dictionary learning methods for sparse representation of hyperspectral super-resolution. SIViP **15**(6), 1099–1106 (2021). https://doi.org/10.1007/s11760-020-01836-8
34. Tan, B., Li, Y., Zhao, H., Li, X., Ding, S.: A novel dictionary learning method for sparse representation with nonconvex regularizations. Neurocomputing **417**, 128–141 (2020)
35. Tan, B., Li, Y., Ding, S., Paik, I., Kanemura, A.: DC programming for solving a sparse modeling problem of video key frame extraction. Digit. Sign. Process. **83**, 214–222 (2018)
36. Wang, S., Chen, X., Dai, W., Selesnick, I.W., Cai, G., Benjamin, C.: Vector minimax concave penalty for sparse representation. Digit. Sign. Process. **83**, 165–179 (2018)

37. Yaghoobi, M., Nam, S., Gribonval, R., Davies, M.E.: Constrained overcomplete analysis operator learning for cosparse signal modelling. IEEE Trans. Signal Process. **61**(9), 2341–2355 (2013)
38. Zhang, C.H.: Nearly unbiased variable selection under minimax concave penalty. Ann. Stat. **38**(2), 894–942 (2010)
39. Zhao, B., Li, F., Xing, E.P.: Online detection of unusual events in videos via dynamic sparse coding. In: Computer Vision & Pattern Recognition (2011)

Data Reconstruction from Gradient Updates in Federated Learning

Xiaoxue Zhang[1], Junhao Li[1], Jianjie Zhang[1], Jijie Yan[1], Enmin Zhu[1], and Kongyang Chen[2,3,4](✉)

[1] School of Computer Science and Cyber Engineering, Guangzhou University, Guangzhou, China

[2] Institute of Artificial Intelligence and Blockchain, Guangzhou University, Guangzhou, China

kychen@gzhu.edu.cn

[3] Pazhou Lab, Guangzhou, China

[4] Jiangsu Key Laboratory of Media Design and Software Technology, Jiangnan University, Wuxi, China

Abstract. Federated learning has become an emerging technology to protect data privacy in the distributed learning area, by keeping each client user's data locally. However, recent work shows that client users' data might still be stolen (or reconstructed) directly from gradient updates. After exploring the attack and defense techniques of these data reconstruction methods, we discover that the attacker cannot steal the victim's data unless it has prior knowledge about the victim's data size. Thus, the attacker can hardly reconstruct any useful information without these prior knowledge. In this paper, we provide a novel data reconstruction method to obtain a high-dimensional compressed data from the gradient updates, without these prior knowledge. Experiment results show that our reconstructed data can be used to attack the model, with high attack accuracy.

Keywords: Federated learning · Data reconstruction · Gradient

1 Introduction

In recent years, the federated machine learning approach serves as an important approach to protect user privacy by keeping each user's data locally. To increase the data privacy, Federated learning is usually applied to keep user's data locally, only transmitting the model parameters to a centralized server for model aggregation [1,2,6]. Due to its excellent data privacy protection, Federated learning has been widely used in many vertical applications [4,5,9,13]. For example, in the medical field, Sui et al. [8] et al. proposed a method based on knowledge distillation that can reduce communication consumption to train the central model. Wang et al. [11] proposed a framework that combines GAN and multi-task discriminator, which can realize very effective user-level privacy leakage. So et al. [7] proposed a fully-decentralized framework that can encode a

Y. Xu et al. (Eds.): ML4CS 2022, LNCS 13655, pp. 586–596, 2023.
https://doi.org/10.1007/978-3-031-20096-0_44

single data securely, thereby simultaneously achieving achievements scalability and privacy protection. Kang et al. [12] proposed a new framework based on the concept of differential privacy (DP), which can effectively prevent information leakage. Filip et al. [3] proposed an optimization formula for training a joint learning model to seek a clear trade-off between the traditional global model and the local model.

However, there are still many security threats in Federally learning. Zhu et al. [14] proposed that an attack can steal the victim's local data with the gradient updates only, which confirms that the attack results are almost 100% the same with the victim's local data. By exploiting the limit of such data leakage attack, we find several drawbacks. That is to say, this method also has many limitations. First, the attacker cannot steal all the victim's local data for training, unless the victim's local data is very small. Second, the attacker needs to know the exact size of the victim's local data, which is almost impossible in reality.

To deal with the drawbacks of existing data leakage in Federated learning, we aim to provide a novel data reconstruction method without these prior knowledge such as the size of the victim's local data. Generally, we will reconstruct a high-dimensional compressed data from the gradient updates, which is equivalent to the victim's local data.

In this paper, we make the following contributions: 1) we propose a new data reconstruction method with no prior knowledge; 2) experiment results show that our reconstructed data can be used to attack the model, with high attack accuracy.

2 Motivation

In recent years, the federated machine learning approach has become increasingly popular as a solution to address the data privacy problem. In federated learning, many individual users obtain an initial model and model parameters from a server, and train its model locally using its local data. After that, the server will choose several users, and ask them to upload their parameter updates (e.g., gradients). In the server, these parameter updates from individual users are aggregated into global parameters to generate an updated global model. After several iterations among the server and participant users, the federated learning will achieve a stable global model. The intuition of federated learning is that the participant users only upload their model parameter updates, rather than their original individual data. In other words, the original data from individual users are not exposed to any participant users as well as the server. Thus, the federated learning serves as an excellent distributed machine learning method to avoid local data leakage and protect data privacy.

However, recent research found that the federated learning will also lead to data leakage in some cases. For example, the original data can be recovered only with the gradient updates in [14]. When the victim puts an image into the model, it obtains an updated gradient W_0 as well as the model's discriminant error. With this gradient, the attacker locally generates a noisy image according to the victim's data size. This noisy image is also marked with a randomly label, which is also considered as an initial value of the final reconstructed data. After that, the victim could obtain an updated gradient W_1 from the noisy image. The variance between the two gradients is determined as:

$$D = ||W_0 - W_1||^2 \tag{1}$$

Finally, the noise data and noise labels are updated using the derivative.

This method can steal the victim's data almost indiscriminately, but it still has some drawbacks. First, it works only for a small amount of data reconstruction (e.g., 1 to 8 images), that is to say, it fails to steal a large amount of data effectively. Second, the size of the victim's training data should be known in advance. For example, if the victim uses 10000 images to train the model to get a gradient, the attack should also set the size of the noise data to 10000. From a practical point of view, such prior knowledge is almost impossible to acquire.

Due to the above drawbacks, we propose a new method to reconstruct a meaningful high-dimensional compressed data from the victim's gradient even without knowing the number of images, which is equivalent to the original data in some sense. Our reconstructed data also has some advantages compared with distilled data. Data distillation is proposed by Wang et al. [10]. This method is to transfer knowledge from a large training dataset into a small distilled dataset by keeping a fixed model. The distillation data performs far better than the original one. Specifically, using distillation data on the network only requires a few gradient descent steps to achieve the training effect of the original dataset on the network. However, the acquisition of distillation data needs to access to the original data, which is difficult to achieve in a federal learning attack. In contrast, our method does not access to the original data during acquisition process. Because we are able to recover it by ourselves, only requiring the victim's gradients and the structure of central model. Moreover, our reconstructed data is almost equivalent to the original one, and it needs no overfitting condition in training process.

3 Our Approach

The goal of our attack method is to recover the data, which is extremely closed to the original one via shared gradients after model training. As we have introduced, the client users send gradients to the central model in federated learning. Since the up-loaded information can be easily leaked during transmission, it is an opportunity for the malicious user to reconstruct private data with the help of stolen gradients. First, noisy images are generated randomly. Then, we make them gradually similar to the training inputs of the victim users by simulating the victims' gradients that are stolen in advance. The whole private data can be recovered until convergence. Our method framework is shown in Fig. 1, and our algorithm for deep reconstruction from gradients is listed in Algorithm 1.

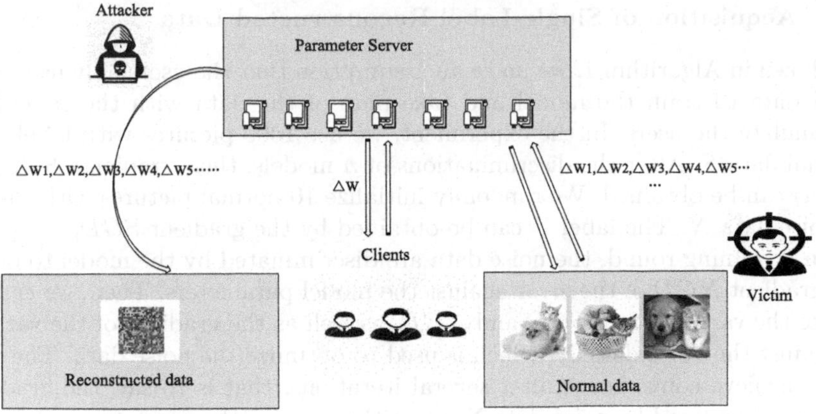

Fig. 1. The Framework of Our Attack Method.

3.1 Label Selection for Reconstructed Data

Considering the classification tasks, it is supposed to mark each training input with a label before model training. However, there are some obstacles for us to get the ground truth labels because of having no access to the original data of victims. To address this problem, we perform label reconstruction algorithm before recovering inputs, which is proposed by [14] et al., helping us to set the label of single-label samples. For mixed-label data, we collect all the possible labels in the dataset, and run the experiments for several times.

Algorithm 1. Data Reconstruction from Gradients Updates in Federated Learning (DRGU)

Input: S: Normal data, N: Reconstructed data, T: training rounds, $F(X;W)$: Differentiable learning model, W: parameters weights, SGD: The gradients calculated by normal data, NGD: the gradients calculated by reconstructed data, L: the loss of SGD and NGD, η: Learning rate.

Output: Reconstructed data N

```
Initialize N, W randomly
for i ← 1 to n do
    SGD_i ← ∂F(S, W_i)/∂W_i        ▷ Compute the gradient of normal data.
end for
for each training round t ← 1 to T do
    for i ← 1 to n do
        NGD_i ← ∂F(N, W_i)/∂W_i    ▷ Compute the gradient of reconstructed data.
        L_i = ||SGD_i − NGD_i||^2   ▷ Calculate the loss of SGD_i and NGD_i
        N = N − η∇_N L_i            ▷ Update reconstructed data.
    end for
end for
```

3.2 Acquisition of Single-Label Reconstructed Data

As shown in Algorithm 1, we make an assumption that the users only use single-label data to train the model and take part of the data with the same label to simulate the users. In the experiment, we use 1000 pictures with label $'7'$ as normal data S. After the discriminations of n models, their gradients $SGD_i(i \in 1 \sim n)$ can be obtained. We randomly initialize 10 normal pictures with the size of noise data N. The label Y can be obtained by the gradient SGD_i.

In a training round, the noise data are discriminated by the model to obtain the gradient NGD of the error against the model parameters. Then, we can calculate the variance L of SGD and NGD, as well as the gradient of the variance L against the noise data N, which is used to optimize the noise data. The algorithm achieve convergence after several iterations, that is to say, the gradients that are calculated by noise data N are as the same as the ones of nomal data S.

3.3 Acquisition of Mixed-Label Reconstruction Data

It is common that the local data of client users contains multiple categories in reality, which hinders us from stealing each data completely. Unlike the compression of single-label data, whose corresponding ground truth labels can be obtained via gradients, the labels of data that mixed categories can not be leaked by the same method directly. Therefore, we need to make some changes in the compression of mixed-label data. For example in MNIST dataset, we choose the label Y of the noisy data N, which is set as $[0, 1, 2, 3, 4, 5, 6, 7, 8, 9]$. If the given label is not accurate enough, for example a label with $[7, 7, 7, 7, 7, 7, 7, 7, 7, 7, 7, 7, 7, 7, 7]$, the variance between SGD and NGD can hardly be reduced effectively after many iterations.

4 Experiment

We present our experimental results on the MNIST dataset. The reconstructed data can be used for backdoor attack or local model training. In our experiment, we evaluate the attack performance and training performance of the reconstructed data. We also use the reconstructed data to conduct the training experiments about Non-IID data. In our experiment, we randomly select 1000 pictures with label 7 and 3000 pictures with various labels in the whole MNIST dataset as the test set of model training. We call them *data1* and *data2* for short, respectively.

4.1 Single-label Data Reconstruction

As shown in Fig. 2, there are some data samples for label '7' in MNIST dataset.

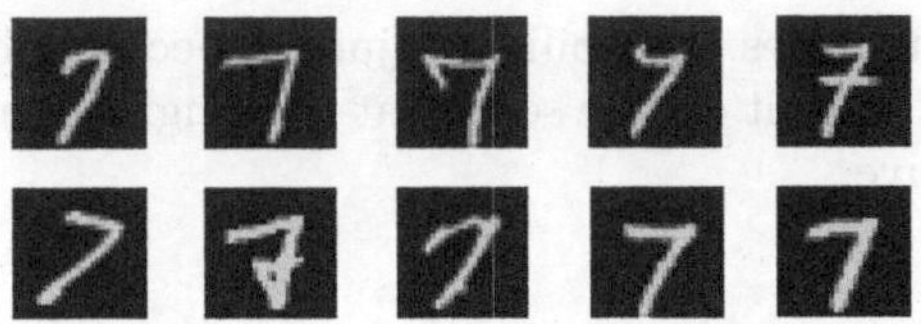

Fig. 2. The Original Data Samples.

Single-label reconstructed data (with label '7') is shown in Fig. 3. From the visualization of the two images, the reconstructed images roughly show the digital outline of the real data from the appearance, which means that the reconstructed data has learned the data characteristics of the original data.

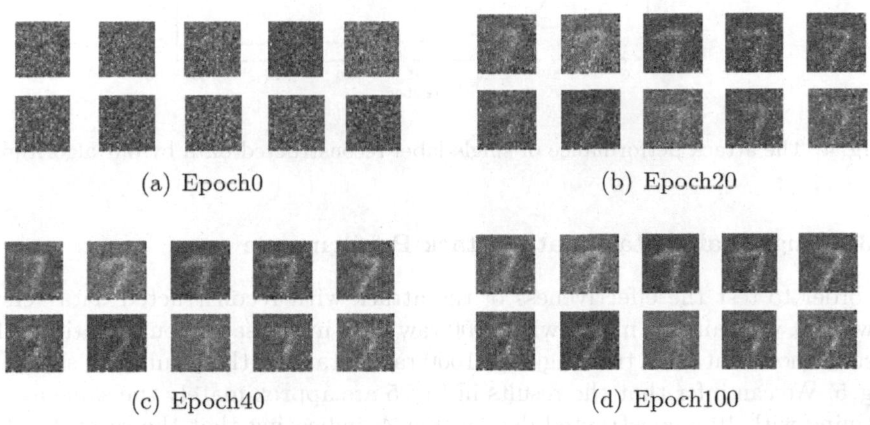

(a) Epoch0 (b) Epoch20 (c) Epoch40 (d) Epoch100

Fig. 3. Single-label reconstructed data.

In the experiment, 1000 images labeled '7' were randomly selected from the whole MNIST dataset. These images are compressed into 10 reconstructed data with label '7', and getting much clearer after several iterations.

4.2 Single Label Reconstructed Data Attack Performance

In the attack on the single-label reconstructed data, we first import the trained model, which achieves an original accuracy of about 98% for the MNIST dataset and an accuracy of about 98% for a specific label '7'. We then apply the targeted attack on this model using the reconstructed data.

In our experiments, we change the label of the reconstructed data with label '7' to '2', and then the learning rate is adjusted to the size of the value when training the model with the original data for 30 rounds. The results are shown in Fig. 4. The accuracy of the model dropped to 0% for the data with label '7' at the end of the training and was around 76% for the overall data. From the results, the model loses the ability to judge specific labels after the attack process is completed, and it can be seen that the single-label reconstructed data is extremely aggressive.

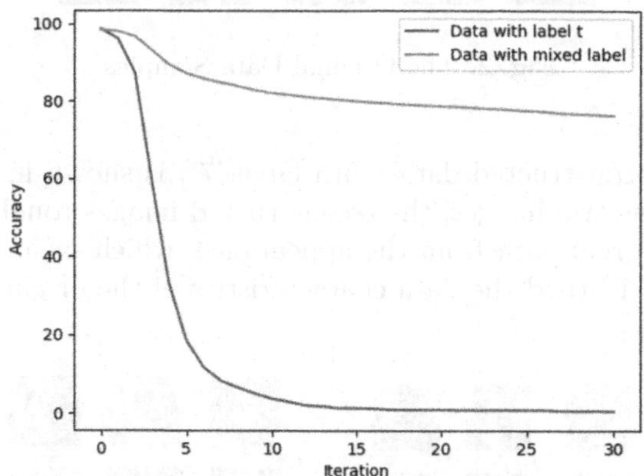

Fig. 4. The attack performance of single-label reconstructed data by our algorithm.

4.3 Single Label Raw Data Attack Performance

In order to test the effectiveness of the attack with reconstructed data versus raw data, we train the model with 1000 raw data in the same configuration. The results show that after training with 1000 raw data, and the results are shown in Fig. 5. We can infer that the results in Fig. 5 are approximately the same as the training with 10 reconstructed data in Fig. 4, indicating that the reconstructed data has the same effect as the raw data in attacking the central server model.

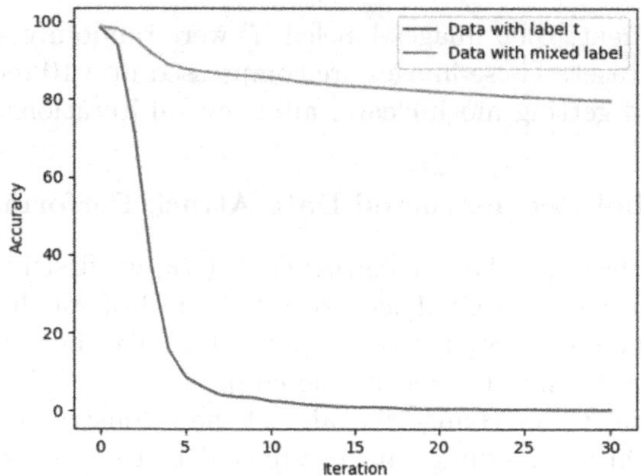

Fig. 5. The attack performance of single-label raw data.

4.4 Single Label Noise Attack Performance

To highlight the attack performance of our reconstructed data, we use the same method. We use noise data instead of reconstructed data to attack the model. The results are shown in Fig. 6. At the beginning, the accuracy rate of model for data1 and data2 are 98% and 98%, respectively. We randomly generated 10 noise images, labeled '2' and then trained the model for 30 rounds . The accuracy rate of MNIST dataset is 91% and that of specific label data is 64%. The results show that the attack using noisy data is not as powerful as that of reconstructed data.

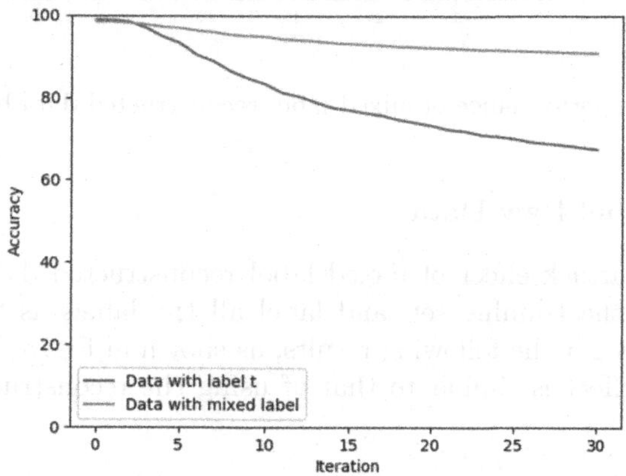

Fig. 6. The attack performance of single-label raw data with noises.

4.5 Mixed Labels Reconstruction Data

Before using mixed Labels reconstruct data to attack the model, the original accuracy rate of the model is about 98% for MNIST dataset and 98% for specific label '7'. In this part, we change the labels of the reconstructed data from $[0, 1, 2, 3, 4, 5, 6, 7, 8, 9]$ to $[2, 2, 2, 2, 2, 2, 2, 2, 2, 2]$. After the training process, The results are shown in Fig. 7. The accuracy rate of the model for the data1 with label '7' drops to about 8%, and the accuracy rate for the data2 drops to 15%. The results show that the model almost loses the ability to judge the whole MNIST dataset which means that the mixed labels reconstructed data also has a strong attack performance.

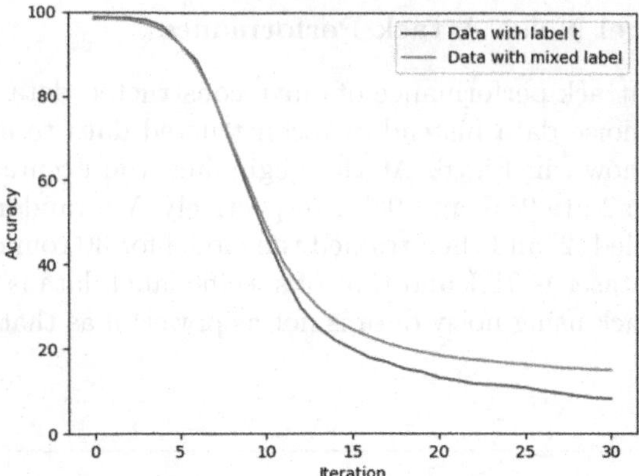

Fig. 7. The attack performance of mixed-label reconstructed data by our algorithm.

4.6 Mixed Label Raw Data

To compare the attack effect of mixed label reconstructed data, we take 1000 random data as the training set, and label all the labels as '2' to attack the model, and finally get the following results, as shown in Fig. 8. The results show that the attack effect is similar to that of using the reconstructed data attack model.

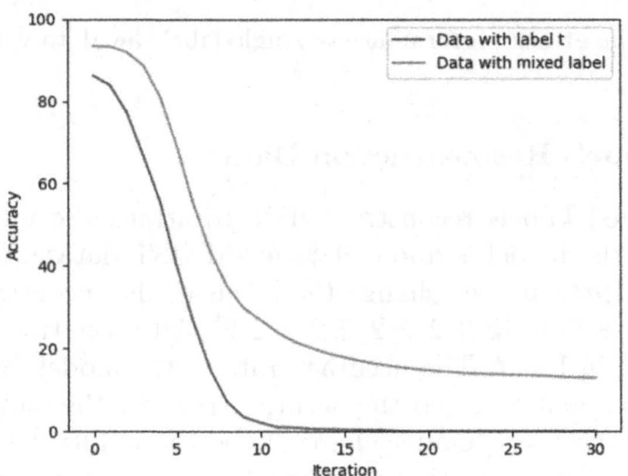

Fig. 8. The attack performance of mixed-label raw data.

4.7 Mixed Label Noise Data

We verified the attack effect of noisy data under the same specification as that for mixed-labels reconstructed data, which is to use 1 noisy data for each label, a total of 10 data to attack the model. The results are shown in Fig. 9. The accuracy of the original model on specific label and total data is around 98%. After the attack, the accuracy of the model on the overall data was around 85%. It can be seen that the attack effect of using noise data under the same specification is not ideal.

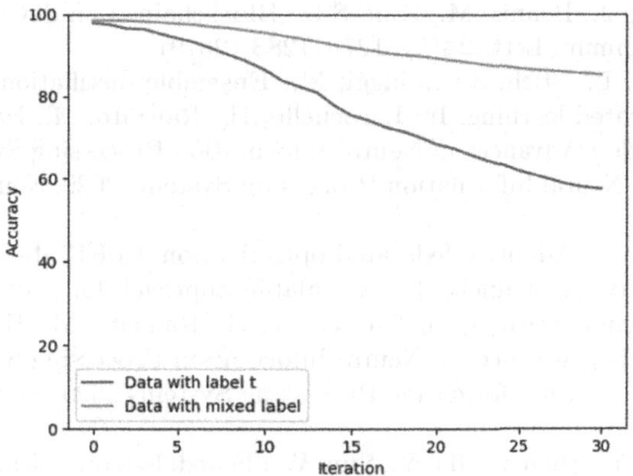

Fig. 9. The attack performance of mixed-label raw data with noises.

5 Conclusion and Future Work

In this paper, we further exploit the idea of data leakage form gradients in Federated learning, and provide an efficient solution when the attacker doesn't have prior knowledge about the victim, such as the size of the training set. We have evaluated our methods and experiment results show that our reconstructed data fits well with the original data. We believe that our method will contribute to the privacy enhanced computing area with more detailed data leakage phenomenon.

Acknowledgments. This work is supported by National Natural Science Foundation of China (No. 61802383), Research Project of Pazhou Lab for Excellent Young Scholars (No. PZL2021KF0024), Guangzhou Basic and Applied Basic Research Foundation (No. 202201010330, No. 202201020162), Guangdong Philosophy and Social Science Planning Project (No. GD19YYJ02), Research on the Supporting Technologies of the Metaverse in Cultural Media (No. PT252022039), Jiangsu Key Laboratory of Media Design and Software Technology (No. 21ST0202).

References

1. Albaseer, A., Ciftler, B.S., Abdallah, M.M., Al-Fuqaha, A.I.: Exploiting unlabeled data in smart cities using federated edge learning. In: 16th International Wireless Communications and Mobile Computing Conference, IWCMC 2020, Limassol, Cyprus, pp. 1666–1671. IEEE (2020)

2. Hamer, J., Mohri, M., Suresh, A.T.: FedBoost: a communication-efficient algorithm for federated learning. In: III, H.D., Singh, A. (eds.) Proceedings of the 37th International Conference on Machine Learning. Proceedings of Machine Learning Research, vol. 119, pp. 3973–3983. PMLR (2020)
3. Hanzely, F., Richtárik, P.: Federated learning of a mixture of global and local models. CoRR abs/2002.05516 (2020)
4. Kim, H., Park, J., Bennis, M., Kim, S.L.: Blockchained on-device federated learning. IEEE Commun. Lett. **24**(6), 1279–1283 (2019)
5. Lin, T., Kong, L., Stich, S.U., Jaggi, M.: Ensemble distillation for robust model fusion in federated learning. In: Larochelle, H., Ranzato, M., Hadsell, R., Balcan, M., Lin, H. (eds.) Advances in Neural Information Processing Systems 33: Annual Conference on Neural Information Processing Systems 2020, NeurIPS 2020, virtual (2020)
6. Reddi, S.J., et al.: Adaptive federated optimization. CoRR abs/2003.00295 (2020)
7. So, J., Güler, B., Avestimehr, S.: A scalable approach for privacy-preserving collaborative machine learning. In: Larochelle, H., Ranzato, M., Hadsell, R., Balcan, M., Lin, H. (eds.) Advances in Neural Information Processing Systems 33: Annual Conference on Neural Information Processing Systems 2020, NeurIPS 2020, virtual (2020)
8. Sui, D., Chen, Y., Zhao, J., Jia, Y., Sun, W.: Feded: federated learning via ensemble distillation for medical relation extraction. In: Proceedings of the 2020 Conference on Empirical Methods in Natural Language Processing (EMNLP) (2020)
9. Wang, H., Yurochkin, M., Sun, Y., Papailiopoulos, D.S., Khazaeni, Y.: Federated learning with matched averaging. CoRR abs/2002.06440 (2020)
10. Wang, T., Zhu, J., Torralba, A., Efros, A.A.: Dataset distillation. CoRR abs/1811.10959 (2018)
11. Wang, Z., Song, M., Zhang, Z., Song, Y., Wang, Q., Qi, H.: Beyond inferring class representatives: user-level privacy leakage from federated learning. CoRR abs/1812.00535 (2018)
12. Wei, K., et al.: Federated learning with differential privacy: algorithms and performance analysis. IEEE Trans. Inf. Forensics Secur. **15**, 3454–3469 (2020)
13. Xie, M., Long, G., Shen, T., Zhou, T., Wang, X., Jiang, J.: Multi-center federated learning. CoRR abs/2005.01026 (2020)
14. Zhu, L., Han, S.: Deep leakage from gradients. In: Yang, Q., Fan, L., Yu, H. (eds.) Federated Learning. LNCS (LNAI), vol. 12500, pp. 17–31. Springer, Cham (2020). https://doi.org/10.1007/978-3-030-63076-8_2

Natural Backdoor Attacks on Speech Recognition Models

Jinwen Xin, Xixiang Lyu(✉), and Jing Ma

School of Cyber Engineering, Xidian University, Xian, China
xxlv@mail.xidian.edu.cn

Abstract. With the rapid development of deep learning, its vulnerability has gradually emerged in recent years. This work focuses on backdoor attacks on speech recognition systems. We adopt sounds that are ordinary in nature or in our daily life as triggers for natural backdoor attacks. We conduct experiments on two datasets and three models to validate the performance of natural backdoor attacks and explore the effects of poisoning rate, trigger duration and blend ratio on the performance of natural backdoor attacks. Our results show that natural backdoor attacks have a high attack success rate without compromising model performance on benign samples, even with short or low-amplitude triggers. It requires only 5% of poisoned samples to achieve a near 100% attack success rate. In addition, the backdoor will be automatically activated by the corresponding sound in nature, which is not easy to be detected and will bring severer harm.

Keywords: Deep learning · Backdoor attacks · Speech recognition · Natural trigger

1 Introduction

Over the past years, with the rapid development of deep learning, human beings have entered the era of AI. Deep learning systems have become prevalent in various fields, including face recognition [1,2], object detection [3], machine translation [4] and speech recognition [5]. However, with the implementation of various deep learning applications, the vulnerability of deep neural networks (DNNs) has gradually emerged. For example, the adversary can fool the DNNs with adversarial examples [6,7].

Compared with adversarial attacks, which mainly occur in the inference stage of DNNs, backdoor attacks occur in the training stage, which needs large datasets and powerful computing resources. To reduce costs, users may adopt third-party datasets and third-party platforms, or directly adopt models provided by third parties [8]. Meanwhile, transfer learning [9] and federated learning [10] are becoming more prevalent. In these untrustworthy scenarios, backdoor attacks can pose a huge threat to the security of DNNs. In general, backdoor attacks work by implanting a backdoor in DNNs during the training stage so that the infected

Y. Xu et al. (Eds.): ML4CS 2022, LNCS 13655, pp. 597–610, 2023.
https://doi.org/10.1007/978-3-031-20096-0_45

DNNs perform well on benign samples, whereas their predictions will be maliciously changed if the buried backdoor is activated by the preset trigger [8].

Speech recognition (SR) plays a key role in many fields, such as voice input, automatic drive and human-computer interaction. At present, most of the researches on backdoor attacks focus on the field of computer vision (CV), but few on SR. However, DNNs of SR are easily disturbed by the noise, which makes them more vulnerable to backdoor attacks. For some security-sensitive applications, such as voice commands in autonomous driving, the existence of backdoor will pose a huge threat. So backdoor attacks on SR deserve attention.

We focus on the design of triggers for backdoor attacks. To the best of our knowledge, there are mainly two types of triggers used in the existing backdoor attacks on SR. One is injecting random noise as a trigger into raw audio samples [11–13], and the other is injecting a sound wave of a certain frequency into the original audio [14], which can be an ultrasonic pulse that humans cannot hear [15]. Almost all existing backdoor attack methods for SR adopt random or meaningless noise as triggers. In order to activate the backdoor in the inference stage, the above works require the adversary to play the sound wave corresponding to the trigger, which undoubtedly increases the risk of being detected.

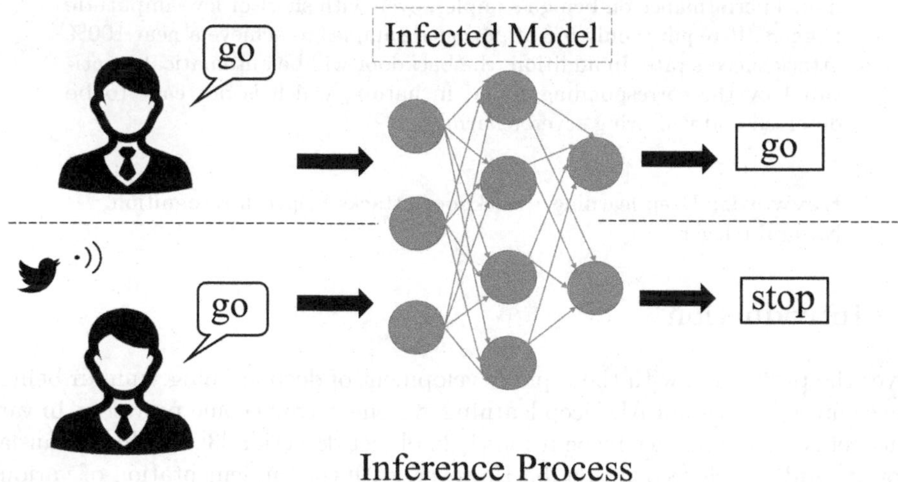

Fig. 1. A natural backdoor attack on SR models.

In this work, we propose to adopt sounds that exist in nature or in our daily life as natural triggers, such as sound of rain, whistle and bird call, to implement a natural backdoor attack on SR models (Fig. 1). Compared with the current methods, our method has the following advantages: Firstly, triggers are hidden. Sounds in nature or in our daily life do not attract human attention because these sounds are ordinary. And our experiments show that few poisoning samples can achieve a high attack success rate, so natural backdoor attacks are covert.

Secondly, it is easier to activate the backdoor in SR models during the inference phase. Our method can cause the backdoor to be automatically activated by sounds in nature or in our daily life, which poses a greater threat to SR systems. Our main contributions are as follows:

1. We propose to adopt sounds that exist in nature or in our daily life as natural triggers to implement a natural backdoor attack on SR models, which is stealthy and harmful.
2. We verify that natural backdoor attacks are still effective in real physical scenarios and are suitable for Clean-label attacks.
3. We evaluate the performance of backdoor attacks with natural triggers and explore the influence of various factors on natural backdoor attacks.

The rest of this paper is organized as follows: Sect. 2 provides the existing works related to backdoor attacks. Implementation method of natural backdoor attacks is presented in Sect. 3. The experimental setup and results are demonstrated in Sect. 4. Our summary is arranged in Sect. 5.

2 Related Work

The concept of the backdoor attack against DNNs was first proposed by Gu et al. [16]. Recently, many works have been proposed to implement the backdoor attack on image domain [16–18]. Liu et al. utilize the natural phenomena (i.e., the reflection) common in life as the trigger to make the attack method stealthy [18]. Meanwhile, backdoor attacks on natural language processing (NLP) are also explored in [19,20]. Qi et al. proposed adopting the syntactic structure as the trigger in textual backdoor attacks, in which trigger-embedded samples are not easily detected [20].

Compared to the above works of backdoor attacks on image and NLP domains, there are relatively few works on speech recognition (SR). Initially, some studies tried to apply backdoor attack methods suitable for CV to SR [11–13]. Liu et al. implanted a backdoor in the SR model by injecting background noise to the raw audio samples and retrained the model to recognize the poisoned audio as an adversary-specified word [11]. Xu et al. conducted a backdoor attack on SR system by generating a random sound signal as a trigger [12]. Tang et al. directly stamped the trigger pattern which was initially designed for image recognition on the spectrogram of the raw audio sample [13]. Experiments in the above works have proved that SR models are also vulnerable to backdoor attacks. However, these studies are not specific to SR. For example, the method of directly stamping the trigger pattern on the spectrogram of raw audio samples is difficult to implement attacks in the inference stage. Subsequently, some backdoor attack methods for SR were proposed. Koffas et al. implemented a backdoor attack on SR systems using an inaudible trigger which was an ultrasonic pulse [15]. Zhai et al. designed a clustering-based attack scheme to implement a backdoor attack on speaker verification models [14]. Ye et al. proposed a dynamic backdoor attack method against SR models, named

DriNet [21]. In order to activate the backdoor in the inference stage, the above works require the adversary to play the sound wave corresponding to the trigger, which undoubtedly increases the risk of being detected.

In contrast, our method can cause the backdoor to be automatically activated by sounds in nature or in our daily life, which poses serious threats to SR systems. Moreover, similar to random noise and the ultrasonic pulse, which are not noticed or even heard by humans, sounds in nature or in our daily life do not attract human attention as these sounds are ordinary, so our method is covert.

3 Methodology

Threat Model. The attacker follows the grey box setting: has no knowledge about the model architecture, parameters and training process of the DNNs, but can control a small number of training samples. This kind of threat exists in real scenarios, speech recognition systems often adopt the dataset collected in the form of crowdsourcing, so that malicious participants can upload malicious data to implement attacks.

Attack Target. In general, the attacker adopts data poisoning to generate an infected model. It will be predicted as the ground-truth label for benign voice input, but for voice input mixed with the preset trigger, it will be predicted as the attacker-specified label.

3.1 Poisoning-based Backdoor Attacks on Speech Recognition

DNNs for Speech Recognition. In general, define $D_{train} = \{(x_i, y_i)\}_{i=1}^{N}$ as an original training dataset for a classification task, which contain N benign audio samples, $x_i \in X$ and $y_i \in Y = \{1, 2, \cdots, K\}$, y_i is the ground-truth label of the input x_i. The target of DNNs for SR is to learn a benign model $F_\omega : X \to Y$ where X is the input space and Y is the label space. The purpose of model training is to find the optimal parameter ω to minimize the distance between the output predicted by the model F_ω and the ground-truth labels, distance is usually measured with a loss function $\mathcal{L}$. The specific calculation formula is as follows:

$$\omega^* = \arg\min_{\omega} \sum_{i=1}^{N} \mathcal{L}(F_\omega(x_i), y_i) \tag{1}$$

Formulation of Data Poisoning. In the poisoning-based backdoor attack, the poisoned samples dataset is generated by revising part of samples from the original training dataset: $D_{poison} = \{(G_t(x_i), y^*)\}_{i=1}^{P}$, where $G_t : X \to X$ indicates the attacker-specified poisoned audio sample generator with the trigger audio t, y^* is the attacker-specified target label. Then the poisoned training set $D^*_{train} = D_{train} \bigcup D_{poison}$ is used to train an infected model F^*_λ. For a test dataset $D_{test} = \{(x_i, y_i)\}_{i=1}^{M}$, infected model will correctly predict the benign test samples: $F_{\lambda}^{*}(x_t) = y_t$, but would classify the trigger-embedded inputs as the target label: $F_{\lambda}^{*}(G_t(x_i)) = y^*$. Let $\frac{P}{N}$ indicates the poisoning rate.

Measure Metrics. To measure the performance of backdoor attacks, two common metrics are introduced [8]: (1) Benign Accuracy (BA), which indicates the prediction accuracy of the infected model on benign test samples; and (2) Attack Success Rate (ASR), which indicates the proportion of trigger-embedded samples that are successfully predicted as the target label by the infected model. In general, higher ASR and BA mean better performance of backdoor attacks. Besides, a lower poisoning rate and unnoticed triggers are needed to make attacks stealthier.

3.2 Backdoor Attacks with Natural Trigger

Generation of Natural Triggers. We adopt sounds that are ordinary in nature or in our daily life as triggers. For sounds in nature, there are sound of rain, thunder, bird call and so on. For sounds in daily life, we can choose whistle, ringtone, etc. Sounds with a high probability of occurrence are easy to activate the backdoor, but are easier to detect, such as rain, whistle. Sounds with a low probability of occurrence are converse, such as thunder. We directly adopt the open source data to obtain natural trigger audio. The sampling rate of the trigger audio is the same as the original audio samples.

Embedding of Triggers. We adopt the method of Time Domain Synthesis Strategy: The audio file is loaded to get the waveform, which is a one-dimensional vector. $x = \{a_1, a_2, a_3 \cdots a_{l_1}\}$ is defined as the waveform of the original audio sample, and $\delta = \{b_1, b_2, b_3 \cdots b_{l_2}\}$ is defined as the waveform of the trigger audio. l_1 and l_2 represent the length of x and δ, respectively, $l_1 \geq l_2$. $G_\delta(x) = x^*$, define x^* as the trigger-embedded inputs. The specific calculation process is as follows.

Algorithm 1. Calculation process: $G_\delta(x) = x^*$

Require: Variables: x, δ, l_1, l_2
Ensure: Variables: x^*
for $i = 1$ to l_1 **do**
  if $i \leq l_2$ **then**
    $x_i^* \leftarrow x_i + \delta_i$
  else
    $x_i^* \leftarrow x_i$
  end if
end for

The poisoning-based backdoor attack is the most commonly adopted attack method in backdoor attacks. We adopt the poisoning-based natural backdoor attack scheme that requires three steps to implement the attack. (1) Select sounds that are ordinary in nature or in our daily life as triggers, such as sound of rain, whistle and bird call, which can be obtained from open-source audio. (2) To generate poisoning samples, we add natural triggers to the original audio samples. Here we adopt the Time Domain Synthesis Strategy. (3) Add the poisoning samples to the training dataset to train an infected model. The spectrogram of the poisoned audio samples with different natural triggers is shown in Fig. 2. Here we set the trigger duration to 0.2 s and the original audio duration to 1 s.

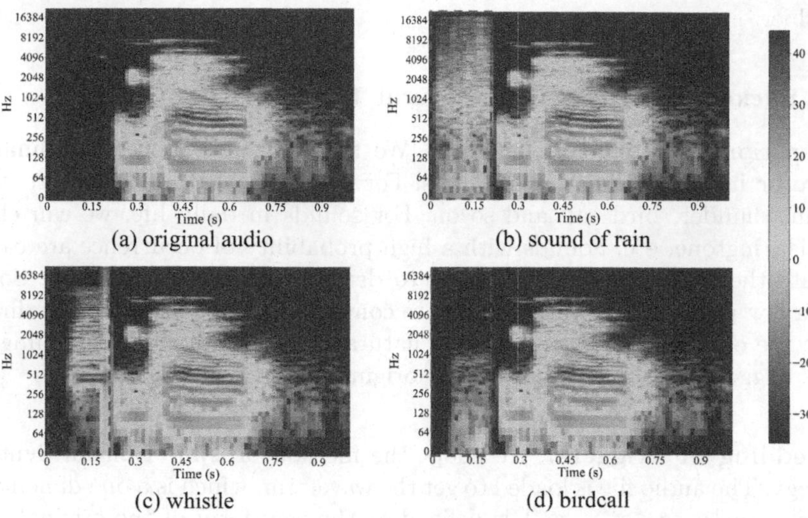

Fig. 2. Poisoned audio samples with different natural triggers: (a) original audio sample; (b) natural trigger of sound of rain; (c) natural trigger of whistle; (d) natural trigger of bird call.

4 Experiments of Natural Backdoor Attacks

4.1 Experimental Setup

Baseline Datasets and Models. We conduct experiments on two datasets for speech classification tasks. One is Speech Commands Dataset Version 2 (SCDv2) [22], also used as a benchmark dataset in other works [15,21,23]. Source audio adopts 44.1 kHz sampling rate, we selected 10 keywords in this dataset to form a 10-classes task. Since DNNs require inputs of consistent length, after discarding audio which are less than 1 s, we get 22384 audio samples. The other is Eating Sound Collection (ESC) [24], which is a 20-classes task to identify the sounds of eating different foods. Source audio use 16 kHz sampling rate. Similarly, we discard audio samples which are less than 3 s. For ESC, we adopt mini-CNN which is used as the baseline model in Ali Tianchi Competition [25]. For SCDv2, we use CNN and LSTM. The CNN was also adopted in [15,23], and the LSTM was introduced in [26]. In addition, we set the epoch to 300 and the learning rate to 0.0001.

Feature Extraction. In the training stage of DNNs, the first step is to extract features from the original input samples. Mel frequency cepstrum coefficient (MFCC) is one of the most commonly used features in SR. The specific process of extracting MFCC is shown in Fig. 3. Firstly, preprocess the raw audio, including pre-emphasis, framing and windowing. After that, the frequency domain features are obtained after the fast Fourier transform (FFT). After the Mel filter banks, logarithmic and discrete cosine transform (DCT), we get MFCCs which are the input of DNNs.

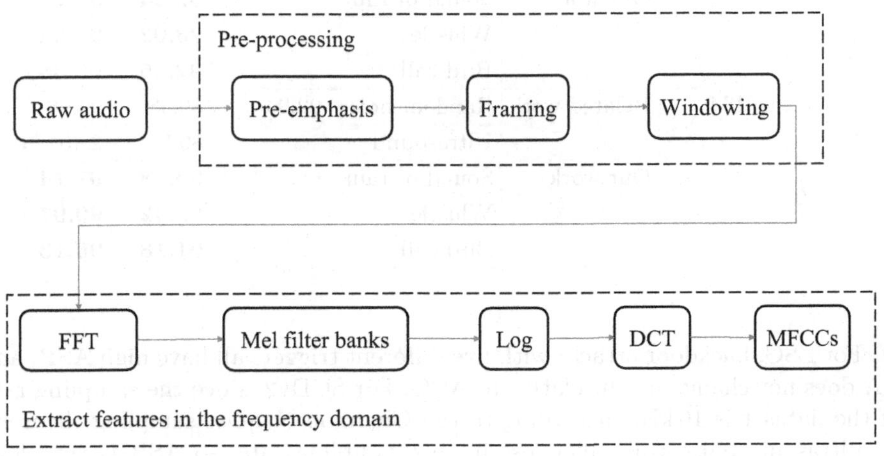

Fig. 3. Extract MFCCs as features from raw audio.

4.2 Evaluation of Natural Backdoor Attacks

We adopt three sounds that are ordinary in nature or in our daily life as natural triggers, including the sound of rain, whistle and bird call. In addition, we add random noise and ultrasound whose frequency is 21 kHz in related work [11,15] as comparative experiments. We utilize the above five triggers to conduct the poisoning-based backdoor attack. Here we set the duration of the trigger to be the same as the duration of the original audio, the poisoning rate to 5%. And we employ ASR and BA to measure the performance of backdoor attacks with different triggers. The results are shown in Table 1. ACC represents the prediction accuracy of the test dataset on the benign model.

Table 1. Evaluation of natural backdoor attacks.

Dataset	Model	Type	Trigger	ACC (%)	BA (%)	ASR (%)
ESC	mini-CNN	Related work	Random noise	97.32	96.70	100.00
			Ultrasound		96.81	99.79
		Our work	Sound of rain		**96.75**	**99.79**
			Whistle		**97.53**	**99.19**
			Bird call		**96.96**	**96.78**
SCDv2	CNN	Related work	Random noise	92.82	92.68	100.00
			Ultrasound		90.88	14.58
		Our work	Sound of rain		**92.24**	**99.22**
			Whistle		**93.02**	**99.94**
			Bird call		**92.95**	**99.38**
	LSTM	Related work	Random noise	92.94	89.98	99.98
			Ultrasound		89.54	2.45
		Our work	Sound of rain		**90.78**	**97.74**
			Whistle		**92.42**	**99.97**
			Bird call		**91.18**	**96.13**

For ESC, backdoor attacks with five different triggers all have high ASR, and BA does not change much relative to ACC. For SCDv2, since the sampling rate of the dataset is 16 kHz, according to the Channon Nyquist sampling theorem, an ultrasonic pulse will suffer loss in this sampling rate, so ASR is very low. Natural triggers have good performance, and the ASR for the CNN model has reached more than 99%. For the LSTM model, ASR can also reach more than 96%.

According to the experimental results, natural backdoor attacks have a high ASR without compromising model performance on benign samples. Compared with related works, our scheme has no restriction on the sampling rate of raw audio samples. Considering that the SCDv2 dataset is a more complicated speech recognition task compared to ESC, the following experiments are all for SCDv2. We choose CNN and LSTM as the infected models and the sound of rain as the natural trigger.

In addition, we also verify the effectiveness of our method in real physical scenarios where we use the sound of cicadas in summer as the natural trigger. We recorded human voices accompanied by sound of cicadas as poisoned training samples. The results of our experiments are shown in Fig. 4. The experimental results show that our method can still maintain a high ASR in real physical scenarios. The buried backdoor can be triggered by the sound in natural, which poses a challenge to the security of speech recognition systems.

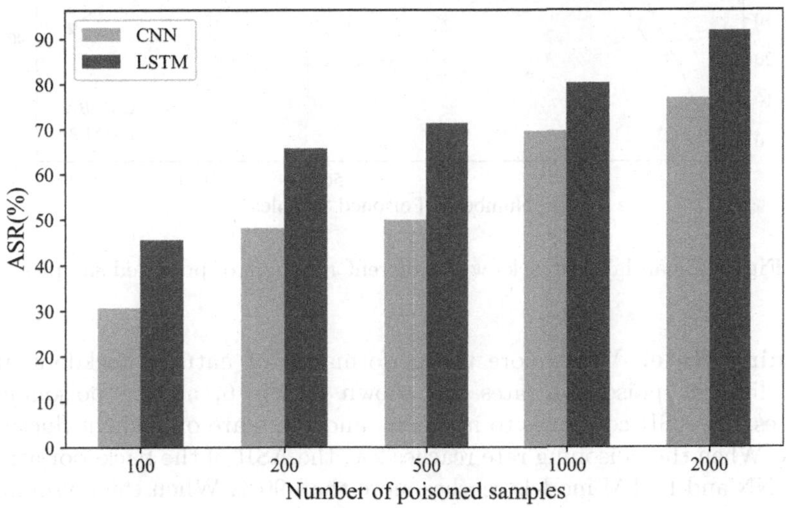

Fig. 4. A natural backdoor attack in real physical scenarios.

In our above experiments, the generation of poisoned samples requires modifying the labels of the samples, which makes the poisoned samples easily detected upon human inspection. Our attack method can also be extended to Clean-label attacks [27], which means the adversary can insert a trigger without modifying the label of the samples, thus making our attack more invisible. Our experimental results are shown in Fig. 5. Compared with Poison-label attacks, Clean-label attacks require more poisoned samples. When the poisoning rate reaches 5% (1000 poisoned samples), the ASR of the backdoor attack on CNN reaches more than 90%. Clean-label attacks on LSTM models require a higher poisoning rate.

4.3 Effect of Different Factors on ASR

We examine the impact of different factors on the performance of natural backdoor attacks, including poisoning rate, trigger duration and blend ratio.

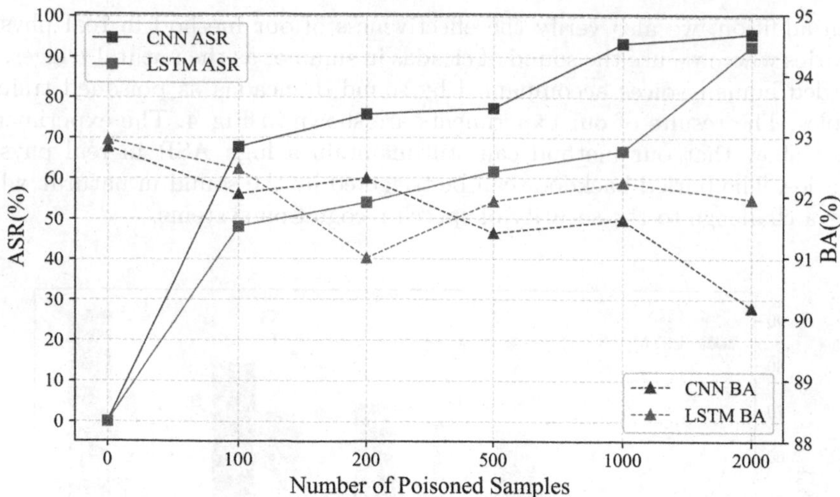

Fig. 5. Clean-label attacks with different numbers of poisoned samples.

Poisoning Rate. We explore the performance of natural backdoor attacks under different poisoning rates. As shown in Fig. 6, as the poisoning rate increases, the ASR continues to in-crease, and there are only slight fluctuations for BA. When the poisoning rate reaches 2%, the ASR of the backdoor attack on both CNN and LSTM models reaches more than 90%. When the poisoning rate reaches 5%, ASR is close to 100%. Compared to CNN, implementing attacks on LSTM requires a larger poisoning rate.

Trigger Duration. In Sect. 4.2, the duration of the trigger we set is the same as the audio samples, which is 1 s. Here we explore the effect of natural trigger duration on the performance of natural backdoor attacks. The results are shown in Fig. 7. As the trigger duration increases, the ASR continues to increase, BA has only minor changes. And the change curve of the ASR for the two infected models remains consistent. When the trigger duration reaches 0.1 s, the ASR exceeds 90%. When it reaches 0.8 s, the ASR is close to 100%.

Blend Ratio. We employ the Blended Injection Strategy [17] to generate poisoned samples. The parameters s and t represent the one-dimensional vector representation of the original audio sample and the trigger signal, respectively.

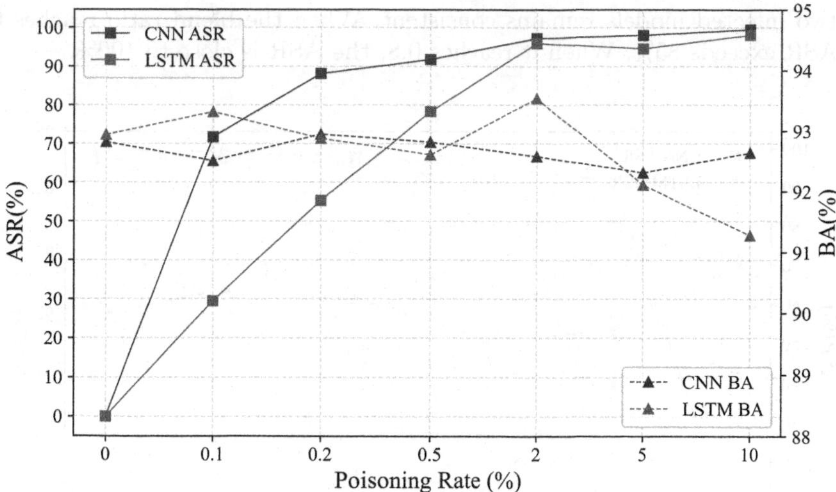

Fig. 6. The performance of natural backdoor attacks under different poisoning rates.

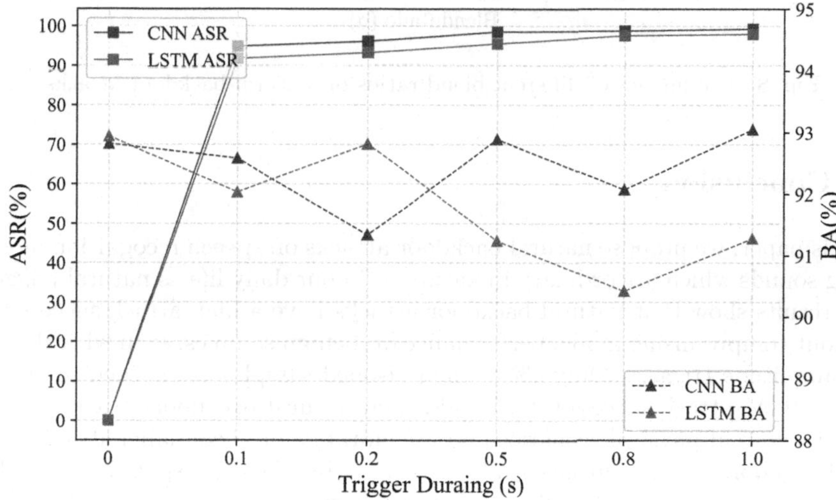

Fig. 7. The performance of natural backdoor attacks under different trigger duration.

The parameter α represents the blend ratio. The poisoned samples are generated as follows:

$$\prod_{\alpha}^{blend}(s,t) = s + \alpha \cdot t \qquad (2)$$

We explore the impact of different blend ratios on natural backdoor attacks, the result is shown in Fig. 8. As the blend ratio increases, the ASR continues to increase, and BA has only minor changes. And the change curve of the ASR for the two infected models remains consistent. When the blend ratio reaches 0.1, the ASR exceeds 85%. When it reaches 0.8, the ASR is close to 100%.

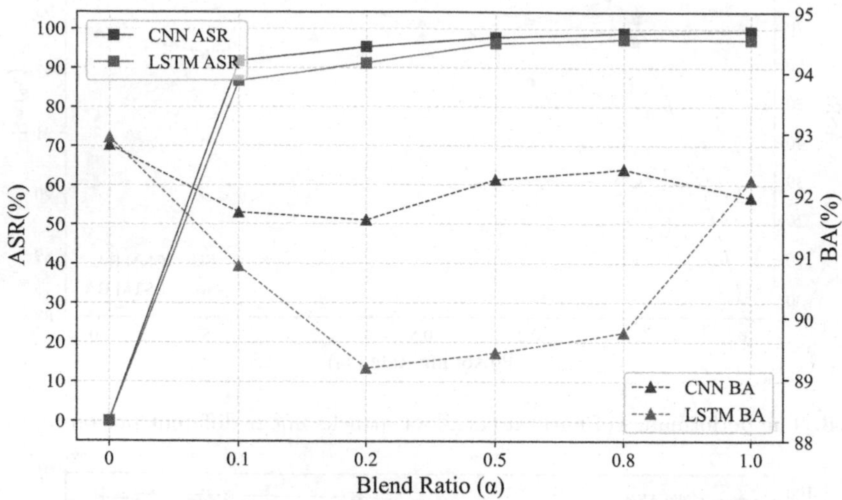

Fig. 8. The impact of different blend ratios on natural backdoor attacks.

5 Conclusion

In this paper, we propose natural backdoor attacks on speech recognition models using sounds which are ordinary in nature or in our daily life as natural triggers. Our results show that natural backdoor attacks have a high attack success rate without compromising model performance on benign samples, even with short or low-amplitude triggers. Only 5% of the poisoned samples are needed to achieve a near 100% attack success rate. In addition, natural backdoor attacks are still effective in real physical scenarios and are suitable for Clean-label attacks. And the backdoor can be automatically activated by the corresponding sound in nature as a trigger, which will bring severer harm.

References

1. Parkhi, O.M., Vedaldi, A., Zisserman, A.: Deep face recognition (2015)
2. Sun, Y., Wang, X., Tang, X.: Deep learning face representation from predicting 10,000 classes. In: Proceedings of the IEEE Conference on Computer Vision and Pattern Recognition, pp. 1891–1898 (2014)
3. Redmon, J., Divvala, S., Girshick, R., Farhadi, A.: You only look once: unified, real-time object detection. In: Proceedings of the IEEE Conference on Computer Vision and Pattern Recognition, pp. 779–788 (2016)

4. Wu, Y., et al.: Google's neural machine translation system: bridging the gap between human and machine translation. arXiv preprint arXiv:1609.08144 (2016)
5. Yu, D., Deng, L.: Automatic Speech Recognition. SCT, Springer, London (2015). https://doi.org/10.1007/978-1-4471-5779-3
6. Akhtar, N., Mian, A.: Threat of adversarial attacks on deep learning in computer vision: a survey. IEEE Access **6**, 14410–14430 (2018)
7. Madry, A., Makelov, A., Schmidt, L., Tsipras, D., Vladu, A.: Towards deep learning models resistant to adversarial attacks. arXiv preprint arXiv:1706.06083 (2017)
8. Li, Y., Jiang, Y., Li, Z., Xia, S.T.: Backdoor learning: a survey. IEEE Trans. Neural Netw. Learn. Syst. 1–18 (2022)
9. Weiss, K., Khoshgoftaar, T.M., Wang, D.D.: A survey of transfer learning. J. Big Data **3**(1), 1–40 (2016). https://doi.org/10.1186/s40537-016-0043-6
10. Bonawitz, K., et al.: Towards federated learning at scale: system design. Proc. Mach. Learn. Syst. **1**, 374–388 (2019)
11. Liu, Y., et al.: Trojaning attack on neural networks (2017)
12. Xu, X., Wang, Q., Li, H., Borisov, N., Gunter, C.A., Li, B.: Detecting AI trojans using meta neural analysis. In: 2021 IEEE Symposium on Security and Privacy (SP), pp. 103–120. IEEE (2021)
13. Tang, R., Du, M., Liu, N., Yang, F., Hu, X.: An embarrassingly simple approach for trojan attack in deep neural networks. In: Proceedings of the 26th ACM SIGKDD International Conference on Knowledge Discovery & Data Mining, pp. 218–228 (2020)
14. Zhai, T., Li, Y., Zhang, Z., Wu, B., Jiang, Y., Xia, S.T.: Backdoor attack against speaker verification. In: ICASSP 2021–2021 IEEE International Conference on Acoustics, Speech and Signal Processing (ICASSP), pp. 2560–2564. IEEE (2021)
15. Koffas, S., Xu, J., Conti, M., Picek, S.: Can you hear it? backdoor attacks via ultrasonic triggers. arXiv preprint arXiv:2107.14569 (2021)
16. Gu, T., Liu, K., Dolan-Gavitt, B., Garg, S.: BadNets: evaluating backdooring attacks on deep neural networks. IEEE Access **7**, 47230–47244 (2019)
17. Chen, X., Liu, C., Li, B., Lu, K., Song, D.: Targeted backdoor attacks on deep learning systems using data poisoning. arXiv preprint arXiv:1712.05526 (2017)
18. Liu, Y., Ma, X., Bailey, J., Lu, F.: Reflection backdoor: a natural backdoor attack on deep neural networks. In: Vedaldi, A., Bischof, H., Brox, T., Frahm, J.-M. (eds.) ECCV 2020. LNCS, vol. 12355, pp. 182–199. Springer, Cham (2020). https://doi.org/10.1007/978-3-030-58607-2_11
19. Qi, F., Chen, Y., Zhang, X., Li, M., Liu, Z., Sun, M.: Mind the style of text! adversarial and backdoor attacks based on text style transfer. arXiv preprint arXiv:2110.07139 (2021)
20. Qi, F., et al.: Hidden killer: invisible textual backdoor attacks with syntactic trigger. arXiv preprint arXiv:2105.12400 (2021)
21. Ye, J., Liu, X., You, Z., Li, G., Liu, B.: DriNet: dynamic backdoor attack against automatic speech recognization models. Appl. Sci. **12**(12), 5786 (2022)
22. Warden, P.: Speech commands: a dataset for limited-vocabulary speech recognition. arXiv preprint arXiv:1804.03209 (2018)
23. Samizade, S., Tan, Z.H., Shen, C., Guan, X.: Adversarial example detection by classification for deep speech recognition. In: ICASSP 2020–2020 IEEE International Conference on Acoustics, Speech and Signal Processing (ICASSP), pp. 3102–3106. IEEE (2020)

24. Eating sound collection (2020). https://www.kaggle.com/datasets/mashijie/eating-sound-collection
25. Baseline model (2021). https://tianchi.aliyun.com/competition/entrance/531887/forum
26. De Andrade, D.C., Leo, S., Viana, M.L.D.S., Bernkopf, C.: A neural attention model for speech command recognition. arXiv preprint arXiv:1808.08929 (2018)
27. Turner, A., Tsipras, D., Madry, A.: Clean-label backdoor attacks (2018)

Boarding Pass Positioning with Jointly Multi-channel Segmentation and Perspective Transformation Correction

Jiahui Wu[1,2], Zuoyong Li[2], Pantea Keikhosrokiani[3], and Yuanzheng Cai[2](✉)

[1] College of Computer and Data Science, Fuzhou University, Fuzhou 350108, China

[2] Fujian Provincial Key Laboratory of Information Processing and Intelligent Control, College of Computer and Control Engineering, Minjiang University, Fuzhou 350121, China
yuanzheng_cai@mju.edu.cn

[3] School of Computer Sciences, Universiti Sains Malaysia, 11800 Minden Penang, Malaysia

Abstract. To solve the problem of boarding pass positioning with image tilt and sticking, we proposed a jointly boarding pass positioning and correction algorithm using multi-channel color components. First, a local threshold segmentation is performed on red and blue components in RGB color space to determine the general area of the boarding pass. Then, edge detection is performed on the blue component and pixel value standardization statistics on the three components to obtain partial edges and internal information of the boarding pass to refine the binary image. Next, the watershed algorithm is used to achieve precise positioning of the boarding pass. Finally, the segmentation and the boarding pass are completely rectified through perspective transformation. The results of segmentation and correction of boarding passes in actual scenarios show that the proposed algorithm can complete segmentation and correction under complex conditions such as boarding pass images sticking to each other, uneven illumination, and large-angle tilt. The average time spent on the test set is 0.049s, and the segmentation and correction success rate is 95.16%. The proposed algorithm has high application value.

Keywords: Jointly multi-channel · Threshold segmentation · Boarding pass positioning · Perspective transformation

1 Introduction

The boarding pass is vital boarding document provided by the airport for passengers, which records important information such as the name, flight, date, class, destination, gate and seat. These information need to be entered into the database for future query. In the past, this work required a lot of manpower to complete. The manual input method not only has problems such as high cost

Y. Xu et al. (Eds.): ML4CS 2022, LNCS 13655, pp. 611–623, 2023.
https://doi.org/10.1007/978-3-031-20096-0_46

and slow input, but also has many errors, which is difficult to meet the service requirement. Therefore, it is necessary to develop an automatic identification system for boarding pass information [1]. With the development of computer vision technology, character recognition technology has become quite mature [2]. Before performing character recognition on the boarding pass information, positioning and correcting the boarding pass can improve the accuracy of character recognition and reduce the difficulty of subsequent steps. However, due to the algorithm of boarding pass positioning and correction, only a few scholars have studied it. Therefore, similar to the positioning and identification method of ship name [3], the identification of boarding pass information can also refer to the identification method of license plate.

In similar field such as license plate recognition, Lu Huazhang et al. [4] proposed a method to locate the license plate according to the mean square error of the longitudinal distance from the license plate characters to the straight line, which improved the accuracy of the license plate location under different degrees of inclination. Wang Nannan [5] used the texture feature of the license plate, combined the information of edge detection and morphological operation to locate the license plate, which improved the effectiveness of the license plate location. [6] proposed a tilt correction algorithm based on Radon transform, using the geometric and texture features of the license plate, which not only improves the effectiveness of the license plate location, but also greatly improves the speed. Liu WenFeng et al. [7] proposed a license plate location and correction method based on RGB color space for license plate images with complex backgrounds and different lighting conditions, which improved the overall performance of the license plate recognition system. Guo Dabo et al. [8] proposed a license plate location method that combines texture features and color features of license plates, which overcomes the problem that the license plate area becomes larger, which is difficult to solve when only texture or shape features are used. To sum up, the license plate location method is relatively mature, and the algorithm is mainly based on the color, edge, texture and geometric features of the license plate.

Different from the uniform font and shape of the license plate, the boarding passes of different airlines are not the same in shape, color and other characteristics, the font size is also inconsistent, and there are many characters, which appear in different positions. Therefore, the license plate recognition algorithm cannot be well applied to the localization of the boarding pass. To this end, we propose a method for quickly positioning and correcting boarding passes.

2 The Proposed Method

Firstly, according to the color features of the boarding pass, the red (R) channel and the blue (B) channel are separately extracted from the RGB color space, and the initial area of the boarding pass is obtained by using the method of local threshold segmentation respectively. Then, we exploit the edge detection algorithm [9] on the B channel and pixel value standardization statistical operation on the three channels to obtain part of the edge and internal information of the boarding pass which is acted as a threshold image to realize preliminary rough-positioning. Next, each different boarding pass areas are individually marked by the watershed algorithm [10] to realize the fine-positioning. Finally, perspective transformation [11] is used to further rectify boarding pass image according to the segmentation result.

The positioning and correction method of boarding pass proposed in this paper, the flow chart of which is shown in Fig. 1. Following sub-sections will describe the theory and implementation of the proposed method.

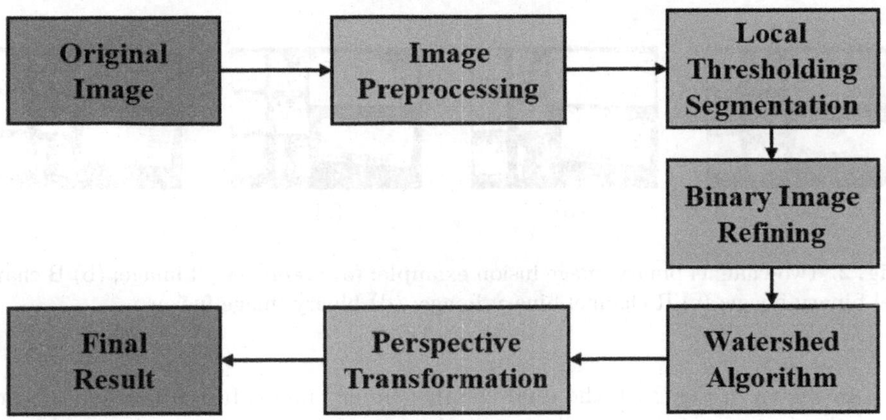

Fig. 1. Flow chart of the proposed method

2.1 Boarding Pass Coarse Positioning

The boarding pass image collected by the image acquisition device usually has some inevitable glare or shadow interference, and negligence in these problems will cause the threshold segmentation error. Follow sub-section will describe the solution.

Image Preprocessing. The original picture is first scaled according to Eq. (1). The purpose of scaling operation is to speed up the calculation, and retain most of the image information at the same time. In this paper, the scaling ratio of the width and height of the image is set to 0.5, which is the trade-off between the time and memory overhead. This scaling method ensures that the input images are consistent in size, and improve the validity and applicability of the parameters set in the algorithm. The boarding pass images shown below are all pre-scaled images.

$$w_i, h_i = w_0 * 0.5, h_0 * 0.5, \tag{1}$$

where w_0 and h_0 are the width and height of the input image, respectively, and w_i and h_i are the width and height of the scaled image.

Local Thresholding Segmentation. Similar to the traditional license plate localization algorithm, the RGB color features of the license plate are used to extract more information for image threshold segmentation by using the method of channel combination or channel separation [7]. Unlike the common license plates with white letters on a blue background, boarding passes are mostly composed of blue top or red top and black letters on a white background. Therefore, using this color feature, the preprocessed boarding pass is channel-separated, and its R channel and B channel are binarized using Otsu algorithm [12] respectively to obtain the binary image of the R channel and the B channel of the boarding pass. Finally, the binary image is fused.

(a) (b) (c) (d)

Fig. 2. Two-channel binary image fusion example: (a) preprocessed image; (b) B channel binary image; (c) R channel binary image; (d) binary image fusion

As shown in Fig. 2(d), the dual-channel binary image fusion method utilizes the color features of the boarding pass. Compared with the single-channel binary image, the extracted boarding pass area is more complete. However, this method cannot obtain a complete boarding pass area under complex conditions such as uneven illumination and alternating light and dark. This is because the method of directly using the Otsu algorithm [12] to binarize the entire image is to calculate the binarization threshold considering the global information of the image. Therefore, the effect is slightly worse for uneven lighting and shadows that may occur in real scenes. In order to solve the problem in this step, we will use the local Otsu algorithm for the R and B channels obtained by channel separation. The specific steps are to divide the image into blocks, and then use the Otsu algorithm to perform threshold segmentation respectively by Eq. (2), and finally save the result.

$$I_{ij} = \begin{cases} 255, & if\ P > T \\ 0, & otherwise \end{cases}, \tag{2}$$

where P are the R and B channel components of the divided image. In this paper, the height and width of the segmented image are taken as 1/5 of the original image. T is the threshold determined by the classical threshold segmentation algorithm Otsu on the corresponding channel. I_{ij} is the final result of the binary image fusion, and the result in Fig. 3(c) is obtained.

Binary Image Refining. As can be seen from Fig. 3(c), compared with the method of directly thresholding the entire image, local threshold segmentation

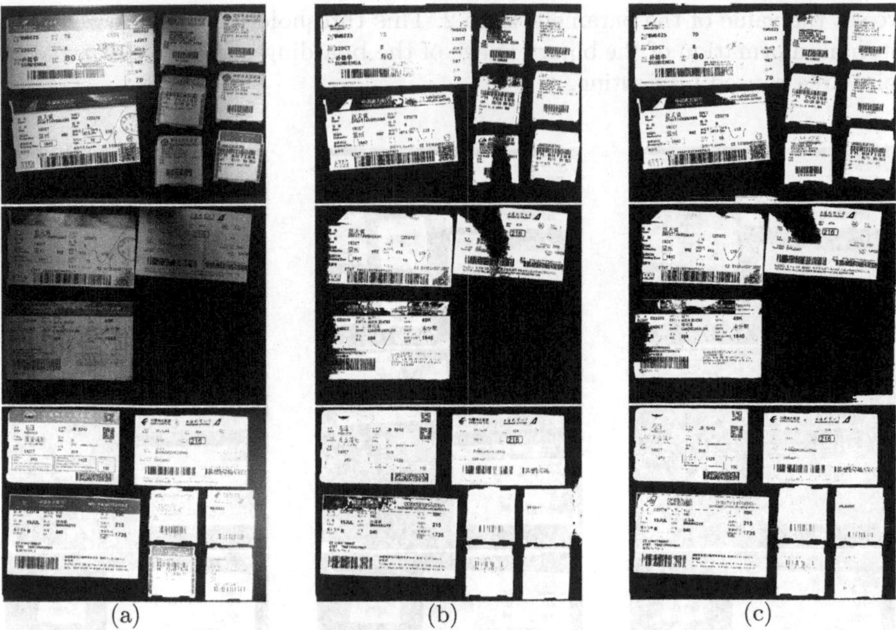

Fig. 3. Local threshold segmentation examples: (a) preprocessed images; (b) global threshold segmentation; (c) local threshold segmentation

can effectively suppress the loss of local information or the appearance of noisy areas due to uneven illumination. However, some edge or internal information of the boarding pass is still lost. For the edge information of the boarding pass, the Canny edge detection algorithm [9] is used for the B channel to obtain the edge information variable e_{ij} of the boarding pass. For the internal information of the boarding pass, first use the standard deviation function on the original image to calculate the standard deviation value x_{ij} of each pixel for the three channel components as sample data. The z-score standardization is carried out by Eq. (3), and the sample data conforming to the standard normal distribution is obtained.

$$z_{ij} = (x_{ij} - x_i) / s_i, \tag{3}$$

where x_i is the mean of x_{ij}, s_i is the standard deviation of x_{ij}, and z_{ij} is the standardized variable value. After obtaining the binary map variable e_{ij} of boarding pass edge information and the sample data variable z_{ij} after internal standardization of boarding pass, the local threshold segmentation result of Fig. 3(c) is refined by Eq. (4):

$$I_{ij} = \begin{cases} 255, & if\ e_{ij} \neq 0\ or\ z_{ij} > \alpha \\ I_{ij}, & otherwise \end{cases}. \tag{4}$$

We set the value of the parameter α to 2. This threshold can not only refine the internal information of the binary image of the boarding pass, but also avoid the noise area caused by lighting.

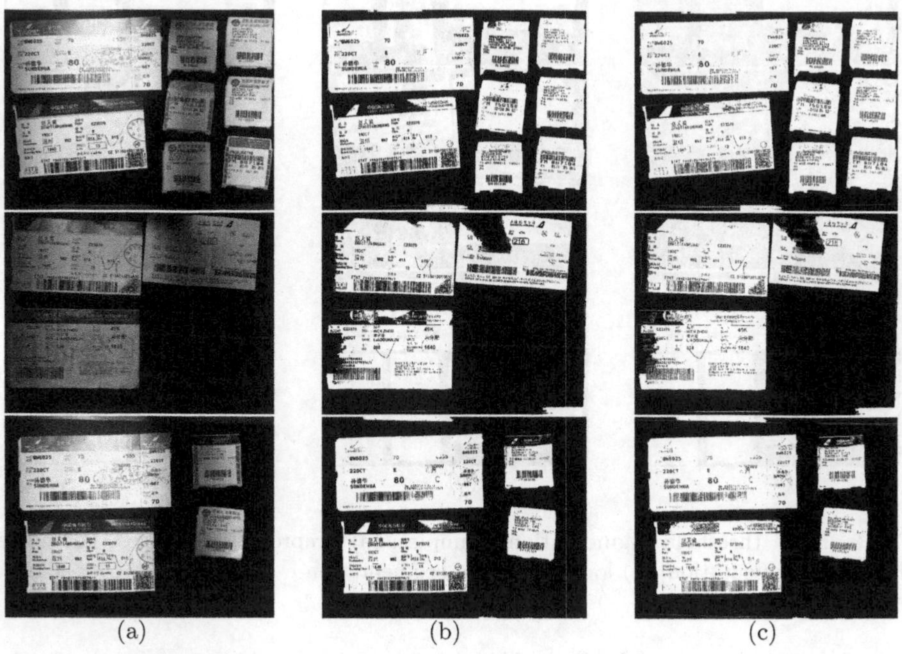

(a) (b) (c)

Fig. 4. Binary image refining example: (a) preprocessed images; (b) local threshold segmentation; (c) binary image refining

As shown in Fig. 4(c), we get more binary maps about the boarding pass area, but the method also leads to some additional noise areas, and it is necessary to formulate a certain screening strategy to get qualified boarding pass area.

- Step1: Find all outer contours in the binary image I_{ij}.
- Step2: Calculate each outer contour area value $area_i$.
- Step3: It is judged whether each outer contour area conforms to the format Eq. (5), and the conformity is the boarding pass area.

$$I_{ij} = \begin{cases} fill(I_c), & if\ area_i > K \\ I_{ij}, & otherwise \end{cases}. \tag{5}$$

In this paper, the value of K is 5000, I_c is the point set of the outer contour corresponding to the $area_i$, and $fill$ is the filling operation for the outer contour, that is, the value of the entire contour area is set to 255. The reason for the value of K is that the main contour area of the boarding pass is large and the noise area is small. The purpose of this step is to ensure that the target area is better preserved in subsequent morphological operations.

2.2 Boarding Pass Precise Positioning

The watershed algorithm [10] is a commonly used image region segmentation algorithm, and each segmented object will not be merged, which is suitable for the situation where the boundaries of the objects to be segmented are stuck. Before using the watershed algorithm, we need to determine the foreground area and background area of the image, then process the connected areas, and finally use the watershed algorithm to label each boarding pass.

First, invert the binary image I_{ij} of the previous step to obtain the background area binary image I_{bg} of the image according to Eq. (6):

$$I_{bg} = \begin{cases} 0, & if\ I_{ij} \neq 0 \\ 255, & otherwise \end{cases} . \tag{6}$$

Then, by constructing a element matrix E of size (5, 5), the initial values are all 1. Erosion operation is performed on the binary image I_{ij}, and the number of iterations is 7. The purpose is to remove some small noise areas while separating the boarding passes with slight adhesion.

However, there may still be some large noise areas in the image, and a certain screening strategy needs to be used to obtain a certain foreground image. The filtering strategy is defined as follows:

- Step1: Find all outer contours in the binary image I_{ij} after erosion.
- Step2: Find the smallest enclosing rectangle R of each outer contour.
- Step3: Calculate the area C_a of each contour and the geometric properties of the corresponding bounding rectangle R including width R_w, height R_h and area R_a.
- Step4: It is judged whether the above variables conform to Eq. (7), if not, it is the background area, which is removed.

$$I_{fg} = \begin{cases} fill(R), & if\ C_a > \alpha \wedge \frac{R_h}{R_w} > \beta \wedge \frac{R_w}{R_h} > \gamma \wedge \frac{C_a}{R_a} > \delta \\ 0, & otherwise \end{cases} , \tag{7}$$

where the parameters α, β, γ and δ are set to 5000, 3, 3.4 and 0.75, respectively. The values of β and γ are based on the characteristics of the shape of the boarding pass, and the values of the other two parameters are because the general area of the boarding pass has been obtained, and the contour area and its proportion to the enclosing rectangle will be relatively large. I_{fg} is the foreground area binary image after filtering. As shown in Fig. 5(c), the binary image obtained through the filtering strategy is the foreground area binary image.

Now we have the foreground and background areas of the image, but there are still some areas that we are not sure about which are the areas that are connected or superimposed between the boarding pass and the boarding pass in the original image, that is, the border. By Eq. (8):

$$I_u = \begin{cases} 255, & if\ \sim I_{fg} - I_{bg} = 255 \\ 0, & otherwise \end{cases} , \tag{8}$$

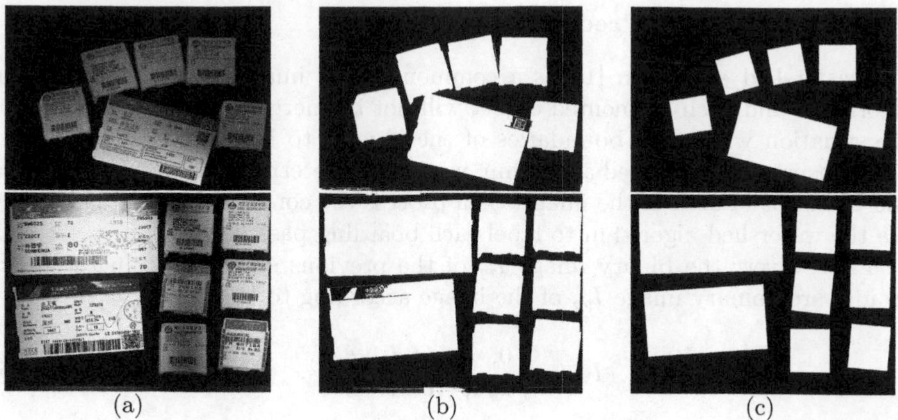

Fig. 5. Filter example: (a) preprocessed images; (b) coarse positioning binary images; (c) filter results

we can roughly obtain these unknown area binary image I_u. Where the background area binary image I_{bg} is obtained by inverting the binary image I_{ij}. So we need to invert the foreground area binary image I_{fg} first and then subtract the background area binary image I_{bg} to get the unknown area binary map I_u of the boarding pass.

Then use the connected domain processing function [13] to mark and classify the boarding pass in the foreground area binary image I_{fg}, and obtain the label matrix M_{ij}. The background pixels are marked as 0, and the non-background pixels are marked up from 1 and marked respectively. Before using the watershed algorithm, we also need to set the label matrix M_{ij} corresponding to the unknown area binary image I_u to 0 by Eq. (9):

$$M_{ij} = \begin{cases} 0, & if\ I_u \neq 0 \\ M_{ij}, & otherwise \end{cases} . \quad (9)$$

Finally, we use the obtained label matrix M_{ij} and the preprocessed image to achieve precise localization of the boarding pass using the watershed algorithm.

As shown in Fig. 6, for the new label obtained by using the watershed algorithm, there is a problem that the obtained label matrix M_{ij}. There is a target area that will be integrated into the background area for marking. Therefore, we traverse the qualified labels and make the corresponding mask image I_m. The segmentation and correction of the boarding pass is completed through perspective transformation, and is removed from the binary map of the rough positioning of the boarding pass in the corresponding area by Eq. (10):

$$I_{ij} = \begin{cases} 0, & if\ I_m \neq 0 \\ I_{ij}, & otherwise \end{cases} . \quad (10)$$

For the last target, segmentation and correction are performed from the binary image I_{ij} after clearing the corresponding mask area.

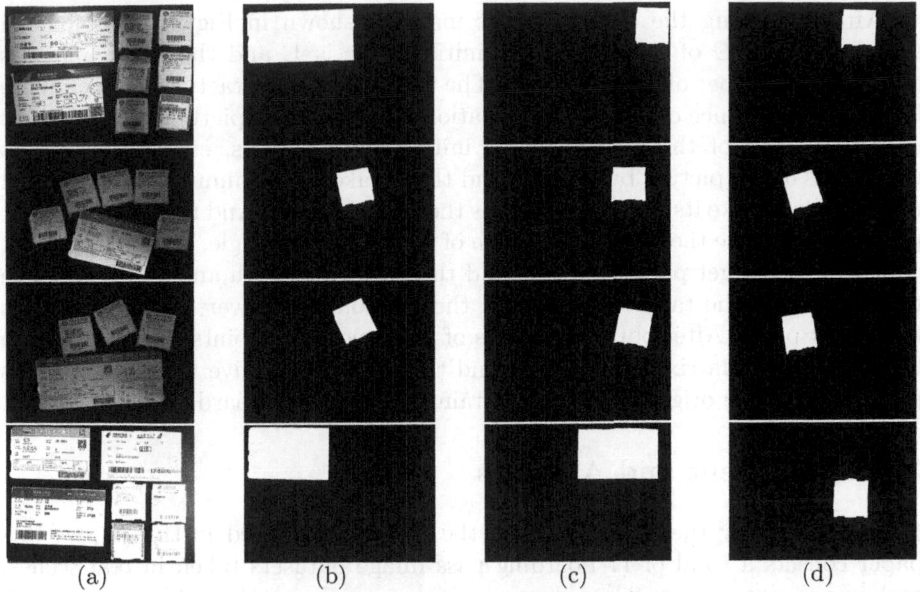

Fig. 6. Watershed algorithm results: (a) preprocessed images; (b), (c), (d) partial mask images

2.3 Segmentation and Correction

Perspective Transformation [11] is to project the image to a new perspective or plane. Its transformation formula is Eq. (11):

$$\begin{bmatrix} \mathrm{X} \\ \mathrm{Y} \\ \mathrm{Z} \end{bmatrix} = \begin{bmatrix} a_{11}\ a_{12}\ a_{13} \\ a_{21}\ a_{22}\ a_{23} \\ a_{31}\ a_{32}\ a_{33} \end{bmatrix} \begin{bmatrix} x \\ y \\ 1 \end{bmatrix}. \tag{11}$$

The point to be moved is (x, y), the target point is (X, Y, Z), and the intermediate matrix A of Eq. (11) forms the perspective transformation matrix. The scope of perspective transformation is a three-dimensional space, but the image is in two-dimensional space. So it needs to be divided by Z, $\left(X^{'}, Y^{'}, Z^{'}\right) = (X \div Z, Y \div Z, Z \div Z)$, and $\left(X^{'}, Y^{'}, Z^{'}\right)$ is the real target point that we need to obtain in the end. The real target point is calculated according to Eq. (12):

$$\begin{bmatrix} a_{33} \\ X^{'} \\ Y^{'} \end{bmatrix} = \begin{bmatrix} 1 \\ a_{11}x + a_{12}y + a_{13} - a_{31}xX^{'} - a_{32}yX^{'} \\ a_{21}x + a_{22}y + a_{23} - a_{31}xY^{'} - a_{32}yY^{'} \end{bmatrix}, \tag{12}$$

and the final purpose is to obtain the transformation matrix, except that 8 unknowns need to be solved, so 8 equations are needed to solve.

After obtaining the boarding pass mask as shown in Fig. 6, we define an element matrix E of size (5, 5), the initial value is 1, and the mask image is dilated, the number of iterations is 3. The purpose is to extract a more complete boarding pass. Since our previous operation has scaled the picture, we must first restore the size of the picture to the initial value, that is, enlarge the x-axis and y-axis of the picture by 2 times, and then make the minimum circumscribed rectangle, and take its 4 corner points as the source points. And use these 4 corner points to calculate the length and width of the target rectangle, set the upper left corner of the target point as (0, 0), and then use the length and width to make the 4 points of the target rectangle in the horizontal and vertical directions as the target point. After obtaining 4 sets of corresponding points, the perspective transformation matrix is calculated, and then the perspective transformation is performed on the original image to obtain the corrected boarding pass image.

3 Experiment and Analysis

In order to verify the effectiveness of the method proposed in this paper, this paper collects a total of 17 boarding pass image datasets taken in real scenes, each image contains 1 to 8 boarding pass images, and a total of 62 images contain various boarding passes and receipt. These 17 pictures are all taken with a fixed camera or mobile phone in real scenes, including non-tilted pictures and horizontally tilted pictures under complex conditions such as uneven illumination, large-angle tilt, and multiple small ticket edges stuck together.

The software and hardware environment running on AMD Ryzen 5800 H 3.20 GHz processor, 16 GB RAM, and Windows 10 operating system is implemented, using Pycharm integrated development environment, Python language for programming, and the open source library OpenCV for auxiliary programming.

3.1 Separate Experimental Analysis

In the segmentation and correction experiments of 17 boarding pass image datasets with different conditions and different situations, a total of 62 various boarding passes and receipts, 59 were correctly segmented and corrected, 1 was incorrectly segmented, 2 were not segmented and corrected. The success rate of segmentation and correction is 95.16%, and the average segmentation and correction time of each boarding pass or receipt is 0.049s in the results of multiple experiments. One of the error segmentation correction is because there are 8 target images on that picture, occupying most of the area of the picture. As a result, when traversing the markers of the watershed algorithm, when one of the images is a background image, the determination of the image area ratio is passed, and it is also segmented. The reason for the failure of complete segmentation and correction of two boarding passes is that there is strong light interference in some areas, which makes other boarding passes in one image relatively dark, and it is difficult to obtain a complete binary image of the boarding pass area.

Fig. 7. Partial segmentation correction results

Part of the segmentation correction results are shown in Fig. 7. The first and fourth groups of results prove that even in the presence of strong light interference or uneven illumination, the algorithm in this paper can complete the segmentation correction task well. Other sets of pictures also verify the effectiveness of the algorithm in the case of boarding pass distribution images with sticking, tilted angles, etc.

3.2 Comparative Experimental Analysis

In the boarding pass character recognition test experiment, there are 16 test images in total, including 3 unsegmented and uncorrected images and 13 corresponding segmented and corrected images. Mainly for a total of 33 pieces of information on the boarding pass, such as name, flight number, date, seat, etc., and a total of 60 pieces of information on the receipt, such as name and luggage number, use Tencent character recognition tool to identify. The experimental results are shown in Table 1.

Table 1. Character recognition results comparison.

	Boarding pass(33 pieces)	Receipt(60 pieces)
Before correction	90.91%	83.33%
After correction	93.94%	86.67%

In test experiments, we found that when performing character recognition on uncorrected images, the greater the tilt of the image, the more difficult it is to locate the characters and lead to recognition errors. For an image with a small slope, it is easy to recognize the number 8 as the character B and the character R as the character A and so on. Moreover, for the identification of continuous line of information, there will be problems such as identifying continuous information as discrete information because the image is tilted. Here, we only conduct a comparative experiment on the character recognition effect of whether the corresponding image is corrected or not. If the entire unsegmented and uncorrected image is directly subjected to character recognition, the effect will be even worse. Therefore, the method proposed in this paper helps to improve the accuracy of subsequent character recognition.

4 Conclusion

This paper proposes a method for quickly positioning and correcting boarding passes. Firstly, channel separation and local threshold segmentation are used to determine the general location of boarding passes. Then, edge detection is performed on the blue component and pixel value standardization statistics on the three components to obtain part of the edge and interior information of the boarding pass to refine the target area. Next, the watershed algorithm is used to accurately locate the boarding pass. Finally, use perspective transformation to complete the segmentation and correction of the boarding pass.

The experimental results show that the method in this paper has good timeliness and high success rate, and can meet the requirements of real-time monitoring in real scenarios. At the same time, the boarding pass positioning correction method in this paper has good robustness, and is effective in the case of uneven illumination, partial adhesion, and large-angle tilt. In the future work, the method of this paper will be expanded, and the positioning correction algorithm will continue to be studied for documents other than boarding passes, such as ID cards and passports, so that the algorithm in this paper has better generalization ability.

Acknowledgment. This work is partially supported by National Natural Science Foundation of China (61972187), Natural Science Foundation of Fujian Province (2020J02024, 2020J01828, 2022J011112).

References

1. Niandong, L.: Research on air ticket information recognition technology with complex background, Ph. D. thesis, University of Electronic Science and Technology of China (2012)
2. Jiao, W.: Design of automatic license plate character recognition system based on machine vision. Automa. Instrum. **8**, 5 (2019)
3. Jiang, Q., Guirong, Z., Jiang, Y., Jianzhong, J., Ping, H., Songhua, G.: The most stable extreme value region and edge-enhanced ship name localization method. Comput. Appl. Softw. **36**(2), 5 (2019)
4. Huazhang, L., Hao, W.: License plate positioning and license plate correction method under different degrees of inclination. Mod. Ind. Econ. Inform. **6**(5), 3 (2016)
5. Nannan, W.: Research on license plate positioning and tilt correction method. Ind. control comput. **27**, 2 (2014)
6. Haijiang, G., Jiangjiang, F., Xiang, Z.: Research on license plate location and tilt correction algorithm in license plate recognition system. J. Hangzhou Dianzi Univ. Natural Sci. Edition **27**(2), 4 (2007)
7. Wenfeng, L., Xueyi, W., Changfu, L.: License plate location and correction algorithm based on RGB chromaticity space. J. Wuhan Univ. (Inf. Sci. Edition) **31**(9), 785–787 (2006)
8. Dabo, G., Limin, C., Chaoyang, L., Liping, H.: License plate location method based on license plate background color recognition. Comput. Eng. Design **24**(5), 5 (2003)
9. Canny, J.: Collision detection for moving Polyhedra. IEEE Trans. Pattern Anal. Mach. Intell. **8**(2), 200 (1986)
10. Meyer, F.: Color image segmentation. In: 1992 International Conference on Image Processing and its Applications, pp. 303–306. IET (1992)
11. Yan, N.: Research on perspective transformation. J. Comput. Aided Des. Graph. **13**(6), 3 (2001)
12. Otsu, N.: A threshold selection method from gray-level histograms. IEEE Trans. Syst. Man Cybern. **9**(1), 62–66 (2007)
13. He, L., Chao, Y., Suzuki, K., Wu, K.: Fast connected-component labeling. Pattern Recogn. **42**(9), 1977–1987 (2009)

AP-GCL: Adversarial Perturbation on Graph Contrastive Learning

ZiYu Zheng[1(✉)], HaoRan Chen[2], and Ke Peng[3]

[1] School of Computer Science and Cyber Engineering, Guangzhou University, Guangzhou, China
1907700034@e.gzhu.edu.cn

[2] School of Electronics and Communication Engineering, Guangzhou University, Guangzhou, China
1904200038@e.gzhu.edu.cn

[3] School of Economics and Statistics, Guangzhou University, Guangzhou, China
2064200075@e.gzhu.edu.cn

Abstract. A serious ecological hazard of illegal transactions (money laundering, financial fraud, etc.) on the Bitcoin trading network. Anti-money laundering and fraud detection are essential instruments to address the problem. However, such datasets are generally extremely unbalanced in terms of positive and negative samples, and most of the data are unlabelled, with the illegal class accounting for just a minimal fraction of the total, which prevents supervised learning from learning a well-represented feature. We propose a self-supervised learning framework based on contrastive learning, in which two different augmented transformations are applied to the original graph data, perturbations are randomly attached to the node features of the upgraded views, and the model parameters and perturbations are updated by gradient descent to maximize the consistency of the single node in different views. The experimental result demonstrates that our model achieves excellent performance in all metrics and is comparable to supervised methods, which verifies the efficiency of the perturbation-based contrastive learning model.

Keywords: Contrastive learning · Adversarial training · Anomaly detection

1 Introduction

Anti-money laundering (AML) and fraud detection are key financial fraud concern, and Bitcoin [11], a P2P structured digital currency, is also subject to money laundering and fraudulent transactions in the Bitcoin network. Anti-money laundering is the process of detecting money laundering in the Bitcoin network by identifying illegal transaction flows in the network to determine which users are illegal. As the class of illegal transactions often represents such a narrow segment of all transactions, and the illegal transactions are not isolated but hidden

Y. Xu et al. (Eds.): ML4CS 2022, LNCS 13655, pp. 624–633, 2023.
https://doi.org/10.1007/978-3-031-20096-0_47

in clusters of legitimate behaviour. The accuracy and efficiency of determining the legitimacy of a transaction directly through the transaction stream is incredibly inefficient.

The Bitcoin network could essentially be mapped as a graph of transaction streams consisting of a number of nodes and edges, with the nodes representing transactions and the edges representing transaction streams. The challenge of detecting offending transaction is then transformed into a problem of node classification on the graph [7,20]. The graph neural network generates node representations through aggregating information about neighbours to update the central node. Current methods mostly learn node representations from deepwalk [14] or by global node embeddings [3], which often resulted in hyper-parameter dependence of the model, while over-smoothing can emerge for models that have gone excessively in depth [5]. In addition, dataset such as the Bitcoin, which is mapped from the physical world to the graph, has extremely unbalanced positive and negative samples and absent labels, with most nodes being unlabelled. How to ensure optimal node representation during the training process and reduce the impact of noise are challenge that require consideration.

In this work, we obtain node representations by introducing contrastive learning [2,10,15], which is a self-supervised method for graph, where an encoder is learned from a given unlabelled data. We focus more on the local representation of the nodes and consider more the subgraphs of the illegal nodes. Perturbations are also randomly added to the data-enhanced features, and the model is updated based on the perturbations during Backpropagation. Experimental result shows that contrastive learning-based training can effectively derive low-dimensional embedding representations of nodes and reduce the impact of oversmoothing. Back propagation based on feature perturbation can improve the interference of noise on the model and increase the performance.

In summary our main contributions are as follows.

- instead of using random walks we use contrastive learning to learn node representations, focusing more on node representations of subgraphs, which is experimentally shown to be better for on bitcoin networks compared to global embeddings.
- Backpropagation based on feature perturbation, by adding random perturbations to the node features, performing a higher order propagation of the perturbed node, and updating the parameters based on the perturbations, can improve the impact of the inherent noise on the classification. It also reduces the dependence of nodes on certain neighbour and enhances the robustness of the model.

The rest of the paper is as follows, Sect. 2 presents the related work, Sect. 3 focuses on our model and methods, while the results and analysis of the experiments are provided in Sect. 4, and then finally, our conclusion is illustrated in Sect. 5.

2 Related Work

In this section, we mainly present the study of some graph models related to this work.

Weber et al. proposed the application of graph neural networks to cryptocurrency forensics, particularly Bitcoin, and made publicly available the Elliptic dataset [20], currently the world's largest publicly available dataset of labelled transactions in cryptocurrencies.

The deepwalk proposed by Perozzi B et al. [14] used the co-occurrence of nodes in the graph to learn the nodes representation, which focusing on the neighbourhood information at the expense of the structural information of the graph. Node2vec by Aditya Grover [3] was a biased random walk algorithm that expands on deepwalk by improving on the homogeneity and structure of the network through BFS and DFS.

Presently, label propagation [5,6,16] is the major way to alleviate the data imbalance and label scarcity problem in real-world graph data, where few labels are used to predict the label information of surrounding nodes through neighbour aggregation. On the other hand, Joana Lorenz used active learning to manually mark the rest of the nodes with known labels [9]. Label usage [18] was proposed by Yangkun Wang, who used label information as feature input and achieved better results.

The initial application of contrastive learning was in image match [4,10], where Chen, Ting et al. [2] proposed a new contrastive learning paradigm. Graph contrastive learning is based on the above studies, Velickovic proposed to maximize the mutual information of global graph embedding and local embedding [15]. Zhu, Yanqiao et al. [22] proposed to maximize the node consistency based on this and You, Yuning et al. used various data augmentation techniques [21] on graph contrast learning.

There are currently two main directions for fraud detection contrastive learning [8,19] and dynamic graphs [1,12,13,17]. Pre-training based on contrastive learning requires fraudulent nodes to be distinct from normal nodes in the graph structure. Dynamic graphs, on the other hand, use historical information from the graph, but training based on dynamic graphs is time consuming.

3 Our Method

In this section, we introduce the basic concept of graph contrastive learning and the relevant symbols and formulas, followed by the improvements and innovations implemented.

3.1 Graph Contrastive Learning

The ultimate goal of graph contrastive learning is to maximize the consistency of positive pairs and the inconsistency of negative pairs through graph encoders to learn node representations. Assuming a graph $G = (\mathbf{A}, \mathbf{X})$ and V, $\mathbf{X}$ is the feature matrix and $\mathbf{A}$ is the adjacency matrix. $V = \{v_1, v_2, \ldots, v_n\}$ denotes the set of nodes of the graph. For a feature matrix $\mathbf{X} = \{x_1, x_2, \ldots, x_n\}$, n denotes the number of nodes and x_i denotes the characteristic representation of node v_i. For an adjacency matrix $\mathbf{A}$, $A_{ij} = A_{ji} = 1$ if there exists v_i to v_j.

With graph contrastive learning, the original graph is typically augmented with multiple different data to obtain a new view.

$$\mathbf{X_i}, \mathbf{A_i} = \mathcal{T}(\mathbf{X}, \mathbf{A}); i = 1, 2, 3, \cdots, k \tag{1}$$

where $\mathbf{X_i}$, $\mathbf{A_i}$ indicate the feature matrix and adjacency matrix after data augmentation. The transformed $\mathbf{X_i}$, $\mathbf{A_i}$, learning a graph encoder to obtain a higher-order representation of node by aggregating information about its neighbours.

$$\mathbf{H_i} = f_\theta(\mathbf{X_i}, \mathbf{A_i}); i = 1, 2, 3, \cdots, k \tag{2}$$

where $\mathbf{H_i} = \{h_1, h_2, \ldots, h_n\}$, h_i is the vector representation of node v_i. $f_\theta(\cdot)$ is the encoder. Once the representation of the node is obtained, we can calculate the mutual information of the different views.

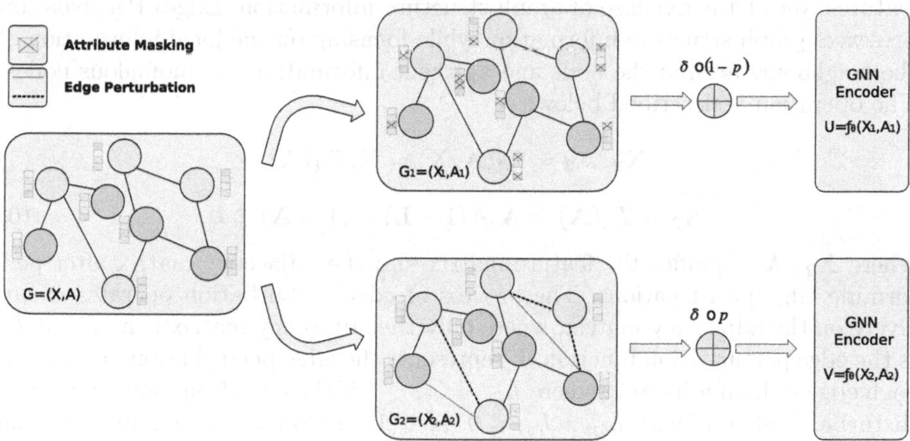

Fig. 1. Our proposed model and representation of adversarial perturbation on graph contrastive learning

3.2 Models and Frameworks

This subsection focuses on our graph contrastive learning framework AP-GCL and the adversarial training method based on feature perturbation. The diagram of the model framework is shown in Fig. 1.

Attribute Masking and Edge Perturbation are adopted in our model to augment the original graph.

Attribute Masking: Randomly masking a portion of the attributes of the feature matrix $\mathbf{X}$, each node in the graph contains multi-dimensional features, but not each dimension of the features is considered valuable for the prediction of results. The use of Attribute Masking in contrastive learning facilitates focusing on important features and ignoring irrelevant features where possible. The equation is expressed as follows:

$$\mathbf{X_1}, \mathbf{A_1} = \mathcal{T_X}(\mathbf{A}, \mathbf{X}) = \mathcal{T_X}(\mathbf{X}), \mathbf{A} \tag{3}$$

$$\mathbf{X_1} = \mathcal{T_X}(\mathbf{X}) = \mathbf{X} \odot (1 - \mathbf{M}) \tag{4}$$

where $\mathbf{X_1}, \mathbf{A_1}$ indicate the feature matrix and adjacency matrix after data augmentation, where the mask only transforms the feature matrix, so the adjacency matrix remains unaffected. $\mathcal{T_X}(\cdot)$ is the feature enhancement function, $\mathbf{M}$ is the masking location matrix, $M_{ij} = 1$ when the last j elements of node v_i is hidden, otherwise $M_{ij} = 0$.

Edge Perturbation: Randomly add or remove a certain percentage of edges to the graph. The random walk focuses on obtaining a representation of node features, yet at the expense of graph structure information. Edges Perturbation preserves graph structure information while focusing on the local information of the neighbours around the node and adjacent information for anomalous nodes. The operation is described below:

$$\mathbf{X_2}, \mathbf{A_2} = \mathcal{T_A}(\mathbf{A}, \mathbf{X}) = \mathbf{X}, \mathcal{T_A}(\mathbf{A}) \tag{5}$$

$$\mathbf{A_2} = \mathcal{T_A}(\mathbf{A}) = \mathbf{A} \odot (1 - \mathbf{L}) + (1 - \mathbf{A}) \odot \mathbf{L} \tag{6}$$

where $\mathbf{X_2}$, $\mathbf{A_2}$ signifies the feature matrix and the adjacency matrix after performing edge perturbations. The process of edge perturbation operates exclusively on the adjacency matrix, where only the adjacency matrix is modified.$\mathcal{T_A}$ is the edge perturbation function. $\mathbf{L}$ represents the edge perturbation matrix and each edge to be undirected, where $L_{ij} = L_{ji} = 1$ if the edge from node v_i to v_j is disturbed, but otherwise $L_{ij} = L_{ji} = 0$. $\mathbf{A} \odot (1 - \mathbf{L})$ refers to randomly deleting existing edges for the graph, and $(1 - \mathbf{A}) \odot \mathbf{L}$ means randomly constructing new edges for the graph.

Perturbation Based on Node Features: Node features contain embedded noise, and we want the encoder to learn node representation that avoids acquiring too much redundant information that is irrelevant as far as possible to the downstream task, instead attention is paid to information about the features of the node linked to the assignment. We randomly add to the node-feature input space of the data-augmented views a perturbation $\boldsymbol{\delta}$. No more than one data-augmented view will be perturbed in each training step, and the corresponding nodes under different views are required to be consistent. Enhancing the smoothness between the original and adversarial nodes by disturbing the node features.

In addition, the gradient accumulation and calculation of the perturbations we performed during the backpropagation process required updating the perturbation as well as upgrading the model parameters. The model will increasingly concentrate on rewarding and strongly relevant features through adversarial training of different views. The perturbation process is represented as follows:

$$\widetilde{\mathbf{X_1}} = \mathbf{X_1} + \boldsymbol{\delta} \odot (1 - \mathbf{M}) \odot (1 - \mathbf{p}) \tag{7}$$

$$\widetilde{\mathbf{X_2}} = \mathbf{X_2} + \boldsymbol{\delta} \odot \mathbf{p} \tag{8}$$

where $\widetilde{\mathbf{X_1}}$ is the feature matrix after perturbation for the view after attribute masking. $(1 - \mathbf{M})$ indicates the unmasked feature location matrix, in this case we only attach perturbations to the unmasked features. $\widetilde{\mathbf{X_2}}$ is the feature matrix after adding feature perturbations to the view after edge perturbations. $\mathbf{p}$ serves to identify the view to which a perturbation has been attached. The perturbation $\boldsymbol{\delta}$ satisfied by $\boldsymbol{\delta} \sim U(-a, a)$, a being the perturbation range.

After obtaining the feature inputs of the two transformed views, we can learn the node embedding through the graph encoder to obtain the node representations $\mathbf{U}$, $\mathbf{V}$ of the two views, and we compute the node pair representations of different views at the same position to maximize the consistency of similar nodes when computing the contrastive loss. The loss function is calculated by maximizing the node consistency, which is described as follows:

$$\ell(\boldsymbol{u}_i, \boldsymbol{v}_i) = \log \frac{e^{sim(\boldsymbol{u}_i, \boldsymbol{v}_i)/\tau}}{e^{sim(\boldsymbol{u}_i, \boldsymbol{v}_i)/\tau} + \sum\limits_{k=1}^{N} \mathbb{1}_{[k \neq i]} [e^{sim(\boldsymbol{u}_i, \boldsymbol{v}_k)/\tau} + e^{sim(\boldsymbol{u}_i, \boldsymbol{u}_k)/\tau}]} \tag{9}$$

where $\boldsymbol{u_i}$, $\boldsymbol{v_i}$ is the embedding generated by the node u_i,v_i. $sim(\cdot)$ computes the cosine similarity of two node pairs. $\mathbb{1}_{[k \neq i]} \in \{0, 1\}$ is the indicator function when $k \neq i$ parameter is 1. τ is the temperature parameter. The contribution of τ is equivalent to a linear scaling on the exponential function. $e^{sim(\boldsymbol{u}_i, \boldsymbol{v}_k)}$ represents the inter-view negative pairs and $e^{sim(\boldsymbol{u}_i, \boldsymbol{u}_k)}$ represents the intra-view negative pairs. Thus to maximize node consistency is to maximize the average of all positive pairs, with the overall objective expressed as follows:

$$\mathcal{J} = \frac{1}{2N} \sum_{i=1}^{N} [\ell(\boldsymbol{u}_i, \boldsymbol{v}_i) + \ell(\boldsymbol{v}_i, \boldsymbol{u}_i)] \tag{10}$$

After the loss is calculated, the gradient is accumulated and updated for each backpropagation process for the perturbation, and the perturbation added to the view is updated at each training session, and finally the perturbation make the model tend to be updated in a task-relevant direction to identify the small number of negative samples in the data. The following is the detailed training process as illustrated in Algorithm 1.

Algorithm 1: AP-GCL training algorithm

for *epoch* $\leftarrow 1,2,\cdots$ **do**
  Generate two new views G_1 and G_2 by augmenting the original graph G with $\mathcal{T}_{\mathcal{X}}(\mathcal{G})$ and $\mathcal{T}_{\mathcal{A}}(\mathcal{G})$
  Randomly add node-based feature perturbation δ to one of the views
  Obtain node embdding $\mathbf{U}$ of G_1 using the encoder $f_\theta(\cdot)$
  Obtain node embdding $\mathbf{V}$ of G_2 using the encoder $f_\theta(\cdot)$
  Compute the contrastive loss J by maximizing the mean value of the positive pair of nodes with $Eq(10)$
  Update parameters θ and δ by gradient descent to maximize J
end

4 Experiments

4.1 Datasets

The dataset we have adopted is the Bitcoin Trading Network dataset published by Elliptic, a global company. The Elliptic dataset maps bitcoin transactions to real entities that belong to the legal class the illegal class. A node in the graph represents a transaction, and an edge can be regarded as a bitcoin stream between one transaction and another. The transaction graph consists of 203,769 nodes and 234,355 edges, of which two percent of the nodes were labelled as illegal. Twenty-one percent were labelled as legal and the rest of the nodes were unlabelled. The illegal types include mainly scams, malware, terrorist organisations, ransomware and Ponzi schemes. There are 166 features per node in the graph, consisting of 94 transaction-related features and 72 aggregated features. The assignment of the dataset is to perform a classification of legal and illegal nodes on the graph.

4.2 Experiment Setup

We split the dataset in 60:20:20 ratio into a training set, a validation set, and a test set. To evaluate the capability of our model to identify anomalous transactions on the Bitcoin trading network, both traditional machine learning models and graph neural network models were used for comparison.

As for the machine learning model, we employed all 166 features for training on the training set and evaluation on the test set, using Logistic Regression(LR), Random Forests(RF) and XGBoost, where the model parameters were set with reference to weber's work [20]. In the case of graph models, we measured them on GCN, Skip-GCN, evolveGCN and DGI. To better compare the performance of the models, a 3-layer network architecture was implemented for both the network layer and the encoder, with an adam optimiser learning rate of 0.001.

Since the dataset is unbalanced with positive and negative samples, the ratio of positive to negative samples is about 10:1; we use Precision, Recall,F1 score to evaluate the model. The objective is to identify the illegal transactions, thus the output is an indicator for the illegal class. Also we expected the model to identify as many illegal transactions as possible, in addition to correctly identifying the illegal transaction, which requires the model to improve recall while ensuring high precision.

4.3 Results and Analysis

The experimental results are shown in Table 1. Among the machine learning models, the best results are obtained from random forests, while among the graph network models, our proposed AP-GCL shows strong performance in all metrics, ensuring high precision coupled with high recall. With our model as a self-supervised learning method, we demonstrate superior performance over supervised learning on the test set. Furthermore, DGI, which is also based on the idea of contrastive learning, has not performed well in identifying illegal transactions. The central focus of DGI is to maximise local mutual information and no consideration is made of node consistency through the transformations. We verified the superiority of our contrastive learning framework in disposing of positive and negative sample imbalances by maximizing node consistency and updating based on perturbations, and also demonstrated that node-based feature perturbations is both simple and effective for improving node representation.

Table 1. Classification metrics for the illegal class

Method	Precision	Recall	F_1
Logistic Regression	0.404	0.593	0.481
RandomForest	0.956	0.670	0.788
Xgboost	0.952	0.552	0.699
GCN	0.812	0.512	0.628
Skip-GCN	0.812	0.623	0.705
EvolveGCN	0.850	0.624	0.720
DGI	0.970	0.448	0.613
AP-GCL	**0.976**	**0.799**	**0.879**

We have shown the variation of the curves for each metric when the sample is tested in the validation set, as shown in Fig. 2. It can be observed that the value of recall is continuously increasing, indicating that the number of all negative samples identified by the model is progressively improving, while the value of precision remains basically the same and maintains a high value, which indicates that the model is more capable of identifying positive and negative samples. As the recall curve in the figure depicts, after 60 epochs, the improvement is slower, but the model is still improving towards a positive direction. Perturbation based on the node features can effectively prevent the model from falling into overfitting, while each update will pay more attention to negative sample-related information to obtain a model-friendly node representation.

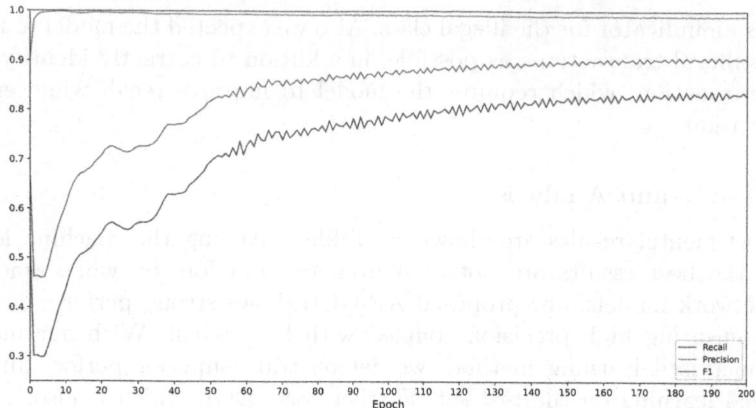

Fig. 2. Transformation curve of our model tested on the validation set

5 Conclusion

In this work, we propose a contrastive learning framework based on perturbation of node features to address the problem of unbalanced samples and sparse labels on the data, which is based on the problem of identifying illegal transactions in the Bitcoin trading network. There are two new views obtained by augmenting the original view with an augmented transformation, randomly adding perturbations to the node features of the new view and maximizing the consistency of the same nodes by the perturbations. Our experimental results indicate that node-feature-based perturbation can effectively improve the node representations achieved in self-supervised learning, thus enabling the model to yield performance comparable to that of supervised learning.

References

1. Cai, L., et al.: Structural temporal graph neural networks for anomaly detection in dynamic graphs. In: Proceedings of the 30th ACM International Conference on Information & Knowledge Management, pp. 3747–3756 (2021)
2. Chen, T., Kornblith, S., Norouzi, M., Hinton, G.: A simple framework for contrastive learning of visual representations. In: International Conference on Machine Learning, pp. 1597–1607. PMLR (2020)
3. Grover, A., Leskovec, J.: node2vec: scalable feature learning for networks. ACM (2016)
4. Hoffer, E., Ailon, N.: Deep metric learning using triplet network. In: Feragen, A., Pelillo, M., Loog, M. (eds.) SIMBAD 2015. LNCS, vol. 9370, pp. 84–92. Springer, Cham (2015). https://doi.org/10.1007/978-3-319-24261-3_7
5. Huang, Q., He, H., Singh, A., Lim, S.N., Benson, A.R.: Combining label propagation and simple models out-performs graph neural networks. arXiv preprint. arXiv:2010.13993 (2020)

6. Iscen, A., Tolias, G., Avrithis, Y., Chum, O.: Label propagation for deep semi-supervised learning. In: Proceedings of the IEEE/CVF Conference on Computer Vision and Pattern Recognition, pp. 5070–5079 (2019)
7. Kipf, T.N., Welling, M.: Semi-supervised classification with graph convolutional networks. arXiv preprint. arXiv:1609.02907 (2016)
8. Liu, Y., Li, Z., Pan, S., Gong, C., Zhou, C., Karypis, G.: Anomaly detection on attributed networks via contrastive self-supervised learning. IEEE Trans. Neural Netw. Learn. Syst. **33**(6), 2378–2392 (2021)
9. Lorenz, J., Silva, M.I., Aparício, D., Ascensão, J.T., Bizarro, P.: Machine learning methods to detect money laundering in the bitcoin blockchain in the presence of label scarcity. In: Proceedings of the First ACM International Conference on AI in Finance, pp. 1–8 (2020)
10. Melekhov, I., Kannala, J., Rahtu, E.: Siamese network features for image matching. In: 2016 23rd International Conference on Pattern Recognition (ICPR), pp. 378–383. IEEE (2016)
11. Nakamoto, S.: Bitcoin: a peer-to-peer electronic cash system. Decentralized Bus. Rev. 21260 (2008)
12. Noorshams, N., Verma, S., Hofleitner, A.: Ties: temporal interaction embeddings for enhancing social media integrity at facebook. In: Proceedings of the 26th ACM SIGKDD International Conference on Knowledge Discovery & Data Mining, pp. 3128–3135 (2020)
13. Pareja, A., et al.: Evolvegcn: evolving graph convolutional networks for dynamic graphs. In: Proceedings of the AAAI Conference on Artificial Intelligence, pp. 5363–5370 (2020)
14. Perozzi, B., Al-Rfou, R., Skiena, S.: Deepwalk: online learning of social representations. ACM (2014)
15. Velickovic, P., Fedus, W., Hamilton, W.L., Liò, P., Bengio, Y., Hjelm, R.D.: Deep graph infomax. ICLR (Poster) **2**(3), 4 (2019)
16. Wang, F., Zhang, C.: Label propagation through linear neighborhoods. IEEE Trans. Knowl. Data Eng. **20**(1), 55–67 (2007)
17. Wang, X., et al.: Apan: asynchronous propagation attention network for real-time temporal graph embedding. In: Proceedings of the 2021 International Conference on Management of Data, pp. 2628–2638 (2021)
18. Wang, Y., Jin, J.: Bag of tricks of semi-supervised classification with graph neural networks. arXiv abs/2103.13355 (2021)
19. Wang, Y., Zhang, J., Guo, S., Yin, H., Li, C., Chen, H.: Decoupling representation learning and classification for gnn-based anomaly detection. In: Proceedings of the 44th International ACM SIGIR Conference on Research and Development in Information Retrieval, pp. 1239–1248 (2021)
20. Weber, M., et al.: Anti-money laundering in bitcoin: experimenting with graph convolutional networks for financial forensics. arXiv preprint. arXiv:1908.02591 (2019)
21. You, Y., Chen, T., Sui, Y., Chen, T., Wang, Z., Shen, Y.: Graph contrastive learning with augmentations. Adv. Neural. Inf. Process. Syst. **33**, 5812–5823 (2020)
22. Zhu, Y., Xu, Y., Yu, F., Liu, Q., Wu, S., Wang, L.: Deep graph contrastive representation learning. In: ICML Workshop on Graph Representation Learning and Beyond (2020). http://arxiv.org/abs/2006.04131

An Overview of Opponent Modeling for Multi-agent Competition

Lu Liu, Jie Yang, Yaoyuan Zhang, Jingci Zhang, and Yuxi Ma(✉)

Beijing Institute of Technology, Beijing 100081, China

mayucc@126.com

Abstract. Multi-agent system (MAS) is an area of distributed artificial intelligence that emphasizes the joint behaviors of agents with some degree of autonomy and the complexities arising from their interactions. Multi-agent systems can solve problems that are difficult or impossible for an individual agent or a monolithic system to solve. Opponent modeling is generally used in competitive multi-agent systems, in which an agent models the actions, behaviors, and strategies of other agents (adversaries) to get better rewards and train stronger strategies for playing against each other. In this survey, we give an overview of multi-agent learning research in a spectrum of areas, including reinforcement learning, evolutionary computation, game theory, and agent modeling.

Keywords: Multi-agent system · Opponent modeling · Behavior modeling

1 Introduction

With the rapid development of a new generation of information technology innovation and application, from the perspective of artificial intelligence (AI) technology development, the dynamic game problem of incomplete information in complex environments has become a hot frontier problem to be solved, and the multi-agent real-time strategy confrontation technology is one of its core keys. The current AI technology represented by Deep Learning (DL) [1] and Reinforcement Learning (RL) [2] has made a big breakthrough, and the problem of the dynamic game with complete information represented by Go and Xiangqi has been solved; the development of AI technology has changed from computational intelligence and perceptual intelligence to more research focus on group The development of AI technology has shifted from computational intelligence and perceptual intelligence to more research focusing on group and cognitive intelligence; the solution of multi-agent real-time strategy confrontation problem has shifted from the traditional pre-programming rule-based approach to the autonomous reinforcement learning-based approach.

In recent years, due to the rapid development of deep learning, Deep Reinforcement Learning (DRL) has performed well in the fields of autonomous unmanned systems, robot control, and intelligent transportation. For example, AlphaGo [3] and AlphaZero [4] have defeated Li Shishi and Ke Jie in Go tournaments, and cities such as Shanghai and

Y. Xu et al. (Eds.): ML4CS 2022, LNCS 13655, pp. 634–648, 2023.
https://doi.org/10.1007/978-3-031-20096-0_48

Hangzhou have used deep reinforcement learning algorithms to solve traffic congestion and road planning problems [5].

In a realistic scenario, there are two roles in the adversarial environment, the number, state, and strategy of the opponent are unknown, and the environment is full of various uncertainties and interference information, which is complex and dynamic.

While the environment remains stable in a single-agent system, in a multi-agent system, all agents share a common environment and their behaviors form part of this environment, with each intelligence having full visibility of the environment but no direct knowledge of the goals of the other agents. At the same time, as the "game" progresses, each agent is greatly influenced by the behavior of the other agents due to changes in their behavior and strategies, leading to non-stationarity in the multi-agent system. In particular, in the game scenario of a competitive multi-agent system, an intelligence may learn a robust strategy by overfitting the current strategy of the opponent, but the learned strategy is usually prone to fail when the opponent changes its strategy [6].

Prior to advances in deep reinforcement learning algorithm research, tracking and context detection approaches were proposed to adapt faster to non-stationary environments [7]. Both approaches take a more proactive and reactive approach in dealing with non-stationary, i.e., they use learning methods that try to quickly change the policy or environment model once the environment dynamics change.

An alternative approach to handling non-stationary is called the self-play algorithm [8]. This approach takes a trained neural network, using each agent's observations as input, and learns strategies that can be generalized to any opponent by comparing them with current or previous versions. It has beaten human champions in backgammon and has been extended to more complex domains, even complex motion environments with continuous states and action spaces.

One way to deal with non-stationary based on deep reinforcement learning is to use a centralized critic architecture [9]. This architecture uses an actor-critic algorithm, where the training of the critic is centralized, which gives access to the observations and actions of all agents, while the training of the actor is decentralized. The strategy computation is done independently by each actor, and the structure corresponding to the critic is removed during testing. Because of the exposure to the opponent's observations and actions during training, the agent does not experience unexpected changes in the environment dynamics, which makes the learning process more stable.

The last mainstream way to deal with non-stationary is to model the opponent's behavior [10, 11]. By modeling the behavior, intentions, and strategies of other agents, the training process of the master agent is stabilized. Modeling other agents in multi-agent systems has been extensively studied.

This paper provides a systematic introduction to the research areas of multi-agent adversarial environment, agent behavior modeling, and agent behavior prediction, mainly containing techniques for multi-agent systems, multi-agent game adversarial, multi-agent reinforcement learning, deep reinforcement learning, and adversary modeling for competitive multi-agent systems.

2 Multi-agent Competition Environment

2.1 Multi-agent System

The theory of multi-agent systems originated in the 1970s with distributed artificial intelligence, whose goal was to create precise conceptual models to describe natural and social systems, mainly Distributed Problem Solving (DPS) [12] and multi-agent systems. The core of multi-agent systems theory is to divide the system into intelligent, autonomous subsystems that are physically and geographically dispersed and can perform tasks independently, but at the same time communicate and coordinate with each other to accomplish tasks together. Compared with traditional AI research, multi-agent systems consider not only the intelligence of individuals but also the autonomy and sociality of the whole system. Since the 1980 s, multi-agent systems theory and other fields have borrowed from each other and gained wider applications, the most important of which is reinforcement learning. Multi-agent systems are often used to solve problems that are difficult to solve by independent agents and single-layer systems. Because of their practicality and scalability, they are often used in robotics cooperation, distributed control, resource management, collaborative decision support systems, autonomous combat systems, data mining, and other fields.

The most common definition of a multi-agent system is a computing system consisting of multiple autonomous interacting agents in the same environment, including both the environment and the agents. Among them, agents can be implemented by methods, functions, processes, algorithms, or reinforcement learning, and can be classified into a variety of types. Including (1) passive agents or "goal-less agents" such as obstacles, apples, or keys in any simple simulation; (2) Active agents with simple goals, such as birds in plants, or wolf-sheep in predator-prey models; and (3) Cognitive agents requiring complex computational cognition, such as intelligent robots, autonomous unmanned systems, etc.

Environments can then be classified as virtual, discrete, and continuous environments. An agent's environment can also be classified according to the properties it contains, such as accessibility (whether complete information about the environment can be collected), determinism (whether actions produce definite effects), dynamism (how many entities currently affect the environment), discrete (whether the number of possible actions in the environment is limited), episodic (whether the actions of actors in certain periods affect other periods), and dimensionality (whether spatial features are important factors in the environment and whether the agent considers space when making decisions).

In a multi-agent system, the agents cooperate or compete with each other, and exhibit regular coordinated movements or competitive behaviors at the group level. Compared with single-agent systems, multi-agent systems have individual behaviors of each agent, and there are both cooperative and competitive relationships among the agents. The optimal solutions of individual agents are constrained not only by the environmental variables but also by the behaviors of other agents, so multi-agent systems have a natural complexity. In addition, individual agents often cannot solve problems independently, and multiple agents need to cooperate to accomplish tasks. If the number of agents is large, the solution space of the algorithm will be too large, and the optimal strategy will not be solved.

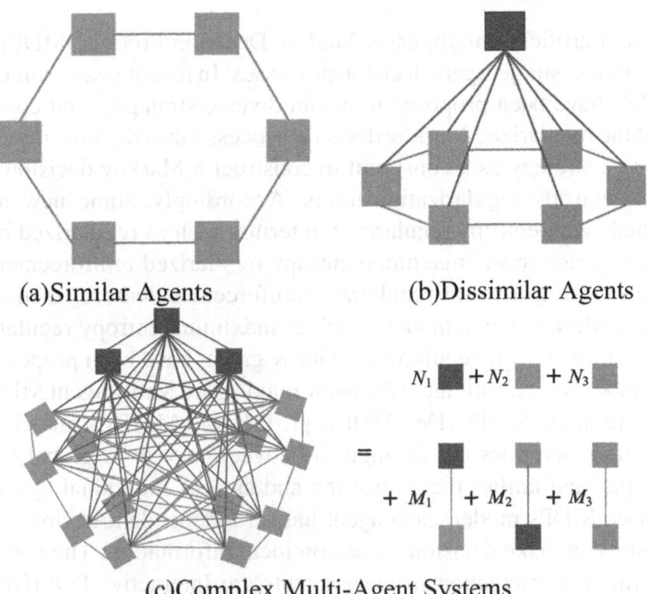

Fig. 1. Multi-agent system classification

Based on the type of agent and the behavioral space, agents can be divided into two types: similar agents and dissimilar agents, as shown in Fig. 1. Other more complex cases can be considered as multiple groups of similar or dissimilar agents, as shown in Fig. 1(c) (with three types of agents). Where N1, N2, N3 denote the number of three types of agents, and M1, M2, M3 denote the number of interactions of the three agents, respectively. The same class of agents is relatively simple because their behavior space is similar and the objects, they interact with are the same agents as themselves, so the agent detection process can be ignored and the behavior of the interacting objects can be predicted when there is enough information to choose the most optimal strategy for themselves. The dissimilar agent environment is a bit more complex. When an agent interacts, the interaction object must first be detected to determine the type of agent body and then select a strategy. In more complex scenarios, the number of agents may cause changes in the environment.

2.2 Multi-agent Game

Multi-intelligence game confrontation is to use a new AI paradigm to design AI and study the problems related to computer games through human-machine confrontation, machine-machine confrontation, human-machine cooperative confrontation, etc. Its essence is to explore the process of human cognitive decision-making intelligence acquisition through game learning methods and to study the intrinsic generation mechanism and technical pathway for AI to upgrade and evolve and defeat human intelligence, which is the necessary way for human-like intelligence research to embark on strong AI.

In the field of artificial intelligence, Markov Decision Process (MDP) [13] is commonly used to model single-agent decision processes. In recent years, some new Markov decision models have been proposed to obtain diverse strategies and cope with sparse feedback, and the regularized Markov decision process takes the information or entropy associated with a strategy as a constraint to construct a Markov decision process with information or entropy regularization terms. Accordingly, some new reinforcement learning methods with entropy regularization terms, such as regularized reinforcement learning in time series space, maximum entropy regularized reinforcement learning in strategy space and Taillis entropy regularized reinforcement learning methods, and some new regularized Markov game models, such as maximum entropy regularized Markov game and migration entropy regularized Markov game, have been proposed.

The main models for multi-agent decision-making are Multi-agent MDPs (MMDPs) [14] and Decentralized MDPs (Dec-MDPs) [15]. In the MMDPs model, a centralized strategy is used, which does not distinguish between private or global information of individual agents, and unifies the processing and assigns individual agents to execute, while in the Dec-MDPs model, each agent has an independent environment and state observation, and can make decisions based on local information. The main models that focus on information interaction between agents are Interactive POMDP (I-POMDP) [16], which mainly use Recursive Reasoning [17] to model the behavior of other agents explicitly, infer the behavioral information of other agents, and then act in response. The decision-theoretic-based learning models of agents are shown in Fig. 2, and they all belong to the category of Partial Observation Stochastic Game (POSG) [18] models.

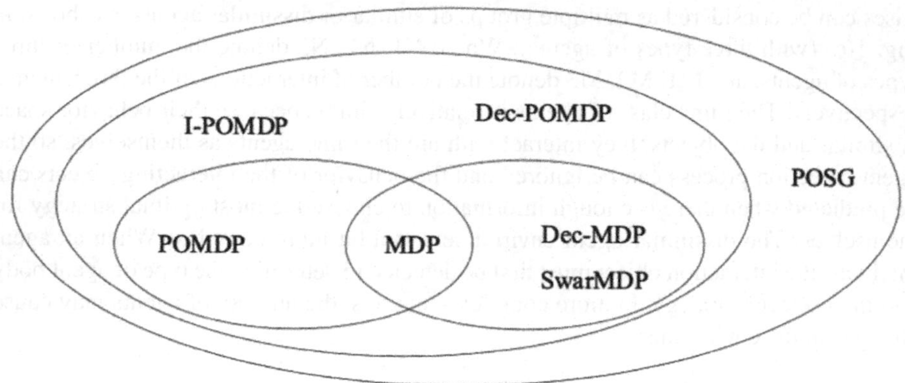

Fig. 2. Factored observation stochastic game

Currently, multi-agent game models directly based on game theory have received a lot of attention. As shown in Fig. 3, there are two typical types of multi-intelligent game models, Stochastic Game [19] (also known as Markov Game) [20] models for modeling problems such as real-time strategy games and unmanned cluster confrontations, and Extensive Form Game (EFG) [21] models for infrastructure protection, sequential interactions in mahjong, bridge, turn-based strategy games [22], and multi-stage military confrontation decisions. Some recent studies have sought to unify the two types of models by modeling the Extended Form Game model as a Factored Observation Stochastic Game (FOSG) [23] model.

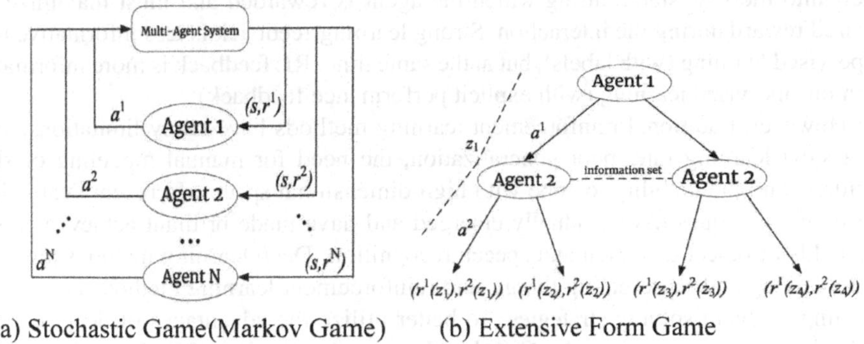

Fig. 3. Typical multi-agent game model

The multi-agent game faces the challenges of incomplete information, uncertain action, large-scale confrontation space, and difficult solution of the multi-party game. During the game, the strategy of each agent changes constantly with time, so the transfer probability distribution and reward function perceived by each agent also change, so its action strategy is non-stationary. Currently, the non-stationary problem is mainly modeled by online learning, reinforcement learning, and game theory. There are five main categories of approaches for agents to deal with non-equilibrium problems: Ignore, which assumes a smooth environment; Forget, which uses a model-free approach to forget past information while updating the latest observations; Fix (Target) opponent model, which optimizes for a predefined opponent; Learn (Learn) opponent model approach, which uses a model-based learning approach, which uses a model-based learning approach to learn the opponent's action strategy; and the Theory of Mind (ToM) [24] approach, where there is recursive reasoning between the agent and the opponent. Facing the adversary with finite rational deceptive strategies, the adversary modeling has become a must-have capability for the intelligent body gaming confrontation, which provides technical support for the processing of non-smooth problems together with distributed execution centralized training, meta-learning, and multi-agent communication modeling.

3 Multi-agent Deep Reinforcement Learning

3.1 Deep Reinforcement Learning

Reinforcement learning is an important branch of machine learning, which essentially describes and solves the problem of learning strategies to maximize the reward or achieve a specific goal as an agent interacts with its environment [25]. Unlike supervised learning, reinforcement learning does not tell an agent how to produce the correct action; it only evaluates the good or bad action and corrects the action choice and strategy based on the feedback signal, so the reward function of reinforcement learning requires less information and is easier to design for solving more complex decision problems. In reinforcement learning, an agent learns by interacting with its environment. At each time step, the agent perceives the state of the environment and takes action to transform itself into the new state, during which the agent is rewarded and must maximize the desired reward during the interaction. Strong learning feedback is less informative than supervised learning (with labels), but at the same time, RL feedback is more informative than unsupervised learning (with explicit performance feedback).

However, traditional reinforcement learning methods have many limitations, such as a slow learning rate, poor generalization, the need for manual modeling of state features, and the inability to cope with high-dimensional spaces. In recent years, deep learning techniques have gradually emerged and have made brilliant achievements in the fields of object detection and speech recognition. Deep learning methods are good at perceiving and representing things, and reinforcement learning methods are good at learning problem-solving strategies. To better utilize the advantages of deep learning and reinforcement learning, the Google AI research team DeepMind creatively fuses deep neural networks and reinforcement learning and uses deep learning algorithms in reinforcement learning to define the field of deep reinforcement learning.

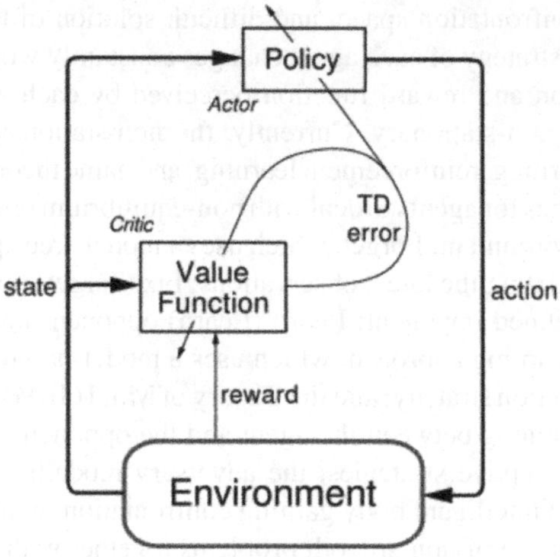

Fig. 4. The actor-critic framework for deep reinforcement learning

For DRL, the current algorithms can be included in the actor-critic framework. Actor-critic belongs to the Time Difference (TD) learning approach, which explicitly represents the policy independent of the value function in a separate memory structure. The policy structure is called actor because it is used to select actions, and the estimated value function is called critic because it evaluates the actions performed by the actor, as shown in Fig. 4. Consider the DRL algorithm as the brain of the agent, i.e., it contains two parts:

the actor action module and the critic judgment module, both consisting of deep neural networks. In the actor-critic framework, Google DeepMind combines CNN with Q-learning [26] to form Deep Q- Network (DQN) [27], which uses deep neural networks to approximate Q-functions and policies, not only allowing the agent to face a high-dimensional state space, but also solving the problem that state features are difficult to model, as shown in Fig. 5.

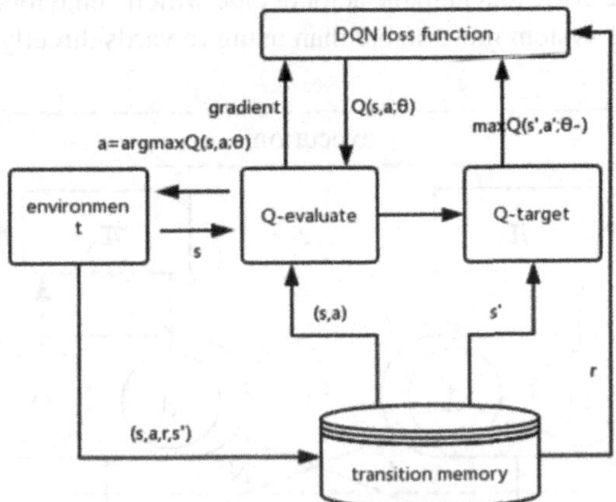

Fig. 5. DQN algorithm training process

DQN is similar to Q-learning in that it is a value-based iterative algorithm, but in normal Q-learning, Q-Table can be used to store Q-values for each state-action pair when the state and action space is discrete and not high-dimensional, while it is difficult to use Q-Table without the action space and states being too large when the state and action space is high-dimensional and continuous. Therefore, a Q-table update can be transformed into a function fitting problem by fitting a function to generate Q-values instead of a Q-table, so that similar states get similar output actions. Since deep neural networks are very effective in extracting complex features, Deep Learning can be combined with Reinforcement Learning to form the DQN algorithm.

The success and widespread application of DRL methods have led to a new interest in using high-capacity models such as neural networks to solve multi-agent reinforcement learning problems, and they have boldly tried to incorporate DRL methods into multi-agent systems to accomplish numerous complex tasks in multi-intelligent environments. After several years of development and innovation, MADRL has produced many algorithms, rules, and frameworks, and has been widely used in various real-world domains. From single to multiple, simple to complex, and low to high dimensional, MADRL is becoming the hottest research and application direction in the field of machine learning and artificial intelligence and has great research value and significance.

One representative algorithm is the Multi-Agent Deep Deterministic Policy Gradient [9] (MADDPG) algorithm proposed by the OpenAI research team, as shown in Fig. 6. When using deep neural networks to solve the MADRL problem, one approach that has worked well in the past is to use a decentralized actor for each agent and a centralized critic with shared parameters among the agents. MADDPG is developed from the DRL algorithm DDPG [28] and is an extension of the actor-critic policy gradient approach based on the actor-critic, with the critic adding additional information about the strategies of other agents, and the actor has access only to the agent's information. Typically, a suggestion is an attempt by the critic to predict the value of an action in a given state (e.g., the expected reward), which will be used by the actor to update its action strategy. The algorithm treats each agent in a multi-agent scenario as an actor, and each actor receives suggestions from the critic that help the actor decide which behaviors to reinforce during training, making the system more stable than using rewards directly.

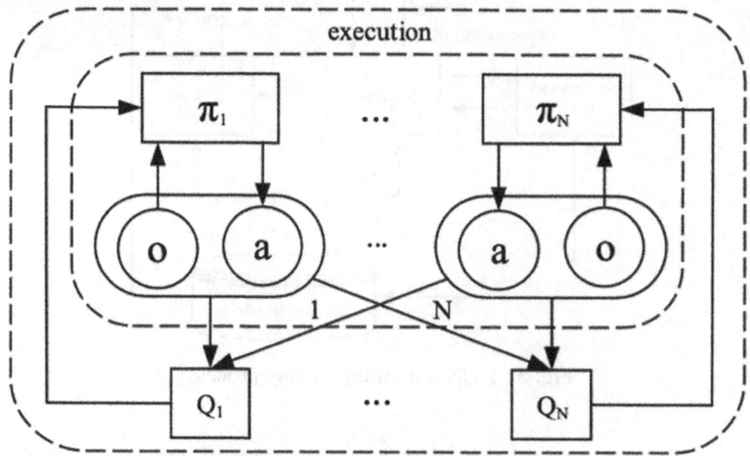

Fig. 6. MADDPG algorithm network structure

In addition, the MADDPG algorithm allows agents to learn to collaborate and compete with each other and reinforces the level of a critic to allow multiple agents to act in a globally coordinated manner so that they have access to the behavior and status of all agents. After the MADDPG algorithm is uniformly trained, the actor no longer needs to listen to the advice from the critic and will act independently based on its observations. Since each agent has its independent centralized critic, the method can be used to simulate multi-agent systems with different target strategies, including adversarial systems with conflicting strategies.

3.2 Multi-agent Reinforcement Learning

Multi-agent reinforcement learning refers to a group of self-controlled, interacting agents that perceive and operate through sensors and actuators in the same environment, resulting in a fully cooperative, fully competitive, or hybrid multi-agent system. In such a system, the rewards of the actions performed by each agent are influenced by the actions of the other agents, so learning a strategy to achieve equilibrium homeostasis is the goal of the multi-agent system.

In a single-agent system, there is only one agent and the environment remains constant. The agent interacts with the environment and optimizes its behavior using returns.

Formally, the single-agent reinforcement learning process can usually be described using a Markov decision process, described by a five-tuple as (S, A, P, r, γ). Where S is the state space, A is the action space, the state transfer probability is $P{:}S \times A \times S \rightarrow [0,1]$, and the immediate payoff is : $r{:}S \times A \rightarrow R$.

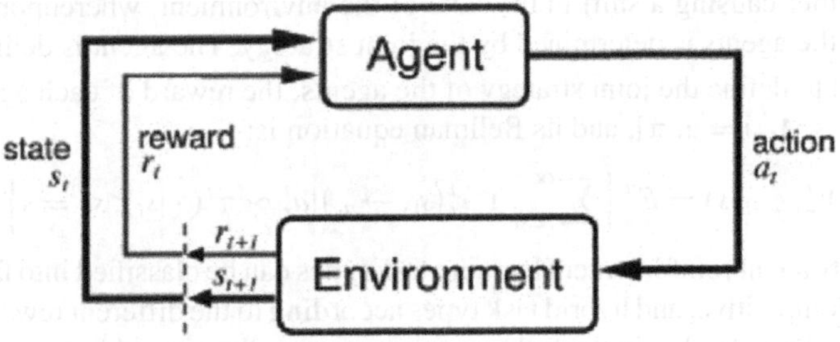

Fig.7. Single-agent reinforcement learning framework

The process of multi-agent reinforcement learning is, in most cases, based on Markovian decision processes as in single-agent reinforcement learning, but since each agent in a multi-agent system is affected not only by the environment but also by the actions of other agents. The single-agent reward in a multi-agent system is not only related to its actions, but also to the actions of other agents. Therefore, a Markov game is usually used to describe a multi-agent system, described by the tuple: (n, S, A1, A2,…, An, T, r1,…, An, T, r1, r2, …, rn, γ).

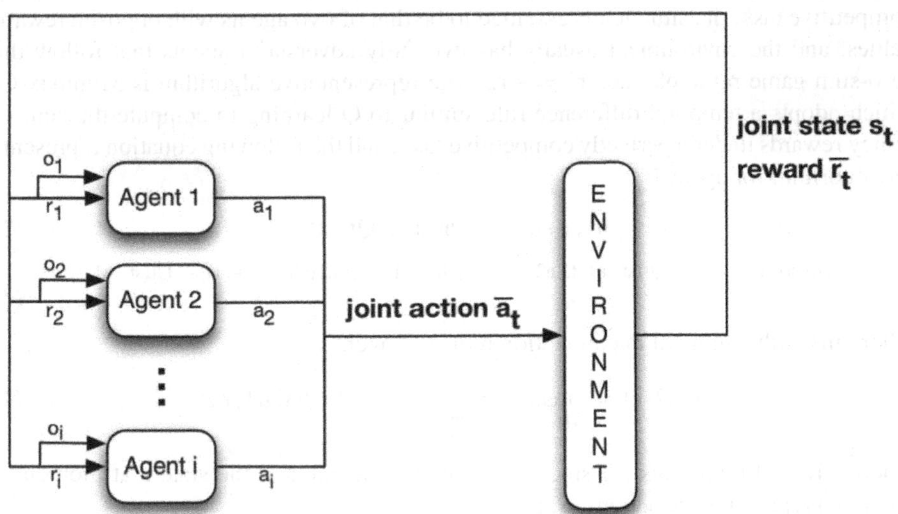

Fig.8. Multi-agent reinforcement learning framework

Where n is the number of multiple agents, S is the joint state space, A is the set of joint action spaces of all agents $A = A1 \times A2 \times An$, ri is the reward function ri: S $\times$

A1, A2,... For each agent, T is the state transfer function T :S × A1, A2,...,An → R and T is the state transfer function T:S × A1, A2,..., An × S → [0,1], and $\gamma \in [0,1]$ denotes the discount factor, which guarantees that the later the reward, the smaller the effect on the reward function, which portrays the uncertainty of future rewards and also makes the reward function bounded. In a multi-intelligent scenario, all the agents take actions together causing a shift in the state of the environment, whereupon the reward received by the agents is determined by the joint strategy. The agent is defined by $\vec{\pi} = (\overrightarrow{\pi 1}, \ldots, \overrightarrow{\pi n})$ to define the joint strategy of the agents, the reward of each agent is: $r_i^{\pi} = E[r_{t+1} | S_t = s, A_t, i = a, \pi]$, and its Bellman equation is:

$$V^i_{\pi^i,\pi^{-i}}(s) = E^{\pi}\left\{\sum\nolimits_{t=0}^{\infty} \Upsilon^t r^i_t(s_t, \to_{a_t}) | a^i_t \sim \pi^i(\cdot\,|s_t), s_0 = s\right\} \tag{1}$$

The multi-agent reinforcement learning task types can be classified into fully cooperative, fully competitive, and hybrid task types according to the different reward functions of the agents. Specifically, in the fully cooperative task, the reward function is the same for all the agents, i.e., r1 = r2 =... = rn, so that the reward value is the same for all the agents. = rn, so that the reward value is the same for all the agents, so that the goal of multi-agent reinforcement learning becomes simple, and only the common reward needs to be maximized. In a fully competitive task, the goals between the agents are adversarial, so the reward values are generally opposite. In addition, many task types, which are neither fully competitive nor fully cooperative, are called hybrid, where the reward values of the agents are often different but interrelated so that the reward values of each agent cannot be maximized independently.

In this paper, we focus on the modeling of agents under game theory, and therefore, only fully competitive multi-agent reinforcement learning is elaborated here. In a fully competitive task, the situation is assumed to be that of two agents with opposite reward values, and the environment usually has two fully adversarial agents that follow the zero-sum game principle, i.e., r1 = −r2. The representative algorithm is Minimax-Q, which adopts a temporal difference rule similar to Q-learning to compute the sum of policy rewards under a perfectly competitive task, and the following equation represents the algorithm for agent 1:

$$\text{h1, t(st, } \cdot) = \text{argm1(Qt, xt)} \tag{2}$$

$$\text{Qt} + 1(\text{st, a1, t, a2, t}) = \text{Qt(st, a1, t, a2, t)} + \alpha\left[\text{rk} + 1 + \gamma\text{m1(Qt, at} + 1) - \text{Qt(st, a1, t, a2, t)}\right] \tag{3}$$

where m1 is the minimal maximization return of agent 1:

$$m_1(Q, s) = \max_{h1(s_{t,\cdot})} \min_{a2} \sum_{a1} h1(x, a1)Q(s, a1, a2) \tag{4}$$

where h1(st, ·) represents the stochastic policy of agent 1 at the state s at moment t, where (·) represents the action parameter.

4 Opponent Modeling for Multi-agent Competition

In an agent interaction environment, the payoff of an agent depends not only on the environment but also on the actions of other agents. Therefore, reasoning about the strategies, beliefs and other characteristics of other agents is essential for effective decision-making. At the same time, the interacting agents often reveal some behavioral characteristics or strategic biases when interacting. If an agent can make use of the features of other agents by modeling them when making interaction decisions, it can help the agent to make better decisions. This approach to modeling other agents involved in the interaction is called adversary modeling. Classical adversary modeling is to build an adversary model based on the interaction history of an agent and to treat the model as a function that inputs information and data about the interaction history of an agent and outputs predictions about its actions, preferences, goals, and plans, etc.

Reasonable prediction of the opponent's behavior and safe exploitation of the opponent's weaknesses can provide a valid basis for the decision-making of the opponent. To solve the problem of incomplete information in games, the most straightforward idea is to approximate it using information complementation and other means to transform it into a complete information game model. In this paper, adversary modeling mainly refers to the way of modeling the behavior of an agent using the interaction information between agents, then reasoning to predict the behavior of the adversary, reasoning to discover the weakness of the adversary and exploit it.

An important function of agent modeling is to infer the action behavior of other agents. By constructing an agent model, predictions can be made about attributes of interest to the agent, including actions, goals, and beliefs. Typically, a model is a function that takes as input a portion of the observed interaction history, and the output is a prediction of some relevant property of the agent. The interaction history contains information such as the past actions taken by the modeling agent in various situations. Nowadays, various modeling approaches exist in multi-agent environments, but the methods and underlying assumptions are quite different.

4.1 Explicit Opponent Modeling

Explicit modeling means building an explicit opponent model, such as decision trees, neural networks, Bayesian networks, etc. The commonly used explicit opponent modeling methods can be broadly classified into planning action intention identification methods, behavior classification and type inference methods, strategy reconstruction methods, cognitive reasoning methods, and game-best response methods.

Hong et al. [29] proposed two models, called the deep policy inference Q-network DPIQN and the recurrent version DRPIQN. Their approach uses an auxiliary implicit adversary modeling goal to update Q learning. Both DPIQN and DRPIQN are trained through an adaptive training process, where the attention of the network is adjusted at different stages of the training process to learn its Q values and policy features.

4.2 Implicit Opponent Modeling

Implicit modeling, on the other hand, implicitly encodes certain features of the opponent's behavior into other structures or reasoning processes. Implicit modeling is mainly classified into meta-learning-based implicit modeling, online learning-based implicit modeling, and opponent-perception-based implicit modeling.

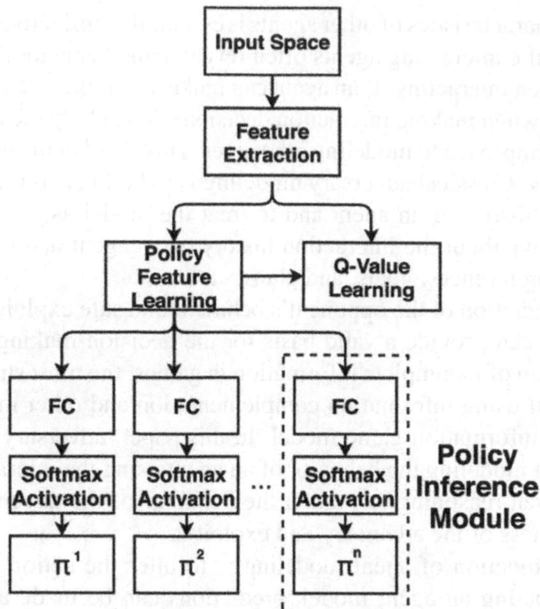

Fig.9. DPIQN explicit opponent modeling network

Raileanu [30] et al. consider a multi-agent reinforcement learning setup with incomplete information, where the reward function depends on the hidden goals of two agents, and thus the agents must infer the goals of other players from their observed behavior to maximize their rewards. They propose a new approach to learning in these domains: Self Other-Modeling (SOM), in which agents use their strategies to predict the behavior of other agents and update their beliefs about their hidden goals in an online fashion. They evaluate this approach on three different tasks and show that agents are able to use their estimates of other participants' goals to learn better strategies in both cooperative and competitive settings.

5 Conclusion

This paper introduces the theory of opponent modeling for multi-agent competition. It introduces the concepts and classical algorithms of multi-agent reinforcement learning, especially the neural network-based multi-agent deep reinforcement learning methods. On this basis, adversarial modeling for multi-agent adversaries is introduced. Finally, we discuss other areas of knowledge related to reinforcement learning.

References

1. LeCun, Y., Bengio, Y., Hinton, G.: Deep learning. Nature **521**(7553), 436–444 (2015)
2. Li, Y.: Deep reinforcement learning: An overview. arXiv preprint arXiv:1701.07274(2017)

3. Wang, F.Y., Zhang, J.J., Zheng, X., et al.: Where does alphago go: From church-turing thesis to alphago thesis and beyond. IEEE/CAA J. Autom. Sinica **3**(2), 113–120 (2016)
4. Holcomb, S.D., Porter, W.K., Ault, S.V., et al.: Overview on deepmind and its alphago zero ai. In: Proceedings of the 2018 International Conference on Big Data and Education, pp. 67–71 (2018)
5. Li, L., Lv, Y., Wang, F.Y.: Traffic signal timing via deep reinforcement learning[J]. IEEE/CAA J. Autom. Sinica **3**(3), 247–254 (2016)
6. Li, S., Chi, H., Xie, T.: Multi-agent combation-stationary environments. In: 2021InternationalJoint Conference on Neural Networks (IJCNN). Shenzhen, China: IEEE, pp. 1–8 (2021)
7. Da Silva B.C., Basso, E.W., Bazzan, A.L., et al.: Dealing with non-stationary environments using context detection. In: Proceedings of the 23rd International Conference on Machine learning, pp. 217–224 (2006)
8. Weinberg, M., Rosenschein, J.S.: Best-response multiagent learning in non-stationary environments Proceedings of the Third International Joint Conference on Autonomous Agents and Multiagent Systems-Volume **2**, 506–513 (2004)
9. Lowe, R., Wu, Y.I., Tamar, A., et al.: Multi-agent actor-critic for mixed cooperative-competitive envi- ronments. In: Advances in Neural Information Processing systems, vol. 30 (2017)
10. Everett, R., Roberts, S.: Learning against non-stationary agents with opponent modelling and deep reinforcement learning. In: 2018 AAAI spring symposium series, (2018)
11. Cohen, M.X., Ranganath, C.: Reinforcement learning signals predict future decisions. J. Neurosci. **27**(2), 371–378 (2007)
12. Yeoh, W., Yokoo, M.: Distributed problem solving. AI Mag. **33**(3), 53 (2012)
13. Puterman, M.L.: Markov decision processes. Handbooks Oper. Res. Management Sci. **2**, 331–434 (1990)
14. Kumar, A., Zilberstein, S.: Event-detecting multi-agent mdps: Complexity and constant-factor approximation (2009)
15. Melo, F.S., Veloso, M.: Decentralized mdps with sparse interactions. Artif. Intell. **175**(11), 1757–1789 (2011)
16. Gmytrasiewicz, P.J., Doshi, P.: Interactive pomdps: Properties and preliminary results. In: International Conference on Autonomous Agents: Proceedings of the Third International Joint Conference on Autonomous Agents and Multiagent Systems, vol. 3, pp. 1374–1375 (2004)
17. Wen, Y., Yang, Y., Luo, R., et al.: Probabilistic recursive reasoning for multi-agent reinforcement learning. arXiv preprint arXiv:1901.09207. (2019)
18. Chatterjee, K., Doyen, L.: Partial-observation stochastic games: How to win when belief fails. ACM Transactions on Computational Logic (TOCL) **15**(2), 1–44 (2014)
19. Shapley, L.S.: Stochastic games. Proc. Natl. Acad. Sci. **39**(10), 1095–1100 (1953)
20. Littman, M.L.: Markov games as a framework for multi-agent reinforcement learning. Machine learning proceedings,: New Brunswick. NJ, USA: Elsevier pp. 157–163 (1994)
21. McCabe, K.A., Rassenti, S.J., Smith, V.L.: Game theory and reciprocity in some extensive form experimental games. Proc. Natl. Acad. Sci. **93**(23), 13421–13428 (1996)
22. Hinrichs, T.R., Forbus, K.D.: Analogical learning in a turn-based strategy game. IJCAI, pp. 853–858 2007
23. Kovařík, V., Schmid, M., Burch, N., et al.: Rethinking formal models of partially observable multiagent decision making. Artif. Intell. **303**, 103645 (2022)
24. Frith, C., Frith, U.: Theory of mind. Curr. Biol. **15**(17), R644–R645 (2005)
25. Kaelbling, L.P., Littman, M.L., Moore, A.W.: Reinforcement learning: a survey. J.Artif. Intell. Res. **4**, 237–285 (1996)

26. Watkins, C.J., Dayan, P.: Q-learning. Mach. Learn. **8**(3), 279–292 (1992)
27. Mnih, V., Kavukcuoglu, K., Silver, D., et al.: Human-level control through deep reinforcement learning. Nature **518**(7540), 529–533 2015
28. Lillicrap, T.P., Hunt, J.J., Pritzel, A., et al.: Continuous control with deep reinforcement learning. arXiv preprint arXiv:1509.02971. (2015)
29. Hong, Z.W., Su, S.Y., Shann, T.Y., et al.: A deep policy inference q-network for multi-agent systems. arXiv preprint arXiv:1712.07893. (2017)
30. Raileanu, R., Denton, E., Szlam, A., et al.: Modeling others using oneself in multi-agent reinforcement learning. In: International Conference on Machine Learning. Stockholm, Sweden: PMLR, pp. 4257–4266 (2018)

Research on Potential Threat Identification Algorithm for Electric UAV Network Communication

Gebiao Hu(✉), Zhichi Lin, Zheng Guo, Ruiqing Xu, and Xiao Zhang

Construction Branch of State Grid Jiangxi Electric Power Co., Ltd., 330001 Nanchang, China
z0220dd@163.com

Abstract. Potential threat identification of network communication can improve the reliability of power grid, and an algorithm for potential threat identification of power UAV (Urban Assault Vehicle) network communication is designed. In order to identify the potential threat of power UAV network communication, we should collect the data of power UAV network communication, establish the evaluation index of potential threat, decompose the data, establish attack graph and identify malicious node. Experimental results show that the proposed algorithm can improve the recognition accuracy, and the recognition rate of errors and omissions is low, which meets the design requirements.

Keywords: UAV network · Signal communication · Potential threats · Distinguish · Acquisition · Indicators

1 Introduction

Power communication network is a special communication network for the operation and management of power system, which is to ensure the safe and stable operation of power system. The resulting important infrastructure of the power system has obvious industry characteristics and special safety and reliability requirements. As an indispensable part of the secondary system of power grid, power communication network provides services such as production, operation and management for the power system, and also ensures the safe operation of the power system. With the development of the power communication network, a large number of power system businesses need to transmit information through the power communication network, and the risk and fault of the power communication network have increasingly serious impact on the power system. The power system production department has higher and higher requirements for the reliability of the power communication network, so it is of great significance to carry out risk assessment on the power communication network.

Li et al. [1] proposed a method for identifying abnormal behavior in mobile wireless sensor network communication. This method groups the overlapping time in the network, and effectively controls the amount of data collected by network nodes based on the overlapping time allocation mechanism. Using the dissimilarity analysis method to

Y. Xu et al. (Eds.): ML4CS 2022, LNCS 13655, pp. 649–663, 2023.
https://doi.org/10.1007/978-3-031-20096-0_49

collect data and analyze the results to complete the identification of abnormal communication behavior, but this method is vulnerable to external factors in the identification process, resulting in the reduction of identification accuracy. Kang et al. [2] proposed a communication signal anomaly detection method based on deep learning. The feasibility of ad is verified by constructing a deep learning network architecture and using time-frequency in-phase/orthogonal sampling data. Deep learning support vector description and modulation recognition ad methods are proposed to complete the detection of communication signals. This method can detect abnormal signals, but the detection time is long.

Therefore, this paper proposes a method of risk identification to optimize the design. By collecting the network communication data of electric UAV, the potential threat assessment index is established, the data is decomposed, the attack graph is established, and the malicious nodes are identified. In order to complete the identification of potential threats to the network communication of electric unmanned aerial vehicles.

2 Data Acquisition of Electric UAV Network Communication

Big data technology exists in every space of data management and data processing. It can provide complete information for data operation and standardize management data mode in the adjustable range [3].

Firstly, the data management information obtained by Big Data Technology will be stored in a centralized manner to obtain the grid data to be manipulated, and the data acquisition equation will be constructed according to the management criteria as follows:

$$C = \left(1 - \frac{U}{I}\right)e^{\frac{l}{K}} \tag{1}$$

In the above formula, C is the data acquisition parameter, U is the internal control spatial information data, I is the number of management data, K is the central management criteria coefficient, and l is the internal information integration data.

After the above operations, the abnormal data will be centrally obtained, and the specific conditions required for monitoring will be studied according to the storage and transmission path of the abnormal data. Based on the above data mining, the data stream is preprocessed. The data stream generated after UAV mapping is an unbounded sequence data, and there are also some old data. Therefore, the data is preprocessed, mainly including data stream blocking, vertical normalization and time slicing.

In terms of data flow block, the data flow generated by UAV is regarded as a series of infinite points, which are relatively difficult to store. Therefore, it is divided into the form of data block and the size of data block is defined as n. Based on this point, data blocks are divided into several categories and standardized for different data specifications and collection ranges. Some data have too large attribute dimensions or collection ranges, which may lead to attribute domination [4]. In order to reduce the impact of data attributes on data detection, this paper introduces the concept of attribute normalization, which is expressed as:

$$\tilde{a}_{ij} = \frac{a_{ij} - \min(a_j)}{\max(a_j) - \min(a_j)} \tag{2}$$

In formula (2), a_{ij} represents the characteristic value of a certain data in the collected data set, a_j represents the set of data dimension attributes, and $\max(a_j)$ and $\min(a_j)$ respectively represent the maximum and minimum values of the data in the collected data set.

Because there are many parameters involved, a single standardized processing cannot meet the requirements. Therefore, the processing formula for data scale transformation and scale change is as follows:

$$\overline{y}_i = \frac{y_i - \overline{Y}}{S} \tag{3}$$

In formula (3), y_i represents the signal parameters of time series data during data collection, $\overline{Y}$ represents the average value of collected signals, and S represents the standard deviation of collected information.

On this basis, for time slice processing, in order to better process data, the original data is created into fixed-size segments and divided into equal-interval time series segments [5], as shown in the following formula:

$$S = \begin{bmatrix} s_1 \\ s_2 \\ \vdots \\ s_j \\ \vdots \\ s_{\overline{N}} \end{bmatrix} = \begin{bmatrix} [t_1(x_1, y_1) : t_L(x_L, y_L)] \\ [t_{l+1}(x_{l+1}, y_{l+1}) : t_{L+l}(x_{L+l}, y_{L+l})] \\ \vdots \\ \left[t_{b-l+1}(x_{b-l+1}, y_{b-l+1}) : t_{\tilde{b}+L-l}(x_{lj+L-l}, y_{b+L-l})\right] \\ \vdots \\ [t_{N-L+1}(x_{N-L+1}, y_{N-L+1}) : t_N(x_N, y_N)] \end{bmatrix} \tag{4}$$

In formula (4), S represents the data set obtained after data slice processing, s_j represents the data segment processed in j, $\overline{N}$ represents the total amount of data, and N represents the total number of fragments.

After the above preprocessing, the potential rules of the data are mined. In this part, convolutional neural network is used for mining. This method has strong local feature extraction ability and can reduce the computational complexity of the network. The whole process is as follows:

Firstly, input layer, which is the beginning and input part of the entire network [6], can mine one-dimensional or two-dimensional data.

Second, the excitation layer function is established, which mainly describes the relationship between the input and output of the network layer and can be expressed as:

$$A = f\left(Z_{i,j,k}^{l}\right) \tag{5}$$

In formula (5), $Z_{i,j,k}^{l}$ represents the description parameter of i, j and k data respectively, and f represents the rectification parameter.

Thirdly, the pooling layer is built, which mainly compresses the feature data, extracts the data more abstractly, and generates the statistics of the surrounding area by the values generated by pooling window.

Fourthly, the full connection layer, which mainly provides the function of transmitting signals in the calculation process, through which the eigenvalues of data are connected and connected into a long vector [7];

Fifth, Backpropagation, which aims primarily at minimizing functions, is able to analyze all data points at minimal cost, with the following expressions:

$$L = -\sum_{T}^{j=1} y_j \lg S_j \tag{6}$$

In formula (6), y_j represents the output value of the i-th data, S_j represents the data probability, and T represents the total number of data categories.

The above calculation can reduce the learning parameters, and is faster than the traditional network training, and can reduce the complexity of the calculation.

3 Establishment of Potential Threat Evaluation Index for Electric UAV Network Communication

Based on the above process, the data are further processed by hyper-network, which is helpful to understand the complexity of special networks not only in scale, but also in attribute. Researchers hope to model the network with multi-layer, multi-level, multi-dimensional network flow characteristics, so as to conduct in-depth analysis and research. The existing methods of hyper-network theory are still limited, so we need to improve them or find new methods to define weights in hyper-network, study flows in hyper-network or use new parameters to measure topology of hyper-network. A hypergraph can be regarded as a generalization of graph theory, and its edges can include any number of nodes. These finite sets of nodes with the same attributes are hyperedges. Compared with the basic graph theory, the connection between nodes is ignored in the definition of hypergraph. But in both the definition of weights and the study of flows, the connection between nodes is of great significance [8].

Therefore, this paper improves the definition of hypergraphs by increasing the connection between nodes, including the definition of nodes and edges in basic graph theory and hypergraph theory. Thus, more details of complex networks can be shown in the logical structure modeling of SAS with improved hypergraph. It should be noted that the practical problems studied in this paper will not be represented by rings or parallel edges, that is, only simple graphs or simple hypergraphs will be used. Represent the hypercorrelation matrix as:

$$b_i^{HG} = \begin{cases} 1, v_i \in e_j^{HG} \\ 0, v_i \notin e_j^{HG} \end{cases} \tag{7}$$

In the above formula, v_i represents the node weight and e_j^{HG} represents the adjacency matrix.

After the abovementioned treatment, an evaluation index shall be established and the influencing factors shall be analyzed, and the risk index set of the network information flow of environmental emergencies shall be recorded as $U = (U_1, U_2 \cdots, U_m)$, among which U_1, U_2 and U_m represent the indexes to be considered for evaluation respectively, and the factor set shall be expressed as $F = (F_1, F_2 \cdots, F_n)$. After the potential hazard evaluation index and influencing factors are constructed, the weight of the indexes shall be determined by adopting the analytic hierarchy process, and be recorded as $B = (B_1, B_2 \cdots, B_m)$, and the weight of the risk evaluation index of a certain layer in the functional layer shall be recorded as:

$$\sum_{j=1}^{m} B_j = 1 \tag{8}$$

The weight matrix of the evaluation index is written as:

$$B = \begin{Bmatrix} B_{11} & B_{12} & \cdots & B_{1n} \\ B_{21} & B_{22} & \cdots & B_{2n} \\ \cdots & \cdots & B_{ij} & \cdots \\ B_{m1} & B_{m2} & \cdots & B_{mn} \end{Bmatrix} \tag{9}$$

In the above matrix, B represents the importance of the weight obtained by the i expert's judgment of the j indicator.

In order to ensure a more scientific weight, the similarity among the weights of each index is analyzed, so the index weights are discretized and the similarity coefficient matrix is formed after processing [9], and the calculation formula is expressed as follows:

$$M_{ij} = 1 - \sqrt{\frac{1}{n}\sum_{i=1}^{n}(B_{ik} - B_{jk})^2} \tag{10}$$

In the above formula, B_{ik} and B_{jk} are dimensions of i and j indexes respectively.

In order to better reflect the correlation between various information elements [10], the early warning indicators need to be fully weighted to make the weighted matrix more stable and normalized. Establish sample matrix:

$$V = \begin{pmatrix} v_{111} & v_{112} & \cdots & v_{11x} \\ v_{121} & v_{122} & \cdots & v_{12x} \\ \vdots & \vdots & & \vdots \\ v_{y1} & v_{y2} & \cdots & v_{yx} \end{pmatrix} \tag{11}$$

In the above formula, the parameters involved are evaluation parameters.

Through the above process, the evaluation indicators are established, and the indicators and influencing factors are given weights to provide the basis for subsequent hazard identification.

4 Data Decomposition

The specific process is as follows:

Step1: Considering the basic principle of N-LMS algorithm [11], set the sampling of power grid reference voltage signal as u, suppose there are N objects in the data set, each object contains M characteristic dimensions;

Step2: Using the random sampling method, in M characteristic dimension, obtains the current data on this characteristic dimension value;

Step3: N-LMS algorithm is convergent under the condition of limited iterative step length, but it will be unbalanced in practical application. In order to converge, the step size must meet the following conditions:

$$0 < \mu < \frac{2}{\lambda_{\max}} \tag{12}$$

where $\lambda_{\max}$ represents the maximum step size.

Step4: the overall average error of the algorithm is expressed as:

$$J = J_{\min} + J_{ex}(\infty) \tag{13}$$

where $J_{\min}$ represents the minimum objective function and $J_{ex}(\infty)$ represents the mathematical expectation.

It can be seen from the above calculation that this method can not meet the performance requirements of the minimum average error, and there is a certain error. Therefore, the offset factor is defined, which is expressed as:

$$U = \frac{J_{ex}(\infty)}{J_{\min}} = \sum_{i=1}^{N} \frac{\mu\lambda_i}{2 - \mu\lambda_i} \tag{14}$$

where λ_i represents the convergence parameter of the i-th coefficient.

Step5: after the above steps are repeated, the basic characteristic data are obtained, and the data are processed by the equal width method. The statistical formula is expressed as:

$$P = \frac{P(OC = 1, U_{lm} = V_i)}{P(U_{lm} = V_i)} \tag{15}$$

In the above formula, $P(OC = 1, U_{lm} = V_i)$ represents the joint probability that the U_{lm}-th data falls into the V_i interval in the statistical period, and $P(U_{lm} = V_i)$ represents the probability that the effective value of the data falls into the V_i interval in the statistical period.

Step6: Function fitting, using Sigmoid function on voltage RMS fitting U_{lm} and alarm between the function relationship between the probability $P(OC = 1, U_{lm} = V_i)$, fitting, the regression coefficient, recorded as β_0, β_1;

Step 7: According to the above steps, find out the corresponding relationship between the data sets, and produce the corresponding eigenvalues, it is recorded as O;

Step 8: Generate key feature data points, detect daily sample data, and calculate anomaly scores for all elements in O.

Through the above process to decompose the data signal, the basic power UAV network communication abnormal data feature points are obtained.

5 Establishment of Attack Graph

Based on the above analysis, an important step in constructing generalized Bayesian attack graphs is to compute the local conditional probability distribution function of nodes [12]. The local conditional probability distribution mediates the interaction between adjacent nodes. In the generalized Bayesian attack graph, we need to calculate the local conditional probability distribution of each class of nodes: attack condition node, atomic node, attack benefit node and threat state variable node.

For any atomic attack node *e*, its parent node is mainly composed of several attack condition nodes, and the set of attack condition nodes in its parent node is set as $C_{pre}(e)$. An atomic attack can occur only when all of its preconditions are true, but it may not occur when all of its preconditions are true. Whether the atomic attack is successfully exploited by the attacker is mainly affected by the difficulty of using the corresponding vulnerability of the atomic attack, that is, the greater the difficulty of the attack, the less likely it is to be successfully exploited by the attacker, and vice versa. The local conditional probability distribution function of the atomic attack node is:

$$\Pr\left(e = TrueC_{pre}(e)\right)\begin{cases} Dif(e), \forall c_j \in C_{pre}(e), c_j = True \\ 0, otherwise \end{cases} \tag{16}$$

For any initial attack condition node c_0, its parent set is an empty set, so its local condition probability distribution is its own probability distribution. According to the actual situation of the evaluation network or information system, the subjective prior probability of the node is determined by the probability distribution of the initial attack condition node. For large attack graph, the probability distribution of initial attack condition nodes can also be determined by template method.

For example, depending on the actual situation of the network or information system, the default initial probability of the initial attack condition node is set to p_0, the probability of Flash is set to $1 - p_0$, and the default local condition probability distribution function of the initial attack condition node is:

$$P_r = (c_0 = True) = p_0 \tag{17}$$

$$P_r = (c_0 = False) = 1 - p_0 \tag{18}$$

The value of p_0 depends on the actual network situation. The special initial attack condition node is set according to the specific condition of the initial condition node.

For any non-initial attack condition node *c*, its parent set is composed of several atomic attack nodes, whose parent set is $Pa[c]$. As long as *e* is successfully exploited, *c* may be exploited. According to this characteristic of non-initial attack condition node, we define its local condition probability distribution function as:

$$\Pr(c = TruePa[c]) = \begin{cases} \Pr(A(e_i, c)) \\ \theta, oth \end{cases} \tag{19}$$

In the above formula, $(A(e_i, c))$ represents the event.

The higher the frequency of atom attack node's threat state, the higher the probability of atom attack node's future occurrence, namely, the higher the probability of atom attack node.

Suppose that the grade of the threat state variable is *m*, and for any threat state variable node *t*, the local conditional probability distribution function of the threat state variable node is expressed as:

$$\Pr(t = w_i \mid e = True) = \frac{1 - \frac{m_t(m_t-1)}{2}d_t}{m_t} + (m_t - 1)d_t \tag{20}$$

In the above formula, *d* represents the set parameter.

Based on the above process, the attack probability graph is constructed to provide a basis for risk assessment.

6 Potential Threat Identification Process of Electric UAV Network Communication

Based on the above process, the attack graph is established, and on this basis, the malicious nodes are identified. The identification results are shown in Fig. 1:

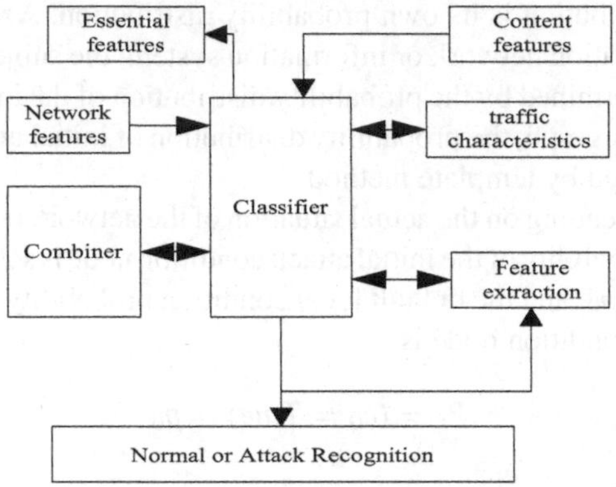

Fig. 1. Identification structure

Malicious nodes can attack independently according to their own decision values, that is, whether malicious nodes attack each other independently. An independent attack by a malicious node indicates that there is no collusion between the malicious nodes, and that they are independent of each other in terms of whether and in what form they attack. Malicious nodes can also attack by conspiracy.

That is, malicious nodes in the attack, first in the malicious data fusion between nodes, get the status of the primary user, and then attack according to attack strategy. It is assumed that all the secondary nodes in CRN have the same local awareness, that is, the local false alarm probability is the same as the local detection probability, regardless of whether the node has honest or malicious attributes.

The false alarm probability of malicious nodes is:

$$P = P(u_i = 1H_0) \tag{21}$$

H indicates that the node is an honest node, and u_i indicates that the secondary node is a malicious node.

Describe the attack behavior of malicious nodes:

$$\Omega = \begin{bmatrix} P_{11} & P_{12} & \cdots & P_{1M} \\ P_{21} & P_{22} & \cdots & P_{2M} \\ \cdots & \cdots & \cdots & \cdots \\ P_{M1} & P_{M2} & \cdots & P_{MM} \end{bmatrix} \tag{22}$$

On this basis, the quantitative evaluation of network or information system attacks is not only a very important quantitative indicators, but also an important basis for further calculation of risk values. According to the different levels, the attack probability is divided into node attack probability, host attack probability and network attack probability. This part calculates the probability of node attack, host attack and network attack according to the generalized Bayesian attack graph.

In the generalized Bayesian attack graph, the node attack probability refers to the probability of the attack condition node or the atomic attack node obtained and utilized by thc attacker.

$$\Pr(v_1, v_2, \ldots, v_n) = \prod_{n}^{i=1} \Pr(v_i Pa[v_i]) \tag{23}$$

In formula (23), v_i represents the node and Pr represents the attack probability of the node.

In the calculation of host attack probability, host attack probability is determined by attack probability of all attack condition nodes, and its value can be determined by attack probability of all attack condition nodes. Its calculation expression is:

$$P_{host}(w) = 1 - \prod_{a \backslash incNode(w)} (1 - P_v(c)) \tag{24}$$

In formula (8), w represents any host.

After the calculation of attack probability is completed, the identification flow is proposed, and the security risk of network attack probability is evaluated by artificial intelligence. In artificial intelligence, when assessing network security risks, it is necessary to initialize such risks:

$$Env(v) = P_v(v) \tag{25}$$

By defining the initial condition node, the attacker can get and use the corresponding initial condition at any time. Therefore, set the prediction support factor of all initial condition nodes to 1 and to 0. The posterior support factor is initialized to zero in the attack graph. Capabilities to initialize AI support:

$$\begin{cases} Sup_d(\emptyset) = 0 \\ Sup_d(\{h\}) = 0 \\ Sup_d(\{-h\}) = 0 \\ Sup_d(h, -h) = 1 \end{cases} \tag{26}$$

The above process is the initial stage, enters the real-time update stage, on this basis, the real-time evaluation system regularly evaluates the network. The time interval for each update calculation shall be set according to the actual situation of the network or information system, and the next update calculation may be determined according to whether the following inequality is true:

$$\sum_{n}^{i=1} w_{di} * w_{hi} * w_{ei} \geq w_c \tag{27}$$

In formula (27), w_c represents the set time interval threshold.

Compared with other regression algorithms, logistic regression algorithm is simple and efficient, with fast parallel processing speed and easy interpretation of results. Its main contents are as follows:

Assuming that p is the probability of customer risk, the logistic regression model is as follows:

$$y = \ln\left(\frac{p}{1-p}\right) = \beta_0 + \beta_1 x_1 + \beta_2 x_2 + \cdots + \beta_s x_s \tag{28}$$

In statistical evaluation of the model, pseudo-R2 statistics were used to evaluate the overall validity of the model. Nagelkerke-r2 is the ratio of independent variables, which is used to explain the difference of dependent variables. The value ranges from 0 to 1. When the Nagelkerke-R2 value is greater than 0.2, the model fitting effect is acceptable. When the Nagelkerke-R2 value is greater than 0.4, the model fitting effect is very good. When the Nagelkerke-R2 value is greater than 0.5, the model fitting effect is very good. For nagelkerke-R2 statistics, the following formula is used:

$$R_N^2 = R_{CS}^2 / \max\left(R_{CS}^2\right) \tag{29}$$

$$\max\left(R_{CS}^2\right) = 1 - [l(0)]^2 \tag{30}$$

$$R_{CS}^2 = 1 - \left[\frac{l(0)}{l(\hat{\beta})}\right]^2 \tag{31}$$

In Formula (31), $\frac{l(0)}{l(\hat{\beta})}$ represents the likelihood value of the original model, and $l(\hat{\beta})$ represents the likelihood value of the current pattern.

Through WOE transformation, substitute WOE value for original attribute value for model training, so as to better distinguish risk levels, and obtain the score of each user as follows:

$$score = \sum_{n}^{i=1} \left((woe_i \times \beta_i) \times factor + \frac{offset}{n} \right) \tag{32}$$

In formula (32), n represents the number of explanatory variables, and woe represents that the value variable is the substitute of the original attribute and is the regression coefficient of the corresponding variable.

Through the above process, the risk score is divided into three risk categories: high, medium and low, and the potential threat identification of UAV network communication is completed. The risk classification is shown in Table 1.

Table 1. Classification of UAV network communication risk level

Risk level number	Level	Value	Specific description
1	Very low	0–0.2	No impact
2	Low	0.2–0.4	Little impact
3	Medium	0.4–0.6	It has a certain impact, but not much
4	High	0.6–0.9	Have a great impact
5	Very high	0.9–1	The impact is very serious

7 Experimental Comparison

In order to verify the application effect of the proposed potential threat identification algorithm for power UAV network communication in the actual scene, experimental comparisons are carried out, and the traditional identification algorithm is compared with the proposed algorithm.

The experimental comparison indexes are as follows:

$$D = \frac{P}{N} \times 100\% \tag{33}$$

$$A = \frac{F}{K} \times 100\% \tag{34}$$

$$R = \frac{F}{B} \times 100\% \tag{35}$$

In the above formula, D, A and R respectively represent the recognition success rate of human intrusion signal, the false recognition rate of human intrusion signal and the missing recognition rate of human intrusion signal, P and Nrespectively represent the accurate intrusion sample data, IV is the total number of samples, *F* and *K* respectively represent the correct number of samples for false recognition intrusion and the total number of normal samples, and *B* is the total number of samples for intrusion.

The success rate of intrusion signal recognition of the recognition algorithm, the recognition method based on mobile wireless sensor and the recognition method based on deep learning in this study is shown in Fig. 2:

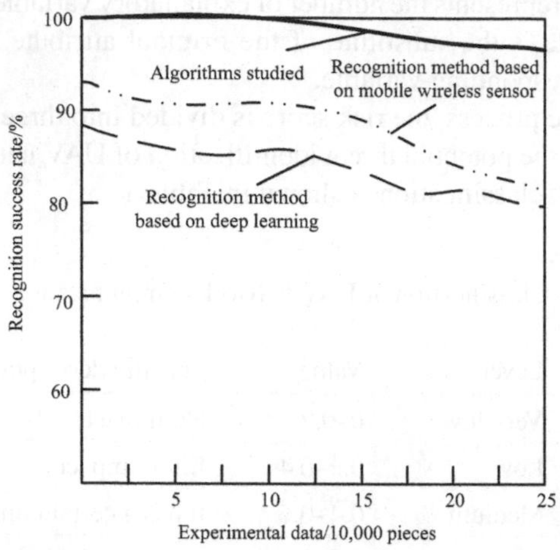

Fig. 2. Comparison of success rate of intrusion signal recognition

When the amount of data is 250000, the recognition success rate fluctuates, but it is still above 95%. The other two methods have a recognition rate of 85% - 90% when the amount of data is 250000. Therefore, it can be concluded that the recognition success rate of the recognition method in this study is the best.

The error recognition rate of the recognition algorithm, the recognition method based on mobile wireless sensor and the recognition method based on deep learning in this study is shown in Fig. 3:

Based on Fig. 3, it can be seen that the error recognition rate of this research method is less than 5%, and the recognition effect is good. The error recognition rate of the recognition method based on mobile wireless sensor and the recognition method based on deep learning is between 5% and 15%. It can be concluded that this research method has a good error recognition rate.

The missing identification rate can affect the identification accuracy. In case of missing identification, the intrusion will be successful, resulting in data loss, damage and serious harm. Therefore, it is necessary to strictly control the missing recognition rate. The sketch results of the recognition algorithm, the recognition method based on mobile wireless sensor and the recognition method based on deep learning in this study are shown in Fig. 4:

As can be seen from Fig. 5, the missing recognition rate of the method in this paper does not have any missing recognition when the data is small, but it still occurs with the increase of data, but the probability is very low. This is mainly because after extracting

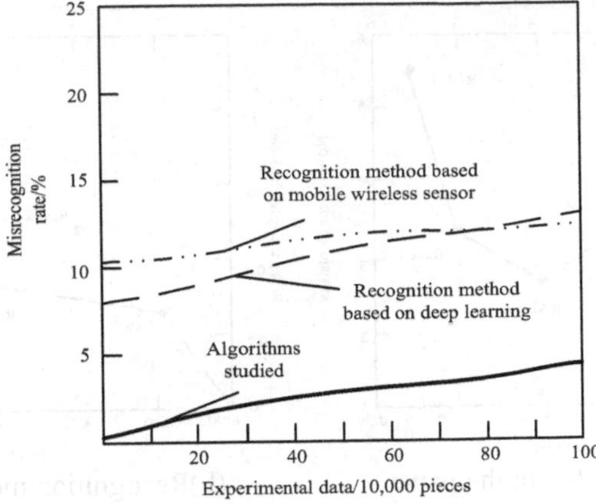

Fig. 3. Comparison of error recognition rate

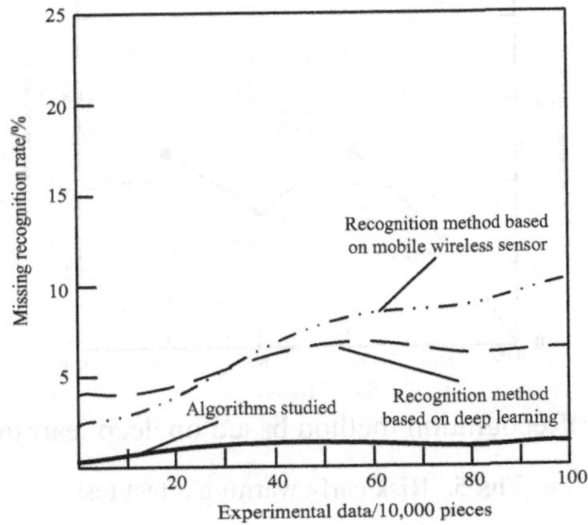

Fig. 4. Comparison of missed recognition rate

the characteristics of the communication network intrusion signals, the nonlinear spatio-temporal actions between the neighborhood signals are captured, so as to predict the working state of the follow-up behaviors, complete the intrusion signal recognition, reduce the missed recognition rate to a minimum, and avoid the normal sample data being affected.

In order to verify the prediction effect of different risks, the recognition algorithm in this study is compared with the recognition method based on mobile wireless sensor and the recognition method based on deep learning. In the experiment, it is preset that there are five risk nodes with different distances in the communication network, and whether the three methods can achieve risk early warning is compared. The experimental results are shown in Fig. 5.

It can be seen from Fig. 5 that my method can accurately identify five risk nodes with different distances, while the identification method based on mobile sensing and

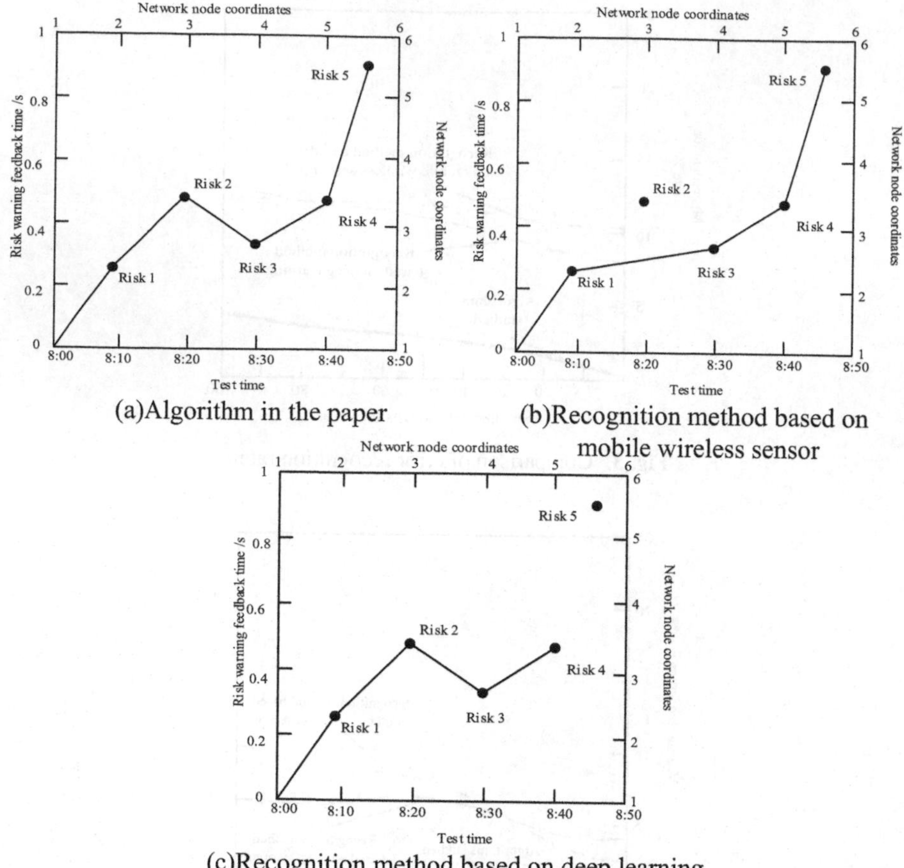

(a)Algorithm in the paper

(b)Recognition method based on mobile wireless sensor

(c)Recognition method based on deep learning

Fig. 5. Risk early warning effect test

the identification method based on deep learning have different degrees of deficiencies, and all risks are not identified. Therefore, it can be concluded that the risk early warning identification effect of this paper is the best.

The above experimental results show that the proposed method has a certain accuracy in the identification of communication network intrusion signals, indicating that the performance of the proposed method is good. However, it is still difficult to process a large amount of data. In the future, optimization iterative method can be used to further improve the recognition performance of intrusion signals for communication network processing a large amount of data.

8 Conclusion

Based on the above process, the potential threat identification algorithm of power UAV network communication is studied. Experimental results show that the proposed algorithm has high recognition accuracy and good recognition effect. Although this method can recognize the intrusion signal effectively, there still exists the situation of mistaken recognition and missing recognition. Based on this, this paper needs to pay attention to the development of network technology.

References

1. Hongying, L., Tianrong, Z.: Research on recognition method of abnormal communication behavior in mobile wireless sensor network. Chinese J. Sens. Actuators **35**(2), 240–245 (2020)
2. Ying, K., Zhihua, Z., Hao, W., Yaxing, L., Jin, M.: Deep SVDD-based anomaly detection method for communication signals. Syst. Eng. Electron. **44**(7), 2319–2328 (2022)
3. Taoufik, A., Defoort, M., Busawon, K., Dala, L., Djemai, M.: A distributed observer-based cyber-attack identification scheme in cooperative networked systems under switching communication topologies. Electronics **9**(11), 1912 (2020)
4. Liu, S., Wang, S., Liu, X.Y., Lin, C.T.: Fuzzy detection aided real-time and robust visual tracking under complex environments. IEEE Trans. Fuzzy Syst. **29**(1), 90–102 (2021)
5. Gupta, K., Sahoo, S., Panigrahi, B.K., Blaabjerg, F., Popovski, P.: On the assessment of cyber risks and attack surfaces in a real-time co-simulation cybersecurity testbed for inverter-based microgrids. Energies **14**(16), 4941 (2021)
6. Hussain, B., Du, Q., Sun, B., Han, Z.: Deep learning-based ddos-attack detection for cyber-physical system over 5g network. IEEE Trans. Industr. Inf. **17**(2), 860–870 (2021)
7. Yang, G.Y., Li, X.J.: Complete stealthiness false data injection attacks against dynamic state estimation in cyber-physical systems. Inf. Sci. **586**, 408–423 (2022)
8. Liu, S., Liu, D., Muhammad, K., Ding, W.P.: Effective template update mechanism in visual tracking with background clutter. Neurocomputing **458**, 615–625 (2021)
9. Liu, S., et al.: Human memory update strategy: a multi-layer template update mechanism for remote visual monitoring, IEEE Trans. Multimedia **23**, 2188–2198 (2021)
10. Fang, L., Yin, C., Zhou, L., Li, Y., Xia, J.: A physiological and behavioral feature authentication scheme for medical cloud based on fuzzy-rough core vector machine. Inf. Sci. **507**, 143–160 (2020)
11. Ahmad, U., Song, H., Bilal, A., Alazab, M., Jolfaei, A.: Securing smart vehicles from relay attacks using machine learning. J. Supercomput. **76**(4), 2665–2682 (2019). https://doi.org/10.1007/s11227-019-03049-4
12. Yan, X.J., Liu, F.J., Yan, Y.Z.: Simulation analysis of end to end delay upper bound in anti jamming communication network. Comput. Simul. **38**(07), 176180 (2021)

Author Index

Printed in the United States
by Baker & Taylor Publisher Services